# THE NEW ERA OF

# TERRORISM

# SELECTED READINGS

### EDITOR

# GUS MARTIN

California State University, Dominguez Hills

**SAGE Publications**
*International Educational and Professional Publisher*
Thousand Oaks ■ London ■ New Delhi

*For information:*

Sage Publications, Inc.
2455 Teller Road
Thousand Oaks, California 91320
E-mail: order@sagepub.com

Sage Publications Ltd.
1 Oliver's Yard
55 City Road
London EC1Y 1SP
United Kingdom

Sage Publications India Pvt. Ltd.
B-42, Panchsheel Enclave
Post Box 4109
New Delhi 110 017  India

Printed in the United States of America

**Library of Congress Cataloging-in-Publication Data**

Martin, Gus.
The new era of terrorism: Selected readings / [edited by] Gus Martin.
    p. cm.
Includes bibliographical references and index.
ISBN 0-7619-8873-4 (pbk.)
1. Terrorism. 2. War on Terrorism, 2001-  I. Martin, Gus. II. Title.
HV6431.M366 2004
303.6′25—dc22              2003026839

This book is printed on acid-free paper.

04  05  06  07  10  9  8  7  6  5  4  3  2  1

| | |
|---|---|
| *Acquisitions Editor:* | Jerry Westby |
| *Editorial Assistant:* | Vonessa Vondera |
| *Production Editor:* | Denise Santoyo |
| *Typesetter:* | C&M Digitals (P) Ltd. |
| *Indexer:* | Kathy Paparchontis |
| *Cover Designer:* | Michelle Lee Kenny |

# THE NEW ERA OF
# TERRORISM

# CONTENTS

# INTRODUCTION

September 11, 2001 was a turning point in the history of political violence. At the beginning of an otherwise routine workday, four civilian airliners were hijacked by 19 terrorists, and three of these aircraft were crashed into buildings in New York City and Washington, D.C. The fourth aircraft crashed in rural Pennsylvania after an apparent struggle on board between passengers and the terrorists. The sheer scope of the attack was stunning: Dedicated religious terrorists from the Middle East used the commercial technology of the world's remaining superpower to destroy or severely damage several centers of power, all for the promise of attaining "martyrdom" in defense of their faith. The outcome of the assault was thousands of deaths and the declaration of a longterm global war on terrorism.

In the United States, this war affected every sector of society, and culminated in the largest reorganization of government in the post-war era. The duties of 22 agencies were concentrated under the authority of a new Department of Homeland Security, which at its inception employed 117,000 personnel. New legislation such as the USA Patriot Act established the legal authority to create an unprecedented domestic security environment. Internationally, governments cooperated to disrupt terrorist cells and their support apparatuses as part of a global effort to break up extremist networks. The solidarity of this effort continued through the allied invasion of Afghanistan, but was severely tested in the spring of 2003 during the invasion and subsequent occupation of Iraq. Nevertheless, this global effort symbolizes the worldwide response to an extraordinary threat from mass casualty political violence that has become a hallmark of the new era of terrorism.

The purpose of this reader is to stimulate critical discussion about the attributes of the new era of terrorism and the policy options available to societies and governments in this era. The reader is organized into three thematic parts, each of which is comprised of three chapters. The parts and chapters are preceded by an introductory discussion and recommended readings. Three articles are included in each chapter: The first articles have been selected from reputable scholarly journals, and the remaining two articles have been selected from policy-oriented political and legal journals, and mass-market publications. The latter publications are recognized for their insightful and often provocative commentary.

The topics of discussion are arranged as follows: Chapter 1 is a prologue chapter which presents some of the theoretical and policy issues that have arisen in the new era of terrorism. After this introduction, the chapters in Part I frame the threat posed by the new terrorist environment. Chapter 2 establishes a contextual framework for understanding modern terrorism. This framework is followed by an updated examination in

Chapter 3 of the definitional debate that has existed since the height of the Cold War. Chapter 4 discusses causes of terrorist behavior among three cultural and demographic groups. Part II assesses several features of the new era of terrorism. The threat from weapons of mass destruction and asymmetrical methods is reviewed in Chapter 5. Chapter 6 outlines the problem of religious motivations for terrorist violence, and Chapter 7 discusses the near future of terrorism from several perspectives. Part III raises the question of counterterrorist options and cooperation in the new era. Problems associated with securing society and waging the war on terrorism are addressed in Chapter 8. Chapter 9 offers assessments of counterterrorist strategies and options in the new terrorist environment. As the terminal chapter for the reader, Chapter 10 assesses the problem of creating and sustaining alliances in the new era.

# ACKNOWLEDGMENTS

For permission to reprint from the following, grateful acknowledgment is made to the publishers and copyright holders.

## Chapter 1

Copyright © 2002. From *Studies in Conflict and Terrorism* by Bruce Hoffman. Reproduced by permission of Taylor & Francis, Inc., http://www.routledge-ny.com.

Krauthammer, Charles. "The Unipolar Moment Revisited." *The National Interest* (Winter 2002/03). Reprinted with permission.

Dinh, Viet. "Foreword: Freedom and Security After September 11." *Harvard Journal of Law & Public Policy,* 25:2 (Spring 2002). Reprinted with permission.

## Chapter 2

Copyright © 2002. From *Studies in Conflict and Terrorism,* Vol. 25, pp. 279–292. Reproduced by permission of Taylor & Francis, Inc., http//www.routledge-ny.com.

Reprinted with permission. Copyright © *The National Interest,* No. 69 (Fall 2002), Washington, DC.

Delpech, Thérèse. "The Imbalance of Terror." *The Washington Quarterly,* 25:1 (Winter 2002). Reprinted with permission.

## Chapter 3

Cooper, H.H.A. "Terrorism: The Problem of Definition Revisited." *American Behavioral Scientist,* Vol. 44, No. 6. Copyright © 2001 Sage Publications, Inc. Used by permission.

Al Sayyid, Mustafa. "Mixed Message: Arab and Muslim Response to 'Terrorism.'" *The Washington Quarterly,* 25:2 (Spring 2002). Reprinted with permission.

Feldman, Noah. "Choices of Law, Choices of War." *Harvard Journal of Law & Public Policy,* 25:2 (Spring 2002). Reprinted with permission.

## Chapter 4

Copyright © 2002. From *Studies in Conflict and Terrorism* by Karla J. Cunningham. Reproduced by permission of Taylor & Francis, Inc., http://www.routledge-ny.com.

## Chapter 5

## Chapter 6

## Chapter 7

## Chapter 8

## Chapter 9

Deutch, John and Jeffrey H. Smith. "Smarter Intelligence." From the January/ February 2002 (#128) issue of *Foreign Policy.* Reprinted with permission.

## Chapter 10

Reprinted by permission of Sage Publications Ltd from Smith, Steve, "The End of the Unipolar Moment? September 11 and the Future of World Order." In *International Relations, 16*(2), 2002.

Dibb, Paul. "The Future of International Coalitions: How Useful? How Manageable?" *The Washington Quarterly, 25:*2 (Spring 2002). Reprinted with permission.

Reprinted by permission of *The New Republic.* Copyright © 2003, The New Republic, LLC.

# 1

# PROLOGUE

## *Rethinking Policy and Theory In the New Era Of Terrorism*

The events of September 11, 2001 awakened the international community to the reality of mass-casualty violence perpetrated by suicidal terrorists. These terrorists were motivated by an uncompromisingly sectarian worldview that allowed for the murder of large numbers of innocent civilians in the name of their faith. The attacks confirmed warnings from experts that a new breed of terrorist would transform available technologies into weapons of enormous destructive power. In the United States, the attacks on the Twin Towers and the Pentagon immediately engendered a thorough reexamination and enhancement of the nation's domestic security environment. This process occurred simultaneously with an unprecedented reorganization of government and the passage of sweeping security laws. As these measures fundamentally changed how Americans would respond to future threats of terrorist violence, they also reflected a basic adaptation of policy and theory to a new era of terrorism. Many experts revisited, and continue to revisit, the questions of which policies are best suited to address the new terrorist threat, as well as how to define and characterize terrorism in the new era.

The articles in this chapter introduce policy and theoretical questions posed by the events of September 11, 2001. In "Rethinking Terrorism and Counterterrorism Since 9/11," Bruce Hoffman explores the lessons of the September 11, 2001 terrorist attacks. The article examines the nature of the new era of terrorism, its impact on the contemporary global community, and the problem of adapting counterterrorism to the new environment. A contextual discussion of these issues is developed to posit existing and future trends in terrorist violence. In "The Unipolar Moment Revisited," Charles Krauthammer revisits his 1990 thesis that the post-Cold War international environment will be unipolar and centered around U.S. predominance, rather than multipolar and centered around several regional powers. The article discusses unipolarity in the aftermath of September 11, 2001, centering on the meaning of American global power in the new era of terrorism. Viet Dinh's article, "Foreword: Freedom and Security After September 11," examines the security environment in the United States from a legalistic perspective. The primary points of discussion are the contention that there exists a dichotomy between freedom and security, and the challenge of how to frame and analyze this debate. It is a provocative article.

## Rethinking Terrorism and Counterterrorism Since 9/11

Bruce Hoffman
*RAND, Arlington, VA, USA*

A few hours after the first American air strikes against Afghanistan began on 7 October 2001, a pre-recorded videotape was broadcast around the world. A tall, skinny man with a long, scraggly beard, wearing a camouflage fatigue jacket and the headdress of a desert tribesman, with an AK-47 assault rifle at his side, stood before a rocky backdrop. In measured, yet defiant, language, Usama bin Laden again declared war on the United States. Only a few weeks before, his statement would likely have been dismissed as the inflated rhetoric of a saber-rattling braggart. But with the World Trade Center now laid to waste, the Pentagon heavily damaged, and the wreckage of a fourth hijacked passenger aircraft strewn across a field in rural Pennsylvania, bin Laden's declaration was regarded with a preternatural seriousness that would previously have been unimaginable. How bin Laden achieved this feat, and the light his accomplishment sheds on understanding the extent to which terrorism has changed and, in turn, how our responses must change as well, is the subject of this article.

## THE SEPTEMBER 11 ATTACKS BY THE NUMBERS

The enormity and sheer scale of the simultaneous suicide attacks on September 11 eclipsed anything previously seen in terrorism. Among the most significant characteristics of the operation were its ambitious scope and dimensions; impressive coordination and synchronization; and the unswerving dedication and determination of the 19 aircraft hijackers who willingly and wantonly killed themselves, the passengers, and crews of the four aircraft they commandeered and the approximately 3,000 persons working at or visiting either the World Trade Center and the Pentagon.

Indeed, in lethality terms alone the September 11 attacks are without precedent. For example, since 1968, the year credited with marking the advent of modern, international terrorism, one feature of international terrorism has remained constant despite variations in the number of attacks from year to year. Almost without exception,[1] the United States has annually led the list of countries whose citizens and property were most frequently attacked by terrorists.[2] But, until September 11, over the preceding 33 years a total of no more than perhaps 1,000 Americans had been killed by terrorists either overseas or even within the United States itself. In less than 90 minutes that day, nearly three times that number were killed.[3] To put those uniquely tragic events in context, during the entirety of the twentieth century no more than 14 terrorist operations killed more than 100 persons at any one time.[4] Or, viewed from still another perspective, until the attacks on the World Trade Center and Pentagon, no single terrorist operation had ever killed more than 500 persons at one time.[5] Whatever the metric, therefore, the attacks that day were unparalleled in their severity and lethal ambitions.

Significantly, too, from a purely terrorist operational perspective, *spectacular* simultaneous attacks—using far more prosaic and arguably conventional means of attack (such as car bombs, for example)—are relatively uncommon. For reasons not well understood, terrorists typically have not undertaken coordinated operations. This was doubtless less of a choice than a reflection of the logistical and other organizational hurdles and constraints that all but the most sophisticated terrorist groups are unable to overcome. Indeed, this was one reason why we were so galvanized by the synchronized attacks on the American embassies in Nairobi and Dar-es-Salaam three years ago. The orchestration of that operation, coupled with its unusually high death and casualty tolls, stood out in a way that, until September 11, few other terrorist attacks had. During the 1990s, perhaps only one other terrorist operation evidenced those same characteristics of coordination and high lethality: the series of attacks that occurred in Bombay in March 1993, when 10 coordinated car bombings rocked the city, killing nearly 300 people and wounding more than 700 others.[6] Apart from the attacks on the same morning in October 1983 of the U.S. Marine barracks in Beirut (241 persons were killed) and a nearby French paratroops headquarters (where 60 soldiers perished); the 1981 hijacking of three Venezuelan passenger jets by a mixed commando of Salvadoran leftists and Puerto Rican *independistas;* and the dramatic 1970 hijacking of four commercial aircraft by the PFLP (Popular Front for the Liberation of Palestine), two of which were brought to and then dramatically blown up at Dawson's Field in Jordan, there have been few successfully executed, simultaneous terrorist spectaculars.[7]

Finally, the September 11 attacks not only showed a level of patience and detailed planning rarely seen among terrorist movements today, but the hijackers stunned the world with their determination to kill themselves as well as their victims. Suicide attacks differ from other terrorist operations precisely because the perpetrator's own death is a requirement for the attack's success.[8] This dimension of terrorist operations, however, arguably remains poorly understood. In no aspect of the September 11 attacks is this clearer than in the debate over whether all 19 of the hijackers knew they were on a suicide mission or whether only the 4 persons actually flying the aircraft into their targets did. It is a debate that underscores the poverty of our understanding of bin Laden, terrorism motivated by a religious imperative in particular, and the concept of martyrdom.

The so-called *Jihad Manual,* discovered by British police in March 2000 on the hard drive of an al Qaeda member's computer, is explicit about operational security (OPSEC) in the section that discusses tradecraft. For reasons of operational security, it states, only the leaders of an attack should know all the details of the operation and these should only be revealed to the rest of the unit at the last possible moment.[9] Schooled in this tradecraft, the 19 hijackers doubtless understood that they were on a one-way mission from the time they were dispatched to the United States. Indeed, the video tape of bin Laden and his chief lieutenant, Dr. Ayman Zawahiri, recently broadcast by the Arabic television news station *al Jazeera* contains footage of one of the hijackers acknowledging his impending martyrdom in an allusion to the forthcoming September 11 attacks.

The phenomenon of martyrdom terrorism in Islam has a course long been discussed and examined. The act itself can be traced back to the Assassins, an off-shoot of the Shia Ismaili movement, who some 700 years ago waged a protracted struggle against the European Crusaders' attempted conquest of the Holy Land. The Assassins embraced an ethos of self-sacrifice, where martyrdom was regarded as a sacramental act—a highly desirable aspiration and divine duty commanded by religious text and communicated by clerical authorities—that is evident today. An important additional motivation then as now was the promise that the martyr would feel no pain in the commission of his sacred act and would then ascend immediately to a glorious heaven, described as a place replete with "rivers of milk and wine . . . lakes of honey, and the services of 72 virgins," where the martyr will see the face of Allah and later be joined by 70 chosen relatives.[10] The last will and testament of Muhammad Atta, the ringleader of the September 11 hijackers, along with a "primer" for martyrs that he wrote, titled, "The Sky Smiles, My Young Son," clearly evidences such beliefs.[11]

Equally as misunderstood is the attention focused on the hijackers' relatively high levels of education, socioeconomic status, and stable family ties.[12] In point of fact, contrary to popular belief and misconception, suicide terrorists are not exclusively derived from the ranks of the mentally unstable, economically bereft, or abject, isolated loners. In the more sophisticated and competent terrorist groups, such as the LTTE (Liberation Tigers of Tamil Eelam, or Tamil Tigers), it is precisely the most battle-hardened, skilled, and dedicated cadre who enthusiastically volunteer to commit suicide attacks.[13] Observations of the patterns of recent suicide attacks in Israel and on the West Bank and Gaza similarly reveal that the bombers are not exclusively drawn from the maw of poverty, but have included two sons of millionaires. Finally, in the context of the ongoing Palestinian-Israeli conflict, suicide attacks—once one of the more infrequent (though albeit dramatic, and attention-riveting, tactics)—are clearly increasing in frequency, if not severity, assuming new and more lethal forms.

## WHERE THE UNITED STATES WENT WRONG IN FAILING TO PREDICT THE 9/11 ATTACKS

Most importantly, the United States was perhaps lulled into believing that mass, simultaneous attacks in general and those of such devastating potential as seen in New York and Washington on September 11 were likely beyond the capabilities of most terrorists—including those directly connected to, or associated with, Usama bin Laden. The tragic events of that September day demonstrate how profoundly misplaced such assumptions were. In this respect, the significance of past successes (e.g., in largely foiling a series of planned terrorist operations against American targets between the August 1998 embassy bombings to the November 2000 attack on the *U.S.S. Cole,* including more than 60 instances when credible evidence of impending attack forced the temporary closure of American embassies and consulates around the world) and the terrorists' own incompetence and propensity for mistakes (e.g., Ahmad Ressam's bungled attempt to enter the United States from Canada in December 1999) were perhaps overestimated. Both impressive and disturbing is the likelihood that there was considerable overlap in the planning for these attacks and the one in November 2000 against the *U.S.S. Cole* in Aden, thus suggesting al Qaeda's operational and organizational capability to coordinate major, multiple attacks at one time.[14]

Attention was also arguably focused too exclusively either on the low-end threat posed by car and truck bombs against buildings or the more exotic high-end threats, against entire societies, involving biological or chemical weapons or cyberattacks. The implicit assumptions of much of American planning scenarios on mass casualty attacks were that they would involve germ or chemical agents or result from widespread electronic attacks on critical infrastructure. It was therefore presumed that any conventional or less extensive incident could be addressed simply by planning for the most catastrophic threat. This left a painfully vulnerable gap in antiterrorism defenses where a traditional and long-proven tactic—like airline hijacking—was neglected in favor of other, less conventional threats and where the consequences of using an aircraft as a suicide weapon seem to have been ignored. In retrospect, it was not the 1995 sarin nerve gas attack on the Tokyo subway and the nine attempts to use bioweapons by Aum that should have been the dominant influence on our counterterrorist thinking, but a 1986 hijacking of a TWA flight in Karachi, where the terrorists' intention was reported to have been to crash it into the center of Tel Aviv and the 1994 hijacking in Algiers of an Air France passenger plane by terrorists belonging to the Armed Islamic Group (GIA), who similarly planned to crash the fuel-laden aircraft with its passengers into the heart of Paris. The lesson, accordingly, is not that there need be unrealistic omniscience, but rather that there is a need to be able to respond across a broad technological spectrum of potential adversarial attacks.

We also had long consoled ourselves—and had only recently began to question and debate the notion—that terrorists were more interested in publicity than killing and therefore had neither the need nor the interest in annihilating large numbers of people.[15] For decades, there was widespread acceptance of the observation made famous by Brian Jenkins in 1975 that, "Terrorists want a lot of people watching and a lot of people listening and not a lot of people dead."[16] Although entirely germane to the forms of terrorism that existed in prior decades, for too long this antiquated notion was adhered to. On September 11, bin Laden wiped the slate clean of the conventional wisdom on terrorists and terrorism and, by doing so, ushered in a new era of conflict.

Finally, before September 11 the United States arguably lacked the political will to sustain a long and determined counterterrorism campaign. The record of inchoate, unsustained previous efforts effectively retarded significant progress against this menace. The carnage and shock of the September 11 attacks laid bare America's vulnerability and too belatedly resulted in a sea change in national attitudes and accompanying political will to combat terrorism systematically, globally, and, most importantly, without respite.[17]

## TERRORISM'S CEO

The cardinal rule of warfare, "know your enemy," was also violated. The United States failed to understand and comprehend Usama bin Laden: his vision, his capabilities, his financial resources and acumen, as well as his organizational skills. The broad outline of bin Laden's curriculum vitae is by now well known: remarkably, it attracted minimal interest and understanding in most quarters prior to September 11.[18] The scion of a porter turned construction magnate whose prowess at making money was perhaps matched only by his countless progeny and devout religious piety, the young Usama pursued studies not in theology (despite his issuance of *fatwas,* or Islamic religious edicts), but in business and management sciences. Bin Laden is a graduate of Saudi Arabia's prestigious King Abdul-Aziz University, where in 1981 he obtained a degree in economics and public administration. He subsequently cut his teeth in the family business, later applying the corporate management techniques learned both in the classroom and on the job to transform the terrorist movement he founded, al Qaeda, into the world's preeminent terrorist organization.[19]

Bin Laden achieved this by cleverly combining the technological munificence of modernity with a rigidly puritanical explication of age-old tradition and religious practice. He is also the quintessential product of the 1990s and globalism. Bin Laden the terrorism CEO could not have existed—and thrived—in any other era. He was able to overcome the relative geographical isolation caused by his expulsion from the Sudan to Afghanistan, engineered by the United States in 1996, by virtue of the invention of the satellite telephone. With this most emblematic technological artifice of 1990s global technology, bin Laden was therefore able to communicate with his minions in real time around the world.[20] Al Qaeda operatives, moreover, routinely made use of the latest technology themselves: encrypting messages on Apple PowerMacs or Toshiba laptop computers, communicating via e-mail or on Internet bulletin boards,[21] using satellite telephones and cell phones themselves and, when travelling by air, often flying first class. This "grafting of entirely modern sensibilities and techniques to the most radical interpretation of holy war," Peter Bergen compellingly explains in *Holy War, Inc.,* "is the hallmark of bin Laden's network."[22]

For bin Laden, the weapons of modern terrorism critically are not only the guns and bombs that they have long been, but the minicam, videotape, television, and the Internet. The professionally produced and edited two hour al Qaeda recruitment videotape that bin Laden circulated throughout the Middle East during the summer of 2001—which according to Bergen also subtly presaged the September 11 attacks—is exactly such an example of bin Laden's nimble exploitation of "twenty-first-century communications and weapons technology in the service of the most extreme, retrograde reading of holy war."[23] The tape, with its graphic footage of infidels attacking Muslims in Chechnya, Kashmir, Iraq, Israel, Lebanon, Indonesia, and Egypt; children starving under the yoke of the United Nations economic sanctions in Iraq; and most vexatiously, the accursed presence of "Crusader" military forces in the holy land of Arabia, was subsequently converted to CD-ROM and DVD formats for ease in copying onto computers and loading onto the World Wide Web for still wider, global dissemination. An even more stunning illustration of his communications acumen and clever manipulation of media was the pre-recorded, pre-produced, B-roll, or video clip, that bin Laden had queued and ready for broadcast within hours of the commencement of the American air strikes on Afghanistan on Sunday, October 7.

In addition to his adroit marrying of technology to religion and of harnessing the munificence of modernity and the West as a weapon to be wielded against his very enemies, bin Laden has demonstrated uncommon patience, planning, and attention to detail. According to testimony presented at the trial of three of the 1998 East Africa embassy bombers in Federal District Court in New York last year by a former bin Laden lieutenant, Ali Muhammad,[24] planning for the attack on the Nairobi facility commenced nearly five years before the operation was executed. Muhammad also testified that bin Laden himself studied a surveillance photograph of the embassy compound, pointing to the spot in front of the building where he said the truck bomb should be positioned. Attention has already been drawn to al Qaeda's ability to commence planning of another operation before the latest one has been executed, as evidenced in the case of the embassy bombings and the attack 27 months later on the *U.S.S. Cole.* Clearly, when necessary, bin Laden devotes specific attention—perhaps even to the extent of micromanaging—various key aspects of al Qaeda "spectaculars." In the famous "home movie"/ videotape discovered in an al Qaeda safe house in Afghanistan that was released by the U.S. government in December 2001, bin Laden is seen discussing various intimate details of the September 11 attack. At one point, bin Laden explains how "we calculated in advance the number of casualties from the enemy, who would be killed based on the position of the tower. We calculated that the floors that would be hit would be three or four floors. I was the most optimistic of them all. . . . due to my experience in this field. . . ." alluding to his knowledge of construction techniques gleaned from his time with the family business.[25] Bin Laden also knew that Muhammad Atta was the operation's leader[26] and states that he and his closest lieutenants "had notification [of the attack] since the previous Thursday that the event would take place that day [September 11]."[27]

The portrait of bin Laden that thus emerges is richer, more complex, and more accurate than the simple caricature of a hate-filled, mindless fanatic. "All men dream: but not equally," T. E. Lawrence, the legendary Lawrence of Arabia, wrote. "Those who dream by night in the dusty recesses of their minds wake in the day to find that it was vanity: but the dreamers of the day are dangerous men, for they may act their dream with open eyes, to make it possible."[28] Bin Laden is indeed one of the dangerous men that Lawrence described. At a time when the forces of globalization, coupled with economic determinism, seemed to have submerged the role of the individual charismatic leader of men beneath far more powerful, impersonal forces, bin Laden has cleverly cast himself as a David against the American Goliath: one man standing up to the world's sole remaining superpower

and able to challenge its might and directly threaten its citizens.

Indeed, in an age arguably devoid of ideological leadership, when these impersonal forces are thought to have erased the ability of a single man to affect the course of history, bin Laden—despite all efforts—managed to taunt and strike at the United States for years even before September 11. His effective melding of the strands of religious fervor, Muslim piety, and a profound sense of grievance into a powerful ideological force stands—however invidious and repugnant—as a towering accomplishment. In his own inimitable way, bin Laden cast this struggle as precisely the "clash of civilizations" that America and its coalition partners have labored so hard to negate. "This is a matter of religion and creed; it is not what Bush and Blair maintain, that it is a war against terrorism," he declared in a videotaped speech broadcast over *al Jazeera* television on 3 November 2001. "There is no way to forget the hostility between us and the infidels. It is ideological, so Muslims have to ally themselves with Muslims."[29]

Bin Laden, though, is perhaps best viewed as a "terrorist CEO": essentially having applied business administration and modern management techniques to the running of a transnational terrorist organization. Indeed, what bin Laden apparently has done is to implement for al Qaeda the same type of effective organizational framework or management approach adapted by corporate executives throughout much of the industrialized world. Just as large, multinational business conglomerates moved during the 1990s to flatter, more linear, and networked structures, bin Laden did the same with al Qaeda.

Additionally, he defined a flexible strategy for the group that functions at multiple levels, using both top down and bottom up approaches. On the one hand, bin Laden has functioned like the president or CEO of a large multinational corporation: defining specific goals and aims, issuing orders, and ensuring their implementation. This mostly applies to the al Qaeda "spectaculars": those high-visibility, usually high-value and high-casualty operations like September 11, the attack on the *Cole,* and the East Africa embassy bombings. On the other hand, however, he has operated as a venture capitalist: soliciting ideas from below, encouraging creative approaches and "out of the box" thinking, and providing funding to those proposals he thinks promising. Al Qaeda, unlike many other terrorist organizations, therefore, deliberately has no one, set modus operandi, making it all the more formidable. Instead, bin Laden encourages his followers to mix and match approaches: employing different tactics and different means of operational styles as needed. At least four different levels of al Qaeda operational styles can be identified:

1. *The professional cadre.* This is the most dedicated, committed, and professional element of al Qaeda: the persons entrusted with only the most important and high-value attacks—in other words, the "spectaculars." These are the terrorist teams that are predetermined and carefully selected, are provided with very specific targeting instructions, and who are generously funded (e.g., to the extent that during the days preceding the September 11 attacks, Atta and his confederates were sending money back to their paymasters in the United Arab Emirates and elsewhere).

2. *The trained amateurs.* At the next level down are the trained amateurs. These are individuals much like Ahmed Ressam, who was arrested in December 1999 at Port Angeles, Washington State, shortly after he had entered the United States from Canada. Ressam, for example, had some prior background in terrorism, having belonged to Algeria's Armed Islamic Group (GIA). After being recruited into al Qaeda, he was provided with a modicum of basic terrorist training in Afghanistan. In contrast to the professional cadre, however, Ressam was given open-ended targeting instructions before being dispatched to North America. All he was told was to attack some target in the United States that involved commercial aviation. Ressam confessed that he chose Los Angeles International Airport because at one time he had passed through there and was at least vaguely familiar with it. Also, unlike the well-funded professionals, Ressam was given only $12,000 in "seed money" and instructed to raise the rest of his operational funds from petty thievery—for example, swiping cell phones and lap tops around his adopted home of Montreal. He was also told to recruit members for his

terrorist cell from among the expatriate Muslim communities in Canada and the United States. In sum, a distinctly more amateurish level of al Qaeda operations than the professional cadre deployed on September 11; Ressam clearly was far less steeled, determined, and dedicated than the hijackers proved themselves to be. Ressam, of course, panicked when he was confronted by a Border Patrol agent immediately upon entering the United States. By comparison, 9 of the 19 hijackers were stopped and subjected to greater scrutiny and screening by airport personnel on September 11. Unlike Ressam, they stuck to their cover stories, did not lose their nerve and, despite having aroused suspicion, were still allowed to board. Richard Reid, the individual who attempted to blow up an American Airlines passenger plane en route from Paris to Miami with an explosive device concealed in his shoe, is another example of the trained amateur. It should be emphasized, however, that as inept or even moronic as these individuals might appear, their ability to be lucky even once and then to inflict incalculable pain and destruction should not be lightly dismissed. As distinctly second-tier al Qaeda operatives, they are likely seen by their masters as expendable: having neither the investment in training nor the requisite personal skills that the less numerous, but more professional, first-team al Qaeda cadre have.

3. *The local walk-ins.* These are local groups of Islamic radicals who come up with a terrorist attack idea on their own and then attempt to obtain funding from al Qaeda for it. This operational level plays to bin Laden's self-conception as a venture capitalist. An example of the local walk-in is the group of Islamic radicals in Jordan who, observing that American and Israeli tourists often stay at the Radisson Hotel in Amman, proposed, and were funded by al Qaeda, to attack the tourists on the eve of the millennium. Another example is the cell of Islamic militants who were arrested in Milan in October 2001 after wiretaps placed by Italian authorities revealed discussions of attacks on American interests being planned in the expectation that al Qaeda would fund them.

4. *Like-minded insurgents, guerrillas, and terrorists.* This level embraces existing insurgent

or terrorist groups who over the years have benefited from bin Laden's largesse and/or spiritual guidance; received training in Afghanistan from al Qaeda; or have been provided with arms, materiel, and other assistance by the organization. These activities reflect bin Laden's "revolutionary philanthropy": that is, the aid he provides to Islamic groups as part of furthering the cause of global jihad. Among the recipients of this assistance have been insurgent forces in Uzbekistan and Indonesia, Chechnya, and the Philippines, Bosnia and Kashmir, and so on. This philanthropy is meant not only hopefully to create a jihad "critical mass" out of these geographically scattered, disparate movements, but also to facilitate a quid pro quo situation, where al Qaeda operatives can call on the logistical services and manpower resources provided locally by these groups.

Underpinning these operational levels is bin Laden's vision, self-perpetuating mythology and skilled acumen at effective communications. His message is simple. According to bin Laden's propaganda, the United States is a hegemonic, status quo power; opposing change and propping up corrupt and reprobate regimes that would not exist but for American backing. Bin Laden also believes that the United States is risk and casualty averse and therefore cannot bear the pain or suffer the losses inflicted by terrorist attack. Americans and the American military, moreover, are regarded by bin Laden and his minions as cowards: cowards who only fight with high-tech, airborne-delivered munitions. The Red Army, he has observed, at least fought the mujahedin in Afghanistan on the ground; America, bin Laden has maintained, only fights from the air with cruise missiles and bombs. In this respect, bin Laden has often argued that terrorism works—especially against America. He cites the withdrawal of the U.S. Marines, following the 1983 barracks bombing, from the multinational force deployed to Beirut and how the deaths of 18 U.S. Army Rangers (an account of which is described in the best-selling book by Mark Bowden, *Black Hawk Down,* and current film of the same title)—a far smaller number—prompted the precipitous U.S. withdrawal from Somalia a decade later.[30]

Finally, it should never be forgotten that some 20 years ago bin Laden consciously sought to make his own mark in life as a patron of *jihad*—holy war. In the early 1980s, he was drawn to Afghanistan, where he helped to rally—and even more critically, fund—the Muslim guerrilla forces resisting that country's Soviet invaders. Their success in repelling one of the world's two superpowers had a lasting impact on bin Laden. To his mind, Russia's defeat in Afghanistan set in motion the chain of events that resulted in the collapse of the U.S.S.R. and the demise of communism. It is this same self-confidence coupled with an abiding sense of divinely ordained historical inevitability that has convinced bin Laden that he and his fighters cannot but triumph in the struggle against America. Indeed, he has often described the United States as a "paper tiger" on the verge of financial ruin and total collapse—with the force of Islam poised to push America over the precipice.

Remarkably, given his mindset, bin Laden would likely cling to the same presumptions despite the destruction of the Taliban and liberation of Afghanistan during this first phase of the war against terrorism. To him and his followers, the United States is doing even more now than before to promote global stability (in their view, to preserve the status quo) and ensure the longevity of precisely those morally bankrupt regimes in places like Egypt, Saudi Arabia, the Gulf, Pakistan, Uzbekistan, and elsewhere whom bin Laden and his followers despise. In bin Laden's perception of the war in Afghanistan, most of the fighting has been done by the Northern Alliance—the equivalent of the native levies of imperial times; though instead of being led by British officers as in the past, they are now guided by U.S. military special operations personnel. Moreover, for bin Laden—like guerrillas and terrorists everywhere—not losing is winning. To his mind, even if terrorism did not work on September 11 in dealing the knockout blow to American resolve that bin Laden hoped to achieve, he can still persuasively claim to have been responsible for having a seismic effect on the United States, if not the entire world. Whatever else, bin Laden is one of the few persons who can argue that they have changed the course of history. The United States, in his view, remains fundamentally corrupt and weak, on the verge of collapse, as bin Laden crowed in the videotape released last year about the "trillions of dollars" of economic losses caused by the September 11 attacks. More recently, Ahmed Omar Sheikh, the chief suspect in the killing of American journalist, Daniel Pearl, echoed this same point. While being led out of a Pakistani court in March, he exhorted anyone listening to "sell your dollars, because America will be finished soon."[31]

Today, added to this fundamental enmity is now the even more potent and powerful motivation of revenge for the destruction of the Taliban and America's "war on Islam." To bin Laden and his followers, despite overwhelming evidence to the contrary, the United States is probably still regarded as a "paper tiger," a favorite phrase of bin Laden's, whose collapse can be attained provided al Qaeda survives the current onslaught in Afghanistan in some form or another. Indeed, although weakened, al Qaeda has not been destroyed and at least some of its capability to inflict pain, albeit at a greatly diminished level from September 11, likely still remains intact. In this respect, the multiyear time lag of all prior al Qaeda spectaculars is fundamentally disquieting because it suggests that some monumental operation might have already been set in motion just prior to September 11.

## FUTURE THREATS AND POTENTIALITIES

Rather than asking what could or could not happen, it might be more profitable to focus on understanding what has not happened for the light this inquiry can shed on possible future al Qaeda attacks. This approach actually remains among the most under-studied and in turn conspicuous lacunae of terrorism studies. Many academic terrorism analyses—when they venture into the realm of future possibilities if at all—do so only tepidly. In the main, they are self-limited to mostly lurid hypotheses of worst-case scenarios, almost exclusively involving CBRN (chemical, biological, radiological or nuclear) weapons, as opposed to trying to understand why—with the exception of September 11—terrorists have only rarely realized their true killing potential.

Among the key unanswered questions include:

- Why haven't terrorists regularly used man-portable surface-to-air missiles (SAMs/MANPADS) to attack civil aviation?
- Why haven't terrorists employed such simpler and more easily obtainable weapons like rocket-propelled grenades (RPGs) to attack civil aviation by targeting planes while taking off or landing?
- Why haven't terrorists used unmanned drones or one-person ultra-light or micro-light aircraft to attack heavily defended targets from the air that are too difficult to gain access to on the ground?
- Why haven't terrorists engaged in mass simultaneous attacks with very basic conventional weapons, such as car bombs, more often?
- Why haven't terrorists used tactics of massive disruption—both mass transit and electronic (cyber)—more often?
- Why haven't terrorists perpetrated more maritime attacks, especially against cruise ships loaded with holidaymakers or cargo vessels carrying hazardous materials (such as liquefied natural gas or [LNG])?
- Why haven't terrorists engaged in agricultural or livestock terrorism (which is far easier and more effective than against humans) using biological agents?
- Why haven't terrorists exploited the immense psychological potential of limited, discrete use of CBRN weapons and cyberattacks more often?
- Why haven't terrorists targeted industrial or chemical plants with conventional explosives in hopes of replicating a Bhopol with thousands dead or permanently injured?
- And, finally, why—again with the exception of September 11—do terrorists generally seem to lack the rich imaginations of Hollywood movie producers, thriller writers, and others?

Alarmingly, many of these tactics and weapons have in fact already been used by terrorists—and often with considerable success. The 1998 downing of a civilian Lion Air flight from Jaffna to Colombo by Tamil Tigers using a Russian-manufactured SA-14 is a case in point. The aforementioned series of car bombings that convulsed Bombay in 1993 is another. The IRA's effective paralyzing of road and rail-commuting traffic around London in 1997 and 1998 is one more as were the similar tactics used by the Japanese Middle Core to shut down commuting in Tokyo a decade earlier. And in 1997, the Tamil Tigers launched one of the few documented cyber-terrorist attacks when they shut down the servers and e-mail capabilities of the Sri Lanka embassies in Seoul, Washington, D.C., and Ottawa. As these examples illustrate, terrorists retain an enormous capability to inflict pain and suffering without resorting to mass destruction or mass casualties on the order of the September 11 attacks. This middle range, between worst-case scenario and more likely means of attack is where the United States remains dangerously vulnerable. Terrorists seek constantly to identify vulnerabilities and exploit gaps in U.S. defenses. It was precisely the identification of this vulnerability in the middle range of America's pain threshold that led to the events of that tragic day.

## CONCLUSION

Terrorism is perhaps best viewed as the archetypal shark in the water. It must constantly move forward to survive and indeed to succeed. Although survival entails obviating the governmental countermeasures designed to unearth and destroy the terrorists and their organization, success is dependent on overcoming the defenses and physical security barriers designed to thwart attack. In these respects, the necessity for change in order to stay one step ahead of the counterterrorism curve compels terrorists to change—adjusting and adapting their tactics, modus operandi, and sometimes even their weapons systems as needed.[32] The better, more determined, and more sophisticated terrorists will therefore always find a way to carry on their struggle.

The loss of physical sanctuaries—the most long-standing effect that the U.S.-led war on terrorism is likely to achieve—will signal only the death knell of terrorism as it has been known. In a new era of terrorism, "virtual" attacks from "virtual sanctuaries," involving anonymous cyberassaults may become more appealing for a new generation of terrorists unable to absorb the means and methods of conventional assault

techniques as they once did in capacious training camps. Indeed, the attraction for such attacks will likely grow as American society itself becomes ever more dependent on electronic means of commerce and communication. One lesson from last October's anthrax cases and the immense disruption it caused the U.S. Postal Service may be to impel more rapidly than might otherwise have been the case the use of electronic banking and other online commercial activities. The attraction therefore for a terrorist group to bring down a system that is likely to become increasingly dependent on electronic means of communication and commerce cannot be dismissed. Indeed, Zawahiri once scolded his followers for not paying greater attention to the fears and phobias of their enemy, in that instance, Americans' intense preoccupation with the threat of bioterrorism. The next great challenge from terrorism may therefore be in cyberspace.

Similarly, the attraction to employ more exotic, however crude, weapons like low-level biological and chemical agents may also increase. Although these materials might be far removed from the heinous capabilities of true WMD (weapons of mass destruction) another lesson from last October's anthrax exposure incidents was that terrorists do not have to kill 3,000 people to create panic and foment fear and insecurity: five persons dying in mysterious circumstances is quite effective at unnerving an entire nation.

This article has hitherto discussed and hypothesized about terrorism. What, in conclusion, should be done about it? How should it be viewed? First, it should be recognized that terrorism is, always has been, and always will be instrumental: planned, purposeful, and premeditated. The challenge that analysts face is in identifying and understanding the rationale and "inner logic"[33] that motivates terrorists and animates terrorism. It is easier to dismiss terrorists as irrational homicidal maniacs than to comprehend the depth of their frustration, the core of their aims and motivations, and to appreciate how these considerations affect their choice of tactics and targets. To effectively fight terrorism, a better understanding of terrorists and terrorism must be gained than has been the case in the past.

Second, it must be recognized that terrorism is fundamentally a form of psychological warfare. This is not to say that people do not tragically die or that assets and property are not wantonly destroyed. It is, however, important to note that terrorism is designed, as it has always been, to have profound psychological repercussions on a target audience. Fear and intimidation are precisely the terrorists' timeless stock-in-trade. Significantly, terrorism is also designed to undermine confidence in government and leadership and to rent the fabric of trust that bonds society. It is used to create unbridled fear, dark insecurity, and reverberating panic. Terrorists seek to elicit an irrational, emotional response. Countermeasures therefore must be at once designed to blunt that threat but also to utilize the full range of means that can be brought to bear in countering terrorism: psychological as well as physical; diplomatic as well as military; economic as well as persuasion.

Third, the United States and all democratic countries that value personal freedom and fundamental civil liberties will remain vulnerable to terrorism. The fundamental asymmetry of `the inability to protect all targets all the time against all possible attacks ensures that terrorism will continue to remain attractive to our enemies. In this respect, both political leaders and the American public must have realistic expectations of what can and cannot be achieved in the war on terrorism and, indeed, the vulnerabilities that exist inherently in any open and democratic society.

Fourth, the enmity felt in many places throughout the world towards the United States will likely not diminish. America is invariably seen as a hegemonic, status quo power and more so as the world's lone superpower. Diplomatic efforts, particularly involving renewed public diplomacy activities are therefore needed at least to effect and influence successor generations of would-be terrorists, even if the current generation has already been missed.

Finally, terrorism is a perennial, ceaseless struggle. Although a war against terrorism may be needed to sustain the political and popular will that has often been missing in the past, war by definition implies finality. The struggle against terrorism, however, is never-ending. Terrorism has existed for 2,000 years and owes its survival to an ability to adapt and adjust to challenges and countermeasures and to continue to identify and exploit its opponent's vulnerabilities. For success against terrorism, efforts must be as tireless, innovative, and dynamic as that of the opponent.

## NOTES

1. The lone exception was 1995, when a major increase in non-lethal terrorist attacks against property in Germany and Turkey by PKK (Kurdistan Workers' Party) not only moved the US to the number two position but is also credited with accounting for that year's dramatic rise in the total number of incidents from 322 to 440. See Office of the Coordinator for Counterterrorism, *Patterns of Global Terrorism 1999*. Washington, D.C., U.S. Department of State Publication 10321, April 1996, p. 1.

2. Several factors can account for this phenomenon, in addition to America's position as the sole remaining superpower and leader of the free world. These include the geographical scope and diversity of America's overseas business interests, the number of Americans traveling or working abroad, and the many U.S. military bases around the world.

3. See "Timetables of the Hijacked Flights," in Reporters, Writers, and Editors of Der Spiegel Magazine, *Inside 9–11: What Really Happened* (NY: St. Martin's, 2002), pp. 261–262.

4. Brian M. Jenkins, "The Organization Men: Anatomy of a Terrorist Attack," in James F. Hoge, Jr. and Gideon Rose, *How Did This Happen? Terrorism and the New War* (NY: Public Affairs, 2001), p. 5.

5. Some 440 persons perished in a 1978 fire deliberately set by terrorists at a movie theater in Abadan, Iran.

6. Celia W. Dugger, "Victims of '93 Bombay Terror Wary of U.S. Motives," *New York Times*, 24 September 2001.

7. Several other potentially high lethality simultaneous attacks during the 1980s were averted. These include, a 1985 plot by Sikh separatists in India and Canada to simultaneously bomb three aircraft while in flight (one succeeded: the downing of an Air India flight while en route from Montréal, Québec, to London, England, in which 329 persons were killed); a Palestinian plot to bomb two separate Pan Am flights in 1982 and perhaps the most infamous and ambitious of all pre-September 11 incidents: Ramzi Ahmed Yousef's "Bojinka" plan to bring down 12 American airliners over the Pacific. See Jenkins, "The Organization Men: Anatomy of a Terrorist Attack," p. 6.

8. See Yoram Schweitzer, "Suicide Terrorism: Development and Main Characteristics," in The International Policy Institute for Counter-Terrorism at the Interdisciplinary Center Herzliya, *Countering Suicide Terrorism: An International Conference*

(Jerusalem and Hewlett, NY: Gefen, 2001), p. 76.

9. See bin Laden's comments about this on the videotape released by the U.S. Government in November 2001, a verbatim transcript of which is reproduced in ibid., pp. 313–321.

10. "Wedded to death in a blaze of glory—Profile: The suicide bomber," *The Sunday Times* (London), 10 March 1996; and Christopher Walker, "Palestinian 'Was Duped into Being Suicide Bomber,'" *The Times* (London), 27 March 1997.

11. See Reporters, Writers, and Editors, *Inside 9–11,* on pp. 304–313.

12. See, for example, Jenkins, "The Organization Men," p. 8.

13. See in particular the work of Dr. Rohan Gunaratna of St. Andrews University in this area and specifically his "Suicide Terrorism in Sri Lanka and India," in International Policy, *Countering Suicide Terrors,* pp. 97–104.

14. It is now believed that planning for the attack on an American warship in Aden harbor commenced some two to three weeks before the August 1998 attacks on the East Africa embassies. Discussion with U.S. Naval Intelligence Service agent investigating the Cole attack. December 2001.

15. See Steven Simon and Daniel Benjamin, "American and the New Terrorism," *Survival,* vol. 42, no. 1, Spring 2000, pp. 59–75 and the "America and the New Terrorism: An Exchange" by Olivier Roy, Bruce Hoffman, Reuven Paz, Steven Simon and Daniel Benjamin, *Survival,* vol. 42, no. 2, Summer 2000, pp. 156–172. In it Simon and Benjamin aver that I had become "too closely bound to the academic fashion of the moment . . ." (p. 171). As I told both Simon and Benjamin after September 11: their observation was indeed correct.

16. Brian Michael Jenkins, "International Terrorism: A New Mode of Conflict," in David Carlton and Carlo Schaerf (eds.), *International Terrorism and World Security* (London: Croom Helm, 1975), p. 15.

17. See, for example, the discussion of two former members of the U.S. National Security Staff, Daniel Benjamin and Steven Simon, on the effects of the al-Shifa on the Clinton Administration and its counterterrorism policy post the August 1998 embassy bombings. Daniel Benjamin and Steven Simon, "A Failure of Intelligence?" in Robert B. Silvers and Barbara Epstein (eds), *Striking Terror: America's New War* (NY: New York Review of Books, 2002), pp. 279–299.

18. It should be noted that on many occasions, the Director of Central Intelligence, George Tenent, warned in Congressional testimony and elsewhere of the profound and growing threat posed by bin Laden and al Qaeda to US national security.

➤19. See Peter L. Bergen, *Holy War, Inc.: Inside the Secret World of Osama bin Laden* (NY: Free Press, 2001), pp. 14–15.

20. Bruce Hoffman, "Terrorism's CEO: An On-Line Interview with Peter Bergen, author of *Holy War, Inc.,*" at http://www.theatlantic.com, January 2002.

21. Bergen, *Holy War, Inc.,* p. 28.

22. Ibid., p. 28.

23. Ibid., p. 27.

24. Ali Muhammad, a former major in the Egyptian Army, enlisted in the U.S. Army, where he served as a non-commissioned officer at Fort Bragg, North Carolina, teaching U.S. Special Forces about Middle Eastern culture and politics. Muhammad, among other al Qaeda operatives, like Wadi el-Hoge, demonstrates how al-Qaeda found the U.S. a comfortable and unthreatening operational environment. See Hoffman, "Terrorism's CEO," www.theatlantic.com/unbound/interviews/int2002–01–09.html.

25. Reporters, Writers, and Editor, *Inside 9–11,* p. 317.

26. Ibid., p. 319.

27. Ibid., p. 317.

28. T. E. Lawrence, *Seven Pillars of Wisdom* (Harmondsworth: Penguin Books, 1977), p. 23.

29. Neil MacFarquhar with Jim Rutenberg, "Bin Laden, in a Taped Speech, Says Attacks in Afghanistan Are a War Against Islam," *New York Times,* November 4, 2001, p. B2.

29. Mark Bowden, *Black Hawk Down: A story of Modern War* (NY: Atlantic Monthly Press, 1999).

31. Raymond Bonner, "Suspect in Killing of Reporter Is Brash and Threatening in a Pakistani Court," *New York Times,* 13 March 2002.

32. Bruce Hoffman, *Inside Terrorism* (London: Orion and NY: Columbia Univ. Press, 1998), pp. 180–183.

33. My colleague at St. Andrews University, Dr Magnus Ranstorp's, formulation.

# The Unipolar Moment Revisited

Charles Krauthammer

> *It has been assumed that the old bipolar world would beget a multipolar world with power dispersed to new centers in Japan, Germany (and/or "Europe"), China and a diminished Soviet Union/Russia. [This is] mistaken. The immediate post-Cold War world is not multipolar. It is unipolar. The center of world power is an unchallenged superpower, the United States, attended by its Western Allies.*
>
> "The Unipolar Movement," 1990[1]

In late 1990, shortly before the collapse of the Soviet Union, it was clear that the world we had known for half a century was disappearing. The question was what would succeed it. I suggested then that we had already entered the "unipolar moment." The gap in power between the leading nation and all the others was so unprecedented as to yield an international structure unique to modern history: unipolarity.

At the time, this thesis was generally seen as either wild optimism or simple American arrogance. The conventional wisdom was that with the demise of the Soviet empire the bipolarity of the second half of the 20th century would yield to multipolarity. The declinist school, led by Paul Kennedy, held that America, suffering from "imperial overstretch," was already in relative decline. The Asian enthusiasm, popularized by (among others) James Fallows, saw the second coming of the Rising Sun. The conventional wisdom was best captured by Senator Paul Tsongas: "The Cold War is over; Japan won."

They were wrong, and no one has put it more forcefully than Paul Kennedy himself in a classic recantation published earlier this year. "Nothing has ever existed like this disparity of power; nothing," he said of America's position today. "Charlemagne's empire was merely western European in its reach. The Roman empire stretched farther afield, but there was another great empire in Persia, and a larger one in China. There is, therefore, no comparison."[2] Not everyone is convinced. Samuel Huntington argued in 1999 that we had entered not a unipolar world but a "uni-multipolar world."[3] Tony

Judt writes mockingly of the "loud boasts of unipolarity and hegemony" heard in Washington today.[4] But as Stephen Brooks and William Wohlforth argue in a recent review of the subject, those denying unipolarity can do so only by applying a ridiculous standard: that America be able to achieve all its goals everywhere all by itself. This is a standard not for unipolarity but for divinity. Among mortals, and in the context of the last half millennium of history, the current structure of the international system is clear: "If today's American primacy does not constitute unipolarity, then nothing ever will."[5]

A second feature of this new post-Cold War world, I ventured, would be a resurgent American isolationism. I was wrong. It turns out that the new norm for America is not post-World War I withdrawal but post-World War II engagement. In the 1990s, Pat Buchanan gave 1930s isolationism a run. He ended up carrying Palm Beach.

Finally, I suggested that a third feature of this new unipolar world would be an increase rather than a decrease in the threat of war, and that it would come from a new source: weapons of mass destruction wielded by rogue states. This would constitute a revolution in international relations, given that in the past it was great powers who presented the principal threats to world peace.

Where are we twelve years later? The two defining features of the new post-Cold War world remain: unipolarity and rogue states with weapons of mass destruction. Indeed, these characteristics have grown even more pronounced.

> *The true geopolitical structure of the post-Cold War world . . . [is] a single pole of world power that consists of the United States at the apex of the industrial West. Perhaps it is more accurate to say the United States and behind it the West.*
>
> "The Unipolar Moment," 1990

Contrary to expectation, the United States has not regressed to the mean; rather, its dominance has dramatically increased. And during our holiday from history in the 1990s, the rogue state/WMD problem grew more acute. Indeed, we are now on the eve of history's first war over weapons of mass destruction.

## UNIPOLARITY AFTER SEPTEMBER 11, 2001

There is little need to rehearse the acceleration of unipolarity in the 1990s. Japan, whose claim to power rested exclusively on economics, went into economic decline. Germany stagnated. The Soviet Union ceased to exist, contracting into a smaller, radically weakened Russia. The European Union turned inward toward the great project of integration and built a strong social infrastructure at the expense of military capacity. Only China grew in strength, but coming from so far behind, it will be decades before it can challenge American primacy—and that assumes that its current growth continues unabated.

The result is the dominance of a single power unlike anything ever seen. Even at its height Britain could always be seriously challenged by the next greatest powers. Britain had a smaller army than the land powers of Europe and its navy was equaled by the next two navies combined. Today, American military spending exceeds that of the next *twenty* countries combined. Its navy, air force, and space power are unrivaled. Its technology is irresistible. It is dominant by every measure: military, economic, technological, diplomatic, cultural, even linguistic, with a myriad of countries trying to fend off the inexorable march of Internet-fueled MTV English.

American dominance has not gone unnoticed. During the 1990s, it was mainly China and Russia that denounced unipolarity in their occasional joint communiqués. As the new century dawned it was on everyone's lips. A French foreign minister dubbed the United States not a superpower but a hyperpower. The dominant concern of foreign policy establishments everywhere became understanding and living with the 800-pound American gorilla.

And then September 11 *heightened* the asymmetry. It did so in three ways. First, and most obviously, it led to a demonstration of heretofore latent American military power; Kosovo, the first war ever fought and won exclusively from the air, had given a hint of America's quantum leap in military power (and the enormous gap that had developed between American and European military capabilities). But it took September 11 for the United States to unleash, with concentrated fury, a fuller display of its power in Afghanistan. Being a relatively pacific, commercial republic, the United States does not go around looking for demonstration wars. This one was thrust upon it. In response, America showed that at a range of 7,000 miles and with but a handful of losses, it could destroy within weeks a hardened, fanatical regime favored by geography and climate in the "graveyard of empires."

Such power might have been demonstrated earlier, but it was not. "I talked with the previous U.S. administration," said Vladimir Putin shortly after September 11,

> and pointed out the bin Laden issue to them. They wrung their hands so helplessly and said, "the Taliban are not turning him over, what can one do?" I remember I was surprised: If they are not turning him over, one has to think and do something.[6]

Nothing was done. President Clinton and others in his administration have protested that nothing could have been done, that even the 1998 African embassy bombings were not enough to mobilize the American people to strike back seriously against terrorism. The new Bush Administration, too, did not give the prospect of mass-casualty terrorism (and the recommendations of the Hart-Rudman Commission) the priority it deserved. Without September 11, the giant would surely have slept longer. The world would have been aware of America's size and potential, but not its ferocity or its full capacities. (Paul Kennedy's homage to American power, for example, was offered in the wake of the Afghan campaign.)

Second, September 11 demonstrated a new form of American strength. The center of its economy was struck, its aviation shut down, Congress brought to a halt, the government sent underground, the country paralyzed and fearful. Yet within days the markets reopened, the economy began its recovery, the president mobilized the nation, and a united Congress immediately underwrote a huge new worldwide campaign against terror. The Pentagon started planning the U.S. military response even as its demolished western facade still smoldered.

America had long been perceived as invulnerable. That illusion was shattered on September 11, 2001. But with a demonstration of its recuperative powers—an economy and political system so deeply rooted and fundamentally sound that it could spring back to life within days—that sense of invulnerability assumed a new character. It was transmuted from impermeability to resilience, the product of unrivaled human, technological, and political reserves.

The third effect of September 11 was to accelerate the realignment of the current great powers, such as they are, behind the United States. In 1990, America's principal ally was NATO. A decade later, its alliance base had grown to include former members of the Warsaw Pact. Some of the major powers, however, remained uncommitted. Russia and China flirted with the idea of an "anti-hegemonic alliance." Russian leaders made ostentatious visits to pieces of the old Soviet empire such as Cuba and North Korea. India and Pakistan, frozen out by the United States because of their nuclear testing, remained focused mainly on one another. But after September 11, the bystanders came calling. Pakistan made an immediate strategic decision to join the American camp. India enlisted with equal alacrity, offering the United States basing, overflight rights, and a level of cooperation unheard of during its half century of Nehruist genuflection to

anti-American non-alignment. Russia's Putin, seeing both a coincidence of interests in the fight against Islamic radicalism and an opportunity to gain acceptance in the Western camp, dramatically realigned Russian foreign policy toward the United States. (Russia has already been rewarded with a larger role in NATO and tacit American recognition of Russia's interests in its "near abroad.") China remains more distant but, also having a coincidence of interests with the United States in fighting Islamic radicalism, it has cooperated with the war on terror and muted its competition with America in the Pacific.

The realignment of the fence-sitters simply accentuates the historical anomaly of American unipolarity. Our experience with hegemony historically is that it inevitably creates a counterbalancing coalition of weaker powers, most recently against Napoleonic France and Germany (twice) in the 20th century. Nature abhors a vacuum; history abhors hegemony. Yet during the first decade of American unipolarity no such counterbalancing occurred. On the contrary, the great powers lined up behind the United States, all the more so after September 11.

---

> *The most crucial new element in the post-Cold War world [is] the emergence of a new strategic environment marked by the proliferation of weapons of mass destruction.... The proliferation of weapons of mass destruction and their means of delivery will constitute the greatest single threat to world security for the rest of our lives. That is what makes a new international order not an imperial dream or a Wilsonian fantasy but a matter of the sheerest prudence. It is slowly dawning on the West that there is a need to establish some new regime to police these weapons and those who brandish them.... Iraq ... is the prototype of this new strategic threat.*
>
> "The Unipolar Moment," 1990

---

The American hegemon has no great power enemies, an historical oddity of the first order. Yet it does face a serious threat to its dominance, indeed to its essential security. It comes from a source even more historically odd; an archipelago of rogue states (some connected with transnational terrorists) wielding weapons of mass destruction.

The threat is not trivial. It is the single greatest danger to the United States because, for all of America's dominance, and for all of its recently demonstrated resilience, there is one thing it might not survive: decapitation. The detonation of a dozen nuclear weapons in major American cities, or the spreading of smallpox or anthrax throughout the general population, is an existential threat. It is perhaps the only realistic threat to America as a functioning hegemon, perhaps even to America as a functioning modern society.

> *It is of course banal to say that modern technology has shrunk the world. But the obvious corollary, that in a shrunken world the divide between regional superpowers and great powers is radically narrowed, is rarely drawn. Missiles shrink distance. Nuclear (or chemical or biological) devices multiply power. Both can be bought at market. Consequently, the geopolitical map is irrevocably altered. Fifty years ago, Germany—centrally located, highly industrial, and heavily populated— could pose a threat to world security and to the other great powers. It was inconceivable that a relatively small Middle Eastern state with an almost entirely imported industrial base could do anything more than threaten its neighbors. The central truth of the coming era is that this is no longer the case: relatively small, peripheral, and backward states will be able to emerge rapidly as threats not only to regional, but to world, security.*
>
> "The Unipolar Moment," 1990

Like unipolarity, this is historically unique. WMD are not new, nor are rogue states. Their conjunction is. We have had fifty years of experience with nuclear weapons—but in the context of bipolarity, which gave the system a predictable, if perilous, stability. We have just now entered an era in which the capacity for inflicting mass death, and thus posing a threat both to world peace and to the dominant power, resides in small, peripheral states.

What does this conjunction of unique circumstances—unipolarity and the proliferation of terrible weapons—mean for American foreign policy? That the first and most urgent task is protection from these weapons. The catalyst for this realization was again September 11. Throughout the 1990s, it had been assumed that WMD posed no emergency because traditional concepts of deterrence would hold. September 11 revealed the possibility of future WMD-armed enemies both undeterrable and potentially undetectable. The 9/11 suicide bombers were undeterrable; the author of the subsequent anthrax attacks has proven undetectable. The possible alliance of rogue states with such undeterrables and undetectables—and the possible transfer to them of weapons of mass destruction—presents a new strategic situation that demands a new strategic doctrine.

> *Any solution will have to include three elements: denying, disarming, and defending. First, we will have to develop a new regime, similar to COCOM (Coordinating Committee on Export Controls) to deny yet more high technology to such states. Second, those states that acquire such weapons anyway will have to submit to strict outside control or risk being physically disarmed. A final element must be the development of antiballistic missile and air defense systems to defend against those weapons that do escape Western control or preemption. . . . There is no alternative to confronting, deterring and, if necessary, disarming states that brandish and use weapons of mass destruction. And there is no one to do that but the United States, backed by as many allies as will join the endeavor.*
>
> "The Unipolar Moment," 1990

## THE CRISIS OF UNIPOLARITY

Accordingly, not one but a host of new doctrines have come tumbling out since September 11. First came the with-us-or-against-us ultimatum to any state aiding, abetting, or harboring terrorists. Then, pre-emptive attack on any enemy state developing weapons of mass destruction. And now, regime change in any such state.

The boldness of these policies—or, as much of the world contends, their arrogance— is breathtaking. The American anti-terrorism ultimatum, it is said, is high-handed and permits the arbitrary application of American power everywhere. Pre-emption is said to violate traditional doctrines of just war. And regime change, as Henry Kissinger has argued, threatens 350 years of post-Westphalian international practice. Taken together, they amount to an unprecedented assertion of American freedom of action and a definitive statement of a new American unilateralism.

To be sure, these are not the first instances of American unilateralism. Before September 11, the Bush Administration had acted unilaterally, but on more minor matters, such as the Kyoto Protocol and the Biological Weapons Convention, and with less bluntness, as in its protracted negotiations with Russia over the ABM treaty. The "axis of evil" speech of January 29, however, took unilateralism to a new level. Latent resentments about American willfulness are latent no more. American dominance, which had been tolerated if not welcomed, is now producing such irritation and hostility in once friendly quarters, such as Europe, that some suggest we have arrived at the end of the opposition-free grace period that America had enjoyed during the unipolar moment.[7]

In short, post-9/11 U.S. unilateralism has produced the first crisis of unipolarity. It revolves around the central question of the unipolar age: Who will define the hegemon's ends?

The issue is not one of style but of purpose. Secretary of Defense Donald Rumsfeld gave the classic formulation of unilateralism when he said (regarding the Afghan war and the war on terrorism, but the principle is universal), "The mission determines the coalition." We take our friends where we find them, but only in order to help us in accomplishing the mission. The mission comes first, and we decide it.

Contrast this with the classic case study of multilateralism at work: the U.S. decision in February 1991 to conclude the Gulf War. As the Iraqi army was fleeing, the first Bush Administration had to decide its final goal: the liberation of Kuwait or regime change in Iraq. It stopped at Kuwait. Why? Because, as Brent Scowcroft has explained, going further would have fractured the coalition, gone against our promises to allies, and violated the UN resolutions under which we were acting. "Had we added occupation of Iraq and removal of Saddam Hussein to those objectives," wrote

Scowcroft in the *Washington Post* on October 16, 2001, " . . . our Arab allies, refusing to countenance an invasion of an Arab colleague, would have deserted us." The coalition defined the mission.

Who should define American ends today? This is a question of agency but it leads directly to a fundamental question of policy. If the coalition—whether NATO, the wider Western alliance, *ad hoc* outfits such as the Gulf War alliance, the UN, or the "international community"—defines America's mission, we have one vision of America's role in the world. If, on the other hand, the mission defines the coalition, we have an entirely different vision.

> *A large segment of American opinion doubts the legitimacy of unilateral American action but accepts quite readily actions undertaken by the "world community" acting in concert. Why it should matter to Americans that their actions get a Security Council nod from, say, Deng Xiaoping and the butchers of Tiananmen Square is beyond me. But to many Americans it matters. It is largely for domestic reasons, therefore, that American political leaders make sure to dress unilateral action in multilateral clothing. The danger, of course, is that they might come to believe their own pretense.*
>
> "The Unipolar Moment," 1990

## LIBERAL INTERNATIONALISM

For many Americans, multilateralism is no pretense. On the contrary: It has become the very core of the liberal internationalist school of American foreign policy. In the October 2002 debate authorizing the use of force in Iraq, the Democratic chairman of the Senate Armed Services Committee, Carl Levin, proposed authorizing the president to act only with prior approval from the UN Security Council. Senator Edward Kennedy put it succinctly while addressing the Johns Hopkins School of Advanced International Studies on September 27: "I'm waiting for the final recommendation of the Security Council before I'm going to say how I'm going to vote."

This logic is deeply puzzling. How exactly does the Security Council confer moral authority on American action? The Security Council is a committee of great powers, heirs to the victors in the Second World War. They manage the world in their own interest. The Security Council is, on the very rare occasions when it actually works, realpolitik by committee. But by what logic is it a repository of international morality? How does the approval of France and Russia, acting clearly and rationally in pursuit of their own interests in Iraq (largely oil and investment), confer legitimacy on an invasion?

That question was beyond me twelve years ago. It remains beyond me now. Yet this kind of logic utterly dominated the intervening Clinton years. The 1990s were marked by an obsession with "international legality" as expressed by this or that Security Council resolution. To take one long forgotten example: After an Iraqi provocation in February 1998, President Clinton gave a speech at the Pentagon laying the foundation for an attack on Iraq (one of many that never came). He cited as justification for the use of force the need to enforce Iraqi promises made under post-Gulf War ceasefire conditions that "the United Nations demanded—not the United States—the United Nations." Note the formulation. Here is the president of the most powerful nation on earth stopping in mid-sentence to stress the primacy of commitments made to the UN over those made to the United States.

This was not surprising from a president whose first inaugural address pledged American action when "the will and conscience of the international community is defied." Early in the Clinton years, Madeleine Albright formulated the vision of the liberal internationalist school then in power as "assertive multilateralism." Its principal diplomatic activity was the pursuit of a dizzying array of universal treaties on chemical weapons, biological weapons, nuclear testing, global environment, land mines and the like. Its trademark was consultation: Clinton was famous for sending Secretary of State Warren Christopher on long trips (for example, through Europe on Balkan policy) or endless shuttles (uncountable pilgrimages to Damascus) to consult; he invariably returned home empty-handed and diminished. And its principal objective was good international

citizenship: It was argued on myriad foreign policy issues that we could not do $X$ because it would leave us "isolated." Thus in 1997 the Senate passed a chemical weapons convention that even some of its proponents admitted was unenforceable, largely because of the argument that everyone else had signed it and that failure to ratify would leave us isolated. Isolation, in and of itself, was seen as a diminished and even morally suspect condition.

A lesson in isolation occurred during the 1997 negotiations in Oslo over the land mine treaty. One of the rare holdouts, interestingly enough, was Finland. Finding himself scolded by his neighbors for opposing the land mine ban, the Finnish prime minister noted tartly that this was a "very convenient" pose for the "other Nordic countries" who "want Finland to be their land mine."

In many parts of the world, a thin line of American GIs is the land mine. The main reason we oppose the land mine treaty is that we need them in the DMZ in Korea. We man the lines there. Sweden and France and Canada do not have to worry about a North Korean invasion killing thousands of their soldiers. As the unipolar power and thus guarantor of peace in places where Swedes do not tread, we need weapons that others do not. Being uniquely situated in the world, we cannot afford the empty platitudes of allies not quite candid enough to admit that they live under the umbrella of American power. That often leaves us "isolated."

Multilateralism is the liberal internationalist's means of saving us from this shameful condition. But the point of the multilateralist imperative is not merely psychological. It has a clear and coherent geopolitical objective. It is a means that defines the ends. Its means—internationalism (the moral, legal and strategic primacy of international institutions over national interests) and legalism (the belief that the sinews of stability are laws, treaties and binding international contracts)—are in service to a larger vision: remaking the international system in the image of domestic civil society. The multilateralist imperative seeks to establish an international order based not on sovereignty and power but on interdependence—a new order that, as Secretary of State Cordell Hull said upon returning from the Moscow

Conference of 1943, abolishes the "need for spheres of influence, for alliances, for balance of power."

Liberal internationalism seeks through multilateralism to transcend power politics, narrow national interest and, ultimately, the nation-state itself. The nation-state is seen as some kind of archaic residue of an anarchic past, an affront to the vision of a domesticated international arena. This is why liberal thinkers embrace the erosion of sovereignty promised by the new information technologies and the easy movement of capital across borders. They welcome the decline of sovereignty as the road to the new globalism of a norm-driven, legally-bound international system broken to the mold of domestic society.[8]

The greatest sovereign, of course, is the American superpower, which is why liberal internationalists feel such acute discomfort with American dominance. To achieve their vision, America too—America especially—must be domesticated. Their project is thus to restrain America by building an entangling web of interdependence, tying down Gulliver with myriad strings that diminish his overweening power. Who, after all, was the ABM treaty or a land mine treaty going to restrain? North Korea?

This liberal internationalist vision—the multilateral handcuffing of American power—is, as Robert Kagan has pointed out, the dominant view in Europe.[9] That is to be expected, given Europe's weakness and America's power. But it is a mistake to see this as only a European view. The idea of a new international community with self-governing institutions and self-enforcing norms—the vision that requires the domestication of American power—is the view of the Democratic Party in the United States and of a large part of the American foreign policy establishment. They spent the last decade in power fashioning precisely those multilateral ties to restrain the American Gulliver and remake him into a tame international citizen.[10] The multilateralist project is to use—indeed, to use up—current American dominance to create a new international system in which new norms of legalism and interdependence rule in America's place—in short, a system that is no longer unipolar.

> *There is much pious talk about a new multilateral world and the promise of the United Nations as guarantor of a new post-Cold War order. But this is to mistake cause and effect, the United States and the United Nations. The United Nations is guarantor of nothing. Except in a formal sense, it can hardly be said to exist. Collective security? In the Gulf, without the United States leading and prodding, bribing and blackmailing, no one would have stirred. . . . The world would have written off Kuwait the way the last body pledged to collective security, the League of Nations, wrote off Abyssinia.*
>
> "The Unipolar Moment," 1990

## REALISM AND THE NEW UNILATERALISM

The basic division between the two major foreign policy schools in America centers on the question of what is, and what should be, the fundamental basis of international relations: paper or power. Liberal internationalism envisions a world order that, like domestic society, is governed by laws and not men. Realists see this vision as hopelessly utopian. The history of paper treaties—from the prewar Kellogg-Briand Pact and Munich to the post-Cold War Oslo accords and the 1994 Agreed Framework with North Korea—is a history of naiveté and cynicism, a combination both toxic and volatile that invariably ends badly. Trade agreements with Canada are one thing. Pieces of parchment to which existential enemies affix a signature are quite another. They are worse than worthless because they give a false sense of security and breed complacency. For the realist, the ultimate determinant of the most basic elements of international life—security, stability and peace—is power.

Which is why a realist would hardly forfeit the current unipolarity for the vain promise of goo-goo one-worldism. Nor, however, should a realist want to forfeit unipolarity for the familiarity of traditional multipolarity. Multipolarity is inherently fluid and unpredictable. Europe practiced multipolarity for centuries and found it so unstable and bloody, culminating in 1914 in the catastrophic collapse of delicately balanced alliance systems, that Europe sought its permanent abolition in political and economic union. Having abjured multipolarity for the region, it is odd in the extreme to then prefer multipolarity for the world.

Less can be said about the destiny of unipolarity. It is too new. Yet we do have the history of the last decade, our only modern experience with unipolarity, and it was a decade of unusual stability among all major powers. It would be foolish to project from just a ten-year experience, but that experience does call into question the basis for the claims that unipolarity is intrinsically unstable or impossible to sustain in a mass democracy.

I would argue that unipolarity, managed benignly, is far more likely to keep the peace. Benignity is, of course, in the eye of the beholder. But the American claim to benignity is not mere self-congratulation. We have a track record. Consider one of history's rare controlled experiments. In the 1940s, lines were drawn through three peoples—Germans, Koreans, and Chinese—one side closely bound to the United States, the other to its adversary. It turned into a controlled experiment because both states in the divided lands shared a common culture. Fifty years later the results are in. Does anyone doubt the superiority, both moral and material, of West Germany vs. East Germany, South Korea vs. North Korea, and Taiwan vs. China?[11]

Benignity is also manifest in the way others welcome our power. It is the reason, for example, that the Pacific Rim countries are loath to see our military presence diminished: They know that the United States is not an imperial power with a desire to rule other countries—which is why they so readily accept it as a balancer. It is the reason, too, why Europe, so seized with complaints about American high-handedness, nonetheless reacts with alarm to the occasional suggestion that America might withdraw its military presence. America came, but it did not come to rule. Unlike other hegemons and would-be hegemons, it does not entertain a grand vision of a new world. No Thousand Year Reich. No New Soviet Man. It has no great desire to remake human nature, to conquer for the extraction of natural resources, or to rule for the simple pleasure of dominion. Indeed, America is the first hegemonic power in history to be obsessed with "exit strategies." It could not wait to get out of Haiti and Somalia; it

would get out of Kosovo and Bosnia today if it could. Its principal aim is to maintain the stability and relative tranquility of the current international system by enforcing, maintaining and extending the current peace.

The form of realism that I am arguing for— call it the new unilateralism—is clear in its determination to self-consciously and confidently deploy American power in pursuit of those global ends. Note: global ends. There is a form of unilateralism that is devoted only to narrow American self-interest and it has a name, too: It is called isolationism. Critics of the new unilateralism often confuse it with isolationism because both are prepared to unashamedly exercise American power. But isolationists *oppose* America acting as a unipolar power not because they disagree with the unilateral means, but because they deem the ends far too broad. Isolationists would abandon the larger world and use American power exclusively for the narrowest of American interests: manning Fortress America by defending the American homeland and putting up barriers to trade and immigration.

The new unilateralism defines American interests far beyond narrow self-defense. In particular, it identifies two other major interests, both global: extending the peace by advancing democracy and preserving the peace by acting as balancer of last resort. Britain was the balancer in Europe, joining the weaker coalition against the stronger to create equilibrium. America's unique global power allows it to be the balancer in every region. We balanced Iraq by supporting its weaker neighbors in the Gulf War. We balance China by supporting the ring of smaller states at its periphery (from South Korea to Taiwan, even to Vietnam). Our role in the Balkans was essentially to create a microbalance: to support the weaker Bosnian Muslims against their more dominant neighbors, and subsequently to support the weaker Albanian Kosovars against the Serbs.

Of course, both of these tasks often advance American national interests as well. The promotion of democracy multiplies the number of nations likely to be friendly to the United States, and regional equilibria produce stability that benefits a commercial republic like the United States. America's (intended) exertions on behalf of pre-emptive non-proliferation, too, are clearly in the interest of both the United States and the international system as a whole.

Critics find this paradoxical: acting unilaterally but for global ends. Why paradoxical? One can hardly argue that depriving Saddam (and potentially, terrorists) of WMD is not a global end. Unilateralism may be required to pursue this end. We may be left isolated in so doing, but we would be acting nevertheless in the name of global interests—larger than narrow American self-interest and larger, too, than the narrowly perceived self-interest of smaller, weaker powers (even great powers) that dare not confront the rising danger.

What is the essence of that larger interest? Most broadly defined, it is maintaining a stable, open, and functioning unipolar system. Liberal internationalists disdain that goal as too selfish, as it makes paramount the preservation of both American power and independence. Isolationists reject the goal as too selfless, for defining American interests too globally and thus too generously.

A third critique comes from what might be called pragmatic realists, who see the new unilateralism I have outlined as hubristic, and whose objections are practical. They are prepared to engage in a pragmatic multilateralism. They value great power concert. They seek Security Council support not because it confers any moral authority, but because it spreads risk. In their view, a single hegemon risks far more violent resentment than would a power that consistently acts as *primus inter pares,* sharing rule-making functions with others.[12]

I have my doubts. The United States made an extraordinary effort in the Gulf War to get UN support, share decision-making, assemble a coalition and, as we have seen, deny itself the fruits of victory in order to honor coalition goals. Did that diminish the anti-American feeling in the region? Did it garner support for subsequent Iraq policy dictated by the original acquiescence to the coalition?

The attacks of September 11 were planned during the Clinton Administration, an administration that made a fetish of consultation and did its utmost to subordinate American hegemony and smother unipolarity. The resentments were hardly assuaged. Why? Because the extremist rage against the United States is engendered by the very structure of the international system, not by the details of our management of it.

Pragmatic realists also value international support in the interest of sharing burdens, on the theory that sharing decision-making enlists others in our own hegemonic enterprise and makes things less costly. If you are too vigorous in asserting yourself in the short-term, they argue, you are likely to injure yourself in the long-term when you encounter problems that require the full cooperation of other partners, such as counterterrorism. As Brooks and Wohlforth put it, "Straining relationships now will lead only to a more challenging policy environment later on."[13]

If the concern about the new unilateralism is that American assertiveness be judiciously rationed, and that one needs to think long-term, it is hard to disagree. One does not go it alone or dictate terms on every issue. On some issues, such as membership in and support of the WTO, where the long-term benefit both to the American national interest and to global interests is demonstrable, one willingly constricts sovereignty. Trade agreements are easy calls, however, free trade being perhaps the only mathematically provable political good. Others require great skepticism. The Kyoto Protocol, for example, would have harmed the American economy while doing nothing for the global environment. (Increased emissions from China, India, and Third World countries exempt from its provisions would have more than made up for American cuts.) Kyoto failed on its merits, but was nonetheless pushed because the rest of the world supported it. The same case was made for the chemical and biological weapons treaties—sure, they are useless or worse, but why not give in there in order to build good will for future needs? But appeasing multilateralism does not assuage it; appeasement merely legitimizes it. Repeated acquiescence to provisions that America deems injurious reinforces the notion that legitimacy derives from international consensus, thus undermining America's future freedom of action—and thus contradicting the pragmatic realists' own goals.

America must be guided by its independent judgment, both about its own interest and about the global interest. Especially on matters of national security, war-making, and the deployment of power, America should neither defer nor contract out decision-making, particularly when the concessions involve permanent structural constrictions such as those imposed by an International Criminal Court. Prudence, yes. No need to act the superpower in East Timor or Bosnia. But there is a need to do so in Afghanistan and in Iraq. No need to act the superpower on steel tariffs. But there is a need to do so on missile defense.

The prudent exercise of power allows, indeed calls for, occasional concessions on non-vital issues if only to maintain psychological good will. Arrogance and gratuitous high-handedness are counterproductive. But we should not delude ourselves as to what psychological good will buys. Countries will cooperate with us, first, out of their own self-interest and, second, out of the need and desire to cultivate good relations with the world's superpower. Warm and fuzzy feelings are a distant third. Take counterterrorism. After the attack on the U.S.S. *Cole,* Yemen did everything it could to stymie the American investigation. It lifted not a finger to press terrorism. This was under an American administration that was obsessively accommodating and multilateralist. Today, under the most unilateralist of administrations, Yemen has decided to assist in the war on terrorism. This was not a result of a sudden attack of good will toward America. It was a result of the war in Afghanistan, which concentrated the mind of heretofore recalcitrant states like Yemen on the costs of non-cooperation with the United States.[14] Coalitions are not made by superpowers going begging hat in hand. They are made by asserting a position and inviting others to join. What "pragmatic" realists often fail to realize is that unilateralism is the high road to multilateralism. When George Bush senior said of the Iraqi invasion of Kuwait, "this will not stand," and made it clear that he was prepared to act alone if necessary, that declaration—and the credibility of American determination to act unilaterally—in and of itself created a coalition. Hafez al-Asad did not join out of feelings of good will. He joined because no one wants to be left at the dock when the hegemon is sailing.

Unilateralism does not mean *seeking* to act alone. One acts in concert with others if possible. Unilateralism simply means that one does not allow oneself to be hostage to others. No unilateralist would, say, reject Security Council support for an attack on Iraq. The nontrivial question that separates unilateralism from multilateralism—and that tests the "pragmatic realists"—is this: What do you do if, at the end of the day, the Security Council refuses to back you? Do you allow yourself to be dictated to on issues of vital national—and international—security?

When I first proposed the unipolar model in 1990, I suggested that we should accept both its burdens and opportunities and that, if America did not wreck its economy, unipolarity could last thirty or forty years. That seemed bold at the time. Today, it seems rather modest. The unipolar moment has become the unipolar era. It remains true, however, that its durability will be decided at home. It will depend largely on whether it is welcomed by Americans or seen as a burden to be shed—either because we are too good for the world (the isolationist critique) or because we are not worthy of it (the liberal internationalist critique).

The new unilateralism argues explicitly and unashamedly for maintaining unipolarity, for sustaining America's unrivaled dominance for the foreseeable future. It could be a long future, assuming we successfully manage the single greatest threat, namely, weapons of mass destruction in the hands of rogue states. This in itself will require the aggressive and confident application of unipolar power rather than falling back, as we did in the 1990s, on paralyzing multilateralism. The future of the unipolar era hinges on whether America is governed by those who wish to retain, augment and use unipolarity to advance not just American but global ends, or whether America is governed by those who wish to give it up—either by allowing unipolarity to decay as they retreat to Fortress America, or by passing on the burden by gradually transferring power to multilateral institutions as heirs to American hegemony. The challenge to unipolarity is not from the outside but from the inside. The choice is ours. To impiously paraphrase Benjamin Franklin: History has given you an empire, if you will keep it.

## NOTES

1. This quotation, and all subsequent boxed quotations in this essay, are from Charles Krauthammer, "The Unipolar Moment," *Foreign Affairs: America and the World* (1990/91), which introduced the idea of American unipolarity. That essay was adapted

from the first annual Henry M. Jackson Memorial Lecture, September 18, 1990.

2. Kennedy, "The Eagle has Landed," *Financial Times,* February 2, 2002.

3. Huntington, "The Lonely Superpower," *Foreign Affairs* (March/April 1999). By uni-multipolar Huntington means a system with a pre-eminent state whose sole participation is insufficient for the resolution of international issues. The superpower can still serve as a veto player, but requires other powers to achieve its ends.

4. Judt, "Its Own Worst Enemy," *New York Review of Books,* August 15, 2002.

5. Brooks and Wohlforth, "American Primacy in Perspective," *Foreign Affairs* (July/August 2002).

6. Interview with the German newspaper *Bild,* translated and reported in the *Interfax News Bulletin,* September 21, 2001.

7. A Sky News poll finds that even the British public considers George W. Bush a greater threat to world peace than Saddam Hussein. The poll was conducted September 2–6, 2002.

8. See my "A World Imagined," *The New Republic,* March 15, 1999, from which some of the foregoing discussion is drawn.

9. Kagan, "Power and Weakness," *Policy Review* (June 2002).

10. In "A World Imagined," I noted the oddity of an American governing elite adopting a goal—a constrained America—that is more logically the goal of foreigners: "The ultimate irony is that this is traditionally the vision of small nations. They wish to level the playing field with the big boys. For them, treaties, international institutions, and interdependence are the great equalizers. Leveling is fine for them. But for us? The greatest power in the world—the most dominant power relative to its rivals that the world has seen since the Roman empire—is led by people who seek to diminish that dominance and level the international arena."

11. This is not to claim, by any means, a perfect record of benignity. America has often made and continues to make alliances with unpleasant authoritarian regimes. As I argued recently in *Time* ("Dictatorships and Double Standards," September 23, 2002), such alliances are nonetheless justified so long as they are instrumental (meant to defeat the larger evil) and temporary (expire with the emergency). When Hitler was defeated, we stopped coddling Stalin. Forty years later, as the Soviet threat receded, the United States was instrumental in easing Pinochet out of power and overthrowing Marcos. We withdrew our support for these dictators once the two conditions that justified such alliances had disappeared: The global threat of Soviet communism had receded, and truly democratic domestic alternatives to these dictators had emerged.

12. This basic view is well represented in *The National Interest*'s Fall 2002 symposium, "September 11th One Year On: Power, Purpose, and Strategy in U.S. Foreign Policy."

13. Brooks and Wohlforth, "American Primacy in Perspective."

14. The most recent and dramatic demonstration of this newfound cooperation was the CIA killing on November 4 of an Al-Qaeda leader in Yemen using a remotely operated Predator drone.

## Foreword: Freedom and Security After September 11

Viet D. Dinh

An oft-repeated refrain since the September 11 terrorist attacks is that Americans must now choose between a robust national defense and their vital civil liberties. Security versus freedom: the underlying assumption is that the two can coexist only uneasily in times of national crisis. The loss of certain freedoms, so goes the prevailing wisdom, is the price that must be paid for additional security. Some are eager to make that exchange, while others consider the price too dear. Both sides, however, seem to agree that freedom and security are competing virtues, and that the expansion of one necessarily entails the contraction of the other.

This is not a new dichotomy. In 1759, Benjamin Franklin reminded his fellow colonists that "they that can give up essential liberty to obtain a little temporary safety deserve neither liberty nor safety."[1] For Franklin, liberty is the supreme good, and a people capable of surrendering its freedoms in exchange for security is not fit for self-governance, or even "safety." A century later, Abraham Lincoln appeared before Congress to justify his unilateral decision to suspend the writ of habeas corpus. "[A]re all the laws, but one," the president asked, "to go unexecuted, and the government itself go to pieces, lest that one be violated?"[2] For Lincoln, the Great Emancipator, liberty was an obstacle to the government's proper functioning and, worse, a threat to the government's very existence.

The dichotomy between freedom and security is not new, but it is false. For security and freedom are not rivals in the universe of possible goods; rather, they are interrelated, mutually reinforcing goods. Security is the very precondition of freedom. Edmund Burke teaches that civil liberties cannot exist unless a state exists to vindicate them: "[t]he only liberty I mean is a liberty connected with order; that not only exists along with order and virtue, but which cannot exist at all without them."[3] In the same way that an individual's moral right to property would be meaningless unless the government establishes courts of law in which those rights can be declared and enforced, so too Americans' civil liberties would be a nullity unless they are protected from those who seek to destroy our way of life.

If much post-September 11 commentary mistakenly casts security as a rival to freedom, it also exhibits an unduly narrow understanding of freedom itself. "Freedom" does not refer simply to the absence of governmental restraint; it also refers, at a more fundamental level, to the absence of fear. Terrorists do not measure success with a body count. Their objective is to spread fear among all Americans, preventing our nation from playing an active part on the world's stage and our citizens from living their lives in the manner to which they are accustomed. Without confidence in the safety of their persons and the security of their Nation, Americans will not be able to go about doing those ordinary things that make America an extraordinary nation.

As the Department of Justice prosecutes the war on terror, we have committed to protect Americans not just against unwarranted governmental intrusion, but also against the incapacitating fear that terrorists seek to engender. To ensure the safety of our citizens and the security of our Nation, the Department has fundamentally redefined our mission. The enemy we confront is a multinational network of evil that is fanatically committed to the slaughter of innocents. Unlike enemies that we have faced in past wars, this one operates cravenly, in disguise. It may operate through so-called "sleeper" cells, sending terrorist agents into potential target areas, where they may assume outwardly normal identities, waiting months, sometimes years, before springing into action to carry out or assist terrorist attacks.[4] And unlike garden-variety criminals the Department has investigated and prosecuted in the past, terrorists are willing to give up their own lives to take the lives of thousands of innocent citizens. We cannot afford to wait for them to execute their plans; the death toll is too high; the consequences too great. We must neutralize terrorists *before* they strike.

To respond to this threat of terrorism, the Department has pursued an aggressive and systematic campaign that utilizes all available information, all authorized investigative techniques, and all legal authorities at our disposal. The overriding goal is to prevent and disrupt terrorist activity by questioning, investigating, and arresting those who violate the law and threaten our national security. In doing so, we take care to discharge fully our responsibility to uphold the laws and Constitution of the United States. All investigative techniques we employ are legally permissible under applicable constitutional, statutory, and regulatory standards. As the President and the Attorney General have stated repeatedly, we will not permit, and we have not permitted, our values to fall victim to the terrorist attacks of September 11.

The Department of Justice has taken a number of concrete steps to advance the goal of incapacitating terrorists before they are able to claim another innocent American life. First, the Department has detained a number of persons on immigration or federal criminal charges. Second, in cooperation with our colleagues in state and local law enforcement, the Department's Anti-Terrorism Task Forces have conducted voluntary interviews of individuals who may have information relating to our investigation. Third, the Bureau of Prisons has promulgated a regulation that permits the monitoring of communications between a limited class of detainees and their lawyers, after providing notice to the detainees. And fourth, the President has exercised his congressionally delegated authority to establish military commissions, which would try non-citizen terrorists for offenses against the laws of war.

With respect to detentions, the Department has taken several hundred persons into custody in connection with our investigation of the September 11 attacks. Every one of these detentions is consistent with established constitutional and statutory authority. Each of the detainees has been charged with a violation of either immigration law or criminal law, or is the subject of a material witness warrant issued by a court. The aim of the strategy is to reduce the risk of terrorist attacks on American soil, and the Department's detention policy already may have paid dividends. These detentions may have incapacitated an Al Qaeda sleeper cell that was planning to strike a target in Washington, DC—perhaps the Capitol building—soon after September 11.[5]

The detainees enjoy a variety of rights, both procedural and substantive. Each of them has the right of access to counsel. In the criminal cases and in the case of material witnesses, the person has the right to a lawyer at the government's expense if he cannot afford one. Persons detained on immigration violations also have a right of access to counsel, and the Immigration and Naturalization Service provides each person with information about available pro bono representation. Every person detained has access to telephones, which they may use to contact their family members or attorneys, during normal waking hours.

Once taken into INS custody, aliens are given a copy of the "Detainee Handbook," which details their rights and responsibilities, including their living conditions, clothing, visitation, and access to legal materials. In addition, every alien is given a comprehensive medical assessment, including dental and mental health screenings. Aliens are informed of their right to communicate with their nation's consular or diplomatic officers, and, for some

countries, the INS will notify those officials that one of their nationals has been arrested or detained. Finally, Immigration Judges preside over legal proceedings involving aliens, and aliens have the right to appeal any adverse decision, first to the Board of Immigration Appeals, and then to the federal courts.

Second, the Department of Justice has conducted voluntary interviews of individuals who may have information relating to terrorist activity. On November 9, the Attorney General directed all United States Attorneys and members of the joint federal and state Anti-Terrorism Task Forces, or "ATTFs," to meet with certain noncitizens in their jurisdictions. That same day, the Deputy Attorney General issued a memorandum outlining the procedures and questions to be asked during those interviews. The names of approximately 5,000 individuals that were sent to the ATTFs as part of this effort are those who we believe may have information that is helpful to the investigation or to disrupting ongoing terrorist activity. The names were compiled using common-sense criteria that take into account the manner, according to our intelligence sources, in which Al Qaeda traditionally has operated. Thus, for example, the list includes individuals who entered the United States with a passport from a foreign country in which Al Qaeda has operated or recruited; who entered the United States after January 1, 2000; and who are males between the ages of 18 and 33.

The President and Attorney General continually have emphasized that our war on terrorism will be fought not just by our soldiers abroad, but also by civilians here at home. The Department instituted a program that would enable our nation's guests to play a part in this campaign. Non-citizens are being asked, on a purely voluntary basis, to come forward with useful and reliable information about persons who have committed, or who are about to commit, terrorist attacks. Those who do so will qualify for the Responsible Cooperators Program. They may receive S visas or deferred action status that would allow them to remain in the United States for a period of time. Aliens who are granted S visas may later apply to become permanent residents and, ultimately, American citizens. The Responsible Cooperators Program enables us to extend America's promise of freedom to those who help us protect that promise.

Third, the Bureau of Prisons on October 31 promulgated a regulation permitting the monitoring of attorney-client communications in very limited circumstances. Since 1996, BOP regulations have subjected a very small group of the most dangerous federal detainees to "special administrative measures," if the Attorney General determines that unrestricted communication with these detainees could result in death or serious bodily harm to others. Those measures include placing a detainee in administrative detention, limiting or monitoring his correspondence and telephone calls, restricting his opportunity to receive visitors, and limiting his access to members of the news media.[6] The pre-existing regulations cut off all channels of communication through which detainees could plan or foment acts of terrorism, except one: communications through their attorneys. The new regulation closes this loophole. It permits the monitoring of attorney-client communications for these detainees only if the Attorney General, after having invoked the existing special administrative measures authority, makes the additional finding that reasonable suspicion exists to believe that a particular detainee may use communications with attorneys to further or facilitate acts of terrorism.[7] Currently, only 12 of the approximately 158,000 inmates in federal custody would be eligible for monitoring.

The Department has taken steps to protect the attorney-client privilege and the detainees' Sixth Amendment right to the effective assistance of counsel. As an initial matter, not all communications between a lawyer and his client are protected by the attorney-client privilege; statements that are designed to facilitate crimes, including acts of terrorism, are not privileged. The "crime/fraud exception" applies even if the attorney is not aware that he is being used to facilitate crime,[8] and even if the attorney takes no action to assist the client.[9]

Moreover, the monitoring regulation includes a number of procedural safeguards to protect privileged communications.[10] First and foremost, the attorney and client would be given written advance notification that their communication will be monitored pursuant to the regulation. Second, the regulation erects a "firewall" between the team monitoring the communications and the outside world, including persons involved with any ongoing prosecution of the client. Third, absent imminent violence or terrorism, the government would have to obtain court approval before any information from monitored communications is used for any purpose, including for investigative purposes. And fourth, no privileged information would be retained by the monitoring team; only information that is not privileged may be retained.

Finally, the President has authorized military commissions to try members of Al Qaeda and other non-citizen terrorists for violations of the laws of war. Trying terrorists before military commissions offers a number of practical advantages over ordinary civilian trials. First, commissions enable the government to protect classified and other sensitive national security information that would have to be disclosed publicly before an Article III court. Second, ordinary criminal trials would subject court personnel, jurors, and other civilians to the threat of terrorist reprisals; the military is better suited to coping with these dangers. And third, military commissions can operate with more flexible rules of evidence, which would allow the introduction all relevant evidence regardless of whether, for example, it has been properly authenticated.

The Supreme Court has unanimously upheld the constitutionality of military commissions,[11] and since its founding our Nation has used them to try war criminals, as have our international allies. During World War II, President Roosevelt ordered eight Nazi saboteurs tried by military commission. After the Civil War, a commission was used to try Confederate sympathizers who conspired to assassinate President Lincoln. And during the Revolutionary War, General Washington convened a military commission to try British Major Andre as a spy. Moreover, the President's authority to convene military commissions is confirmed by Article 21 of the Uniform Code of Military Justice.[12] In 1942, the Supreme Court interpreted identical language, then appearing in the Articles of War, as recognizing the President's power to try war crimes before military commissions.[13] And America and her allies made liberal use of military commissions after World War II to try war criminals both in the European and Pacific theater.[14]

After September 11, Americans in their own ways have sought answers to the seemingly unfathomable question: why? Because Americans are somehow different from and better than the people of the world? I do not think so. We *are* the people of the world. We are not, as individuals, different from those who would rain terror upon us. But there is something special that defines us as Americans—the benefits and responsibilities of living in this nation. America gives to people who come to her shores the freedom to achieve extraordinary things. Our uniqueness lies in our ability as ordinary people to do extraordinary ordinary things as Americans. It was this foundation of freedom that was under attack.

America's tradition of freedom thus is not an obstacle to be overcome in our campaign to rid the world of individuals capable of the evil we saw on September 11. It is, rather, an integral objective of our campaign to defend and preserve the security of our nation and the safety of our citizens. Indeed, as the images of liberated Afghan men shaving their beards and freed Afghan women shedding their burquas eloquently testify, freedom is itself a weapon in our war on terror. Just as we unleash our armed forces abroad, and empower our law-enforcement officers here at home, America's campaign against terrorism will extend freedom for our citizens, as well as for the people of the world.

## Notes

1. Benjamin Franklin, Historical Review of Pennsylvania (1759), *quoted in* The Oxford Dictionary of Political Quotations 141 (Anthony Jay ed., 1996).

2. Abraham Lincoln, Message to Congress in Special Session (July 4, 1861), *reprinted in* 4 Collected Works of Abraham Lincoln 421, 430 (Roy P. Basler ed., 1953).

3. Edmund Burke, Speech at His Arrival at Bristol Before the Election in That *City (1774)*, *quoted in* Robert H. Bork, Slouching Towards Gomorrah: Modern Liberalism and American Decline 64 (1996).

4. *See, e.g.,* Karen DeYoung, *"Sleeper Cells" of Al Qaeda Are Next Target,* Wash. Post, Dec. 3, 2001, at A1.

5. *See* Jeffrey Bartholet, *Al Qaeda Runs for the Hills,* Newsweek, Dec. 17, 2001, at 21, 23.

6. *See generally* 28 C.F.R. pt. 500 (2001).

7. *See* 28 C.F.R. § 501.3(d) (2001).

8. *See* United States v. Soudan, 812 F.2d 920, 927 (5th Cir. 1986).

9. *See In re* Grand Jury Proceedings, 87 F.3d 377, 382 (9th Cir. 1996).

10. *See generally* 28 C.F.R. § 501.3(d)(1), (2), (3) (2001).

11. *See In re* Yamashita, 327 U.S. 1 (1946); *Ex parte* Quirin, 317 U.S. 1 (1942).

12. *See* 10 U.S.C. § 821 (2001).

13. *See Quirin,* 317 U.S. at 27, 29.

14. *See generally* Dep't of Army, Pam. 27–161–2, International Law, Vol. II, at 235 (1962); Philip R. Piccigallo, The Japanese on Trial; Allied War Crimes Operations in the East, 1945–1951 (1979).

## Review Questions

- Why was September 11, 2001 a turning point for international security policy and theory?
- How did the attacks on the American homeland affect the global community?
- What is the role of the United States in the new security environment? What is the role of the international community?
- In what manner has the debate about freedom and security been shaped by the new era of terrorism?
- Is the new era of terrorism one of permanent domestic and international security realignment, or will this era evolve and ultimately be supplanted by another environment?

The following books and articles are suggested for further information about understanding issues affecting policy and theory in the new era of terrorism:

## Books

Bergen, Peter L. *Holy War, Inc.: Inside the Secret World of Osama bin Laden.* New York: Free Press, 2001.
Gunaratna, Rohan. *Inside Al Qaeda: Global Network of Terror.* New York: Columbia University Press, 2002.
Howard, Russell D. and Reid L. Sawyer, eds. *Terrorism and Counterterrorism: Understanding the New Security Environment, Readings & Interpretations.* Guilford, CT: McGraw-Hill/Dushkin, 2003.


## Articles

Embar-Sedden, Ayn. "Cyberterrorism: Are We Under Siege?" *American Behavioral Scientist.* 45:6 (February 2002).
Hoffman, Bruce. "Change and Continuity in Terrorism." *Studies in Conflict & Terrorism.* 24:5 (September 2001).
Hugo, Slim. "Why Protect Civilians? Innocence, Immunity, and Enmity in War." *International Affairs.* 79:3 (April 2003).

# Part I

# Conceptualizing the Threat in the New Era

*Today, our fellow citizens, our way of life, our very freedom came under attack in a series of deliberate and deadly terrorist acts. The victims were in airplanes or in their offices: secretaries, businessmen and -women, military and federal workers, moms and dads, friends and neighbors. Thousands of lives were suddenly ended by evil, despicable acts of terror. The pictures of airplanes flying into buildings, fires burning, huge structures collapsing have filled us with disbelief, terrible sadness and a quiet, unyielding anger.*

—President George W. Bush
Address to the Nation
September 11, 2001

# 2

---

# THE NEW ERA IN PERSPECTIVE

Prior to the events of September 11, 2001, terrorism was an instrument of revolutionary violence emanating mostly from the political grievances of secular extremists. Terrorist threats to governments and "enemy peoples" usually originated in Marxist-inspired ideologies, rightist reaction, ethno-nationalist imperatives, or idiosyncratic amalgams of these tendencies. Religious terrorism certainly occurred, but until the mid-1990s such violence was largely a sideshow to the predominance of secular ideologies and ethno-nationalist tensions. This older, Cold War-influenced era was gradually supplanted by a newer, deadlier, and primarily sectarian terrorist environment—at first sporadically and then principally. Aside from several seemingly intractable (and localized) ethno-nationalist conflicts in Africa, the Middle East, and Asia, religion has become the driving force behind international terrorist violence in the new era. It is therefore critical to develop a contextual understanding of the characteristics of this transformation.

The articles in this chapter discuss the characteristics of the terrorist environment in the new era. Chris Quillen examines an important characteristic of the new era from a historical perspective in "A Historical Analysis of Mass Casualty Bombers." In particular, an analysis is made of the modern pattern of mass casualty terrorist attacks as a central characterization of the new terrorism. His provocative discussion unfolds within the contexts of modern terrorist typologies. John Mueller's essay, "Harbinger or Aberration? A 9/11 Provocation," critiques the predominant assumption that the September 11, 2001 attacks were an overture to an era of similar attacks. He instead offers an "outlier" position which argues that such attacks are aberrational in the overall history of international conflict and political violence. In "The Imbalance of Terror," Thérèse Delpech summarizes the nature of the terrorist threat in the new era. The essay discusses the agenda of the New Terrorism, new challenges for counterterrorism, and points of instability in the contemporary international environment.

# A Historical Analysis of Mass Casualty Bombers

Chris Quillen
*Oak Ridge Associated Universities, Washington, DC, USA*

*The truth is, I blew up the Murrah building and isn't it kind of scary that one man could reap this kind of hell?*

—Timothy McVeigh[1]

In a world where airliners bring down skyscrapers and anthrax is delivered in the mail, it is important to not forget the devastating effects of conventional explosives in the hands of terrorists. Until the attacks on the World Trade Center and the Pentagon, the deadliest terrorist attacks were all bombings. In spite of the events of 11 September 2001 conventional bombings remain the most likely terrorist method of inflicting mass casualties as evidenced by the recent suicide bombings of an Israeli shopping mall. As such, this particular terrorist tactic is worthy of study as its own unique form of terrorism. Although it is impossible to discuss terrorism without recognizing the September 11 attacks, this article deals with the longer-term trend of mass casualty bombings that is likely to continue and not with the hopefully unique events of that tragic day.

Over the past two decades many "new" forms of terrorism have been identified. In the 1980s it was the state-sponsored terrorist who reportedly represented an entirely new form of warfare. The state-sponsored terrorist had access to a larger, more technologically sophisticated arsenal and, therefore, was alleged to be more deadly than his "freelance" counterpart. Beginning in 1983, the suicide terrorist also became a great concern. With the attack on the U.S. Marine's barracks in Lebanon, suicide terrorism appeared to be an unstoppable and exceedingly deadly new form of terrorism. In the 1990s, with the rise of Christian Identity violence in the United States and the Aum Shinrikyo attack in Japan, religious terrorists received renewed attention especially with regard to possible use of "weapons of mass destruction" (WMD).

The key to each of these new forms of terrorism lay in their ability and their desire to kill large numbers of people. This article argues that the principal thread running through each of these differing aspects of terrorism over the past two decades is that of the mass casualty bomber. Mass casualty bombers are unique in that they possess both the technological and logistical sophistication to construct and employ a large, powerful bomb *and* the willingness to use that bomb to kill large numbers of people—regardless of their state-sponsorship, suicidal tendencies, or religious beliefs.

## DEFINING MASS CASUALTY BOMBERS

The phrase "mass casualty" is clearly a relative term, a fact made obvious by the events of September 11.[2] Until that date, the single deadliest terrorist attack was the 1985 destruction of an Air India flight off the coast of Ireland that killed 329 people.[3] Although mass casualty bombings are more likely to yield deaths in the hundreds rather than the thousands, no one can deny the very real significance of such attacks.

For the purposes of this article an admittedly arbitrary number must be chosen as a cutoff point for mass casualties. That number must be high enough to genuinely reflect the devastation wrought by such attacks, but low enough to yield a useful sample given the traditional terrorist tendency to scare rather than kill. As terrorism expert Brian Jenkins argued in 1985,

Arbitrarily taking 100 deaths as the criterion, it appears that only a handful of incidents of this scale have occurred since the beginning of the century. Lowering the criterion to 50 deaths produces a dozen or more additional incidents. To get even a meaningful sample, the criterion has to be lowered to 25.[4]

Choosing 25 or more casualties does admittedly eliminate many of the most significant terrorist bombings of recent years from the discussion. The 1993 World Trade Center bombing had a significant impact on the American psyche by seriously undermining the belief in U.S. immunity from terrorism at home in spite of the fact that only six people were killed. Recent deadly attacks on U.S. forces in Saudi Arabia and Yemen also fall below this threshold, despite their important implications for American military forces deployed abroad. Not even the assassination of Rajiv Gandhi by the Tamil Tigers or the attempted assassination of the South Korean cabinet by North Korean gents rises to this level of mass casualties.

Obviously then, there is a considerable difference between significance and casualties. Mass casualty bombings will no doubt yield massive attention from the authorities and from the media (in those states with a free press, at least), but may not necessarily yield similarly large effects. Terrorist audiences (the general public) can become desensitized to the violence and push terrorists into increasingly deadly attacks with decreasing effects.[5] Such desensitization may have occurred in Lebanon during the 1980s and is likely still playing itself out in Sri Lanka. High casualties can also yield the wrong kind of effects for a terrorist group. Inadvertently or purposefully killing large numbers of people may cause a backlash among the group's supporters or potential supporters. Such a backlash no doubt led to the swift decline in militia group membership after the Oklahoma City bombing. Similarly, the Real IRA was forced to apologize for the Omagh bombing that killed 28 people (the single most deadly IRA terrorist attack in its history) after a public outcry. High death tolls may also elicit an unexpectedly harsh government response. The Russian government's crackdown in Chechnya after a series of Moscow apartment bombings and the U.S. war in Afghanistan may be examples of this trend.

Even after choosing a number, there are considerable difficulties in conducting the count.

First, identifying the number of persons killed in any given attack is extremely difficult. Prior to an explosion it is generally unknown how many people are in a building or a busy marketplace. (A significant exception is onboard airliners). After an explosion, identifying the number of victims amid the carnage is extremely complicated.

Beyond the actual inability of the authorities to quantify the number of victims is their occasional unwillingness. A government that does not wish to appear weak or does not want to admit to any terrorism on its territory will be tempted to downplay the number of casualties to lessen the perception of terrorist strength.[6] On the other hand, a government wishing to justify the institution of ever more repressive tactics may actually inflate the number of casualties in a terrorist attack.[7] This is a challenge for the analyst that has no easy answer.

Second, there is the issue of suicide terrorists. Although certainly not victims, do they nevertheless count as casualties? Do they not, at least partially, indicate the willingness of the terrorist group to shed blood—including its own? What about the unintentional suicide bomber? Some terrorists have been tricked into becoming martyrs for their cause.[8] Others have inadvertently found themselves in the middle of a car bomb attack while driving their packages to their intended destinations. In many cases it is impossible to separate victims from terrorists among the dead and so it is necessary to count simply casualties without drawing moral distinctions between them. As a practical matter, this tends to drive up the perceived death toll of such attacks. For example, under this methodology the October 2000 bombing of the *U.S.S. Cole* did not simply kill 17 U.S. sailors, but rather killed a total of 19 people.

Third, multiple bombs pose a challenge to quantification of casualties. Many terrorist bombings, especially those yielding large numbers of casualties, involve more than one explosive device. Do 2 bombs that each killed 15 people on the same day count as separate incidents (thus falling below this definition of mass casualty) or as a single incident (thus rising to the level of mass casualty)? In this analysis the casualties from multiple bombings are counted together if they occur on the same day (although not necessarily in the same location) and appear to be part of a coordinated effort. Thus, the bombings of the two U.S. embassies in East Africa in 1998 count as one incident with 224 casualties, even though the attack in Tanzania killed only 11 people and, thus, falls below the mass casualty threshold.

Of course, it is not always clear the terrorists intended to kill such large numbers of people. As a practical matter, terrorists who place a bomb on an airplane can reasonably be suspected of seeking the death of all of its passengers. In other attacks, however, it is not nearly so easy to determine the group's intentions. Just as terrorists sometimes kill fewer than intended, no doubt on occasion they kill more. Terrorists often claim such a "mistake" when their supporters and potential supporters express displeasure at an especially high body count or they fear a harsh government reprisal.

Next is the definition of "terrorism." Far too many trees have been slain and far too much ink spilled already debating the exact definition of terrorism. In the interest of simplicity, the definition used by the Federal Bureau of Investigation will be used: "Terrorism is the unlawful use of force or violence against persons or property to intimidate or coerce a government, the civilian population, or any segment thereof, in furtherance of political or social objectives."[9]

This task is, of course, made somewhat easier by focusing exclusively on the act of bombings and not engaging in a debate about which tactics are indeed terrorist by nature. The challenge lies in separating purely criminal or military bombings from the terrorist ones. For our purposes, criminal bombings perpetrated solely for profit are not included, but those with a wider audience in mind are. An example should suffice. In November 1955, Jack Gilbert Graham placed a bomb on board a passenger plane that killed all 44 persons on board. Graham's reason was simple: he wanted to collect the life insurance policy on one of the passengers—his mother.[10] By comparison, the "Extraditables" (a front for the Medellin drug cartel) blew up an Avianca airliner in 1989 that killed 110 people. Their immediate goal was to silence a police informant on board. However, their broader goal was to intimidate other potential informants and to convince the Colombian government of the danger of extraditing its drug lords to the United States. Thus, although the tactics were essentially the same—blowing up an entire airliner in order to kill one person—the reasons make all the difference between the terrorist and the criminal. Of course, divining a bomber's rationale is not always so easy.

Differentiating between terrorism and covert military operations is similarly difficult. Added to the bomber's motivation is the context of the attack as well as the identity of the attackers and their victims. Are bombings necessarily "military" if the attackers or the targets are of a military nature? Does a state of war need to exist in order for covert attacks to be declared military rather than terrorist? A particularly nettlesome issue involves state-sponsored terrorism and the concomitant blurring of distinctions between state and substate actors. Generally, bombings will be considered terrorist if they are carried out outside of a state of war or if the targets are of a nonmilitary character regardless of the nature or motivations of the attackers. Thus, the July 1987 car bomb attacks in Karachi, Pakistan, which were likely carried out by Soviet-backed Afghan intelligence, are considered terrorist because the target was a civilian marketplace. A similar covert bombing by the Afghans the following April on a Pakistani ammunition dump that supplied the mujahedin, however, is considered a covert military attack because the attack was clearly linked to the ongoing Afghan civil war.[11]

Finally, the time period involved must be delineated and explained. The period selected runs from the end of World War II (14 August 1945) to the end of the twentieth century (31 December 2000). This period was chosen because it contains all of the known modern terrorist motivations from anticolonialism to religious fundamentalism.

## MASS CASUALTY BOMBERS

Mass casualty bombings were carried out on 76 separate occasions in the second half of the twentieth century. In those attacks a total of 5,690 persons were killed for an average killed per attack of nearly 75 people.[12] Perhaps more disturbingly, at least 19 different terrorist groups have been identified as having carried out these bombings.[13]

Not surprisingly, the Tamil Tigers of Tamil Eelam (LTTE) are the most prolific users of the mass casualty bombing attack.[14] The Tigers have been waging an intense guerilla war/terrorist campaign for a separate homeland in the Jaffna peninsula of Sri Lanka since 1983, a conflict that has claimed nearly 60,000 lives to date. In many ways the Tamil Tigers are a unique organization. Their use of suicide bombers is unmatched; until the attack on the *U.S.S. Cole,* the LTTE was virtually the only group to use explosive-laden boats in their attacks; and the Tiger movement itself is probably best described as a broad-based cult rather than an insurgent or terrorist group. These issues, particularly the relationship between cults, religion, and suicide attacks, will be explored further.

*Hezbollah* (Party of God) has perpetrated fewer attacks, but with a higher total killed and a higher average killed per attack than the LTTE.[15] Hezbollah is a Shi'ite Muslim terrorist organization at least partially trained and funded by the Iranian government. The group's goal is to destroy the state of Israel and drive the United States out of the Middle East. It is reasonable to assume that its state-sponsorship gives Hezbollah a higher level of training and technological sophistication that has enabled it to inflict such high numbers of casualties and that its religious orientation has seemingly permitted its attacks to be so deadly.

A similarly state-sponsored terrorist group is the *Mujahedeen-e-Khalq* (MEK), also known as the People's Mujahedeen. Essentially an arm of Iraqi foreign policy, the group has long attacked Iraq's main regional rival, Iran.[16] The most significant and most deadly attack by MEK was the June 1981 bombing of the Islamic Republic Party headquarters in Tehran. Among the 72 people killed was the second most powerful figure in Iran at the time, Supreme Court Chief Justice Ayatollah Mohammed Behesti. Although both Iran and Iraq have recently taken to launching mortar and rocket raids on each other's capitals, their capabilities to carry out such mass casualty bombings remain intact.

The Lebanese civil war in the 1980s saw a disproportionately large number of mass casualty bombings causing over 1,000 deaths.[17] The most prolific mass casualty bombing group was the Front for the Liberation of Lebanon from Foreigners (FLLF).[18] As their name implies, the FLLF was created to keep "foreigners"—Israel, the United States, the United Nations, and Syria—out of Lebanese affairs in what was portrayed as an entirely nationalist affair. The Lebanese civil war, however, also had a major religious component as Muslim and Christian factions fought for control of the countryside. One of these groups, broadly labeled "Christians," engaged in a back-and-forth war of car bombings with various Muslim factions throughout the 1980s.[19] The Popular Front for the Liberation of Palestine (PFLP) and its offshoot, the PFLP-GC (General Command) were also major players in the Lebanese conflict.[20] The PLFP-GC is also accused of having a role (in the planning if not the actual execution phase) in the bombing of Pan Am Flight 103.

Religious/nationalist separatists in Russia and India have resorted to mass casualty bombings in their struggles for independence. The Chechens have been waging a separatist civil war since the late 1990s. In their campaign to drive Russian troops from what they consider to be their independent homeland, the Chechen terrorists engaged in multiple bombings of Russian military sites in and around Chechnya and have been accused of several devastating bombings in Moscow itself.[21] Similarly, the Sikhs have been quite destructive in their fight for independence within India even though their most significant attack occurred over the Atlantic Ocean—the aforementioned destruction of an Air India flight.[22]

By comparison, the Colombian narcoterrorists, the Extraditables, have not sought an independent homeland. Instead, they have desired simply to maintain their existing power base within Colombia and avoid extradition to the United States for prosecution on drug charges. Toward this end, the Extraditables have engaged in both airplane and car bombings in Colombia.[23] Finally, the Afghan government—via its intelligence services—is blamed by Islamabad for two mass casualty car bombings in Pakistan in 1987 and 1995.[24]

A rather long list of terrorist groups has engaged in only one mass casualty bombing for obviously differing reasons. The most prominent is Osama bin Laden's al Qaida organization for the dual bombings of U.S. embassies in East Africa that killed 224 people. The Jewish terrorist group, Irgun, killed 91 British soldiers in their 1946 truck bombing of the King David Hotel in Israel. The neofascist Armed Revolutionary Nuclei (NAR) killed 84 in their attack on a Bologna, Italy train station that they were later forced to repudiate. The Palestine Liberation Organization (PLO) killed 80 in their 1978 attack on the headquarters of the pro-Iraq Palestine Liberation Front. In an apparent assassination attempt on Saddam Hussein (then-Deputy Chairman of the Revolutionary Command Council in Iraq), Free Iraq killed 40 in a bombing attack at the Baghdad airport. The Real IRA killed 28 at Omagh. The Croats, long before the current Yugoslav civil war, killed 27 in a 1972 airliner attack. Hamas also has only one mass casualty bombing—a 1996 suicide bus bombing that killed 26—included here, but carried out a second attack that killed 25 in December 2001.

Significantly, many of the "traditional" terrorist organizations such as the IRA and the PLO are also on this one-time-only list. In the IRA case at least (the Omagh bombing carried out by the Real IRA), the group was forced to apologize after a public backlash. The Irgun also tried to distance themselves from the bombing of the King David Hotel, by citing British failure to evacuate after being warned in advance. The fact that al Qaida appears only once is obviously more a testament to millennial counter-terror actions and heroic efforts to keep the *U.S.S. Cole* afloat than to any restraint or inability on that group's part. Hamas's single appearance would appear to counter the belief that suicide bombers are inherently more deadly (more on this later).

Conspicuous by their absence from this list of mass casualty bombing groups are other "traditional" groups such as the ETA in Spain, the Red Brigades in Italy, the Red Army Faction in Germany, and the Japanese Red Army (JRA). Over the lifetime of the organization, the ETA is responsible for over a thousand deaths; but its single deadliest bomb attack remains the 21 people killed in a car bombing of a Barcelona parking garage in 1987. The other groups have not gone even that far (although the JRA did participate in the Lod Airport Massacre that

claimed 26 lives). Writing in 1975, Jenkins no doubt had such groups in mind when he coined his famous phrase that "Terrorists want a lot of people watching and not a lot of people dead."[25] These "traditional" political terrorist groups clearly were not capable of or not interested in causing mass casualties. Today, unfortunately, too many groups have failed to follow this tradition.

As these examples demonstrate, mass casualty bombers cover a wide range of terrorist groups of varying size, sophistication, and, importantly, motivations. These differences will now be explored in comparison to the other identified "new" forms of terrorism in an attempt to determine what effect state-sponsorship, suicidal tendencies, religious belief, and interest in chemical, biological, radiological, and nuclear (CBRN) weaponry has had and may have on mass casualty bombings.

## STATE-SPONSORED TERRORISTS

In the past two decades the possibility of states sponsoring terrorists has become a serious international concern.[26] Such devastating attacks as the destruction of Pan Am Flight 103 and the bombing of two U.S. embassies in East Africa have been ascribed, at least in part, to national governments. The United States, for one, has responded to such state-sponsorship with military force in Libya, Iraq, Sudan, and, in particular, Afghanistan. After September 11, the battle against state-sponsors has broadened from those providing direct support to terrorist operations to include those states accused of harboring terrorists and providing them safe haven from which to carry out their attacks.

In all, states are implicated in at least 17 mass casualty bombings, killing 1,905 people for an average of 112 dead per attack (compared to 75 for mass casualty bombings generally). Thus, state-sponsored terrorists would appear both more able and more willing to kill in large numbers. As a point of departure for analysis, the U.S. State Department's annual list of terrorism's sponsors will be used.[27]

Iran—via Hezbollah and other groups—leads the list of state-sponsors of mass casualty bombings with six attacks.[28] The single most devastating attack ascribed to Tehran is the simultaneous truck bombing of the U.S. Marines barracks and the French paratroopers headquarters in 1983 that killed a total of 301 people. Also in Beirut in 1983, Tehran is accused of backing mass casualty bombings of the U.S. embassy and the Israeli army headquarters. Iran is also implicated in attacks on two Israeli/Jewish targets in Argentina in the 1990s. Iran's archrival, Iraq—generally via the Mujahedeen e-Khalq—comes in next with four mass casualty bombings.[29] Of those, no fewer than three were perpetrated in Iran including the afore-mentioned assassination of Iran's Supreme Court Chief Justice. Baghdad is also implicated in a 1986 truck bombing in Damascus, Syria that killed 60.

Syria—acting through Hamas, the PFLP-GC, and the Palestinian Islamic Jihad (PIJ)—has allegedly perpetrated three mass casualty bombing attacks.[30] Two of these attacks were airline bombings conducted by the PFLP-GC in the 1970s, the other is the 1996 Hamas suicide bus bombing that killed 26. Libya, which was bombed by the United States for its support of terrorist groups in 1986, has only two mass casualty attacks on its record, but they are two of the deadliest.[31] The downing of Pan Am Flight 103 over Lockerbie, Scotland killed 270 and the destruction of a French UTA airliner over Niger killed 171. Rounding out the list is North Korea with its bombing of a South Korean airliner in 1987 that killed 117 people. Neither Cuba nor Sudan appears to be a sponsor in any of the mass casualty cases.

Other nations not on the State Department's list, however, do appear to have participated in mass casualty bombings. Afghanistan (classified as merely "failing to cooperate" on counterterrorism issues in the State Department's most recent report) is implicated three times. However, to be fair, two of those were under the previous Soviet-backed regime (117 dead in Pakistan) and only one was during the Taliban's watch (224 killed in East Africa). Pakistan also appears to be responsible for sponsorship of two mass casualty bombings. Both of Islamabad's attacks were against India including a devastating series of bombs in Bombay in 1993 that killed 317. Islamabad, however, does not yet appear anywhere on State's list because of its support for U.S. efforts in Afghanistan in opposing the Soviet Union in the 1980s and recent assistance in ousting the Taliban and destroying al Qaida.

Although state-sponsorship does appear to yield better technology and training for terrorists and more suffering for their victims, it is not at all clear that state-sponsorship itself is necessary for mass casualty bombings. Out of 76 cases, a state sponsor can only be identified in 20 attacks. The remaining 56 were apparently carried out without the knowledge or resources of any national government. In addition, of the 19 identified groups that have conducted mass casualty bombings, only 5 (Hezbollah, MEK, PFLP-GC, al Qaida and Hamas) did so with any degree of state sponsorship. National governments generally do not create terrorist groups for their attacks (the obvious exception is North Korea), but use existing groups that have already demonstrated their capability and willingness in such attacks. Thus, for the terrorist seeking to conduct casualty attack state-sponsorship is useful, but far from required.

## SUICIDE TERRORISTS

Although not a new phenomenon, suicide terrorism became a major concern beginning in 1983.[32] In that year the buildings housing the U.S. Marine's peacekeeping force in Beirut were destroyed by an explosive-laden truck driven by a suicide bomber, killing 241 Marines. A few minutes after the explosion took place at the U.S. compound, the building housing the French peacekeeping troops was hit in the same manner, resulting in the death of 58 French paratroopers. The total killed in the simultaneous suicide missions came to 301 (including the suicide bombers).

The United States blamed the attack on Hezbollah and, by extension, Iran. Hezbollah's leader, Hussein Mussawi, praised the attacks against U.S. and French forces, but denied responsibility.[33] Within months U.S. and UN forces withdrew from Lebanon and the civil war continued to rage for several more years (and, in some ways, continues to this very day).

To many, it appeared that a new wave of terrorism had indeed been born in which the terrorists were not only willing to fight, but also willing to die, for their cause. Some blamed the trend on radical Islamic fundamentalism, but the Hindu Tamil Tigers (who coincidentally also began their struggle in earnest in 1983) embraced the method of suicide terrorism quickly and completely. In fact, according to Yoram Schweitzer, since 1983 the LTTE has engaged in more suicide terrorist attacks than all other terrorist organizations *combined*.[34]

Ehud Sprinzak has argued that suicide terrorism, "guarantees mass casualties and extensive damage (since the suicide bomber can choose the exact time, location, and circumstances of the attack)"[35] and that "the most devastating terrorism of our time has been suicide bombing."[36] However, a closer look at the facts reveals far less than Sprinzak believes. Using terrorism expert Yoram Schweitzer's data on suicide terrorism from April 1983 to February 2000,[37] an examination can be made of the same time period for any overlap between suicide terrorism and mass casualty bombings. In that timeframe Schweitzer finds "about 275 suicide incidents" (not necessarily all bombings). During the same dates there were 47 mass casualty bombings of which only 6 (7 if one counts the 1983 Beirut bombings as separate events as Schweitzer does) were suicide attacks. Put another way, during this time period all mass casualty bombings averaged 85 people killed per incident, and the suicide bombings alone averaged 95 killed in each attack. Thus, the average death toll of a suicide attack is somewhat higher, but not surprisingly so. However, after the atypical 301 deaths from the 1983 Beirut bombings are taken out, the average mass casualty suicide attack averages a much lower 54 dead.

Thus, although suicide terrorism may have a major psychological effect (which probably explains its continued use and effectiveness at garnering attention), it does not necessarily involve a higher death toll. There are, of course, two major exceptions: the 1983 Beirut bombings and the September 11 attacks, but they are only that—exceptions. As demonstrated earlier, the vast majority of suicide terrorist attacks are not inherently more devastating than other forms of terrorism. It appears that suicide terrorism and mass casualties may now be forever linked in the popular imagination, but without a strong analytical basis in fact. After all, it is more important that the terrorist is willing to kill than that he is willing to die.

## RELIGIOUS TERRORISTS

More recent concerns have focused on religious terrorists.[38] The close correlation in time of the Aum Shinrikyo attack on the Tokyo subway and the Oklahoma City bombing have led many to make the perceptual connection between religion and mass casualties (and also with WMD as discussed later). Religious terrorism is by no means a new phenomenon,[39] but it seems to have taken on a new fervor in recent years to justify an ever-increasing body count. In this study of mass casualty bombings, a religious motivation can be identified in not only the majority of cases (47), but also in a majority of the casualties (3,952).[40]

Within these cases, Islam is the most common motivating religious tradition, and within Islam, the Sunni branch—not the Shi'a branch so often associated with terrorism because of the Iranian regime—is the most deadly.[41] Much of the Sunni body count comes from five terrorism "spectaculars": the 1988 bombing of Pan Am Flight 103, the 1989 bombing of a French UTA airliner, the 1993 series of bombings in Bombay, the 1998 simultaneous truck bombing of two U.S. embassies, and the 1999 bombing of a Moscow apartment building.

The Shi'a branch of Islam, by comparison, has motivated terrorists to conduct fewer mass casualty bombings, but with a higher average killed per bombing.[42] Virtually all of these attacks were carried out by Hezbollah and supported by the government of Iran. The most devastating was the 1983 simultaneous suicide truck bombing of the U.S. Marine barracks and the French paratroopers headquarters in Beirut.

However, Islam is not the only religious tradition that can be cited for mass casualty bombings—far from it. Sikhism has proven particularly deadly, especially in connection with the Air India disaster that killed 329.[43] Hinduism—via the Tamil Tigers—can be held responsible for an especially high incidence of mass casualty bombings as well.[44] Christianity—including Protestants, Catholics,

Maronites, and even Christian Identists—has motivated at least five mass casualty bombings including its single most deadly attack in Oklahoma City.[45] Finally, Judaism can be cited in only one case, but a significant one: the 1946 bombing of the King David Hotel that killed 91.

Thus, an empirical argument can seemingly be made that religious terrorists are inherently more deadly than other terrorist groups. Such a conclusion, however, suffers from several significant and interconnected flaws.

First, assigning motivations to individual acts of terror is inherently subjective and open to considerable interpretation. (This fact becomes all the more problematic as terrorist groups move away from explicitly claiming their attacks and prefer instead to let their actions speak for themselves.) A particularly apt example comes out of Oklahoma City. Timothy McVeigh could have been (and was) described as a terrorist motivated by religion for his adherence to the Christian Identity movement.[46] However, it now appears that McVeigh viewed himself more as a political terrorist acting in response to the botched federal raids at Ruby Ridge and Waco and out of his virulent opposition to gun control measures.[47] Less often cited, but still possible, is the contention that McVeigh acted on ethnic principles based on his alleged belief in the White supremacy movement.[48]

If identifying the motivation of a single actor in such a heavily analyzed attack as Oklahoma City is so problematic, identifying group motivations across multiple bombings is no doubt an even more daunting challenge. Like the individual actor, the same group can be motivated by different factors at different times from the religious to the nationalist to the political. Moreover, not all bombings are a direct result of the group's principal motivation. Simple retaliatory attacks are common, especially during the Lebanese civil war when car and truck bombs were sent back and forth at a furious pace. Other attacks may focus on assassination in line with or even separate from the group's larger goals.

Second and related to the first is the virtual impossibility of separating religious from ethno-nationalist or separatist motivations. The Palestinian terrorists, for example, could conceivably fall into any (or all) of these categories. Were the Jewish terrorists in British Palestine fighting for religion or against colonialism? Do the Tamil Tigers want their own homeland because they are Hindus in a Muslim nation or because they are Tamils in a Sinhalese country? Divining terrorist intentions in these cases is all but impossible.

Even distinguishing the religious from the political runs into considerable difficulty at times, usually when state-sponsors become involved. Iraqi bombings in Iran and Iranian bombings in Iraq could be expressions of either centuries-old religious animosities or more recent political battles for regional hegemony. Similarly, Pakistani bombings within India reflect both a religious and a political battle over Kashmir.

Cults, which would seemingly offer religious motivation devoid of ethnic or political entanglements, are also not immune to confused motivations. The cultlike Black Tigers within LTTE that carry out the suicide missions of the organization also possess broader religious, ethnic, nationalist, and political goals. Even Aum Shinrikyo, the prototypical terrorist cult (that, to be clear, did not ever engage in mass casualty bombings) also harbored political ambitions including the complete takeover of the Japanese government.

Although it is true that "religious" terrorists are indeed much more willing to kill in large numbers, it is far from clear how one can differentiate the religious from the other terrorists. Given these limitations on identifying motivations, any analysis of "religious" terrorism as a distinct entity is intrinsically suspect. Many of these questions about terrorist motivations are simply unanswerable. In fact, seeking definitive answers may obscure more than it reveals. It is arguably more productive—and considerably less difficult—to study terrorist actions such as mass casualty bombings that are empirically provable rather than terrorist motivations such as religion that are inherently unknowable.

## CBRN TERRORISTS

Finally, the most recently identified "new" form of terrorism involves terrorist use of so-called weapons of mass destruction: chemical, biological, radiological, and nuclear weapons (CBRN).[49]

To date, the examples of terrorist use of CBRN weapons are exceedingly thin. Only two terrorist groups have apparently ever killed with such weapons. The first was Aum Shinrikyo with their sarin gas attack in the Tokyo subway that killed 12 people. The second is the recent wave of anthrax mailings in the United States by an as-yet-unknown group (or individual) that has killed, as of this writing, five people. As psychologically powerful as these events have been, it is worth noting that had they been conventional bombings, these attacks would not have made it onto the list of cases presented here—even if their death tolls were combined.

Nevertheless, there is considerable value in exploring whether or not mass casualty bombers are more or less likely to use CBRN weapons in the future. Any insight into such potential actions must be considered important due to the possible consequences of a CBRN attack. An examination of a potential mass casualty bomber shift from conventional explosives to CBRN weapons largely hinges on the degree to which mass casualty bombers are innovative.

The debate over the degree of terrorist innovation has been raging for years and has no doubt intensified in recent months. Terrorism expert Paul Wilkinson has argued that terrorists are quite innovative and cites advances "such as the barometric pressure bomb to sabotage airliners in flight, the drogue grenade developed by the IRA . . . , and the use of the photo-electric device to fire a bicycle bomb (as used by the Red Army Faction in Germany)."[50] RAND terrorism expert Bruce Hoffman, on the other hand, has argued that terrorists are not innovative and are likely to stick with the gun and the bomb for the foreseeable future. Hoffman counters that, "What innovation does occur is mostly in the methods used to conceal and detonate explosive devices, not in their tactics or in their use of nonconventional weapons."[51] Hoffman is undoubtedly correct when it comes to terrorist innovation regarding conventional explosives, but terrorist tactics do, in fact, appear to have shifted considerably over the past few decades with considerable implications for CBRN terrorism.

Significantly, a major terrorist innovation in tactics was the shift *to* bombings. Terrorists only truly began to focus on bombings after

their preferred targets were hardened. As Jenkins has observed,

> In the 1970s, seizing embassies and kidnapping diplomats were common terrorist tactics. With better security and growing resistance to meeting terrorist demands, embassy takeovers declined but assassinations and bombings increased. Overall, attacks on diplomats went up. . . . If embassies cannot be seized, embassies can be blown up.[52]

Hoffman agreed when it came to airliners (in this now dated quote):

> While these [aviation security] measures were successful in reducing airline hijackings, they did not stop terrorist attacks on commercial airlines altogether. Instead, prevented from smuggling weapons on board to hijack aircraft, terrorists merely continued to attack them by means of bombs hidden in carry-on or checked baggage.[53]

Thus, anti- and counterterrorism policies and measures instituted in response to terrorism forced the terrorists to move away from one set of tactics and toward another.

The probability that countermeasures for terrorism may actually lead terrorists to more deadly avenues of attack must be kept in mind when recommending or adopting such changes. "In many cases, . . . new technologies will be exploited by *both* sides in a kind of high-tech intelligence war between terrorists and counterterrorists." (Italics in original.)[54] Closing down one avenue of attack will then invariably create interest in another. If the terrorist ability to use conventional explosives effectively is significantly curtailed and if aviation security is now truly impossible to penetrate, will these groups now seek to employ CBRN weapons that bypass these defenses altogether? As Wilkinson has noted,

> We should already be anticipating the tactics that the terrorists are likely to use once the method of sabotage bombing [of airliners] has been blocked. For example, we should already be devising ways of preventing terrorists from obtaining and using surface-to-air missiles against civil aviation. And we should be planning defensive and countermeasures to deal with the possible terrorist use

of chemical and biological weapons against such targets as airport terminals.[55]

A final point on the possible terrorist use of CBR (but not necessarily nuclear) weapons should also be made. Conventional explosives have proven to be most deadly when employed against airliners (where most people die from the crash of the plane rather than the explosion) and against multistory buildings (where most people die from the collapse of the building)—two tactics that were combined to devastating effect on September 11. It is precisely this same concentration of large numbers of people in small, confined spaces that is most likely to benefit the terrorist using chemical, biological, or radiological materials. Rather than use an airplane crash or a building collapse to his benefit, this terrorist would theoretically use the limited and controlled air supply in such venues to concentrate his agent to an effective level to produce mass casualties. As Jenkins has noted, "The most plausible scenarios involving chemical or biological weapons in a contained environment—a hotel, a convention, a banquet—would produce deaths in the hundreds."[56] Such attacks are far more likely—and more likely to be deadly—than the much-ballyhooed citywide attack where high concentrations of agent would be exceedingly difficult. Thus, although the principles will be different for mass casualty attacks with conventional explosives and unconventional weapons, the settings will likely be the same.

The connection between the mass casualty bomber and the CBRN terrorist is by no means definitive. The attacks on September 11 were a terrible demonstration of terrorist innovation that, nevertheless, relied on conventional technology to kill on an unprecedented scale. Clearly, terrorists do not have to use CBRN weapons to get to the "next level" of terrorism, but the possible crossover remains worthy of serious consideration. Mass casualty bombers are the most technologically and logistically sophisticated terrorist groups and have repeatedly demonstrated their willingness to kill indiscriminately and in large numbers. Moreover, terrorist innovation in tactics and weaponry is almost exclusively driven by the adoption of anti- and counterterror strategies by national governments. As those governments continue to improve their defenses against conventional explosives, mass casualty bombers will increasingly begin to look elsewhere for their needs. CBRN weapons may provide them an answer.

## CONCLUSIONS

Mass casualty bombers do not have to be sponsored by a government, willing to die, inspired by a god, or interested in exotic weapons in order to kill large numbers of people. Mostly, they just have to be willing to kill. State-sponsorship undoubtedly benefits terrorist groups, but most mass casualty bombings occur, and most such groups exist, without it. Despite significant examples of suicide terrorism, a terrorist's willingness to die is rarely indicative of his ability to kill. Religious motivations, too, may indeed be significant, but it is at best difficult and at worst counterproductive to seek to identify religious motivations as the most important aspect of terrorist activity. Finally, although there would appear to be little link between mass casualty bombers and CBRN terrorists at present, the hardening of targets to conventional explosives may inspire terrorists to expand their arsenal in the future.

## NOTES

1. Timothy McVeigh as quoted in Lois Romano, "McVeigh Admits Bombing That Killed 168," *Washington Post,* 30 March 2001, p. A2.

2. The term "mass casualty" is used throughout this article in accordance with that term's use in the growing literature on "mass casualty terrorism." However, because this article deals solely with fatalities an argument can be made that the term "mass fatality" would be more precise.

3. This number rises to 331 when the 2 casualties from the simultaneous, but failed attack at the Narita airport in Japan are included.

4. Brian Michael Jenkins, *The Likelihood of Nuclear Terrorism,* RAND Paper P-7119 (July 1985), p. 7.

5. Brian Michael Jenkins, *The Future Course of International Terrorism,* RAND Paper P-7139 (September 1985), p. 5. September 11 may be offered as proof of terrorist efforts to counteract this trend.

6. Uighur separatists in Xinjiang Province in China have apparently put Beijing authorities in this position many times.

7. Similar accusations have been leveled against the Russian government by Boris Kagarlitsky, "Terrorism Benefits the State," *The Moscow Times,* 4 September 2001, p. 13.

8. It now appears likely that many, if not most, of the hijackers on September 11 were unaware they were on a suicide mission.

9. 28 Code of Federal Regulations (C.F.R.) Section 0.85.

10. Jay Robert Nash, *Terrorism in the 20th Century* (New York: M. Evans and Company, 1998), p. 327.

11. These incidents, but not this analysis, are taken from the RAND Chronology of International Terrorism.

12. As further testament to the unique nature of the September 11 attacks, twentieth century terrorists took more than 50 years and over 75 different attacks to kill as many people as the four simultaneous hijackings did *in a single day.*

13. This list of cases is principally drawn from the following sources: the RAND Chronology of International Terrorism for international incidents between 1968 and 1998; Jay Robert Nash, "A Chronology of 20th Century Terrorism, 1900–1998" in *Terrorism in the 20th Century: A Narrative Encyclopedia from the Anarchists through the Weathermen to the Unabomber* (New York: M. Evans and Co., 1998), pp. 289–412 for domestic and international events from 1946 to 1998; and author research of open news sources, principally the *New York Times,* for all incidents from 1946 to 2000. A complete chronology with specific references is also available on the website of the Terrorism Research Center (www.terrorism.com).

14. The LTTE is implicated in 13 incidents with 622 casualties—an average of 48 killed per attack.

15. Hezbollah has perpetrated 6 attacks with a death toll of 671 and an average killed per attack of 112. This, however, is a grayer area than with the Tamil Tigers. Hezbollah is a far more amorphous organization with a less set membership and many other competing organizations within the same area of operations. As a practical matter, virtually all bombings in Sri Lanka (especially the mass casualty ones) can be ascribed to the LTTE with reasonable certainty. This is far from the case, however, in the Middle East, where Hezbollah operates. Other organizations within the

area have undoubtedly claimed Hezbollah operations as their own and Hezbollah may have also claimed operations it did not, in fact, carry out.

16. In three attacks within Iran, MEK has killed 157 people for 52 per attack.

17. From 1978 to 1988, Lebanon suffered no fewer than 14 mass casualty bombings for a death toll of 1,113 people. Virtually all of these bombings were carried out in the context of the Lebanese civil war, in which all sides engaged in terrorist bombings as a regular course of action.

18. In only 4 attacks, the FLLF was able to kill 232 people for an average of 58 per attack.

19. These Christian groups killed 155 people in only 3 attacks (51 deaths per bombing).

20. In 3 attacks, the Palestinian organization claimed 405 lives with an average of 135 per attack.

21. The Chechens are blamed for taking 314 lives in only 4 bombings (78 per attack).

22. In only 2 attacks the Sikhs have killed 411 people in mass casualty bombings.

23. 162 killed in 2 separate attacks.

24. Total killed in 2 attacks was 117.

25. Brian Michael Jenkins, *Will Terrorists Go Nuclear?,* RAND Paper P-5541 (November 1975), p. 4.

26. See, for example, Steven Simon and Daniel Benjamin, "America and the New Terrorism," *Survival* 42(1) (Spring 2000).

27. United States Department of State, *Patterns of Global Terrorism* (Washington, DC: U.S. Government Printing Office, 2000), pp. 33–37.

28. 6 mass casualty attacks and 671 killed for an average of almost 112.

29. 4 bombings with a total killed of 217 for an average of 54.

30. 3 bombings killing 161 at an average of nearly 54.

31. 2 attacks with a death toll of 441.

32. See, for example, Yoram Schweitzer, *Suicide Terrorism: Development and Characteristics,* International Policy Institute for Counter-Terrorism, 21 April 2000, available at (www.ict.org.il); Ehud Sprinzak, "Rational Fanatics," *Foreign Policy* (September/October 2000), pp. 66–68; and Harvey Kushner, "Suicide Bombers: Business as Usual," *Studies in Conflict and Terrorism* 19(4) (1996).

33. A tactic very similar to the one used by Osama bin Laden after September 11.

34. 168 compared to 25 each for the next most prolific, Hezbollah/Amal and other Lebanese groups.

Yoram Schweitzer, *Suicide Terrorism: Development and Characteristics.*

35. Sprinzak, "Rational Fanatics," pp. 66–67.

36. Ehud Sprinzak, "Revisiting the Super-terrorism Debate," *Foreign Policy,* available at (www.foreignpolicy.com/issue_SeptOct_2001/sprinzakrevisiting.html).

37. Schweitzer, *Suicide Terrorism.*

38. See, for example, Bruce Hoffman, *Holy Terror: The Implications of Terrorism Motivated by a Religious Imperative,* RAND Paper P-7834 (June 1993); Mark Jurgensmeyer, *Terror in the Mind of God: The Global Rise of Religious Violence* (Berkeley: University of California Press, 2000); and Simon and Benjamin, "America and the New Terrorism."

39. See David Rapoport's seminal article on religious terrorism, "Fear and Trembling: Terrorism in Three Religious Traditions," *American Political Science Review* 78(3) (September 1984), pp. 658–677.

40. Religious terrorists can be claimed in 47 cases out of 76 and for 3,952 deaths out of 5,690 for an average killed per attack of 84 (compared to 75 for all mass casualty bombings).

41. 21 bombings with 1,977 dead for an average of 94 per bombing.

42. 5 bombings that killed 500 people for an average of 100.

43. Sikhs have killed 411 people in only 2 attacks.

44. 622 deaths in the course of 13 attacks.

45. 5 attacks killing 351 people.

46. Jurgensmeyer, *Terror in the Mind of God.*

47. Bruce Hoffman, *Inside Terrorism* (New York: Columbia University Press, 1998), pp. 105–107.

48. Ibid.

49. See, for example, Richard A. Falkenrath, Robert D. Newman, and Bradley A. Thayer, *America's Achilles Heel: Nuclear, Biological, and Chemical Terrorism and Covert Attack* (Cambridge, MA: MIT Press, 1999).

50. Paul Wilkinson, "Editor's Introduction: Technology and Terrorism," *Terrorism and Political Violence,* Special Issue on Technology and Terrorism, 5(2) (Summer 1993), p. 4.

51. Bruce Hoffman, "Terrorist Targeting: Tactics, Trends, and Potentialities," *Terrorism and Political Violence,* Special Issue on Technology and Terrorism, 5(2) (Summer 1993), p. 12.

52. Brian Michael Jenkins, *Some Reflections on Recent Trends in Terrorism,* RAND Paper P-6897 (1983), p. 1.

53. Bruce Hoffman, "Terrorist Targeting: Tactics," p. 21.

54. Wilkinson, "Editor's Introduction," p. 7.

55. Paul Wilkinson, "Designing an Effective International Aviation Security System," *Terrorism and Political Violence,* Special Issue on Technology and Terrorism, 5(2) (Summer 1993), p. 107.

56. Jenkins, *The Future Course,* p. 6.

---

## Harbinger or Aberration? A 9/11 Provocation

John Mueller

The terror attack of September 11, 2001 was quite literally off the charts: no other single act of terrorism has ever done remotely as much damage. Over the course of the entire 20th century, fewer than twenty terrorist attacks managed to kill as many as one hundred people, and none killed more than four hundred. Until September of last year, far more Americans were killed in any given grouping of years by lightning than by all forms of international terrorism combined. Of course, such data beg the central question of the post-9/11 world: Will we revert to the relatively benign levels of the past, or have we really entered a new and nasty era?

Most observers hold to the latter, believing that the September 11 attacks represent a sort of historical step function—the "everything has changed" point of view. Accordingly, they suggest that such extensive destruction to life and property will become common or even routine, particularly if the United States and its allies fail to respond vigorously to the threat. This is hardly a baseless supposition. It is clear that the convergence of certain political and technological trends gives such concerns real logical traction. However, a case can be made that rather than foreshadowing the future, the attacks may turn out to have been a statistical outlier, a kind of tragic blip in the experience of American national security.

One reason to take the outlier thesis seriously is simple enough: There have been several extreme and highly alarming events in recent decades that seemed to imply future patterns, but failed to do so. Indeed, near the beginning of every decade since at least 1930 there came a major shock that many people presumed to mark the beginning of big and very bad trends. The Depression had convinced many by the early 1930s that capitalism was in terminal crisis. At the beginning of the 1940s came World War II; around 1950 came the shock of both the Korean War and the maturation of the balance of thermonuclear terror; in the early 1960s the trauma of the Cuban missile crisis; then the oil crisis and malaise of the early 1970s; then the Iranian hostage crisis and the Soviet invasion of Afghanistan on the very cusp of 1980; then a decade later the seeming prospect of major ethnic warfare around the periphery of former Communist Europe—and now 9/11. It is worth reviewing this record in a bit more detail, and recalling what people had to say about these and other alarming events at the time.

## CRYING WOLF?

World War II was the most destructive war in history. It has yet to inspire a sequel, but that is not how it looked to most in its immediate aftermath when historian Arnold Toynbee confidently argued, "In our recent Western history war has been following war in an ascending order of intensity; and today it is already apparent that the War of 1939–45 was not the climax of this crescendo movement."[1] After V-J Day, Ambassador Joseph Grew, one of America's most perceptive diplomats, concluded that "a future war with the Soviet Union is as certain as anything in this world."[2] Soviet dictator Josef Stalin concurred: "We shall recover in fifteen or twenty years and then we'll have another go

at it."[3] Relatedly, when the Communists successfully fomented a coup in democratic Czechoslovakia in 1948, there were great fears in the West that this would be followed by further Communist takeovers in Europe, especially in Italy and France. Public opinion polls conducted in the United States in the mid-1940s characteristically found 30 to 75 percent opining that, on account of such trends, the next world war would occur within 25 years.[4] Even decades later, the prominent political scientists, Hans J. Morgenthau, announced that "the world is moving ineluctably towards a third world war—a strategic nuclear war. I do not believe that anything can be done to prevent it. The international system is simply too unstable to survive for long."[5]

But something was done to prevent it: It was called the containment policy, carried out more or less skillfully by successive U.S. administrations in the context of the NATO alliance. And thanks in large part to the Marshall Plan, Italy and France were not suborned by Communists.

Communist aggression in Korea in 1950 was deeply alarming. As President Truman put it, "The attack upon Korea makes it plain beyond all doubt that Communism has passed beyond the use of subversion to conquer independent nations and will now use armed invasion and war."[6] Bernard Brodie recalled that the Joint Chiefs "were utterly convinced that the Russians were using Korea as a feint to cause us to deploy our forces there while they prepared to launch a 'general' (i.e., total) war against the United States through a major attack on Europe."[7] The Russians, it turned out, were up to no such thing; there were no other "Koreas" after Korea. (Vietnam arose from Communist insurgency, not direct aggression.)

In the early 1960s, it was widely feared in the United States that Castro's victory in Cuba presaged the embrace of Soviet communism over all Latin America. It didn't. Meanwhile, the Cuban Missile Crisis of October 1962 was the most extreme crisis of the Cold War, and when it was resolved, many felt the Soviets would respond to their failure there by creating trouble somewhere else, probably in Berlin. As Defense Secretary Robert McNamara predicted, "sure as hell they're going to do something there."[8] In other words, the "smart money" postulated that the missile crisis was just the beginning of a more intense phase of confrontation as Soviet military power grew, and so, conditioned by several years of Soviet bluster and swagger, the Americans poised themselves for the next challenge. But it never came: Cuba proved to be the last major direct U.S.-Soviet military-strategic crisis of the Cold War.

When the Soviet Union intervened in Afghanistan in late December 1979, many saw it as an aggressive ploy relevant to the entire Middle East and South Asia. Alarmed that the Soviet probe might be a prologue to further adventures in the oil-rich Persian Gulf area, President Carter sternly threatened to use "any means necessary" to counter a further Soviet military move in the area, a threat reiterated by his successor, Ronald Reagan, the next year.[9] It was the first time Soviet forces had been sent openly into a country outside their empire since 1945. It was also the last.

When ethnic conflicts and warfare broke out on the periphery of Europe in the early 1990s, many expected it to metastasize all over the continent, maybe even leading to a nuclear war between Russia and Ukraine. Even short of such an extreme prediction, many analysts believed that we were in for an age of multiplying ethnonational conflicts in Europe with a terrifying potential to spread and grow. The problems mostly fizzled away, however, and even the larger Balkan conflicts (and the Armenian-Azeri one), ugly as they were, did not spread.

Many other doomsday predictions failed to hold, as well. There was a nearly unanimous expectation in the 1950s and 1960s that dozens of countries would have nuclear weapons by the end of the 20th century. The CIA extrapolated in 1960 that the Soviet GNP might be triple that of the United States by the year 2000.[10] It was widely assumed in the early 1960s that, since the Soviets enjoyed such an overwhelming lead in the space race, they would surely be first to get to the moon. There was a common fear during the Cold War that a nuclear weapon would inevitably explode somewhere and soon; C.P. Snow said in 1960: "Within, at the most, ten years, some of those bombs are going off. I am saying this as responsibly as I can. *That* is the certainty."[11] Then there was the wisdom that the oil shocks of the 1970s proved that world power was shifting to the Middle East, and the series of related predictions after 1974 and again in 1979 that oil prices would rise sharply, and stay high. None of these things happened.

A similar pattern holds with some more recent extreme acts of terrorism. Since its alarming release of poison gas in the Tokyo subway in 1995—an attack that sickened thousands and killed twelve—the apocalyptic group Aum Shinrikyo appears to have abandoned the terrorism business. And Timothy McVeigh's destructive truck bombing in Oklahoma City has failed, at least thus far, to inspire successful American imitators. Even Libya's Muammar Qaddafi, a devil *du jour* of terrorism of the 1980s, seems to have gone on to other, far more innocuous things.

## The Uses of Fear

None of this is to suggest that all extreme events prove to be the last in their line. At the time, World War I—called the Great War for decades—was the worst war of its type. Yet, as many expected, an even more destructive one followed. Nor is it to suggest that deep concern about extreme events is unreasonable or necessarily harmful. Fear has its uses. Aid and alliances in Western Europe surely did help to keep the area out of Communist hands, the forceful response in Korea to dissuade the Communists from further direct military probes, anti-Castro efforts in Latin America to prevent further Communist gains there, the reaction to the Soviets' Cuban venture to discredit crisis as a tactic, intervention in the Balkans to contain or defuse similarly-sourced conflicts nearby. Thus, efforts to confront terrorism and to reduce its incidence and destructiveness are certainly wise and justified.

Moreover, while Aum Shinrikyo and Qaddafi may be under control, Al-Qaeda and like-minded terrorist groups are unlikely to die out any time soon: September 11 was, after all, their second attempt to destroy the World Trade Center. And, of course, terrorism itself will never go away: it has always existed and always will. The central issue is whether such spectacularly destructive terrorist acts will become commonplace. Experience suggests that it is entirely possible that they will not.

As we wait to find out, efforts directed against terrorism might perhaps be more usefully considered a campaign against crime than a war. Now, this is not to say that the initial U.S. government reaction to the events of this past September 11 was wrongheaded. The war imagery rallied American people and it helped to clear up the longstanding legal and psychological fog concerning just what our adversaries have been up to. But from the start there were risks with using such imagery, and we as a society are not compelled to retain it if we conclude, upon reflection, that there is a better way to think about our problems.

One such risk is that war imagery does not fit the facts of the current challenge in a way that most Americans can understand. Wars end, but terrorism and crime, since they are carried out by isolated individuals or by tiny groups at times of their own choosing, never do. One cannot, therefore, "conquer" terrorism. As with crime, one can at best seek to reduce its frequency and destructiveness so that people feel reasonably—if never perfectly—safe from it. Of course, military measures may sometimes be highly useful in the campaign, as they have proved to be in Afghanistan. But to frame the campaign against terror as a "war" risks the danger of raising unreasonable expectations, this despite the administration's repeated efforts to counsel patience and forbearance.

The war imagery also suggests that ordinary people should be asked somehow to make sacrifices. This popular conclusion is at least partly fanciful. Few Americans except those directly involved in the wars in Korea or Vietnam really made much of a sacrifice, and, although there were inconveniences and shortages during World War II, homefront consumer spending by the Greatest Generation generally surged. A goal of terrorism presumably is to hamper the economy, and therefore the best response to it— hardly much of a "sacrifice"—would be to go out and buy a refrigerator or to take an airplane to a vacation resort. The war imagery suggests we should be cutting back; but cutting back, and hunkering down, helps the terrorists.

It makes great sence to heighten security and policing measures, and to ask people to maintain awareness—as with crime, to report any suspicious behavior to authorities. But it is important that this be done without inducing hysteria. In the extreme foreign policy events noted above, the creation of panic was only a by-product of the main concern; in the case of terrorism, it is central because it is integral to terrorism as a strategy.[12] Alarmism can be harmful, particularly economically, because it can create the damaging consequences the terrorists seek but are unable to bring about on their own. As Michael Osterholm of the University of Minnesota Medical School has stressed, there is a big difference between living *with* fear and living *in* fear.

This is a difficult challenge, but not an impossible one. It would help if officials and the press were to assess probabilities more sensibly and put them in some sort of context, rather than simply stress extreme possibilities so much and so exclusively. It is certainly reasonable to point out that an atomic bomb in the hands of a terrorist could kill tens of thousands of people, but it may also be worthwhile to note that making such a bomb is an extra-ordinarily difficult task. And while a "dirty bomb" might raise radiation 25 percent over background levels in an area, and therefore into a range the Environmental Protection Agency officially considers undesirable, there ought to be some discussion about whether that really constitutes "contamination" or, indeed, much of a danger at all given the somewhat arbitrary and exceedingly cautious levels declared to be acceptable by the EPA.

Nor would it necessarily be remiss to note that biological and chemical weapons have not proven so far to be great killers. Although the basic science about them has been well-known for at least a century, both kinds of weapons are notoriously difficult to create, control and focus. Thus far, biological weapons have killed almost no one, and the notion that large numbers of people could be killed by a small number of poison gas explosives is highly questionable. Although they obviously can be hugely lethal when released in gas chambers, their effectiveness as weapons in warfare has been unimpressive. In World War I, for example, gas attacks caused less than one percent of total combat fatalities; on average, it took a ton of gas to produce one fatality. In the conclusion to the official British history of the war, chemical weapons are relegated to a footnote asserting rather mildly that gas "made war uncomfortable . . . to no purpose."[13] A 1993 analysis by the Office of Technology Assessment found that a terrorist would have to deliver a full ton of sarin nerve gas perfectly and under absolutely ideal conditions over a heavily populated area to cause between 3,000 and 8,000 deaths, something that would require the near-simultaneous detonation of dozens, even hundreds, of weapons. Under slightly less ideal circumstances—if there was a moderate wind or if the sun was out, for example—the death rate would be only one-tenth as great.[14]

The problem is that the press and most politicians find that extreme and alarmist possibilities arrest attention more effectively than discussions put in their proper, broader contexts. Moreover, there is more reputational danger in underplaying risks than in exaggerating them. H.G. Wells' prediction that the conflict beginning in 1914 would be "the war that will end war" is often ridiculed in retrospect, but not his equally confident declaration at the end of World War II that "the end of everything we call life is close at hand."[15] Disproved doomsayers can always claim that caution induced by their warnings prevented the predicted calamity from occurring. (Call it the Y2K effect.) Disproved Pollyannas can bank on no such convenient refuge.

Moreover, the record with respect to fear about crime suggests that efforts to deal responsibly with the risks of terrorism will prove difficult. Fear of crime rose notably in the mid-1990s even as statistics were showing it to be in pronounced decline. When Mayor David Dinkins, running for re-election in New York City, pointed to such numbers, he was accused by A.M. Rosenthal of the *New York Times* of hiding behind "trivializing statistics" that "are supposed to convince us that crime is going down."[16] New Yorkers did eventually come to feel safer from crime in the 1990s than they had in the 1980s, but this was probably less because crime rates actually declined than because graffiti, panhandlers, aggressive windshield washers and the homeless were banished or hidden from view. So it makes sense, at least for a while, to have armed reservists parading menacingly around airports. It is not always clear how they prevent terrorist attacks, and pulling them from productive jobs hardly helps the economy. But

if they provide people with a sense of security, their presence may be beneficial.

More extreme forms of alarmism are not reasonable, however. Some commentators are now arguing, for example, that the United States has become "vulnerable," even "fragile." All societies are "vulnerable" to tiny bands of suicidal fanatics, but the United States is hardly "vulnerable" in the sense that it can be toppled by extreme and dramatic acts of terrorist destruction—however grimly, the country can readily absorb that kind of damage. (It does, after all, "absorb" some 40,000 deaths each year from automobile accidents.) There are, as always, dangers out there; as always, too, uncertainties abide and abound. But the sky, as it happens, isn't falling.

No one really knows, of course, whether September 11 will prove to be a blip or a step function. The record suggests, however, that terrorists will find it difficult to match or top it. The extreme destruction of the events of last September 11 has also raised the bar, reducing the psychological and political impact of less damaging attacks. That even ambitious terrorists will fail to deliver as painful a blow seems at least as likely as that they will succeed.

In practical terms, too, Al-Qaeda represents a difficult but still bounded problem: in its concentric circles of evil, from Osama bin Laden and his lieutenants to the thousands of glassy-eyed misfits trained in Taliban-hosted camps, the numbers of terrorists and terrorist adjuncts are finite and probably manageable. Other potential apocalyptic terrorists from other climes are imaginable, and if many of those potential terrorists emerge, then our problem could slip its bounds. But it is not obvious that these potential terrorists will have either the motivation or the resources to murder Americans in large numbers. A vastly exaggerated U.S. global military response to September 11, however, could inadvertently produce enough fear and resentment abroad to increase the possibility of this happening. No chance of that, is there?

## Notes

1. Arnold J. Toynbee, *War and Civilization* (New York: Oxford University Press, 1950), p. 4.

2. Grew quoted in John Lewis Gaddis, *The Long Peace: Inquiries into the History of the Cold War* (New York: Oxford University Press, 1987), p. 218.

3. Quoted in Milovan Djilas, *Conversations with Stalin* (New York: Harcourt Brace, 1962), pp. 114–5.

4. For data, see John Mueller, "Public Expectations of War During the Cold War," *American Journal of Political Science* (May 1979), pp. 303–7.

5. Quoted in Francis Anthony Boyle, *World Politics and International Law* (Durham, NC: Duke University Press, 1985), p. 73.

6. Quoted in Marshall D. Shulman, *Stalin's Foreign Policy Reappraised* (New York: Athenaum, 1963), p. 150.

7. Bernard Brodie, *War and Politics* (New York: Macmillan, 1973), p. 63.

8. Quoted in McGeorge Bundy and James G. Blight, eds., "October 27, 1962: Transcripts of the Meetings of the ExComm," *International Security* (Winter 1987/88), p. 92.

9. Quoted in Morton H. Halperin, *Nuclear Fallacy* (Cambridge, MA: Ballinger, 1987), p. 45.

10. Richard Reeves, *President Kennedy* (New York: Simon & Schuster, 1993), p. 54.

11. "The Mortal Un-Neutrality of Science," *Science,* January 27, 1961, p. 259. (Emphasis in the original.)

12. See David Fromkin's still excellent essay, "The Strategy of Terrorism," *Foreign Affairs* (July 1975).

13. Sir James E. Edmonds and R. Maxwell-Hyslop, eds., *Military Operations: France and Belgium,* 1918, vol. 5 (London: HMSO, 1947), p. 606.

14. Office of Technology Assessment, United States Congress, *Proliferation of Weapons of Mass Destruction: Assessing the Risks,* OTA-559 (Washington, DC: U.S. Government Printing Office, 1993), p. 54.

15. H.G. Wells, *The War That Will End War* (New York: Duffield, 1914); H.G. Wells, The Last Books of H.G. Wells (London: H.G. Wells Society, 1968), p. 67.

16. A.M. Rosenthal, "New York to Clinton," *New York Times,* October 1, 1993. For data showing that crime peaked in New York in 1990 and declined steadily thereafter, see *New York Times,* February 19, 1998.

---

## The Imbalance of Terror

Thérèse Delpech

In the eyes of history, the 10 years from December 25, 1991, until September 11, 2001, may become known as the interwar years. Just as the 20 years from 1919 to 1939 have no organizing principle to define them, so too the last 10 years may be independently unrecognizable to the future. From the day the Soviet flag was lowered from the Kremlin until the day the twin towers collapsed, the shape of the world to come was impossible to imagine. Granted, new trends distinct from the Cold War were emerging. A limited, regional war in the Persian Gulf had gathered together one of the major coalitions in the history of warfare. Three major actors—the United States, Russia, and China—worked with a curious mix of cooperation and confrontation. Intrastate wars were blooming in the Balkans, Indonesia, Central Asia, and Africa, but ethnic rivalries were hardly the only feature of these conflicts, even in the chaos of Africa.. Globalization was an economic, rather than strategic, concept and its very meaning remained elusive. The information revolution was changing the nature of conflict, but exactly how was difficult to assess. Simply stated, no clear picture was emerging from these different elements.

One thing, however, was already clear: by the end of the last century, hopes concerning a "new world order" had vanished. The strategic literature was full of "new threats." Rapid change was indeed feared by many, particularly with the appearance of two additional declared nuclear powers in 1998, with the intractable problems posed by Iraq and North Korea, and with the modernization of the Chinese military. Possible failures of deterrence were often contemplated, and missile defenses were supposed to protect people and troops at home and abroad. The question at the beginning of September 2001 was whether such defenses would increase international security or *in*security.

The vocabulary used to describe the international situation did not reflect the striking difference between expectations at the beginning and at the end of the 1990s. For want of something better, observers retained the term "post-Cold War" as the least imperfect way to name the 10 years that followed the Soviet Union's breakup. Now, something different, something unrecognizable, something irreconcilable with concepts inherited from past experiences of either war or terrorism has come into being. This new phenomenon, however, does have a name: asymmetric warfare. Significant thought had already been given to asymmetric threats before September 11, but it had been nothing but a way of thinking. Such an extraordinary attack, in real time and real space, gave asymmetry a horrific shape.

## THE TERRORIST AGENDA

Those who planned the attacks seem to have operated from a list detailing the striking differences between the United States and themselves and to have played on those differences as much as they could. Their strategy can be described as follows:

- *Have no center and strike at the heart of the superpower.*

Although the United States may have become increasingly non-Clausewitzian in its approach to warfare, the terrorists adhered to the old recipe of warfare's most famous theoretician: inflict the most powerful blow at the center of gravity of your enemy. The World Trade Center, as a symbol of U.S. economic might and U.S.-led globalization, was precisely that point. The decapitation of U.S. political and military power with strikes on the Pentagon and possibly the White House or the Capitol was supposed to finish off the task. President George W. Bush

correctly described the terrorist attack as an act of war. This trauma has been far worse than during the 1950s when Sputnik revealed the vulnerability of U.S. territory. Although that threat was much more serious, putting the entire United States within a fraction of an hour's journey of Soviet nuclear missiles, it remained unreal because it was theoretical. Today's threat is no longer "potential": lower Manhattan lies in ruins. The terrorists correctly calculated the psychological effect.

- *The United States wants life at any cost? Kill as many civilians as possible.*

In his first *fatwa,* or religious declaration, Osama bin Laden in 1996 urged Muslims to kill U.S. military men abroad. In 1998, he expanded this "religious duty" to all U.S. citizens, civilian and military. Shortly after the second *fatwa,* hundreds died in the Kenyan and Tanzanian embassy bombings, most of them Africans. The latest escalation on September 11 is impressive. The terrorists so shocked the U.S. psyche that Bush received unprecedented popular support (91 percent of the U.S. population) even after he said that no victory would be possible without casualties, most probably heavy ones. As the conflict unfolds more frightening scenarios surface, involving unconventional means. This enemy has no moral limits.

- *Reveal U.S. vulnerability to rustic means of war.*

To defeat the high-tech superpower, knives, fuel, and planes would suffice. The hijackers conducted a live demonstration for would-be terrorists. The message is clear: do not fear the United States' power; the United States is a giant with feet of clay. Worldwide eavesdropping can easily be defeated and the most effective missile shield provides no protection against this type of attack. Does this notion mean that the terrorists did not use modern technology? Certainly not. They used the Internet for communication and encryptions. They made electronic money transfers from Dubai to the United States and back until just before the attacks. Moreover, networking, an essential component of postmodern society, was key to the terrorists' strategy. Yet, in the minds of terrorists, highly developed technology cannot defeat those committed to the cause, and willing to die for it, no matter how simple their methods.

- *Fight the kind of war the United States hates: an elusive enemy who uses guerrilla tactics.*

From the terrorists' standpoint, the only possible responses to the September 11 attacks would be either that of 1998, which proved totally ineffective (perhaps because of Pakistani betrayal); a Soviet-style invasion, which would lead to a second disaster for another major power; or guerrilla-style warfare, where the United States is not at its best. Lessons from experiences in Vietnam and more recently in Somalia were not lost on the terrorists. Afghanistan presents a particularly difficult and inhospitable terrain. Even the Soviet "Speznats" were unable to defeat the mujahideen. Granted, the United States has also learned lessons—not just from 1998, but also from Soviet errors—and has new technologies that allow it to destroy key military infrastructures immediately and trace fighters even in difficult terrains. Still, what exactly does the U.S. technological advantage provide in a fight against a tribal army in its mountainous homeland?

- *The United States makes military plans years ahead, so surprise them continuously.*

Surprise has always been the nightmare of the military, but the U.S. military may particularly hate it. If no consistent strategy is recognizable, if no anticipation can be expected, preparation is almost impossible. With strikes both at home and abroad, domestic support may prove more fragile over a long period, particularly if unconventional means are used against unprotected civilians. Adapting to surprise might become an important element of future planning.

- *Because the United States worries about collateral damage, fight unrestricted and total war.*

In February 1999, China's People's Liberation Army published a document entitled "War without Limits." The authors, Qiao Liang and Wang Xiangsui, two senior colonels from the younger generation of Chinese military officers, advocated a multitude of means, military and nonmilitary, to strike at the United States. Liang presented the document with the following description: "The first rule is that there are no rules, with nothing forbidden." At the time of publication, reports implied that the authors,

deliberately ignoring the laws of war, were promoting terrorism. This characterization might have been unfair, but the methods that bin Laden follows do fit conceptual "war without limits." He acknowledges no laws of war whatsoever. Since September 11, numerous articles have been published about biological and chemical threats on U.S. or European soil. They attest to a spreading public fear, but bin Laden's past statements justify it. He has made no mystery about his quest for weapons of mass destruction and his readiness to use them. The danger is therefore a real one.

- *The United States places a premium on transparency, so act like a secret sect.*

In the United States' vision, the networked society, with its global information-sharing ambition, creates transparency and disincentives for conflict. Criminal clandestine networks, however, operating in the midst of postmodern societies, constitute a dark side of globalization that is difficult to detect and destroy. These dispersed units can penetrate, disrupt, and then evade. Nonstate actors can gain a significant edge over state systems if they choose to fight "netwars," as a recent RAND study suggests.[1]

## NEW ASSETS TO FIGHT TERRORISM

The terrorists' conviction in the ultimate success of their plan can be carried too far. The attacks have brought to light new factors with the ability to shift the conflict in a different direction.

- *Impetus for cooperation.*

The commitment of the United States' allies to collective defense has become more assertive. With NATO's first-ever invocation of its founding treaty's Article 5 on September 12, and with Japan's decision to send Self-Defense Forces to the Indian Ocean, the allies have actualized the notion of collective defense in an unprecedented manner. Germany, in a dramatic recasting of its policy, declared that the time had come to show a new international responsibility. Further, the composition of alliances and coalitions is changing. The first telephone call Bush received after the attacks was from Russian president Vladimir Putin. Russia opened its airspace and bases and went so far as to suggest that it might reconsider its negative position on NATO enlargement. Does this response indicate that, in the future, NATO might become a broad political alliance, leaving military operations to "coalitions of the willing?" A new, closer relationship might emerge between the Cold War adversaries. As for China, not only did it vote in favor of the United Nations (UN) Security Council resolutions condemning the attacks, but it also assured Washington of its support. Furthermore, China expressed its understanding of Japan's deployment of an Aegis-type destroyer to the Indian Ocean for monitoring and surveillance. Even if Beijing acts out of the belief that the current conflict will weaken the United States, its political cooperation with Washington is significant. The actions of these major powers set into motion an unprecedented coalition to fight international terrorism, and maintaining it will be as great a challenge as defeating terrorism itself.

- *The world recognizes that extraordinary means are necessary to fight terrorism.*

In the past, counterterrorism has been fought with minimal military involvement, but now Article 51 of the UN Charter, which justifies action in cases of self-defense, backs Washington's military response. There is broad agreement that a campaign on international terrorism, sustained over a long period, must be fought and won. In the process, states sponsoring or supporting terrorism will also face consequences, military or otherwise. Beyond Afghanistan, Somalia and Sudan are nations frequently cited in connection with bin Laden, as well as Iraq, but no hard facts link Baghdad to the September 11 attacks so far.

- *The globalized economic environment allows a worldwide counterattack to eradicate funds of terrorist organizations.*

To win this battle, the banking system is adopting new forms of transparency, and restrictions on the flow of international capital are being contemplated. Governments are likely to alter the freedom of movement of goods and individuals, and even the most liberal of all nations, the United States, will have to accept limits to globalization and free trade. At its October 2001 meeting in Washington, the Group of Seven nations pledged to crack down on the financing of terrorism. It also endorsed making the fight against terrorism a new focus of international agencies that have been combating the laundering of drug money.

- *Concerted intelligence has already begun to play a crucial role in the battle.*

Before September 11, warning signals were few, but immediately after the attacks, intelligence gatherers made substantial breakthroughs in a matter of days, with wide international cooperation in Europe but also in the Middle East, Pakistan (albeit a questionable source), India, and Southeast Asia. Domestic and foreign intelligence are now connected in an unprecedented manner. Because the lines between terrorism and global crime are not very clear, all kinds of illicit trafficking are likely to pay a heavy price in this campaign. A good ploy might well be to enlist the talents of the international criminal world to help apprehend terrorists (just as the underworld was enlisted in Fritz Lang's famous film *M*).

- *Civil defense, long considered secondary, will be reinforced.*

The boundaries between military and civil defense are being blurred. The increasing need to protect civilians from terrorist attacks, possibly involving weapons of mass destruction, will lead the most-developed countries to give a new priority to civil defense, making it harder for the terrorist to strike in the middle of cities and easier for governments to deal with limited unconventional attacks.

- *No country can afford a U.S. defeat, for it would throw the world off balance, into terror and chaos.*

This belief undoubtedly is the main strength on which the United States can rely during this most difficult conflict.

## A DISTURBING NEW WORLD

To where is the new world leading? The September 11 attacks provide confusing messages.

- *A frightening imbalance.*

To think that the leading world power would have found itself in the extraordinary position of needing to mobilize four aircraft carriers and 400 planes to oppose a nonstate threat is astonishing. Since 1991, the trend had been toward interethnic conflicts, even though the Persian Gulf War had been an example to the contrary and Africa had experienced a few cases of bloody state conflicts (between Ethiopia and Eritrea, for instance). To launch such a major military force against al Qaeda is a truly radical version of asymmetrical conflicts. After the Gulf War, the United States came to the conclusion that Saddam Hussein had made the major mistake of confronting the U.S. led coalition on its own terms, ending in Iraq's resounding defeat. This lesson was also not lost on the enemies of the United States.

- *The distinction between state and nonstate actors may not be as relevant as it had been.*

We now face a corruption of state power in Afghanistan by nonstate actors. The possible use of nonstate actors by states to further state ends, however, must now also be seriously considered. In the September 11 attacks, al Qaeda may have received support from foreign intelligence services (reportedly from those of Pakistan and Iraq). Evidence exists that certain terrorists have had contacts with undercover services on several continents (in Europe, the Middle East, South Asia, and Southeast Asia) and that some provided the terrorists with the Social Security numbers of deceased people. The latter is typical of state agents' work. Moreover, the terrorists' ability to defeat U.S. eavesdropping, monitoring, and counterintelligence over an extended period of time also suggests that undercover specialists may have assisted the perpetrators. Thus the attack most probably involved a mixture of state and nonstate action. Incontrovertible evidence of any state complicity might never surface, however, further complicating the mission to eradicate international terrorism. This lesson for the future is a dire one: states may learn that they can use nonstate actors to inflict major blows on an adversary without having to be held accountable for their actions.

- *The strategic challenge of failed states.*

The fact that large expanses of territories in so-called failed states escape government control need no longer be considered a regrettable feature of the postmodern world, but rather a strategic challenge that should be addressed urgently. Anarchic countries are both a breeding ground and a haven for terrorists. Apart from Central Asia, Africa comes to mind as a dramatic illustration of a locale that cannot be left any longer in its too-often chaotic shape. Nation-building and peacemaking, far from being secondary tasks that can be easily dismissed, should become central not only in European but also in U.S. security policy.

- *Possible failures of deterrence.*

Deterrence, in the context of asymmetric warfare, is probably less relevant than in more classical scenarios, because surprise and shock are essential part of asymmetric strategies. Failures of deterrence should particularly be considered in the case of nonstate actors engaged in unrestricted wars, whether they act alone or with the sponsorship of a nation-state, because they have little to lose, particularly when suicide is used as a weapon.

- *Defenses could be equally ineffective.*

This precept is notably true if the main preoccupation in the United States remains long-range ballistic missiles. Long-range ballistic missiles, in fact, appear less threatening than cruise missiles, which have been mentioned only rhetorically so far. About 80,000 cruise missiles are deployed in 70 countries. A dozen countries retain land-attack cruise missiles and antiship cruise missiles; unmanned aerial vehicles are proliferating. All the key cruise-missile technologies are widely available, and the end-products of that technology are all potential delivery systems for chemical and biological agents. Cruise missiles present air defense systems with an enormous challenge, to detect the missile early enough to mount an effective defense. A new emphasis on protection against cruise missiles is needed now.

- *The strength of an absolute ideology against our moderate societies.*

The danger of "religious" wars is greater than that of wars between "civilizations" because religions have a significantly greater power than civilizations. Al Qaeda uses religion not only to be able to recognize God as the sole constituency, but also to use the absolute power of religious faith in countries where literacy does not allow people even to read the Qur'an. Al Qaeda's declared ambition is to annihilate not just religions other than Islam (the destruction of the ancient Bamiyan's Buddhist statues in February 2001 is an eloquent testimony), but also anyone who does not accept its perverse version of Islam (bin Laden's people have burned Shi'ites alive in Afghanistan). No concession, however great, would be enough to end bin Laden's "mission" because, unlike many previous terrorist organizations, it does not intend to create a state nor does it wish to introduce political reforms. Its objective is metaphysical: a titanic struggle between "good" and "evil" forces, in which any means can be used to achieve the end.

- *A new world is taking shape.*

All conflicts have one quality in common: they all contribute to reshaping international relations, sometimes in dramatic ways. This conflict, by starting out to destroy al Qaeda and other terrorist organizations with global reach, may end up reshaping the world. Waging the fight with this new world in mind is essential. An increased potential for miscalculation and surprise will probably occur in the future. Predictability should therefore be improved whenever possible during this conflict, especially in areas where strong tensions exist. In Europe's past, differences in strategic approach have resulted in grave errors, but the odds of misinterpretation between countries with different cultures are incomparably greater. The Bush administration has been wise to refute the vague and dangerous concept of "wars of civilizations," but words are not enough. Second, U.S. security will depend increasingly on its ability to keep alliances alive, to build coalitions, and to sustain multilateralism. The world will be policed collectively or not at all.

Containing violence has always been the key to security. In *Leviathan,* Thomas Hobbes argued that people needed the state to insulate them from violent death. In the twentieth century, one of the most violent in history, the state itself was the major vehicle that produced violence through wars and revolutions. During the Cold War, the concept of mutual assured destruction expressed an unprecedented magnitude of violence between the two superpowers, contained at great risk with nuclear weapons. The world now faces a different, highly dispersed form of radical violence that results most identifiably from the failures of politics throughout the planet. If the ability to contain violence, particularly in its most extreme forms, is a common objective, then those failures should now be addressed. Otherwise, terrorism will destroy society, first in the Muslim world, where it is most threatening, and then elsewhere as well.

Addressing past failures will require significant changes. First, political courage is needed: where terrorism is concerned, there should be no room for ambivalence or tolerance. A dramatic reassessment of past policies in a large number of countries will be necessary. Some Muslim leaders have already dared to say that groups that call themselves Islamic "hijacked" their countries in order to further destructive political goals; the veil of secrecy that covers the activities of such groups should now be removed. On the Western side, the end of support for corrupt and repressive regimes that sponsor terrorism, such as Saudi Arabia, appears essential.

Second, when this campaign is fought, vague confidence in free markets and political liberalism will not meet the challenge of a lasting peace. Nothing less will do than a return to the origins of political values in ethics. A new international order based on justice and arbitration is the only way to avoid clashes liable to unleash the devastating potential of the twenty-first century's violence and war technologies.

## NOTE

1. David Ronfeldt and John Arquilla, eds., *Networks and Netwars: The Future of Terror, Crime, and Militancy* (Santa Monica, Calif.: RAND, 2001).

# REVIEW QUESTIONS

- How and why did the new era of terrorism arise?
- Is the modern terrorist proclivity for indiscriminate mass casualty attacks a new phenomenon, or a new manifestation of an older terrorist profile?
- Are the tactics used for the September 11, 2001 attacks a likely scenario for future attacks, or are they unique to this specific context?
- Is the terrorist threat in the new era more pronounced than in the past? How so? How not?
- What do the characteristics of the New Terrorism bode for the continuation of terrorist violence into the near future?

The following books and articles are suggested for further information about the new era of terrorism in perspective:

## Books

Griset, Pamela L. and Sue Mahan. *Terrorism in Perspective.* Thousand Oaks, CA: Sage Publications, 2003.
Kushner, Harvey W. *Encyclopedia of Terrorism.* Thousand Oaks, CA: Sage Publications, 2003.
Martin, Gus. *Understanding Terrorism: Challenges, Perspectives, and Issues.* Thousand Oaks, CA: Sage Publications, 2003.

## Articles

Huntington, Samuel P. "The Clash of Civilizations?" *Foreign Affairs.* 72:3 (Summer 1993).
Laqueur, Walter. "Terror's New Face." *Harvard International Review.* 20:4 (Fall 1998).
Rubin, Elizabeth. "Gen X." *The New Republic.* (April 2002).

# 3

# DEFINING TERRORISM
# IN THE NEW ERA

Although most lay persons have a fairly instinctive understanding that terrorism is politically-motivated violence deliberately undertaken to affect a target audience, experts have devoted a great deal of intellectual effort toward crafting and refining a definition of terrorism. Governments, academics, and practitioners have designed definitional constructs which often reflect their own political, research, or constituent agendas. Thus, various definitions may emphasize contending legalistic, theoretical, or ideological perspectives. There is also a significant disconnect between how experts in the West and the developing world interpret politically-motivated violence–this is the classic tension between classifying a revolutionary as a terrorist or a freedom fighter. These debates are likely to continue for the foreseeable future, especially as the characteristics of the new era's environment continue to develop.

The articles in this chapter discuss the modern definitional problem, a problem that represents an ongoing debate among practitioners, scholars, and analysts. In "Terrorism: The Problem of Definition Revisited," H.H.A. Cooper presents the ongoing question of how to define terrorism. The article offers a contextual discussion of the seemingly endless debates, frequent discord, temporary consensus, and common disagreements that have characterized recent scholarship and practice. An approach for defining or identifying terrorism in the new era is suggested. Mustafa Al Sayyid's article, "Mixed Message: Arab and Muslim Response to 'Terrorism,'" provides a non-Western context for the issue of defining terrorism. An explanation, grounded in perceptions on what is or is not terrorist behavior, is given for the sometimes tepid support from the Arab and Muslim world for the Western war on terrorism. Noah Feldman's article "Choices of Law, Choices of War," examines the policy implications of definitional "choice of framework" considerations in the new era of terrorism. The central question is whether to conceptualize terrorism within war-fighting or crime-fighting frameworks.

## Terrorism: The Problem of Definition Revisited

H.H.A. Cooper
*Nuevevidas International, Inc.*

> *A living language has no existence independent of culture. It is not the loom of culture but its data bank. As such, it serves the needs, past and present, of a given community. As those needs change, language evolves to accommodate them.*
>
> —Raymond Cohen (1990, pp. 41–42)[1]

With the advent of the new millennium, whatever one's preference for the mathematics of the event, a certain nostalgia for the past is inevitable. Although it is still difficult for many of us to adjust to no longer living in the 20th century, it seems even harder for others to let go of even the most recent of bygone memories. As the century raced to its anticlimactic close, a wave of recall swept through the media worldwide, made possible by new technologies that have given potent meaning to the yet ill-defined term *globalization*. Amid this feverish search for the most memorable this and the most renowned that, the sensitive observer might discern a hankering for earlier times, a kind of golden age in which everything was simpler, much easier to understand and, to use appropriate *fin de siècle* terminology, less stressful. No examination of these impressions in general is essayed here. Yet, it is of some importance to notice them in relation to the present topic if for no other reason than to offer a pertinent rejoinder. It can be stated with absolute certainty that there has never been, since the topic began to command serious attention, some golden age in which terrorism was easy to define or, for that matter, to comprehend. And, as we plunge gaily into the brave new world of the 21st century, there is not the slightest reason to suppose that the problem of definition, or as it was once described, the problem of the problem of definition (Cooper, 1978), will come any closer to sensible resolution. With that solemn caveat in place, let us proceed to consider how, variously, we may come to define terrorism or at least know it when we see it in the coming decades.

## DEFINITION IS TRULY AN ART

Parenthetically, we must deal here with what is implied in the process of definition itself. Definition is truly an art. The artist seeks to represent, in concrete or abstract terms, something he or she has conceptualized or observed so as to give it some meaning of a distinctive character. The resultant work is a vehicle of communication for the thought or revelation that the artist seeks to convey to others. The central problem in the process is that no two human beings ever see the same thing, however simple, in exactly the same light or from the same standpoint. There is rarely, if ever, an exact correspondence of interpretation, and the introduction of but the slightest complexity can alter the meaning intended by the artist. Most ordinary, social communication is imprecise by nature. It simply is not necessary that we define our terms with exactitude; it suffices that we are generally understood. Of course, misunderstandings abound, especially between the genders[2] and persons of differing status, culture, occupation, education, and the like. This is sometimes a source of irritation and occasionally cause for amusement, but it is not often of great consequence. Yet, in serious discourse, especially on matters involving a potential for substantial disagreement or those bearing controversial or emotional overtones, the closest correspondence of understanding as to the meaning of the language employed is imperative. If we are discussing fruit, and I believe you are talking about apples when in fact you are trying to convey to me that your are referring to oranges, we are not going to get very far without timely clarification. With respect to terrorism, there is among the many participants to the discussion no agreement on the basic nature of the fruit under consideration. For some, it will always, unalterably be apples; for others, with equal rigor, it will remain oranges. No amount of sophistry or the introduction of other varietals will be helpful in resolving the issue of meaning. One person's terrorist will ever remain another's freedom fighter. The process of definition is wholly frustrated by the presence of irreconcilable antagonisms.

## A DEFINITION OF TERRORISM

Hope springs eternal in the human breast, and perhaps for this reason alone, so many conferences and writings on the subject of terrorism begin with the obligatory, almost ritualistic recitation by the presenter of some preferred definition of terrorism.[3] This is not wholly an exercise in futility; whatever the discrepancies detected by others, the definitions at least provide starting points for debate. The search has always been for one all-embracing statement that could stand at least a chance of gaining a high degree of acceptance by others as well as covering a majority of the bases. It can be reasonably confidently asserted that this procedure will continue unaltered as we transit the 21st century. In a similar spirit, then, the following definition of terrorism is offered here so that we may have a basis for reflection on the problems of terrorism and how it is likely to present itself in the new millennium.

> Terrorism is the intentional generation of massive fear by human beings for the purpose of securing or maintaining control over other human beings.

This definition evolved over some 25 years of teaching about the topic of terrorism in a university setting, and during that time, it has undergone a number of small refinements as experience has suggested. Other definitions have similarly been subject to modification as those who propounded them sought to meet criticisms extended by others and to perfect the concepts enshrined in the words employed. In a very real sense, all the earlier definitions had to be subject to this process of refinement if they were to survive at all. Even the most assiduous wordsmiths were humbled by the task of encapsulating such powerful, at their simplest, contradictory ideas in one all-embracing sentence. It is no surprise, then, to encounter definitions that run for paragraphs, even pages, in frantic attempts to capture the elusive meaning embodies in the word *terrorism*. This is dialectic rather than definition, but it is an inescapable part of the process whether it is reduced to writing or articulated only in discussion. The above definition, in the form it is presented here, owes much to classroom discussion and the acuity of the students to whom it was offered as a starting point for an exploration of the subject. Before examining its components in detail, it seems helpful to explain the underlying philosophy orienting its construction. Although it is always dangerous to generalize, it may be observed that university students tend to be an unforgiving bunch. They are quick to seize on any errors or inconsistencies they detect in the formula. And, if they have cause to doubt as a result, their overall confidence in the instruction and the instructor is shaken. In particular, in the matter of defining terrorism, the product offered had necessarily to address succinctly the thorny issue of "one person's terrorist is another's freedom fighter"; hence the formulation offered here.

Again, a further thought has to be inserted at this juncture. However much you may buy into the freedom fighter argument, you are forced, if you are intellectually honest, to the conclusion that whatever label it might bear, terrorism is a bad thing. All you can sensibly say in its defense is that sometimes it may be necessary to do bad things to other people, most usually with the apologetic justification that it is done to prevent or deter them from doing bad or worse things to you. If it is conceded that there is no "good" terrorism, that such an import would be a contradiction in terms, any definition must unambiguously take this into account, for it goes to the fundamental nature of the concept. In practice, the definition of terrorism has been consistently plagued by an ever increasing need to justify the reprehensible. This has proved the biggest obstacle to the production of anything approaching a widely acceptable definition, especially in the international arena. It must be stressed that there is a basic antinomy here: What *I* do, however unpleasant is not terrorism; what *you* do is terrorism. From the point of view of definition, this is not a question of degrees such as dogs, for example, the term *high crimes and misdemeanors* in the impeachment realm (see Posner, 1999, pp. 98–105). What is asserted is a difference in kind; *I* don't commit terrorism, *you* do. You can no more have a little bit of terrorism than you can be a little bit pregnant. From a definitional perspective, it ought not to matter who does what to whom. Terrorism should be defined solely by the nature and quality of what is done. Difficult as this is, definition should strive for impartiality in this field, or the exercise must fail in its purposes.

## IS TERRORISM A FREESTANDING CONCEPT?

Is terrorism, then, a freestanding concept? In terms of penal policy or normative configuration, is it something autonomous or simply a constituent element of certain kinds of criminal behavior that are already defined? What is offered above certainly has to be carefully considered in that light. An examination of any coherent legal system will reveal many crimes where the creation of great fear in the victim (e.g., rape) is a central, defining feature. Many would agree that rape is a terroristic act, especially when it is employed in warfare as an instrument of subjugation or humiliation. In any unbiased analysis, it might reasonably be put forward as terrorism par excellence. Yet, it is not the crime of rape that comes readily or immediately to mind in any discussion of the meaning of terrorism. This is not to deny the terroristic content within what is understood about the crime of rape, at least in its violent manifestation, but rather an unexpressed preference for seeing terrorism as something separate, distinct, and having an existence all its own. For those taking such a position, and no objection is taken

to it here, terrorism seems to inhabit a different universe from the ordinary, from even the most heinous of otherwise criminal behavior. That it can or should do so comes as no surprise to the legal positivist. Although norms cannot be simply conjured up out of thin air, the power to create new crimes in response to altered circumstances is an inherent faculty of any legal system. At this point, it must be made clear that what has been offered above as a conceptualization of terrorism is in no way to be regarded as an inchoate norm awaiting the interposition of the legal system's authority to give it independent being. And, herein lies the central dilemma, which cannot be readily overcome by recourse to any legal artifice. It is only possible to construct a freestanding penal figure denominated *terrorism* out of elements borrowed from preexisting crimes already defined as such in their own right. Thus, rape can in this view be seen as a constituent element of an autonomous crime of terrorism, just as terrorism can be seen as a necessary ingredient in a violent rape. Although this does little to advance the process of definition per se, it does serve to expose a critical problem that cannot be evaded.

Even the most cursory examination of the many definitions of terrorism on offer should quickly persuade the critic how many of these rely for any sort of precision on the adjectives employed in their elaboration. These definitions tend to focus on purpose, and that, in each of them, is primarily political. Reduced to its simplest terms, terrorism is seen as extreme political coercion. This, truth to tell, is the *raison d'être* of virtually all these definitional exercises. For it is only in the realm of the political that these definitions have any useful employment; hence their adversarial nature. Yet, assuredly, the abused child knows exactly what terrorism is, even though he or she might be quite unable to enunciate the word. More is revealed in this of the purposes of the definers, or refiners, than of the nature of terrorism itself. All who seek to find a meaning in the term *terrorism* would have to agree on the centrality of the massive fear, or terror,[4] it inspires in those on whom it is inflicted, as well as its coercive nature. What is in dispute is whether there is anything in the nature of a right to inflict such misery on others and, if so, in whom it inheres. Here, we come to another dilemma that cannot escape the notice of anyone seeking to define terrorism. In its nature, terrorism, by reason of its coercive aspects, has a marked similarity to the corrective and deterrent functions vested by common understanding and political theory in the state—and the responsible parent. The distinction is in degree rather than anything else. Consider, for example, the ultimate sanction permitted the nation-state seeking to exercise its authority internally to control crime, namely the death penalty. Those who subscribe to a belief in its efficacy, whether by way of deterrence or social hygiene, can only rely on its intimidatory effect; if it does not frighten others by way of example, its value is very limited. The state's power to wage war to maintain its integrity against external foes can be viewed in much the same way. Clearly, effectiveness turns on the ability to secure the desired result through intimidation. Here lies the road to Dresden, Hiroshima, and Nagasaki, but we accord the nation-state considerable latitude in these maters. But, there comes a point when the line is crossed and we would say that the state has begun to rule by terror. There are issues of proportionality involved of a most delicate kind, but they are the ones that perturb the definitional process in most awkward ways. Terrorism becomes, for those in power, an affront to established authority. Power, when stretched to its limits is, to many, no more than a reign of terror. Any definition that ignores this is open to attack as pure cant. The point there is that the way in which these things are done has always assumed lesser importance from the point of view of their characterization as terrorism than who does them and to whom.[5]

It should be observed that there is a kind of parallel in this regard with what have come to be known in recent times as "hate crimes." Those who oppose the promulgation, altogether, of such a category argue simply that it is otiose; murder is murder is murder. What can be done to increase the gravity with which certain matters seem to clamor for attention? Is any greater protection afforded potential victims by this increment? Nothing is added, for example, to the crime of murder that might serve as a special

deterrent to those who would commit it against some class supposedly in need of particular protection. Many behaviorists and mental health professionals would argue, with considerable force on their side, that an individual who kills any victim in a singularly vicious way is exhibiting a hatred of that person regardless of the class to which that person belongs; in fact, so personalized may be the hatred that no issue of a class character enters into the matter (see Gourevich, 2000). None of this would satisfy those who argue for special hate crime legislation. Once more, the focus is plainly on who does what to whom and why. Hatred is an emotion and one that in civilized society is regarded as reprehensible, unhealthy, and socially harmful. It is the "why" of the matter that is troubling to those who see themselves as likely to be victimized by those who bear and exhibit these ugly emotions. The problem resides herein: The feelings we characterize as hatred cannot be punished unless they are exhibited in a way that is criminal in itself or in association with conduct that is already criminalized. If the device of making the element of hate is a way of making this latter punishable in a more severe fashion than would otherwise be the case, the position has something to commend it, but in the case of the most serious crimes, such as murder, they are already punishable to the limit; the rest is merely posturing. As with terrorism, we should define by reference to what is done rather than by shifting our focus to those who are victimized and the reasons they are targeted.

## Good News/Bad News

Viewed in the formulation set down here, terrorism is a game of fixed quantities. It is cold comfort, but comfort nevertheless, that as we enter the new millennium, no new terrorism is possible. How can this be? Creating massive fear in human beings is based on the same principles that have always informed the process: You can kill them, you can mutilate them or otherwise damage their physical or mental integrity, you can deprive them of their liberty, you can damage or destroy their relationships with people and things, you can adversely alter the quality of their lives by affecting their environment or their economic prospects or by imposing onerous burdens on them, or you can achieve your ends by credibly threatening to do all or any of these things. It is not possible to conceive of anything else that might accomplish the goal of creating the massive fear, or terror that is at the heart of terrorism. That is the good news. The bad news—and it is very, very bad— is that with each passing moment ever newer and more horrible ways of undertaking these things are being imagined and made possible by the implacable, onward sweep of technology. That is the awful prospect that looms before us as we proceed into the new millennium. The 19th-century terrorist, if he or she were lucky, might have anticipated a body count in the hundreds, although none attained that target. It was probably easier for the terrorist, especially the anarchist, to concentrate on trying to effect change through coercion against selected individual targets, for example, the assassination of key members of the ruling classes. The 20th-century terrorist never truly reached his or her potential, for which we should be devoutly grateful. The ingredients were there, but somehow, the deadly brew was never administered to its deadliest effect. With regard to the concept and the resources available to it, the attack by Aum Shinrikyu on the Tokyo subway, judged on its results, was puny in the extreme; a 19th-century anarchist operating alone with black powder might have accomplished much more. The World Trade Center bombing in New York, similarly from the terrorists' point of view, produced a pathetically small death toll and nothing like the property damage that was possible. Although the horrific attack on the Murrah Building in Oklahoma City stands above them all in terms of execution, magnitude, and a lasting impression on the psyche of the American people, it is not difficult to imagine how much worse it might have been. This is the frightening face of the future, but in the matter of definition, it is no different from what we have struggled with in the past. This is the fact that is urged here on those who will have to cope with the practical implications of terrorism in the new millennium.

## COMPREHENDING TERRORISM

We seek to define terrorism so as to be better able to cope with it. We cannot begin to counter effectively that which we are unable to fully comprehend or agree on as to its nature. Some 50-odd years have been wasted in trying to disentangle the topic of terrorism from the much grander subject of wars of national liberation.[6] A great deal of time and effort has been expended in trying to make the truly reprehensible politically respectable. As the awesome possibilities of the new millennium are translated into ever more frightening realities, we can no longer afford the fiction that one person's terrorist may yet be another's freedom fighter. Fighting for freedom may well be his or her purpose, but if the mission is undertaken through the employment of terroristic means, a terrorist he or she must remain; we ought not to confuse the sophistry of refinement for the process of definition. This assumes considerable importance as the older forms of terrorism give way, as they must, before the newer and more horrible ways of going about this grim business. For the advances of technology have not all aided the terrorist's purposes. As in so many other departments of modern life, the audience has become increasingly difficult to shock. Indeed, the terrorist nowadays has to struggle mightily against a kind of ennui affecting those he or she would seek to impress. The audience, with the ever present assistance of television reporting of the contemporaneous, has become sated on a diet of death and destruction. The misery of others is fast losing its ability to horrify or, at least, to horrify for very long. Terroristic violence on the screen, whether fact or fiction, has become commonplace; much of the mystery has faded. This has made the terrorist's task increasingly difficult: How do you recapture and refocus the jaded attention of such an audience? The possibilities are really quite limited. You can strive to increase the toll in terms of the body count; compared to conventional warfare, deaths resulting from acts of terrorism have been numerically insignificant. To measure the true potential of terrorism, one would have to look to, say, Rwanda. Alternatively, the terrorist has to imagine novel, strikingly horrible means for doing the traditional things; and, significantly, the execution must match the imaginings. Clearly, whichever course is chosen, some of the mystery has to be reintroduced. Fear feeds off the unknown. We must be careful not to allow this development to warp the process of definition.

## From Weapons of Mass Destruction to Cyberterrorism

The expression "weapons of mass destruction" has now entered firmly into common currency. The expression conjures up visions of lots and lots of casualties and people dying in horrid ways as a result of the employment of such weapons. Because of its awesome, proved potential, nuclear weaponry is perhaps the first type to come to mind when the expression is used. Credible fears of the terrorist nuclear bomb go back at least to the 1970s; much fiction has been written around the theme of the "basement nuclear bomb." The concept has dominated futuristic theorizing about the direction terroristic escalation might take. Nuclear terrorism has, thankfully, remained in the realm of fiction. But, as we stand on the threshold of the new millennium, we would be most unwise to conclude that it will be ever thus. Indeed, it is little short of a miracle that we have not had to face the realities of nuclear terrorism to date. The knowledge and the materials have long been available to those who might have been tempted to engage in some feat of superterrorism (see Schweitzer, 1998). The point here is that if and when this awful eventuality materializes, it will not require any redefinition of terrorism; it will simply sharpen the terms with which it is drawn. We might remind ourselves at this juncture that it matters little to the instant victims whether they are done to death with a hatpin or consigned to perish in a nuclear conflagration. But, viewed in prospect, which is the more fearful, which the more likely to produce social nightmares? Even serially, you cannot account for a great many victims with hatpins. A simple nuclear device in the possession of a competent terrorist would demolish much

property, alter the landscape, and kill and horribly maim a great many human beings. Its employment would alter forever the face of terrorism, and the way we have come to think about it. It would not, however, require us to alter the way we define it.

Until the late 1980s, many tended to think of terrorism in almost climatological terms, as though it were blown by a cold wind out of the East. It was, for the most part, an indelibly Cold War phenomenon; terrorism was often referred to as a form of surrogate warfare. Unpleasant it undoubtedly was, especially for the instant victims, but there did exist a useful measure of control applied by the patron states. The euphoria of the early 1990s blinded us to the dangers inherent in the collapse of the control factor. Whether or not one subscribed to the mutually assured destruction theory, it was very unlikely that the principal antagonists would encourage their surrogates to use weapons of mass destruction that they would be unwilling themselves to employ. The disintegration of the "evil empire" had another unpleasant consequence for terrorism: It unleashed deadly material and put a lot of disengaged experts on the "free" market. Now, we have to face the real possibility of a revitalized Cold War with old Cold Warriors such as Vladimir Putin in the driver's seat. What is uncertain is whether the old controls will be reimposed, or even whether they can. Although none of this is likely to unleash fresh fears of small-group nuclear terrorism in the West, it is likely to have an impact in other areas of perhaps greater concern. The fearful instruments of chemical and biological warfare, largely eschewed by a majority of civilized nations, have acquired the sobriquet of "the poor man's nuclear bomb." Certainly, as death-dealing implements, the term is well applied. There is a kind of inevitability about the employment of these weapons by terrorists. The amount of publicity they have received over the past decade or so alone would have assured that outcome. It is worthy of note, yet again, that these possibilities encouraged by technological advances and political shifts have no definitional significance. The alterations have been simply adjectival. But, they will change the way we think about terrorism as well as about those whose job it is to undertake countermeasures. Sooner maybe than later, one of those packets or envelopes is going to contain anthrax spores, the real thing, rather than the miscellaneous hoax powders that have turned up so far. There is a kind of fearfulness about handling this stuff that, as much as anything else, has probably protected society until now. The fears are not misplaced. Considering the number of terrorist who have blown themselves up with their own bombs, the very unfamiliarity with the handling of some of these substances, especially the nerve gases, suggests perils of an entirely different order from those previously experienced. The first successful employment of chemical and biological agents by terrorists will doubtlessly overcome any lingering inhibitions.

Now, yet another term has to be employed by those seeking to give precision to their particular definitions of terrorism. Not long after heaving a sigh of relief and congratulating ourselves at having avoided the catastrophes of Y2K predicted by the doomsayers, we have been hit with a wave of what is being called "cyberterrorism." Modern society is becoming more and more computer dependent. Everything from electronic commerce to the supply of energy is vulnerable, and although this may not be the immediate objective of the perpetrators, the potential for the associated loss of human life is not inconsiderable.[7] This cyberterrorism is still very much in its infancy; the methods are primitive and unsophisticated but effective. This is not "virtual" terrorism or Game Boy stuff. Cyberspace is a real place; real operations and real functions take place there, and real interests are at risk. The methods are new, but the principles behind their application are as old as terrorism itself. The technology employed has enabled the terrorists to reintroduce a useful, from their point of view, element of mystery into the process. They can, for a little while at least, operate from a considerable distance, concealing their identities and their purposes. The authorities, for the moment, can only confess to a sense of bafflement and try to reassure the affected public that everything possible is being done to protect the systems at risk and to apprehend the culprits. All this is going to generate a new lexicon, and already familiar terms such as

*hackers, computer viruses, trap doors,* and the like will gain greater currency. Yet, we could as easily say these cybersystems were being "kidnapped," "hijacked," or "taken hostage," and when demands are presented to desist, the term *extortion* will come into play. Of greatest interest, perhaps, for the present purposes, a participant in an online discussion opined, "Hackers are freedom fighters for cyberspace" (Weise, 2000, p. 2A). Those who do not learn the lexical lessons of history are obbliged to repeat the semester!

Terrorism, by its nature, seeks out and exploits its opponents' weaknesses. Again, a well-known aphorism has it that "terrorism is the weapon of the weak." This was a definitional device intended to characterize those tarnished with the terrorist label as being those who challenged rightful authority rather than those who abused it through practices that smacked of vicious cruelty. The nation-state has always been ultrasensitive to accusations that it is guilty of terrorism, whether against its own lawful residents or others (see, e.g., Herman & O'Sullivan, 1989). Where these cruelties are egregious, as in the case of Nazi Germany, few would cavil at defining what is done as terrorism. Yet, even that awful regime would claim its actions were in the nature of self-defense, a deterrent to behavior that threatened its cohesiveness and purposes.[8] "Unhappily, such state terrorism is very far from being a thing of the past. As we proceed into the new millennium, we shall be confronted more and more with terrorism that proceeds from the mighty rather than the weak. A practical consequence of this delicacy in the matter of labeling can be seen by studying in any particular year the nations that find themselves on the U.S. State Department's list of "terrorist states," and those that do not. There is a kind of hypocrisy about this process that no definitional sophistry can hide; it simply highlights the perennial difficulty of describing forthrightly what terrorism is, for fear of upsetting those we might find it inconvenient to criticize. This is unfortunate on much more than a linguistic level. Definition is dictated under such circumstances by the harsh realities of power: None dare call it by its rightful name. This is surely the road to

Tiananmen Square, and the consequences of ignoring the route are much more than merely academic.

Terrorism is a naked struggle for power, who shall wield it, and to what ends. The coercive character of what is done is plain enough to require little beyond description. Where the process does not produce the requisite submission, escalation is inevitable; action begets reaction. This is the real challenge to the high-minded. It is here that the state finds it especially needful to characterize what its opponents do as terrorism while seeking to distinguish its own counteraction as something quite different, lacking in reprehensible qualities. While looking at the conduct of those whose political philosophies we do not share, we ought not to disregard too cavalierly the mote in our own eye. No nation-state can relinquish its sovereign authority to an adversary, attempting to seize it by force, and retain its own integrity. Retaliation is an imperative in such cases, but one of the objectives of the adversary is to produce an overreaction. Brutal repression serves the adversary's purposes, so as to give rise to the charge, "See, you are as bad, or worse, than we are. Who is the terrorist now?" The audience is the community of nation-states, which has become increasingly censorious in judging the responses of others, especially when the judges are not directly confronted, for the moment, with terrorism problems of their own. In an ideal world, responses would be measured by much the same criteria as those against which an individual's rights of self-defense at law are evaluated, namely that the response should be necessary, reasonable, and proportionate to the harm suffered or apprehended (Cooper, 1998). We are forced to recognize that the real world in which modern-day terrorism takes place is very far from ideal. It is, rather, a Hobbesian universe in which all life is to be regarded as "nastie, brutish and shorte"—and cheap in the bargain. Terrorism thus becomes a battle for the moral high ground, with those in legitimate power trying to preserve their positions against opponents bent on dragging them into the gutter. The outcome is yet another phenomenological element in the process of defining terrorism that is likely to be of increasing importance in coming decades.

## THE PROBLEM OF DEFINITION REMAINS UNALTERED THROUGHOUT

Thus, at the start of the new millennium, we can say with a high degree of certainty that the definition of terrorism is as needful and as illusory as ever. The fine minds that have engaged in the task over the past three decades or so have provided much fuel for the crucible and a great deal of raw material for the process, but a truly pure ingot has eluded all. Once again, the focus here has been on the problem of definition, which remains unaltered throughout. It is realism rather than pessimism that prompts the observation that this is really a problem without a solution, for none can voluntarily yield the high ground to the others. Terrorism is not a struggle for the hearts and minds of the victims nor for their immortal souls. Rather, it is, as Humpty Dumpty would have said, about who is to be master, that is all. Yet, withal, no one who has experienced terrorism in the flesh has the slightest doubt about what it is or the sensations that it engenders.[9] Ask any concentration camp survivor. Ask those fortunate enough to have returned from the gulag. Ask those who have experienced the more recent examples of ethnic cleansing in the former Yugoslavia or in East Timor. They may not be able to encapsulate the horrors of their respective experiences in a finely turned phrase or two, but what they have undergone is to them and countless others not in the slightest doubt, for it is indelibly engraved on their psyches. Although this cannot suffice for the purposes of the polemic, it does help to focus the debate. As with obscenity, we know terrorism well enough when we see it. For the minds and bodies affected by it, this suffices; definition for these is otiose. This will not and cannot change in the years to come, strive as we may to give precision to the concept. It is diffidently opined here that we would be better employed in refocusing our efforts on what is done, the terrible acts themselves, whether by way of original initiative or retaliation. It might be more admirable to call a spade a spade, in the hands of whoever might be wielding it. These pathetic attempts at making the contemptible respectable will seem as ridiculous to those approaching the end of the present millennium as efforts to rehabilitate Attila the Hun or Genghis Khan would appear in our own times. So we are left, as we began, with our own imperfect formulas and the ever insistent need to explain and expound. As the incomparable Ludwig Wittgenstein (1921/1961) instructed us, "There are, indeed, things that cannot be put into words. *They make themselves manifest.* They are what is mystical" (p. 151). Terrorism is one of those things.

## NOTES

1. Cohen's (1990) *Culture and Conflict in Egyptian-Israeli Relations: A Dialogue of the Deaf* is an excellent scholarly work that deserves to be more widely known.

2. See, for example, the excellent scholarly works of Deborah Tannen, especially *You Just Don't Understand: Women and Men in Conversation* (1990).

3. Representative of these worthy efforts is *International Terrorism: National, Regional, and Global Perspectives* (1976), edited by Yonah Alexander.

4. Terror and terrorism tend to be confused, somewhat awkwardly, in Frederick J. Hacker's (1976) well-known work *Crusaders, Criminals, Crazies: Terror and Terrorism in Our Time.*

5. See, generally, the thoughtful arguments of Noam Chomsky, especially his chapter "International Terrorism: Image and Reality" in *Western State Terrorism* (1991z), edited by Alexander George.

6. One of the more thoughtful and eclectic symposia on this subject was held in 1976 at Glassboro State College. The splendidly edited proceedings volume, *International Terrorism in the Contemporary World* (Livingston, 1978), contains the following, written by the author, on its first page: "Many nations have recognized the great potential of terrorism; the terrorist is now the spearhead of a developing theory and practice of surrogate warfare."

7. Such an attack on the air traffic control system, for example, has long been feared.

8. "Terrorism was the chief instrument of securing the cohesion of the German people in war purposes" (Office of the Chief Counsel for the Prosecution of Axis Criminality, 1946, p. 144).

9. There is something faintly paradoxical about this that is reminiscent of the renowned cat of Schrödinger, seemingly capable of being alive and dead at the same time.

## REFERENCES

Alexander, Y. (Ed.). (1976). *International terrorism: National, regional, and global perspectives.* New York: Praeger.

Cohen, R. (1990). *Culture and conflict in Egyptian-Israeli relations: A dialogue of the deaf.* Bloomington: Indiana University Press.

Cooper, H.H.A. (1978). Terrorism: The problem of the problem of definition. *Chitty's Law Journal, 26*(3), 105–108.

Cooper, H.H.A. (1998). Self-defense. In *Encyclopedia Americana* (Vol. 25, pp. 532). Danbury, CT: Grolier.

Chomsky, N. (1991). International terrorism: Image and reality. In A. George (Ed.), *Western state terrorism* (pp. 12–38). New York: Routledge.

Gourevich, P. (2000, February 14). A cold case. *The New Yorker,* 42–60.

Hacker, F.J. (1976). *Crusaders, criminals, crazies: Terror and terrorism in our time.* New York: Norton.

Herman, E., & O'Sullivan, G. (1989). The Western model and semantics of terrorism. In *The "terrorism industry: The experts and institutions that shape our view of terror.* New York: Pantheon.

Livingston, M.H. (with Kress, L.B., & Wanek, M.G.). (Eds.). (1978). *International terrorism in the contemporary world.* Westport, CT: Greenwood.

Office of the Chief Counsel for the Prosecution of Axis Criminality. (1946). *Nazi conspiracy and aggression.* Washington, DC: Government Printing Office.

Posner, R.A. (1999). *An affair of state: The investigation, impeachment, and trial of President Clinton.* Cambridge, MA: Harvard University Press.

Schweitzer, G.E. (with Dorsch, C.C.). (1998). *Superterrorism: Assassins, mobsters, and weapons of mass destruction.* New York: Plenum.

Tannen, D. (1990). *You just don't understand: Women and men in conversation.* New York: Ballantine.

Weise, E. (2000, February 10). Online talk is of conspiracy, crime and punishment. *USA Today,* p. 2A.

Wittgenstein, L. (1961). *Tractatus logico-philosophicus.* London: Routledge Kegan Paul. (Original work published 1921)

## Mixed Message: The Arab and Muslim Response to 'Terrorism'

Mustafa Al Sayyid

Many Arab and Muslim countries sympathized with the victims of September 11 and offered valuable support to the United States in its campaign against Osama bin Laden's organization and the Taliban regime in Afghanistan. Yet large sections of the Arab and Muslim public, as well as many of their governments, cannot offer the United States full support in its fight against terrorism because they do not share with the United States the same definition of terrorism and suspect a hidden agenda behind the future phases of this campaign. The general public in the West, particularly in the United States, may not realize that the earliest victims of armed groups claiming to be inspired by certain interpretations of Islam were themselves Muslims—intellectuals, senior officials of government, ordinary citizens, and security police. These people lived in Muslim countries such as Algeria, Egypt, Yemen, and Saudi Arabia years before a small group of alleged members of an Islamic organization launched its deadly attacks of September 11 in New York City and Washington, D.C. Arab and Muslim countries, therefore, did not need any particular preaching on the part of Washington to join an international campaign against terrorism because many of them had long been involved. Arab people have learned, however, that terrorism cannot be defeated if those who fight it rely exclusively on military force.

## ISLAM AND TERRORISM

To start this story at its inception, reflection on any possible link between Islam and terrorism is important. Because some Western media tend to label those individuals involved in terrorist actions "Muslim terrorists," the positions taken by Arab and Muslim states on the White House's "war on terrorism" should be analyzed. One should consider that the U.S. State Department's list of terrorist organizations mostly includes organizations that are active in Muslim countries, which becomes the focus of

media reporting, while ignoring organizations in non-Muslim countries, such as Spain, Northern Ireland, and Latin America, and reinforcing a perception in Western public opinion that terrorism is exclusively Islamic. Western media also uses jihad to convey the notion of an armed struggle launched by Muslims against people of other religions in order to compel them to renounce their religions and adopt Islam. Based on these observations, examining if there is an unbroken link between Islam and terrorism is necessary.

Popular Western media tends to misconstrue the relationship between Islam and terrorism significantly. Attributing a particular policy position on the use of armed struggle for political ends to any religion as a whole is difficult. Among Christians, one can find militant priests in Latin America, such as Colombia's Camillo Torres, who justify armed struggle in terms of a theology of liberation. Islam, as any other world religion, can be interpreted in various ways.

More importantly, those who believe that Islam can guide and inspire a political order do not necessarily seek to establish that political order by force. Many Islamic political movements try to seek political power using peaceful methods. The Rafah Party in Turkey is one; others can be found in Jordan, Yemen, Lebanon, Indonesia, Malaysia, Pakistan, and Bangladesh. Islamic organizations such as the Muslim Brothers in Egypt, the Islamic Salvation Front in Algeria, and the Nahda Party in Tunisia accept a pluralist political system and an electoral path to political power. The government in each of these countries bans these parties, however, because they constitute serious contenders for power that the ruling groups, who are reluctant to accept any transfer of power through the ballot box, reject.

Furthermore, the notion of forced conversion is alien to Islam. Although explaining their religion to others is a duty incumbent on Muslims, Islam considers the question of faith a personal matter. Most Muslims recognize and respect the religions of Christians and Jews and consider their holy and respect the religions of Christians and Jews and consider their holy books sacred texts for Muslims as well. Indeed, the Prophet Muhammad married a Coptic Christian from Egypt. When the notion of jihad was applied during the early days of the Prophet Muhammad, it meant armed struggle against the enemies of the new faith who were launching war against it. Once the new faith triumphed with Muhammad's entry into Mecca, jihad acquired a new meaning. In Muhammad's words, the "greater jihad" meant an inner struggle to suppress one's evil desires and elevate one's soul.

According to the most authoritative statements on the Islamic theory of international relations, the so-called division of the world into the realm of war (*dar al-harb*) and the realm of Islam (*dar al-islam*) does not hold in the modern world because reciprocal commitments to maintain friendly relations tie Muslim states to other countries. The mere establishment of diplomatic relations with other nations signals that the other country has become part of the realm of commitment (*dar al-'ahd*).[1]

Yet, political Islam—just like Arab nationalism and Marxism—can be interpreted in several ways. Some versions would call for the use of exclusively peaceful methods of political action. Other versions of the same ideologies would justify and legitimize armed struggle against those domestic and foreign powers that seem to pose an obstacle to the realization of the political strategy inspired by these ideologies. Thus, some Muslim activists would interpret verses of the Qur'an or traditions of the Prophet Mohammed to serve their own political ends, however they conceive them. Nevertheless, just as no one in his or her right mind would charge all Protestants or Catholics of being terrorists because certain Protestant or Catholic groups in Northern Ireland resort to armed action, by the same logic, the presence of certain terrorist groups that call themselves Islamic does not make Islam and all its adherents potential terrorists and a threat to the rest of humanity.

As this introduction conveys, Arab and Muslim states do not feel that they bear any special responsibility in the battle against terrorism. Even if one accepts the claims bin Laden made in his televised statements—as well as the

charges of the U.S. government that the perpetrators of the tragic and condemnable attacks on September 11 are all Arabs and Muslims—terrorism has nothing to do with Islam and Arabism because these individuals cannot, by any stretch of the imagination, be considered representative of approximately one billion Muslims.

Not reflecting on the reasons that would lead people to commit such acts, however, would be completely irresponsible. Inquiring about the motivations is not an attempt to justify or excuse what happened on September 11, as commonly assumed in the United States, but just the opposite. If the causes of such acts are not understood, the victims of the tragic events of September 11, as well as the victims of any future terrorist acts, will be disserved. Those who do not learn from history are bound to pay a bitter price in the future.

Arab and Muslim governments also do not feel that they bear more responsibility than other countries in the fight against terrorism. Not only have a number of these governments been engaged in the fight against terrorism for many years, but they have also not received much support from the governments of the United States and the United Kingdom. At different times during the 1980s, Egypt, Algeria, Jordan, Syria, Saudi Arabia, and even Iraq and Libya were engaged in a fight against Islamic organizations that were using armed struggle in an attempt to overthrow or at least destabilize their governments. The extent of the armed insurrection has varied from country to country—sporadic in Jordan, Libya, Iraq, and Tunisia; more serious in Saudi Arabia; quite protracted in Egypt; and bloodiest, but short-lived, in Syria and Algeria. Pointing the finger at these countries and accusing them of not doing enough to curb terrorism would simply be ignoring well-established facts.

Moreover, leaders of these countries, particularly President Hosni Mubarak of Egypt, have called on Western governments not to provide easy asylum to well-known key figures in militant Islamic organizations who are wanted for trial for their involvement in terrorist acts. For example, Shaykh Omar Abdel-Rahmanthe—spiritual leader of the Islamic Group, or *Al-Jama'a al-Islamiyyah,* who calls on members to launch armed attacks to topple the Egyptian government—was given an entry visa to the United States, where he stayed and continued to agitate against the Egyptian government until he was arrested for his role in the 1993 attempt to blow up the World Trade Center. Members of the Islamic Group, including two of the shaykh's sons, joined the International Islamic Front led by bin Laden in Afghanistan. The United Kingdom gave political asylum to Yasser Al-Sirri, suspected mastermind of the assassination of Ahmed Shah Mas'oud, the former leader of Afghanistan's Northern Alliance. Many leaders of Islamic organizations in Tunisia and Algeria, such as Rashid Al-Ghanoushi, have also found asylum in the United Kingdom. Habib Al-Adli, the Egyptian minister of interior, pointed out that, of all Western countries that were warned about the presence of Egyptian terrorists on their territories, only Italy was willing to offer some cooperation.[2]

## REACTIONS OF ARAB AND MUSLIM COUNTRIES TO SEPTEMBER 11

As with any broad discussion, examining "the" Arab and Muslim response to terrorism in general, and the September 11 attacks in particular, is difficult. The positions of Arab and Muslim countries on these issues cover a large spectrum. These positions, moreover, have not been consistent from the beginning of the crisis with the attacks of September 11 through the U.S. military operations that led to the fall of the Taliban regime in Afghanistan and the installment of a provisional administration in late December 2001. In addition, Arab governments' formal positions have not always truly reflected public opinion in these countries. Indeed, a major dilemma for U.S. commentators has been not just the indifference but the open hostility with which the public in a number of Arab and Muslim countries met the U.S. war against terrorism.[3]

When news of the September 11 events reached the capitals of Arab and Muslim countries, their reactions were varied. On the whole, all Arab and Muslim governments condemned the attacks and expressed sympathy for the American people. Holding ranks with other Arab governments, Iraq's President Saddam Hussein, Deputy Prime Minister Tariq Aziz, and Permanent Representative to the United Nations (UN) Mohammed al-Douri all deplored these attacks and expressed sympathy with their victims. Aziz in particular categorically rejected any link between Iraq and the perpetrators of the attacks.[4] When U.S. authorities first revealed the identities of those suspected of hijacking the planes, public opinion in Arab countries was generally skeptical of the reliability of such information, particularly because some of the names were of people who were either still alive in Saudi Arabia and the United Arab Emirates or who had died years earlier.

Numerous Arab commentators believed it to be unlikely that bin Laden, whom U.S. authorities declared a prime suspect in the attacks, could have been capable of masterminding such an elaborate, well-timed, and well-synchronized attack from his hideout in the mountains of Afghanistan. Many people in Arab countries remained perplexed about why bin Laden declared his support for the attacks in later televised statements relayed to the Arab world through Qatar's Al Jazeera television network. Even when he suggested in another televised videotape that he knew in advance of the attacks and its details, Arab public opinion continued to be divided between those who believed that he masterminded the attacks and condemned him and those who thought that the attacks were the acts of the enemies of Arabs and Muslims who wanted to drive a wedge between the Arabs and Muslims and Western people. The conversation on that televised tape, for them, was simply fake.[5]

When the U.S. government resolved to undertake military action against Al Qaeda—the organization believed to be led by bin Laden and supported by the Taliban regime in Afghanistan, where bin Laden has been living—most Arab and Muslim governments reluctantly joined what the U.S. government called "a worldwide coalition against terror." The degree of support varied, however, from total support (Kuwait, Bahrain, Qatar, and Jordan), to verbal support (Tunisia, Algeria, and Morocco), and support coupled with criticism (Saudi Arabia and Egypt).

Apart from Pakistan, Uzbekistan, Turkey, and Jordan, few Arab and Muslim governments adopted a position of total support for U.S. military action in Afghanistan. Pakistan, which had been the Taliban's major source of economic, military, and diplomatic aid, shifted its posture completely—first, by attempting to persuade Afghanistan's Taliban leaders to agree to hand bin Laden over to U.S. authorities; later, by offering logistical and intelligence support to the U.S. military; and finally, by withdrawing diplomatic recognition of the Taliban regime following its retreat from Kabul in November when it seemed that its days were numbered. Pakistan's alignment with the United States was a major risk for its head of state, General Pervez Musharraf, who faced difficult foreign and domestic policy choices. On the one hand, India, Pakistan's traditional rival, was offering the United States varied military assistance in the war against the Taliban regime. Had Pakistan denied the United States the same assistance, it would have incurred the United States' wrath, enabling India to gain a diplomatic advantage. On the other hand, if Pakistan aided the United States, Musharraf's government would face serious domestic opposition and would be sacrificing a friendly neighboring regime in Afghanistan. Musharraf decided to take the risk of increased domestic tension to gain some U.S. diplomatic and economic support, deny India its monopoly of U.S. favors in the subcontinent, and hopefully ensure a voice for Pakistan in deciding the future of Afghanistan.

Uzbekistan also took a major risk by allowing the United States to use its air bases to launch operations in northern Afghanistan, to provide areas from which U.S. special forces could undertake underground operations into northern Afghanistan in the early phases of the war, and to assist Northern Alliance troops. Uzbekistan's strategic location and the Northern Alliance's early successes, gaining control over Mazar-e Sharif as well as Kabul, reduced the strategic importance of Pakistan in the later stages of the U.S. military effort in Afghanistan. Other countries of the Commonwealth of Independent States, such as Tajikistan, Turkmenistan, Kyrgyzstan, and Kazakhstan, offered logistical services, later acknowledged by Secretary of State Colin Powell in his tour of these countries following the fall of the Taliban regime in December. Some of them faced internal opposition by Islamic movements that the Taliban regime supported; all were hoping to benefit from U.S. generosity after the war.

Turkey's support for the United States surprised no one. The Turkish government offered to send a small contingent of troops to train Northern Alliance forces and expressed its readiness to send troops to participate in a future peacekeeping force in Afghanistan. The Turkish government's position is consistent with the domestic and foreign policy it has pursued in recent years, which the country's military establishment firmly supports. The Turkish government has been adopting an extremely secular stance in its relations toward its domestic Islamic parties, to the extent that it has outlawed even those Islamic parties that abide by the rules of democratic politics. In foreign policy, the Turkish government considers alignment with U.S. policies the best way to get the Bush administration to use its leverage to persuade European countries to relax the requirements for Turkey's admission into the European Union. Moreover, Turkey views a military presence in Afghanistan as a way to strengthen its position as a key player in the regional politics of Central Asia, a region in which it shows great interest.

Thus far, the Jordanian government has been the only other Arab government to offer to send troops to partake in a future peacekeeping force in Afghanistan. Jordan's King Abdullah, standing next to President George W. Bush at the White House in mid-September 2001, was eager to announce Jordan's total solidarity with the American people as well as its willingness to offer all the aid it could under the present circumstances. The young king has been careful to pursue the policy that his father, who tried to safeguard the independence of his country by allying Jordan with the dominant powers in the Middle East and in the world, had laid down. King Abdullah wants to maintain cordial relations with the United States and avoid deteriorating relations with Israel, despite the intransigent policies of the government of Prime Minister Ariel Sharon. Algerian president Abdul-Aziz Bouteflika's forceful position in support of U.S. actions should occasion no surprise.

Many other countries in the Arab and Muslim world support the United States in its political and military campaign against both bin Laden and Al Qaeda as well as the Taliban regime, as clearly indicated in statements issued by the Organization of the Islamic Conference in its Doha summit in October 2001.[6] Their support, however, is limited to backing the U.S. effort diplomatically, sharing intelligence, and freezing funds that individuals and organizations suspected of sympathizing with terrorists allegedly used, steps that follow UN Security Council Resolution 1373.

Another group of Arab and Muslim countries did not hesitate to condemn the terrorist attacks on the United States or to share intelligence with U.S. authorities, but these states—Egypt and Saudi Arabia, in particular—were critical of certain aspects of the U.S. response to the attacks. The *Washington Post* and the *New York Times,* among other U.S. newspapers, have published editorials that were quite critical of the positions of these two governments, accusing them of not providing the United States with sufficient support in its battle against terrorism.

Before the United States began military operations in Afghanistan, Mubarak, who is skeptical about using massive force to deal with terrorism, suggested that terrorism is a complex problem, one that is rooted in frustrations caused by a lack of progress in resolving issues affecting Arab peoples and one that requires an international solutions. He reiterated a proposal he made for the first time in 1995 following a failed attempt on his life by Egyptian Islamists in Addis Ababa, Ethiopia. Mubarak attenuated his reservations against the use of force to deal with the problem of terrorist attacks on the United States, but he emphasized that no Egyptian troops would be sent to fight in Afghanistan. He added that Egypt would not participate in a peacekeeping force in Afghanistan. Mubarak was careful to point out, however, that the Egyptian government supported the U.S. military effort. He even expressed delight that the problem of bin Laden would finally vanish.[7]

Some Saudi officials were more outspoken in their disapproval and concern about the suffering of the civilian population in Afghanistan as a result of the U.S. military campaign. The Arab media, especially Al Jazeera, which is widely watched in Saudi Arabia, kept its viewers well informed about reports of the extent of civilian casualties in Afghanistan, particularly sensitive issue for Saudi Arabia not only because of the country's claims to leadership in the Muslim world but also because of Saudi Arabia's close relationship with the Taliban regime. Saudi Arabia was one of three countries (along with Pakistan and the United Arab Emirates) that had recognized and maintained diplomatic relations with the Taliban government. (Only Pakistan maintained diplomatic relations with the Taliban regime after the fall of Kabul, allegedly on advice from the United States, as a way to maintain a channel of communication with the Taliban leadership.) Some Saudi officials also expressed displeasure that some of the personalities and organizations whose assets were frozen at the request of the UN Security Council committee in charge of implementing the resolution on fighting terrorism were included on that list on very shaky and suspicious grounds. Prince Nayef, the minister of interior, reiterated several times that U.S. authorities did not provide any convincing evidence about the involvement of Saudis in the September 11 attacks; the Saudi government revoked bin Laden's Saudi nationality some time ago. Although some Saudis criticized the civilian casualties in Afghanistan, U.S. officials nevertheless declared their appreciation of the cooperation they received from Saudi authorities in the war.

Other voices in the Arab and Muslim world were critical of the U.S. military campaign, but this reaction came from quarters that are critical of U.S. policy in general. Iran's president Muhammed Ali Khatami, for example, did not like the two choices that Bush put to the rest of the world—"Either you are with the United States, or you are with the terrorists."—arguing that Iran was neither with the United States nor with terrorists. The Iranian government also condemned the use of military force against the Afghan people. Nevertheless, the Iranian government has been careful not to take any practical steps to thwart U.S. military action in Afghanistan.

## PUBLIC OPINION: DIVIDED OR CRITICAL?

Despite the overall supportive positions taken by governments in Arab and Muslim countries toward the United States in its campaign against terrorism, reading a U.S. newspaper would give one the impression that public opinion in those countries is quite critical of the United States and even sympathetic toward bin Laden and his followers. Because most of these countries have no reliable polls to gauge public opinion, one can only attempt to do so by looking at media coverage in these countries. Some judgments can be made by examining a sampling of what has appeared in the mainstream media in the Arab world.

Public opinion in many Arab countries has been quite divided on the issue of what happened in New York City and Washington, D.C., on September 11, as well as the U.S. response to these events and the impact of the attacks on Arab and Muslim countries. Some have been concerned that these events would have a negative impact on relations between Arab as well as Muslim countries on the one hand and Western countries on the other, particularly the United States. Others were concerned about the projected images of Islam and Muslims, which certain media and prominent Western politicians immediately linked with terrorism and the absence of freedom. Some in the business sector were apprehensive that they might be punished twice—first by the economic forces of a deepened recession, then as a result of prejudices against Muslims that would be the natural outcome of the association some in the West try to establish between Islam and terrorism. Finally, some political strategies believed that Muslim countries had a great deal to gain from the West by aligning completely on the side of the United States at the moment when it most needed their moral support. Turkish, Pakistani, and Jordanian government supporters were among these groupings, as were those who called on the Egyptian government to endorse the U.S. position more forthrightly.

Nevertheless, many people in Arab and Muslim countries presumably were not convinced of any of the evidence that the U.S. government presented to prove that bin Laden and his organization organized the September 11 events. Many did not see any reason to insist 25 million Afghan people pay the price for something that was allegedly done by an individual or a small group of people. The release of two bin Laden videotapes, in which he came close to admitting knowledge of and even inspiration for the September 11 attacks, did not change these initial positions. According to one school of thought, no matter how distasteful the Taliban regime was, the war that the United States launched in Afghanistan has disrupted the lives of millions of Afghans who should have been spared that heavy price—notwithstanding the airdrops of food packages in the same areas that U.S. warplanes had bombed. For these segments of Arab and Muslim public opinion, the belief that an end to terrorism could be sought through the use of military means is quite naive. The use of force by the United States would breed more terrorism in the future, fed by the frustrations of victims of the U.S. attacks, many of whom perhaps had not been involved with the Taliban regime but suffered as a result of the so-called collateral damage of U.S. military operations.

Moreover, these same segments of Arab and Muslim public opinion consider the U.S. administration's definition of terrorism to be rather selective. One can understand that the United States considers bin Laden and members of Al Qaeda—who have acknowledged their responsibility for attacks on the U.S. embassies in Nairobi and Dar es Salaam as well as U.S. military bases and a warship in Saudi Arabia and the Persian Gulf region—to be terrorists. The same standard would no doubt apply to those who perpetrated the September attacks. Arabs, Muslims, and many others around the world, however, question the U.S. criteria that categorize groups that are fighting against foreign military occupation as terrorist organizations, even though U.S. State Department experts know fully well that international law recognizes the legitimate right of all people to self-defense. Thus, many Middle Easterners feel that the White House adapts its concept of terrorism to whatever suits its needs at the moment and considers those fighting Israeli military occupation of the Palestinian territories in the West Bank and Gaza Strip and what remains in southern Lebanon to be terrorists.

From this viewpoint, the U.S. administration prefers to ignore real terrorist practices when its closest friends, foremost Israel, conduct them. The Israeli government not only has persisted in its military occupation of Arab territories in Palestine, the Golan Heights, and the Sheb'a farms in southern Lebanon, but it also has consolidated this occupation by building settlements in defiance of several UN resolutions that the U.S. government itself supported. Reneging on its promise to negotiate an end to occupation, the Israeli government has declared the Oslo Accords dead and, in the face of Palestinians' legitimate resistance to the occupation, has proceeded to carry out a policy of siege, closure of Palestinian towns, economic blockade, and targeted assassination of Palestinian leaders. Any objective observer would find that state terrorism is the only name that can be used to describe this Israeli policy. The U.S. administration's reaction has been at best a mild reproach of Israel that rarely comes at the worst moment of Israeli atrocities and is usually pronounced by a junior member of the administration. In the eyes of the Arab and Muslim public, this course of action amounts to a double standard.

Another major cause for concern among Arab and Muslim people has been the mystery the U.S. administration has fostered about its plans for the duration of the campaign against terrorism. Bush has stated a number of times that the campaign against terrorism would be a long one that would continue for years and involve other countries and organizations. Initial reports in the U.S. press and later statements by senior U.S. officials suggested that some Arab countries were indeed targeted for future phases of the campaign, the prime candidate being Iraq. Bush himself threatened the use of force if Hussein refused to allow UN arms inspectors to return to Iraq. Powell said on December 5 that the United States had not yet decided whether to launch a strike against Iraq.

Such statements have been so alarming that many world leaders, including the German chancellor and French president as well as Egyptian and Saudi senior officials, have warned that striking at Iraq would be a mistake. It is doubtful that any of those leaders have much sympathy for the Iraqi regime, but implicating Iraq in this war against terrorism casts serious doubts on U.S. intentions underlying the whole enterprise. In fact, immediately after the September 11 attacks, some U.S. officials suggested that Iraqi intelligence services had had contact with some of the people who hijacked the planes that struck the World Trade Center, but the officials did not offer any convincing evidence and did not repeat the allegation. More importantly, talk of toppling Saddam was an open secret in Washington in the spring of 2001, months before the September attacks. Large segments of the Arab and Muslim world, including some policymakers, believe that the U.S. administration is using the campaign against terrorism as a pretext to carry out its own hidden agenda, which has nothing to do with the war against terrorism.

## WHERE WE GO FROM HERE

In the wake of the fall of the Taliban regime, the vast majority of Arab and Muslim countries are abiding by the Security Council resolution on fighting terrorism and cooperating with the established committee to implement the different measures included in that resolution. Four Muslim countries reportedly expressed interest in participating in the peacekeeping force in Afghanistan, namely Jordan, Turkey, Bangladesh, and Indonesia. Saudi Arabia is participating in the financial effort to help rebuild Afghanistan. Arab and Muslim and other concerned countries are expected to continue sharing intelligence on terrorist organizations.

Continued talk by U.S. officials of other phases in the war, however, causes much concern in the Arab and Muslim world for two reasons. First, the U.S. definition of terrorism does not distinguish between those launching a just armed struggle against the illegal occupation of their land and those using force against elected, legitimate governments. Accordingly, the U.S. administration considers Palestinians fighting Israeli troops inside the occupied West Bank and Gaza Strip to be terrorists. Second, the U.S. administration does not condemn state terrorism. U.S. spokespersons did not recognize the Israeli government's siege of Palestinian towns and villages and targeted assassination of Palestinian officials by Israeli secret services, which provoked suicide attacks on the part of Palestinian groups, as terrorist actions. That the United States provides Israel with the economic and military means through which it executes such policies but protects Israel from any UN condemnation is even more frustrating for Arabs. For example, in early December the United States thwarted a resolution supported by 12 members of the UN Security Council to send international observers to monitor the safety of the civilian population in the West Bank and Gaza Strip.

Under these conditions, for most Arab and Muslim governments to extend more support to the United States for future phases of its war against terror becomes difficult. Of course, Yemen, concerned that it might become a possible target in a second phase in this so-called war, did begin its own internal efforts against alleged members of Al Qaeda, with the help of special forces trained by the United States and under the personal guidance of President Ali Abdallah Saleh's son. Somalia, another possible target in a future phase in this war, offered to cooperate with the United States while denying any presence of Al Qaeda members on its territory.

These two examples demonstrate that, although the governments of a few countries had incomplete control over their territories, such as Afghanistan, Yemen, and Somalia, no Muslim government encouraged terrorist activities against U.S. citizens or officials. Many Arab and Muslim governments did face problems with their own terrorists. They spared no effort fighting them and did not always receive the timely support they expected from the international community. Ironically, the U.S. government played a role in encouraging the groups of young people who went to Afghanistan in the 1980s to fight the Soviet military presence there and who ended up fighting the United States.

Even before the events of September 11, a gulf of mistrust separated the United States from large sections of the Arab and Muslim public and policymakers. What the U.S. administration is contemplating at present—launching a second phase of this war against other Arab and Muslim countries while doing very little to stop state terrorism practiced, for example, by Israel—risks widening this gulf even further and does not bode well for friendly relations between the United States and Arab and Muslim nations in the future.

Apart from exchanging intelligence, participating in a peacekeeping force in Afghanistan, and contributing to the rebuilding of Afghanistan, the best service that Arabs and Muslims can offer to the U.S. administration and to the U.S. people is its advice for the United States to cooperate with Arab and Muslim peoples and governments to find nonmilitary solutions for the profound causes that push some young people to take up arms against their own governments and those of other countries. This approach could perhaps be the best way to promote the ideals of the American Revolution: life, liberty, and the pursuit of happiness, by all people.

## NOTES

1. Majid Khadduri, "The Islamic Theory of International Relations and Its Contemporary Relevance," in Harris Proctor, ed., *Islam and International Relations* (London and Dunmow, England: Pall Mall Press, 1964), pp. 26–27, 35–38.

2. *Mussawwar,* December 28, 2001, p. 8.

3. See in particular articles by Thomas Friedman in the *New York Times* and several editorials in the *Washington Post* during October 2001.

4. *Iraqi News Agency,* October 21, 2001; *Al-Ahram,* September 18 and October 7, 2001.

5. For examples of press reactions in the Arab world, see "Slalma Ahmed Salama," *Al-Ahram,* December 2001.

6. Statement of the Secretary General of the Organization of the Islamic Conference, October 11, 2001.

7. Mubarak became more forthcoming in his support of the U.S. preparation to launch military action in Afghanistan following his visit to Paris and his meeting with President Jacques Chirac on September 24, 2001. Prior to that date, he was critical of both the notion of an international alliance against terrorism, arguing that it would be divisive, and of the use of massive military force against terrorist organizations. His statements were reported in *Al-Ahram* and *Al-Hayat* newspapers.

## Choices of Law, Choices of War

Noah Feldman

Is terrorism crime, or is it war? What conceptual framework will or should the United States use to conceptualize its fight against terror? The distinction between crime and war, embodied in international and domestic legal regimes, institutional-administrative divisions, and in such legislation as the Posse Comitatus Act,[1] requires serious rethinking in the light of the terrorist attacks of September 11, 2001.[2] Whether we choose the framework of war, the framework of criminal pursuit and prosecution, or, as is more likely, some complicated combination of the two will have major ramifications in the spheres of law, politics, and policy.

This essay proposes to examine a few of the most important and interesting problems associated with the choice of framework, and to address in a preliminary way the central question of how the crime/war distinction should be treated, developed, preserved, or revised. Part I investigates the distinction between crime and war and proposes four criteria that underlie that intuitive distinction. Applying these criteria shows that some cases, such as international terrorism, can plausibly be characterized as both crime and war and that these cases therefore undermine the binary character of the crime/war distinction. Part II considers the practical consequences of the crime/war distinction for the pursuit and capture of international terrorists, paying particular attention to a striking asymmetry; on the one hand, criminals generally may not be killed by their pursuers if they pose no immediate threat, but may be punished after capture; adversaries in war, on the other hand, may generally be killed in pursuit without giving quarter, but generally cannot be punished after they are captured. (War criminals constitute a complicated hybrid category.) There is therefore reason to think that U.S. policy can and will treat international terrorists as war adversaries while they are being pursued and as criminals of some sort after they are captured. Part III briefly considers the institutional and administrative implications of the breakdown of the crime/war distinction in the case of

combating international terror and dicusses the sorts of institutional changes that may be appropriate. The general suggestion of the Essay is that it may not be necessary to choose either crime was as an exclusive general framework for addressing problems of international terror. Rather, the framework itself may require reexamination—a reexamination perhaps long overdue, but in any case prompted in the United States by the events of September 11.

## I. WAR AND CRIME: A BRIEF EXCURSUS

What sort of distinction is the familiar one between war and crime? Begin with the traditional distinction between crimes against domestic law and acts of war against a state. Both crime and war involve acts that in some sense offend against the state—after all, crime was long said to violate "the king's peace."[3] But a crime violates the laws of the state, whereas a war involves a violation of, or a challenge to, a state's sovereignty more generally. What are the constitutive elements of this distinction?

The first element of the crime/war distinction, which interacts in complicated ways with the other elements I shall discuss, is the identity of the actor. International law traditionally took the view that only a sovereign state could perform an act of war. Reciprocally, the domestic law of jurisdiction has traditionally incorporated the view that sovereign states are immune from criminal (and civil) prosecution, as indeed are their leaders.[4] Call this the *identity* criterion: the actor's identity plays a role in determining the difference between war and crime. The identity criterion may not have an independent logical basis,[5] but it certainly plays a key role in our intuitive understanding of the differences between crime and war. Our intuition tells us that states make wars and individuals commit crimes.

A second salient element of the distinction lies in jurisdictional provenance. For an act to count as a crime, it must be committed by someone who falls within the relevant jurisdiction. The standard view of jurisdiction, embodied in, for example, *Restatement (Third) of Foreign Relations Law,* gives a state jurisdiction over actions taken within its borders; actions intended to have substantial effects within its borders (even if taken outside the borders); actions against its nationals, even nationals abroad under some circumstances; and actions taken outside the state that are directed against the security of the state.[6]

This view of jurisdiction builds on the basic intuition that crimes are archetypically committed within the state itself. Expansion of criminal jurisdiction outside the geographical boundaries of the state is designed to protect persons and property that are either within the state or so closely associated with the state as to count as within it. By contrast, war is typically waged by some force or power that is located outside the state's jurisdiction, although in the course of war, the outside power may make incursions into the state's jurisdiction. Notwithstanding that such incursions harm the state's interests and authorize self-defense and the use of force, it is difficult to imagine a domestic law that prohibits invasion by a foreign power. It would be very strange, for example, for the United States to pass a domestic law making it a crime for Canada or Mexico to invade the United States. Part of the reason appears to be that no one state possesses the supranational jurisdiction to prohibit war. If crime violates the king's peace, then war violates a peace that (in the traditional view) does not belong to anybody, since no one state has the supranational jurisdiction to prohibit war. Call this jurisdictional element the *provenance* criterion of the crime/war distinction.

A third salient element of the crime/war distinction has to do with the intent of those who commit crime or wage war. A criminal typically intends to achieve some prohibited end and to get away with it by avoiding discovery, prosecution, and punishment. He normally does not deny the state's legitimate right to enact the law that he violates. By contrast, the body that commits an act of war against a state normally intends to contest the state's legitimate right to something.[7] Perhaps the war-maker contests the attacked state's sovereignty over some piece of land, or contests the legitimacy of some act

of alleged aggression by the attacked state. Sometimes, though not always, the attacker contests the very legitimacy of the attacked state's government, and seeks to replace it. In any case, it will be rare (though not unimaginable) for those who wage war to acknowledge the complete legitimacy of the attacked state's identity and actions and to say simply that the war is aimed at expanding territory or seeking revenge. Shakespeare's Henry V launches his invasion of France after his legal advisers reassure him that he is the legitimate heir to the French throne, notwithstanding the Salic law prohibition on inheritance through the female line.[8] The War of Jenkins's Ear took place some eight years after Captain Jenkins lost the ear in question to a Spanish knife, but as the eponym suggests, even that war was said to have a *casus belli* grounded in the illegitimate actions of Spain.[9] Call this the *intentionality* criterion of the crime/war distinction.

Finally there is a fourth element, one relating to the scale of the hostile action taken. Call it the *scale* criterion. This criterion is even less susceptible to precise characterization than the other three criteria, but nonetheless it matters in some way. Large-scale hostilities seem more plausibly to constitute war than do small-scale ones. A shot fired in anger across a hostile border by a single enemy soldier with the intent to challenge the legitimacy of the government on the other side—even if the shot were ordered through the chain of command—would not normally be considered an act of war unless it were followed by lots more shooting. Although occasionally a *casus belli* may be small (consider Jenkins's ear again), usually such as *casus belli* suggests that the attacked party is looking for an excuse to say that war has begun against it. When the hostilities mount in scale, the escalation looks more like war. Similarly crime on a large enough scale—an organized syndicate's robbing, for example, thousands of banks in a day, killing hundreds of guards and police— begins to resemble war.

The hard cases on the border of the crime/war distinction show the importance of all four criteria: identity, provenance, intentionality, and scale. Is treason under the U.S. Constitution war or a crime? The Constitution does not resolve the question satisfactorily. It says that treason may consist in "levying war against," or in "adhering to" the enemies of, the United States, but it also, of course, prescribes a trial for charges of treason.[10] The very notion of treason requires action by someone within the state's jurisdiction, whether geographical or personal;[11] this is a provenance argument for viewing treason as a crime. However, while those who commit treason do not themselves normally constitute a state (except in the contested case of secession), they may be "adhering to" an aggressor state, which will complicate matters and make their act look like war. The identity criterion therefore raises tricky problems. Treason will often involve a challenge to the legitimacy of the state's rule, and so the intentionality criterion also makes treason look like an act of war. Finally, treason by thousands of people looks more like war than does the treason of one or two. Perhaps the way to resolve this puzzle is to say that treason is the prohibited crime of war against the state waged by a citizen or another person within the state's jurisdiction.[12]

Rebellion poses a related problem. Rebels generally claim to be engaged in war, and they certainly challenge the state's legitimacy, thereby satisfying the intentionality criterion for war. They also often claim to have a state of their own, which would make them state actors under the identity criterion. The state, on the other hand, often insists on treating rebels as common criminals, presumably on the theory that because they fall within the state's jurisdiction and lack the state that would make them state actors, they are therefore criminals under the provenance criterion. What we think of the categorization will likely depend on whether we think the rebels' claims are justified. The American Civil War featured a classic version of this problem: the Union saw secessionist Southerners as criminals, while the Confederate States of America saw itself as a legitimate state involved in a war for its independence. It is no surprise that the crime/war distinction was often unstable during the Civil War.

Civil disobedience also poses interesting problems. The individual engaging in civil disobedience commits a crime under the provenance criterion. She is not typically a state actor. But whether she does or does not intend to challenge the legitimacy of the state depends on

circumstances. In his *Letter from Birmingham City Jail,* Martin Luther King, Jr. went to great lengths to argue that he did not intend his actions to challenge the legitimacy of the United States or the rule of law but only the moral correctness of the law in question.[13] Under the intentionality criterion, King's disobedience looks nothing like war. He was imprisoned for an act that challenged the legitimacy of one law, not the legitimacy of the state per se. By contrast, Mahatma Gandhi's non-violent opposition to British rule in India, undertaken on a massive scale, seems to have been intended in significant part to challenge the very legitimacy of imperial rule and colonial domination. Gandhi did not directly represent a government-in-exile, so he probably was not a state actor. Nonetheless, if the leader of a civil disobedience movement were to claim to represent a legitimate government, her actions might look more like war under the intentionality and identity criteria. (This would still be war of a non-violent sort, if such a thing is possible to conceive.)[14]

The identity, provenance, intentionality, and scale criteria provide the beginnings of an account of the crime/war distinction. But what of that hybrid being, the war crime? How does the war crime fit into the crime/war distinction under these criteria? The war crime is a crime committed within the rubric of war; it is not, or is not primarily, a crime against the laws of any one particular state. Rather, the war crime violates some legal norm that exists outside the rubric of domestic law—a legal norm belonging to that set of norms known as the law of war.[15] Where does the law of war come from? This question appears to be a subset of the general question of the origins of international law. Suffice it to say, for our purposes, that the law of war derives either from international agreements and custom, implicit and explicit, or else from the natural law firmament. One's general theory of international law will probably determine one's view of the law of war.

Conceptually, a war crime therefore is an act in violation of laws laid down by some supranational source of sovereignty, whether human (international agreement or common custom) or metaphysical (natural law). Recall that under the provenance criterion, actions that fall within the jurisdictional reach of the law-making capacities of an identifiable sovereign count as crime, while those that do not count as war. It follows that, under the provenance criterion, a war crime is an instance of crime. If one accepts the existence of war crimes (which one need not logically do), then one surely has the view that war crimes fall within some relevant sovereign's jurisdictional capacity to prohibit the action in question. That jurisdiction may include all those areas upon which international actors agree or all those areas to which natural law speaks.

Under the intentionality criterion, is a war crime to be considered as crime or war? The question is close. One answer is that a war crime normally is a crime as a matter of intentionality, because one who commits a war crime typically does not intend by that act to challenge the legitimacy *of the relevant sovereign that has prohibited the act.* Rather, the war crime is an act undertaken to further the local ends of winning the war in which the war criminal is engaged. A war criminal may, for example, massacre non-combatants or use gas against troops in order to defeat the adversary and achieve his war aims. He may also commit war crimes that do not serve his war aims but simply result from cruelty or lack of discipline. Such actions do not make war against the international order—they simply violate the law of war that derives from that order.

Of course, because the war crime is committed in the act of making war, there will always be another layer that corresponds to the intentionality of war *against the attacked party.* But this layer of making war against the adversary is incidental (at least usually) to the criminal aspect of the act, which has to do with choice of some means of behavior that happens to violate the law of war. The war criminal normally would like to avoid being held responsible for the war crime, and he normally does not intend, at the moment of commission of the crime, to challenge the legitimacy of the source of the law of war.

Regarding identity, one might observe that one who commits a war crime will normally be some sort of state actor, to the extent that an individual fighting in a war represents a state. The identity criterion then might be said to make the war crime into an act of war. But

on the other hand, the war criminal is not normally the state itself but rather someone acting under the state's putative authority. Finally, a war crime can be small or large. The scale criterion therefore does not place it squarely within the category of war.

From this analysis, it emerges that the war crime is a special case of a crime, committed in violation of the international order of the law of war, while in pursuit of war against a particular enemy. The adjective in the phrase "war crime" is the word "war," which tells us when the crime was committed and which law the offender violated. The provenance criterion and the intentionality criterion point in this direction, and the force of the identity criterion does not seem sufficient to push in a different direction here.

War crimes, I have just said, imply the existence of some supranational source of law, even if that source consists of no more than an abstract truth of the law of nations that each country applies through its own legal institutions. The rise of war-crimes discourse may therefore be an interesting example of the growth of the practice of speaking as if there were some settled supranational framework for assessing the legitimacy of action.[16] If one has sympathy for the ideal of supranational law, whether created by consent, custom, or some natural law source, one will likely be sympathetic to invoking war crimes both generally and in the case of terrorism in particular. If, to the contrary, one wishes to reject the view that there exists supranational law regulating action in war, then one will be disinclined to invoke the notion of war crimes.

## II. THE FUNCTIONAL CONSEQUENCES OF THE CRIME/WAR DISTINCTION: PURSUIT, CAPTURE, SANCTION

Why does it matter whether we characterize a given act as a crime or an act of war? The functional consequences of the crime/war distinction matter in several spheres. The first has to do with the paradigmatic models of pursuit, capture, and sanction that attach differentially to crime and war. Some of these models are required by domestic laws, constitutional or otherwise, and some by international law norms. Some, and perhaps all, may be avoided or avoidable as a matter of practical reality. The purpose of this discussion will be less to detail these requirements with legal precision—such an attempt would in any case involve details that would differ from case to case—than to capture in the broadest terms how these paradigms differ, and why it matters.

The paradigm of crime normally requires that the criminal be pursued by means aimed at his capture, not at his death. Death of the criminal at the hands of an unruly mob is, or is supposed to be, a thing of the past.[17] Under some circumstances, the criminal may be injured or killed in the pursuit, but it is generally thought that this should happen only if the criminal resists capture by violent means. The paradigmatic requirement that pursuit be aimed at capture, not death, gives rise to the notion that capture itself should be preceded by some opportunity for the criminal to give himself up. The criminal's failure to give himself up does not mean that he may be killed, however. The fleeing criminal may normally be killed only if he actively endangers his pursuers or other persons.[18] The implicit reason seems to be that otherwise we do not fear that the fleeing criminal poses an immediate mortal danger to others.[19] Or perhaps we are simply confident that he will be captured soon.

Another reason not to kill the fleeing criminal may have to do with the presumption of innocence that attaches to the criminal suspect. This presumption plays its major role in the trial that is meant to follow capture and precede sanction. The crime paradigm requires due process, aimed at ascertaining that the person to be punished actually is the criminal. Detention is permitted only pending trial and determination of guilt. Even if intended to avoid recidivism, pre-trial detention is thought to be preventive, rather than punitive. The criminal trial itself is associated with a high standard of proof, partly because we have the leisure of trying the criminal at our "speedy" convenience, and partly because our sense of justice requires it.

Finally, the punishment that follows conviction of the criminal can be very harsh, and can even include death, at least in the United States of 2002. The punishment is meant to be carried out coldly and deliberately. Although theories of criminal punishment abound, on nearly every contemporary theory the punishment is to be determined and meted out by an agent of the sovereign against whom the crime initially offended. The people make the law, and the people, through their judicial or jury delegates, punish the law-breakers.

The norms surrounding pursuit, capture, and sanction are very different in the context of war.[20] First of all, subject to rather loose international law norms of necessity and proportionality, pursuit may normally take the form of pursuit with the intent to kill.[21] There is no requirement of warning. There is also no obligation to give the enemy an opportunity to surrender. Wartime rules of engagement as practiced by the U.S. typically permit fire on all identified targets, regardless of whether there exists an immediate threat to U.S. forces.[22] Capture (as opposed to killing) is usually required only when the enemy actively surrenders; that is, the burden to give way rests on the enemy, not on the pursuer. After surrender, the norms are also sharply divergent. Normally there can be no sanction for participating in war. The captured combatant becomes a prisoner of war, and must not be harmed.[23] He must be returned at the end of hostilities. He is detained not as a matter of sanction, but only so he will not fight again.

Notice the fascinating asymmetry between the paradigms of crime and war, especially with respect to killing. In crime, one generally cannot kill until after capture, but at that point, cold-blooded execution is legally permissible. In war, one may kill almost at will before surrender and capture, but after capture, the prisoner cannot be killed or otherwise sanctioned.

This striking asymmetry gives rise to serious complications in cases where there is some reason for uncertainty about which paradigm is appropriate. Consider the case of the terrorist who, from abroad, masterminds a terrorist act in the United States or another nation. What will be the position of the United States with respect to whether the act should be treated as a crime or as an act of war?

The criterion of intentionality lends weight to the view that a terrorist act is an act of war. Terrorists generally intend to contest the legitimacy of actions of the U.S. government, and this is apparently true of those who appear to have been responsible for the attacks of September 11, 2001. The terrorists—assuming they were members of Al Qaeda—deny the legitimacy of American support of local governments in the Middle East, of U.S. intervention against Iraq in the Gulf War, of the continued presence of U.S. troops in the region, and perhaps even of the U.S. government's fundamental right to govern its own country.

The criterion of provenance is a bit trickier. By hypothesis, we are speaking of a terrorist who plans his actions outside the U.S. But let us assume that those who carried out the attacks did so within the jurisdiction of the U.S., or attacked U.S. nationals abroad. Normal principles of jurisdiction certainly extend criminal jurisdiction to terrorist-planners whose actions abroad have effects within the United States or against its nationals. There is thus good reason to say that applying the provenance criterion leads to the conclusion that the terrorist act is a crime. The terrorist mastermind, in other words, is different with respect to provenance than a general who plans an attack that will be made on the U.S. by an army attacking from without.[24] The reason, under the provenance criterion, is that no standard principles of domestic jurisdiction would reach the general. Even though his actions will have effects within the U.S., we have the intuition that the United States cannot, in its domestic law, prohibit war being waged against it from without.

Next, consider the identity criterion. The party who planned the terrorist action may or may not be a state actor—indeed the question is open even with respect to the September 11 attacks. It may, furthermore, be difficult to determine if a person who planned terrorist acts did so in concert with or at the behest of a state until after the person has been captured; and even then the facts may remain unclear. In light of this uncertainty, the identity criterion will not help us much in choosing a framework for pursuit, capture, and prosecution.

Finally, there is scale. Terrorist actions that are very large, like the attacks of September 11, seem to authorize a discourse of war much more than do smaller attacks. (Of course, small attacks that intentionally follow a large attack would seem to be continuing parts of the war—it is not a transaction-by-transaction analysis.) Yet some acts of international terrorism may be isolated, relatively small, and not part of a larger campaign. It would clearly be more difficult, though not impossible, to classify such smaller attacks as war.

It follows from this analysis that terrorist attacks on the United States, planned from without, cannot definitively be categorized as either war or crime. They are crime from the perspective of provenance, war from the perspective of intentionality, probably crime from the perspective of identity, and very possibly war from the perspective of scale. So what course should be followed—or will be followed—in pursuing, capturing, and sanctioning terrorists? Will it be the paradigm of crime or the paradigm of war?

Applying either paradigm in its ideal form might contingently lead to results that are politically difficult, and perhaps undesirable. If the framework is war, then the terrorist—for example, Osama bin Laden and those close to him—can probably be pursued and killed as enemies, so long as he does not surrender. Of course, since the law of war is being applied here, the killing must be necessary to achieve the aims of the war. But this requisite condition should not be too difficult to achieve. The terrorist leader is analogous to the general of an opposing army in wartime—that is, a combatant who would be a fair target for attack.

But what if bin Laden, or any other terrorist leader for that matter, surrenders or is captured alive? It is easy to imagine that, as a last resort, a terrorist might surrender. Even someone who sincerely seeks martyrdom might prefer to defer that martyrdom to an opportune time and place. A media-savvy terrorist might show the white flag while video cameras were running, with a live feed to CNN or Al-Jazeera or the cable network of the moment. If the war paradigm applied in its purest form, then the Geneva Convention would, in the first instance, mandate prisoner-of-war treatment. This would not be a politically acceptable outcome, nor would it make very much sense as a matter of legal logic. Not only is there no counterpart to whom the non-state-actor terrorist might be returned at the cessation of hostilities; there is no obvious counterpart with whom peace might logically be concluded at all. Indefinite detainment would seem silly and, in any case, would not be a proper form of sanction under the war paradigm.

If the terrorist is captured alive or surrenders, then it is near certain that some other solution would have to be found than applying the paradigm of war. We would expect, at that point, for the paradigm of crime to come into play. The crime paradigm could be deployed in one of several ways. It would be possible to be the charge the terrorist with war crimes.[25] This appears to be the current policy of the United States in relation to at least some international terrorists, particularly those associated with Al Qaeda, the organization that the U.S. holds accountable for the attacks of September 11. On November 13, 2001, President Bush issued a Military Order authorizing the Secretary of Defense to constitute "military commissions" for the purposes of trying non-citizens whom the President determines there is reason to believe either (1) are or were members of Al Qaeda, (2) engaged in, aided or abetted, or conspired to commit "acts of international terror," or (3) knowingly harbored Al Qaeda members or international terrorists.[26]

The crime/war distinction is at work here as a matter of constitutional and statutory law. The Military order, like the World War II-era proclamation and order on which it is in part based,[27] apparently purports to rely implicitly on the executive's power as Commander in Chief. Its preamble invokes not only this constitutional power but also the Use of Military Force Joint Resolution passed by Congress after the September 11 attacks, as well as the federal statutes that refer to the existence of military commissions and that have in the past been held to authorize the creation of such commissions.[28] The Military Order then begins by finding that international terrorists, "including members of Al Qaeda," have attacked U.S. citizens at home ad abroad "on a scale that has created a state of armed conflict that requires the use of U.S. armed forces."[29] To begin with, then, the Military Order invokes the executive branch's war powers and the congressional authorization of their use. Although the order does not expressly use the word "war," it invokes the idea of scale, presumably in order to contextualize the use of military commissions, which in the past have been used by the U.S. only in wartime and in its immediate aftermath.[30]

The predicate of punishment, however, is not war but crime; what crimes are the President's commissions intended to punish? The Military Order, unlike the World War II-era proclamation, does not specifically speak of punishing war crimes. The earlier proclamation applied to citizens or others obedient to nations at war with the U.S., who entered the U.S. and who attempted or committed "sabotage, espionage, hostile or warlike acts, or violations of the law of war."[31] The Military Order purports to authorize trial and punishment of Al Qaeda members, of international terrorists, and of those who harbor them, for "all offenses triable by military commission."[32] The Military Order does not specify what these offenses" triable by military commission" are. The implication, however, is surely that that the persons triable by military commission must be both involved in some act of war and accused of committing some war crime in the process. For military commissions do not, presumably, try offenses other than those against the law of war.[33] If it were not so, it would be entirely unclear on what basis such persons could be tried by military commissions.

The crime element of the war crimes that the Military Order sets out to try and punish is thus under-specified. The order never identifies what crimes the commission may try or what crimes the terrorists affected by the order have allegedly committed. The order also does not draw an explicit line between acts of terrorism and war crimes. Instead, the crime element is implicitly incorporated by reference to the jurisdiction of military commissions generally. Because of its vagueness, this may be a defect of constitutional proportions but perhaps it could be remedied by subsequent orders creating particular military commissions and specifying what crimes they may try. International terror is surely a crime of some sort, and for reasons discussed above, as well as others beyond the scope of this essay, it is not implausible to say it is a war crime.

There are a variety of serious and interesting constitutional and legal questions associated with this order, and these should receive significant consideration from scholars and the courts.[34] Still, the war crimes position at least has the benefit of being legally and logically compatible with initially treating the terrorist as an enemy in war. The military commissions also avoid the question of whether Article III courts have jurisdiction to hear war crimes cases.[35] There is precedent in the United States for trying war criminals before military commissions specially constituted by the executive branch and for administering capital sentences to the convicted.[36] Of course, logical work would still have to be done to show that international terrorism is in fact a species of war crime.[37]

Yet there are reasons to doubt the constitutionality of military commissions for prosecuting terrorists. There was no direct appeal from the World War II tribunals, nor does the Military Order allow for judicial review on the merits. Habeas review of the sort allowed in the World War II-era cases will surely lie, but it may not suffice as a constitutional matter. It is also conceivable that such tribunals may only be constitutional once a declaration of war has been made, although an authorization of use of military force might suffice.[38]

Moreover, the cases upholding the use of such tribunals are of doubtful continuing weight. Although the decisions have not been overturned, the cases arose in the same wartime atmosphere that produced *Korematsu v. United States,*[39] which famously justified the detention of Japanese-Americans during World War II. One of the decisions was accompanied by a stinging dissent that declared, in no uncertain terms, that due process had been deeply compromised by the dispatch with which the proceedings had occurred, by the procedures that were employed, and even by the substantive law that was applied.[40] There is reason, therefore, to wonder whether courts today would be prepared to treat these cases as good law and to suggest that they ought not be treated as such.

Alternatively, an international war crimes tribunal might be constituted for the purpose of trying captured terrorists. It is very possible that political sentiment in the U.S. would balk at allowing a tribunal located abroad and not under the jurisdiction or direction of the U.S. to judge the perpetrator of a major terrorist act in the U.S. It is likely that American pride would demand trial in the U.S. by American judges.[41] Some in the U.S. would probably be uncomfortable with an international war crimes tribunal simply because it would implicitly acknowledge the presence of supranational authority that superseded the American desire to punish those who have injured the U.S. (Other Americans would, of course, welcome such a tribunal for the very same reason.)[42]

At a pragmatic political level, there would be a real risk that a tribunal might find the terrorist not guilty for lack of sufficient proof of causation between the terrorist's plan and its execution at a distance of time and space.[43] Even if the terrorist were found guilty, since Nuremberg, international tribunals have not administered the death penalty, and the statutes governing international tribunals uniformly exclude capital punishment as an option.[44] The divergence between American law and the law of most other countries of the world (including all of Europe) would seem to rule out the death penalty, yet for better or for worse American popular sentiment surely demands a capital sentence. Again, the view that a supranational authority has the power to decide sentencing would disturb some Americans, and please others.

If an international war crimes tribunal is thought to be an unsatisfactory solution by many Americans, the next logical possibility would be to try the terrorist for murder in federal or state court.[45] This is the crime paradigm with a vengeance. Finding a venue for a fair trial might be a problem in the case of a major attack. But even leaving aside the delicate question of proper venue for a fair trial, there is again the problem of proof. It is possible that the chain of causal connections between a terrorist mastermind and the crimes of his associates might never be established with sufficient strength to satisfy the demands of the U.S. justice system. Nonetheless, assuming these problems could be overcome, in most states the death penalty would probably be available, albeit after appeals. The federal death penalty might also apply in many situations where, for example, federal workers were killed. Public demand for capital justice could therefore be satisfied, although getting to that stage might be very difficult.

If politically popular views about justice would be best satisfied by criminal prosecution, conviction, and sanction, and if we suppose for the moment that all these steps could be achieved morally and lawfully, why not just begin with the paradigm of crime? After all, it looks very awkward to set out with a paradigm of war while pursuing the terrorists and then shift to the paradigm of crime if the terrorists should be lucky enough to avoid being killed.

The short and perhaps heartless answer is that under the crime paradigm, it would be far more difficult legally to kill terrorists before apprehending them than it would be under the war paradigm. Presumably terrorists could be treated like other dangerous fugitives. There is also at least some possibility that the U.S. Constitution would not bar the killing of a suspect outside the U.S.[46] But at the level of logic and political discourse, there is a real difference between battle against an enemy and hot pursuit of a criminal, especially at the crucial moments surrounding capture. Even if the Constitution does not require it outside the U.S., a criminal suspect is normally warned to surrender, whereas an enemy at war need receive no such warning. To call someone a criminal, moreover, is already to place him in the category of people who must be tried and afforded due process. (This may be one reason why we go through the motions of trying war criminals and don't simply execute them summarily.) This rhetorical norm may have force even if the Constitution technically does not.

In practice, the strategy of the U.S. in a situation like the one I am describing will probably be to keep its options open. To maximize flexibility, the U.S. government would probably try to give itself the option of invoking either the crime paradigm or the war paradigm at any moment. If the terrorist can be killed, and is killed, then the U.S. will call that war. If the terrorist surrenders or is captured, the paradigm will be crime.[47] Whatever happens operationally can then be justified according to one of the two paradigms in question.

What are we to make of this pragmatically likely solution of preserving both paradigms and deploying the most convenient? We must consider several possibilities. First, it may be that as a matter of logic and law, there is nothing wrong with considering the same act to be both a crime and an act of war. After all, the identity, provenance, intentionality, and scale criteria are not technical requirements of law but heuristic devices intended to make sense of our use of the two concepts of crime and war. Surely Congress could lawfully declare an act of hostility like a massive terrorist attack to be an act of war. Similarly there is no doubt that an act of terror qualifies as a crime under the laws of the states and the United States. So perhaps there is nothing wrong with the lawyerly strategy of keeping all theories of the case on the table at all times and of being prepared to argue in the alternative should it be necessary.

There would be something troubling about this approach if we were committed to the view that the value of the rule of law somehow requires a state always to act on the basis of a specified and specific legal theory. One could imagine the Office of Legal Counsel, or the Office of the Legal Advisor at the State Department, producing a learned opinion on the crime/war distinction that privileges one paradigm over the other. And this undertaking would not seem preposterous to the legally-trained mind. There are good and independent reasons for government to set out to act according to one legal theory at a time.

On the other hand, perhaps the content of the concept "rule of law" does not demand that governments stick to one legal theory at a time. Sometimes even the government has to argue theories in the alternative. After all, as long as each paradigm is independently justified and justifiable under domestic and international law, we are still committed to the rule of law even if we apply each paradigm only in some circumstances and not in others. It is simply that the law gives us two options. We could deploy either at any moment, and still be within our legal rights. This argument, too, resonates with the legal mind, at least any legal mind that is prepared to tolerate, for example, subsequent state and federal prosecutions for the same act under different legal theories.[48] Such prosecutions, too, constitute examples of government (albeit nominally two different sovereigns) relying on alternative legal theories for the same factual situation. The very fact that we are on the border of crime and war itself means that our legal judgments may need to be drawn cautiously and with our eyes on the real world.

More generally, however, what can we say about the use and the meaning of the categories of crime and war in this complicated situation of pursuing, capturing, and sanctioning terrorists? The key point of this Part of my argument is surely that terror fits both categories—and neither. Terror defies easy categorization under the four criteria proposed here. Although terror itself has always existed, terror against the United States on the scale of the September 11 attacks is unprecedented. Law is resourceful; it can adapt old categories to new situations or create new categories to address them. But the fact that old paradigms may be malleable does not mean that they are conceptually adequate. We may need new paradigms for thinking about actions of mass terror. That would mean specifying, ex ante, both the criteria for terror and the rules for confronting it. This task will require work and time. But it is work that can, and perhaps must, be done.

## III. INSTITUTIONS AND THE CRIME/WAR DISTINCTION

In Part II, I pointed out that the crime/war distinction could break down in the case of international terrorism. I suggested, however, that maintaining that distinction may still be possible to the extent that we are willing to pursue two simultaneous, alternative theories of action. This sort of post-hoc rationalization is less easily available with respect to a second problem emerging from the uneasy status of terror: the institutional question of what agencies and instrumentalities of government will play what role in the fight against terror.

The crime/war distinction has traditionally played a key role in determining what parts of the U.S. government do what. Broadly speaking, the Department of Justice fights crime. Although FBI agents sometimes operate abroad, they do so as part of an effort to prosecute—and to a lesser extent, preemptively prevent—crimes committed against the United States. On the other hand, the CIA and the military, in subtly different ways, operate abroad. The CIA is arguably statutorily barred from domestic intelligence collection under the Central Intelligence Agency Act.[49] The Agency gathers intelligence

that serves the national interest, often (although not only) in the sphere of defense against those who might wage war against the U.S. The CIA does not fight crime; it is not a police agency. Its primary mission is directed abroad, not within. Under some relatively well-publicized circumstances, the CIA's mission has even placed it at odds with crime prevention and law enforcement.[50]

The military, even more obviously than the CIA, is designed to fight wars, not domestic crime. A Reconstruction-era statute called the Posse Comitatus Act[51] actually codifies this principle into law. The Posse Comitatus Act bars use of the military "as a posse comitatus or otherwise to execute the laws."[52] This formulation effectively stops the military from pursuing criminals or fighting crime, and it has been so interpreted by the courts, despite an absence of prosecutions under the act.[53] A related enabling statute directs the Secretary of Defense to enact regulations to prevent military personnel from participating in "search, seizure, arrest, or other similar activity."[54] This statute makes it even clearer than the Posse Comitatus Act that the military is barred from fighting domestic crime.

Leaving aside the particular Reconstruction history of the enactment of the Posse Comitatus Act, we should pause to notice that the rationale for the devotion of the military to matters of war, not domestic crime, runs deep in the history and theory of republicanism. For our purposes it should suffice to say that the republican fear of standing armies plagued the Framers.[55] The Third Amendment stands as a monument to this fear, even if this Amendment now does little else.[56] One element of the response to the concern that a standing army might influence domestic politics was to direct the military outward, to the defense of the country from external threats. Preventing the military from fighting crime is consistent with the republican impulse to maintain a separation between the military and potential domestic political involvement.

How does the crime/war distinction operate in the institutional context? Broadly speaking, as I have said, the domestic agencies fight crime, and the CIA and the military fight and prepare for war. The provenance criterion seems to be doing most of the work with respect to intelligence gathering, in the sense that the FBI generally acts domestically, while the CIA and the military typically act against persons and places that are outside U.S. jurisdiction. The domestic/foreign distinction is normally the main vehicle for discussing the respective roles of the FBI and CIA. As for the military's role, the provenance criterion might also be doing some work. It might be argued that the Posse Comitatus Act implicitly applies only within the U.S. and not abroad (though the statute is silent on this point). But the intentionality criterion may also be at work when it comes to the military. The laws that bar the military from fighting crime do not operate on the basis of geographic provenance, but rather on the basis of categorizing the action to be opposed as crime. The military could doubtless pursue and capture foreign troops on U.S. soil, if those troops were (deemed to be) engaged in an act of war. Surely defending the U.S. against such an incursion by foreign troops would be an instance of defense, not an instance of the military's "executing the laws." The implicit premise in this reasoning is that it is possible to distinguish acts of war on U.S. soil from mere crimes. As I argued above, the basis for that distinction must be some version of the intentionality criterion.

In the wake of the September 11 attacks, there is near universal agreement that the separation of roles among crime-fighting agencies, like the FBI, and war-oriented or foreign-oriented institutions, like the military and the CIA, has ill served the objective of preventing domestic terror. There is an emerging consensus that fighting terror will require deeper coordination than existed heretofore between law enforcement agencies, the CIA, and the military. Although there have been many earlier efforts at effecting such coordination, there is now reason to think that the very distinction is misplaced when it comes to terror. The creation of a new institutional mechanism for coordination under the rubric of Homeland Security may have some effect on coordination, but as the example of the Drug Czar position has shown, that effect is not easily predictable ex ante. There are numerous ways to allocate administrative authority, and many of these may not deliver coordination.

Such coordination of agencies requires the recognition that terrorism undercuts the crime/war distinction. If terrorism is crime under the provenance criterion, then it falls within the ambit of the FBI. But the FBI is, understandably, better at investigation and arrest than it is at prevention, especially when that prevention would require action against individuals who have not yet committed crimes. The institutional focus of the FBI is on capture and arrest.[57] The FBI has had relatively little success investigating terror abroad,[58] in large part because the FBI is conceived on a provenance model of fighting crime. More basically than this, the statutory mandate of the Attorney General, the Department of Justice, and the FBI is directed toward fighting crime, rather than toward providing intelligence for or fighting war.

There may be a need for a statutory—and a conceptual—fix that would reframe the respective roles of the FBI and the CIA on terms less dependent on the crime/war distinction, at least with respect to terrorism. Merely calling for coordination will not change the basic institutional orientation of the two agencies. On this view, the FBI should conceive its role as including the adoption of means directed not only at reaction, capture, and conviction, but also at prevention and at the transfer of information to the CIA or the military for sanctioning terrorists outside the domestic legal system. At present, the FBI "succeeds" when criminals are captured and punished. This notion of success may have to be altered to incorporate prevention and non-conventional (but legal) sanction abroad, outside the sphere of the U.S. justice system.[59] For its part, the CIA may need to be freed of even the possibility of a statutory disability barring it from domestically-oriented surveillance, so long as the surveillance is directed at preventing terror at home or abroad.

The objections to such proposals will be deep and reasonable. If the FBI finds itself no longer oriented solely toward criminal prosecution, this may develop habits of investigation and action that will be detrimental in enforcing domestic law and in punishing crime. The law-abiding ethos of the FBI may be damaged, perhaps irrevocably. As for the CIA, there is a real constitutional danger in encouraging domestic surveillance by an agency *not* expected to present its findings to a jury under judicially-mandated rules of procedure and constitutional protections. Expansion of the role of the CIA may actually reduce our privacy and our freedoms, even if we never become aware of it.

To say that these costs are real, though, is not to say that they are costs that should never be borne. Deciding how to proceed in the fight against terrorism requires serious, concentrated thought, and some empirical experimentation as well. Ex ante, it is difficult to anticipate all of the benefits and all of the potential harmful results that might come from acknowledging that the crime/war distinction creates problems in the sphere of fighting terror. But it is worth noticing that the crime/war distinction is not *itself* a fundamental value. It is, rather, a heuristic we have used to distinguish certain forms of institutional action from others. The true values here are liberty, privacy, the rule of law, and safety. As an instrumental distinction, the crime/war distinction is only good so long as it serves our purposes. We need to balance the underlying values to make as wise a decision as we can.

Now consider the situation of the military. Under the intentionality criterion, terrorism looks more like war than like crime. Can the military act against terror domestically without violating the Posse Comitatus Act? There is an institutional problem here that cannot be resolved as easily as the problem of pursuit and capture discussed in Part II. To the extent that terrorism is conceived as crime, the military cannot legally fight it, at least within the U.S.

One partial solution here would be the repeal of the Posse Comitatus Act, or at least the passage of legislation that would circumvent the Posse Comitatus Act by specifically authorizing the military to be used domestically in the fight against terror. Such legislation would have some significant costs. In particular, allowing the military to execute the laws, even in limited situations, undercuts the republican value of distancing the military from involvement with civilian political affairs. The costs might be warranted under conditions in which terror is a serious threat. It also might, however, prove difficult to repeal such legislation when the threat

recedes because of the powerful bureaucratic interests of the military. Again, the crucial point is that the crime/war distinction is not *itself* the value to be protected. Here republicanism is the value we wish to protect, and when making our institutional analysis, we should try to balance that value against the apparent pragmatic requirement of fighting terror.

It is tempting to conclude by proposing some new, comprehensive theory that would definitively categorize international terror as crime or as war. But like judgments made in the crucible of crisis, theories concocted for the occasion can look unwise when seen in retrospect. What we need now is caution tempered by common sense. If we begin by delineating the structures of how we think about the problem, and identify the weaknesses of our approach and its capacities for flexibility, then we may begin on the right track.

## NOTES

1. 18 U.S.C § 1385 (1994) ("Whoever, except in cases and under circumstances expressly authorized by the Constitution or Act of Congress, willfully uses any part of the Army or the Air Force as a posse comitatus or otherwise to execute the laws shall be fined under this title or imprisoned not more than two years, or both.").

2. According to former Attorney General William Barr: "There's a basic tension as to whether to treat this as a law enforcement issue or a national security/military issue." Douglas W. Kmiec, *Infinite Justice,* NATIONAL REVIEW ONLINE (Oct. 11, 2001), *at* http://www.nationalreview.com/comment/comment-kmiec101101.shtml.

3. The common law writs recited the phrase *contra pacem regis* not only in cases of crime but also in cases of tort. In any case the basic notion is surely a violation of legal conditions specified by the sovereign. See Morris S. Arnold, *Accident, Mistake, and Rules of Liability in the Fourteenth-Century Law of Torts,* 128 U. Pa. L. REV. 361, 370–71 (1979) (associating the phrase with crime even in the tort context).

4. See, *e.g.,* Restatement (Third) of Foreign Relations Law § 451–52 (1987) [hereinafter Restatement].

5. Notice that the identity criterion might be understood as implicit within the other two criteria. If jurisdiction is necessary for something to count as a crime, and there is no domestic jurisdiction over sovereign states, then one could plausibly find that the identity criterion is already present within the provenance criterion. Similarly, if one were to take the view that only a sovereign state can meaningfully be said to intend to challenge the legitimacy or sovereignty of another state, then the identity criterion would be built into the intentionality criterion.

6. See RESTATEMENT, *supra* note 4, § 402. The so-called protective jurisdiction is embodied in 18 U.S.C. § 2332 (1994), which criminalizes killing U.S. nationals abroad, and which is invoked to try, for example, terrorists who attack U.S. embassies. These sorts of jurisdiction do not necessarily depend on international agreement or consensus. Greater expansions of jurisdiction—for example, universal jurisdiction over certain crimes against humanity—do derive in some way from international law. *See* RESTATEMENT, *supra* note 4, § 404.

7. Compare the definition of "aggression" adopted by the U.N. General Assembly in 1974: "the use of armed force by a State against the sovereignty, territorial integrity or political independence of another State, or in any other manner inconsistent with the Charter of the United Nations. . . ." G.A. Res. 3314 (XXIX), U.N. GAOR, 29th Sess., Supp. No. 31, annex, at 143, U.N. Doc. A/9631 (1974). This definition focuses upon intentionality, but by describing aggression as an act of one state against another, the definition implicitly adverts to provenance as well. In my view, it is too restrictive to limit aggression or war to actions of states.

8. William Shakespeare, Henry V act 1, sc. 2 See Theodor Meron, Henry's Wars and Shakespeare's Laws: Perspectives on the Law of War in the Later Middle Ages (1993).

9. Parliament declared war on October 19, 1739. Jenkins claimed his ear was taken in 1731.

10. U.S. CONST, art. III, § 3. One can commit treason under the U.S. Constitution by levying war against the United States—presumably, while being a citizen of the U.S.—or by adhering to "enemies" of the U.S. See *id.* These enemies are presumably state actors, but they might also include non-state actors.

11. Treason extends to events committed outside the U.S. See Tomoya, Kawakita v. United States, 343 U.S. 717, 732–33 (1952). Nonetheless, the theory must be that the U.S. maintains jurisdiction over its citizens wherever they go.

12. Citizenship and treason interact in interesting ways. Yet a person must actually be a citizen to be convicted of treason for acts committed outside the United States. *Kawakita,* 343 U.S. at 723–33. The treason statute extends to persons "owing allegiance to the U.S." 18 U.S.C. § 2381 (1994). This strongly suggests that its reach is limited to citizens. United States v. Stephan, 50 F. Supp. 445 (E.D. Mich. 1943), *aff'd,* 139 F.2d 1022 (6th Cir, 1943). Of course it is not inconceivable that this language might be extended to, say, permanent residents.

13. See MARTIN LUTHER KING, JR., LETTER FROM BIRMINGHAM CITY JAIL (1994). See also RONALD DWORKIN, TAKING RIGHTS SERIOUSLY 186, 207 (1978) (arguing that civil disobedience derives from moral duty to conscience in conflict with law, and suggesting that punishment for civil disobedience may be inappropriate); MICHAEL WALZER, OBLIGATION: ESSAYS ON DISOBEDIENCE, WAR, AND CITIZENSHIP 43 (1970) (distinguishing direct disobedience to a law that is thought immoral from indirect disobedience to a law—like a trespassing law—in the course of engaging in protest).

14. Must war be violent to count as war? The question is beyond the scope of this Essay, but notice that one could imagine a sustained non-violent attempt to overthrow a government, waged from outside. It might be unlikely to succeed, but what would we call it? Larry Kramer suggested to me the example of economic sanctions as an instance of non-violent—or at least not always directly violent—acts that might constitute aggression against a state. There is of course a large political science literature on economic sanctions, but the literature does not focus on the essentially legal question of whether such sanctions count as "war."

15. In Grotian terms, a war crime may be a crime against *jus in bello* or *jus ad bellum*—that is, either a crime committed by an act against the law of war during the prosecution of war, or a crime committed by the fact of the unjust prosecution of the war. For a sophisticated modern exposition, see MICHAEL WALZER, JUST AND UNJUST WARS: A MORAL ARGUMENT WITH HISTORICAL ILLUSTRATIONS (1992). This essay focuses on war crimes as violations of *jus in bello,* although many war crimes are violations of *jus ad bellum.*

16. It is the impulse to act and speak in terms of supranational sovereignty that Antonio Negri and Michael Hardt mean to identify in their

widely-discussed book, EMPIRE (2000). The "empire" exists insofar as it justifies and organizes supranational authority for prohibiting actions by states and individuals.

17. See 2 SIR FREDERICK POLLOCK & FREDERIC WILLIAM MAITLAND, HISTORY OF ENGLISH LAW 579 (2d ed. 1959) ("Now if a man is overtaken by hue and cry while he has still about him the signs of his crime, he will have short shrift. Should he make any resistance, he will be cut down."); see also Garner v. Memphis Police Dep't, 710 F.2d 240, 243–44 (6th Cir. 1983), *aff'd*, Tennessee v. Garner, 471 U.S. 1 (1985) (citing POLLOCK & MAITLAND, *supra*).

18. See *Garner*, 471 U.S. at 1.

19. If we did have good reason to believe that the fleeing felon were very likely to kill innocent persons before being captured, it would be doubtful as a moral matter that we should let him escape rather than kill him straightaway. Of course we want to be certain that the fleeing felon is actually the guilty party, but imagine that someone has just fired into a crowd of people, has dropped his gun, and has then fled. If there were reason to believe he might have ready access to another gun and could be likely to kill other persons with it, then surely it would be justified, and maybe even morally compulsory, to shoot at him in order to stop him from harming others imminently.

20. For a useful review of the issue, see Mark S. Martins, *Rules of Engagement for Land Forces: A Matter of Training. Not Lawyering*, 142 MIL. L. REV. 1 (1994).

21. See *id.* at 29 n.84 (describing necessity and proportionality requirements).

22. *Id.* at 27. Peacetime rules of engagement may differ.

23. See *id.* at 28 n.82 (citing Department of the Army regulation mandating instructing on "basic law of war rules").

24. Of course some states have adopted universal jurisdiction over war crimes, so if terrorism is in fact a species of a war crime, then jurisdiction might lie in any of these states. But universal jurisdiction, it must be noted, is itself a challenge to the very idea of the provenance criterion. If I have jurisdiction over any event that occurs anywhere, then provenance is essentially irrelevant.

25. For an extended proposal to this effect regarding domestic terrorists, see Spencer J. Crona & Neal A. Richardson, *Justice for War Criminals of Invisible Armies: A New Legal and Military Approach to Terrorism*, 21 OKLA. U. L. REV. 349 (1996).

26. Military Order, Detention, Treatment, and Trial of Certain Non-Citizens in the War against Terrorism § 2(A)(1)(i)-(iii), 66 Fed. Reg. 57,833, 57,834 (Nov. 13, 2001) [hereinafter Military Order].

27. See Proclamation 2561, Denying Certain Enemies Access to the Courts of the United States, 7 Fed. Reg. 5101 (July 7, 1942); Appointment of a Military Commission, 7 Fed. Reg. 5103 (July 7, 1942).

28. See Military Order, *supra* note 26, preamble, at 57,833 (citing Joint Resolution to Authorize the Use of United States Armed Forces Against Those Responsible for the Recent Attacks Launched Against the United States, Pub. Law 107–40, 115 Stat. 224 (2001), and 10 U.S.C. §§ 821,836 (1994)). In *In re* Yamashita, 327 U.S. 1, 7–8 (1946), the Court held that a mere statutory reference to "military commissions" authorized the existence of these commissions. And here, § 821 would appear to do the trick:

> The provisions of this chapter conferring jurisdiction upon courts-martial do not deprive military commissions, provost courts, or other military tribunals of concurrent jurisdiction with respect to offenders or offenses that by statute or by the law of war may be tried by military commissions, provost courts, or other military tribunals.

10 U.S.C. § 821. As Professor Fletcher suggests in his article in this special issue, this is a slender reed on which to rest the claim of authority. See George P. Fletcher, *On Justice and War: Contradictions in the Proposed Military Tribunals*, 25 HARV. J.L. & PUB. POL'Y 635 (2002). But nonetheless, the fact remains that the same rationale offered in *Yamashita* could be offered here.

29. Military Order, *supra* note 26, § 1(a), at 57,833.

30. See *Ex parte* Quirin, 317 U.S. 1, 12–13 & nn.9–10 (1942) (reviewing use of military commissions in U.S. history prior to World War II).

31. 10 U.S.C. § 906 (1994).

32. Military Order, *supra* note 26, § 4(a), at 57,834.

33. Cf. Quirin, 317 U.S. at 28–29, 30–31.

34. To name just one important constitutional problem, the order bars an "individual subject to the order" of any remedy, direct or indirect, in U.S., foreign, or international courts. Military Order, *supra* note 26, § 7(b)(2), at 57,835. What sort of habeas remedy does this leave for such individuals? One

possible argument is that a petitioner should be able to claim on habeas that he is not an "individual subject to the order," because he is either a citizen or else does not fall within the category of Al Qaeda member, international terrorist, or person who has harbored either. This would have the effect of introducing meaningful judicial review in many cases, at least where the accused denies that he belongs to Al Qaeda or has committed terrorist acts. Two arguments support this reading. First, in *Quirin,* 317 U.S. at 25, the Court said there was "nothing in the Proclamation to preclude access to the courts for determining its applicability to the particular case." This could be read to suggest that the World War II order, at least, preserved this sort of review. Second, under the admittedly complicated decision in *Crowell v. Benson,* 285 U.S. 22 (1932), it could be argued that jurisdictional facts must always be determined by an Article III court, not by the executive. At a minimum this would apply to the fact of citizenship. *See* Ng Fung Ho v. White, 259 U.S. 276, 285 (1922) (stating persons claiming citizenship "are entitled to judicial determination of their claims"). On the other side of this argument, it could perhaps be maintained that unlike the World War II order, the Military order makes citizenship the only jurisdictional fact and then allows the president to determine of non-citizens whether they are Al Qaeda members, international terrorists, or persons who harbored either.

35. But see Crona & Richardson, *supra* note 25, at 371–72 (arguing that since U.S. law incorporates international law, U.S. courts have universal jurisdiction over war crimes).

36. See *In re* Yamashita, 327 U.S. 1 (1946); *Quirin,* 317 U.S. at 10–12 (holding that Congress conferred power on President to create military tribunals to try and execute infiltrators). Crona & Richardson, *supra* note 24, argue for the application of the *Yamashita* model to terrorists. See also Kmiec, *supra* note 1 (same). For the FBI's official account of the capture of the *Quirin* infiltrators, see *George John Dasch and the Nazi Saboteurs, at* http://www.fbi.gov/fbinbrief/historic/famcases/nazi/nazi.htm (last visited Feb. 1, 2002).

37. Professor Fletcher makes the point that the President cannot remove from the Article III courts the power to try offenses within their jurisdiction. See Fletcher, *supra* note 28, at 639–40; *cf. Ex parte* Milligan, 71 U.S. 2 (1866). Fletcher adds that the offenses committed by Yamashita in the Philippines

were not triable in Article III courts. Yet in *Quirin,* the offenses were committed inside the U.S., and the Court found that is suffced to avoid the *Milligan* problem that the defendants were belligerents who entered the U.S. out of uniform. The Court distinguished *Milligan* by saying that Milligan was a non-belligerent. *Quirin,* 317 U.S. at 45–46. If it could conceivably be said that international terrorists are non-belligerents, then the reasoning of *Quirin,* such as it is, could suffice to avoid the *Milligan* problem. But of course that would be a tricky argument: if the terrorists are not belligerents then who is?

38. Due process is also rudimentary in such tribunals: all evidence thought to be probative is admitted, and a two-thirds majority may convict and sentence. Military Order, *supra* note 26, §§ 7(c)(3), 7(c)(7), at 57,835. Even if due process is satisfied by these procedures, they are hardly the stuff of which confident judgments are made.

39. 323 U.S. 214 (1944).

40. See *Yamashita,* 327 U.S. at 42–61 (Rutledge, J., dissenting).

41. The same feeling might exist in other countries, too, if they were subject to attack. The solution reached in the Lockerbie bombing trial, in which Scottish judges presided over a Scottish-procedure trial that took place in the Hague, suggests both that some European countries might demand the primacy of their law and institutions, and that Europeans may be prepared to compromise in ways that Americans might not be with respect to terrorism that occurs domestically.

42. There have also been proposals to try Islam-inspired terrorists before an Islamic court applying Islamic law. The trouble with such a proposal is, again, largely one of domestic U.S. politics. It is extremely unlikely that the American public would be prepared to tolerate judgment being passed by a court applying law particular to the defendants. Other proposals include the suggestion that whatever court might try Muslim terrorists include one Muslim judge. It seems unlikely that such a solution would satisfy anyone.

43. Acquittal of a major figure in Al Qaeda, for example, could have serious repercussions for international opinion about U.S. actions in Afghanistan.

44. See, *generally,* William A. Schabas, *War Crimes, Crimes Against Humanity, and the Death Penalty,* 60 ALB. L. REV. 733 (1997) (reviewing history and statutes).

45. For an especially thoughtful version of this argument, see Harold Hongju Koh, *We Have the Right Courts for Bin Laden,* N.Y. TIMES, Nov. 23, 2001, at A39. One cannot but agree with Professor Koh's view of the U.S. courts as the most desirable and appropriate venue for trial of terrorists who have committed crimes against U.S. citizens, but the difficulty of proving guilt beyond a reasonable doubt may be greater than he anticipates.

46. *Cf.* United States v. Verdugo-Urquidez, 494 U.S. 259 (1990) (holding that the Fourth Amendment does not apply to search and seizure by United States agents of property owned by a nonresident alien and located in a foreign country).

47. Something similar seems to have happened to Manuel Noriega, who was captured in war but was then tried in a domestic criminal trial. The difference is that Noriega was tried for actions that preceded the war against him (or against Panama, whichever one prefers). See United States v. Noriega, 746 F. Supp. 1506 (S.D. Fla. 1990), *aff'd,* 117 F.3d 1206 (11th Cir. 1997). The hypothetical terrorist I am describing is being tried for the very act that put him into the position of either enemy or criminal. (And indeed, although Osama bin Laden could be tried for earlier crimes for which he is under indictment, there would surely be great pressure to try him for the crimes of September 11).

48. For classic statements of the constitutionality of successive prosecutions by different sovereigns, see United States v. Wheeler, 435 U.S. 313 (1978); Bartkus v. Illinois, 359 U.S. 121 (1959); and United States v. Lanza, 260 U.S. 377 (1922).

49. Central Intelligence Agency Act of 1949, 50 U.S.C. §§ 403a–403j (1994). The legislative history included the statement that the CIA's focus would be "purely and completely and wholly and singly in the external or foreign field.... Its sole effort is outside the United States." 95 CONG. REC. 6948 (1949) (statement of Rep. Tydings). There has nonetheless always been debate about whether the CIA could gather intelligence in the U.S. for use regarding external operations. See Sherri J. Conrad, Note, *Executive Order 12,333: 'Unleashing' the CIA Violates the Leash Law,* 70 CORNELL L. REV. 968, 972–73 (1985) (citing FINAL REPORT OF THE SENATE SELECT COMMITTEE TO STUDY GOVERNMENTAL OPERATIONS WITH RESPECT TO INTELLIGENCE ACTIVITIES, BOOK 1, S. REP. NO. 94–755, at 97–98, 138 (1976) [hereinafter CHURCH COMM. REPORT]). The so-called Church Committee took the view that Congress in the National Security Act was "codifying the prohibition against police and internal security functions...." CHURCH COMM. REPORT, *supra,* at 138.

50. Again, the example of Manuel Noriega is apt. See *supra* note 47. The CIA kept Noriega on its payroll even when Noriega was engaged, to the CIA's apparent knowledge, in some of the criminal acts for which he was later convicted.

51. 18 U.S.C. § 1385 (1994).

52. *Id.*

53. See Roger Blake Hohnsbeen, *Fourth Amendment and Posse Comitatus Act Restrictions on Military Involvement in Civil Law Enforcement,* 54 GEO. WASH. L. REV. 404, 409–13 (1986) (reviewing judicial interpretations of the Posse Comitatus Act).

54. See 10 U.S.C. § 375 (1994) ("The Secretary of Defense shall prescribe such regulations as may be necessary to ensure that any activity (including the provision of any equipment or facility or the assignment or detail of any personnel) under this chapter does not include or permit direct participation by a member of the Army, Navy, Air Force, or Marine Corps in a search, seizure, arrest, or other similar activity unless participation in such activity by such member is otherwise authorized by law.").

55. See GORDON S. WOOD, THE CREATION OF THE AMERICAN REPUBLIC 1776–1787 (1998).

56. U.S. CONST. amend. III. For the republican associations of the Amendment, see William S. Fields & David T. Hardy, *The Third Amendment and the Issue of the Maintenance of Standing Armies,* 35 AM. J. LEGAL HIST. 393 (1991). See also Morton Horwitz, *Is the Third Amendment Obsolete?,* 26 VAL. U. L. REV. 209, 211–13 (1991).

57. *Cf.* LAURIE MYLROIE, STUDY OF REVENGE: SADDAM HUSSEIN'S UNFINISHED WAR AGAINST AMERICA 4–6 (2000) (arguing that, for institutional reasons, the FBI had little interest in pursuing antecedents of terror in the first World Trade Center bombing investigation).

58. Consider, for example, the frustrations faced by the FBI in pursuing the investigation into the bombings of the U.S.S. Cole in Yemen and the al-Khobar towers in Saudi Arabia.

59. The institutional changes that have been proposed or introduced in this direction are so far not deep. On November 8, 2001, Attorney General John Ashcroft announced what he called a "wartime reorganization" of the Department of Justice. The

plan called for reassignment of 10% of the current headquarters-based personnel to "the field," for better coordination with local law enforcement and for non-duplication of resources. The proposals for the FBI did specifically state that the FBI should focus on prevention of terror but left that project to future strategic planning to be carried out by the FBI itself. It remains to be seen what this will bring. *See* Press Release, U.S. Dep't of Justice, Attorney General Ashcroft and Deputy Attorney General Thompson Announce Reorganization and Mobilization of the Nation's Justice and Law Enforcement Resources (Nov. 8, 2001), http://www.usdoj.gov/ag/speeches/2001/agcrisis remarks11_08.htm. For the strategic plan itself, see U.S. Dep't of Justice, *Strategic Plan*

*2001–2006* (2001), http://www.usdoj.gov/jmd/mps/strategic2001–2006/ entiredoc.htm. A few days later, the Attorney General announced the reorganization of the Immigration and Naturalization Service into two separate bureaus, one for immigration services, the other for immigration enforcement. Although Ashcroft described this as useful for preventing terror, he also acknowledged that the plan, with its lengthy report, had been substantially completed before September 11, 2001. Press Release, U.S. Dep't of Justice, Attorney General John Ashcroft and INS Commissioner Ziglar Announce INS Restructuring Plan (Nov. 14, 2001), http://www.usdoj.gov/ag/speeches/2001/agcrisisremarks11_14.htm.

## REVIEW QUESTIONS

- Why has there been so much debate and occasional discord about defining terrorism?
- Because of the emergence of the New Terrorism, has the time finally come for a unified definition of terrorism?
- In what ways does the perception of "terrorism" differ in the West and Middle East? Is one perception more valid or more correct than the other?
- Is the War on Terrorism truly a "war?"
- What are the implications of designing a war-fighting framework in the new era of terrorism, vis-à-vis using a crime-fighting framework?

The following books and articles are suggested for further information about defining terrorism in the new era:

## Books

Laqueur, Walter. *The New Terrorism: Fanaticism and the Arms of Mass Destruction.* New York: Oxford University Press, 1999.
Snow, Donald. *September 11, 2001: The New Face of War?* New York: Pearson Higher Education, 2001.
Talbott, Strobe, and Nayan Chandra, eds. *The Age of Terror: America and the World After September 11.* New York: Basic Books, 2002.

## Articles

Howard, Michael. "What's in a Name? How to Fight Terrorism." *Foreign Affairs.* 81:1 (January-February 2002).
Gearson, John. "The Nature of Modern Terrorism." *The Political Quarterly.* 73:4, Supplement 1 (August 2002).
Hassner, Pierre. "Definitions, Doctrines, and Divergences." *The National Interest.* (Fall 2002).

# 4

# CAUSES OF TERRORISM IN THE NEW ERA

A number of theories have been developed to explain why people, movements, and governments choose to engage in terrorist violence. Most theories are grounded in political science, sociological, and psychological research agendas that attempt to identify the cultural, political, and individual idiosyncratic factors that lead to political violence. Some theories reflect the biases of researchers or commentators, especially when they sympathize with a particular cause. Nevertheless, it is uncontroversial to conclude that all terrorists are extremists, and can be motivated by a number of theoretical factors. These factors include extremist political or religious ideologies, violent intergroup conflict, blaming enemy interests for their plight, or a perceived need to defend an established order from supposed insurgents. It is clear that no single causal model can be applied to explain all terrorist behavior. Rather, contextual approaches recognizing the idiosyncratic quality of each environment are most adequate. For this reason, it is important to investigate the question of causation from many perspectives.

The articles in this chapter discuss the motives for, and sources of, contemporary terrorism. In "Cross-Cultural Trends in Female Terrorism," Karla Cunningham investigates the under-studied subject of women who engage in terrorist violence, an issue that has received secondary attention in the literature and commentary on terrorism. The article discusses the increase in terrorist violence by women, and identifies several reasons for this increase. Reasons for the recruitment of women by terrorist groups are also addressed. Daniel Pipes offers an overview of economic factors in the rise militant Islam in "God and Mammon: Does Poverty Cause Militant Islam?" He argues that poverty is not the primary causal factor for Islamist violence, but rather issues of identity. Thus, a great deal of radical Islamist activism is found among relatively competent and educated associations of extremists. The article by Daniel Levitas, entitled "The Radical Right After 9/11," updates the case of the fringe right wing in the United States. The essay discusses the radical right in the era of the war on terrorism, and presents telling commentary from leaders of the movement in the immediate aftermath of the attacks.

## Cross-Regional Trends in Female Terrorism

Karla J. Cunningham
*Department of Political Science, SUNY Geneseo*
*Geneseo, New York, USA*

Although women have historically been participants in terrorist groups[1] in Sri Lanka, Iran, West Germany, Italy, and Japan, to name a few cases, very little scholarly attention has been directed toward the following questions: first, why women join these groups and the types of roles they play; and second, why terrorist organizations recruit and operationalize women and how this process proceeds within societies that are usually highly restrictive of women's public roles. Answering these questions may facilitate the creation of a comprehensive strategy for combating terrorism and limiting political violence. Regardless of region, women's involvement with politically violent organizations and movements highlights several generalizable themes. First, there is a general assumption that most women who become involved with terrorist organizations do so for personal reasons, whether a personal relationship with a man or because of a personal tragedy (e.g., death of a family member, rape). This assumption mirrors theories about female criminal activity in the domestic realm, as well as legitimate political activity by women,[2] and diminishes women's credibility and influence both within and outside organizations.

Second, because women are not considered credible or likely perpetrators of terrorist violence, they can more easily carry out attacks and assist their organizations. Women are able to use their gender to avoid detection on several fronts: first, their "non-threatening" nature may prevent in-depth scrutiny at the most basic level as they are simply not considered important enough to warrant investigation; second, sensitivities regarding more thorough searches, particularly of women's bodies, may hamper stricter scrutiny; and third, a woman's ability to get pregnant and the attendant changes to her body facilitate concealment of weapons and bombs using maternity clothing, as well as further impeding inspection because of impropriety issues. Finally, popular opinion typically considers women as victims of violence, including terrorism, rather than perpetrators, a perspective that is even more entrenched when considering women from states and societies that are believed to be extremely "oppressed" such as those in the Middle East and North Africa (MENA). Such a perspective is frequently translated into official and operational policy, wherein women are not seriously scrutinized as operational elements within terrorist and guerilla organizations because of limited resources and threat perception.

This analysis contends that female involvement with terrorist activity is widening ideologically, logistically, and regionally for several reasons: first, increasing contextual pressures (e.g., domestic/international enforcement, conflict, social dislocation) creates a mutually reinforcing process driving terrorist organizations to recruit women at the same time women's motivations to join these groups increases; contextual pressures impact societal controls over women thereby facilitating, if not necessitating, more overt political participation up to, and including, political violence; and operational imperatives often make female members highly effective actors for their organizations, inducing leaders toward "actor innovation" to gain strategic advantage against their adversary.[3]

## CONTEXTUAL PRESSURES AND INNOVATION

Since 11 September, 2001, United States law enforcement and national security efforts have been aggressively targeted at identifying current and potential terrorist actors who threaten the country's interests. This activity has largely centered on Muslim males because of the types of terrorist attacks that have threatened the United States over the past decade (e.g., the World Trade Center (1993), the African Embassy bombings (1998), and the USS *Cole* bombing (2000) to name a few). All of the incidents were planned and implemented by Muslim, and predominantly Arab, males residing within the United States or abroad.

Terrorist organizations tend to be highly adaptive and although there are fundamental differences among terrorist groups along ideological lines (e.g., ethnonationalist, religious, Marxist-Leninist) that influence the types of ends these organizations seek, they are typically unified in terms of the means (e.g., political violence) they are willing to employ to achieve their goals. The means/goals dichotomy is reflected by the absence of a single definition of terrorism with which all can agree.[4] Nevertheless, an ancient Chinese proverb quickly gets to the heart of terrorism noting that its purpose is "to kill one and frighten 10,000 others."[5]

Problematic, and evidenced by the evolving nature of campaigns in Sri Lanka and Israel/Palestine, as well as historical examples from Ireland and Lebanon, is that terrorist organizations tend to adapt to high levels of external pressure by altering their techniques and targets. Terrorist organizations learn from each other and "[t]he history of terrorism reveals a series of innovations, as terrorists deliberately selected targets considered taboo and locales where violence was unexpected. These innovations were then rapidly diffused, especially in the modern era of instantaneous and global communications."[6] Corresponding to existing terrorism theory, the use of suicide campaigns is an example of one type of tactical adaptation utilized by terrorist organizations, especially in the Arab—Israeli conflict and Sri Lanka, and both cases have also witnessed an evolution in targets (e.g., combatant to civilian).

This analysis suggests that terrorist organizations "innovate" on an additional level, particularly under heavy government pressure or to exploit external conditions, to include new actors or perpetrators.[7] In both Sri Lanka[8] and Palestine, female participation within politically violent organizations has increased and women's roles have expanded to include suicide terrorism. Sri Lanka's "Black Tigers," composed of roughly 50 percent women, is symbolic of this adaptation. In 2002, the Al-Aqsa Martyrs Brigade in the Occupied Territories began actively recruiting women to act as suicide bombers in its campaign against Israeli targets. Other organizations have demonstrated efforts to recruit and employ women. For example, the Algerian-based Islamic Action Group (GIA) operation planned for the Millennium celebration in 1999 reportedly had a woman, Lucia Garofalo, as a central character. The Revolutionary Armed Forces of Columbia (FARC) and Peru's Shining Path have growing levels of female operatives, and even right-wing extremist groups in the United States, such as the World Church of the Creator (WCOTC), are reportedly witnessing high female recruitment levels and one woman associated with the rightist movement, Erica Chase, went on trial in summer 2002 with her boyfriend in an alleged plot to bomb symbolic African-American and Jewish targets.

## WOMEN'S POLITICAL VIOLENCE AND THE ROLE OF SOCIETY: THE CASE OF ALGERIA

Almost universally, women have been considered peripheral players by both observers and many terrorist organizations, typically relegated to support functions such as providing safe houses or gathering intelligence. However, women have been central members of some organizations, such as Shigenobu Fusako, founder and leader of the Japanese Red Army (JRA), and Ulrike Meinhof, an influential member of the West German Baader-Meinhof Gang. In Iran, Ashraf Rabi was arrested in 1974 by the SAVAK, the country's secret police, after a bomb accidentally detonated in her headquarters. In Sri Lanka, women have been effective suicide bombers for the Liberation Tigers for Tamil Eelam (LTTE) and interestingly, their role is modeled after women's participation in the Indian National Army (INA) during the 1940s war with Britain, which included female suicide bombers.[9] Women have also historically been active, albeit less visible members, of a range of right-wing organizations including the Ku Klux Klan (KKK)[10] and the Third Reich.[11] If women's involvement with political violence is interpreted more broadly to include revolutionary movements, then scholarly discourse clearly demonstrates the importance of women like Joan of Arc and women during the Russian Revolution.[12]

Thus, even a cursory look at history provides numerous examples of a diverse array of cases and roles of women's involvement with political violence. Despite historical evidence though, most observers remain surprised and baffled by women's willingness to engage in political violence, especially within the context of terrorism. Importantly, the "invisibility" of women both within terrorist organizations, and particularly their assumed invisibility within many of the societies that experience terrorism, makes women an attractive actor for these organizations, an advantage that female members also acknowledge. This invisibility also makes scholarly inquiry of the phenomenon more difficult and may lull observers into the false assumption that women are insignificant actors within terrorist organizations.

An analysis of the role of "veiled" and "unveiled" women during the 1950s Algerian resistance against the French provides insights into the process by which women were consciously mobilized into "terrorist" roles within a MENA case by both politically violent organizations and the women who chose to join these organizations. Significantly, "[t]he Algerian woman's entrance into the Revolution as political agent was simultaneous with the deployment of the necessarily violent 'technique of terrorism,'" and the veil became "both a dress and a mask," facilitating women's operational utility during the Revolution.[13] Mirroring scholarly discourse on the "popular upsurge" in transitions against authoritarian rule in which civil society "surges" and then retreats, women's incorporation into the Algerian resistance movement emerged within a process of resistance to international oppression, suggesting that the societal sector may have been momentarily, albeit effectively, mobilized to include women.[14]

The phased mobilization of women into the Algerian resistance movement, and the societal environment that facilitated it, is argued to have had three distinct junctures. Prior to 1956, Algerian resistance led to the "cult of the veil" and women's decisions to veil were an active response to colonial attempts to unveil them and thereby dominate society even further. Only men were involved in armed struggle during this period but French adaptation to resistance tactics prompted male leaders to hesitantly transform their strategy and include women in the "public struggle." This initiated the second phase of women's mobilization, wherein "terrorist tactics are first fully utilized" and the conflict moved to urban areas and women unveiled in order to exploit their opponent. The final phase occurred when "woman . . . was transformed into a 'woman-arsenal': Carrying revolvers, grenades, hundreds of false identity cards or bombs, the unveiled Algerian woman move[d] like a fish in the Western waters."[15] "By 1957, the veil reappeared because everyone was a suspected terrorist and the veil facilitated the concealment of weapons." Further, "[r]esistance [wa]s generated through the manipulation, transformation, and reappropriation of the traditional Arab woman's veil into a 'technique of camouflage' for guerilla warfare."[16]

The societal process(es) that facilitated the coalescence of organizational and individualist interests in Algeria is significant. There occurred "[a] transformation of the Muslim notion of femininity, even if only momentarily during decolonization, [which] is central to theorizing the general range of *possibilities* for Algerian women's subjectivity and agency."[17] Significantly, this same type of process has been visible within the Palestinian context for at least three decades. Although women were not actively visible in the earlier periods of the Arab—Israeli conflict, with the creation of the General Union of Palestinian Women (1969) and the spread of education, there was a growing idea among Palestinian leaders "that women constitute half the available manpower resource, one that a small, embattled nation cannot afford to waste. Women began to participate, publicly, in every crisis, from Wahdat camp in the 1970 Amman battles to the latest Israeli invasion in South Lebanon." Although women were willing to participate, and Palestinian leaders were clearly willing to rely on them, Arafat's conception of their role conflicted with societal conceptions of women's roles, thereby making it difficult for women to fully participate in the conflict.[18]

The Algerian case is illustrative of a number of themes that will be developed in this article. First, there was a mutually reinforcing process driving both women and organizations using political violence together. The revolutionary features of Algerian resistance against external, colonial control led to broad political mobilization that included women, a process engendered not only by the promise of socialist "equality" but also by the colonial state's efforts to regulate the veil. Furthermore, the entrenched features of a war for independence inextricably involves virtually every societal segment and ensures that the conflict extends to the household level. Second, the deepening sociopolitical process of the resistance increasingly overlapped with operational imperatives within the all-male resistance movement that indicated the utility of using women against the French.

Third, Algerian men and women generally shared the same political objective—freedom from French colonial domination. Equally significant, however, is that women and men held a secondary, albeit divergent, goal regarding social change; women clearly wished for greater equality, albeit not in the Western feminist sense, whereas men saw social change as asserting more authentic cultural forms (e.g., Islam). The articulation of the latter's vision of social change is captured in *La Charte d'Alger* (1964) wherein women's inferiority under colonialism resulted from poor interpretations of Islam to which women "naturally" reacted. As a result, "[t]he war of liberation enabled the Algerian woman to assert herself by carrying out responsibilities *side by side* with man and taking part in the struggle. . . . In this sense the charter reveals its unwillingness discursively to allow women's participation in the war to be the product of their chosen activity. Women's historical action is legitimized by their proximity to men . . . not by their agency."[19]

This process led to two outcomes that are visible in other cases. First, upon achieving the group's ends, women's participation therein is reinterpreted or reframed as less authentic, which allows women to be legitimately politically peripheralized (i.e., because they were not full and "authentic" participants) and their objectives, particularly with respect to social change, to be dismissed. Second, women's participation is not individually chosen; rather, it is facilitated by relationships with others or structural factors (e.g., poverty) that distance women from the violence they participated in, allowing society (and emergent political leaders) to not only separate women from the citizenship rights inherent in military-type service but also placing women's violence within a more palatable context. Importantly, this process mirrors women's participation in war and even instances of political mobilization within more limited (i.e., less violent) environments of political change, suggesting that it is not unique to terrorist or revolutionary structures and rather reflects more embedded features of female citizenship and political participation.

## PATTERNS OF OPERATIONAL FEMALE TERRORISM

Not only have women historically been active in politically violent organizations, the regional and ideological scope of this activity has been equally broad. Women have been operational (e.g., regulars) in virtually every region and there are clear trends toward women becoming more fully incorporated into numerous terrorist organizations. Cases from Colombia, Italy, Sri Lanka, Pakistan, Turkey, Iran, Norway, and the United States suggest that women have not only functioned in support capacities, but have also been leaders in organization, recruitment, and fund-raising, as well as tasked with carrying out the most deadly missions undertaken by terrorist organizations—suicide bombings. Regardless of the region, it is clear that women are choosing to participate in politically violent organizations irrespective of their respective organizational leaders' motives for recruiting them.[20]

### European Female Terrorism

European terrorist organizations are among the oldest groups to examine and offer the first insights into women's roles in these organizations. Women have been drawn to leftist and rightist organizations in Europe, and have thus been involved in groups with goals ranging from separatism to Marxist-Leninism. Women have been, and in certain cases continue to be, active members of several terrorist organizations within Europe including the Euskadi Ta Askatasuna (ETA, Basque Homeland and Unity), the Irish Republican Army (IRA), and the Italian Red Brigades (RD), to name a few.

Mirroring the Palestinian conflict, which will be discussed later, Irish women, particularly mothers, have been widely active in their conflict with the British, which was waged close to home in their neighborhoods and communities.

One examination of the operational role of women in Italy's various terrorist factions during the 1960s and 1970s identifies several important tendencies. Although women generally accounted for no more than 20 percent of terrorist membership during this period, Italian women who participated in terrorist organizations were overwhelmingly drawn to leftist and nationalist organizations. This corresponded to a general period of social change, evidenced by movement in areas such as divorce, abortion, education, and employment, which allowed the Italian left to recruit and mobilize the country's women.[21] Women within the Italian left had a good chance of functioning as "regulars" and occasionally in leadership roles, particularly during the later stages of the organization's operations.[22]

The Italian experience correlates with a general trend[23] in which leftist organizations tend to attract more female recruits not only because their ideological message for political and social change (e.g., equality) resonates with women, but also because those ideas influence leadership structures within the groups. As a result, "[w]omen tend to be overrepresented in positions of leadership in left-wing groups and to be underrepresented in right-wing groups."[24] Conversely, rightist organizations have more limited recruitment of women and they have historically been characterized by an almost uniform absence of female leaders. In Norway, male domination of rightist organizations, and the inability of women to obtain leadership positions, prompted the creation of Valkyria, an all-women rightist organization that allowed members to develop leadership skills and opinions.[25]

## North American Female Terrorism

Women's roles North American-based terrorist organizations mirrors the variability of Europe but includes an international element that is distinguishing, at least at this juncture. First, there is an important division between women based on "origination," for lack of a better word. One group of women involved in alleged terrorist organizations are members of, or closely tied with, an expatriate or immigrant community that has links to international terrorism. The other group of women has links to domestic terrorist organizations,[26] and within this category there are three subsets: those belonging to right-wing organizations that include the WCOTC[27] and the Aryan Nation, as well as militia movements and "patriot" organizations; those belonging to "leftist" groups typically linked to Puerto Rican nationalism;[28] and those belonging to "special interest" terrorist groups that range from leftist to rightist including the Animal Liberation Front (ALF), the Earth Liberation Front (ELF), and anti-abortion activists.[29] Second, women's roles in North American terrorist organizations are highly influenced by their organization's target. For most international terrorist organizations, North America is less a theater of operation than an extremely important locus of financial, logistical, and ideological support for operations in other parts of the world. Obviously, for domestic terrorist organizations this is not a limiting factor. Third, readily available social and political freedoms in the region facilitate travel, communication, and organizational advancement that may be unattainable in other states. Finally, most connections involve both Canada and the United States, particularly with respect to legal entry and residency status for international terrorist groups.

Both the Mujahadeen-e-Khalq (MEK) and the Kurdistan Workers' Party (PKK) have attracted official attention in both the United States and Canada since 2000 for incidents involving female members. Mahnaz Samadi became a member of the MEK in 1980 and was an active fighter for the organization against Iranian targets in the 1980s, including alleged terrorist attacks in Tehran in 1982. After becoming leader of the National Liberation Army and the National Council of Resistance (NCR), a MEK civilian front, she replaced Robab Farahi-Mahdavieh in 1993 to head NCR fundraising in North America. Mahdavieh is alleged to have been involved with the 1992 attack against the Iranian embassy in Ottawa, leading to her deportation from Canada in 1993. Samadi was arrested in 2000 by Canadian officials and was deported to the United States where senior officials became involved to prevent her deportation to Iran.[30] A similar fund-raising role was allegedly carried out by Zehra Saygili (a.k.a. Aynur Saygili, Beser Gezer)[31] and Hanan Ahmed Osman (a.k.a. Helin Baran)[32] both with the PKK. Osman allegedly entered Canada in 1984 and was granted refugee status. She then turned to recruiting, fund-raising, and propaganda activities on behalf of the PKK. Saygili arrived in Canada in 1996 and allegedly became active with the Kurdish Cultural Association in Montreal to raise money and support for the PKK.[33]

Another woman suspected of having ties with terrorist networks, but later cleared by the U.S. government under somewhat vague circumstances, was a Montreal woman born in Italy, Lucia Garofalo. Garofalo was allegedly linked to Ahmed Ressam, who was found guilty in U.S. federal court of plotting a terrorist attack within the United States around the Millennium celebrations. Garofalo pled guilty to two counts of illegally transporting individuals into the United States, including her attempt to smuggle Bouabide Chamchi through an unstaffed border crossing in Vermont. She also admitted to providing him with a stolen French passport. Garofalo and Chamchi were arrested after explosive-sniffing dogs positively indicated on the vehicle she was driving. One week before attempting to transport Chamchi into the United States, Garofalo reportedly successfully transported a Pakistani man into the country, raising speculation at the time that she was transporting aliens into the United States. Phone records linking Garofalo with Ressam and other members of the conspiracy, vehicle ownership by a reported member of the Algerian Islamic League, travel records showing numerous trips to Europe, Morocco, and Libya without apparent funding to support such travel, and personal ties linked Garofalo to several individuals indicted in the Millennium operation.[34] Because terrorist charges have been dropped against Ms. Garofalo, her overall role in the Millennium plot is unknown and likely minimal; however, she is reported to have had contact with a large number of individuals linked to the plot and is married to Yamin Rachek who was deported from Canada and has been wanted by both German and British officials for theft and passport fraud. In an effort to secure counsel for her husband, Garofalo allegedly was in contact with one of the individuals linked to the Millennium plot.

Both the Anti-Defamation League (ADL)[35] and the Southern Poverty Law Center (SPLC) have noted an emerging trend in U.S. right-wing movements involving the growing mobilization of female members, particularly on the Internet. According to the SPLC, women now make up 25 percent of right-wing groups in the United States and as much as 50 percent of new recruits, and these young women want a greater role in their organizations, including leadership, than their predecessors have demanded.[36] Considering that domestic terrorism remains the most likely source of terrorist activity in the United States, according to the Federal Bureau of Investigation (FBI), and that right-wing terrorist groups are among the most active domestic terrorists in the country, this trend is noteworthy.

Lisa Turner, founder of the "Women's Frontier" of the WCOTC, provides insights into the perceived role of women for this and other White supremacist organizations.[37] Although acknowledging the role of women in combat and as martyrs for the organization (particularly Vicki Weaver and Kathy Ainsworth[38]), Turner states that "most women are not 'Shining Path' guerilla fighters." She rejects the use of women as suicide bombers ("cannon fodder") by the LTTE not on the basis that such a role is beyond women, but that it emanates from male exploitation of women that appears conjoined with their "non-White" status. Turner concentrates on avoiding a generalized understanding of what is, or is not, a revolutionary and from this argument she asserts that women's roles within the organization should be a function of their unique talents and abilities. This includes leadership positions and she notes that women can become Reverends within the organization as well as Hasta Primus, the second highest position within the organization and the main assistant to the group's leader, the Pontifex Maximus.[39] Female leadership within right-wing groups is not isolated to the WCOTC; Rachel Pendergraft is reportedly a lieutenant in the Ku Klux Klan, an organization that has clearly targeted potential and current members with a women's website.[40] Women have also been associated with potentially more violent activities, such as Erica Chase, who went on trial in summer 2002 for an alleged plot to bomb prominent African-American and Jewish targets.

Women have played a central and important role in the Puerto Rican nationalist movement, particularly the Puerto Rican Armed Forces of National Liberation (FLAN) and *Los Macheteros* (The Machete Wielders or the Puerto Rican Peoples' Army), both designated as terrorist organizations by the FBI. Women such as Blanca Canales and Adelfa Vera were significant leaders in the early nationalist movement and women are significantly represented in nonterrorist, but "supportive" entities like the Puerto Rican New Independence Movement (NMIP) and various demonstrations surrounding U.S. military exercises on Vieques. Additionally, women have been tried and incarcerated in the United States for their affiliation and actions with Puerto Rican nationalist movements. For example, 5 of 15 individuals arrested and tried by the United States between 1980 and 1985 for sedition, conspiracy, and illegal weapons possession were women (Dylcia Pagan, Alejandrina Torres, Carmen Valentin, and Alicia and Ida Luz Rodriguez) with Pagan (a.k.a. Dylcia Pagan Morales) considered the leader of the group by the government.[41]

For both the ALF and ELF, the most visible members are male, as evidenced by spokespeople (e.g., Craig Rosebraugh of the ELF) and arrests. However, this surface impression is likely not indicative of the actual rosters of these organizations and the individuals who take part in their operations. According to the FBI, the ELF and ALF have committed 600 criminal acts since 1996 amounting to more than US$42 million in damages.[42] Neither the ALF nor ELF disseminate lists of their members and members' names tend to only come to the surface based on arrest records.[43] In a report documenting actions undertaken by the ELF and ALF in 2001, of the 23 individuals associated with various legal actions ranging from arrest, imprisonment, and subpoenas only 3 were women.[44] However, this should not be construed as totally representative of female participation rates within these organizations, based upon historical trends that clearly demonstrate higher female participation rates within leftist organizations.

To date women affiliated with designated terrorist organizations in North America, both international and domestic, have played mixed roles in their respective organizations. International organizations appear to have incorporated women into more important structures, particularly those associated with fundraising and recruitment, although cases remain few and far between. Domestic terrorist groups are increasingly targeting females for recruitment, and are attracting a diverse occupational and generational group of women. However, their roles within the leadership structures of their respective organizations is either minimal (right wing) or unknown (special interest). Leftist organizations have traditionally centered on Puerto Rican independence and have frequently involved women in a variety of capacities, including leadership positions, mirroring trends visible in Latin America and other "nationalist" settings.

## Latin American Female Terrorism

Women have historically been involved in numerous revolutionary movements in Latin America (e.g., Cuba, El Salvador, Nicaragua, Mexico) so their more visible role in groups like the FARC and Shining Path is not surprising.[45] Within Latin America, two of the most notable terrorist organizations designated by the U.S. Department of State, Colombia's FARC and the Shining Path of Peru, have increasingly incorporated women into their organizations. Figures on total female membership within the FARC vary from 20 to 40 percent, with a general average of 30 percent.[46] Although the FARC's senior leadership structure, particularly the Secretariat, remains all male, women have been ascending throughout the group's ranks, with women now reportedly bearing the title "Commandante." Like Shining Path, the FARC has recruited and retained women for more than a dozen years. Unlike the FARC, the Shining Path's senior leadership structure, the Central Committee, is composed of 8 women (out of 19).[47] The Latin American phenomenon of "machismo" is noted as responsible for the continuation of senior male leadership for the FARC and the "cult of personality" that is said to surround the Shining Path's former leader, Abimael Guzman. As with the LTTE, women of both groups experience the same types of training and expectations as their male counterparts and women have been increasingly used in intelligence roles by the FARC.[48]

In Latin America, female activism in politically violent organizations remains concentrated within leftist movements, corresponding to themes seen in Europe and North America. In both Columbia and Peru, the revolutionary features of the respective movements movements is significant, mirroring processes in Palestine and Sri Lanka, as well as Iran, South Africa, and Eritrea. For the most part, women join the FARC and Shining Path while young, engage in all facets of the organization, and often remain members for life, although activism rates may alter with age, as is true with their male counterparts. Also noteworthy is that cases drawn from three regions (South Asia, Middle East, Latin America) confront more generalized poverty and "youth bulges" than is true of North America and Europe. Between 1983 and 2000, the percentage of the population living on less than US$2 per day was 45.4 for Sri Lanka, 36 for Colombia, and 41.4 for Peru. Data released by the Palestinian Central Bureau of Statistics in early 2002 showed that 57.8 percent of those living in the West Bank and 84.6 percent of those living in the Gaza Strip were living below the poverty line. In addition to poverty, each of these states is confronting some form of "youth bulge" evidenced by the percentage of their populations between 0 and 14 as reported in 2001. These figures ranged from 25.9 percent in Sri Lanka, 31.88 percent in Colombia, 34.41 percent in Peru, 49.89 percent in the Gaza Strip, and 44.61 percent in the West Bank.[49] Thus, the fact that poor, young individuals are frequently drawn to terrorist organizations and politically violent groups is neither regionally limited nor gendered.

## South Asian Female Terrorism

The Sri Lankan case shares some parallels with MENA terrorist organizations, including the structural imperatives that favor the use of women as suicide bombers, the intersection of political and sociocultural goals of liberation, and sociocultural norms that idealize sacrifice.[50] As of 2000, roughly half of the LTTE's membership[51] were females, who are frequently recruited as children into the Black Tigers, an elite bomb squad composed of women and men.[52] Women enjoy equivalent training and combat experience with their male counterparts and are fully incorporated into the extant structure of the LTTE. Women's utility as suicide bombers derives from their general exclusion from the established "profile" of such actors employed by many police and security forces (e.g., young males), allowing them to better avoid scrutiny and reach their targets. The 1991 assassination of Rajiv Gandhi, then leader of India, by a young Tamil woman who garlanded him, bowed at his feet, and then detonated a bomb that killed them both, provides proof of the power of this terrorist weapon. However, that woman, identified as Dhanu (a.k.a. Tanu), suggests some of the contradictory themes that arise when considering women's roles in the LTTE.

Reportedly prompted to join the LTTE because she was gang-raped by Indian peacekeeping forces who also killed her brothers,[53] Dhanu has become an important mythical force utilized for further recruitment as rape has been identified as one of the primary reasons motivating young women to join the LTTE. The goal of *eelam* (freedom) pursued by the LTTE is said to be conjoined with the pursuit of similar personal, and perhaps even societal, freedom for female recruits as "[f]ighting for Tamil freedom is often the only way a woman has to redeem herself."[54] Also inherent in the struggle is the idea (1) of sacrifice, particularly for Tamil rape victims who are said to be socially prohibited from marriage and childbearing. Equating the sacrifice of the female bomber as an extension of motherhood, suicide bombings become an acceptable "offering" for women who can never be mothers, a process that is reportedly encouraged by their families.[55] "As a rule, women are represented as the core symbols of the nation's identity" and the "Tamil political movements have used women's identity as a core element in their nationalism."[56]

According to *Jane's Intelligence Review,* "suicide terrorism is the readiness to sacrifice one's life in the process of destroying or attempting to destroy a target to advance a political goal. The aim of the psychologically and physically war-trained terrorist is to die while destroying the enemy target."[57] It is also on the increase. Aside from the LTTE, the main groups that employ suicide terrorism in pursuit of their objectives are located in, or linked to, the Middle East, such as Hamas, Hizballah, and Islamic Jihad. The LTTE is the only current example of a terrorist organization that has permanently adopted "suicide terrorism as a legitimate and permanent strategy."[58] Suicide terrorism in this context is the result of a "cult of personality" rather than a religious cult, demonstrating that "under certain extreme political and psychological circumstances secular volunteers are fully capable of martyrdom."[59]

Sri Lanka is not the only place in South Asia, however, where women are, or have been, allegedly involved with terrorism. Among Sikh militants, women have participated in an array of roles including armed combat. Importantly, Sikhism does not distinguish between male and female equality forming a religio-societal grounding that neither precludes female combat nor categorizes that role as uniquely masculine (or "unfeminine"). Rather, societal resistance to female combat roles is fostered by well-founded fears of sexual abuse, rape, and sexual torture of women if captured. Within the Sikh case, women's "support" roles are not viewed as peripheralized or indicative of women's marginalization within the political sphere. Instead, women's support of their husbands and sons is seen to critically enable their ability to fight and die for the nation, and women's roles as mothers producing future fighters for that nation is also recognized. As a result, "[w]hile it is obvious that the celebrated virtues of courage, bold action, and strong speech are consonant with masculinity as understood in the West, among Sikhs these qualities are treated as neither masculine nor feminine, but simply as Sikh, values. Women may be bound to the kitchen and may have babies in their arms, but they are still fully *expected* to behave as soldiers, if necessary."[60]

Additional examples of women's participation with politically violent organizations relate to the Indian-Pakistan confrontation over Kashmir. According to Indian sources, Shamshad Begum

was arrested by Indian security forces in October 2001 for allegedly acting as a guide responsible for identifying safe travel routes for members of Hizbul Mujahadeen.[61] Another female member of the same organization was reportedly killed by Lashker-e-Taiyaba members. Indian sources claim that women are drawn to the organization for financial motives, and women's roles as couriers have been improved by a "requirement" to wear a *burqa*.[62] Reports of female involvement in terrorist groups expanded by December 2001 as the Indian press reported female bomb squads were being prepared by Pakistan-supported groups in Kashmir for attacks against senior officials during the Republic Day Parade.[63]

Several themes arise from the South Asian context that provide additional insight into female terrorists, particularly suicide terrorism. First, personal motives (e.g., family, rape, financial) are argued to greatly influence women to join organizations like the LTTE and, even more importantly, into becoming suicide bombers (e.g., rape). Second, freedom and liberation are key themes at both the collective and individualistic levels. Collectively, freedom and liberation capture the legitimating ideology of the LTTE vis-à-vis the Sinhalese and the Indian governments, the mujahadeen in Kashmir vis-à-vis India, and the Sikhs vis-à-vis India for Khalistan. Liberation also appears to be conceptualized individualistically as, according to one Tamil Tiger, "the use of women in war is part of a larger vision of the guerrilla leadership to liberate Tamil women from the bonds of tradition."[64] However, this has led to accusations that women are less committed to *eelam* as their primary motivation for participating in the LTTE, joining instead for personal vengeance.[65] The idea of sacrifice as an ideal is the third theme and it centers both on the role of women within society as a whole (e.g., motherhood) as well as for suicide bombers more particularly. Female sacrifice for her family, and particularly for her male children, is seen as a generalized cultural norm that is usefully extended to female self-sacrifice for her community and family, particularly if she is unable (e.g., because of rape), to undertake her role as wife and mother within the society. In both the Sikh and Sri Lankan examples, female martyrdom is viewed as necessary to overcome the individual and—more importantly—collective shame of dishonor caused by rape. Fourth, the personalism of women's motives that arguably drive them to join organizations like the LTTE is both responsible for somehow diminishing the overall "authenticness" of women's roles in these organizations, particularly for outside observers, and allowing for charges of LTTE exploitation of its female cadre who are used as "throw-aways" or "as artillery."[66]

## Middle East and North African Female Terrorism

From the earliest days of the Palestinian resistance, women have been involved in both the leftist and rightist sides of the Palestinian struggle against Israel.[67] The events of 2002 suggest that this pattern remains intact. Through April 2002 four Palestinian women have become suicide bombers on behalf of the Al-Aqsa Martyrs Brigade, an offshoot of Fatah, prompting, in part, a major Israeli military offensive against the Palestinians begun in March 2002. However, although these attacks have shocked Israeli security analysts, there is a sustained, and varied, history of Palestinian women who have been involved with terrorist organizations, particularly since the nationalist-based movements began to increasingly carry out violent activities in the 1960s. One of the most well-known female terrorists is Leila Khaled, affiliated with the Popular Front for the Liberation of Palestine (PFLP), who hijacked a plane in 1969. Another woman convicted of planting a bomb in a Jerusalem supermarket during 1969, Randa Nabulsi, was sentenced to 10 years imprisonment.[68] Although there has been a low probability that women will be used by Islamist terrorist groups, continuing the trend of lower female representation among rightist organizations, there is precedent for such inclusion in Palestine. Etaf Aliyan, a Palestinian woman who is also a member of Islamic Jihad, was scheduled to drive a car loaded with explosives into a Jerusalem police station in 1987 but was apprehended before the attack could take place. If the attack had occurred, it would have represented "the first suicide vehicle bombing in Israel"[69] and significantly, it would have been implemented by a woman.

Women's roles were increasing among secular and Islamist Palestinian organizations before 2002, suggesting a warning sign of the impending escalation of Palestinian violence against Israeli targets. In particular, there was an apparent trend in women's growing roles within the Palestinian resistance that was initiated with examples of male/female collaboration (e.g., suggesting female training by more experienced males), followed by individual women planting explosive devices but not detonating them, to the culmination wherein women were tasked with actually detonating bombs on their own persons. Thus, in hindsight suicide bombing by women appeared to be a logical progression in women's operations within various organizations, and suggests that women may be tasked with tandem suicide bombing and other operations in the future.

For example, Ahlam Al-Tamimi was arrested by Israel's Shabak in 2001, charged with extending logistical support to the Hamas cell that attacked the Sbarro pizzeria in West Jerusalem. She reportedly worked with Mohamed Daghles, a member of the Palestinian Authority security body. The two are linked to at least two incidents in summer 2001. In July, Al-Tamimi reportedly carried a bomb disguised as a beer can into a West Jerusalem supermarket that detonated but did not injure anyone. In August, Al-Tamimi was linked to a Hamas bomber who carried a bomb in a guitar case into a Sbarro pizzeria that killed the bomber and 15 others.[70] In another instance, on 3 August 2001, Ayman Razawi (a.k.a. Imman Ghazawi, Iman Ghazawi, Immam Ghazawi), 23,[71] a mother of 2, was caught before she could plant an 11-pound bomb packed with nails and screws hidden in a laundry detergent box in a Tel Aviv bus station. However, despite the escalating role of women in the *intifada,* the prospect of a female suicide bomber remained remote through the first weeks of 2002 because "[t]here have been very few cases of Arab women found infiltrating Israel on a mission to murder civilians."[72]

That perception changed dramatically in the wake of 28 January 2002 when Wafa Idris (a.k.a. Wafa Idrees, Shahanaz Al Amouri),[73] 28, detonated a 22-pound bomb in Jerusalem that killed her, an 81-year-old Israeli man, and injured more than 100 others. Confusion punctuated the immediate aftermath of the attack given that heretofore women had only helped plant bombs and it was not clear whether Idris had intended to detonate the explosive or whether the explosion was accidental. Equally unclear was whether she was acting on behalf of some group or how she had obtained the explosives. This confusion made the Israelis reticent to confirm that the attack constituted the first "official" case of a female suicide bomber related to the Arab-Israeli conflict and, therefore, a significant shift in the security framework within which the Israelis would have to operate. As Steve Emerson is quoted as stating in the wake of Idris's attack, if true the bombing "opens a whole new demographic pool of potential bombers."[74] By early February the Israelis declared that Wafa Idris was a suicide bomber[75]—a first. The Fatah-linked Al-Aqsa Martyrs Brigade (a.k.a. Al Aqsa Brigades) claimed responsibility for her attack and described Idris as a "martyr."

Idris's motivation to commit a suicide operation was arguably prompted by a sense of hopelessness under occupation and rage, not heaven as promised to her male counterparts.[76] As a result, her action is seen "to have been motivated more by nationalist than religious fervor,"[77] a motivation that is frequently attributed to her male counterparts. In addition to not being a "known" member of a terrorist organization, and therefore more likely to be identified as a potential suicide bomber, Idris did not carry out the attack in the "normal" fashion. She carried the bomb in a backpack, rather than strapped to her waist, raising widespread speculation that she did not intend to detonate the bomb and the explosion was accidental.[78] Another cause for skepticism about Idris's role in the attack arose from the lack of a note and martyr's video, which are typically left behind by one engaging in a "martyr's operation."

The response by secular and Islamist Palestinian leaders to the attack is important. Although the Al-Aqsa Martyrs Brigade claimed responsibility for the attack, it did not do so immediately. The strong reaction by the "Arab street" to the attack, and the heightened sense of insecurity noted by Israeli officials, provide two excellent reasons why women's operational utility increased for Al-Aqsa's leaders. First, Idris's action resonated strongly throughout the Arab world. Egypt's weekly *Al-Sha'ab* published an editorial on 1 February 2002 entitled "It's a Woman!" that is reflective of the general tone that emanated throughout the Arab press regarding the attack. The editorial stated, in part, "It is a woman who teaches you today a lesson in heroism, who teaches you the meaning of Jihad, and the way to die a martyr's death. . . . It is a woman who has shocked the enemy, with her thin, meager, and weak body. . . . It is a woman who blew herself up, and with her exploded all the myths about women's weakness, submissiveness, and enslavement."[79]

The profound reaction to her attack by the masses both within and outside Palestine created a turning point for the Al-Aqsa Martyrs Brigade that had two effects: first, a willingness to use both men and women in terrorist attacks and second, an acknowledgement of the utility of using suicide bombers against civilian targets within Israel to undermine Israeli security and force Israel to negotiate from a position of weakness. Within days of the attack, Abu-Ahman, founder and leader of Al-Aqsa, showed signs of a tactical shift, asserting that there would be a "qualitative military operation by Al-Aqsa Battalions (*sic*) against Israeli targets," within a short period of time[80] that was clearly designed to take advantage of the psychological and tactical significance of female members of the organization. By the end of February, the Al-Aqsa Martyrs Brigade reportedly confirmed it had created a "special women's unit" named after Wafa Idris[81] to carry out attacks. Subsequent attacks by female suicide bombers over the next three months did not confirm the existence of a "special unit," but it did signify the group's willingness to utilize female members for suicide operations was not a fluke.

Reactions by Islamists were more mixed and muted, but not rejective in the immediate aftermath of the attack, Sheikh Ahmad Yassin, spiritual leader of Hamas, initially opposed Idris's action citing personnel imperatives, stating that "in this phase (of the uprising), the participation of women is not needed in martyr operations, like men." He went on to note that "[w]e can't meet the growing demands of young men who wish to carry out martyr operations," and "women form the second line of defence (*sic*) in the resistance to the occupation." However, he later qualified his objection when he added that if a Hamas woman wanted to carry out a "martyr operation," she should be accompanied by a man if the operation required her to be away more than a day and a night. Hamas leaders Sheikh Hassan Yusef and Isma'eel Abu Shanab noted that there was no *fatwa* (religious decree) that prevented a woman from being a martyr, ostensibly against Israeli occupation in the Palestinian territories.[82] Sheikh Abdullah Nimr Darwish, spiritual leader of Arabs in Israel, was more forceful in advocating the new role for women, driven in large part by the extension of the occupation to the home. He stated "the women will fight. Now the Palestinians prefer to be killed at the front rather than wait and be killed at home. . . . Israel has the Dimona nuclear plant, but we Palestinians have a stronger Dimona—the suiciders. We can use them on a daily basis. He also pointed, with pride, at the sight of Palestinian women in white shrouds at funerals—a sign of their readiness to become shuhada, or martyr." Further, women lined up to become martyrs, shouting "make a bomb of me, please!"[83] All of these reactions were in keeping with the August 2001 *fatwa* issued by the High Islamic Council in Saudi Arabia urging women to join the fight against Israel as martyrs.

Despite Israeli assertions that Idris's attack was a planned suicide bombing, significant uncertainty surrounds the authenticity of this attack as an Al-Aqsa Martyrs Brigade-planned suicide attack. More likely is that Idris was to plant the bomb as Al-Tamimi and Razawi were to have done in 2001. Nevertheless, Al-Aqsa learned an important lesson about the utility of female suicide bombers, and the uncertainties of the Idris case were addressed in subsequent attacks by female martyrs: Darin Abu Aysheh (a.k.a. Dareen Abu Ashai, dareen Abu Eishi), 21, detonated an explosive device on 27 February 2002 at an Israeli checkpoint in the West Bank;[84] Ayat Akhras, 18, blew herself up on 29 March 2002 at a Jerusalem neighborhood grocery store in a wave of Passover attacks that followed Israeli attacks against Arafat's headquarters;[85] and Andalib Takafka blew herself up in a crowded Jerusalem market, killing 6 and wounding more than 50 people on 12 April 2002, undermining efforts by the U.S. Secretary of State Colin Powell to move ahead with peace talks.[86]

Historical and recent cases of female Palestinian terrorism suggest several trends. First, female activism has tended to be more active within the secularist context (e.g., leftist) rather than among Islamists (e.g., rightist), reflecting a general global trend. However, although women have been more active with the nationalist/secular side of the Palestinian movement, women have been linked to Islamist groups either directly or in terms of their overall support. Second, as the conflict with Israel deepened, the scope of activism widened to include women in an increasing array of activities, up to and including suicide bombing, and women pushed for these expanded roles. Third, women activists have tended to be young, with one or more politically active family members (male), and exposed to some form of loss (e.g., within their family or immediate community) that arguably contributed to their mobilization. Importantly, marital, educational, and maternal status were not uniform factors. Also, these factors are not radically divergent from males who undertake suicide operations within this context. Fourth, Palestinian secular leaders' willingness to include women in martyr operations was influenced by security assessments (e.g., an ability to evade security scrutiny and travel more deeply into Israel), operational constraints (e.g., growing Israeli pressure on male operatives), and publicity. Female suicide bombers represent one way to overcome Israeli security pressures, heighten Israeli insecurity, and exhaust Israeli security resources by significantly increasing the operational range and available pool for suicide operations. Akhras is an exemplary case as witnesses noted she looked "European," and dressed like any Israeli schoolgirl.[87] Trying to protect against that type of terrorist represents a fundamental challenge for any security apparatus.

## CONCLUSION: PRELIMINARY TRENDS AND THEMES

Although there is a tendency to dismiss the overall threat of women suicide bombers, or female terrorists more broadly, because they have historically engaged in such a small percentage of terrorist activities, contextual pressures are creating a convergence between individual women, terrorist organization leaders, and society that is not only increasing the rate of female activity within terrorist and politically violent organizations, but is also expanding their operational range. The tactical advantage of this convergence is apparent particularly with respect to female suicide bombers, a tactic designed to attract attention and instill widespread fear in the target audience, because as one observer noted in the wake of Idris's attack, "it's the women we remember."[88] Because suicide terrorism is designed to attract attention and precipitate fear, in an increasingly charged atmosphere it takes more and more to attract attention, increasing the utility of female suicide bombers. Female suicide bombers also fundamentally challenge existing security assessments and socially derived norms regarding women's behavior, heightening the fear factor. Finally, and more significantly, the small number of women who have, to date, been used in such operations suggests that they will be able to better evade detection than their male counterparts.

Leftist organizations may be more likely to initially recruit or attract women because their goals tend to conform more easily to general processes of social change in society. Nevertheless, security, operational, and publicity assessments inducing secular organizations to recruit and operationalize women in a variety of roles, including as suicide bombers, may spread to rightist organizations including Islamist groups and rightwing organizations. This process may first be visible in Palestine if violence is prolonged or deepens for four reasons: first, women are operationally significant to achieve the over-all goals of the *intifada* in a manner that at least immediately overrides potential social costs of their mobilization; second, given the nascent "public" political roles of women in the region, and sociocultural factors that facilitate this role, women could very well be "demobilized" back into the private realm with little effort; third, nothing in Islam precludes women from serving in this function; and fourth, as the conflict has progressed the lines between the secular/nationalists (e.g., Fatah) and the Islamists (e.g., Hamas) has blurred.[89] Furthermore, it is also possible that groups like Al Qaeda may see women as operationally useful, as enabling conditions abound, including: the horizontal structure and loose affiliations of these organizations, the "war on terrorism" and its escalating enforcement efforts, and no overt religious prohibition against women's activity.

There is a real fascination for many observers with why women join and participate in groups like the FARC, Shining Path, the LTTE, and even the Palestinian groups, perhaps in part because this membership is fairly visible and sizable within their respective organizations. This focus is not overly surprising "[b]ecause politics, and especially revolutionary politics, has traditionally been regarded as a male affair . . . [and as a result] the historian has never really had to 'explain' why an individual man chose to enter political activity."[90] Ergo, trying to "explain" why an individual woman engages in not just political activity but violent political activity becomes quite necessary because there is something not quite "natural" about it.

Both women and men join politically violent organizations, and engage in an array of activities within those organizations, for similar reasons. Most frequently, individuals want to achieve some form of political change, whether revolutionary or more limited in nature. At the most basic level, groups that use political violence as a tactic have as their end-goal a right to draw up and implement new rules of the political game. In revolutionary or nationalist contexts like Palestine, Colombia, and Sri Lanka, the potential political change is far-reaching and typically involves replacing some form of external (or externally linked) leadership. However, political institutions do not arise in a cultural vacuum and often necessitate some form of social change.

Typically women are said to have engaged in political violence for personal (private) reasons, whether because of a male family member, poverty, rape, or similar factors. Importantly, this argument suggests women do not choose their participation consciously, but are rather drawn in as reluctant, if not victimized, participants. Even women who join for ideological (public) reasons are suspect, especially in revolutionary contexts. Here, women's motivations for "freedom" are viewed dualistically as both collective (e.g., independence) and individualistic (e.g., equality) or their ideological motivations are not fully developed, making them "helpers" to men rather than ideologues in their own right. The Algerian case suggests dualistic goals for both men and women, differing only with respect to their conceptualization of social change, the secondary goal, not political change, the primary goal. Nevertheless, there remains an entrenched belief that women's motives are more personal (and private), leaving behind an impression of insincerity and shallowness that prevents women from having any fundamental voice in creating new structures.

In addition to determining why women join organizations there is an equal effort to untangle what women do once they join. Although women have historically been involved with politically violent organizations, most of their activities have been in "support" capacities; thus, their presence has been seen as passive. Usually, this support has come from mothers, who have moral authority, a certain degree of safety vis-à-vis the adversary, and fairly clear boundaries within which they operate (both with respect to their own societies and the adversary).[91] Such action is typically viewed as initiated by the women themselves, and while resistance or terrorist leaders may exploit this activity through propaganda, the role is so natural, if not expected in a highly conflictual context, that very few finds this type of activity threatening (e.g., Ireland, Sri Lanka, and Palestine).

This is not true of the "warrior" women. Even a cursory review of interviews with these women demonstrates that women are pushing for expanded roles within their respective organizations, from leadership to combat, and that a growing number of younger women are joining organizations and staying. However, what is equally clear is that for most observers (e.g., academic, journalistic, policymakers) this choice seems so foreign and unnatural to women that there must be an explanation beyond simply that women want to fight for their respective causes.[92] As a result, women are duped into being "cannon fodder" as they are tasked with the most dangerous missions because they are expendable to their leaders. Additionally, history is replete with cases where women's support and service have not produced extended political freedom. But here is the rub, and the significance of the expanding roles of women in various organizations on both the left and right. As female "warriors," women are able to carve out roles themselves both within their respective organizations and with the hope of doing so in the structures that result from the struggle. Significantly, the women who are being drawn to these movements may be attracted by political opportunities implied by combatant (public) roles regarding citizenship that were denied their mothers who remained altogether private during earlier conflicts. Although it is safer and easier to simply dismiss "warrior" women as pawns of male leaders, as "dupes," and as misguided women who have lost sight of their femininity, this obscures the more interesting issue of why and how women have concluded that political violence will help them achieve desired political (and perhaps social) ends.

In evaluating the roles of women in terrorist and politically violent organizations, it remains prudent to be cognizant of the following: first, the implications of limited data; second, the possibility of denial and deception; third, that invisibility does not necessarily equate with passivity or powerlessness; and fourth, organizational versus societal imperatives. The secretiveness of many of the groups addressed in this study underscores the difficulties with obtaining reliable information related to both male and female recruitment, leadership, and operational roles. Furthermore, group leaders may mislead observers regarding the depth and breadth of female participation in their groups, either through inflation or under-inflation, to gain strategic advantages vis-à-vis their adversaries. Relatedly, just because women are not necessarily visible participants within organizations does not correlate with their absence or passivity within said organizations. Women's operational strengths and tactical advantages may induce leaders to keep female participants well-hidden until contextual pressures necessitate the group show its hand. Finally, it should not be immediately concluded that societal structures that traditionally limit female public roles will hold under tremendous conflict, nor that such structures will necessarily dictate women's roles once within politically violent organizations.

As a result, academic and policy observers must be extremely cautious in how they approach and frame female activism within terrorist or politically violent organizations. Women have been, and will continue to be, willing to serve in a variety of groups, including right wing/religious and, significantly, they may very well be tasked in combatant roles. Terrorist or politically violent organizations are extremely aware of the potential utility of female members because this actor allows them to play on established biases and assumptions in their adversary. Terrorist organizations engage in "actor innovation" because women are able to penetrate more deeply into their targets to gather intelligence or carry out violent operations than many of their male counterparts. These organizations are interested in immediate results; the system that results will be dealt with later. This same imperative drives both female members of these organizations and the societies within which this process occurs. Societies that are under extreme strain due to occupation or conflict will often loosen their constraints on women to facilitate the convergence of individual and terrorist organizational interests. The aftermath of this process remains generally uncertain, as many of the cases discussed herein remain unresolved.

## NOTES

1. Organizations labeled as "terrorist" are derived from the United States Department of State listing of designated terrorist organizations through either support or operational activities (see *Patterns of Global Terrorism 2000,* available at (http://www.state.gov/s/ct/rls/pgtrpt/2000/2450.htm). This analysis will utilize this designation for the sake of simplicity.

2. Because a woman's place is "naturally" private her motivation to become "public" would have to be personal. This suggests as well that once this personal reason has been resolved she will willingly and naturally return to her normal, private, role.

3. The common belief that women's participation in political violence is quite limited is not supported by even a cursory examination of history. However, what is clear from that cursory look is that women's experiences with political violence have not received sustained attention, and what examination has occurred has often been heavily influenced by established Western norms of appropriate female behavior. Given the constraints of any article-length analysis, certain limitations were necessary in approaching the subject matter. As a result, this work should not be construed as an exhaustive inventory of women's participation in politically violent or terrorist organizations, past or present, but rather a selective examination of primarily current critical cases.

4. Several of the most oft-quoted terrorism definitions include those used by the United States Federal Bureau of Investigation (FBI), the United States Department of State, and the United States Department of Defense (DoD). The FBI defines terrorism as "the unlawful use of force and violence against persons or property to intimidate or coerce a government, the civilian population, or any segment thereof, in furtherance of political or social objectives" (28 Code of Federal Regulations Section 0.85). The State Department defines terrorism as "premeditated, politically motivated violence perpetrated against noncombatant targets by subnational groups or clandestine agents, usually intended to influence an audience" (United States Department of State, *Patterns of Global Terrorism 2000,* available at (http://www.state.gov/s/ct/rls/pgtrpt/2000/), 13 April 2001). Problematic with both definitions, however, is that they fail to capture organizations motivated by religious or economic motives, such as Islamist organizations in the Middle East and North Africa (MENA) or narcoterrorist organizations such as the Revolutionary Armed Forces of Columbia (FARC) and National Liberation Army (ELN) in Columbia. The DoD partially overcomes this deficiency by widening the goal orientation of terrorist organizations as it defines terrorism as "the calculated use of violence or the threat of violence to inculcate fear; intended to coerce or to intimidate governments or societies in the pursuit of goals that are generally political, religious, or ideological" (Department of Defense, "DoD Combating Terrorism Program," Directive Number 2000.12, available at (http://www.defenselink.mil/pubs/downing_rpt/annx_e.html), 15 September 1996).

5. Jamie L. Rhee, "Comment: Rational and Constitutional Approaches to Airline Safety in the Face of Terrorist Threats," *DePaul Law Review* 49(847) Lexis/Nexis (Spring 2000).

6. Martha Crenshaw, "The Logic of Terrorism: Terrorist Behavior as a Product of Strategic Choice," in Walter Reich, ed., *Origins of Terrorism: Psychologies, Ideologies, Theologies, States of Mind* (Washington, DC: Woodrow Wilson Center Press, 1998), p. 15.

7. If we examine state behavior with respect to military recruitment, we see a similar process. Samarasinghe notes "most nations have increased women's military roles only when there has been a shortage of qualified men and a pressing need for more warriors. . . . The decision to permit women into combat is made by men. . . . [And] the allowable space within which women could operate in military units is also determined by them." (Vidyamali Samarasinghe, "Soldiers, Housewives and Peace Makers: Ethnic Conflict and Gender in Sri Lanka," *Ethnic Studies Report* XIV(2) (July 1996), p. 213).

8. As of early 2002, a cease-fire deal was secured between the Tamil Tigers and the government of Sri Lanka, halting the type of violence that will be discussed in this article. However, even if this activity is now a matter of historical record, rather than a current phenomenon, it offers important insights into how women were (are) mobilized into a politically violent movement.

9. Peter Schalk, "Women Fighters of the Liberation Tigers in Tamil Ilam. The Martial Feminism of Atel Palacinkam," *South Asia Research* 14(2) (Autumn 1994), pp. 174–175.

10. See Kathleen M. Blee's *Women of the Klan: Racism and Gender in the 1920s* (Berkeley: University of California Press, 1991) for an interesting study of this widely overlooked phenomenon.

11. See Claudia Koonz, "Women in Nazi Germany," in Renate Bridenthal and Claudia Koonz, eds., *Becoming Visible, Women in European History* (Boston: Houghton Mifflin, 1977).

12. Marie Marmo Mullaney, "Women and the Theory of the 'Revolutionary Personality': Comments, Criticisms, and Suggestions for Further Study," *The Social Science Journal* 21(2) (April 1984), pp. 49–70.

13. Jeffrey Louis Decker, "Terrorism (Un)Veiled: Frantz Fanon and the Women of Algiers," *Cultural Critique* 17 (Winter 1990), pp. 180–181.

14. Although O'Donnell and Schmitter's argument centers around mobilization against domestic authoritarian rule, there are parallels in the decolonization process that makes this comparison useful. See Guillermo O'Donnell and Philippe C. Schmitter, *Transitions from Authoritarian Rule: Tentative Conclusions About Uncertain Democracies* (Baltimore, MD: The Johns Hopkins University Press, 1986). With respect to civil society, O'Donnell and Schmitter argue that "private" civil society mobilizes only temporarily to become "public" to achieve its goal (transition from authoritarianism). Once that goal is achieved, civil society willingly returns to its "natural" private sphere. This conceptualization bears striking parallels to the role of women wherein Algeria's "private" women (a role physically visible through the veil) are temporarily mobilized into "public" action to achieve independence. However, once the aim of the mobilization is completed (e.g., independence) they are assumed to willingly and naturally return to their private role. However, not all scholars (Karla J. Cunningham, "Regime and Society in Jordan: An Analysis of Jordanian Liberalization," Dissertation, University at Buffalo, 1997; Peter P. Ekeh, "Historical and Cross-Cultural Contexts of Civil Society in Africa," Paper presented at the United States Agency for International Development (USAID)—Hosted Workshop on *Civil Society, Democracy, and Development in Africa,* 9–10 June 1994) are convinced that the rigid conceptual boundaries between "public" and "private" in transition are meaningful, with important ramifications for transition.

15. The account of these phases are taken from Decker, "Terrorism (Un)Veiled," pp. 190–192. The first quotation is located on p. 191, the second is on p. 192.

16. Ibid., p. 193.

17. Ibid., p. 183, emphasis in original.

18. This account of the conflicting interests of Palestinian women, leaders, and society was discussed by Soraya Antonius, "Fighting on Two Fronts: Conversations with Palestinian Women," *Journal of Palestine Studies* 5 (October 1979), pp. 28–30.

19. Marnia Lazreg, "Citizenship and Gender in Algeria," in Saud Joseph, ed., *Gender and Citizenship in the Middle East* (Syracuse, NY: Syracuse University Press, 2000), p. 62, emphasis in original.

20. The regional cases that are discussed later are utilized to demonstrate these developments given the constraints of an article. However, it should be understood that this is not, and is not intended to be, an exhaustive inventory of cases in which women have engaged in political violence or terrorism. Cases from Africa (Eritrea, South Africa) and East Asia (Japan, Korea, Vietnam) are also worth investigating.

21. Leonard Weinberg and William Lee Eubank, "Italian Women Terrorists," *Terrorism: An International Journal* 9(3) (1987), p. 247.

22. Weinberg and Eubank, 1987, pp. 250–252. The authors' conclusions are based on biographical reviews of female terrorists reported in two major Italian newspapers. Concentrating on individuals identified and arrested by the Italian government, the authors admit that their information "does not represent a sample of terrorists" (Ibid., p. 248). A point to consider is that women's roles and representation may remain somewhat skewed, even in this worthwhile study, because one of the apparent operational advantages of female members to terrorist organizations, at least in other contexts, is that they tend to go unnoticed by officials. As a result, relying on official recognition of key women may not provide the fullest picture of women's roles in varying terrorist organizations.

23. For a good analysis of female participation in left- and right-wing organizations within the United States during the 1960s and 1970s please see Jeffrey S. Handler, "Socioeconomic Profile of an American Terrorist: 1960s and 1970s," *Terrorism* 13(3) (May–June 1990), pp. 195–213.

24. Ibid., 1990, p. 204.

25. Katrine Fangen, "Separate or Equal? The Emergence of an All-Female Group in Norway's Rightist Underground," *Terrorism and Political Violence* 9(3) (Autumn 1997), pp. 122–164. In contrast, leftist women tend to organize their own organizations to pursue a particular objective (Ibid., p. 122).

26. According to the FBI, domestic terrorism is "the unlawful use, or threatened use, of force or violence by a group or individual based and operating entirely within the United States or Puerto Rico without foreign direction committed against persons or property to intimidate or coerce a government, the civilian population, or any segment thereof in furtherance of political or social objections" (United States Department of Justice Federal Bureau of Investigation, Terrorism in the United States 1999, Counterterrorism Threat Assessment and Warning Unit, Counterterrorism Division, available at http://www.fbi.gov/publications/terror/terror99.pdf, 1999). For the purposes of this study, FBI official designations of domestic terrorist status will be utilized in characterizing a group as terrorist. Between 1980–1999 there were 327 incidents or suspected incidents of terrorism within the United States, of which 239 were attributed to domestic terrorism (Ibid.). The analysis of domestic terrorism offered in this article is focused on groups or categories the FBI deems as generally active. As a result, historical examples of female participation may not be included, particularly if the group is no longer actively identified by the FBI as a terrorist threat.

27. According to the FBI, the WCOTC has been linked to acts of domestic terrorism including the July 1999 shootings of several racial minorities by Benjamin Nathaniel Smith in Illinois and Indiana (United States Department of Justice Federal Bureau of Investigation, 1999).

28. Women's participation with left-wing movements is long-standing, with prominent examples from the 1960s and 1970s including the Weathermen, the Black Panthers, and the Symbionese Liberation Army. The discussion of left-wing terrorism in this article does not focus on these examples because they have diminished or disappeared, at least with respect to FBI reporting of left-wing terrorism.

29. Please note that these three generalized categories have been created to facilitate discussion within the limited confines of this article. There is tremendous variation within the three categories that such grouping tends to obscure.

30. Background on Samadi and Mahdavieh were drawn from: Aaron Sands, "Secret Arrest of Saddam Ally," Ottawa Citizen 1 February 2000, Lexis/Nexis, 3 March 2002; Moira Farrow, "Woman Ordered Deported Not a Terrorist Lawyer Says," *The Vancouver Sun,* 8 April 1993 Lexis/Nexis, 3 March 2002.

31. See *Zehra Saygili v. The Minister of Citizenship & Immigration and Solicitor General for Canada,* Court No. DES-6–96, available at (http://decisions.fct-cf.gc.ca/cf/1997/des-6–96.html).

32. Tom Godfrey, "Lax Security Screening Has Allowed 'Sleeper' Terrorists to Infiltrate Canada for Years," *Toronto Sun,* 7 October 2001, available at (http://www.canoe.ca/TorontoNews/04n1.html).

33. The PKK reportedly used women as suicide bombers in Turkey during 1998, but ended the tactic thereafter, suggesting that suicide terrorism was used temporarily to achieve a specific objective (Ehud Sprinzak, "Rational Fanatics," *Foreign Policy* 120 (September/October 2000), ProQuest, 25 March 2002, pp. 4–5). For more information on the PKK's use of suicide bombing during 1998 please see "Female Separatist Rebel Captured in Southeastern

Turkey," *BBC Worldwide Monitoring,* 15 August 1998, Lexis/Nexis, 31 January 2002; "Female 'Terrorist' Reportedly Carries Out Suicide Bombing," *BBC Worldwide Monitoring,* 24 December 1998, Lexis/Nexis, 31 January 2002; and "Child Wounded in Female Suicide Bombers' Attack in Southeastern Turkey," *BBC Worldwide Monitoring,* 17 November 1998, Lexis/Nexis, 31 January 2002.

34. For the ups and downs of this particular case see Neil MacFarquhar, "Woman Freed After Pleading in Border Case," *The New York Times,* 16 February 2000, Lexis/Nexis, 25 March 2002; Michael G. Crawford, "MILNET: The Algerian Y2K Bomb Case," 2001, available at (http://www.milnet.com/milnet/y2kbomb/y2kbomb.htm), 7 March 2002; Cindy Rodriguez, "Stress Line US Tries to Tighten Security on Canadian Border," *The Boston Globe,* 7 November 2001, Lexis/Nexis, 6 March 2002; Lloyd Robertson, "Lucia Garofalo Pleaded Guilty to Immigration Charges Today But Was Cleared of Terrorism Charges," *CTV Television, Inc.,* 15 February 2000, Lexis/Nexis, 6 March 2002; David Arnold, "Garofalo Might Go Free: U.S. to Recommend Release of Montrealer Suspected of Terrorism Link," *The Gazette* (Montreal), 15 February 2000, Lexis/Nexis, 6 March 2002; "Special Report: The Future of Terror: On Guard: America is the Dominant Nation Entering the New Century— and the Top Target for Extremists," *Newsweek International,* 10 January 2000, Lexis/Nexis, 6 March 2002; "Canadian Police Search Apartment of Accomplice of Terrorism Suspect," *Agence France Presse,* 24 December 1999, Lexis/Nexis, 6 March 2002; Butler T. Gray, "U.S. Prosecutors Link Arrests in Vermont and Washington State," *Washington File, United States Department of State International Information Programs,* 1999, available at (http://usinfo.state.gov/topical/pol/terror/99123004.htm), 15 March 2002; and "Canadian Woman Has Ties to Washington Bomb Suspect, 2 Algerian Terrorist Groups," *CNN.com,* 30 December 1999, available at (http://www.cnn.com/2000/US/01/12/border.arrest.02), 15 March 2002.

35. "Feminism Perverted: Extremist Women on the World Wide Web," Anti-Defamation League, 2000, available at (http://www.adl.org/special_reports/extremist_women_on_web/print.html), 18 February 2002.

36. "All in the Family," Southern Poverty Law Center, n.d., available at (http://www.splcenter.org/intelligenceproject/ip-4k2.html), 28 March 2002. Also see Jim Nesbitt, "The American Scene: White Supremacist Women Push for Greater Role in Movement," Newhouse News Service, 1999, available at (http://www.newhousenews.com/archive/story1a1022.html) accessed 24 July 2002.

37. Turner's efforts to create a women's organization within the larger movement is noteworthy and parallels Norwegian experiences (see Fangen, "Separate or Equal?," especially pp. 124–127, 128–140, 144–155).

38. Vicki Weaver, wife of Randy Weaver, was shot by an FBI sniper in August 1992. Randy Weaver, a white separatist, was accused by the government of illegal weapons sales. Kathy Ainsworth was killed by the FBI in 1968 when she and another man tried to plant a bomb at the house of an ADL leader in Mississippi, allegedly on behalf of the Ku Klux Klan. She is one of the only known women affiliated with the white supremacy movement in the United States to be tasked with this type of mission. Interestingly, an additional woman often noted as a "martyr" is Hanna Reitsch who was reportedly a leading proponent of suicide plane missions on behalf of the Nazis during World War II (see http://www.sigrdrifa.com/sigrdrifa/67hanna.html for a sample biography). For additional information on "martyrs" identified by the white supremacist movement (see http://www.volksfrontusa.org/martyrs. shtml).

39. Turner's argument regarding women's roles in the WCOTC were taken from Sister Lisa Turner, "The Women of the Creativity Revolution," ChurchFliers.com, n.d., available at (http://www.churchfliers.com/sub_articles/women.html), 2 April 2002. In looking at the WCOTC site over a period of several months, there have been clear changes in the positioning of women's sites. In April 2002, women's issues were clearly not a priority but there was a direct link on the main page directing women to four white women's movement sites: Elisha Strom: A Woman's Voice, available at (http://www.elishastrom.com), Free Our Women Campaign (FOW), available at (http://www.midhnottsol.org/fow/index.html). Mothers of the Movement (MOTM), available at (http://www.sigrdrifa.com/motm), and Sigrdrifa.com—Premier Voice of the Proud White Women, available at (http://www.sigrdrifa.com). Sigrdrifa publishes a journal that addresses a wide range of issues important to women in the movement including feminism, women's roles in the organizations,

recruitment, and prison outreach. Elisha Strom's "Angry White Woman" site covers an array of issues clearly central to women in the movement, including debates over feminism and the importance of motherhood. She is also extremely critical of Kathleen M. Blee's works on the white power movement (see Blee, Women of the Clan, 1991 and *Inside Organized Racism: Women in the Hate Movement,* Berkeley: University of California Press, 2002). The WCOTC links, however, are not fully representative of the websites oriented toward women in the white power movement. Stormfront has a women's page as well which links into a variety of profiles of women who have joined the white power movement (see http://www.stormfront.org). Through their links page Women for Aryan Unity can be assessed at (http://www.wau14.cjb.net/), which features a picture of a white woman holding her baby that acts as the site's gateway to a site dedicated to the more pagan side of the white power movement, pictures of the Aryan sisterhood including tatoos, childrearing tips, and similar features. By July 2002, the WCOTC had removed the linkage to women's sites from their main page for unknown reasons, although this author speculates that the growing outside scholarly and activist scrutiny of these women is unwelcome by the organization for various reasons, including operational. Attempts to find the Women's Frontier using the WCOTC search engine as of July 2002 were ineffectual, bringing up only four articles apparently targeted to women, including the aforementioned article, none of which was accessible.

40. See (http://www.kukluxklan.org/lady4.htm) for the KKK's "Woman to Woman" Website, which covers a range of issues including children, attacks against the feminist movement, and even women's roles in combat.

41. In 1999 President Clinton offered the individuals arrested and convicted during this time, known by many Puerto Rican activists as the "independentistas," clemency. All but two accepted the offer.

42. Dale L. Watson, "The Terrorist Threat Confronting the United States," Statement before the Senate Select Committee on Intelligence, Washington, D.C., 6 February 2002, available at (http://www.fbi.gov/congress/congress02/watson020602.htm), 18 February 2002.

43. See "What is the Earth Liberation Front (ELF)?" available at (http://www.animalliberation.net/library/facts/elf.html) for details on organizational features of the group.

44. "2001 Year End Direct Action Report Released by ALF Press Office," 2001, available at (http://www.earthliberationfront.com/library/2001 DirectActions.pdf), 30 March 2002.

45. For a useful examination of women's roles in Latin American guerilla movements please see Linda M. Lobao, "Women in Revolutionary Movements: Changing Patterns of Latin American Guerilla Struggle," *Dialectical Anthropology* 15 (1999), pp. 211–232.

46. For varying figures see Jeremy McDermott, "Girl Guerillas Fight Their Way to the Top of Revolutionary Ranks," *Scotland on Sunday,* 23 December 2001, Lexis/Nexis, 2 April 2002; Karl Penhaul, "Battle of the Sexes: Female Rebels Battle Colombian Troops in the Field and Machismo in Guerilla Ranks," *San Francisco Chronicle* 11 January 2001, Lexis/Nexis, 2 April 2002; and Martin Hodgson, "Girls Swap Diapers for Rebel Life," The Christian Science Monitor, 6 October 2000, available at (http://www.csmonitor.com/durable/2000/10/06/p6s1.htm), 2 April 2002. Aside from a fascination with the makeup habits of the female FARC members, these articles offer some insights into the motivations driving women into the FARC's ranks.

47. M. Elaine Mar, "Shining Path Women," n.d., *Harvard Magazine,* available at (http://www.harvard magazine.com/issues/mj96/right.violence.html), 2 April 2002. During the late 1980s, "approximately 35 percent of the military leaders of . . . [the Shining Path], primarily at the level of underground cells . . . [were] also women" (Juan Lazaro, "Women and Political Violence in Contemporary Peru," *Dialectical Anthropology* 15(2–3) (1990), p. 234). Additionally, by 1987 roughly 1,000 women had been arrested on suspicion of terrorism in Peru including four senior Shining Path female leaders: Laura Zambrano ("Camarada Meche"), Fiorella Montano ("Lucia"), Margie Clavo Peralta, and Edith Lagos (Ibid., p. 243).

48. This position is advanced by McDermott, "Girl Guerillas Fight Their Way to the Top."

49. This data was drawn from several sources. Poverty rates for Colombia, Peru, and Sri Lanka were taken from the United Nations Development Programme, *Human Development Report 2002,* available at (http://www.undp.org/hdr2002/) whereas the data for the Gaza Strip and the West Bank were found in "More Than Two Thirds of Palestinian Children Living on Less than US$1.90/day," 21 May 2002, available at (http://www.iap.org/newsmay

213.htm). The demographic data can be found in the Central Intelligence Agency's *The World Factbook 2001,* available at (http://www.cia.gov/cia/publications/factbook/index.html).

50. Interestingly, the LTTE's creation of an organized squad of female suicide bombers is said to be mirrored after the Indian National Army's (INA) activities against the British during the early to mid-1940s (see Schalk, "Women Fighters of the Liberation," p. 174).

51. United States Department of State, *Patterns of Global Terrorism 2000,* "Asia Overview," 30 April 2001, available at (http://www.state.gov/s/ct/rls/pgtrpt/2000/2432.htm), 2 April 2002.

52. Some observers further identify the female cadre of the Black Tigers as the "Birds of Freedom." See, for example, Charu Lata Joshi, "Sri Lanka: Suicide Bombers," *Far Eastern Economic Review,* 1 June 2000, available at (http://www.feer.com/_0006_01/p64currents.html), 11 March 2002. The idea of a bird carrying the soul of the martyr to paradise is a theme seen in Islamist discourse on martyr operations.

53. Ana Cutter, "Tamil Tigresses: Hindu Martyrs," n.d., available at (http://www.columbia.edu/cu/sipa/PUBS/SLANT/SPRING98/article5.html), 11 March 2002. Also see Frederica Jansz, "Why Do They Blow Themselves Up?" *The Sunday Times,* 15 March 1998, available at (http://www.lacnet.org/suntimes/980315/plus4.html), 3 April 2002.

54. Cutter, "Tamil Tigresses."55. Ibid.

55. Ibid.

56. Joke Schrijvers, "Fighters, Victims and Survivors: Constructions of Ethnicity, Gender and Refugeeness among Tamils in Sri Lanka," *Journal of Refugee Studies* 12 (3 September 1999). The quotation on women as core national symbols is on p. 308; the quote on Tamil use of women's identity is on p. 311; and the quote on purity and suicide bombing is on p. 319 with emphasis in the original.

57. "Suicide Terrorism: A Global Threat," *Jane's Intelligence Review,* 20 October 2000, available at (http://www.janes.com/security/regional_security/news/usscole/jir001020_1_n.shtml), 11 November 2001.

58. Sprinzak, "Rational Fanatics," p. 6.

59. Ibid.

60. The discussion of the role of Sikh women was drawn from Cynthia Keppley Mahmood, *Fighting for Faith and Nation: Dialogues with Sikh Militants* (Philadelphia: University of Pennsylvania Press,

1996), pp. 213–234. The quotation is located on pp. 230–231, emphasis added.

61. "Veiled Women Show the Way to Terrorists in the Kashmir," *The Statesman* (India), 20 October 2001, Lexis/Nexis, 31 January 2002.

62. Ibid. This line of reasoning is very reminiscent of Decker's discussion of Algerian women during the Resistance.

63. For example see "Indian Intelligence Agencies Warn of Possible Female Suicide Squad Attacks," *BBC Worldwide Monitoring,* (originally published in *The Asian Age,* Delhi), 14 December 2001, Lexis/Nexis, 31 January 2002. Although no attacks occurred during the 26 January 2002 festivities, security was reportedly tight.

64. "Female Fighters Push on for Tamil Victory," *Michigan Daily.com* CX (93) 10 March 2000, available at (http://www.pub.umich.edu/daily/2000/mar/03–10–2000/news/09.html), 2 April 2002.

65. Jansz, "Why Do They Blow Themselves Up?"

66. The artillery reference was reportedly made by a Sri Lankan military source ("Female Fighters Push on for Tamil Victory").

67. For two good studies on the role of women in Palestinian resistance both before and during the first *intifada* see Antonius, "Fighting on Two Fronts," pp. 26–45 and Graham Usher, "Palestinian Women, the *Intifada* and the State of Independence," *Race & Class* 34(3) (January-March 1993), pp. 31–43.

68. Majeda Al-Batsh, "Mystery Surrounds Palestinian Woman Suicide Bomber," *Agence France Presse,* 28 January 2002, Lexis/Nexis, 6 February 2002.

69. David Sharrock, "Women: The Suicide Bomber's Story," *The Guardian,* 5 May 1998, Lexis/Nexis, 30 March 2002.

70. For more information on Al-Tamimi and the Summer 2001 incidents that appear linked to her see Wafa Amr, "Palestinian Women Play Role in Fighting Occupation," *Jordan Times,* 29 January 2002, available at (http://www.jordantimes.com/tue/news/news6.htm), 3 February 2002; also see "Shabak Accuses Young Palestinian Woman of Assisting Hamas Cell," The Palestinian Information Center, 17 September 2001, available at (http://www.palestine-info.com/daily_news/prev_editions/2001/ep01/17sep01.htm), 3 February 2002. As of 12 February 2002, Al-Tamimi remains in Israeli custody awaiting trial (see http://www.palestinemirror.org/Other%20Updates/palestinian_women_political_prisoners.htm).

71. Ghazawi's age has been quoted as either 23 or 24 (see Majeda Al-Batsh, "Palestinian Mother, 24, Is Among Loners Mounting Attacks On Israel," *Agence France Presse,* 6 September 2001, Lexis/Nexis, 30 March 2002; David Rudge, "Alert Security Guard Foils TA Bombing," *The Jerusalem Post,* 5 August 2001, Lexis/Nexis, 30 March 2002; "Palestinians' New Weapon: Women Suicide Bombers," *The Straits Times (Singapore),* 6 August 2001, Lexis/Nexis, 30 March 2002; Uzi Mahnaimi, "Israeli Fear As Women Join Suicide Squad," *Sunday Times (London),* 5 August 2001, Lexis/Nexis, 30 March 2002; and Douglas Davis, "Women Warriors," *Jewish World Review,* 9 August 2001, available at ⟨http://www.jewishworldreview.com/0801/women. warriors.asp⟩, 30 March 2002).

72. Phil Reeves, "The Paramedic Who Became Another 'Martyr' for Palestine," *The Independent,* 31 January 2002, available at ⟨http://www.ccmep.org/ hotnews/parameic013102.html⟩, 6 March 2002.

73. Hizbollah television identified the bomber as Shahanaz Al Amouri following the attack See Imigo Gilmore, "Woman Suicide Bomber Shakes Israelis," *The Daily Telegraph* (London), 28 January 2002, Lexis/Nexis, 6 March 2002.

74. William Neuman, "Femmes Fatales Herald New Terror Era," *The New York Post,* 28 January 2002, Lexis/Nexis, 11 March 2002.

75. James Bennet, "Israelis Declare Arab Woman Was In Fact a Suicide Bomber," *The New York Times,* 9 February 2002, Lexis/Nexis, 11 March 2002.

76. Lamis Andoni, "Wafa Idrees: A Symbol of a Generation," *Arabic Media Internet Network* (AMIN), 23 February 2002, available at ⟨http://www. amin.org/eng/uncat/2002/feb/feb23.html⟩, 6 March 2002.

77. Reeves, "The Paramedic Who Became Another 'Martyr'"; James Bennet, "Filling in the Blanks on Palestinian Bomber," *The New York Times,* 31 January 2002, Lexis/Nexis, 6 March 2002; and Wafa Amr, "Palestinian Woman Bomber Yearned for Martyrdom," *The Jordan Times,* 31 January 2002, available at ⟨http://www.jordantimes.com⟩, 31 January 2002.

78. Peter Beaumont, "From an Angel of Mercy to Angel of Death," *The Guardian,* 31 January 2002, available at ⟨http://www.guardian.co.uk/Print/ 0,3858,4346503,00.html⟩, 6 March 2002.

79. Quoted in "Inquiry and Analysis No. 84: Jihad and Terrorism StudiesWafa Idris: The Celebration of the First Female Palestinian Suicide Bomber—Part II,"

*The Middle East Media and Research Institute,* 13 February 2002, available at ⟨http://www. memri.org⟩, 6 March 2002. Also see James Bennet, "Arab Press Glorifies Bomber as Heroine," *The New York Times,* 11 February 2002, Lexis/Nexis, 6 March 2002.

80. "Militant Palestinian Leader on Imminent Operations with 15-km Rockets," *BBC Monitoring Middle East,* 4 February 2002, Lexis/Nexis, 4 March 2002.

81. Sophie Claudet, "More Palestinian Women Suicide Bombers Could Be On the Way: Analysts," Agence France Presse, 28 February 2002, Lexis/ Nexis, 16 March 2002.

82. Yassin and Yusef's points were taken from "We Don't Need Women Suicide Bombers: Hamas Spiritual Leader," *Agence France Presse,* 2 February 2002, Lexis/Nexis, 6 March 2002; "Islam Not (sic) Forbid Women From Carrying Out Suicide Attack," *Xinhua,* 28 February 2002, Lexis/Nexis, 31 January 2002. For further accounts of the range of religious responses to Idris' action please see "Inquiry and Analysis No. 83: Jihad and Terrorism Studies—Wafa Idris: The Celebration of the First Female Palestinian Suicide Bomber—Part I," *The Middle East Media and Research Institute,* 12 February 2002, available at ⟨http://www.memri.org⟩, 6 March 2002.

83. Darwish's statements were taken from "Palestinians' New Weapon: Women Suicide Bombers," *The Straits Times (Singapore),* 6 August 2001, Lexis/Nexis, 31 January 2002.

84. Mohammed Daraghmeh, "Woman Suicide Bomber Rejected by Hamas," *The Independent,* 1 March 2002, Lexis/Nexis, 6 March 2002; Mohammad Daraghmeh, "Woman Bomber Wanted to Carry Out Sbarro-Like Attack," T*he Jerusalem Post,* 1 March 2002, Lexis/Nexis, 6 March 2002; "Woman Suicide Bomber was 21-Year Old Palestinian Student," *Agence France Presse,* 28 February 2002, Lexis/Nexis, 6 March 2002; Sandro Contenta, "Student 'Had a Wish to Become a Martyr,'" *Toronto Star,* 1 March 2002, Lexis/Nexis, 13 March 2002; Stephen Farrell, "Daughter's Dedication Was Beyond Doubt," *The Times* (London), 1 March 2002, Lexis/Nexis, 13 March 2002.

85. See "Deadly Secret of Quiet High School Girl Who Became a Suicide Bomber," *The Herald* (Glasgow) 30 March 2002, Lexis/Nexis, 1 April 2002; Anton La Guardia, "The Girl Who Brought Terror to the Supermarket," *The Daily Telegraph* (London), 30 March 2002, Lexis/Nexis, 1 April

2002; and Cameron W. Barr, "Why a Palestinian Girl Now Wants to Be a Suicide Bomber," *The Christian Science Monitor,* 1 April 2002, Lexis/Nexis, 1 April 2002; Eric Silver, "Middle East Crisis: Schoolgirl Suicide Bomber Kills Two in Supermarket," *The Independent* (London), 30 March 2002, 1 April 2002; Philip Jacobson, "Terror of the Girl Martyrs," *Sunday Mirror,* 31 March 2002, Lexis/Nexis, 1 April 2002. The reference to the militia linked to Arafat is a thinly disguised reference to the Al-Aqsa Martyrs Brigade.

86. David Lamb, "The World; Gruesome Change from the Ordinary; Conflict: A Quiet, Young Seamstress Further Widened the Mideast Breach When She Joined the Ranks of Palestinian Suicide Bombers," *The Los Angeles Times,* 14 April 2002, ProQuest, 3 June 2002; "Jerusalem Shocked by Suicide Bomb; Woman Bomber Kills Six in Attempt to Derail Powell Peace Talks," Belfast News Letter, 13 April 2002, Lexis/Nexis, 3 June 2002.

87. Jacobson, "Terror of the Girl Martyrs."

88. Melanie Reid, "Myth That Women Are the Most Deadly Killers of All," *The Herald (Glasgow)* 29 January 2002, Lexis/Nexis, 6 February 2002.

89. This last point is reinforced by reports emanating from the territories that suggest at least a temporary "alignment" between the two sides. For example, in Jenin Hamas and Fatah reportedly joined together to distribute "explosive belts" and hand grenades to individuals in the camp for self defense. A woman, Ilham Dosuki, reportedly blew herself up on 6 April 2002 as soldiers approached the door to her home ("Fierce Battles in Jenin, Nablus: Unconfirmed Reports: Scores of Palestinians Killed and Injured in Jenin Refugee Camp," 2002, *Al-Bawaba,* 6 April 2002, available at ⟨http://www.albawaba.com/⟩, 6 April 2002.

90. Mullaney, "Women and the Theory of the "Revolutionary Personality,'" p. 54.

91. See Antonius, "Fighting on Two Fronts," pp. 26–45 and Juliane Hammer, "Prayer, *Hijab* and the *Intifada:* The Influence of the Islamic Movement on Palestinian Women," *Islam and Christian-Muslim Relations* 11(3) (October 2000), pp. 299–320 for additional information on the role of mothers in the Palestinian resistance to Israeli occupation.

92. This argumentation is directed from a number of sources, including feminist scholars who view violent women as "unnatural" because women are naturally peaceful, a feminine attribute that is superior and morally virtuous. Thus, violent women are either duped by male leaders or have internalized masculine (violent) traits in lieu of female traits (nonviolence). This reasoning is shared, interestingly enough, by many conservative thinkers.

---

## God and Mammon: Does Poverty Cause Militant Islam?

Daniel Pipes

The events of September 11 have intensified a long-standing debate: What causes Muslims to turn to militant Islam? Some analysts have noted the poverty of Afghanistan and concluded that herein lay the problem. Jessica Stern of Harvard University wrote that the United States "can no longer afford to allow states to fail." If it does not devote a much higher priority to health, education and economic development abroad, she writes, "new Osamas will continue to arise." Susan Sachs of the *New York Times* observes: "Predictably, the disappointed youth of Egypt and Saudi Arabia turn to religion for comfort." More colorfully, others have advocated bombarding Afghanistan with foodstuffs not *along with* but *instead of* explosives.

Behind these analyses lies an assumption that socioeconomic distress drives Muslims to extremism. The evidence, however, does not support this expectation. Militant Islam (or Islamism) is not a response to poverty or impoverishment; not only are Bangladesh and Iraq not hotbeds of militant Islam, but militant Islam has often surged in countries experiencing rapid economic growth. The factors that cause militant Islam to decline or flourish appear to have more to do with issues of identity than with economics.

## ALL OTHER PROBLEMS VANISH

The conventional wisdom—that economic stress causes militant Islam and that economic growth is needed to blunt it—has many well-placed adherents. Even some Islamists themselves accept this connection. In the words of a fiery sheikh from Cairo, "Islam is the religion of bad times." A Hamas leader in Gaza, Mahmud az-Zahar, says, "It is enough to see the poverty-stricken outskirts of Algiers or the refugee camps in Gaza to understand the factors that nurture the strength of the Islamic Resistance Movement." In this spirit, militant Islamic organizations offer a wide range of welfare benefits in an effort to attract followers. They also promote what they call an "Islamic economy" as the "most gracious system of solidarity in a society. Under such a system, the honorable do not fall, the honest do not perish, the needy do not suffer, the handicapped do not despair, the sick do not die for lack of care, and people do not destroy one another."

Many secular Muslims also stress militant Islam's source in poverty as an article of faith. Süleyman Demirel, the former Turkish president, says, "As long as there is poverty, inequality, injustice, and repressive political systems, fundamentalist tendencies will grow in the world." Turkey's former prime minister, Tansu Çiller, finds that Islamists did so well in the 1994 elections because "People reacted to the economy." The chief of Jordanian Army Intelligence holds, "Economic develop may solve almost all of our problems [in the Middle East]." Including militant Islam, he was asked? Yes, he replied: "The moment a person is in a good economic position, has a job, and can support his family, all other problems vanish."

Leftists in the Middle East concur, interpreting the militant Islamic resurgence as "a sign of pessimism. Because people are desperate, they are resorting to the supernatural." Social scientists sign on as well: Hooshang Amirahmadi, an academic of Iranian origins, argues that "the roots of Islamic radicalism must be looked for outside the religion, in the real world of cultural despair, economic decline, political oppression, and spiritual turmoil in which most Muslims find themselves today." The academy, with its lingering Marxist disposition and disdain for faith, of course accepts this militant Islam-from-poverty thesis with near unanimity. Ervand Abrahamian holds that "the behavior of Khomeini and the Islamic Republic has been determined less by scriptural principles than by immediate political, social and economic needs." Ziad Abu-Amr, author of a book on militant Islam (and a member of the Palestine Legislative Council), ascribes a Palestinian turn toward religiosity to "the sombre climate of destruction, war, unemployment, and depression [which] cause people to seek solace, and they're going to Allah."

Western politicians also find the argument compelling. For former President Bill Clinton, "These forces of reaction feed on disillusionment, poverty and despair," and he advocates a socioeconomic remedy: "spread prosperity and security to all." Edward Djerejian, once a top State Department figure, reports that "political Islamic movements are to an important degree rooted in worsening socio-economic conditions in individual countries." Martin Indyk, another former high-ranking U.S. diplomat, warns that those wishing to reduce the appeal of militant Islam must first solve the economic, social and political problems that constitute its breeding grounds.

Militant Islam reflects "the economic, political, and cultural disappointment" of Muslims, according to former German Foreign Minister Klaus Kinkel. Former Interior Minister Charles Pasqua of France finds that this phenomenon "has coincided with despair on the part of a large section of the masses, and young people in particular." Prime Minister Eddie Fenech of Malta draws an even closer tie: "Fundamentalism grows at the same pace as economic problems." Israel's Foreign Minister Shimon Peres flatly asserts that "fundamentalism's basis is poverty" and that it offers "a way of protesting against poverty, corruption, ignorance, and discrimination."

Armed with this theory of cause and effect, businessmen on occasion make investments with an eye to political amelioration. The Virgin Group's chairman, Richard Branson, declared as he opened a music store in Beirut: "The region will become stable if people invest in it, create jobs and rebuild the countries that need rebuilding, not ignore them."

Somewhere
Near the Stratosphere

But the empirical record evinces little correlation between economics and militant Islam. Aggregate measures of wealth and economic trends fall flat as predictors of where militant Islam will be strong and where not. On the level of individuals, too, conventional wisdom points to militant Islam attracting the poor, the alienated and the marginal—but research finds precisely the opposite to be true. To the extent that economic factors explain who becomes Islamist, they point to the fairly well off, not the poor.

Take Egypt as a test case. In a 1980 study, the Egyptian social scientist Saad Eddin Ibrahim interviewed Islamists in Egyptian jails and found that the typical member is "young (early twenties), of rural or small-town background, from the middle or lower middle class, with high achievement and motivation, upwardly mobile, with science or engineering education, and from a normally cohesive family." In other words, Ibrahim concluded, these young men were "significantly above the average in their generation"; they were "ideal or model young Egyptians." In a subsequent study, he found that out of 34 members of the violent group *At-Takfir w'al-Hijra,* fully 21 had fathers in the civil service, nearly all of them middle-ranking. More recently, the Canadian Security Intelligence Service found that the leadership of the militant Islamic group Al-Jihad "is largely university educated with middle-class backgrounds." These are not the children of poverty or despair.

Other researchers confirm these findings for Egypt. In a study on the country's economic troubles, Galal A. Amin, an economist at the American University in Cairo, concludes by noting "how rare it is to find examples of religious fanaticism among either the higher or the very lowest social strata of the Egyptian population." When her assistant in Cairo turned Islamist, the American journalist Geraldine Brooks tells of her surprise: "I'd assumed that the turn to Islam was the desperate choice of poor people searching for heavenly solace. But Sahar [the assistant] was neither desperate nor poor. She belonged somewhere near the stratosphere

of Egypt's meticulously tiered society." And note this account by the talented journalist Hamza Hendawi: In Egypt,

> a new breed of preachers in business suits and with cellular phones are attracting increasing numbers of the rich and powerful away from Western lifestyles and into religious conservatism. The modern imams hold their seminars over banquets in some of Cairo's most luxurious homes and in Egypt's seaside resorts to appeal to the wealthy's sense of style and comfort.

What is true of Egypt holds equally true elsewhere: Like fascism and Marxism-Leninism in their heydays, militant Islam attracts highly competent, motivated and ambitious individuals. Far from being the laggards of society, they are its leaders. Brooks, a much-traveled journalist, found Islamists to be "the most gifted" of the youth she encountered. Those "hearing the Islamic call included the students with the most options, not just the desperate cases. . . . They were the elites of the next decade: the people who would shape their nations' future."

Even Islamists who make the ultimate sacrifice and give up their lives fit this pattern of financial ease and advanced education. A disproportionate number of terrorists and suicide bombers have higher education, often in engineering and the sciences. This generalization applies equally to the Palestinian suicide bombers attacking Israel and the followers of Osama bin Laden who hijacked the four planes of September 11. In the first case, one researcher found by looking at their profiles that: "Economic circumstances did not seem to be a decisive factor. While none of the 16 subjects could be described as well-off, some were certainly struggling less than others." In the second case, as the Princeton historian Sean Wilentz sardonically put it, the biographies of the September 11 killers would imply that the root cause of terrorism is "money, education and privilege." More generally, Fathi ash-Shiqaqi, founding leader of the arch-murderous Islamic Jihad, once commented, "Some of the young people who have sacrificed themselves [in terrorist operations] came from well-off families and had successful university careers." This makes sense, for suicide bombers who hurl themselves against foreign enemies offer their lives not to protest financial deprivation but to change the world.

Those who back militant Islamic organizations also tend to be well off. They come more often from the richer city than the poorer countryside, a fact that, as Khalid M. Amayreh, a Palestinian journalist, points out, "refutes the widely-held assumption that Islamist popularity thrives on economic misery." And they come not just from the cities but from the upper ranks. At times, an astonishing one-quarter of the membership in Turkey's leading militant Islamic organization, now called the Saadet Party, have been engineers. Indeed, the typical cadre in a militant Islamic party is an engineer in his forties born in a city to parents who had moved from the countryside. Amayreh finds that in the Jordanian parliamentary elections of 1994, the Muslim Brethren did as well in middle-class districts as in poor ones. He generalizes from this that "a substantial majority of Islamists and their supporters come from the middle and upper socio-economic strata."

Martin Kramer, editor of the *Middle East Quarterly,* goes further and sees militant Islam as

> the vehicle of counter-elites, people who, by virtue of education and/or income, are potential members of the elite, but who for some reason or another get excluded. Their education may lack some crucial prestige-conferring element; the sources of their wealth may be a bit tainted. Or they may just come from the wrong background. So while they are educated and wealthy, they have a grievance: their ambition is blocked, they cannot translate their socio-economic assets into political clout. Islamism is particularly useful to these people, in part because by its careful manipulation, it is possible to recruit a following among the poor, who make valuable foot-soldiers.

Kramer cites the so-called Anatolian Tigers, businessmen who have had a critical role in backing Turkey's militant Islamic party, as an example of this counter-elite in its purest form.

## NOT A PRODUCT OF POVERTY

The same pattern that holds for individual Islamists exists on the level of societies, as well. That social pattern can be expressed by four propositions.

First, wealth does not inoculate against militant Islam. Kuwaitis enjoy a Western-style income (and owe their state's very existence to the West) but Islamists generally win the largest bloc of seats in parliament (at present, twenty out of fifty). The West Bank is more prosperous than Gaza, yet militant Islamic groups usually enjoy more popularity in the former than the latter. Militant Islam flourishes in the member states of the European Union and in North America, where Muslims as a group enjoy a standard of living *higher* than the national averages. And of those Muslims, as Khalid Durán points out, Islamists have the generally higher incomes: "In the United States, the difference between Islamists and common Muslims is largely one between haves and have-nots. Muslims have the numbers; Islamists have the dollars."

Second, a flourishing economy does not inoculate against radical Islam. Today's militant Islamic movements took off in the 1970s, precisely as oil-exporting states enjoyed extraordinary growth rates. Muammar Qaddafi developed his eccentric version of proto-militant Islam then; fanatical groups in Saudi Arabia violently seized the Great Mosque of Mecca; and Ayatollah Khomeini took power in Iran (though, admittedly, growth had slacked off several years before he overthrew the Shah). In the 1980s, several countries that excelled economically experienced a militant Islamic boom. Jordan, Tunisia and Morocco all did well economically in the 1990s—as did their militant Islamic movements. Turks under Turgut Özal enjoyed nearly a decade of particularly impressive economic growth even as they joined militant Islamic parties in ever larger numbers.

Third, poverty does not generate militant Islam. There are many very poor Muslim states but few of them have become centers of militant Islam—not Bangladesh, not Yemen, and not Niger. As an American specialist rightly notes, "economic despair, the oft-cited source of political Islam's power, is familiar to the Middle East"; if militant Islam is connected to poverty, why was it not a stronger force in years and centuries past, when the region was poorer than it is today?

Fourth, a declining economy does not generate militant Islam. The 1997 crash in Indonesia and Malaysia did not spur a large turn toward militant Islam. Iranian incomes have gone down by half or more since the Islamic Republic came to power in 1979; yet, far from increasing support for the regime's militant Islamic ideology, impoverishment has caused a massive alienation from Islam. Iraqis have experienced an even more precipitous drop in living standards: Abbas Alnasrawi estimates that per capita income has plummeted by nearly 90 percent since 1980, returning it to where it was in the 1940s. While the country has witnessed an increase in personal piety, militant Islam has not surged, nor is it the leading expression of anti-regime sentiments.

Noting these patterns, at least a few observers have drawn the correct conclusion. The outspoken Algerian secularist, Saïd Sadi, flatly rejects the thesis that poverty spurs militant Islam: "I do not adhere to this view that it is widespread unemployment and poverty which produce terrorism." Likewise, Amayreh finds that militant Islam "is not a product or by-product of poverty."

## Providing a Decent Living

If poverty causes militant Islam, broad-based economic growth is the solution. And indeed, in countries as varied as Egypt and Germany, officials argue for a focus on building prosperity and fostering job formation to combat militant Islam. At the height of the crisis in Algeria during the mid-1990s, when the government pled for Western economic aid, it implicitly threatened that without this aid, the Islamists would prevail. This interpretation has practical results: for example, the government in Tunisia has taken some steps toward a free market but has not privatized for fear that the swollen ranks of the unemployed would provide fodder for militant Islamic groups. The same goes for Iran, where Europe and Japan mold policies premised on the notion that their economic ties to the Islamic Republic tame it and discourage military adventurism.

This emphasis on jobs and wealth creation also transformed efforts to end the Arab-Israeli conflict during the Oslo era. Prior to 1993, Israelis had insisted that a resolution would require Arabs to recognize that the Jewish state is a permanent fact of life. Achieving that was thought to lie in winning acceptance of the Jewish state and finding mutually acceptable borders. Then, post-1993, came a major shift: increasing Arab prosperity became the goal, hoping that this would diminish the appeal of militant Islam and other radical ideologies. A jump start for the economy was expected to give Palestinians a stake in the peace process, thereby reducing the appeal of Hamas and Islamic Jihad. In this context, Serge Schmemann of the *New York Times* wrote (without providing evidence) that Arafat "knows that eradicating militancy will ultimately depend more on providing a decent living than on using force."

The Israeli analyst Meron Benvenisti agreed: Islam's "militant character derived from its being an expression of the deep frustration of the underprivileged. . . . Hamas's rise was directly linked to the worsening economic situation and to the accumulated frustration and degradation of the ongoing occupation." Shimon Peres weighed in as well: "Islamic terror cannot be fought militarily but by eradicating the hunger which spawns it." Guided by this theory, the Western states and Israel contributed billions of dollars to the Palestinian Authority. Even more remarkably, the Israeli government fought against efforts by pro-Israel activists in the United States to make U.S. aid to the PLO contingent on Arafat's fulfilling his formal written promises to Israel.

At this late date, one hardly needs to point out the falsehood of Oslo's assumptions. Wealth does not resolve hatreds; a prosperous enemy may simply be one more capable of making war. Westerners and Israelis assumed that Palestinians would make broad economic growth their priority, whereas this has been a minor concern. What has counted instead are questions of identity and power, but so strong is the belief in the militant Islam-from-poverty thesis that Oslo's failure has not managed to discredit the faith in the political benefits of prosperity. Thus, in August 2001, a senior Israeli officer endorsed the building of a power station in northern Gaza on the grounds that it would supply jobs, "and every [Palestinian] working is one less pair of hands for Hamas."

## A DIFFERENT ARGUMENT

If poverty is not the driving force behind militant Islam, several policy implications follow. First, prosperity cannot be looked to as the solution to militant Islam and foreign aid cannot serve as the outside world's main tool to combat it. Second, Westernization also does not a provide a solution. To the contrary, many outstanding militant Islamic leaders are not just familiar with Western ways but are expert in them. In particular, a disproportionate number of them have advanced degrees in technology and the sciences. It sometimes seems that Westernization is a route to hating the West. Third, economic growth does not inevitably lead to improved relations with Muslim states. In some cases (for example, Algeria), it might help; in others (Saudi Arabia), it might hurt.

Could it be, quite contrarily, that militant Islam results from wealth rather than poverty? It is possible. There is, after all, the universal phenomenon that people become more engaged ideologically and active politically only when they have reached a fairly high standard of living. Revolutions take place, it has often been noted, only when a substantial middle class exists. Birthe Hansen, an associate professor at the University of Copenhagen, hints at this when she writes that "the spread of free market capitalism and liberal democracy . . . is probably an important factor behind the rise of political Islam."

Moreover, there is a specifically Islamic phenomenon of the faith having been associated with worldly success. Through history, from the Prophet Muhammad's time to the Ottoman Empire a millennium later, Muslims usually had more wealth and more power than other peoples, and were more literate and healthy. With time, Islamic faith came to be associated with worldly well-being—a kind of Muslim Calvinism, in effect. This connection appears still to hold. For example, as noted in the formulation known as Issawi's law ("Where there are Muslims, there is oil; the converse is not true"), the 1970s oil boom mainly benefited Muslims; it is probably no coincidence that the current wave of militant Islam began then.

Seeing themselves as "pioneers of a movement that is an alternative to Western civilization," Islamists need a strong economic base. As Galal Amin writes, "There may be a strong relationship between the growth of incomes that have the nature of economic rent and the growth of religious fanaticism."

Conversely, poor Muslims have tended to be more impressed by alternative affiliations. Over the centuries, for example, apostasy from the religion has mostly occurred when things have gone badly. That was the case when Tatars fell under Russian rule or when Sunni Lebanese lost power to the Maronites. It was also the case in 1995 in Iraqi Kurdistan, a region under double embargo and suffering from civil war:

> Trying to live their lives in the midst of fire and gunpowder, Kurdish villagers have reached the point where they are prepared to give up anything to save themselves from hunger and death. From their perspective, changing their religion to get a visa to the West is becoming an increasingly more important option.

There are, in short, ample reasons for thinking that militant Islam results more from success than from failure.

## THE ELEVATOR TO POWER

That being the likely case, it is probably more fruitful to look less to economics and more to other factors when seeking the sources of militant Islam. While material reasons deeply appeal to Western sensibilities, they offer little guidance in this case. In general, Westerners attribute too many of the Arab world's problems, observes David Wurmser of the American Enterprise Institute, "to specific material issues" such as land and wealth. This usually means a tendency "to belittle belief and strict adherence to principle as genuine and dismiss it as a cynical exploitation of the masses by politicians. As such, Western observers see material issues and leaders, not the spiritual state of the Arab world, as the heart of the problem." Or, in Osama bin Laden's ugly formulation, "Because America worships money, it believes that [other] people think that way too."

Indeed, if one turns away from the commentators on militant Islam and instead listens to the

Islamists themselves, it quickly becomes apparent that they rarely talk about prosperity. As Ayatollah Khomeini memorably put it, "We did not create a revolution to lower the price of melon." If anything, they look at the consumer societies of the West with distaste. Wajdi Ghunayim, an Egyptian Islamist, sees it as "the reign of *décolleté* and *moda* [fashion]" whose common denominator is an appeal to the bestial instincts of human nature. Economic assets for Islamists represent not the good life but added strength to do battle against the West. Money serves to train cadres and buy weapons, not to buy a bigger house or a late-model car. Wealth is a means, not an end.

Means toward what? Toward power. Islamists care less about material strength than about where they stand in the world. They talk incessantly of this. In a typical statement, 'Ali Akbar Mohtashemi, the leading Iranian hard-liner, predicts that "ultimately Islam will become the supreme power." Similarly, Mustafa Mashhur, an Egyptian Islamist, declares that the slogan "God is Great" will reverberate "until Islam spreads throughout the world." Abdessalam Yassine, a Moroccan Islamist, asserts "We demand power"—and the man standing in his way, the late King Hassan, concluded that for Islamists, Islam is "the elevator to take power." He was right. By reducing the economic dimension to its proper proportions, and appreciating the religious, cultural and political dimensions, we may actually begin to understand what causes militant Islam.

---

### It's the Clash, Not the Cash

It is quite astonishing how little we have understood, or empathised with, the huge crisis that has faced that vast and populous section of the world stretching from the Mahgreb through the Middle East and Central Asia into South and South-East Asia and beyond to the Philippines: overpopulated, underdeveloped, being dragged headlong by the West into the post-modern age before they have come to terms with modernity. This is not a problem of poverty as against wealth, and I am afraid that it is symptomatic of our Western materialism to suppose that it is. It is the far more profound and intractable confrontation between a theistic, land-based and traditional culture, in places little different from the Europe of the Middle Ages, and the secular material values of the Enlightenment.

—Sir Michael Howard,
speech to the Royal United Service Institute,
October 30, 2001

---

## The Radical Right After 9/11

Daniel Levitas

*"Hallelu-Yahweh! May the WAR be started! DEATH to His enemies, may the World Trade Center BURN TO THE GROUND! . . . We can blame no others than ourselves for our problems due to the fact that we allow . . . Satan children, called jews [sic] today, to have dominion over our lives. . . . My suggestion to all brethren, if we are left alone, sit back and watch the death throws [sic] of this Babylonian beast system and later we can get involved in clean up operations. If this beast system looks to us to plunder, arrest and fill their detention camps with, then by all means fight force with force and leave not a man standing."*

—"Pastor" August B. Kries III,
Sheriff's Posse Comitatus

## THE ATTACKS HARDENED THE RESOLVE OF IMMIGRANT BASHERS AND ANTI-SEMITES

The attacks of September 11 focused the nation's attention on terrorist threats from abroad, but even as the World Trade Center towers were collapsing, hate groups were scheming about how to turn the situation to their advantage in the United States. "WONDERFUL NEWS, BROTHERS!!" crowed Hardy Lloyd, the Pittsburgh coordinator of the racist, anti-Semitic World Church of the Creator. Referencing ZOG—the supposed "Zionist Occupied Government" of the United States—Lloyd alerted supporters throughout western Pennsylvania on September 12 that "maybe as many as 10,000 Zoggites are dead." He also called for vigilante street violence. "The war is upon us all, time to get shooting lone wolves!! [September 11] is a wonderful day for us all. . . . Let's kick some Jew ass."

Lloyd and other militants may have been excited by the suicidal hijackers of Al Qaeda, but like the Oklahoma City bombing six years earlier, the events of 9/11 enraged the American public and undermined those on the radical right devoted to criminal violence. Additionally, fear and resentment over the prospect of heightened government surveillance has prompted numerous rightists to denounce the passage of anti-terrorism legislation, while others are mulling over whether to go underground. "The Feds are clamping down with the definition of a domestic terrorist," warned Christopher Kenney, the "Commander" of the Republic of Texas, a "Christian Patriot" group whose original leaders are serving long prison terms for earlier crimes. "I am sure there will be even more restrictions coming down the pike. We must prepare while we can."

Although most of the Christian right has avoided the kind of violent antigovernment rhetoric embraced by many neo-Nazis after 9/11, some have not. Militant antiabortion campaigners were quick to take advantage of public fears by mailing hundreds of letters containing fake anthrax to family planning clinics across the nation. And homophobes like the Rev. Fred Phelps of Topeka, Kansas, celebrated 9/11 by gleefully declaring that "the Rod of God hath smitten fag America!" and "the multitudes slain Sept. 11, 2001 are in Hell—forever!" The response was different from Christian Coalition founder Pat Robertson and other more mainstream leaders of the religious right, but they also tried to turn the tragedy to their political advantage by attacking Arab immigrants, Islam, liberals, feminists, gays and other enemies both secular and allegedly profane. As for militia and "patriot" groups—whose numbers have been dwindling since the late 1990s—some seized on events to unload their inventory of survivalist paraphernalia left over from the marketing bust of Y2K, while others proclaimed their loyalty to the Republic—or threatened to overthrow it.

Bloodthirsty endorsements of 9/11 won't win hate groups many recruits. But like the conspiracy theories hatched after Oklahoma City (i.e., that Timothy McVeigh was a government patsy who killed 168 people to give the New World Order a pretext to repress the patriot movement), many of the statements made by right-wing militants have been aimed at hardening the movement faithful, not attracting those on the outside looking in. As others on the radical right have done, Hardy Lloyd both praised and vilified the September 11 hijackers. "My only concern is that we Aryans didn't do this and that the rag-heads are ahead of us on the Lone Wolf point scale." Other neo-Nazis called the attackers "towel heads" and worse, yet hailed them as "very brave people [who] were willing to die for whatever they believed in."

"We may not want them marrying our daughters. . . . But anyone who is willing to drive a plane into a building to kill Jews is alright by me. I wish our members had half as much testicular fortitude," observed Billy Roper, deputy membership coordinator of the National Alliance. Notwithstanding such anti-Arab bigotry, some leaders of the radical right believe that 9/11 is a good reason to make common cause with radical Islamic fundamentalists and others who share their visceral hatred of Jews and Israel, though it is unlikely a functional alliance will be formed.

Militant anti-Semites like Roper may be willing to join forces with America's enemies in the hopes of overthrowing ZOG, but in the aftermath of the terrorist attacks the targets of vigilante violence were not Jews but Arabs and others mistaken for Middle Easterners. In the ten weeks following 9/11, the American-Arab Anti-Discrimination Committee reported more than 500 violent incidents, including threats, assaults, arsons, shootings and at least a half-dozen murders. Attacks on South Asian immigrants spiked sharply, with about 250 incidents reported in the last three months of 2001 alone.

Bigotry and intolerance have hardly been limited to criminals, mobs and hate groups. On February 21 Pat Robertson denounced Islam on the Christian Broadcasting Network's 700 Club, saying it "is not a peaceful religion that wants to coexist. They want to coexist until they can control, dominate and then if need be destroy." Robertson asserted that US immigration policies are "so skewed to the Middle East and away from Europe that we have introduced these people into our midst and undoubtedly there are terrorist cells all over them."

Robertson's remarks came on the heels of criticism of US Attorney General John Ashcroft for statements he made last November disparaging Islam. In a radio interview with Cal Thomas, a conservative pundit and syndicated columnist, Ashcroft reportedly said that "Islam is a religion in which God requires you to send your son to die for him. Christianity is a faith in which God sends his son to die for you." Thomas published Ashcroft's statements on November 9, but it wasn't until Muslim groups discovered Thomas's column in early February that the resulting controversy reached the pages of the Washington Post. Ashcroft's response—that his reported statements "do not accurately reflect what I believe I said"—has done little to allay Arab-American concerns.

Similar anti-Arab sentiments have been voiced by the Council of Conservative Citizens, a white supremacist group descended from the Citizens' Council movement, which vigorously opposed integration in the 1950s and '60s. Praised by former member Trent Lott, now Senate minority leader, the CCC produces literature and a website overflowing with racist rhetoric venerating the Confederacy and railing against "black militants, alien parasites, queer activists . . . Christ haters" and multiculturalism. Predictably, the council has also taken to spewing anti-Arab and anti-immigrant bigotry, denouncing "Dirty Rotten Arabs and Muslims" and blaming 9/11 on pluralism and the nation's alleged "open door" immigration policy. "America is now drinking the bitter dregs of multiculmralism and diversity," declared the council on its website, which also displayed an essay linking 9/11 to Abraham Lincoln and America's "[sinful] religion of equality and unity."

Former Klan Imperial Wizard David Duke, who won 607,000 votes when he ran for the US Senate in 1990, trumpeted a similar message in October, saying, "If the demographics of America were still the same as in the 1960s we would be absolutely secure." Duke was last seen in Moscow hawking his hate-filled autobiography, *My Awakening,* and he has been raising money to underwrite his next book, *Jewish Supremacism.* In the post-9/11 issue of his newsletter, Duke explained that "reason should tell us that even if Israeli agents were not the actual provocateurs behind the operation [on 9/11], at the very least they had prior knowledge. . . . Zionists caused the attack America endured just as surely as if they themselves had piloted those planes. It was caused by the Jewish control of the American media and Congress."

Although such anti-Semitic canards have been widely endorsed in the foreign Arab press, most Americans have rejected these and other conspiracy theories out of hand.

Still, Duke and others aren't trying to reach a general audience. The anti-Jewish line of the radical right since 9/11 is aimed at the 17 percent of American adults (an estimated 35 million) who, according to a recent survey by Marttila Communications Group and Kiley & Company for the Anti-Defamation League, hold significantly anti-Semitic views—as well as the one but of five people who, as a recent Harris poll reports, blame America's support for Israel for the attacks.

While it might seem counterintuitive for the radical right to be making both anti-Arab and anti-Semitic appeals, hatred of Jews and Arabs has never been mutually exclusive. After all, there have been many Holocaust deniers and other neo-Nazis who have allied themselves with the Arab cause when it comes to denouncing

Jews but who still hold racist views of Arabs. And the radical right stands to gain from denouncing both groups. There are still millions of garden-variety anti-Semites, some of whom will be receptive to the message that 9/11 was a Zionist plot or the result of Jews having "too much power"—or both. Just because some Americans are seething with anti-Arab bigotry doesn't mean the radical right isn't also using September 11 to promote anti-Semitism.

Enter William Pierce, founder of the neo-Nazi National Alliance and author of the racist novel The Turner Diaries. In a September 22, 2001, Internet radio broadcast, the former assistant professor of physics claimed that America was attacked "because we have been letting ourselves be used to do all of Israel's dirty work in the Middle East." The National Alliance distilled this message into a flier that pictured the disintegrating towers and asked the rhetorical question, "Is Our Involvement in the Security of the Jewish State Worth This?" Beyond 9/11, Pierce is investing heavily in the skinhead music business. Although the aging neo-Nazi would much prefer listening to Wagner, he paid $250,000 in 1999 for Resistance Records, a "white power" music label that now generates about $1 million a year for his hard-core National Alliance. According to Justin Massa of the Chicago-based Center for New Community, which has launched a nationwide campaign to counter neo-Nazi bands and hate music (www.turnitdown.com), "White power music has become the number one recruitment tool for organized bigots hoping to turn healthy youth rebellion into white supremacy."

In the minds of most Americans, Osama bin Laden was responsible for 9/11, but leaders of the Christian right tried to put their own self-serving spin on events. In addition to joining the conservative chorus assailing Arabs and immigration, Pat Robertson argued that the attacks occurred because America had insulted God "at the highest levels of our government" through "rampant secularism," pornography and abortion. As punishment, "God Almighty . . . lifted] his protection from us," declared Robertson on The 700 Club on September 13. His guest that day, the Rev. Jerry Falwell, agreed: The ACLU and other godless secularists clearly were to blame. "I really believe that the pagans, and the abortionists, and the feminists, and the gays and the lesbians who are actively trying to make that an alternative lifestyle . . . all of them who have tried to secularize America. I point the finger in their face and say 'you helped this happen.'"

"Well, I totally concur," said Robertson. Both men spent the next two months trying to undo the damage to their reputations incurred by these remarks. Among other factors, the embarrassment contributed to Robertson's December 5 resignation as director of the Christian Coalition.

Robertson and others on the Christian right have also rushed to the defense of Israel—though such support is strongly rooted in the perverse theological notion that Israel must be supported to prepare for the Second Coming of Christ, when Jews will either convert or be destroyed [see Deanne Stillman, "Onward, Christian Soldier," June 3].

If the hijackers of 9/11 believed they would be rewarded in heaven, so, too, did the antiabortion zealot who sent fake anthrax through the mail. The first round of hoax letters—more than 280 of them—began arriving at family planning and abortion clinics in seventeen states in the second week of October 2001 (coincidentally, the same week that staffers in the office of Senate majority leader Tom Daschle unleashed a plume of real anthrax spores when they opened an envelope sent from a fictitious fourth-grade class in Franklin Park, New Jersey). The envelopes, containing harmless white powder, were marked "Time Sensitive" and "Urgent Security Notice Enclosed," bore the return address of the US Marshals Service or the Secret Service, and included threatening messages signed by the Army of God, a well-known militant antiabortion group. Still, it took two more weeks for the FBI to open a national investigation. And despite demands from abortion advocates and healthcare providers, Attorney General Ashcroft has yet to designate the Army of God a domestic terrorist group.

A few weeks later another round of threats was delivered to clinics via Federal Express using account numbers stolen from abortion rights groups. The man now under federal indictment for these crimes is Clayton Lee Waagner, a self-described "antiabortion warrior" and federal fugitive who had escaped from an Illinois jail eight months earlier while he was awaiting sentencing on federal weapons (and stolen vehicle) charges. The father of nine children, Waagner, 45, once testified that God told him to kill abortion doctors. Waagner was arrested in early December after an alert employee at a Kinko's copy shop in suburban Cincinnati recognized him. It was a lucky break for the FBI, which missed the chance to nab Waagner a week earlier when he showed up on the doorstep of Neal Horsley, a Georgia man who posts detailed personal information on the Internet about anyone he deems responsible for abortion. Using different typefaces, Horsley indicates whether the "criminals" have been killed (crossed out), wounded (gray) or remain unscathed (plain black type). Given the severity of the violence carried out by the antiabortion movement, as well as the government resources that have been consumed in responding to anthrax hoaxes, it's odd that the FBI did not have avowed militants like Horsley under closer surveillance. Then again, one should not be too surprised that Ashcroft's Justice Department has ordered the interrogation of thousands of Arabs and Arab-Americans yet failed to quiz those who endorse the murder of abortion providers.

Twenty years ago, the self-described Christian Patriot movement spread across rural America, recruiting thousands of bankrupt farmers with bogus rhetoric about an "International Jewish Banking Conspiracy." Those were hard times, and fear mongering speeches about the Trilateral Commission and the Federal Reserve fell on receptive ears. While organizations like the Posse Comitatus were trying to build a mass movement, racist militants associated with the underground group the Order deluded themselves into believing they could instigate a race war by robbing banks, counterfeiting money and assassinating their enemies. But right-wing criminality has always cut both ways. On the one hand, it has been used to inspire followers to take action, it has helped finance the movement and it has resulted in plenty of publicity, which these groups often crave. On the other hand, the movement's crimes often mobilize its opposition, lead to public disgust and can prompt more aggressive government surveillance and prosecution. While the violence of

the Order in the 1980s inspired a generation of militant skinheads and others, the crackdown that followed pushed some hate-group leaders to explore different options, especially in the electoral arena. Organizations like the Populist Party—an offshoot of the far-right Liberty Lobby, based in Washington, DC—canvassed the radical right for contributions and candidates. Among the latter was David Duke, who ran a lackluster third-party presidential campaign as a Populist in 1988. But Duke was elected to the Louisiana State House a year later, and in 1990 he won the support of 60 percent of Louisiana's white voters in his Senate bid.

The militia movement of the early 1990s was fed not by hard times but by hard-core ideological opposition to gun control, "big government" and globalization. It was easy to parody the paranoid rants about invasions by black helicopters and blue-helmeted UN troops, but the same nationalist fears about America's waning stature in an increasingly global world were shared by millions of mainstream Americans who had nothing to do with the militias. The deaths of Branch Davidians in Waco—and of family members of hardened white supremacist Randy Weaver in Idaho—also helped fuel the militia movement at the same time as they inspired Timothy McVeigh and Terry Nichols to commit mass murder. But regardless of how many hard-core militiamen bought one or more of the myriad conspiracy theories about who was really behind the Oklahoma City bombing, the sight of nine stories of the Alfred P. Murrah building reduced to rubble, juxtaposed with regular news reports about the escapades of militia groups, doomed any hope the paramilitary right might have had for translating antigovernment sentiment into popular support. The approaching millennium and fears of Y2K offered doomsday-preaching patriots a temporary reprieve, but when nothing happened after midnight on December 31, 1999, the movement again lost recruits.

Although the radical right never reached a consensus about supporting Pat Buchanan in the 2000 presidential race, his message of white Christian nationalism was well received by many militants. Buchanan managed to seize the Reform Party and $12.6 million in federal matching funds, even as he fared dismally on Election Day. Buchanan's recent book, The Death of the West, which laments the demise of white Anglo-Saxon culture (and its accompanying gene pool), enjoyed twelve weeks on the New York Times' bestseller list.

Long before September 11, large numbers of Americans held negative views of Arabs and immigrants. One ABC News poll, conducted in 1991, found that majorities of Americans saw Arabs as "terrorists" (59 percent), "violent" (58 percent) and "religious fanatics" (56 percent). And a Gallup poll conducted two years later found that two-thirds of Americans believed that there were "too many" Arab immigrants in the United States. A Newsweek poll conducted immediately in the wake of 9/11 revealed that 32 percent of Americans favored putting Arabs under special surveillance like that of Japanese-Americans during World War II. Sixty-two percent of Americans disagreed, but the fact that nearly one-third supported the idea indicates the untapped potential of anti-immigrant and right-wing groups. Anti-Arab attitudes have not softened much since.

True, the radical right suffers from a lack of stable, well-funded organizations as well as a shortage of leaders, finances and organizational vehicles capable of penetrating very far into the political mainstream. But in the wake of 9/11 there are plenty of highly charged racial issues for the far right to inflame and exploit, especially when it comes to questions of immigration, racial profiling and national security. Be on the lookout, then, for more hardened underground activity as well as a concerted effort to recruit and mobilize new supporters based on fear and distrust of Arabs, immigrants, Israel and American Jews.

## REVIEW QUESTIONS

- Why have gender issues about terrorism received relatively secondary attention from terrorism experts?
- What accounts for the increased participation of women in terrorist violence?
- Why is it simplistic to presume that poverty alone is the primary cause of religious terrorism? What is the role of identity?
- What is the nature of the threat from the radical right in the United States?
- Is there a possibility of common cause between the American radical right and militant Islamists?

The following books and articles are suggested for further information about the causes of terrorism in the new era:

### Books

Michel, Lou and Dan Herbeck. *American Terrorist: Timothy McVeigh & the Oklahoma City Bombing*. New York: ReganBooks, 2001.
Khalid, Harub. Hamas: *Political Thought and Practice*. Washington, D.C.: Institute for Palestine Studies, 2000.
Rashid, Ahmed. *Taliban: Militant Islam, Oil and Fundamentalism in Central Asia*. New Haven: Yale University Press, 2000.

### Articles

Berman, Paul. "The Philosopher of Islamic Terror." *The New York Times Magazine*. (March 23, 2003).
Parachini, John V. "Comparing Motives and Outcomes of Mass Casualty Terrorism Involving Conventional and Unconventional Weapons." *Studies in Conflict and Terrorism*. 24:5 (September 2001).
Taylor, Max and John Horgan. "The Psychological and Behavioral Bases of Islamic Fundamentalism." *Terrorism and Political Violence*. 13:4 (Winter 2001).

# Part II

## TERRORIST BEHAVIOR
## IN THE NEW ERA

*The confrontation that we are calling for with the apostate regimes does not know Socratic debates, . . . Platonic ideals, . . . nor Aristotelian diplomacy . . . But it knows the dialogue of bullets, the ideals of assassination, bombing and destruction, and the diplomacy of the cannon and machine gun . . . The main mission for which the Military Organization is responsible is the overthrow of the godless regimes and the replacement with an Islamic regime . . . Cell or cluster methods should be adopted by the Organization. It should be composed of many cells whose members do not know one another.*

—From the Al Qaeda "Terrorist Manual"
U.S. Department of Justice Web site

# 5

---

# Exotic Terrorism

A vigorous discussion occurred during the post-Cold War and pre-September 11, 2001 period about whether a "New Terrorism" had supplanted the previous terrorist environment. Participants in this dialogue argued that the conversion of new technologies into weapons and the acquisition of chemical, biological, radiological and nuclear weapons would characterize the New Terrorism. According to many experts, creative organizational models based on cells and "leaderless resistance" rather than hierarchical leadership would typify the new era of terrorism. One critical dimension of this scenario was that terrorists would be motivated by apocalyptic religious and mystical ideologies. The attacks on September 11, 2001 effectively confirmed that the era of the New Terrorism had begun. This new era threatens violence from small semi-autonomous cells of revolutionaries motivated by fringe religious agendas. It seems clear from the September 11 terrorists' conversion of airliners into ballistic missiles that modern terrorists would think nothing of inflicting mass casualties using weapons of mass destruction.

The articles in this chapter discuss the newly emerging behaviors of modern terrorists. In "What it Takes to Become a Nuclear Terrorist," Fredrich Steinhausler points out that modern concern about terrorists' acquisition of radioactive material is quite justified. The essay addresses several scenarios and attack modes to illustrate the inherent difficulty in acquiring radioactive materials and converting them into a viable weapon. However, the article also warns that committed terrorists can successfully act out each scenario. Thomas Homer-Dixon argues in "The Rise of Complex Terrorism" that modern societies are particularly vulnerable to devastating disruption from terrorists. He hypothesizes that the primary threat from terrorists is not the use of weapons of mass destruction, but rather sophisticated attacks against nodes that concentrate financial, communications, power, or other resources. In a short essay entitled "The Culture of Martyrdom: How Suicide Bombing Became not Just a Means but an End," David Brooks argues that the uptick in the incidence of suicide bombing around the turn of the millennium reflects a fundamental shift in the purpose of such attacks. Rather than seeking measurable policy outcomes from these attacks, suicide terrorists in the new era tend to view these attacks and subsequent "martyrdom" as acceptable ends in themselves.

# What It Takes to Become a Nuclear Terrorist

Friedrich Steinhausler
*Center for International Security and Cooperation, Stanford
University/Institute of Physics and Biophysics, University of Salzburg*

## THE NUCLEAR AGENDA OF TERRORISM

Traditionally, terrorism has resorted to the use of conventional weapons, such as explosives, guns, and knives. These weapons have been used to threaten, maim, or kill the victim. Data collected since 1991 indicate that some groups involved in terrorist activities have been interested in acquiring fissile material to terrorize society with nuclear devices in the form of a weapon of mass destruction (WMD) or obtaining other radioactive material to be used as a radiological weapon causing mass disturbance (McCloud & Osborne, 2001).

For example, members of the terrorist organization al Qaeda reportedly tried to acquire weapons-usable nuclear material on a number of occasions in the period 1993 to 2001 (CNS Web site). Chechen separatists have repeatedly threatened to use radioactive material against Russian soldiers and the civilian population. They have pilfered a radioactive waste depository site near Grozny and allegedly used the recovered radiation sources to make powerful bombs. Dozens of radiation sources were found in parts of Grozny during the second military campaign in Chechnya between 2000 and 2002 (Database on Nuclear Smuggling, Theft and Orphan Radiation Sources [DSTO], 2002).

In the following, the objectives, as well as logistical and technical prerequisites for terrorists to engage in such activities, are reviewed for different terrorist activities involving fissile and other radioactive material. This is primarily intended to improve the understanding of possible modes of operation by terrorists and to provide assistance to the members of the security community in assessing the significance of suspicious activities, thereby preempting any planned nuclear terrorism activities.[1]

## RADIOACTIVE DISPERSION WITH CRIMINAL INTENT

It has become evident that—as one of the possible malevolent acts involving radioactive material—terrorists want to disperse radioactive material. In May 2002, the suspected member of al Qaeda, Jose Padilla, was arrested in Chicago and charged with plotting a terrorist attack using a radiological dispersion device (RDD), the so-called dirty bomb (Hanley, 2002). The objectives of deploying such a weapon are twofold:

- contamination of persons in the target area due to the incorporation of radioactive isotopes and external deposition of these isotopes on the skin, hair, and clothes of the victims, and
- contamination of the environment of the target area and its surroundings due to radioactive isotopes deposited on the soil, surfaces of buildings, roads, and vegetation.

These objectives can be achieved by either causing the contamination in a rather controlled manner (e.g., using an aerosol generator or releasing radioactive gas) or less uncontrolled by combining the radioactive material with conventional explosives and detonating them together (dirty bomb).

A terrorist aiming at the dispersal of radioactive material does not need to acquire nuclear fissile material because the main purpose is to cause mass panic rather than mass destruction, as is the case with the detonation of a nuclear weapon. There are a variety of locations worldwide where potentially suitable radioactive sources for such a purpose are in use, such as research establishments, medical institutions, industry, and the military (Gonzalez, 2001):

- some caesium (Cs-137) sources (activity: about 10E14 Becquerel[2]) used in medicine can contain caesium chloride, which is a highly dispersible powder; no precise data available on the total number still in service or awaiting disposal;

- teletherapy cobalt (Co-60) sources contain typically 1,000 metal pellets (activity: 10E11 Becquerel each); more than 10,000 sources in use worldwide;
- industrial radiography sources use mostly metallic iridium (Ir-192), to a lesser extent cobalt (Co-60), selenium (Se-75), or ytterbium (Yt-169), with a typical activity of about 3 trillion Becquerel each; several tens of thousands of sources worldwide; and
- industrial gauges and other applications can contain cobalt (Co-60), caesium (Cs-137), or americium (Am-241) (typical activity: 0.1 to 50 × 10E9 Becquerel); several million sources worldwide.

The activity of radiation sources (Co-60, Cs-137) used in industrial irradiators is too high (typically 1 million billion Becquerel) to be considered for criminal diversion because the thief would be incapacitated almost instantaneously due to lethal radiation overexposure.

It is also possible for terrorists to consider an RDD using spent nuclear fuel as the source of radiation. The high exposure for the terrorist resulting from the handling of such a device makes this kind of attack only feasible for a suicide commando.

Physical protection of such radioactive sources against diversion varies considerably between different types of establishments and countries. Security measures are frequently rather lax: Annually, several hundreds of medical and industrial sources are stolen, abandoned, or lost; in the United States alone, on average, more than 200 such incidents are reported (Dicus, 1999). Except for "light security," counterterrorism security measures are missing in general. Despite international consensus documents and supporting legislation, based on an international survey in several countries, major deficits have been revealed in terms of security, questioning their ability to maintain adequate control over radioactive materials under their jurisdiction (Steinhausler, Bremer Maerli, & Zaitseva, 2002). In some of these countries, a central register for the radioactive material in their territory is missing. It is known to them that

unlicensed radioactive material has existed or that some radioactive material was removed from storage sites or end-users without proper authorization; strategies for the detection and the relocation of "orphan" radioactive sources are frequently absent, and some have no radiation monitoring installations at national checkpoints.

Once the radioactive material has been obtained by the terrorist, it can be hidden in practically any type of containment, ranging from a soft-drink bottle to a briefcase, because the volume of the actual radioactive material in a radiation source without the shielding is rather small (typically a few mm$^3$ to about 100 cm$^3$ only). The subsequent release of the material can occur from any type of land-, water-, or air-based vehicle. The three scenarios considered most probable are as follows:

- *Attack mode no. 1*: Radioactive material is dispersed into the environment by using an RDD. Such an RDD can be designed to generate radioactive aerosols over an extended period of time. This aerosol is introduced into a ventilation system (e.g., subway) in a covert manner. Subsequently, all persons present, as well as all surfaces exposed to this aerosol, will be contaminated to a varying degree.
- *Attack mode no. 2*: Radioactive material is combined with conventional explosives (e.g., a truck bomb, loaded with radioactive material blanketed with explosives). The explosion will result in conventional damage due to the blast but also distribute the radioactive material in the environment. As a result, the blast victims, first responders, and the area of the attack will be contaminated. Depending on the prevailing weather conditions at the time of the detonation, adjacent areas also may be contaminated.
- *Attack mode no. 3*: A fully fueled plane is loaded with radioactive material and conventional explosives. Provided the aircraft is under the control of a suicide commando, it could be crashed into a civilian target. The detonation of the explosives on impact, combined with the ignition of the fuel, would result in the release of a significant amount of chemical energy. In case of a large civilian airliner, the total energy released approaches that of a tactical nuclear weapon. Besides the distribution of the radioactive material by the blast

resulting from the plane crash, the heat from the fire would cause hot air, mixed with radioactive particles, to raise several hundred meters (chi-mney effect), thereby contaminating a larger area as compared to the other two scenarios described above.

To achieve these objectives, the terrorist would have to have basic knowledge about different types of radiation, isotope characteristics, and radiation protection to select suitable radioactive materials and to ensure a minimum of radiation protection for those handling the weapon; the latter can be considered of lesser importance in the case of a suicide terrorist. To implement a successful diversion of the material sought after, information about the storage conditions and physical protection practices at the storage site of the radioactive material are needed. No special criminal skills are needed for a break-in into such a storage facility because the security level is typically comparable to that of a jewelry shop or a subsidiary branch of a bank. The successful thief or thieves need transport facilities suitable for the handling of an object potentially weighing several hundred kilograms (i.e., high-activity radioactive source plus large shielding), depending on the type of source diverted. Once the radiation source has arrived at the terrorist workshop, simple mechanical tools are all that are needed to gain access to the radioactive material, typically contained inside massive shielding. Access to a workshop with average technical equipment (DIY-level) would be sufficient to manufacture the RDD itself, using the radioactive material from the source and conventional explosives.

To implement the actual terror attack, the following is required, depending on the attack mode chosen:

- *Attack mode no. 1*: Adequate knowledge about the layout of the ventilation system in the target area to deploy the RDD in a covert manner for an extended period of time.
- *Attack mode no. 2*: Access to a truck for delivering the dirty bomb to the target area and detonating it under remote control; remote staging area for loading the device into the vehicle (e.g., rented garage).

- *Attack mode no. 3*: Access to a plane for delivering the dirty bomb to the target area and detonating it on impact; remote staging area for loading the device onto the aircraft (e.g., small commuter airport in rural area).

After the attack, the degree of radioactive contamination resulting from the dispersion will depend primarily on the amount and type of radioactive material used and the degree of aerosol generation. In the case of attack mode no. 1, the layout of the ventilation system (e.g., in a subway station or large office complex) distributing the radioactive aerosol will be decisive for the extent of the contamination.

For attack mode nos. 2 and 3, the amount of explosives and the pertinent meteorological conditions at the time of the detonation will determine the size of the area contaminated. It can be assumed that typically an area composed of several city blocks would be affected initially. The target areas at highest risk for such an attack would be areas with high population density in order to cause maximum impact, such as shopping malls.

The overall magnitude of the impact on the target society is determined by the timely knowledge about the radioactive contamination. If the use of radioactive material in the terror attack remains undiscovered for a sufficiently long time, then the probability is high that first responders and the victims will assist unknowingly in the further spread of the contamination: People and vehicles moving in and out of the primary affected area will transport the radioactive debris to hospitals, homes, and offices.

Upon realization by members of the public at a later stage of potentially having been contaminated, this is likely to cause widespread panic, as was the case in the incident in the Brazilian city of Goiania in 1987. In this case, the uncontrolled dispersion of Cs-137 from a stolen medical source resulted in about 112,000 persons requiring to be monitored (Steinhausler & Wieland, 1998). Furthermore, the treatment of victims with wounds contaminated by radioactivity will put additional stress on the health services.

The environmental clean-up costs are difficult to estimate without data on the type and size of area affected by the radioactive contamination.

However, the practical experience gained during the clean-up procedures of the city of Goiania (resulting in 5,000 m³ of radioactive waste) and the Ukrainian city of Pripyat (contaminated during the Chernobyl accident in 1986 and finally abandoned) are indicative of the technical and logistical challenges associates with such a task.

Provided the radioactive contamination of the victims and the debris of the terror attack are discovered in the initial stages of the emergency response, cordoning off the impacted area and triage procedures should suffice to keep the situation under reasonable control.

## RADIOLOGICAL MALEVOLENCE

Sufficiently high overexposure to radiation can kill. This fact makes a strong radiation source a potential weapon in the hands of terrorists. Such has already occurred in Russia where a member of the business community became a victim of organized crime due to a source implanted in his chair (Ward, 1994).

Alternatively, terrorists may be tempted to use the widespread inherent fear of anything "radioactive" to blackmail society, as was the case when Chechen terrorists buried a radioactive source in a Moscow park in 1995 and informed the authorities and media about their threat capabilities (DSTO, 2002).

At risk of being diverted are high-activity sources used predominantly in industry (radiography) and medicine (radiotherapy), and to a lesser extent, sources used as industrial gauges (frequently insufficient activity) and those employed in industrial irradiators (food preservation, sterilization of medical supplies) because the handling of the latter sources would cause almost instant death. The sources at risk of diversion number several tens of thousand worldwide, and the security practices have been found lacking in many instances. Therefore, the probability for a terrorist to obtain access to one of them is sufficiently high to warrant uttermost concern.

- *Attack mode no. 4*: Radiation sources without their shielding are usually small, inconspicuous pieces of metal, which can be hidden with relative ease. Our lack of any sensory capability for

ionizing radiation, together with the frequent absence of radiation detectors in the everyday-type environment, makes a strong radiation source a weapon of choice for a terrorist aiming at committing a covert murder. In this case, the hidden source would be positioned in such a manner as to expose the targeted person(s) to an excessively high dose rate for a period of time. Upon application of a lethal dose (exposure period: typically several days), the radiation source would be removed in a clandestine manner.

- *Attack mode no. 5*: Alternatively, hiding a strong radiation source in a public place with a high frequency of pedestrians is less likely to represent a major health hazard due to the presumably short exposure time of people passing by. But it is sure to cause panic in the public upon revelation of the fact, largely independent of the magnitude of the actual radiation dose received.

- *Attack mode no. 6*: The target society is blackmailed by claiming to have placed many such radiation sources at hitherto undisclosed places. It is likely that the terrorist could get a way by bluffing and only placing a few such radiation sources to remain credible. The actual (or fake) locations would only be revealed upon fulfillment of the demand by the terrorist.

A terrorist needs to meet several requirements to succeed with his malevolent act, using radioactive material. The essential prerequisite is to obtain a suitable radiation source either by theft or by unauthorized purchase. There have been at least 370 thefts and seizures of radiation sources worldwide over the past decade (DSTO, 2002). Such a magnitude of illicit trafficking of radiation sources represents a serious threat.

For the terrorist to be able to estimate the duration of the necessary exposure time, it is necessary to have some basic knowledge about radiation dosimetry and radiation-induced health effects. The actual implementation of the malevolent act will require different methods for different modes:

- *Attack mode no. 4*: Covert placement of the source at a location that result in an excessively high dose rate for the victim(s); covert removal of the source.

- *Attack mode no. 5*: Covert placement of the source in a public with high traffic density: simultaneous disclosure of the fact to the authorities and the media.
- *Attack mode no. 6*: Covert placement of several sources in different public places with high traffic density; simultaneous disclosure of the threat to the authorities and the media.

Until now, this form of terrorism has reportedly taken place only in a few cases (see sect. 1). In the case of its more frequent use, this would have a largely different impact on the targeted individual victim as compared to the targeted society.

The individual irradiated as described in mode no. 4 is likely to suffer lethal injuries, although there would be only minor, if any, impact on most other members of the society.

The impact of attack mode nos. 5 and 6 is very different from that of no. 4: significant collective *psychological* impact (fear) on large segments of the targeted society but very likely only minor *health* impact (low additional cancer risk) to the exposed individual.

## ATTACK ON A NUCLEAR POWER PLANT

There are 434 operating nuclear power plants (NPPs) worldwide (International Atomic Energy Agency [IAEA], 1999). Due to their radioactive inventory (in the reactor core, in the spent fuel storage area, to a lesser extent in the fresh fuel depot), they represent an attractive target for a terrorist attack for the following reasons: instilling fear in the public about an uncontrolled release of radioactivity by merely threatening with the possibility of such an attack, that is, another form of "nuclear blackmail"; and conducting an actual terrorist attack on vital areas of an operating nuclear power plant to inflict major damage to the facility, resulting in the loss of control over the plant. This could lead to major radioactive releases into the environment, resulting in elevated health risks and substantial economic losses for society.

In the recent past, such threats have occurred already in the United States (Pasternak, 2001)[3] and in Russia (Cameron, 2001).[4] However, so far, in all cases, the individuals could be neutralized in time by the respective national security forces.

Security risks at NPPs can result from terrorists intruding onto the site of the NPP and through sabotage carried out by insiders. To manage such security risks, major efforts are undertaken by nuclear regulators, NPP operators, and managers to provide adequate physical protection for NPPs worldwide.

The protection against intruders consists typically of a series of fences, CCTV cameras installed on-site and at the site perimeter, as well as inspection of all persons and vehicles entering the site. In many countries, the basis for the specific security features is the *Design Basis Threat*, developed specifically for each NPP. This Design Basis Threat specifies the number of attackers to be assumed, together with the type of vehicle and weapons used in the attack, as well as the kind of assistance provided by the collaborating insider.

The protection against insiders is based on criminal background checks and psychological tests of employees.

Mock attacks on NPPs are carried out in the United States to test the state of readiness of the on-site security forces. However, despite preannouncement of the exercises, guards at half the nation's NPPs failed to repel the attackers (Leventhal, 2001).

Terrorists can seriously threaten the security of an NPP in several manners, for example:

- *Attack mode no. 7*: A heavily armed suicide commando attacks the weakest entry point of an NPP with a truck bomb, followed by additional truck bombs breaking through the damaged barriers. This latter group attacks vital installations of the NPP.
- *Attack mode no. 8*: A suicide commando hijacks a fully fueled large aircraft and crashed it into the spent nuclear fuel storage area of the NPP.

The logistical and technical requirements are such that they are not within the realm of possibility of the average terrorist group but require a certain degree of sophistication. In particular, it would be necessary for this group to foresee that at least some of the members are prepared to die during the attack. Under these conditions, both attack modes could be successful, provided the terrorists succeed in acquisition of heavy weapons and a sufficient amount of explosives to build several truck bombs; obtain detailed knowledge about the layout of the NPP, the location of its vital components, and important plant-specific operational characteristics; succeed in hijacking a large civilian airliner; and inflict sufficient damage to the rather small cross section of vital NPP components either by detonating the truck bombs or by crashing the plane into them.

For both attack modes, it cannot be excluded that—in case of a successful attack—the resulting uncontrolled releases of radioactivity will result in a significant threat to man and the environment (Nuclear Regulatory Commission, 1981). The exact magnitude of any health risks to employees and nearby residents (external and internal radiation exposure), as well as the economic losses to the NPP itself and adjacent areas (production loss in agriculture, clean-up costs, devaluation of property value), cannot be estimated without specific input data characterizing the circumstances of the attack and the resulting radioactive release.

## Nuclear Weapons

Nuclear experts concur that a nuclear weapon in the hands of a terrorist represents the most devastating scenario (IAEA, 2001). So far, this WMD has only been deployed twice by a nation-state since its invention more than 50 years ago: the bombing of an urban environmental by the United States in 1945. Since then, there have been more or less successful attempts by other states (China, France, Israel, India, Iraq, North Korea, Pakistan, Russian Federation, South Africa, United Kingdom) to acquire these weapons as well, but never by terrorists. It became evident in the aftermath of the terror attacks on September 11, 2001, that there is now a real threat from a sophisticated terror organization not only to aim at the use of an illegally acquired nuclear WMD but possibly even to build one.

There are two possible reasons for a terrorist to deploy a nuclear weapon: blackmailing the targeted state with the threat to detonate a hidden nuclear device to obtain concessions from society or detonation of a nuclear device on the territory of the declared adversary to inflict mass casualties and widespread contamination of the territory. These objectives can be met by either diverting an already existing nuclear weapon (*advanced nuclear device*) from a military storage site or by attempting to build a less sophisticated one (*crude nuclear device*).

The prerequisite for any terrorist nuclear weapon program is access to an adequate quality and amount of weapons-usable nuclear material. At present, the following stockpiles of nuclear material exist around the world (Bunn & Bunn, 2001): approximately 30,000 nuclear weapons, about 450 tons of military and civilian separated plutonium (Pu), and more than 1,700 tons of highly enriched uranium (HEU). Physical protection of these materials is the responsibility of the state owning the material. However, national practices and the resulting levels of security vary considerably between states due to the lack of adequate mandatory standards and large differences in the available funds. This results in fortress-like storage facilities with multiple security barriers in nuclear weapon states to facilities housing weapons-usable fissile material protected by unarmed guards, reflecting also cultural differences in national threat perception. Another important reason for this discrepancy is the inadequacy of the current international regulatory framework. The only legally binding international requirements obligate the adherence to the *Convention on the Physical Protection of Nuclear Material*[5] while the nuclear material is in international transport. There is no such obligation while the material is in domestic use, storage, and transit.

However, already there have been several cases of successful diversion of nuclear weapons-grade material, such as the 1992 theft of 1.5 kg of weapons-grade HEU (90% enrichment) from the Luch Scientific-Production Association in Podolsk (Russia) or the 1994 diversion of almost 3 kg of HEU from the Russian Electrostal Machine-Building Plant, which produces fuel for research and naval reactors (DSTO, 2002).

In view of the many difficulties involved in acquiring or building a nuclear weapon, it appears to be considerably less likely that terrorists would use a nuclear device as their weapon of choice as compared to the deployment of an RDD. Nevertheless, after the attacks on September, 11, 2001, it cannot be excluded that terrorists would continue to try to obtain such a weapon. Its deployment could occur in two ways:

- *Attack mode no. 9*: An advanced nuclear device is smuggled into a city harbor and hidden inside a container on a ship. The government is given an ultimatum that the device will be detonated unless certain demands are met.

Approximately 6 million such containers pass through U.S. ports annually, but only about 2% are ever searched (Greenway, 2002). Therefore, the probability for this to go undetected is finite, despite multiple radiation monitors installed, due to intrinsic detection problems associated with the detection of fissile material (caused by radiation shielding, particularly in the case of HEU-based nuclear devices).

- *Attack mode no. 10*: A terrorist group has obtained enough nuclear weapons-grade material to build a crude nuclear device and places it on a truck. This nuclear truck bomb is successfully detonated in a metropolitan area without prior warning.

Some countries have provided for search teams capable of finding nuclear and other radioactive materials (e.g., NEST[6] in the United States). However, unless put into action because of pertinent intelligence information made available about an area under suspicion, these teams would be very limited in their capabilities to provide timely assistance in detecting such a hidden nuclear device. The reason lies in their mode of operation: It is neither continuous nor ubiquitous. In addition, these teams of nuclear specialists also face inherent technical limitations with regard to the detection of well-shielded nuclear devices based on HEU.

The construction of a crude nuclear device requires teamwork, better still tacit government support. Even if the terrorists should have gained possession of sufficient amounts of

weapons-grade nuclear fissile material, it is still a major technical challenge to actually build such a device. Provided that this undertaking is successfully completed, then the terrorists face the problem that the design of the nuclear device cannot be tested by them, that is, it remains uncertain whether it will actually work, and the explosive yield of the nuclear device will not be known for sure. However, it may be possible to counter the former uncertainty by overengineering, whereas the latter may not necessarily matter to a terrorist.

Based on experience gained during the construction of the earlier United States devices in 1945, it can be estimated that the yield of such a terrorist design (crude nuclear device) would be in the order of about 10 kiloton[7] at the most. For comparison, even a nuclear device with a yield of only 0.01 kiloton ("nuclear fizzle") would exceed by far the damage caused by the car bomb destroying the Oklahoma City Federal Building in 1995.

The theft of an advanced nuclear device from a nuclear weapons storage area would overcome all of these problems but would raise other ones with regard to its built-in safeguard features (see below). In addition, multiple technical and logistical challenges have to be met in implementing a terrorist nuclear threat.

In case of planning to stage an attack similar to mode no. 9 with an advanced nuclear device, they would have to succeed in the following:

- Acquisition of an advanced nuclear device from one of the storage sites of the nuclear weapon states (NWS). Officially, all nuclear weapons of NWS are accounted for. However, there are also contradictory statements concerning the former Soviet Union, ranging from questionable accounting practices for tactical nuclear weapons (Potter & Sokov, 2000) to reportedly missing *nuclear suitcases* (Parrish, 1997).
- Importing the weapon into the harbor of the target country without being detected.
- Access to the information on how to override the multiple safeguard features of an advanced nuclear device, which are built into the weapon against its unauthorized use; additional difficulties are the thick bomb case (at least 10 mm of hardened steel) with an (almost) access-resistant hatch.

Should the terrorists intend to use a crude nuclear device instead, following attack mode no. 16, they need to have the following:

- basic knowledge in physical and chemical properties of fissile materials; radiation physics; physical principles of explosive devices, particularly about shaped charges; and electronics;
- access to a workshop with advanced equipment, such as precision calibrated, computer-guided machine tools ($\leq 25,000$ rpm) with laser-interferometer, air-bearing lathe, and artificial room ventilation with built-in air cleaner;
- acquired a sufficient amount of nuclear weapons-grade material needed for building a crude nuclear device (about 25 kg of HEU, respectively, 8 kg Pu) (IAEA, 2001), at least 50 kg of high explosives, and a supply of Kryton switches;
- machining capabilities for the production of complex shapes (tolerance: about 10E-10 m); and
- ceramic (cerium sulfide) crucibles, electric furnace, argon-filled enclosure, Freon gas, and vacuum pumps.

Upon detonation of a nuclear (crude or advanced) device, the targeted population will notice (National Council on Radiation Protection and Measurements [NCRP], 2001) a crater (diameter in dry soft rock for a 10 kt nuclear device: 80m), a strong shock wave (air blast), and a fireball (thermal radiation). Neither the initial nuclear radiation (release of neutrons and gamma rays during the first minute) nor the subsequent residual radiation resulting from the decaying radionuclides would be noticed, unless radiation-monitoring equipment was available to them. Assuming an explosive yield of the nuclear device of about 10 kt, 50% fatality is to be expected (distance from ground zero[8]) from flying glass up to 590 m, from thermal radiation up to 1,800 m, from acute radiation exposure without medical treatment up to 1,200 m, and from residual radiation in the first hour after detonation up to 9,600 m.

If such a device is detonated over a major sport stadium or convention center, tens of thousands of fatal injuries would result even from a "nuclear fizzle"—size yield. In addition, the radioactive cloud drifting away from ground zero could cause considerable radiation doses to some people located downwind or in the air (police and news helicopter crews).

The clean-up cost for the directly affected area at ground zero and the fallout from contaminated areas downwind will be significant, but it is impossible to provide a reliable estimate because it depends on too many variables (population density, number and type of buildings, meteorological conditions).

Initial on-site management of the aftermath will have to address the blast and radiation casualties; persons having inhaled radioactive particles; and those (both injured and unharmed) with contaminated skin, clothes, and hair. In addition, psychosocial effects (radiation psychosis, survivor guilt, physiological stress) will be noticeable among some survivors, not necessarily related to their respective exposure history, as noted after the radiation accident in Goiania (1987) and the nuclear reactor accidents in Three Mile Island (1979) and Chernobyl (1986). The situation will be aggravated further because high rates of post-traumatic stress disorder (PTDS) have been observed frequently after an act of terrorism (National Research Council, 1999).

## CONCLUSIONS

Since the terror attacks in the United States on September 11, 2001, society has to be prepared for terrorists willing and capable of using nuclear or other radioactive materials in their attacks. Taking into account the large differences in actually implementing these threats, the following can be concluded:

- The security community has the opportunity to look for technological and logistical "markers" in the international terrorism scene, which may be indicative of the covert preparation of a nuclear or radiological act of terrorism, because several specific requirements have to be fulfilled for its successful implementation.
- The probability for such a terror attack to be actually happening is largest for a dirty bomb scenario, detonating one of the widely available radiation sources together with conventional explosives.

- A nuclear explosion with a covertly built crude nuclear device is considerably less likely than the dirty bomb scenario; the use of a stolen military weapon for a terror attack is the least likely scenario.
- An attack on a nuclear power plant, resulting in an uncontrolled release of radioactivity, is within the possibilities of a terrorist organization with a certain degree of sophistication.
- Despite the multiple technological and logistical hurdles discussed, many of them are not insurmountable for a determined terror organization, especially if operating with tacit support of a sympathetic state and willing to deploy suicide commandos.

## NOTES

1. For reasons of security, this article will address generic issues only and avoid providing technical details.

2. Becquerel (Bq) is the SI-unit for the activity of radioactive material; 1 Bq = 1/s.

3. "General" Donald Beauregard's (Southwestern Alliance Right-Wing Radical Group) plan of attacking the nuclear power plant at Tampa Bay, Florida, was foiled by the Federal Bureau of Investigation in 2000.

4. In fall 1996, the Russian nuclear regulatory agency, Gosatomnadzor, received a warning that an armed group of Chechens was planning to target the Balakovo Nuclear Power Plant, a facility with four VVER-1000 reactors.

5. Negotiated under the International Atomic Energy Agency (IAEA), with 71 State Parties, and entered into force in 1987.

6. Nuclear Emergency Search Team (NEST), founded in 1976.

7. The unit "kiloton" (kt) refers to the equivalent of 1,000 tons of the explosive TNT (1 kt = $4.2 \times 10E9$ Joule).

8. Denotes the point of detonating the nuclear device.

## REFERENCES

Bunn, M., & Bunn, G. (2001). Nuclear theft & sabotage: Priorities for reducing new threats. *IAEA Bulletin, 43*(4), 20–29.

Cameron, G. (2001, November 2). *Nuclear terrorism: Reactors and radiological attacks after September 11*. Paper presented at the International Atomic Energy Agency (IAEA): Special session on combating nuclear terrorism, Vienna, Austria. Retrieved from http://www.iaea.or.at/worldatom/press/focus/nuclear_terrorism/Cameron.pdf

*Database on Nuclear Smuggling, Theft and Orphan Radiation Sources* (DSTO). (2002). Center for international security and cooperation. Stanford, CA: Stanford University.

Dicus, G. J. (1999). USA perspectives: Safety and security of radioactive sources. *IAEA Bulletin, 41*(4), 43.

Gonzalez, A. J. (2001). Security of radioactive sources: The evolving new international dimension. *IAEA Bulletin, 43*(4), 39–48.

Greenway, H. D. S. (2002, April 30). Scary potential for domestic terrorism. *Boston Globe*. This item can be purchased from the *Boston Globe* Web site: http://www.boston.com/globe/

Hanley, C. J. (2002, June 14). Radioactive markets boom in Central Asia. *New York Times*. Retrieved from http://cgi.wn.com/?action=display&article=14137326&template=worldnews/search.txt&index=recent

International Atomic Energy Agency. (IAEA). (1999, April). *Nuclear power reactors in the world*. Reference Data Series No. 2.

International Atomic Energy Agency (IAEA). (2001). Newsbrief. *IAEA Bulletin, 43*(4), 2.

Leventhal, P.L. (2001, May 17). More nuclear power means more risk. *New York Times*. Retrieved from http://www.nci.org/pl-nyt-oped51701.htm

McCloud, K., & Osborne, M. (2001). *WMD terrorism and Usama Bin Laden*. CNS report. Monterey, CA: Center for Nonproliferation Studies (CNS), Monterey Institute of International Studies.

National Council on Radiation Protection and Measurements (NCRP). (2001). Management of terrorist events involving radioactive material. *NCRP Report, 138*.

National Research Council/Institute of Medicine. (1999). *Potential radiation exposure in military operations: Protecting the soldier before, during and after*. Washington, DC: Committee on Battlefield Radiation Exposure Criteria, National Academy Press.

Nuclear Regulatory Commission. (1981). Supplement to draft environmental statement, San Onofre Units 2 and 3, NUREG-0490, explained in D. Hirsch, *The truck bomb and insider threats to nuclear facilities*. In P. Leventhal & Y. Alexander. (1989). *Preventing nuclear terrorism*. Lexington, MA: Lexington Books.

Parrish, S. (1997). *Are suitcase nukes on the loose? The story behind the controversy*. CNS report. Monterey, CA: Center for Nonproliferation

Studies (CNS), Monterey Institute of International Studies.

Pasternak, D. (2001, September 17). Too many nuclear plants are not prepared to prevent attacks. *U.S. News and World Report*. Retrieved from http://www.nci.org/new/usn1.htm

Potter, W., & Sokov, N. (2000). *Tactical nuclear weapons: The nature of the problem*. CNS report. Monterey, CA: Center for Nonproliferation Studies (CNS), Monterey Institute of International Studies.

Steinhausler, F., Bremer Maerli, M., & Zaitseva, L. (2002). *Assessment of the threat from diverted radioactive material and "orphan sources":*

*An international comparison*. Proceedings of the International Conference on Security of Nuclear Material and Sources, Stockholm, Sweden. Vienna: International Atomic Energy Agency.

Steinhausler, F., & Wieland, P. (1998). Radiological emergencies due to unaccounted sources or failures of the control system in developing countries. *International Atomic Energy Agency*, IAEA-GOCP, "Ten Years Later," Vienna.

Ward, O. (1994, January, 25). Deadly dose of radiation is murder . . . Russian-style, fears on the rise about nuclear terrorism. *The Toronto Star*, p. A-18.

# The Rise of Complex Terrorism

Thomas Homer-Dixon
*University of Toronto*

It's 4 a.m. on a sweltering summer night in July 2003. Across much of the United States, power plants are working full tilt to generate electricity for millions of air conditioners that are keeping a ferocious heat wave at bay. The electricity grid in California has repeatedly buckled under the strain, with rotating blackouts from San Diego to Santa Rosa.

In different parts of the state, half a dozen small groups of men and women gather. Each travels in a rented minivan to its prearranged destination—for some, a location outside one of the hundreds of electrical substations dotting the state; for others, a spot upwind from key, high-voltage transmission lines. The groups unload their equipment from the vans. Those outside the substations put together simple mortars made from materials bought at local hardware stores, while those near the transmission lines use helium to inflate weather balloons with long silvery tails. At a precisely coordinated moment, the homemade mortars are fired, sending showers of aluminum chaff over the substations. The balloons are released and drift into the transmission lines.

Simultaneously, other groups are doing the same thing along the Eastern Seaboard and in the South and Southwest. A national electrical system already under immense strain is massively short-circuited, causing a cascade of power failures across the country. Traffic lights shut off. Water and sewage systems are disabled. Communications systems break down. The financial system and national economy come screeching to a halt.

Sound far-fetched? Perhaps it would have before September 11, 2001, but certainly not now. We've realized, belatedly, that our societies are wide-open targets for terrorists. We're easy prey because of two key trends: First, the growing technological capacity of small groups and individuals to destroy things and people; and, second, the increasing vulnerability of our economic and technological systems to carefully aimed attacks. While commentators have devoted considerable ink and airtime to the first of these trends, they've paid far less attention to the second, and they've virtually ignored their combined effect. Together, these two trends facilitate a new and sinister kind of mass violence—a "complex terrorism" that threatens modern, high-tech societies in the world's most developed nations.

Our fevered, Hollywood-conditioned imaginations encourage us to focus on the sensational possibility of nuclear or biological attacks—attacks that might kill tens of thousands of people in a single strike. These threats certainly deserve attention, but not to the neglect of the likelier and ultimately deadlier disruptions that could result from the clever exploitation by terrorists of our societies' new and growing complexities.

## Weapons of Mass Disruption

The steady increase in the destructive capacity of small groups and individuals is driven largely by three technological advances: more powerful weapons, the dramatic progress in communications and information processing, and more abundant opportunities to divert nonweapon technologies to destructive ends.

Consider first the advances in weapons technology. Over the last century, progress in materials engineering, the chemistry of explosives, and miniaturization of electronics has brought steady improvement in all key weapons characteristics, including accuracy, destructive power, range, portability, ruggedness, ease-of-use, and affordability. Improvements in light weapons are particularly relevant to trends in terrorism and violence by small groups, where the devices of choice include rocket-propelled grenade launchers, machine guns, light mortars, land mines, and cheap assault rifles such as the famed AK-47. The effects of improvements in these weapons are particularly noticeable in developing countries. A few decades ago, a small band of terrorists or insurgents attacking a rural village might have used bolt-action rifles, which take precious time to reload. Today, cheap assault rifles multiply the possible casualties resulting from such an attack. As technological change makes it easier to kill, societies are more likely to become locked into perpetual cycles of attack and counterattack that render any normal trajectory of political and economic development impossible.

High-tech societies are filled with supercharged devices packed with combustibles and poisons, giving terrorists ample opportunities to divert such nonweapon technologies to destructive ends.

Meanwhile, new communications technologies—from satellite phones to the Internet—allow violent groups to marshal resources and coordinate activities around the planet. Transnational terrorist organizations can use the Internet to share information on weapons and recruiting tactics, arrange surreptitious fund transfers across borders, and plan attacks. These new technologies can also dramatically enhance the reach and power of age-old procedures. Take the ancient *hawala* system of moving money between countries, widely used in Middle Eastern and Asian societies. The system, which relies on brokers linked together by clan-based networks of trust, has become faster and more effective through the use of the Internet.

Information-processing technologies have also boosted the power of terrorists by allowing them to hide or encrypt their messages. The power of a modern laptop computer today is comparable to the computational power available in the entire U.S. Defense Department in the mid-1960s. Terrorists can use this power to run widely available state-of-the-art encryption software. Sometimes less advanced computer technologies are just as effective. For instance, individuals can use a method called steganography ("hidden writing") to embed messages into digital photographs or music clips. Posted on publicly available Web sites, the photos or clips are downloaded by collaborators as necessary. (This technique was reportedly used by recently arrested terrorists when they planned to blow up the U.S. Embassy in Paris.) At latest count, 140 easy-to-use steganography tools were available on the Internet. Many other off-the-shelf technologies—such as "spread-spectrum" radios that randomly switch their broadcasting and receiving signals—allow terrorists to obscure their messages and make themselves invisible.

The Web also provides access to critical information. The September 11 terrorists could have found there all the details they needed about the floor plans and design characteristics of the World Trade Center and about how demolition experts use progressive collapse to destroy large buildings. The Web also makes available sets of instructions—or "technical ingenuity"—needed to combine readily available materials in destructive ways. Practically anything an extremist wants to know about kidnapping, bomb making, and assassination is now available online. One somewhat facetious example: It's possible to convert everyday materials into potentially destructive devices like the "potato cannon." With a barrel and combustion chamber fashioned from common plastic pipe, and with propane as an explosive propellant, a well-made cannon can hurl a homely spud hundreds of meters—or throw chaff onto electrical substations. A quick search of the Web reveals dozens of sites giving instructions on how to make one.

Finally, modern, high-tech societies are filled with supercharged devices packed with energy, combustibles, and poisons, giving terrorists ample opportunities to divert such nonweapon technologies to destructive ends. To cause horrendous damage, all terrorists must do is figure out how to release this power and let it run wild or, as they did on September 11, take control of this power and retarget it. Indeed, the assaults on New York City and the Pentagon were not low-tech affairs, as is often argued. True, the terrorists used simple box cutters to hijack the planes, but the box cutters were no more than the "keys" that allowed the terrorists to convert a high-tech means of transport into a high-tech weapon of mass destruction. Once the hijackers had used these keys to access and turn on their weapon, they were able to deliver a kiloton of explosive power into the World Trade Center with deadly accuracy.

## High-Tech Hubris

The vulnerability of advanced nations stems not only from the greater destructive capacities of terrorists, but also from the increased vulnerability of the West's economic and technological systems. This additional vulnerability is the product of two key social and technological developments: first, the growing complexity and interconnectedness of our modern societies; and second, the increasing geographic concentration of wealth, human capital, knowledge, and communication links.

Consider the first of these developments. All human societies encompass a multitude of economic and technological systems. We can think of these systems as networks—that is, as sets of nodes and links among those nodes. The U.S. economy consists of numerous nodes, including corporations, factories, and urban centers; it also consists of links among these nodes, such as highways, rail lines, electrical grids, and fiber-optic cables. As societies modernize and become richer, their networks become more complex and interconnected. The number of nodes increases, as does the density of links among the nodes and the speed at which materials, energy, and information are pushed along these links. Moreover, the nodes themselves become more complex as the people who create, operate, and manage them strive for better performance. (For instance, a manufacturing company might improve efficiency by adopting more intricate inventory-control methods.)

Complex and interconnected networks sometimes have features that make their behavior unstable and unpredictable. In particular, they can have feedback loops that produce vicious cycles. A good example is a stock market crash, in which selling drives down prices, which begets more selling. Networks can also be tightly coupled, which means that links among the nodes are short, therefore making it more likely that problems with one node will spread to others. When drivers tailgate at high speeds on freeways, they create a tightly coupled system: A mistake by one driver, or a sudden shock coming from outside the system, such as a deer running across the road, can cause a chain reaction of cars piling onto each other. We've seen such knock-on effects in the U.S. electrical, telephone, and air traffic systems, when a failure in one part of the network has sometimes produced a cascade of failures across the country. Finally, in part because of feedbacks and tight coupling, networks often exhibit nonlinear behavior, meaning that a small shock or perturbation to the network produces a disproportionately large disruption.

Terrorists and other malicious individuals can magnify their own disruptive power by exploiting

these features of complex and interconnected networks. Consider the archetypal lone, nerdy high-school kid hacking away at his computer in his parents' basement who can create a computer virus that produces chaos in global communications and data systems. But there's much more to worry about than just the proliferation of computer viruses. A special investigative commission set up in 1997 by then U.S. President Bill Clinton reported that "growing complexity and interdependence, especially in the energy and communications infrastructures, create an increased possibility that a rather minor and routine disturbance can cascade into a regional outage." The commission continued: "We are convinced that our vulnerabilities are increasing steadily, that the means to exploit those weaknesses are readily available and that the costs [of launching an attack] continue to drop."

Terrorists must be clever to exploit these weaknesses. They must attack the right nodes in the right networks. If they don't, the damage will remain isolated and the overall network will be resilient. Much depends upon the network's level of redundancy—that is, on the degree to which the damaged node's functions can be offloaded to undamaged nodes. As terrorists come to recognize the importance of redundancy, their ability to disable complex networks will improve. Langdon Winner, a theorist of politics and technology, provides the first rule of modern terrorism: "Find the critical but nonredundant parts of the system and sabotage . . . them according to your purposes." Winner concludes that "the science of complexity awaits a Machiavelli or Clausewitz to make the full range of possibilities clear."

The range of possible terrorist attacks has expanded due to a second source of organizational vulnerability in modern economies— the rising concentration of high-value assets in geographically small locations. Advanced societies concentrate valuable things and people in order to achieve economies of scale. Companies in capital-intensive industries can usually reduce the per-unit cost of their goods by building larger production facilities. Moreover, placing expensive equipment and highly skilled people in a single location provides easier access, more efficiencies, and synergies that constitute an important source of wealth. That is why we build places like the World Trade Center.

In so doing, however, we also create extraordinarily attractive targets for terrorists, who realize they can cause a huge amount of damage in a single strike. On September 11, a building complex that took seven years to construct collapsed in 90 minutes, obliterating 10 million square feet of office space and exacting at least $30 billion in direct costs. A major telephone switching office was destroyed, another heavily damaged, and important cellular antennas on top of the towers were lost. Key transit lines through southern Manhattan were buried under rubble. Ironically, even a secret office of the U.S. Central Intelligence Agency was destroyed in the attack, temporarily disrupting normal intelligence operations.

Yet despite the horrific damage to the area's infrastructure and New York City's economy, the attack did not cause catastrophic failures in U.S. financial, economic, or communications networks. As it turned out, the World Trade Center was not a critical, nonredundant node. At least it wasn't critical in the way most people (including, probably, the terrorists) would have thought. Many of the financial firms in the destroyed buildings had made contingency plans for disaster by setting up alternate facilities for data, information, and computer equipment in remote locations. Though the NASDAQ headquarters was demolished, for instance, the exchange's data centers in Connecticut and Maryland remained linked to trading companies through two separate connections that passed through 20 switching centers. NASDAQ officials later claimed that their system was so robust that they could have restarted trading only a few hours after the attack. Some World Trade Center firms had made advanced arrangements with companies specializing in providing emergency relocation facilities in New Jersey and elsewhere. Because of all this proactive planning—and the network redundancy it produced—the September 11 attacks caused remarkably little direct disruption to the U.S. financial system (despite the unprecedented closure of the stock market for several days).

To maximize their psychological impact, the perpetrators of complex terrorism will carry

out their attacks in audacious, even bizarre, manners—using methods that are unimaginably cruel.

But when we look back years from now, we may recognize that the attacks had a critical effect on another kind of network that we've created among ourselves: a tightly coupled, very unstable, and highly nonlinear psychological network. We're all nodes in this particular network, and the links among us consist of Internet connections, satellite signals, fiber-optic cables, talk radio, and 24-hour television news. In the minutes following the attack, coverage of the story flashed across his network. People then stayed in front of their televisions for hours on end; they viewed and reviewed the awful video clips on the CNN Web site; they plugged phone lines checking on friends and relatives; and they sent each other millions upon millions of e-mail messages—so many, in fact, that the Internet was noticeably slower for days afterwards.

Along these links, from TV and radio stations to their audiences, and especially from person to person through the Internet, flowed raw emotion: grief, anger, horror, disbelief, fear, and hatred. It was as if we'd all been wired into one immense, convulsing, and reverberating neural network. Indeed, the biggest impact of the September 11 attacks wasn't the direct disruption of financial, economic, communications, or transportation networks—physical stuff, all. Rather, by working through the network we've created within and among our heads, the attacks had their biggest impact on our collective psychology and our subjective feelings of security and safety. This network acts like a huge megaphone, vastly amplifying the emotional impact of terrorism.

To maximize this impact, the perpetrators of complex terrorism will carry out their attacks in audacious, unexpected, and even bizarre manners—using methods that are, ideally, unimaginably cruel. By so doing, they will create the impression that anything is possible, which further magnifies fear. From this perspective, the World Trade Center represented an ideal target, because the Twin Towers were an icon of the magnificence and boldness of American capitalism. When they collapsed like a house of cards, in about 15 seconds each, it suggested that American capitalism was a house of cards, too. How could anything so solid and powerful and so much a part of American identity vanish so quickly? And the use of passenger airplanes made matters worse by exploiting our worst fears of flying.

Large gas pipelines, many of which run near urban areas, have huge explosive potential; attacks on them could produce great local damage and wider disruptions in the energy supply.

Unfortunately, this emotional response has had huge, real-world consequences. Scared, insecure, grief-stricken people aren't ebullient consumers. They behave cautiously and save more. Consumer demand drops, corporate investment falls, and economic growth slows. In the end, via the multiplier effect of our technology-amplified emotional response, the September 11 terrorists may have achieved an economic impact far greater than they ever dreamed possible. The total cost of lost economic growth and decreased equity value around the world could exceed a trillion dollars. Since the cost of carrying out the attack itself was probably only a few hundred thousand dollars, we're looking at an economic multiplier of over a millionfold.

## The Weakest Links

Complex terrorism operates like jujitsu—it redirects the energies of our intricate societies against us. Once the basic logic of complex terrorism is understood (and the events of September 11 prove that terrorists are beginning to understand it), we can quickly identify dozens of relatively simple ways to bring modern, high-tech societies to their knees.

How would a Clausewitz of terrorism proceed? He would pinpoint the critical complex networks upon which modern societies depend. They include networks for producing and distributing energy, information, water, and food; the highways, railways, and airports that make up our transportation grid; and our healthcare system. Of these, the vulnerability of the food system is particularly alarming [see sidebar on opposite page]. However, terrorism experts have paid the most attention to the energy and information networks, mainly because they so clearly underpin the vitality of modern economies.

The energy system—which comprises everything from the national network of gas pipelines to the electricity grid—is replete with high-value nodes like oil refineries, tank farms, and electrical substations. At times of peak energy demand, this network (and in particular, the electricity grid) is very tightly coupled. The loss of one link in the grid means that the electricity it carries must be offloaded to other links. If other links are already operating near capacity, the additional load can cause them to fail, too, thus displacing their energy to yet other links. We saw this kind of breakdown in August 1996, when the failure of the Big Eddy transmission line in northern Oregon caused overloading on a string of transmission lines down the West Coast of the United States, triggering blackouts that affected 4 million people in nine states.

Substations are clear targets because they represent key nodes linked to many other parts of the electrical network. Substations and high-voltage transmission lines are also "soft" targets, since they can be fairly easily disabled or destroyed. Tens of thousands of miles of transmission lines are strung across North America, often in locations so remote that the lines are almost impossible to protect, but they are nonetheless accessible by four-wheel drive. Transmission towers can be brought down with well-placed explosive charges. Imagine a carefully planned sequence of attacks on these lines, with emergency crews and investigators dashing from one remote attack site to another, constantly off-balance and unable to regain control. Detailed maps of locations of substations and transmission lines for much of North America are easily available on the Web. Not even all the police and military personnel in the United States would suffice to provide even rudimentary protection to this immense network.

The energy system also provides countless opportunities for turning supposedly benign technology to destructive ends. For instance, large gas pipelines, many of which run near or even through urban areas, have huge explosive

---

**Feeding Frenzies**

Shorting out electrical grids or causing train derailments would be small-scale sabotage compared with terrorist attacks that intentionally exploit psychological vulnerabilities. One key vulnerability is our fear for our health—an attack that exploits this fear would foster widespread panic. Probably the easiest way to strike at the health of an industrialized nation is through its food-supply system.

Modern food-supply systems display many key features that a prospective terrorist would seek in a complex network and are thus highly vulnerable to attack. Such systems are tightly coupled, and they have many nodes—including huge factory farms and food-processing plants—with multiple connections to other nodes.

The recent foot-and-mouth disease crisis in the United Kingdom provided dramatic evidence of these characteristics. By the time veterinarians found the disease, it had already spread throughout Great Britain. As in the United States, the drive for economic efficiencies in the British farming sector has produced a highly integrated system in which foods move briskly from farm to table. It has also led to economic concentration, with a few immense abattoirs scattered across the land replacing the country's many small slaughterhouses. Foot-and-mouth disease spread rapidly in large part because infected animals were shipped from farms to these distant abattoirs.

Given these characteristics, foot-and-mouth disease seems a useful vector for a terrorist attack. The virus is endemic in much of the world and thus easy to obtain. Terrorists could contaminate 20 or 30 large livestock farms or ranches across the United States, allowing the

*(Continued)*

(Continued)

disease to spread through the network, as it did in Great Britain. Such an attack would probably bring the U.S. cattle, sheep, and pig industries to a halt in a matter of weeks, costing the economy tens of billions of dollars.

Despite the potential economic impact of such an attack, however, it wouldn't have the huge psychological effect that terrorists value, because foot-and-mouth disease rarely affects humans. Far more dramatic would be the poisoning of our food supply. Here the possibilities are legion. For instance, grain storage and transportation networks in the United States are easily accessible; unprotected grain silos dot the countryside and railway cars filled with grain often sit for long periods on railway sidings. Attackers could break into these silos and grain cars to deposit small amounts of contaminants, which would then diffuse through the food system.

Polychlorinated biphenyls (PCBS)—easily found in the oil in old electrical transformers—are a particularly potent group of contaminants, in part because they contain trace amounts of dioxins. These chemicals are both carcinogenic and neurotoxic; they also disrupt the human endocrine system. Children in particular are vulnerable. Imagine the public hysteria if, several weeks after grain silos and railway cars had been laced with PCBS and the poison had spread throughout the food network, terrorists publicly suggested that health authorities test food products for PCB contamination. (U.S. federal food inspectors might detect the PCBS on their own, but the inspection system is stretched very thin and contamination could easily be missed.) At that point, millions of people could have already eaten the products.

Such a contamination scenario is not in the realm of science fiction or conspiracy theories. In January 1999, 500 tons of animal feed in Belgium were accidentally contaminated with approximately 50 kilograms of PCBS from transformer oil. Some 10 million people in Belgium, the Netherlands, France, and Germany subsequently ate the contaminated food products. This single incident may in time cause up to 8,000 cases of cancer.

*—T.H.D.*

potential; attacks on them could have the twin effect of producing great local damage and wider disruptions in energy supply. And the radioactive waste pools associated with most nuclear reactors are perhaps the most lethal targets in the national energy-supply system. If the waste in these facilities were dispersed into the environment, the results could be catastrophic. Fortunately, such attacks would be technically difficult.

Even beyond energy networks, opportunities to release the destructive power of benign technologies abound. Chemical plants are especially tempting targets, because they are packed with toxins and flammable, even explosive, materials. Security at such facilities is often lax: An April 1999 study of chemical plants in Nevada and West Virginia by the U.S. Agency for Toxic Substances and Disease Registry concluded that security ranged from "fair to very

poor" and that oversights were linked to "complacency and lack of awareness of the threat." And every day, trains carrying tens of thousands of tons of toxic material course along transport corridors throughout the United States. All a terrorist needs is inside knowledge that a chemical-laden train is traveling through an urban area at a specific time, and a well-placed object (like a piece of rail) on the track could cause a wreck, a chemical release, and a mass evacuation. A derailment of such a train at a nonredundant link in the transport system—such as an important tunnel or bridge—could be particularly potent. (In fact, when the U.S. bombing campaign in Afghanistan began on October 7, 2001, the U.S. railroad industry declared a three-day moratorium on transporting dangerous chemicals.) Recent accidents in Switzerland and Baltimore, Maryland, make clear that rail and highway tunnels are vulnerable because they are choke

points for transportation networks and because it's extraordinarily hard to extinguish explosions and fires inside them.

Modern communications networks also are susceptible to terrorist attacks. Although the Internet was originally designed to keep working even if large chunks of the network were lost (as might happen in a nuclear war, for instance), today's Internet displays some striking vulnerabilities. One of the most significant is the system of computers—called "routers" and "root servers"—that directs traffic around the Net. Routers represent critical nodes in the network and depend on each other for details on where to send packets of information. A software error in one router, or its malicious reprogramming by a hacker, can lead to errors throughout the Internet. Hackers could also exploit new peer-to-peer software (such as the information-transfer tool Gnutella) to distribute throughout the Internet millions of "sleeper" viruses programmed to attack specific machines or the network itself at a predetermined date.

The U.S. government is aware of many of these threats and of the specific vulnerability of complex networks, especially information networks. President George W. Bush has appointed Richard Clarke, a career civil servant and senior advisor to the National Security Council on counterterrorism, as his cyberspace security czar, reporting both to Director of Homeland Security Tom Ridge and National Security Advisor Condoleezza Rice. In addition, the U.S. Senate recently considered new legislation (the Critical Infrastructure Information Security Act) addressing a major obstacle to improved security of critical networks: the understandable reluctance of firms to share proprietary information about networks they have built or manage. The act would enable the sharing of sensitive infrastructure information between the federal government and private sector and within the private sector itself. In his opening remarks to introduce the act on September 25, 2001, Republican Sen. Bob Bennett of Utah clearly recognized that we face a new kind of threat. "The American economy is a highly interdependent system of systems, with physical and cyber components," he declared.

"Security in a networked world must be a shared responsibility."

## Preparing for the Unknown

Shortly following the September 11 attacks, the U.S. Army enlisted the help of some of Hollywood's top action screenwriters and directors—including the writers of *Die Hard* and *McGyver*—to conjure up possible scenarios for future terrorist attacks. Yet no one can possibly imagine in advance all the novel opportunities for terrorism provided by our technological and economic systems. We've made these critical systems so complex that they are replete with vulnerabilities that are very hard to anticipate, because we don't even know how to ask the right questions. We can think of these possibilities as "exploitable unknown unknowns." Terrorists can make connections between components of complex systems—such as between passenger airliners and skyscrapers—that few, if any, people have anticipated. Complex terrorism is particularly effective if its goal is not a specific strategic or political end, but simply the creation of widespread fear, panic, and economic disruption. This more general objective grants terrorists much more latitude in their choice of targets. More likely than not, the next major attack will come in a form as unexpected as we witnessed on September 11.

What should we do to lessen the risk of complex terrorism, beyond the conventional counterterrorism strategies already being implemented by the United States and other nations? First, we must acknowledge our own limitations. Little can be done, for instance, about terrorists' inexorably rising capacity for violence. This trend results from deep technological forces that can't be stopped without producing major disruptions elsewhere in our economies and societies. However, we can take steps to reduce the vulnerabilities related to our complex economies and technologies. We can do so by loosening the couplings in our economic and technological networks, building into these networks various buffering capacities, introducing "circuit breakers" that interrupt dangerous feedbacks, and dispersing high-value assets so that they are less concentrated and thus less inviting targets.

These prescriptions will mean different things for different networks. In the energy sector, loosening coupling might mean greater use of decentralized, local energy production and alternative energy sources (like small-scale solar power) that make individual users more independent of the electricity grid. Similarly, in food production, loosening coupling could entail increased autonomy of local and regional food-production networks so that when one network is attacked the damage doesn't cascade into others. In many industries, increasing buffering would involve moving away from just-in-time production processes. Firms would need to increase inventories of feedstocks and parts so production can continue even when the supply of these essential inputs is interrupted. Clearly this policy would reduce economic efficiency, but the extra security of more stable and resilient production networks could far outweigh this cost.

Circuit breakers would prove particularly useful in situations where crowd behavior and panic can get out of control. They have already been implemented on the New York Stock Exchange: Trading halts if the market plunges more than a certain percentage in a particular period of time. In the case of terrorism, one of the factors heightening public anxiety is the incessant barrage of sensational reporting and commentary by 24-hour news TV. As is true for the stock exchange, there might be a role for an independent, industry-based monitoring body here, a body that could intervene with broadcasters at critical moments, or at least provide vital counsel, to manage the flow and content of information. In an emergency, for instance, all broadcasters might present exactly the same information (vetted by the monitoring body and stated deliberately and calmly) so that competition among broadcasters doesn't encourage sensationalized treatment. If the monitoring body were under the strict authority of the broadcasters themselves, the broadcasters would—collectively—retain complete control over the content of the message, and the procedure would not involve government encroachment on freedom of speech.

If terrorist attacks continue, economic forces alone will likely encourage the dispersal of high-value assets. Insurance costs could become unsupportable for businesses and industries located in vulnerable zones. In 20 to 30 years, we may be astonished at the folly of housing so much value in the exquisitely fragile buildings of the World Trade Center. Again, dispersal may entail substantial economic costs, because we'll lose economies of scale and opportunities for synergy.

Yet we have to recognize that we face new circumstances. Past policies are inadequate. The advantage in this war has shifted toward terrorists. Our increased vulnerability—and our newfound recognition of that vulnerability—makes us more risk-averse, while terrorists have become more powerful and more tolerant of risk. (The September 11 attackers, for instance, had an extremely high tolerance for risk, because they were ready and willing to die.) As a result, terrorists have significant leverage to hurt us. Their capacity to exploit this leverage depends on their ability to understand the complex systems that we depend on so critically. Our capacity to defend ourselves depends on that same understanding.

---

## Want to Know More?

Many of the ideas introduced in this article are discussed further in Thomas Homer-Dixon's *The Ingenuity Gap: How Can We Solve the Problems of the Future?* (New York: Alfred A. Knopf, 2000). See especially Chapter 4, which examines the nature and sources of complexity in our societies and technologies, as well as the discussion of the instabilities of complex technological systems and networks in Chapter 7 and of terrorism in Chapter 13.

A comprehensive technical treatment of complexity theory can be found in *Dynamics of Complex Systems* (Reading: Addison-Wesley, 1997) by Yaneer Bar-Yam. This book is not for the faint-hearted, and some knowledge of mathematics is helpful, but Bar-Yam is quite daring in his treatment of the social, political, and security implications of complexity. A truly groundbreaking discussion of the sources of complexity in biological, technological, and social systems is W. Brian Arthur's **"On the Evolution of Complexity"** in *Complexity: Metaphors, Models, and Reality*, edited by G. Cowan, D. Pines, and D. Meltzer (Reading: Addison-Wesley, 1994).

Countless writings examine the implications of rising complexity in our world, but four are particularly stimulating. The seminal discussion of the perils of complex technological systems is Charles Perrow's ***Normal Accidents: Living With High-Risk Technologies*** (New York: Basic Books, 1984). Gene Rochlin examines the unexpected outcomes of the information revolution in ***Trapped in the Net: The Unanticipated Consequences of Computerization*** (Princeton: Princeton University Press, 1997). Langdon Winner's wonderful article **"Complexity and the Limits of Human Understanding"** is rich with insights on the social and cognitive challenges posed by rising complexity. It can be found in a book that is worth reading in its entirety: ***Organized Social Complexity: Challenge to Politics and Policy*** (Princeton: Princeton University Press, 1975), edited by Todd La Porte. For a far more apocalyptic but tremendously provocative study of the risks of greater social complexity, see Joseph Tainter's ***The Collapse of Complex Societies*** (Cambridge: Cambridge University Press, 1988).

On the vulnerabilities of modern infrastructure, see ***Critical Foundations: Protecting America's Infrastructures*** (Washington: President's Commission on Critical Infrastructure Protection, 1997) and Massoud Amin's **"National Infrastructures as Complex Interactive Networks"** in Tariq Samad and John Weyrauch, eds., ***Automation, Control, and Complexity: An Integrated Approach*** (Chichester: John Wiley & Sons, 2000). For a journalistic account of how New York financial firms protected their critical infrastructure in the aftermath of the September 11 attacks, see Tom Foremski's **"How Business Could Survive"** (*Financial Times*, October 10, 2001).

For links to relevant Web sites, as well as a comprehensive index of related FOREIGN POLICY articles, access www.foreignpolicy.com.

---

## The Culture of Martyrdom: How Suicide Bombing Became not Just a Means but an End

### David Brooks

Suicide bombing is the crack cocaine of warfare. It doesn't just inflict death and terror on its victims; it intoxicates the people who sponsor it. It unleashes the deepest and most addictive human passions—the thirst for vengeance, the desire for religious purity, the longing for earthly glory and eternal salvation. Suicide bombing isn't just a tactic in a larger war; it overwhelms the political goals it is meant to serve. It creates its own logic and transforms the culture of those who employ it. This is what has happened in the Arab-Israeli dispute. Over the past year suicide bombing has dramatically changed the nature of the conflict.

Before 1983 there were few suicide bombings. The Koran forbids the taking of one's own life, and this prohibition was still generally observed. But when the United States stationed Marines in Beirut, the leaders of the Islamic resistance movement Hizbollah began to discuss turning to this ultimate terrorist weapon. Religious authorities in Iran gave it their blessing, and a wave of suicide bombings began, starting with the attacks that killed about sixty U.S. embassy workers in April of 1983 and about 240 people in the Marine compound at the airport in October. The bombings proved so successful at driving the United States and, later, Israel out of Lebanon that most lingering religious concerns were set aside.

The tactic was introduced into Palestinian areas only gradually. In 1988 Fathi Shiqaqi, the founder of the Palestinian Islamic Jihad, wrote a set of guidelines (aimed at countering religious objections to the truck bombings of the 1980s) for the use of explosives in individual bombings; nevertheless, he characterized operations calling for martyrdom as "exceptional." But by the mid-1990s the group Hamas was using suicide bombers as a way of derailing the Oslo peace process. The assassination of the master Palestinian bomb maker Yahya Ayyash, presumably by Israeli agents, in January of 1996, set off a series of suicide bombings in retaliation. Suicide bombings nonetheless remained relatively unusual until two years ago, after the Palestinian leader Yasir Arafat walked out of the peace conference at Camp David—a conference at which Israel's Prime Minister, Ehud Barak, had offered to return to the Palestinians parts of Jerusalem and almost all of the West Bank.

At that point the psychology shifted. We will not see peace soon, many Palestinians concluded, but when it eventually comes, we will get everything we want. We will endure, we will fight, and we will suffer for that final victory. From then on the struggle (at least from the Palestinian point of view) was no longer about negotiation and compromise—about who would get which piece of land, which road or river. The red passions of the bombers obliterated the grays of the peace process. Suicide bombing became the tactic of choice, even in circumstances where a terrorist could have planted a bomb and then escaped without injury. Martyrdom became not just a means but an end.

Suicide bombing is a highly communitarian enterprise. According to Ariel Merari, the director of the Political Violence Research Center, at Tel Aviv University, and a leading expert on the phenomenon, in not one instance has a lone, crazed Palestinian gotten hold of a bomb and gone off to kill Israelis. Suicide bombings are initiated by tightly run organizations that recruit, indoctrinate, train, and reward the bombers. Those organizations do not seek depressed or mentally unstable people for their missions. From 1996 to 1999 the Pakistani journalist Nasra Hassan interviewed almost 250 people who were either recruiting and training bombers or preparing to go on a suicide mission themselves. "None of the suicide bombers—they ranged in age from eighteen to thirty-eight—conformed to the typical profile of the suicidal personality," Hassan wrote in *The New Yorker*. "None of them were uneducated, desperately poor, simple-minded, or depressed." The Palestinian bombers tend to be devout, but religious fanaticism does not explain their motivation. Nor does lack of opportunity, because they also tend to be well educated.

Often a bomber believes that a close friend or a member of his family has been killed by Israeli troops, and this is part of his motivation. According to most experts, though, the crucial factor informing the behavior of suicide bombers is loyalty to the group. Suicide bombers go through indoctrination processes similar to the ones that were used by the leaders of the Jim Jones and Solar Temple cults. The bombers are organized into small cells and given countless hours of intense and intimate spiritual training. They are instructed in the details of *jihad*, reminded of the need for revenge, and reassured about the rewards they can expect in the afterlife. They are told that their families will be guaranteed a place with God, and that there are also considerable rewards for their families in this life, including cash bonuses of several thousand dollars donated by the government of Iraq, some individual Saudis, and various groups sympathetic to the cause. Finally, the bombers are told that paradise lies just on the other side of the detonator, that death will feel like nothing more than a pinch.

Members of such groups re-enact past operations. Recruits are sometimes made to lie in empty graves, so that they can see how peaceful death will be; they are reminded that life will bring sickness, old age, and betrayal. "We were in a constant state of worship," one suicide bomber (who somehow managed to survive his mission) told Hassan. "We told each other that if the Israelis only knew how joyful we were they would whip us to death! Those were the happiest days of my life!"

The bombers are instructed to write or videotape final testimony. (A typical note, from 1995: "I am going to take revenge upon the sons of the monkeys and the pigs, the Zionist infidels and the enemies of humanity. I am going to meet my holy brother Hisham Hamed and all the other martyrs and saints in paradise.") Once a bomber has completed his declaration, it would be humiliating for him to back out of the mission. He undergoes a last round of cleansing and prayer and is sent off with his bomb to the appointed pizzeria, coffee shop, disco, or bus.

For many Israelis and Westerners, the strangest aspect of the phenomenon is the televised interview with a bomber's parents after a massacre. These people have just been told that their child has killed himself and others, and yet they seem happy, proud, and—should the opportunity present itself—ready to send another child off to the afterlife. There are two ways to look at this: One, the parents feel so wronged and humiliated by the Israelis that they would rather sacrifice their children than continue passively to endure. Two, the cult of suicide bombing has infected the broader culture to the point where large parts of society, including the bombers' parents, are addicted to the adrenaline rush of vengeance and murder. Both explanations may be true.

It is certainly the case that vast segments of Palestinian culture have been given over to the creation and nurturing of suicide bombers. Martyrdom has replaced Palestinian independence as the main focus of the Arab media. Suicide bombing is, after all, perfectly suited to the television age. The bombers' farewell videos provide compelling footage, as do the interviews with families. The bombings themselves produce graphic images of body parts and devastated buildings. Then there are the "weddings" between the martyrs and dark-eyed virgins in paradise (announcements that read like wedding invitations are printed in local newspapers so that friends and neighbors can join in the festivities), the marches and celebrations after each attack, and the displays of things bought with the cash rewards to the families. Woven together, these images make gripping packages that can be aired again and again.

Activities in support of the bombings are increasingly widespread. Last year the BBC shot a segment about so-called Paradise Camps—summer camps in which children as young as eight are trained in military drills and taught about suicide bombers. Rallies commonly feature children wearing bombers' belts. Fifth- and sixth-graders have studied poems that celebrate the bombers. At Al Najah University, in the West Bank, a student exhibition last September included a re-created scene of the Sbarro pizzeria in Jerusalem after the suicide bombing there last August: "blood" was splattered everywhere, and mock body parts hung from the ceiling as if blown through the air.

Thus suicide bombing has become phenomenally popular. According to polls, 70 to 80 percent of Palestinians now support it—making the act more popular than Hamas, the Palestinian Islamic Jihad, Fatah, or any of the other groups that sponsor it, and far more popular than the peace process ever was. In addition to satisfying visceral emotions, suicide bombing gives average Palestinians, not just PLO elites, a chance to play a glorified role in the fight against Israel.

Opponents of suicide bombings sometimes do raise their heads. Over the last couple of years educators have moderated the tone of textbooks to reduce and in many cases eliminate the rhetoric of holy war. After the BBC report aired, Palestinian officials vowed to close the Paradise Camps. Nonetheless, Palestinian children grow up in a culture in which suicide bombers are rock stars, sports heroes, and religious idols rolled into one. Reporters who speak with Palestinians about the bombers notice the fire and pride in their eyes.

"I'd be very happy if my daughter killed Sharon," one mother told a reporter from *The San Diego Union-Tribune* last November. "Even if she killed two or three Israelis, I would be happy." Last year I attended a dinner party in

Amman at which six distinguished Jordanians—former cabinet ministers and supreme-court justices and a journalist—talked about the Tel Aviv disco bombing, which had occurred a few months earlier. They had some religious qualms about the suicide, but the moral aspect of killing teenage girls—future breeders of Israelis—was not even worth discussing. They spoke of the attack with a quiet sense of satisfaction.

It's hard to know how Israel, and the world, should respond to the rash of suicide bombings and to their embrace by the Palestinian people. To take any action that could be viewed as a concession would be to provoke further attacks, as the U.S. and Israeli withdrawals from Lebanon in the 1980s demonstrated. On the other hand, the Israeli raids on the refugee camps give the suicide bombers a propaganda victory. After Yasir Arafat walked out of the Camp David meetings, he became a pariah to most governments for killing the peace process. Now, amid Israeli retaliation for the bombings, the global community rises to condemn Israel's actions.

Somehow conditions must be established that would allow the frenzy of suicide bombings to burn itself out. To begin with, the Palestinian and Israeli populations would have to be separated; contact between them inflames the passions that feed the attacks. That would mean shutting down the vast majority of Israeli settlements in the West Bank and Gaza and creating a buffer zone between the two populations. Palestinian life would then no longer be dominated by checkpoints and celebrations of martyrdom; it would be dominated by quotidian issues such as commerce, administration, and garbage collection.

The idea of a buffer zone, which is gaining momentum in Israel, is not without problems. Where, exactly, would the buffer be? Terrorist groups could shoot missiles over it. But it's time to face the reality that the best resource the terrorists have is the culture of martyrdom. This culture is presently powerful, but it is potentially fragile. If it can be interrupted, if the passions can be made to recede, then the Palestinians and the Israelis might go back to hating each other in the normal way, and at a distance. As with many addictions, the solution is to go cold turkey.

## REVIEW QUESTIONS

- Are modern scenarios positing terrorists' acquisition of weapons of mass destruction plausible?
- Which terrorist typologies are most likely to use weapons of mass destruction? Why would they use these weapons?
- What kinds of attacks might be launched against economic or communications nodes? How plausible is this threat?
- What effect do suicide bombings have on victim societies?
- In what way is "martyrdom" a logical and legitimate end from the point of view of some terrorist movements?

The following books and articles are suggested for further information about exotic terrorism:

### Books

Alexander, Yonah, and Milton M. Hoenig, eds. *Super Terrorism: Biological, Chemical, and Nuclear*. New York: Transnational Publishers, 2001.

Miller, Judith, Stephen Engelberg, and William Broad. *Germs: Biological Weapons and America's Secret War*. New York: Simon & Schuster, 2001.

Tucker, Jonathan B., ed. *Toxic Terror: Assessing Terrorist Use of Chemical and Biological Weapons*. Cambridge, MA: The MIT Press, 2000.

## Articles

Keller, Bill. "Nuclear Nightmare." *The New York Times Magazine*. (May 26, 2002).

Kuhr, Steven and Jerome M. Hauer. "The Threat of Biological Terrorism in the New Millennium." *American Behavioral Scientist*. 44:6 (February 2001).

Schmid, Alex P. "Terrorism and the Use of Weapons of Mass Destruction: From Where the Risk?" *Terrorism and Political Violence*. 11:45 (Winter 1999).

# 6

---

# The New Era
# of Religious Terrorism

Violence committed "in the name of the faith" has been a feature of human conflict since the early centuries of the previous millennium. Violence committed in the name of the faith is, from a religious terrorist's perspective, desirable and pleasing to their god. In the new era of terrorism, the belief that one group has discovered, and obeys, the dictates of a single and exclusive spiritual truth has been used to justify incidents of horrific terrorist violence. The perpetrators of this violence are nihilistic in the sense that they have only a vague notion of what kind of religious society will replace the existing "apostate" world. What is important to them is that their violence has been sanctioned by their faith and that victory is inevitable–how can one be defeated when God is on their side? Should apocalyptic terrorists acquire weapons of mass destruction, the risk that they will be used is very real.

The articles in this chapter discuss the characteristics and sources of contemporary religious terrorism. In "Just War, Jihad, and Terrorism: A Comparison of Western and Islamic Norms for the Uses of Political Violence," Adam Silverman presents a comparative discussion of cultural justifications for political violence. Just war doctrine and jihad are investigated and defined prior to a discussion of the definition of terrorism. A contextual examination of just war and jihad is made using examples from both traditions. Haim Malka examines the wave of suicide attacks by religious Palestinian organizations against Israel in "Must Innocents Die? The Muslim Debate Over Suicide Attacks." He discusses the underlying religious and utilitarian rationales for these attacks. The fundamental characteristics of the New Terrorism are presented and discussed in Steven Simon's essay "The New Terrorism: Securing the Nation Against a Messianic Foe." The centrality of religious extremism in the new era is investigated, citing Al Qaeda as the quintessential example of a terrorist movement in the emerging environment. Anti-terrorism, international cooperation, and promoting democracy in the Middle East are cited as viable responses to the New Terrorism.

# Just War, Jihad, and Terrorism: A Comparison of Western and Islamic Norms for the Use of Political Violence

Adam L. Silverman

In the wake of the terrorist attacks of 11 September 2001, the attention of many Americans—both policymakers and ordinary citizens—has been captured by a vision of Islam that appears to be militant, reactionary, and violent. Too often this face of Islam is the only face that many in the U.S. actually perceive. We are deluged with nightly reports of "suicide bombings" in Israel, hostage takings in the Philippines, harsh capital punishment in Afghanistan, and the slave trade between the Sudan and Libya. While what we see on the news does actually happen, it does not represent the reality or totality of Islam and the Islamic experience.

The events of 11 September 2001 have refocused American and world attention upon reactionary Islamic extremism. Osama bin Laden, the expatriate Saudi religious leader, and members of his organization, al-Qaeda, however, have emerged as the prime suspects in the ongoing law enforcement investigations into the World Trade Center and Pentagon attacks. All nineteen of the hijackers have been identified as Arab Muslims with ties to Islamic revivalist movements in Algeria, Egypt, Saudi Arabia, the United Arab Emirates, and Yemen. As a result, Americans have taken on a new interest in Islam, as well as the religious and political histories of the Islamic world.

Scholars and analysts who specialize in the study of terrorism were caught flat-footed by the incidents in New York and Washington, D.C. The Islamic identities of the hijackers, an identity based in a unique and peculiar interpretation of Islam not shared by the majority of Muslims, was so powerful that it allowed them to go willingly to their deaths. Thus, while many Americans view these acts as suicidal aggression against noncombatants, the hijackers likely perceived their actions as *jihad* (struggle) and *shahadat* (martyrdom), on behalf of Islam and against its enemies. The inability to either predict these attacks or to understand the motivations of the terrorists is due to the lack of

attention to the power of identity.[1] In order to better understand the recent events of 11 September 2001, as well as other acts of so called Islamic terrorism and "suicide bombings," it is necessary to review what Islam has to say about the use of political violence, compare these Islamic norms with Western norms, and contrast them with the concept of terrorism. This is especially true as very few Muslims actually subscribe to or believe in the type of Islam that has once again grabbed attention in headlines and news reports. Such a review is necessary in order to dispel some of the myths that have developed regarding Islam's position towards the non-Muslim world—myths that have filtered into academia, analysis, and policymaking. The resulting discussion should enhance our understanding of what really happens when Islamic actors engage in terrorism, as well as how groups recontextualize ideas about "just war" and "jihad" in order to justify terrorism.

I will first introduce the concept of just war theory, then discuss the Islamic norms of *jihad* and *shahadat* and briefly review the definition and etiology of terrorism. I will then present Western and Islamic examples and discuss how both just war and jihad are recontextualized in order to justify terrorism.

## METHODS

One of the most effective methodological tools for the study of cultural and contextual based phenomena is constructivism. There are two types of constructivism: tethered/thin and postmodern/thick constructivism.[2] As this inquiry is intended to present Western and Islamic norms pertaining to the use of warfare and political violence, I have chosen to utilize tethered/thin constructivism, also referred to as positivist constructivism.

This methodology developed within the field of cultural sociology and social anthropology in order to account for cultural and contextual matters, especially in a comparative framework, while also providing some form of empirical results. In tethered constructivism, the researcher attempts to establish a baseline against which comparisons can be made since tethered constructivism begins with the normative assumption that verifiable results can be obtained. Conversely, postmodern/thick constructivism begins with the opposite assumption—that all results are culturally specific and relative.

In this research, I intend to estalish a Western and Islamic baseline. This baseline, the actual norms regarding warfare and political violence in both the Western and Islamic traditions, will then be contrasted with the concept of terrorism. This baseline will develop out of the textual evidence pertaining to these norms. An important part of the discussion of the similarities between just war, *jihad,* and *shahadat,* as well as how these norms are used to justify terrorism and other deviant actions, centers around the concept of recontextualizing an identity group's ideational components. Recontextualization occurs when members of a given tradition foreground[3] portions of their cultural contents. Through recontextualization, leaders and adherents de-emphasize societal and cultural elements perceived to be superfluous. Instead, focus and emphasis is placed on very specific pieces of content and context. Consequently, the conditions of the past that once allowed for certain types of action and behavior are overlaid on the conditions of the present. Through recontextualization, members of identity-based groups are able to maintain their subcultural boundaries while promoting, justifying, and restricting specific behaviors.

## The Just War Tradition[4]

The just war tradition is intimately connected with the development of both the Western Christian tradition and the modern states that have developed from it. Augustine of Hippo was the first theologian to develop a set of criteria for what is termed a just war. Augustine set down these criteria to ensure that if war had to be fought, it would only be fought after deliberate moral consideration of all alternatives.[5]

He partially based his work on that of the Roman statesman Cicero, who attempted to reconcile Socratic, Platonic, and Aristotelian concepts of warfare with those of the Roman legal code.[6] Several centuries after Augustine, Thomas Aquinas developed a four-criteria system in the thirteenth century, based partially on Christian theology and partially on Aristotelian ethics.[7]

In order to create an ethical juxtaposition of the moral uses of force, the just war tradition criteria seek to make a virtue out of an immoral necessity—violence and killing. It is very important, however, that, in an attempt to justify the need for war, necessity is not reduced to utility.[8] When this occurs, it is possible to justify almost anything as being necessary. In attempting to make this point. Michael Walzer has argued that supreme necessity in an emergency can be used to justify a means of war that would not normally be permissible under the just war criteria[9]: the bombings of Dresden and Hiroshima/Nagasaki are examples. Another important reason for the just war tradition is to reassure those who must resort to force that they are not simply committing murder.[10]

Within the just war tradition, three different but interconnected sets of criteria have evolved. The first set, *bellum justum,* contains overarching criteria that apply to both of the other two sets: the *jus ad bellum* and the *jus in bello* criteria. The *bellum justum* requires that (1) the proportion of good from the outcome of the war must outweigh the war's potential for harm, (2) the probability of success must outweigh the probability of defeat, and (3) all reasonable peaceful remedies must be exhausted prior to a state's entering into a given conflict.[11]

The *jus ad bellum* criteria comprise three points that apply to whether or not a just war state can enter into a conflict. These requirements are (1) the war must be called for/initiated by a competent authority, (2) just cause—specifically, either individual or collective self-defense or the offensive protection of one's rights, and (3) right intention prior to initiating war. These criteria, governing a state's entrance into conflict, are intended to ensure that a given war will be entered into lawfully, that it will be fought in a redressive rather than a retaliatory manner, and that the war will be contested on the basis of morally acceptable intentions.[12]

The final three just war criteria are referred to as *jus in bello* and are intended to govern the conduct of the state once a conflict has been joined. These require the state to (1) utilize military means in prosecuting the war that are proportional to the state's political and military ends, (2) discriminate in targeting and tactics (a state may not attack non-combatants and non-military targets), and (3) the prohibition of certain military means—disproportionate types of combat and military conduct are prohibited.[13]

Although the nine criteria of the just war tradition are interconnected, it would appear that several of them make competing and often opposing claims upon a combatant. For instance, the *in bello* criterion of proportionality allows for a reciprocal reprisal by a just war state against a non-just war state. An example of this would be the Allied firebombing of Dresden that was a response to the German aerial blitz on London, Coventry, and other British cities. While the Dresden firebombing appears to be allowable under the proportionality criteria, it seems to violate the prohibitions concerning appropriate targeting and tactics. This example of the often-conflicting nature of the just war criteria is not unique; other examples, such as the atomic bombings of Hiroshima and Nagasaki would also seem to fall outside of the just war tradition's attempt to place force and morality side by side.

If the Dresden firebombing can be covered by the just war tradition, so too can the atomic bombings of Hiroshima and Nagasaki. The Dresden bombings were acceptable because they allowed for a successful prosecution of the war against an enemy that was not adhering to a just war tradition and likely would have continued to engage in horrific acts of evil and depravity had it won that war. In the case of Hiroshima and Nagasaki, it was necessary in the estimations of U.S. decision makers to use the atomic bombs in order to make the Japanese realize that they would not, and could not, win the war and that there was no need to fight to the last man, woman, and child. In the Japanese example, the criteria of proportionality also comes into play: the nuclear destruction of Hiroshima and Nagasaki arguably saved more lives, both Japanese and Allied, than it took, by bringing the war to an end sooner rather than later.[14]

## JIHAD AND SHAHADAT[15]

### Jihad

*Jihad* is an Arabic word that means "struggle." In its Islamic context, it can refer to everything from striving to be a better person to waging war on behalf of G-d. The plasticity of the word, especially in regard to its context, has made it the source for much debate. In the West, however, it has become a synonym for the terms "holy war" and "terrorism." The pigeonholing of both the term and its range of meanings does a disservice and often leads to a misunderstanding of Islamic behavior. In order to understand the meaning of *jihad* in its proper context, one must know how it is used in the *Qur'an*. The oldest reference to *jihad* in the *Qur'an* is in *Sura al-Haj*.[16]

> To those against whom war is made, permission is given to fight, because they are wronged;—and truly, G-d is most powerful for their aid;—They are those who have been expelled from their homes in defiance of right—for no cause except that they say "Our Lord is G-d." Did not G-d check one set of people by means of another, There would surely have been pulled down monasteries and churches, synagogues and mosques, in which the name of G-d is commemorated in abundant measure. G-d will certainly aid those who aid His cause;—for verily G-d is full of strength, exalted in might, and able to enforce his will.

Verses 39–40, the oldest verses revealed regarding *jihad,* establish how, when, and why *jihad* may be waged. In order for one to engage in *jihad,* one must be defending oneself and attempting to redress an unjust action. These verses address two of the criteria for just war: 1) the criterion of right intention, and 2) the criteria of proportionality. They indicate that one can only act in order to right a wrong and in defense.

It is also important to understand the historical context in which these verses were revealed.

Abdullah Yusuf Ali, a translator of and commentator on the *Qur'an,* indicates that these *ayat* were revealed during the Medinan period. It was at this time that the Prophet and his followers were no longer able to avoid violence with the Meccans,[17] avoidance that had taken the form of two types of self imposed exile, to Ethiopia and to Medina. In other words, these verses were revealed on the first occasion when violence was not only necessary for defense of the Muslim community, but also unavoidable.

There is also another verse within *Sura* XXII that is of vital importance to the analysis of the nature of *jihad.* Verse sixty states: "And if one has retaliated to no greater extent then the injury he received, and is again set upon inordinately, G-d will help him: for G-d's is one that blots out sins and forgives again and again."[18] This *ayat* clearly shows that *jihad* includes a concept of proportionality; one may not respond in greater manner then he received.

Two sets of verses in *Sura* VIII, *Sura al-Anfal,* provide instructions about what to do prior to resorting to war. "Against them make ready your strength to the utmost of your power including steeds of war, to strike terror into the hearts of the enemies of G-d and your enemies, and others besides, whom you may not know but G-d does know."[19] This verse seems to instruct Muslims to assemble a force as a deterrent to war. Verse sixty-one of the same *sura* indicates that there should be, whenever possible, an inclination towards peaceful solutions and relations. "But if the enemy incline towards peace, you too should incline towards peace, and trust in G-d: for He is the one that hears and knows all things."[20] These two verses taken together seem to create an analogue to the third criteria of the West's just war theory, that war should be the last resort.

In the second *sura* of the *Qur'an, Sura al-Baqara* there are two verses that provide an Islamic mirror of the second and sixth just war criteria, right intention and moderation. Verse 190 clearly indicates that there are limits that cannot be crossed in the implementation of *jihad.* "Fight in the cause of G-d those who fight you, but do not transgress limits, for G-d loves not those who transgress"[21] clearly declares that there is a limit beyond which Muslims cannot go

in their struggles/wars with others. Verse 193 of the same *sura* delineates just what the struggle is to be fought for. "And fight them until there is no more tumult or oppression, and there prevail justice and faith in G-d; but if they cease let there be no hostility except to those who practice oppression."[22] Moreover, there is a verse that clearly proscribes what *jihad* cannot be used for; it cannot be used to impose faith. *Sura* 2: 256 states "let there be no compulsion in religion." This makes it quite evident that one is not to force faith on another. Similar to this is a verse from *Sura* IX, *Sura al-Tawba,* which states that the Muslim should even fight against "the People of the Book" (Jews and Christians), but only "until they pay the *jizyah* (the head tax)."[23] Here religion cannot be forced, and hostilities must cease once the head tax is paid.

This set of Islamic precepts for the use of political violence, however, has been interpreted and applied in an interesting manner. Shortly after the death of Prophet Muhammad, many of the Arabian tribes that had accepted his authority and converted to Islam began to abandon the Islamic community.[24] The leaders of these tribes argued that since their agreements to enter into Islam and submit to Islamic authority were made with Muhammad, these agreements ceased to be binding after his death. As a result, the Islamic community, the *ummah,* faced a challenge to authority and loss of social, political, economic, and religious cohesion. The response of Abu Bakr, Muhammed's successor as leader of the Muslims, was to declare the Arab tribes apostate. Abu Bakr justified the use of force to bring them back into the *ummah* and under Islamic control as an attempt to control apostasy. These conflicts are referred to as the *ridda* wars or wars of apostasy.[25]

Once these tribes were subdued, Abu Bakr turned the attention of the *ummah,* including the warriors of the Arab tribes, to spreading the message of Islam. Abu Bakr emphasized the *Qur'an*ic imperatives to bring the teachings of Islam to all those who had not received it[26] and de-emphasized the prohibition about forcing adherence to religion. Consequently, Abu Bakr was able to accomplish two very important objectives. He essentially neutralized the internal threat of the Arab tribesmen by directing their energy to those outside of Islam. And by directing the tribesmen's attention towards the frontiers and borders of Islam, he was able to use them to expand Islam's sphere of influence and enlarge the Islamic community.

Abu Bakr's use of the concept of *jihad* is both an example of its normative use and its recontextualization. As caliph, Abu Bakr was empowered to issue the call for *jihad* and in this respect his actions were normative. He recontextualized *jihad,* however, by ignoring the injunction against compulsion in religion. By sending his troops out beyond the borders of Islam in order to subdue these areas and bring Islam to their inhabitants, he seems to have violated one of the provisions that govern the use of *jihad.* The manner in which Abu Bakr understood and used *jihad* was followed by his immediate successors as caliph, Umar and Uthman, who followed his lead in expanding and consolidating Islamic holdings and acquisitions.

All of the Islamic interpretations of *jihad* are ultimately based on the *Qur'an.* While not all of the verses that deal with *jihad* have been presented (a full list would include more than thirty *ayat* in some ten different *suras*), those that have been presented are fairly representative of the nature and tone of the totality of the revelations regarding *jihad.* On this subject, what remains to be done is to explore how Muslims have interpreted these passages about *jihad.* During the medieval Islamic period, several legal scholars advocated a very militant view of *jihad.* For these *mujtahids,*[27] *jihad* is not merely an internal struggle to be a good Muslim, but also an external fight in order to protect Islam from non-Muslim aggression. The first of these advocates was Ibn Hazm al-Andulusi (d. 1064 CE). Al-Andulusi, as well as his contemporaries Ibn Salamah (d. 1032 CE) and *Qadi*[28] Iyadh (d. 1149 CE), called for the waging of *jihad* as a *fard ayn,* a personal obligation.[29] The Hanbali scholar Taqi al-Din ibn Taymiyyah (d. 1328 CE) expanded this belief that every Muslim had to wage an external battle on behalf of Islam. Ibn Taymiyyah seems to be the personal embodiment of the militant theoretician and activist defender of the faith. Not only did he call for *jihad* against the Mongols, *Ismailis,*

*Alawis,* and *Druze,* he wished to place heavy restrictions on non-Muslims living under Muslim rule.[30] Fighting in a *jihad* for Ibn Taymiyyah constituted a higher obligation than *haj*/pilgrimage, *salat*/prayer, or *zom*/fasting.[31]

Ibn Taymiyyah practiced what he preached: he actually went and fought against the Tatars.[32] It is this piece of information that provides us with the vital clue as to why Ibn Taymiyyah adopted such an extreme view of *jihad.* During his lifetime, the Tatars threatened the borders of Islam as they attempted to cut a swath across Central Asia and Asia Minor. Ibn Taymiyyah's call for *jihad* was, at its root, a call for defense against invasion. Moreover, his calls for *jihad* against the *Ismailis, Alawis,* and *Druze* were an attempt to fulfill those revelations about *jihad* that call for *jihad* against disbelief and hypocrisy, symptoms each of these three alternate Islamic systems seem to put forward in the view of traditional Islam. Many of the later scholars who advance a concept of *jihad* against all that is not Islam, such as Muhammad Ibn Abd al-Wahhab, Rashid Rida, Abu al-Ala Mawdudi, Sayyid Qutb, Shakri Mustafa, Abd al-Salam Faraj, and Juhayman al-Utaybi, often call upon the rulings and interpretations of Ibn Taymiyyah. They attempt to achieve what Ibn Taymiyyah did in his jurisprudence: draw a connection between their situation and his, just as he attempted in his time and circumstances and those of the imperiled Medinans.

In many places, the interpretation of *jihad* goes hand in hand with an attempt to implement the *Qur'an*ic injunction to command the good and forbid the evil. The formation of a right and just society is one of the examples of implementing this injunction. Islam tries to establish a society that covers all aspects of human life that has political and economic aspects, and that commands the good and forbids the evil. This struggle is also *jihad.*[33] Murtada Mutahhari posits that while war can be aggressive, *jihad* is a response to aggression that has conditions.[34] The conditions are that the adversary must be in a state of aggression towards an Islamic community and/or that the adversary is unjustly oppressing some group, either Muslim or non-Muslim.[35] Furthermore, *jihad* encompasses the defense of life, property, wealth, land, independence, and principles. The most valuable form of *jihad* is not in defense of oneself, but rather in defense of humanity and human rights.[36] Those that perform this type of *jihad* literally and figuratively enjoin the good and forbid the evil.

## Shahadat

In the *Qur'an,* there are twelve verses that deal directly with the concept of *shahadat/*martyrdom. Among these, the three most interesting and important are verse 169 in *Sura* III, *Sura al-i-Imran,* and verses 58 and 59 of *Sura* XXII, *Sura al-Hajj. Qur'an* 3:169 declares: "Think not of those who are slain in the way of G-d as dead. Nay, they live finding their sustenance in the presence of their Lord."[37] *Ayat* 58 and 59 of *Sura* XXII declare: "Those who leave their homes in the cause of Allah and are then slain or die—on them will G-d bestow verily a good Provision: truly G-d is he who bestows the best Provision. Truly He will admit them to a place with which they shall be well pleased: for G-d is all-knowing, most forbearing."[38] These verses imply that those who become *shahids* do not really die; in fact they are to receive an excellent reward in the afterlife. As a result of what these verses reveal, one of the greatest Western misconceptions about Islamic political behavior can be resolved. Those who participate in self-martyring operations are not committing suicide by doing so, and do not receive the Islamic stigma associated with one who commits suicide. This is supported by many interpretations. Ahmad Ibn Naqib al-Misri writes that:

> There is no disagreement among scholars that it is permissible for a single Muslim to attack battle lines of unbelievers headlong and fight them even if he knows he will be killed. But if one knows that he will not hurt them at all, such as if a blind man were to hurl himself against them, then it is unlawful.[39]

Al-Misri's interpretation further removes the stigma of suicide from the *shahid*. He does indicate, however, that a probable degree of success is a requirement for this type of action. It is this belief that the *shahid* is exalted before the Lord that has long made the *shahid* a model for Islamic behavior. Those companions of the Prophet who threw themselves into battle at the *ghazwas,* raids on behalf of Islam, at Badr and Uhud, did so against amazing odds. At Badr, the Muslim combatants were outnumbered by more than three to one.[40] Some of the most prominent Muslims fell at these early battles while others died later and in other ways; the most notable of these are Ali ibn Abi Talib and his son Husayn. 'Ali survived all of the *ghazwa* only to become a *shahid* much later in his life when he was assassinated by the *kharijites.* Husayn was martyred when he refused to accept the political authority of the Ummayid dynasty, the regime that Muawiya established.

'Ali Shari'ati, using the examples of those who fell in the *ghazwas* and those who became *shahids* later in life, developed two distinct types of *shahadat.* The first type of *shahid* is one who gives up his life through *jihad;* he is chosen by *shahadat.* The second type rebels and consciously welcomes death; he chooses his own *shahadat.*[41] The most revered of the *shahids* that chose *shahadat* was Husayn. He was killed after refusing to avoid a confrontation with a regime, which though illegitimate, vastly outnumbered Husayn's forces. Husayn's example, which only involved injury and death to combatants, has been used to legitimate martyrdom that have inflicted many collateral deaths on non-combatants. The reason that some willingly choose this new type of self-martyrdom is that *shahadat* is seen as a way to draw attention to injustice so that action can be taken against it.

## TERRORISM

Before examining the relationship between religiously inspired violence and terrorism, it is necessary to explore the definition of terrorism. Traditionally, terrorism is defined as the systematic use of violence by individuals to create and utilize the fear and intimidation caused by their actions to bring about socio-political change.[42] While this definition explains terrorism from the law enforcement perspective, it fails to account for many of the important structural components of terrorism. As a result, I suggest the following alternative etiology:

> Terrorism is the systematic use of violence by actors who have a subcultural identity attachment—either subjective or objective. Terrorism is the attempt to bring about social and political change through fear and intimidation. Terrorism is one way that subcultural actors attempt to resolve the disputes between themselves and the larger culture or between themselves and other subcultures. Terrorism is an attempt to assert the constitutive and regulatory subcultural norms of the actors onto the larger culture and/or other subcultures.

This subculturally based definition of terrorism takes into account several important concepts that are left out of the traditional law enforcement perspective. For instance, it places the terrorist within a specific context—the subculture. The subculture provides the terrorist with his identity and his ideational and physical resources, as well as an understanding of the disputes and grievances that need to be resolved. While not all subcultures spawn terrorism, or all subcultural members become terrorists, the literature on terrorism has as one of its primary focuses the identity basis of terrorist groups. Moreover, grievances that need to be addressed also often arise out of one's identity.[43]

The terrorist attacks of 11 September 2001, as well as a good deal of the other terrorist incidents that occur, seem to be related to the identity-based grievances of the terrorists. The martyrs of the *Hamas, Hezbullah,* and Islamic Jihad all have specific identity-based grievances for their actions: the existence of Israel and the lack of an Islamically acceptable society and polity.

Even the terrorism of Timothy McVeigh is based on his adoption of the identity of the American Patriot Movement. This identity calls for the dismantling of the federal government, the social, political, and economic protection of white Christians, and the return of the majority of political power to the local level of government. Moreover, it recontextualizes familiar parts of American social, religious, political, and economic culture in a manner that justifies white supremacy and anti-government sentiment.

It includes the belief that there is an organic constitution, comprised of the Ten Commandments, the Bill of Rights, and the Articles of Confederation.[44] McVeigh's actions were bound within the "patriot" identity that he had adopted—he had a responsibility and obligation to hold the government accountable for its actions. In each of these examples, the identity that is adopted not only provides or reinforces the grievances and issues of the adherents, it also recontextualizes pieces of the identity's tradition in order to justify the acts of terrorism.

It does seem that a large portion of the Islamic motivations for *jihad* and *shahadat* are analogous to Western concepts of just war. In both the West's conception of just war and Islam's conception of *jihad* and *shahadat,* one can find concepts of proportionality, redress, limitations on combat, defense, and the need to exhaust other methods before resorting to violence. Even though these two sets of norms are parallel, they are often used to justify terrorism. A good American example of this is the behavior of Timothy McVeigh in blowing up the Murrah Federal Building in Oklahoma City.

After washing out of special forces training and disputing an IRS audit of his payroll withholding tax while serving in the U.S. Army, McVeigh grew increasingly frustrated with, and angry towards, the U.S. government. After the standoff between federal law enforcement agents and the Branch Davidians at the Mt. Carmel complex in Waco, Texas, McVeigh became convinced that the federal government had become tyrannical and had to be held accountable for its illicit actions. McVeigh justified his behavior by recontextualizing both the American norms for use of political violence, just war, as well as other elements of American political culture. McVeigh viewed the Murrah building as a legitimate target because it housed offices of the Federal Bureau of Investigation and the bombing as proportional to what occurred at Waco. He viewed his actions as legitimate by recontextualizing the meaning of the Declaration of Independence, some of Thomas Jefferson's writings, and parts of the first and second amendments to the Bill of Rights. McVeigh believed in the insurrectionist interpretation of the Second Amendment. This understanding of the right to keep and bear arms, separated from the need to serve in a well-regulated militia, is frequently used in the American Patriot movement to justify armed demonstration and insurrection against the American government.[45]

Similarly, *Hamas,* the Islamic resistance movement for Palestine, also recontextualizes norms, in this case Islamic norms, to justify the actions of some of its members. *Hamas* has established and maintains hospices, food services, and schools to enjoin the good and forbid the evil, all actions that are not only necessary but also very far from armed resistance. *Hamas* also resorts to an interpretational legerdemain in its charter in order to justify its political violence. *Hamas* claims to be waging a *jihad* against what it calls Zionist Israeli aggression. *Hamas* claims that there is no solution to the Palestinian condition except by *jihad.*[46] Article eleven of the *Hamas* charter establishes all of Israel/Palestine as an Islamic *waqf,* an area set aside for G-d. Article fifteen of the *Hamas'* Charter calls for *jihad* to end the usurpation of this particular *waqf* from those who are not permitted by G-d to have it. *Hamas* has attempted to establish its call for armed struggle on the basis that they are defending Islamic territory, and therefore their actions are both legitimate expressions of *jihad* and of attempting to enjoin the good and forbid the evil.

In order to do this, however, *Hamas* has had to stretch the meaning of *waqf.* Eventually, *Hamas* will have to choose which type of enjoining the good and forbidding the evil in which it wishes to participate. By establishing all of Palestine as a *waqf, Hamas* can then make the call to protect it through *jihad* and *shahadat.* Even if this jurisprudential manipulation was unnecessary, the activities of those who choose *shahadat* call their Islamic motivation into question. Shari'ati argues that the *shahid* chooses *shahadat* in order to expose injustice in an unjust society so that others will then know to engage in a *jihad* to end the injustice. He does not, however, posit that when exposing injustice, one should annihilate as many innocents and non-combatants as possible. *Hamas's shahids* would be true *shahids* if they sacrificed only themselves in the enactment of *shahadat.*

By killing innocents and non-combatants, they place themselves within the West's conception of terrorists, regardless of their status vis-à-vis Islam. Throughout history, many men and women have offered up their lives to point out injustice in society and did so without sacrificing the lives of innocents. Among them stand great men and women, both Muslim and non-Muslim. People such as 'Ali ibn Abu-Talib, Husayn, Joan of Arc, and Dr. Martin Luther King, Jr. chose either *shahadat* or their religion's equivalent without sacrificing innocent lives.

A good illustration of this point was made in a CBS Sixty Minutes interview with a Palestinian named Salameh.[47] Mr. Salameh is the man who planned the bombing of *Eged* Bus number eighteen in 1996. When asked why he planned this act. Salameh responded that it was in retaliation for the Israeli assassination of Yehye Ayyash. Ayyash was the *Hamas* member known as the "engineer" for his bomb-making skills. If Salameh had planned an operation where either only the participant died in order to call attention to the assassination of Ayyash, or where the Israeli directly responsible for terminating Ayyash were killed, his actions, while violent, would have fit within both Western justifications for political violence, as well as Islamic concepts of *jihad* and *shahadat.* If the operation had been carried out in either of these two ways, then it would have been redress instead of retaliation, a retaliation in which innocents and non-combatants lost their lives.

Another Islamic example is not quite so neat and clear cut. In Algeria, the Islamic Salvation Front (the FIS) stood poised to win a democratically held and Western monitored election to form a government in 1991. Fearing that it would lose its control over Algeria, the military negated the election results, usurped political authority, and established an illicit regime. Several Islamically motivated groups, most notably the FIS and the Armed Islamic Group (the GIA), began to combat the new regime. At first, the majority of targets were connected with the regime—they were military and government installations and personnel. Up to this point, the majority of the actions in regard to this *jihad* would meet both the West's criteria for acceptable political violence and Islamic concepts of *jihad.*

The battle for the hearts, souls, and power in Algeria, however, quickly deteriorated into senseless bloodshed and horrifying massacre. With the disintegration of acceptable resistance, the insurgency gave way to wholesale slaughter and several thousand Algerian innocents died both in the name of Islam and in the call to protect Algeria from Islam. In 1996, the highest Muslim spiritual leader in Algeria, Shaykh Mezarag, who heads the FIS and is considered to be the national *amir,*[48] announced that the wanton slaughter was a violation of Islam and called for a cease-fire and a search for other options to end what had become a ten-year-old civil war.[49]

Algeria's civil insurgency has clearly had three distinct phases: 1) legitimate *jihad* against an illicit regime, 2) acceptable and unacceptable uses of political violence, and 3) terrorism. The first phase, the phase that can be categorized under the Islamic concept of *jihad,* involved the FIS and the GIA targeting only governmental and military targets. The second phase, begun when the Islamic combatants realized that the insurgency would not be quickly resolved, includes both examples of acceptable and unacceptable political violence. During this phase, the Islamic actors added attacks on non-combatants to their attacks on governmental and military targets. These attacks included violence against members of the media and tourists. It is clear that, in the second phase of the Islamic insurgency, some of the political violence was acceptable while some was not, depending upon the target. The third distinct phase of the Algerian Islamic insurgency is the phase that is currently ongoing. In this, the present phase, the Islamic actors have hijacked airplanes and threatened to blow them up, attacked targets as far afield as Paris, and massacred and slaughtered thousands of Algerians who cannot in any way be considered combatants.

Three large questions still need to be addressed in greater detail. The first is why have past acts of Islamically motivated terrorism largely not been condemned by Muslim leaders, both within and without the Muslim world. There are two fairly straightforward reasons for this: the lack of a hierarchical and centralized Muslim religious authority and fear of reprisal. With the exception of Shi'i Islam, especially twelver shi'ism as practiced in Iran, Islam does not have a centralized clerical structure. As a result, there is no one Muslim cleric or organization of Muslim religious leaders who can be turned to for comment on any given issue. Thus, when an act of terrorism occurs, there are no clerics who have the legitimate authority to step up and condemn these acts of violence.

The lack of centralized authority, however, cannot excuse individual religious scholars who fail to speak out and condemn acts of terrorism committed in the name of Islam. Moreover, many in the Muslim world are intimidated by the violent elements within their communities. As a result, they have said nothing rather than draw attention to themselves. Consequently, non-Muslims are left to wonder if Muslim silence regarding the use of terrorism means Muslim approval. In the wake of the recent attacks on the World Trade Center and Pentagon, a large number of Muslim leaders have come forward to condemn the acts of terrorism and try to explain that they are not really justified by Islam or condoned by most Muslims. One has to wonder if some of these leaders had come forward following earlier terrorist events in Europe, the U.S., the Middle East, and Central Asia, then some of the atrocities committed in the name of Islam might have been prevented.

The second issue is why the reactionary and extremist versions of Islam seem to have such a great mass appeal. It appears that the extreme Islamic revivalist movements thrive in those places that have the least developed and open polities and the worst economic conditions. Reactionary Islamic revivalism seems to be strongest in places like Egypt, which is an authoritarian police state run by a former military officer. It is also present in places where the state and civil society has either failed or has never seemed to exist.[50] Lebanon, Afghanistan, Algeria, and the West Bank and Gaza strip are good examples of the breeding ground for reactionary Islam. Islamic revivalism gives the inhabitants of these areas an identity, a sense of what is expected and allowed in regard to behavior, and focuses the anger and frustration of its adherents at a clear enemy: non-Muslims.[51] It is important to remember that the rise of a Shi'i revivalist regime in Iran was the result of the Shah's authoritarian and despotic rule. Moreover, Iranian Islamic anger at the United States was the result of America's unflinching support for a monarch it viewed as an ally but whose subjects viewed as an oppressive tyrant.

The example of Iran is important to understanding the appeal and spread of reactionary Islam beyond a popular base. In Iran, just as in many other predominantly Muslim countries, many of the leaders and most active adherents within the Islamic movements are from the middle and upper classes (religious leaders, scholars, students, and merchants). They are well educated and often affluent. This also seems to be the case with those involved in the attacks on the World Trade Center and Pentagon. Osama bin Laden is extremely wealthy and from one of the most powerful families in Saudi Arabia. The suspected lead hijacker, Muhammed Atta, is reported as being the son of a highly respected Cairo lawyer. This seems to indicate that the message of reactionary Islam appeals both to the masses and to those in society with significant religious and economic resources.

Another answer to the question of why reactionary Islam is attractive to some Muslims is that it is often the only version of Islam taught.[52] The Saudi regime, in deference to its political partners within Hanbali/Wahhabi Islam, finances the construction of *madrassahs* (Islamic schools) throughout the Islamic world that are dedicated to teaching Wahhabi Islam. Wahhabism is the strictest and most reactionary version of the four schools of Sunni Islam. It is also the type of Islam that has been traditionally practiced in Saudi Arabia. It calls for the adherence to a strict code of conduct in a manner that the other three branches of Sunni Islam does not. The exportation of Wahhabism by the House of Saud is an attempt to appease its own constituency; however, it has had the unanticipated effect of spreading the most inflexible version of Islam to places like Afghanistan. It is important to note that Ibn Taymiyyah, the religious scholar who recontextualized the meaning of *jihad* and *shahadat* during the Tatar invasions, was a

Wahhabi cleric. It should come as no surprise that those Muslims who have engaged in acts of terrorism in the U.S., Algeria, Egypt, the West Bank and Gaza Strip, Pakistan, India, the Philippines, and Indonesia are predominantly adherents of Wahabbi Islam.

The third possible issue to be dealt with is more contentious and problematic than the previous two. Some have argued that the problem is not in Islam and its teachings per se, but rather in the way that they are expressed in Arabic.[53] The argument is that the language that is used to make social, religious, and political points is inherently given to exaggerated, and sometimes extreme, formulations that should not be taken literally. Another related argument is that this political language and rhetoric contains multiple different shades of meaning and nuance. This flexibility within Arabic vocabulary allows Arab and Islamic leaders to make statements that are intended to be understood one way by their followers and another way when translated for non-Arabic speakers and non-Muslims. This is Bernard Lewis's argument in regard to the term *jihad*. He argues that while the Arabic word for war is *harb*, the term *jihad* is used in the *Quran* and the related religious literature (*hadith* and *fiq*) to refer to violent conflict between Muslims and non-Muslims. As a result, Lewis asserts that it is not accurate to state that the primary meaning of *jihad* is the struggle to improve oneself instead of fighting on behalf of, and to spread Islam.[54]

## CONCLUSION

It is possible through a detailed presentation, analysis, and comparison of Western concepts of just war with the Islamic concepts of *jihad* and *shahadat* to conclude that the West and Islam's concepts are both, at their cores, analogous. Both sets of norms of acceptable violence in regard to political behavior incorporate concepts of proportionality, redress, moderation, exploration of other options, and defense within their respective systems. There are also numerous similarities regarding unacceptable political behavior—behavior that the West labels as terrorist. It is very important to note that one of the reasons, if not the most important reason, that *jihad* and *shahadat* strike such a chord in the West is that it clearly reminds Westerners of a religious crusade. This concept makes Westerners uncomfortable because it is a clear indicator of what happens when religion and politics are tightly interwoven, a notion that the West rejected some two to three hundred years ago.

It is clear that much of the so-called Islamic behavior that the West terms terrorism is outside the norms that Islam holds for political violence. A large part of this Islamic terrorism occurs when Islamically motivated actors, both groups and individuals, play fast and loose with Islamic norms. The concept of the *jihad* clearly calls for a redressive action with specific limitations, employed as a last resort. Likewise, the concept of the self-choosing *shahid* calls only for the sacrifice of the *shahid;* it does not call for the killing of innocents and non-combatants. Furthermore, it is curiously frustrating to Western perceptions that Muslims who have any form of authority have rarely denounced terrorist acts that are claimed to be Islamic in nature by their perpetrators. It is often pointed out that when Baruch Goldstein killed over twenty Muslims at the Tomb of the Patriarchs' Mosque in Hebron, Jewish religious and political leaders immediately and resoundingly denounced his actions. Moreover, when the IRA, a Catholic sectarian organization, performs a terrorist act, Catholic leaders, both religious and secular, denounce the acts. The same is true of Protestant leaders in regard to Protestant violence in Ulster. Quite often, non-Muslim observers of supposed Islamic events feel that the lack of a response by Muslim authorities and leaders amounts to condoning the actions through silence.

Playing fast and loose with the rules, as well as descending into barbarism, is not confined to Islamic actors who have slid over the line. There are numerous instances in the West, when Western actors, state, non-state groups, and individuals have willingly walked across the same line. The Spanish Inquisition, the bombings of Dresden, the forcing of an unconditional surrender on the Japanese after World War II,

and the My Lai massacre are just a few items from a long list of violations of the norms of just war and examples of deviant political violence in the West. The best way to proceed in the future is for both the West and Islam to attempt a better understanding of the norms and rules governing the other side. In addition, adherents of each view must police themselves. Furthermore, by emphasizing the similarities in norms between the two views, a more equal and balanced approach toward eliminating human tragedies that result from political violence can be formulated.

## NOTES

1. "Profiling Terrorists," National Public Radio, 9/18/01: Martin Kramer, "The Moral Logic of Hizballah," in *Origins of Terrorism: Psychologies, Ideologies, Theologies, States of Mind,* ed. Walter Reich (Cambridge, Mass.: Cambridge University Press, 1990), 131–60.

2. Joel Best, "But Seriously Folks: The Limitations of the Strict Contructivist Interpretation of Social Problems," in *Constructionist Controversies: Issues in Social Problems Theory,* eds. Gale Miller and James A. Holstein (New York: Aldine de Gruyter, 1993), 109–27.

3. Nathan Katz, "Understanding Religion in Diaspora: The Case of the Jews of Cochin," *Religious Studies and Theology* 15 (June 1996); 7–8.

4. There are numerous variations on just war, just revolution, and crusade in the Western tradition. Among them are Aristotle's, Cicero's Augustine's, Thomas of Aquinas's and Bernard of Claivaux's. The one presented here is a composite of Augustinian, Aquinine, Aristotelian, and other traditions.

5. Jean Bethke Elshtain, "Reflections on Ware and Political Discourse: Realism, Just War, and Feminism in a Nuclear Age," in *Perspectives on World Politics: A Reader,* eds. Richard Little and Michael Smith (London: Routledge, 1991), 460–61.

6. Cicero, *On Duties,* ed. M. T. Griffin and E. M. Atkins (Cambridge, Mass.: Cambridge University Press, 1991), 14–15.

7. Abbott A. Brayton and Stephama J. Landwehr, *The Politics of War and Peace: A Survey of Thought* (Washington D.C.: University Press of America, 1981), 66–67.

8. John Howard Yoder, *When War is Unjust: Being Honest in Just War Thinking* (Minneapolis, Minn.: Augsburg Publishing House, 1984), 59.

9. James Turner Johnson, *Can Modern War be Just?* (New Haven, Conn.: Yale University Press, 1984), 30.

10. Yoder, *When War is Unjust,* 56.

11. William V. O'Brien, *The Conduct of Just and Limited War* (New York: Praeger, 1981), 73.

12. lbid., 16.

13. lbid., 37.

14. This is one of the two traditional views of whether the atomic strikes at Hiroshima and Nagasaki were morally justified. The other view is that the bombings were unethical and unjust since they targeted civilian population in order to bring about a swifter conclusion to the war.

15. I have chosen to focus on these two normative Islamic concepts in creating my comparative analysis. There are, however, other Islamic concepts, that while related to *jihad* and *shahadat,* are outside of the scope of this essay. The most conspicuous of these is *fitnah. Fitnah* has been interpreted to mean everything from the oppression of Muslims by Polytheists to anarchical civil behavior to seditious speech. In terms of Islamic history, it refers to two specific civil insurgencies against the caliphate of Ali.

16. Q 22: 39–40.

17. *The Holy Qur'an: Text, Translation, and Commentary,* trans. Abdullah Yusuf Ali (New York: Thrike Tarsile Qur'an Inc., 1988), 861.

18. Q 22: 60.

19. Q 8: 60.

20. Q 8: 61.

21. Q 2: 190.

22. Q 2: 193.

23. Q 9: 29.

24. Arthur Goldschmidt, Jr., *A Concise History of the Middle East* (Boulder, Colo.: Westview Press, 1988), 55–57.

25. Bernard Lewis, *The Political Language* (Chicago, Ill.: The University of Chicago Press, 1991), 85.

26. Ibid., 73.

27. A *mujtahid* is a master of Islamic jurisprudence. Interestingly, the term is derived from the same root as *jihad.*

28. A *qadi* is an Islamic judge and arbitrator.

29. R. Hrair Dekmejian, *Islam in Revolution: Fundamentalism in the Arab World* (Syracuse, N.Y.: Syracuse University Press, 1985), 39.

30. Ibid., 39–40.

31. Ibid., 40.

32. Ibid.

33. Murtada Mutahhari, *"Jihad* in the *Qur'an,"* in *Jihad and Shahadat: Struggle and Martyrdom in Islam,* eds. Mehdi Abedi and Gary Legenhausen

(Houston, Tex.: Institute for Research and Islamic Studies, 1986), 89.

34. Ibid., 93.

35. Ibid., 96.

36. Ibid., 104–05.

37. Q 3: 169.

38. Q 22: 58–59.

39. Ahmad Ibn Naqib al-Misri, *The Reliance of the Traveler: A Classic Manual of Islamic Sacred Law* (Evanston, Ill.: Sunna Books, 1991), 718, sect. Q2.4(4).

40. "The Great *Ghazwa* of Badr," in *A Reader on Islam; Passages from Standard Arabic Writings Illustrative of the Beliefs and Practices of Muslims,* ed. Arthur Jeffery ('S-Gravenhage: Mouton and Company, 1962), 290–300.

41. Ali Shariati, "A Discussion of *Shahid,"* in *Jihad and Shahadat: Struggle and Martyrdom in Islam,* eds. Mehdi Abedi and Gary Legenhausen (Houston, Tex.: Institute for Research and Islamic Studies, 1996), 234–35 and 240.

42. Alex P. Schmid and Albert J. Jongman, *Political Terrorism: A New Guide to Actors, Authors, Concepts, Databases, Theories, and Literature* (Amsterdam: North Holland Publishing Company, 1988), 37.

43. Ronald L. Akers, *Deviant Behavior: A Social Learning Approach* (Belmont, Calif.: Wadsworth, 1985).

44. Micheal Barkun, *Religion and the Racist Right* (Chapel Hill, N.C.: The University of North Carolina Press, 1994), 103–20.

45. Thomas Halpern and Brian Levin, *The Limits of Dissent: The Constitutional Status of Civilian Militias* (Amherst, N.Y.: Alethia Press), 1996, 83–86.

46. From the *Hamas* Charter, article 13.

47. "The Suicide Bombers," *Sixty Minutes,* CBS, 12 October 1997.

48. *Amir* is Arabic for commander and is short for *amir al-mutminim,* which means the commander of the faithful, and was a title attributed to the *khalifa* since the time of the first successors to Muhammed.

49. *The Miami Herald,* 26 September 1997, 19A.

50. Fareed Zakaria, "The Allies Who Made Our Foes," *Newsweek,* 1 October 2001, 34.

51. Fouad Ajami, *The Arab Predicament: Arab Political Thought Since 1967* (New York: Cambridge University Press, 1989), 177–81.

52. Zakaria, "The Allies Who Made Our Foes," 34.

53. Ajami, *The Arab Predicament,* 26–27.

54. Lewis, *The Political Language,* 70–72.

## Must Innocents Die? The Islamic Debate Over Suicide Attacks

Haim Malka
*Research Analyst, Saban Center for Middle East Policy*

Over the last two years, the issue of suicide attacks or "martyrdom operations" against Israel has dominated public discussion throughout the Arab world. Since the outbreak of the current Palestinian *intifada,* in September 2000, the Palestinian resort to suicide attacks has won widespread Arab public acceptance as a legitimate form of resistance against Israeli occupation. Some Muslim clerics and other commentators justify them on political, moral, and religious grounds. Even those attackers who bomb and kill women and children are hailed as martyrs for their heroism in confronting the enemy.

It is often said that the "martyrdom operations" are acts of religious extremism. The operatives who recruit young men and women to detonate themselves in crowds of Israelis manipulate religious fervor by wedding the ideas of heavenly reward to martyrdom. A young believer who detonates himself in the midst of the enemy will ascend straight to heaven and enter paradise—so he or she is indoctrinated. This is presented as the ultimate sacrifice and reward for a devout young Muslim.

But the operations themselves are very carefully calculated maneuvers. Islamist and other groups launch suicide attacks because they are seen as effective means to demoralize Israel. The "martyrdom operations" are deemed the only answer to the vastly superior military capabilities of the Israeli army. In the words of the founder and spiritual leader of Hamas, Sheikh Ahmad Yasin, "Once we have warplanes and missiles, then we can think of changing our means of legitimate self-defense. But right now, we can only tackle the fire with our bare hands and sacrifice ourselves."[1]

Advocates have described the attacks as the most important "strategic weapon" of Palestinian resistance. And while religious justification of such attacks is important for many Muslims, secular groups related to Fatah

such as the Tanzim and Al-Aqsa Martyrs Brigade have resorted to similar tactics.[2]

Suicide attacks enjoyed almost unquestioning support in the Arab world—until the suicide attacks of September 11, 2001. Overnight, Muslims everywhere found themselves defending their religion against charges of espousing violence and terror. Many Muslim scholars have responded by condemning the assault against America as terrorism. But even as they affirm that the attacks in America were terrorism—because they killed innocent civilians—many of the same scholars still regard attacks carried out against Israeli civilians as "martyrdom operations," a form of legitimate resistance to occupation of holy Muslim land. These scholars now seek to explain the difference between suicide operations in New York and Washington and those perpetrated in Tel Aviv and Jerusalem.

The acceleration of Palestinian suicide bombings against Israeli civilians in spring 2002 complicated the issue still further. The "martyrdom operations" against Israeli civilians, following one another in rapid succession, licensed Israel to launch massive reprisals. Before these reprisals, Arab governments and opinion-makers had been content to let the "suicide fever" run rampant, in the media and in street demonstrations. But as Israeli military responses escalated, Arab governments sent their clients—Muslim clerics, journalists, and officials—to throw cold water on the frenzied enthusiasm of the masses. The specter that such operations might spread to their own countries, threatening their own security, cannot be far from their minds.

In short, three main arguments have emerged: the first, endorsing the attacks of September 11, and against Israeli targets; the second, rejecting attacks like September 11, but supporting attacks against Israeli targets; and the third, rejecting all suicide attacks, wherever they take place. The debate is now fully engaged, yet it is not entirely new. The debate over "martyrdom operations" goes back to the 1980's when various groups employed the technique against U.S., French, and Israeli forces in Lebanon. But the sheer number of Palestinian "martyrdom operations" against Israel and the unprecedented number of Americans killed in New York and Washington have imparted a new urgency to the debate. What follows is a sketch of the recent arguments for and against the operations against Israel. It is important to acknowledge that a debate is underway. It is also crucial to recognize that those who sanction attacks against Israeli civilians seem to be winning it.

## FOR AND AGAINST

The debate began in early December 2001, when a deadly wave of suicide operations struck Jerusalem and Haifa, leaving 26 Israelis dead.

The bombings constituted the first major wave of terrorism, post-September 11. They came at a time when the leadership of Egypt and Saudi Arabia, whose nationals had been implicated in the September 11 attacks, were still reeling from criticism that they had not done enough to battle terrorism and suicide fever in the region.

After September 11, the governments of Egypt and Saudi Arabia faced severe criticism for the role their nationals played in the attacks. They also deemed it in their interest to promote a more conciliatory image of Islam—to argue that it opposes the killing of innocent civilians and is based on ideals of peace and justice. In November, Saudi Arabia's crown prince Abdullah called a meeting of senior Islamic clerics including the grand mufti of the kingdom, to urge them to exercise caution in their public declarations, and to remember that their words were now under unprecedented international scrutiny:

> Brothers, you know that we are passing through crucial days. We must be patient and you must clarify to your brothers in good words since you are now the target of the enemies of the Islamic faith . . . do not be unnerved or provoked by passion.[3]

President Mubarak of Egypt made similar appeals to religious scholars and preachers during the holy month of Ramadan. He stressed the tolerant nature of Islam, calling on the religious figures to "clarify the real nature of Islam's divine message, that it is the religion of tolerance and mercy, that it forbids the killing of innocent civilians."[4]

The December 2001 bombings in Israel immediately put Egypt and Saudi Arabia to the test. Would their religious leaders finally speak out against the widespread glorification and acceptance of "martyrdom" and indiscriminate killing that had taken root in their own societies?

Two of them did. Sheikh Muhammad Sa'id Tantawi, head of Egypt's Al-Azhar mosque and university, had been equivocal about the issue in past declarations. Now he reiterated the government's position, declaring that the shari'a (Islamic law) "rejects all attempts on human life, and in the name of the shari'a, we condemn all attacks on civilians, whatever their community or state responsible for such an attack."[5]

Echoing Tantawi's ruling, Sheikh Muhammad bin 'Abdallah as-Sabil, member of the Saudi council of senior ulema (clerics) and imam at the grand mosque in Mecca, also decried the suicide attacks. "Any attack on innocent people is unlawful and contrary to the shari'a," he announced, adding, "Muslims must safeguard the lives, honor, and property of Christians and Jews, attacking them contradicts the shari'a." The Islamic legal arguments against the operations relied upon three principles of Islamic law: the prohibition against killing civilians, the prohibition against suicide, and the protected status of Jews and Christians.[6]

But would these arguments hold? For centuries, Muslim rulers have paid the salaries of religious figures and used them to boost their own legitimacy. The highest religious leaders of Egypt and Saudi Arabia are government-appointed officials. Any edict emanating from these religious bodies inevitably reflects state policy. Both governments tap their religious establishments whenever they need religious backing for controversial policies. In the past, the Sheikh al-Azhar, the head of the Azhar theological seminary, provided Anwar Sadat with a religious edict, or *fatwa,* in support of the peace treaty Sadat signed with Israel. During the Kuwait war, the late grand mufti of Saudi Arabia, Sheikh 'Abd al-'Aziz bin Baz, ruled that the presence of foreign troops was permitted on Saudi soil to defend the kingdom from Saddam Hussein. He also issued an extremely controversial *fatwa* in 1995, ruling that the shari'a permitted peace with Israel, under certain conditions. The dependence of the clerics on the rulers has sometimes eroded the credibility of state religious officials and their edicts. In any event, no Muslim authority exercises a kind of "papal" authority over his coreligionists. And so it was not surprising that the declarations of Tantawi and Sabil, far from ending the debate, actually intensified it.[7]

The harshest rebuttal came from the Egyptian-born Sheikh Yusuf al-Qaradawi, who currently heads the Sunni studies department at Qatar University. Sheikh Qaradawi is a consistent critic of the United States as well as many pro-Western Arab governments, and is increasingly popular throughout the Muslim world. He was also one of the first religious scholars to sanction the use of suicide attacks by Palestinian militants during the waves of Hamas-led bombings in the mid-1990s. Qaradawi has gained popularity and legitimacy throughout the Arab world by questioning the authority of the state, and he reaches a broad audience through his regular appearances on the Arabic satellite channel, al-Jazeera. Qaradawi has emerged as one of the preeminent Islamic religious figures in the Arab world and arguably represents the mainstream of Arab Muslim society.

"I am astonished that some sheikhs deliver *fatwas* that betray the mujahideen, instead of supporting them and urging them to sacrifice and martyrdom," announced Qaradawi.[8]

Responding specifically to the imam of Mecca, Qaradawi stated, "It is unfortunate to hear that the grand imam has said it was not permissible to kill civilians in any country or state, even in Israel." Qaradawi based his opposition to these *fatwas* on the premise that Israelis were not civilians but rather combatants in a war of occupation waged against the Palestinians. He argued that[9]

> Israeli society was completely military in its make-up and did not include any civilians . . . How can the head of Al-Azhar incriminate mujahideen

who fight against aggressors? How can he consider these aggressors as innocent civilians?[10]

While sanctioning suicide attacks against Israelis, Qaradawi quickly condemned the September 11 attacks against American civilians, claiming that "such martyrdom operations should not be carried out outside of the Palestinian territories." Attempting to differentiate between terrorism and "martyrdom," Qaradawi declared, "The Palestinian who blows himself up is a person who is defending his homeland. When he attacks an occupier enemy, he is attacking a legitimate target. This is different from someone who leaves his country and goes to strike a target with which he has no dispute."[11]

Qaradawi distinguished "martyrdom operations" from terrorism as an act of self-defense and thus a legitimate form of resistance. He continues: "The Palestinians have a right to defend their land and property from which they were driven out unjustly . . . the Palestinians have a right to resist this usurping colonialism with all the means and methods they have. This is a legitimate right endorsed by the divine laws, international laws, and human values."[12]

Qaradawi was also at pains to distinguish between suicide and martyrdom. Islam clearly prohibits suicide, yet views martyrdom as a noble act, assuring individuals a place in heaven. In an interview with Al-Jazeera, Qaradawi rejected the term "suicide operations."

> This is an unjust and misleading name because these are heroic commando and martyrdom attacks and should not be called suicide operations or be attributed to suicide under any circumstances.[13]

He clarified that the term suicide applies to someone who kills himself for personal reasons and is therefore a coward. In contrast, an attack against Israel is defined as martyrdom and therefore legitimized as a brave, unselfish sacrifice carried out on behalf of the entire Muslim community.

Other critics of the edicts issued by Tantawi and Sabil based themselves on the status of Jews and Christians in Islam, considered "people of the covenant"—*ahl adh-dhimma,* or *dhimmis.* There are clear guidelines in the Qur'an and

Sunna for Muslim relations with Jews and Christians, providing for the protection of their lives and property. But as one commentator argued, "preserving the life of the *dhimmis* is conditional on their living under Muslim rule in a Muslim state. This does not apply to the *dhimmis* mentioned by the imam [of Mecca], since they are living in their own state that has usurped the rights of Muslims and occupied their lands." Jews and Christians are protected under Islam, but only when they live under Muslim rule; outside the boundaries of Islamic rule, they are no longer protected. According to this chain of reasoning, it is permissible to kill Jews in Israel who live in their own state, especially as its territory has been usurped from Muslims.[14]

Other religious scholars within the Azhar establishment continued to challenge the prohibition on killing civilians espoused by Tantawi and Sabil. 'Abd al-'Azim al-Mit'ani, a lecturer at Al-Azhar University, rejected arguments differentiating between Israeli civilian and military targets claiming, "They should not make any difference between civilians and military. It is a fact that Israel is one big military camp. There is no real civilian there. It is the Palestinians' rights to hit all the inhabitants of Israel as they can." Al-Mit'ani continued by claiming that the prophet's words prohibiting the killing of children, elderly, or women did not apply in the case of Palestinian suicide bombers, stating, "He was talking about an ordinary war, between two armies. The situation in occupied Arab Palestine is different. We are faced with an enemy that attacks indiscriminately. The Palestinians have every right to return the treatment."[15]

The killing of innocent women and children is often quickly dismissed by advocates of suicide operations as "collateral damage" and an inevitable by-product of the struggle against Israel. Addressing this issue in an interview, Sheikh Qaradawi denied that such casualties contradict Islamic doctrine. "Some children, old people, and women may get hurt in such operations. This is not deliberate. However, we must all realize that the Israeli society is a military society, men and women . . . we cannot say that the casualties were innocent civilians."[16]

'Abd as-Sabur Shahin, a lecturer at the Islamic Dar al-'Ulum College in Cairo, concurred and argued that, "We are at war, as we have never been before throughout history. If civilians are killed in the course of Palestinian operations, this is not a crime."[17]

Islamic scholars who endorse and even promote suicide or "martyrdom" attacks justify their positions by reference to the shari'a. But these rulings are driven more by emotions and television images of Palestinian suffering than by deep immersion in the records of ancient Islamic precedent. These clerics, like many secular enthusiasts of the bombings, seek to champion the Palestinians in their resistance against Israel. And for the Muslim believer, the young men who sacrifice their lives in the name of resistance are not only defending the Palestinian nation, they are also defending the wounded honor of the Arab nation, in a struggle that was lost decades ago by the secular Arab regimes.

## ENTER THE RULERS

Once the clerics had staked out their positions, it was the turn of the rulers to "operationalize" them. Yet it did not take long for the debate to become muddled, as both the Egyptian and Saudi Arabian governments hedged their own condemnations of the operations.

The judgments of Tantawi and Sabil condemning violence against civilians prepped the call by the leaders of Egypt, Saudi Arabia, and Syria to "reject all forms of violence," at a May 2002 tripartite summit meeting in Sharm al-Sheikh. But their final statement did not specifically condemn "martyrdom operations."[18]

Syria soon exploited the loophole. True, Syrian president Bashar al-Assad had attended the meeting and agreed to the text of the final communiqué—this, despite the fact that Syria continues to support suicide attacks carried out by Hamas and the Palestine Islamic Jihad. But after the summit, Syrian foreign minister Faruq ash-Shar' explained why Syria put its name to the summit communiqué, by claiming that the term "violence" referred to "Israeli crimes against the Palestinian people." Syrian sources then confirmed that there would be no change in Syria's political support for "resistance" and for leaders of Hamas and Islamic Jihad.[19]

Saudi Arabia's effort to curb support for violence against Israel was discussed between President George W. Bush and Crown Prince

Abdullah at their meeting in Crawford, Texas, in April 2002, with Abdullah promising to use his influence over both Hamas and Syria.[20]

Widely circulating reports later claimed that Saudi Arabia was attempting to use its influence on Hamas to end suicide attacks through high-level meetings.[21]

But Hamas spokesman Mahmud az-Zahar denied that any meetings occurred, while affirming the movement's willingness to discuss the issue of "martyrdom operations" with any Arab party. Such attempts were renewed later in the year under the auspices of the Egyptian government, yet broke down over the refusal of Hamas to end the attacks.[22]

Moreover, it soon turned out that Saudi Arabia itself had been paying allowances to the families of "martyrs" and funneling money directly for Hamas, which was responsible for a majority of suicide attacks. The Saudi Committee for the Support of Al-Quds Intifada, headed by Saudi interior minister Prince Nayif bin 'Abd al-'Aziz, had been channeling money to Hamas and affiliated organizations. In the words of the Saudi government, the committee "has been extending assistance to the families of Palestinian martyrs, as well as injured and handicapped Palestinians." According to its own figures, published on an official Saudi government website, the family of each suicide bomber is paid 20,000 Saudi riyals (about $5,300).[23]

In addition, money from the Saudi Committee for the Support of Al-Aqsa Intifada was paid to the Tulkarm Charity Committee, an organization cited by the United States as connected to Hamas. While it is clear that the charity committee does administer social work and aid, it is also known to have ties with the military apparatus of Hamas.[24]

Secretary of State Colin Powell acknowledged that Saudi cash was funding Hamas during a hearing of the Foreign Operations Subcommittee of the Senate Appropriations Committee. In response to a question about the destination for funds raised through a series of Saudi telethons which raised millions of dollars, Secretary Powell claimed, "We have seen some indications, and I've even seen in an Arab newspaper—handed to me by Chairman Arafat, I might add—where some of the money, at least according to this Arab newspaper advertisement, would be going to elements of Hamas."[25]

The Saudi embassy in Washington attempted to deflect criticism that it was funding the families of suicide bombers by claiming that the term "martyr" used in relation to official Saudi efforts to raise funds for Palestinians referred not to suicide bombers but to "Palestinians who are victimized by Israeli terror and violence."[26]

Yet the executive manager of the Saudi committee stated otherwise: "We support the families of Palestinian martyrs, without differentiating between whether the Palestinian was a bomber or was killed by Israeli troops."[27]

In the Egyptian case, the weak link in the debate proved to be Sheikh Tantawi. The Sheikh al-Azhar, subjected to withering criticism, began to issue confusing and contradictory statements, effectively abrogating his earlier *fatwa.* In an interview with the Egyptian state-owned magazine *Ruz al-Yusuf,* Tantawi claimed that his earlier rulings had been distorted, stating,

> My words were clear . . . a man who blows himself in the middle of enemy militants is a martyr, repeat, a martyr. What we do not condone is for someone to blow himself up in the middle of children or women. If he blows himself up in the middle of Israeli women enlisted in the army, then he is a martyr, since these women are fighters.[28]

In later statements he reiterated this formula, declaring, "I repeat that those who defend their rights by blowing themselves up in the midst of their enemies who murder his people, occupy their land or humiliate their people, are martyrs, martyrs, martyrs."[29]

Since shifting his position on attacks, Tantawi has continuously sought to clarify the issue by distinguishing between terrorism and jihad, which is the impetus for "martyrdom." "Jihad in Islam was ordained in order to support the oppressed and defend sacred places, human lives, personal funds, occupied land, and so on. Terrorism, on the other hand, is an aggression and an insistence on killing innocent people, civilians, and peaceful people." The distinction rests on the notion of self-defense, which distinguishes martyrdom operations from terrorism. Tantawi intended to cover both angles of the debate, conferring the status of martyr on Palestinian suicide bombers engaged in a struggle of self-defense, while condemning the killing of innocent civilians.[30]

Within Palestinian society there have been calls to half the campaign of suicide attacks. Unfortunately, the majority of these appeals are based on strategic considerations and not on religious or moral arguments. The usual arguments against suicide attacks are that they harm the image of the Palestinian struggle or engender harsh Israeli reprisals—not that the attacks are themselves reprehensible. Some Palestinians support attacks only within the West Bank and Gaza and not in the pre-1967 borders of Israel. But Palestinian critics of the attacks clearly have not persuaded their planners and perpetrators since the attacks continue.

## NEXT PHASE?

If suicide attacks are permissible against Israeli targets, might they be deemed legitimate against repressive Arab leaders accused of being "apostates"? Religious decrees were used to justify the assassination of Egyptian president Anwar Sadat. Various edicts issued against leading intellectuals such as the Egyptian author and Nobel laureate Naguib Mahfouz (who was stabbed by a would-be assassin), and Egyptian secular thinker Farag Foda (who was murdered), have put secularists on notice. All of this raises the prospect that, even if the "suicide fever" subsides among the Palestinians, it could surface elsewhere—not just in the West, where it has already taken a devastating toll, but in Arab capitals ruled by regimes friendly to the West and at peace with Israel.

This would be the point of entry for theological freelancers. In recent years, there has been a proliferation of *fatwas* issued by various religious scholars of dubious authority. These *fatwas* may lack legal soundness, yet they are often accepted and adhered to by many Muslims who are dissatisfied with the status quo. Some of these *fatwas* conform to Islamic law, and some do not. But the crucial point is that the lack of qualifications of those issuing such rulings has become nearly irrelevant.

Usama bin Ladin's so-called *fatwa* of 1998, for example, urged Muslims to "kill the Americans and their allies, civilians and military." Though such a ruling by a person lacking legal training has no authority in Islam, the fact remains that a small group of people who believed these words perpetrated an unprecedented act of terror against the United States on September 11. Thus, is it inconceivable that a disgruntled extremist group, desperate in its confrontation with an authoritarian state in the Middle East, could use such tactics against an Arab regime? Bin Ladin's 1998 call for murder was directed at "Americans and their allies," easily interpreted as the Western-allied states of the Arab world.[31]

Arab governments have struggled against the proliferation of *fatwas* and have taken various measures to limit those issuing religious rulings. The government of Saudi Arabia issued a public statement that only authorized clerics could issue *fatwas*. This was in part a response to a *fatwa* issued by a dissident cleric, calling for jihad against the United States.[32]

The Saudi minister of Islamic affairs also attempted to curb public calls for jihad, which he declared could only be ordered by the government.[33]

In Kuwait, which faces a growing Islamic opposition, the Ministry of Justice, Religious Endowments, and Islamic Affairs issued rules to mosque preachers in an attempt to control religious discourse. The ministry also established a *fatwa* committee to coordinate and approve religious rulings. Similar restrictions and regulations have been enacted throughout the Arab world in an attempt to limit the influence of independent clerics.[34]

Until now, most Islamic groups have refrained from directly confronting the state for ideological or tactical reasons. Generally speaking, those groups that have chosen violence have been crushed. But the widespread legitimacy of the "martyrdom operations" could set extremists to considering the tactic, if and when they revive armed struggle against the state. Egyptian president Hosni Mubarak raised such concerns in an interview with The New York Times: "I am afraid of what's happening in the Middle East for the future . . . the seriousness of the situation may generate new kinds of terrorism against all of us, against the U.S., against Egypt, against Jordan." Arab rulers could find themselves the next target of a new wave of "martyrs."[35]

This suggests that the debate over "martyrdom operations" may continue for a long time to come. And at this moment in time, those in favor of such attacks seem to be scoring points. Cairo and Riyadh remain reluctant to oppose such attacks fully in clear and definitive language, and such attacks continue. Perhaps their hesitation has to do with the answer to this question: Even if they were to call unambiguously for an end to the suicide attacks, would anyone heed them?

## NOTES

1. *The Daily Star* (Beirut), Feb. 8, 2002.
2. 'Abd al-'Aziz Rantisi on "Al-Jazeera This Morning," Al-Jazeera (Doha), May 20, 2002.
3. Saudi Press Agency (SPA), Nov. 28, 2001.
4. *Al-Akhbar* (Cairo), Dec. 16, 2001.
5. Ibid., Dec. 4, 2001.
6 SPA, Dec. 4, 2001.
7. *An-Nahar* (Beirut), Feb. 14, 1995.
8. Agence France-Presse (AFP), Dec. 4, 2001.
9. *Al-Musawwar* (Cairo), Dec. 7, 2001.
10. AFP, Dec. 4, 2001.
11. *Ar-Rayah* (Doha), Oct. 26, 2002.
12. *Ash-Sharq al-Awsat* (London), Dec. 12, 2001.
13. *Al-Jazeera,* Dec. 9, 2001.
14. *Al-Quds al-'Arabi* (London), Dec. 6, 2001.
15. *Al-Ahram al-'Arabi* (weekly magazine, Cairo), Dec. 15, 2001.
16. *Ash-Sharq al-Awsat,* Dec. 12, 2001.
17. *Al-Ahram al-'Arabi,* Dec. 15, 2001.
18. *Al-Ahram al-Masa'i* (Cairo), May 12, 2002.
19. *Al-Hayat* (London), May 15, 2002.
20. *Ha'aretz* (Tel Aviv), May 15, 2002.
21. *Al-Ayyam* (Ramallah), May 15, 2002.
22. *Al-Quds* (Jerusalem), May 16, 2002.
23. *Saudi Arabian Information Resource,* Dec. 1, 2001.
24. *Israel Defense Forces Web site.*
25. *Hearing of the Foreign Operations Subcommittee of the Senate Appropriations* Committee, Apr. 24, 2002, Voice of America.
26. Associated Press (AP), Apr. 11, 2002.
27. *Arab News* (Jidda), May 27, 2002.
28. *Ruz al-Yusuf* (Cairo), Jan. 5, 2001.
29. *Al-Wafd* (Cairo), Feb. 8, 2002.
30. Arab Republic of Egypt Radio General Service (Cairo), Feb. 1, 2002.
31. *Al-Quds al-'Arabi,* Feb. 23, 1998; *The International Policy Institute for Counter-Terrorism.*
32. AP, Jan. 21, 2002.
33. *Al-Watan* (Abha), Oct. 18, 2001.
34. *Al-Qabas* (Kuwait), Oct. 29, 2001.
35. *The New York Times,* June 4, 2002.

---

## The New Terrorism: Securing the Nation Against a Messianic Foe

Steven Simon
*International Institute for Strategic Studies*

In the minds of the men who carried them out, the attacks of September 11 were acts of religious devotion—a form of worship, conducted in God's name and in accordance with his wishes. The enemy was the infidel; the opposing ideology, "Western culture." That religious motivation, colored by a messianism and in some cases an apocalyptic vision of the future, distinguishes al-Qaida and its affiliates from conventional terrorists groups such as the Irish Republican Army, the Red Brigades, or even the Palestine Liberation Organization. Although secular political interests help drive al-Qaida's struggle for power, these interests are understood and expressed in religious terms. Al-Qaida wants to purge the Middle East of American political, military, and economic influence, but only as part of a far more sweeping religious agenda: a "defensive jihad" to defeat a rival system portrayed as an existential threat to Islam.

The explicitly religious character of the "New Terrorism" poses a profound security challenge for the United States. The social, economic, and political conditions in the Arab and broader Islamic world that have helped give rise to al-Qaida will not be easily changed. The maximalist demands of the new terrorists obviate dialogue or negotiation. Traditional strategies of deterrence by retaliation are unlikely to work because the jihadists have no territory to hold at risk, seek sacrifice, and court Western attacks that will validate their claims about Western hostility to Islam. The United States will instead need to pursue a strategy of containment, while seeking ways to redress, over the long run, underlying causes.

## THE FABRIC OF NEW TERRORISM

Religiously motivated terrorism, as Bruce Hoffman of the RAND Corporation first noted in 1997, is inextricably linked to pursuit of mass casualties. The connection is rooted in the sociology of biblical religion. Monotheistic faiths are characterized by exclusive claims to valid identity and access to salvation. The violent imagery embedded in their sacred texts and the centrality of sacrifice in their liturgical traditions establish the legitimacy of killing as an act of worship with redemptive qualities. In these narratives, the enemy must be eradicated, not merely suppressed.

In periods of deep cultural despair, eschatology—speculation in the form of apocalyptic stories about the end of history and dawn of the kingdom of God—can capture the thinking of a religious group. History is replete with instances in which religious communities—Jewish, Christian, Islamic—immolated themselves and perpetrated acts of intense violence to try to spur the onset of a messianic era. Each community believed it had reached the nadir of degradation and was on the brink of a resurgence that would lead to its final triumph over its enemies—a prospect that warranted and required violence on a massive scale.

Such episodes of messianic zeal are not restricted to the distant past. In the mid-1980s, a group of Israeli settlers plotted to destroy the Dome of the Rock, the 8th-century mosque atop the Haram al Sharif in Jerusalem. The settlers appeared to believe that destroying the mosque would spark an Arab invasion, which would trigger an Israeli nuclear response—the Armageddon said by the Bible to precede the kingdom of God. The plot was never carried out because the conspirators could not get a rabbinical blessing. Analogous attempts have characterized Christian apocalypticists and even a Buddhist community whose doctrine was strongly influenced by Christian eschatology—Aum Shinrikyo.

## THE DOCTRINAL POTENCY OF AL-QAIDA

Similar thinking can be detected in narrative trends that inform al-Qaida's ideology and actions. Apocalyptic tales circulating on the web and within the Middle East in hard copy tell of cataclysmic battles between Islam and the United States, Israel, and sometimes Europe. Global battles see-saw between infidel and Muslim victory until some devastating act, often the destruction of New York by nuclear weapons, brings Armageddon to an end and leads the world's survivors to convert to Islam.

The theological roots of al-Qaida's leaders hark back to a medieval Muslim jurisconsult, Taqi al Din Ibn Taymiyya, two of whose teachings have greatly influenced Islamic revolutionary movements. The first was his elevation of jihad—not the spiritual struggle that many modern Muslims take it to be, but physical combat against unbelievers—to the rank of the canonical five pillars of Islam (declaration of faith, prayer, almsgiving, self-purification, and pilgrimage to Mecca). The second was his legitimization of rebellion against Muslim rulers who do not enforce *sharia,* or Islamic law, in their domains.

Ibn Taymiyya's ideas were revived in the 1960s in Egypt, where they underpinned 25 years of violence, including the assassination of Anwar Sadat in 1981. When the Egyptian government vanquished the militants, survivors fled abroad, taking advantage of European laws regarding asylum or of the lawlessness of Yemen, Afghanistan, and Kashmir.

Ibn Taymiyya's teachings have even deeper roots in Saudi Arabia. They became part of the founding ideology of the Saudi state when Muhammad Ibn Abd al Wahhab formed an alliance with Ibn Saud in 1744.

Al-Qaida embodies both the Egyptian and Saudi sides of the jihad movement, which came together in the 1960s when some Egyptian militants sought shelter in Saudi Arabia, which was locked in conflict with Nasserist Egypt. Osama bin Laden himself is a Saudi, and his second-in-command, Ayman al Zawahiri, an Egyptian who served three years in prison for his role in Sadat's assassination.

The jihadist themes in Ibn Taymiyya's teachings are striking an increasingly popular chord in parts of the Muslim world.

## AL-QAIDA'S GEOPOLITICAL REACH

Religiously motivated militants have now dispersed widely to multiple "fields of jihad." The social problems that have fueled their discontent are well known—low economic growth, falling wages and increasing joblessness, poor schooling, relentless but unsustainable urban growth, and diminishing environmental resources, especially water. Political alienation and resentment over the intrusion into traditional societies of offensive images, ideas, and commercial products compound these problems and help account for the religious voice given to these primarily secular grievances. The mobilization of religious imagery and terminology further transforms secular issues into substantively religious ones, putting otherwise negotiable political issues beyond the realm of bargaining and making violent outcomes more likely.

The political power of religious symbols has led some pivotal states, in particular Egypt and Saudi Arabia, to use them to buttress their own legitimacy. In so doing they perversely confer authority on the very clerical opposition that threatens state power and impedes the modernization programs that might, over the long haul, materially improve quality of life. Although the jihadists are unable to challenge these states, Islamists nevertheless dominate public discourse and shape the debate on foreign and domestic policy. For the jihadists, following Ibn Taymiyya's principles, the "near enemy" at home took precedence over the "far enemy," which was once Israel and now includes the United States and the West. In Egypt and Saudi Arabia, Islamists have inextricably intertwined the near and far enemies. The governments' need to cater to the sentiments aroused within mosques and on the Islamist airwaves to keep their regimes secure dictates their tolerance or even endorsement of extreme anti-American views. At the same time, strategic circumstances compel both states to provide diplomatic or other practical support for U.S. policies that offend public sensitivities. It is small wonder that Egyptians and Saudis are the backbone of al-Qaida and that Saudi Arabia spawned most of the September 11 attackers.

The fields of jihad stretch far and wide. In the Middle East, al-Qaida developed ties in Lebanon and Jordan. In Southeast Asia, Indonesians, Malaysians, and Singaporeans trained in Afghanistan, or conspired with those who had, to engage in terror, most horrifically the bombing in Bali. In Central Asia, the Islamic Movement of Uzbekistan became a full-fledged jihadist group. In Pakistan, jihadists with apocalyptic instincts nearly provoked a nuclear exchange between India and Pakistan. Videotapes of atrocities of the Algerian Armed Islamic Group circulate in Europe as recruitment propaganda for the global jihad.

Given its role as a springboard for the September 11 attacks, Europe may be the most crucial field of jihad. Lack of political representation and unequal access to education, jobs, housing, and social services have turned European Muslim youth against the states in which they live. In the United Kingdom, the Muslim prison population, a source of recruits for the radical cause, has doubled in the past decade. Close to a majority of young Muslims in Britain have told pollsters that they feel no obligation to bear arms for England but would fight for bin Laden.

The United States remains al-Qaida's prime target. Suleiman Abu Ghaith, the al-Qaida spokesman, has said that there can be no truce until the group has killed four million Americans, whereupon the rest can convert to Islam.

## THE RECALCITRANCE OF THE JIHADISTS

How should the United States respond to the jihadist threat? To the extent one can speak of the root causes of the new terrorism, they defy direct and immediate remedial action. Population in the Middle East is growing rapidly, and the median age is dropping. The correlation between youth and political instability highlights the potential for unrest and radicalization. In cities, social welfare programs, sanitation, transportation, housing, power, and the water supply are deteriorating. In much of the Muslim world, the only refuge from filth, noise, heat, and, occasionally, surveillance is the mosque. Economists agree that the way out of the morass is to develop institutions that facilitate the distribution of capital and create opportunity; how to do that, they are unsure. The West can offer aid but cannot correct structural problems.

Improving public opinion toward the United States is also deeply problematic. Decades of official lies and controlled press have engendered an understandable skepticism toward the assertions of any government, especially one presumed hostile to Muslim interests. Trust is based on confidence in a chain of transmission whose individual links are known to be reliable. Official news outlets or government spokespersons do not qualify as such links. Nor, certainly, do Western news media.

Moreover, highly respected critics of the United States in Saudi Arabia demonstrate an ostensibly profound understanding of U.S. policies and society, while offering a powerful and internally consistent explanation for their country's descent from the all-powerful, rich supplier of oil to the West to a debt-ridden, faltering economy protected by Christian troops and kowtowing to Israel. These are difficult narratives to counter, especially in a society where few know much about the West.

The prominent role of clerics in shaping public opinion offers yet more obstacles. The people who represent the greatest threat of terrorist action against the United States follow the preaching and guidance of Salafi clerics— the Muslim equivalent of Christian "fundamentalists." Although some Salafi preachers have forbidden waging jihad as harmful to Muslim interests, their underlying assumptions are that jihad qua holy war against non-Muslims is fundamentally valid and that Islamic governments that do not enforce *sharia* must be opposed. No authoritative clerical voice offers a sympathetic view of the United States.

The prognosis regarding root causes, then, is poor. The world is becoming more religious; Islam is the fastest-growing faith; religious expression is generally becoming more assertive and apocalyptic thinking more prominent. Weapons of mass destruction, spectacularly suited to cosmic war, are becoming more widely available. Democratization is at a standstill. Governments in Egypt, Saudi Arabia, Pakistan, and Indonesia are unwilling or unable to oppose anti-Western religiously based popular feeling. Immigration, conversion, and inept social policies will intensify parallel trends in Europe.

At least for now, dialogue does not appear to be an option. Meanwhile, global market forces beyond the control of Western governments hasten Western cultural penetration and generate ever-greater resentment. Jihadists could conceivably argue that they have a negotiable program; cessation of U.S. support for Israel, withdrawal from Saudi Arabia, broader American disengagement from the Islamic world. But U.S. and allied conceptions of international security and strategic imperatives will make such demands difficult, if not impossible, to accommodate.

## REDUCING VULNERABILITY TO NEW TERRORISM

Facing a global adversary with maximal goals and lacking a bargaining option or means to redress severe conditions that may or may not motivate attackers, the United States is confined primarily to a strategy of defense, deterrence by denial, and, where possible and prudent, preemption. Deterrence through the promise of retaliation is impossible with an adversary that controls little or no territory and invites attack.

Adjusting to the new threat entails disturbing conceptual twists for U.S. policymakers. After generations of effort to reduce the risk of surprise attack through technical means and negotiated transparency measures, surprise will be the natural order of things. The problem of warning will be further intensified by the creativity of this adversary, its recruitment of Europeans and Americans, and its ability to stage attacks from within the United States. Thinking carefully about the unlikely—"institutionalizing imaginativeness," as Dennis Gormley has put it—is by definition a paradox, but nonetheless essential for American planners.

With warning scarce and inevitably ambiguous, it will be necessary to probe the enemy both to put him off balance and to learn of his intentions. The United States has done so clandestinely against hostile intelligence agencies, occasionally with remarkable results. Against al-Qaida, a more difficult target, the approach will take time to cohere. Probes could also take the form of military action against al-Qaida-affiliated cantonments, where they still exist. The greater the movement's virtuality, however, the fewer such targets will be available for U.S.

action. Preemptive strikes could target sites that develop, produce, or deploy weapons of mass destruction.

A decade of al-Qaida activity within the United States has erased the customary distinction between the domestic and the foreign in intelligence and law enforcement. The relationship between the Central Intelligence Agency and the Federal Bureau of Investigation must change. Only a more integrated organization can adapt to the seamlessness of the transnational arenas in which the terrorists operate.

Civil liberties and security must be rebalanced. How sweeping the process turns out to be will depend largely on whether the nation suffers another attack or at least a convincing attempt. Americans will have to be convinced that curtailing civil liberties is unavoidable and limited to the need to deal with proximate threats. They will need to see bipartisan consensus in Congress and between Congress and the White House and be sure that politicians are committed to keeping the rebalancing to a minimum.

The distinction between public and private sector has also been vitiated. Al-Qaida has targeted the American population and used our infrastructure against us. A perpetual state of heightened readiness would impose unacceptable opportunity costs on the civilian world, so vulnerabilities must be reduced. Civilian ownership of the infrastructure is a complication. What the U.S. government does not own, it cannot completely defend. Private owners do not necessarily share the government's perception of the terrorist threat and are often able to resist regulation. Where they accept the threat, they view it as a national security issue for which the federal government should bear the cost. The idea of public-private partnership is only now finding acceptance in the cybersecurity realm as concerns over litigation have brought about a focus on due diligence. The pursuit of public-private partnership will have to be extended to all potentially vulnerable critical infrastructures by a government that does not yet understand perfectly which infrastructures are truly critical and which apparently dispensable infrastructures interact to become critical.

Defending these infrastructures will also present hair-raising challenges. The U.S. government is not on the lookout for military formations, but for a lone, unknown person in a visa line. Technology—biometrics, data-mining, super-fast data processing, and ubiquitous video-surveillance—will move this needle-in-the-haystack problem into the just-possible category by providing the means to collect and store detailed and unique characteristics of huge numbers of people and match them to the person in the visa line. The cost will be the need to archive personal information on a great mass of individuals.

The United States must also devise ways to block or intercept vehicles that deliver weapons of mass destruction. It cannot do that alone. The cruise missile threat, for instance, requires the cooperation of suppliers, which means an active American role in expanding the remit of the Missile Technology Control Regime (MTCR). Weapons components themselves must be kept out of terrorists' hands. The recent adoption of MTCR controls on cheap technologies for transforming small aircraft into cruise missiles shows what can be accomplished. Washington has been buying surplus fissile materials from Russia's large stock and helping Russians render them useless for weapons; it will be vital to continue generous funding for that effort.

Remote detection of weapons, especially nuclear ones, that have reached the United States is crucial. Emergency response teams will need to be able to pinpoint the location of a device, identify its type, and know in advance how to render it safe once it has been seized. Local authorities will have to detect and identify biological and chemical agents that have been released. Genetically engineered vaccines must be rapidly developed and produced to stop local attacks from becoming national, and ultimately global, epidemics. Special medical units must be on standby to relieve local health-care personnel who become exhausted or die.

Offensive opportunities will be limited but not impossible. They do, however, require impeccable intelligence, which has been hard to come by. The Afghan nexus in which jihadis initially came together and the cohesion of the groups that constitute the al-Qaida movement have made penetration forbiddingly complicated. But as al-Qaida picks up converts to Islam and Muslims who have long resided in Western countries, penetration may become easier. The more they look like us, the more we look like them.

Another source of potentially vital information is the jihadis picked up by local authorities abroad on the basis of U.S. intelligence and then shipped to their countries of origin for interrogation. Transfers of this sort were carried out frequently during the 1990s and sometimes produced life-saving intelligence on imminent terrorist attacks In some cases, the authorities where a suspect resides will not wish to make an arrest, fearing terrorist retaliation, political problems at home, or diplomatic frictions abroad. The United States has asserted the authority to conduct these operations without the consent of the host government but has generally refrained from acting. In the wake of September 11, Washington may want to reassess the risks and benefits of these unauthorized transfers, or, put more crudely, kidnappings.

Without revoking the longstanding executive order prohibiting assassination, the United States should also consider targeted killing, to use the Israeli phrase, of jihadists known to be central to an evolving conspiracy to attack the United States or to obtain weapons of mass destruction. As a practical matter, the intelligence value of such a person alive would generally outweigh the disruptive benefits of his death, assuming that U.S. or friendly intelligence services could be relied on to keep him under surveillance. But this will not always be so. When it is not, from a legal standpoint, targeted killing falls reasonably under the right to self-defense. Such a policy departure is unsavory. But in a new strategic context, with jihadis intent on mass casualties, unsavory may not be a sensible threshold.

## ALLIED COOPERATION

As the al-Qaida movement dissolves into virtuality in 60 countries worldwide, international cooperation becomes ever more indispensable to countering the threat.

Many countries that host al-Qaida will cooperate with the United States out of self-interest; they do not want jihadis on their soil any more than Americans do on theirs. A durable and effective counterterrorism campaign, however, requires not just bare-bones cooperation, but political collaboration at a level that tells the bureaucracies that cooperation with their American counterparts

is expected. Such a robust, wholesale working relationship is what produces vital large-scale initiatives—a common diplomatic approach toward problem states; a sustainable program of economic development for the Middle East; domestic policy reforms that lessen the appeal of jihadism to Muslim diaspora communities; improved border controls; and tightened bonds among the justice ministries, law enforcement, customs, and intelligence agencies, and special operations forces on the front lines.

Whether this level of burden sharing emerges, let alone endures, depends on the give and take among the players. Since September 11, the United States has fostered allied perceptions that Washington is indifferent to their priorities. Apart from slow progress toward a UN Security Council resolution on Iraq, the United States has not yet paid a serious penalty in terms of allied cooperation. The scale of the attacks and the administration's blend of resolve and restraint in the war on terrorism have offset allies' disappointment in its go-it-alone posture. But as the war grinds on, good will is certain to wear thin. The United States would be wise to forgo some of its own trade- and treaty-related preferences, at least in short term, to ensure allied support in the crises that will inevitably come.

Washington's interests would also be well served by modifying what appears at times to be a monolithic view of terrorist networks that equates the Arafats and Saddams of the world with bin Laden (or his successors). Several European partners regard Arafat and his ilk as considerably more controllable through diplomacy than bin Laden and view countries such as Iran, which has used terrorism against the United States, as amenable to "constructive dialogue." Greater American flexibility may prove essential for ensuring European capitals' military, law-enforcement, and intelligence cooperation. And the fact remains that al-Qaida has killed more Americans than have Iraq, Iran, or Palestinian groups and would use weapons of mass destruction against the United States as soon as it acquired them.

## ISRAEL AND THE PALESTINIANS

Since the heyday of the Middle East peace process under Ehud Barak's Labor government, jihadists have exploited the Israeli-Palestinian conflict to boost their popularity. The strategem has worked: jihadists are seen as sticking up for Palestinian rights, while Arab governments do nothing. Direct, energetic U.S. diplomatic intervention in the conflict would lessen the appeal of jihadi claims and make it marginally easier for regional governments to cooperate in the war on terrorism by demonstrating American concern for the plight of Palestinians.

The Bush administration fears becoming entangled in a drawn out, venomous negotiation between irreconcilable parties. They see it distracting them from higher priorities and embroiling them in domestic political disputes over whether Washington should pressure Israel. Still, the administration has been drawn in by degrees and has announced its support for creating a Palestinian state. If the war on terrorism is now the highest U.S. priority, then more vigorous—and admittedly risky—involvement in the Israeli-Palestinian conflict is required. The jihadi argument that the United States supports the murder of Palestinian Muslims must be defanged.

## DEMOCRATIZATION IN THE MIDDLE EAST

As it continues to engage with the authoritarian regimes in Cairo and Riyadh, Washington should try to renegotiate the implicit bargain that underpins its relations with both. The current bargain is structured something like this: Egypt sustains its commitment to peace with Israel, Saudi Arabia stabilizes oil prices, and both proffer varying degrees of diplomatic support for American objectives in the region, especially toward Iraq. In return, Washington defers to their domestic policies, even if these fuel the growth and export of Islamic militancy and deflect public discontent onto the United States and Israel. With jihadis now pursuing nuclear weapons, that bargain no longer looks sensible.

Under a new bargain, Cairo and Riyadh would begin to take measured risks to lead their publics gradually toward greater political responsibility and away from Islamist thinking (and action) by encouraging opposition parties of a more secular cast and allowing greater freedom of expression. Saudi Arabia would throttle back on its wahhabiization of the Islamic world by cutting its production and export of unemployable graduates in religious studies and reducing subsidies for foreign mosques and madrassas that propagate a confrontational and intolerant form of Islam while crowding out alternative practices. Both countries would be pushed to reform their school curricula—and enforce standards—to ensure a better understanding of the non-Islamic world and encourage respect for other cultures. With increased financial and technical assistance from the West, regimes governing societies beset by economic problems that spur radicalism would focus more consistently on the welfare of their people. In this somewhat utopian conception, leaders in both countries would use their newly won credibility to challenge Islamist myths about America and the supposed hostility of the West toward Islam. In sum, Cairo and Riyadh would challenge the culture of demonization across the board, with an eye toward laying the groundwork for liberal democracy.

In the framework of this new bargain, the United States would establish contacts with moderate opposition figures in Egypt, Saudi Arabia, and perhaps other countries. The benefit would be twofold. Washington would get a better sense of events on the ground and would also gain credibility and perhaps even understanding on the part of critics. For this effort to bear fruit, however, the United States would have to use regional media efficiently—something for which it has as yet no well-developed strategy. Washington would also have to engage in a measure of self scrutiny and explore ways in which its policies contribute—in avoidable ways—to Muslim anti-Americanism. "Rebranding" is not enough.

Change will be slow. The regimes in Cairo and Riyadh face largely self-inflicted problems they cannot readily surmount without serious risks to stability. Nor is the United States entirely free to insist on the new bargain: it will need Saudi cooperation on Iraq as long as Saddam Hussein is in power, if not longer, given the uncertainties surrounding Iraq's future after Saddam leaves the stage. Egyptian support for a broader Arab-Israeli peace will also remain essential. But change has to start sometime, somewhere. It will take steady U.S. pressure and persistent attempts to persuade both regimes that a new bargain will serve their countries' long-term interests. The sooner the new deals are struck, the better.

## Hazardous but Not Hopeless

Western democracies face a serious, possibly transgenerational terrorist threat whose causes are multidimensional and difficult to address. The situation is hazardous, but not hopeless. The United States possesses enormous wealth, has capable allies, and stands on the leading edge of technological development that will be key to survival. A strategy that takes into account the military, intelligence, law-enforcement, diplomatic, and economic pieces of the puzzle will see America through. For the next few years, the objective will be to contain the threat, in much the same way that the United States contained Soviet power throughout the Cold War. The adversary must be prevented from doing his worst, while Washington and its allies wear down its capabilities and undermine its appeal to fellow Muslims. Success will require broad domestic support and a strong coalition abroad.

Prospects are, in many respects, bleak. But the dangers are not disproportionate to those the nation faced in the 20th-century. America's initial reaction to September 11 was and indeed had to be its own self-defense: bolstering homeland security, denying al-Qaida access to failing or hostile states, dismantling networks, and developing a law-enforcement and intelligence network able to better cope with the new adversary. Not all vulnerabilities can be identified and even fewer remedied, and al-Qaida need launch only one attack with a weapon of mass destruction to throw the United States into a profound crisis. Washington and its partners must convince Muslim populations that they can prosper without either destroying the West or abandoning their own traditions to the West's alien culture. That is a long-term project. American and allied determination in a war against apocalyptic—and genocidal—religious fanatics must be coupled with a generous vision about postwar possibilities. Militant Islam cannot be expected to embrace the West in the foreseeable future. But the United States can lay the foundation for a lasting accommodation by deploying its considerable economic and political advantages. It is not too late to begin.

## REVIEW QUESTIONS

- How are the Christian just war and Islamic jihad doctrines distinguishable from each other?
- Is terrorism sometimes justifiable from the perspective of just war and jihad?
- What is the underlying religious rationale used to justify suicide bombing?
- Should movements such as Al Qaeda be classified as organizations or religious ideologies?
- How effective are modern counterterrorist measures against religious terrorism movements?

The following books and articles are suggested for further information about the new era of religious terrorism:

### Books

Barkun, Michael. *Religion and the Racist Right: The Origins of the Christian Identity Movement.* Revised ed. Chapel Hill: University of North Carolina Press, 1997.
Murphy, John F. *Sword of Islam: Muslim Extremism from the Arab Conquests to the Attack on America.* Amherst, NY: Promethius, 2002.
Rashid, Ahmed. *Jihad: The Rise of Militant Islam in Central Asia.* New Haven, CT: Yale University Press, 2002.

### Articles

Fuller, Graham E. "The Future of Political Islam." *Foreign Affairs.* 81:2 (March/April 2002).
Goldberg, Jeffrey. "Inside Jihad U.: The Education of a Holy Warrior." *The New York Times Magazine.* (June 25, 2000).
White, Jonathan. "Political Eschatology: A Theology of Antigovernment Extremism." *American Behavioral Scientist.* 44:6 (February 2001).

# 7

# THE NEAR FUTURE OF TERRORISM

I t is no more possible to predict terrorist violence than it is to predict criminal victimization. However, it is possible to *project* potential scenarios and features of near-term terrorist behavior and the terrorist environment. For example, the discussion among experts during the 1990s about the New Terrorism did project the asymmetrical quality of the new era of terrorism. It is likely that the emerging terrorist profile of terrorism in the new era will continue to be the predominant typology for terrorist violence into the immediate future. This profile will, of course, be shaped by new national and international political environments as the war on terrorism progresses. Therefore, our consideration of the near-future of terrorism is by no means an exact science. It is contingent upon expert analysis of how current trends and behavior may impact the future environment. Thus, examination of the motives and conduct of contemporary terrorists is critical to projecting the near-future of the new era.

The articles in this chapter discuss near-term issues that are likely to characterize the modern terrorist environment. Al Qaeda's calculations for carrying out the September 11, 2001 attacks are analyzed by Brigitte Nacos in "The Terrorist Calculus Behind 9–11: A Model for Future Terrorism?" Al Qaeda's goals and objectives for the attacks are discussed, as is the question of the degree to which the attacks were successful. The article probes the likelihood that terrorists do consider the attacks to be successful, and that these events may be replicated by like-minded extremists. Gary Milhollin outlines the ways that terrorists can obtain nuclear weapons and the feasibility for them doing so in "Can Terrorists Get the Bomb?" The essay investigates several methods for obtaining the requisite materials for constructing bomb components, as well as whether an intact device can be acquired. Ariel Cohen assesses the war on terrorism from Russia's perspective in "Russia, Islam, and the War on Terrorism: An Uneasy Future." An analysis is made of Russia's participation in the war on terrorism, and the danger from militant Islamist terrorism directed against Russian interests.

## The Terrorist Calculus Behind 9–11: A Model for Future Terrorism?

Brigitte L. Nacos
*Columbia University New York, NY, USA*

Before he and his Al Qaeda comrades fled their quarters in the Qandahar region of Afghanistan, probably some time in mid-November 2001, Osama bin Laden discussed the twin attacks on the World Trade Center in New York and the Pentagon in Washington two months earlier. Referring to the kamikaze pilots whom he called "vanguards of Islam," bin Laden marveled, "Those young men ( . . . inaudible . . . ) said in deeds, in New York and Washington, speeches that overshadowed other speeches made everywhere else in the world. The speeches are understood by both Arabs and non-Arabs—even Chinese." With these remarks bin Laden revealed that he considered terrorism first and foremost as a vehicle to dispatch messages—"speeches" in his words—and, with respect to the events of 11 September 2001 (9–11), he concluded that Americans in particular had heard and reacted to the intended communication.[1]

Terrorists used suicide attacks long before the killing of about 3,000 Americans and foreign nationals in New York, Washington, D.C., and near Pittsburgh on that "Black Tuesday" in September. In Sri Lanka the Tamil Tigers have undertaken many suicide missions in their fight against the Sinhala-dominated central government; the Kurdish Workers Party, too, used these terrorist methods against Turkish and Kurdish targets. In 1983 members of the Lebanese Hizbollah drove an explosive-laden truck into the U.S. Marine barracks in Beirut killing 243 American soldiers. Hizbollah and the Palestinian Hamas have used "human bombs" for years to attack Israel. But the scope and impact of the 9–11 terror operations proved more than any other suicide mission before that weak non-state actors can strike hard against even the strongest of today's nation states.

There is no evidence of a direct connection between the terror of 9–11 and the unprecedented wave of suicide strikes against Israelis some six months later. But it is noteworthy that the Al-Aksa Martyrs Brigade, part of Yasir Arafat's Fatah organization and—unlike Hamas, the Palestinian Jihad, and Hizbollah—a secular group, did embrace this strategy for the first time in late 2001—after the 9–11 attacks—and in the process paved the way for female recruits who were not accepted by the religious groups. During the most lethal wave of suicide attacks against Israeli targets this spring, more of these bombers were associated with the Al-Aksa group than with Hamas. It can therefore be asked whether the "human bomb" offensive starting with the Passover massacre on 27 March 2002 that killed 28 and injured 150 Israelis was encouraged by the suicide terror against symbolic targets in New York and Washington and, more importantly, by the impact of those horrific attacks. Whether or not that was the case, the idea of the calculus behind the 9–11 attacks serving as a model for future terrorism is not far fetched, if the operation was and continues to be deemed successful by groups and individuals already involved in or pondering political violence. Although perceptions are often far removed from reality, most terrorists make rational choices and cost-benefit calculations.[2] Thus the need to explore the following questions: Was the terror of 9–11 successful from the terrorist perspective? To what extent did bin Laden and his followers realize or further their various objectives—or fail to do so?

With the "war against terrorism" far from over, it is too early for a definitive answer to such questions. But bin Laden commented repeatedly on the consequences of the 9–11 attacks as if he deemed them a success, for example, when he claimed that "[t]his is the first time the balance of terror has been close between the two parties, between Muslims and Americans, in the modern age."[3]

Terrorism's efficacy, like beauty, is in the eyes of the beholder in that those who commit political violence deliberately targeting civilians believe in the success of their deeds even if the consequences are disappointing from the perpetrators's perspective. In the case of the attacks on New York and Washington, however, there is no doubt that the architects of terror were successful in realizing some of their objectives. It has been suggested that "the success of the military campaign in Afghanistan" in response to 9–11 did hurt Osama bin Laden's reputation among Arabs and Muslims in that he is increasingly perceived as a loser.[4] But the conclusion of bin Laden becoming a hero in the Arab and Muslim world is more plausible. One observer, in fact, cast the United States and its allies in the counterterrorist campaign in a no-win role arguing that "[t]he allies are now in a horrible dilemma. If they 'bring him to justice' and put him on trial they will provide bin Laden with a platform for global propaganda. If, instead, he is assassinated—perhaps 'shot while trying to escape'—he will become a martyr. If he escapes he will become a Robin Hood. Bin Laden cannot lose."[5] But regardless of the Al Qaeda leader's ultimate standing among fellow Muslims, in one respect the success of the 9–11 operation is indisputable: The masterminds behind the attack proved the impotence of the mightiest military power to protect its citizens against these kinds of devastating blows. As one expert concluded, "One of the objectives of the terrorist attack was to prove that the United States was not invulnerable—that it could be hurt by small, relatively weak groups of dedicated fighters. The reaction of most Americans to the attacks have played into their hands."[6] It must be added that the reaction of the U.S. government as well proved that the most lethal act of terror on U.S. soil hit a raw nerve in Washington's power centers. Following the attacks both the legislative and executive branches were preoccupied with anti- and counterterrorist measures apart from the actual "war against terrorism" in Afghanistan. In the four months following the events of 9–11 a stunning "ninety-eight percent of all bills, resolutions, and amendments proposed by the House of Representatives and 97 percent by the Senate related to terrorism. . . . President Bush issued 12 Executive Orders and 10 Presidential Proclamations related to the attacks."[7] With their deadly assault, bin Laden and his followers managed to set America's public agenda for many months, perhaps even years. Given the magnitude of the 9–11 terror, these reactions

were hardly surprising, but from the perspective of bin Laden and company, these responses demonstrated day-in and day-out how they had stung America.

## TERRORISM'S MEDIA-CENTERED GOALS AND 9–11

In a popular culture inundated with images of violence, the horror of the quadruple hijack coup and the deliberate flights into the World Trade Center and Pentagon was as real as in the movies, but it was surreal in life. The novelist John Updike, who witnessed the calamity from a tenth-floor apartment in Brooklyn, felt that "as on television, this was not quite real, it could be fixed; the technocracy the towers symbolized would find a way to put out the fire and reverse the damage."[8]

The greatest irony was that the very terrorists who loathed America's pop culture as decadent and poisonous to their own beliefs and ways of life turned Hollywood-like horror fantasies into real life hell. In that respect they outperformed Hollywood, the very symbol of the American-led Western entertainment that they despise. After visiting the World Trade Center disaster site for the first time New York's Governor George Pataki said: "It's just incomprehensible to see what it was like down there. You know, I remember seeing one of these Cold War movies and after the nuclear attacks with the Hollywood portrayal of a nuclear winter. It looked worse than that in downtown Manhattan, and it wasn't some grade "B" movie. It was life. It was real."[9]

From the terrorists' point of view the attack on America was a perfectly choreographed production aimed at American and international audiences. In the past, terrorism has often been compared to theatre because political violence is staged to get the attention of the audience. Although the theatre metaphor remains instructive, it has given way to that of terrorism as a global television spectacular, as breaking news that is watched by international audiences and transcends by far the boundaries of theatrical events. In the past most, if not all, acts of terrorism resulted in a great deal of publicity in the form of news reporting but 9–11 opened a new chapter in the annals of terrorism as communication because of the choices the planners made with respect to method, target, timing, and scope. To this day the images of airliners crashing as suicide-homicide missiles into the very symbols of America's economic and military might next to the dominant U.S. and global media organizations remain almost incomprehensible. Those responsible for these deeds could have struck at night, spared many lives, and still rake a great deal of publicity. But the bright daylight guaranteed the most "spectacular'" visuals and the loss of life for which they undoubtedly aimed. In all these respects no previous act of terrorism came even close to the events of 9–11.

## THE WHOLE WORLD WATCHING

Those who plan and commit acts of terrorism calculate the consequences of their deeds, the likelihood of gaining media attention, and, most important, the chance of winning entrance— through the media—to what I call The Triangle of Political Communication. The corners of this triangle are the news media, the public, and governmental decision makers. In mass societies in which direct contact and communication between the governors and the mass of the governed are no longer possible, the media provide the links that allow the flow of messages between those in public offices and the general public. Indeed, it has been argued that "politics is communication" and that "[p]olitical communication is therefore the means by which people express both their unity and their differences. Through communication we petition our government, plead our unique and special interests, rally those who agree with us to our causes, and chastise those who do not share our world views."[10]

But groups and individuals who have the urge to communicate their causes and grievances because they do not share the mainstream views may not get any access, or from their point of view not enough access, to the mass media. The fact is, of course, that the news media are not simply neutral and passive communication conduits but rather represent one of the corners in the communication triangle. In

that strategic position the media magnify and minimize, include and exclude. The notion of the news media as gatekeepers is useful to explain the concept of mass-mediated political violence, namely terrorists' expectation that in the face of this sort of political violence, especially spectacular terrorist acts, the media open their gates for all kinds of incident-related reporting to enter the triangle of communication— including the well-calculated messages that terrorists want publicized regardless of whether they claim responsibility for their acts or remain silent. When terrorists strike, their deeds assure them instant media attention and, as a consequence of generous news coverage, of the general public and the government in their particular target country. Moreover, given the global nature of the contemporary communication system, the perpetrators of international and domestic terrorism also tap into the international media and thereby receive the attention of publics and governments beyond their immediate target countries as well.

It has been argued that beginning with the first World Trade Center bombing in 1993 and the Oklahoma City bombing, the world has entered into a new age of mega-terrorism, that this new "terrorism of expression" is no longer dependent on the media, and that therefore claims of responsibility are no longer necessary. However, in most of the recent cases of horrific acts of terrorism the responsible parties either claimed responsibility by contacting the media (i.e., the first World Trade Center case), left clues (e.g., Timothy McVeigh by striking on the second anniversary of the inferno at Waco, Texas), or hinted at their identity and eventually making quasi claims of responsibility (bin Laden and his associates after the bombing of the U.S. Embassies in Kenya and Tanzania in 1998, after the attack on the destroyer U.S.S. Cole in the port of Aden, Yemen, and, most importantly, after the events of 9–11).

Pulitzer Prize winner Thomas Friedman has suggested that Osama bin Laden "is not a mere terrorist" but a "super-empowered" man with geopolitical aspirations who "has employed violence not to grab headlines but to kill as many Americans as possible to drive them out of the Islamic world and weaken their society."[11] But according to a detailed manual of the

The Near Future of Terrorism · 179

Afghan jihad that was used for the instruction of would-be terrorists in Al Qaeda's training camps, publicity was (and most probably still is) an overriding consideration in planning terrorist acts. Thus, the manual advised holy warriors to target "sentimental landmarks" such as the Statue of Liberty in New York, Big Ben in London, and the Eiffel Tower in Paris because their destruction would "generate intense publicity."[12] Whether the extensive terrorism network under the leadership of bin Laden and his associates or a small cell of violent environmentalists, Paul Wilkinson's astute observation holds true:

> When one says "terrorism" in a democratic society, one also says "media." For terrorism by its very nature is a psychological weapon which depends upon communicating a threat to a wider society. This, in essence, is why terrorism and the media enjoy a symbiotic relationship.[13]

To be sure, publicity via the mass media is not an end in itself; it is a means to more important ends, namely the realization of short- and medium-term or long-term political objectives. But like terrorists at all times and in all places, those who planned the 9–11 attacks were well aware that the news about their acts would first of all help them achieve their media-centered publicity goals and in the process could also advance some or all of their political objectives.[14] In particular, massive news coverage assures terrorists the attention of their target audiences, a discussion of their motives, and a status of prominence for their leaders.[15]

If not the perpetrators themselves, the architects of their terror enterprise surely anticipated the immediate media impact: blanket coverage not only in the United States but worldwide. Opinion polls revealed that literally all Americans followed the news of the terrorist attacks (99% or 100% according to surveys) by watching and listening to television and radio and logging on to the Internet. Around the world there was an equally universal awareness of what had happened in the United States. This was a perfect achievement with respect to the "attention getting" goal for which all terrorists strive.

Until 9–11, the terrorist assault on members of Israel's Olympic team by the Palestinian "Black September" group during the 1972 Olympic Games at Munich, Germany, was considered the one terrorist action watched by an estimated audience of 800 million around the world. But the advances in communication technology and the greater availability of television sets, personal computers, and cellular phones today put the events of 9–11 or "Black Tuesday" for sure into the record books as the most watched terrorist coup ever.

## THE INTIMIDATION FACTOR

Closely tied to the objective to get public and elite attention is another terrorist goal, namely to intimidate their target audience, to spread anxiety and fear in a public traumatized by their terror. Opinion polls revealed that the terror attacks on New York and Washington heightened American's fear of more terrorism to come and of the likelihood that they themselves or a member of their family might become victims. This effect on the targeted population was not lost on bin Laden and his associates. In commenting on the impact of the terror attack on the American enemy, the Al Qaeda leader remarked with obvious satisfaction, "There is America, full of fear from north to south, from west to east. Thank God for that."[16]

Moreover, terrorists hope to strike hard enough so that alarmed governments in democracies adopt anti- and counterterrorist laws and regulations that curb highly esteemed civil liberties and thereby weaken the very fabric of liberal democratic societies. Of the more than 20 federal laws adopted in the United States after 9–11 and before the end of 2001, many dealt with domestic anti- and counterterrorist matters. This followed the pattern that liberal democracies take in response to terrorism. But, as one terrorism scholar pointed out, the problem was that "these provisions sought to ensure greater security for Americans, [but] many of them made serious inroads into the individual rights of both citizens and non-citizens."[17] These developments were not lost on bin Laden, who told a correspondent of the Al-Jazeera television network that "freedom and human rights in America are doomed" and predicted that the U.S. government would lead its people and the

West "into an unbearable hell and a choking life."[18] Although few in the general public in the United States and elsewhere in the West believed seriously that civil liberties were doomed as a result of hastily adopted antiterrorism laws, there were uneasy sentiments and outright opposition in some quarters against governments going too far in efforts to protect their citizens from terrorist strikes at the expense of individual rights. It is not clear whether bin Laden seriously aims at provoking political changes in the United States and the West but he certainly wants to demonstrate the hypocritical application of Western values and how easily they are weakened or abandoned. In the wake 9–11 he saw this goal accomplished, explaining:

> The values of this Western civilization under the leadership of America have been destroyed. Those awesome symbolic towers that speak of liberty, human rights, and humanity have been destroyed. They have gone up in smoke.
>
> The proof came when the U.S. government pressured the media not to run our statements that are not longer than a few minutes. They felt that the truth started to reach the American people, the truth that we are not terrorists as they understand it but because we are being attacked in Palestine, Iraq, Lebanon, Sudan, Somalia, Kashmir, the Philippines and everywhere else.[19]

Bin Laden is not the first terrorist and Al Qaeda not the first terrorist organization aiming at trapping liberal states into extreme measures that violate the fundamental values of the state. Indeed, when targeting liberal democracies "terrorism strives and trades on the grave mistakes and misjudgments of the government authorities and security forces, powerful parties and groups within society."[20]

## WHY DO THEY HATE US?

After 9–11 there was a tremendous jump in the quantity of news reports about one or the other aspect of and reasons for anti-American sentiments in the Arab and Muslim world. There was an even greater increase in the stories that explained the teachings of mainstream Islam and how it differs from the extreme

fundamentalist versions. American television news especially had paid little attention to these topics before the terrorist attacks in the United States. But the switch from scarce and modest reporting on Arabs, Muslims, and Islam before 9–11 to far more news coverage thereafter occurred in radio news and in the print press as well. Although many of these stories focused on extreme anti-American actions by Arabs and Muslims, many others explored the roots of these sentiments, the problems caused by U.S. foreign policy in these regions, and the nonviolent essence of mainstream Islam and its teachings.

The point here is not to criticize the news media for publicizing such contextual reports but rather to point out that this coverage and the accompanying mass-mediated debate was triggered by the events of 9–11 and thus was a direct result of terrorist action. Before the terror attacks U.S. American news organizations—with few exceptions—reported far less from abroad than their European counterparts. Moreover, foreign news reporting was predominantly episodic, focused on a particular case at hand, rather than thematic and focused on the underlying conditions, developments, and attitudes. This changed in a rather dramatic fashion after 9–11 when the U.S. media tried to answer the question that President Bush had posed in his speech before a joint session of the U.S. Congress: Why do they hate us? In the process, the perpetrators of violence achieved their perhaps most important media-dependent goal, namely to publicize their causes, grievances, and demands. By striking hard at America, the terrorists forced the mass media to explore their grievances in ways that transcended by far the quantity and narrow focus of the pre-crisis coverage. Again, bin Laden was acutely aware that the attacks had resulted in Americans' and Westerners' sudden interest in Islam and the Muslim world. According to a videotaped conversation bin Laden told associates:

> [I]n Holland, at one of the centers, the number of people who accepted Islam during the days that followed the operations [of 9–11] were more than the people who accepted Islam in the last eleven years. I heard someone on Islamic radio who owns a school in America say: "We don't have time to keep up with the demands of those who are asking about Islamic books to learn more about Islam."

This event made people think which benefited Islam greatly.[21]

Although there is no evidence for the claim of massive conversions to Islam in the West on the heels of the kamikaze attacks of 9–11, many people, especially in America, showed a sudden interest in learning more about Islam—either from books or courses taught in universities and adult education programs. This and the continued coverage of such topics in the mass media increased the American public's knowledge about Islam. According to a CBS News survey, 55% of Americans said at the end of February 2002 that they knew more now about Islam than they did before September 2001. The same survey showed that 30% of the public had a positive, 33% a negative view of this religion. But this was actually a net gain in favor of Americans' positive attitudes toward Islam compared to a 1993 survey conducted by the *Los Angeles Times,* when 14% revealed positive and 22% negative feelings toward Islam.[22]

Unfortunately, the aftermath of 9–11 witnessed hate crimes against Muslims, Arabs, and people who were neither but looked to their attackers like "terrorists." There is no doubt that the news about the identities of the 9–11 perpetrators and the endless news images of bin Laden and his followers perpetuated the negative stereotype of the Muslim and Arab as terrorist that American disaster novels and motion pictures had nourished and exploited for decades. The vast majority of U.S. media organizations reported on and condemned this senseless violence giving representatives of these groups opportunities to speak out on behalf of the Muslim and Arab communities. Strangely, in the process the media also seemed to reveal the emergence of a reverse stereotype in the minds and words of some Arabs and Muslims in the United States—that of the Muslim-hating and Arab-hating American, a stereotype that is just as unreal as that of the Muslim and Arab as terrorist.

## OSAMA BIN LADEN SUPERSTAR

What about the third goal that many terrorists hope to advance, namely to win or increase their standing and support in some publics? Here, the perpetrators' number one audience was not the terrorized American public but rather the population in their homelands and their regions of operation. A charismatic figure among his supporters and his sympathizers to begin with, Osama bin Laden was the biggest winner in this respect. The media covered him as America's number one public enemy and thereby bolstered his popularity, respectability, and legitimacy among millions of Muslims abroad. Although certainly not liked by Americans, bin Laden became a household name in the United States. In the first 10 issues after 9–11, *Newsweek* depicted bin Laden 3 times on its cover, *Time* twice. During this same period *Time* featured the image of President George W. Bush twice, *Newsweek* not at all. This prominent coverage of the Al Qaeda leader was not peculiar to these two leading U.S. news magazines.

In the aftermath of the terrorist attacks on New York and Washington and up to the start of the war in Afghanistan on October 7, the U.S. television networks covered Osama bin Laden more frequently, leading newspapers and National Public Radio only somewhat less frequently than George W. Bush. This was particularly noteworthy because during this period the U.S. president made in one form or another 54 public statements whereas bin Laden did not make any personal appearances at all but relied on a few faxed and videotaped statements by himself and close associates that were delivered to the Arab news network Al-Jazeera.

The same coverage patterns prevailed through the next two months and thus during the military strikes against targets in Afghanistan. Again, although President Bush went public more than 70 times during this period, bin Laden remained in hiding or was on the run and in no position to "go public" apart from several videotaped messages. Yet, the 9–11 terrorism and its aftermath turned the world's most notorious terrorist into one of the leading newsmakers—indeed *the* leading newsmaker. From the terrorists' point of view it did not matter that bin Laden got bad press in the United States and elsewhere. Singled-out, condemned, and warned by leaders such as President Bush and British Prime Minister Tony Blair, Osama bin Laden was covered as frequently and prominently as the world's most influential legitimate leaders, or even more frequently and more prominently. This in itself was a smashing success from the perspective of bin Laden and his associates and supporters. Perhaps the Al Qaeda leader is not a "mere terrorist,"[23] but the attention conferred on him by both the mass media and political leaders elevated him as much to a global figure as did the terror of 9–11 and the fear it struck into Americans.

There is no doubt, then, that the architects of 9–11 had a perfect score with respect to the three media-centered objectives of the calculus of terror: they raked unprecedented media attention, publicized their causes and motives and in the process the grievances of many Muslims, and gained global prominence and notoriety otherwise only accorded to nation-states and their leaders.

## The Ultimate Goals

If accomplished publicity goals are merely the means to far more important ends, as argued earlier, it must be wondered whether bin Laden and Al Qaeda succeeded or failed to advance their intertwined political and religious goals and to what extent the media-centered objectives figured into the results. There is no doubt that the interactions and links between the media, the public, and governmental decision makers are stronger in the United States and other democracies than in the mostly authoritarian Arab and Muslim states. Nevertheless, the increased availability of news sources in the non-Western world has bolstered the opportunities for terrorist propaganda directed at both the masses and the rulers. Although American and Western news organizations—not only CNN— still dominate the global news market, satellite television networks and regional channels have proliferated, especially in the Arab world. And with the exception of Qatar-based Al-Jazeera television that strives for a balance in reporting, the programming is typically one-sided anti-Israel, anti-Jewish, and anti-American—especially in the wake of 9–11 and during the "war on terrorism." Even Al-Jazeera catered to bin Laden for years and certainly after September 11 by airing interviews with the Al Qaeda leader, carrying his statements, publicizing his views and grievances. The Israeli-Palestinian conflict is simply reported in terms of Israelis as aggressors and Palestinians as victims. In addition, the Internet proves an increasingly ideal vehicle for spreading propaganda. Thus, the outlandish idea that thousands of Jews had been warned of the World Trade Center attack and did not go to work on September 11 was spread over the World Wide Web and adopted by many millions of Muslims. This kind of news has incited the masses in Arab and Muslim countries to a degree that governments in the region cannot completely ignore. And this seems to have worked in favor of bin Laden's policy goals.

Strangely, in the United States even months after the shock of 9–11 some observers claimed that the political goals of "these new terrorists were 'not even clear' and remained 'vague.'"[24] The truth is that bin Laden laid out his agenda very clearly in his so-called religious edicts or fatwa of 1996 and 1998 as well as in interviews granted in the years before the terror strikes in the United States. The texts of all of these statements were available on the Internet—and they still are.[25] Moreover, his well-publicized post-9–11 statements and documents retrieved in Afghanistan revealed his views and causes. Three grievances in particular were repeatedly articulated:

1. The presence of U.S. forces on the Arabian peninsula—and especially in Saudi-Arabia.

2. U.S. sanctions and aggression against Iraq and the alleged plan of the "Crusader-Zionist alliance" to "annihilate what is left of this [the Iraqi] people."

3. American support of "the Jews petty state" and for the "spilling of blood in Palestine. . . ."

The claim that bin Laden did not talk about the Palestinian question before the Afghan war and simply jumped on the pro-Palestinian bandwagon in a belated opportunistic move to enlist support in the Arab world needs clarification.[26] It is certainly true that bin Laden spoke more often and more forcefully in support of Palestinians after 9–11, but he had not been silent on this issue before that date. Addressing his Muslim brothers—particularly those on the Arabian peninsula, he wrote in his 1996 fatwa, that the money they paid to buy American goods would be transformed into bullets and used against their brothers in Palestine and tomorrow against their sons in their own lands. Thus, the more immediate political agenda contained three clearly defined goals:

1. The removal of the U.S. military and thus the reduction or removal of U.S. interest from Saudi Arabia and other countries in the region.

2. The end of U.S. pressure on and sanctions against Iraq.

3. The destruction of the U.S.-Israeli alliance and the strengthening of the Palestinians' battle against Israel.

So how did bin Laden and Al Qaeda fare on these accounts? For starters, the once symbiotic relationship between the American and Saudi governments-based on Saudi Arabia's flow of oil to the United States on the one hand and on U.S. military protection of the Saudi rulers on the other, became tense and contentious after 9–11. The revelation that 15 of the 19 9–11 terrorists were Saudi nationals and that the Saudi government financed anti-American, anti-Western, anti-Christian, and anti-Jewish teachings by Wahhabist fundamentalists in Islamic schools and mosques at home and abroad were only the first in a catalogue of grievances on the part of Washington. Once the "war against terrorism" began in Afghanistan, the Al Saud rulers questioned the prudence of continued American military presence inside their borders; later on they declared repeatedly that the United States would not be allowed to use bases on their territory in an attack on Iraq. As Americans prepared to commemorate the first anniversary of the 9–11 catastrophe, the United States retained military bases in Saudi Arabia and other Gulf countries. But considering that bin Laden's initial and most prominent target of discontent was the regime in Saudi Arabia and its alleged collusion with America, the cooling off in the relationship between Saudis and Americans was a move in the direction of his agenda. After all, the U.S. forces on Saudi Arabian soil had been a particular affront all along because of the kingdom's importance as the sacred heartland of the Islamic faith.

Secondly, when President Bush identified Iraq, Iran, and North Korea as terrorist states in what he characterized as an "axis of evil" and potential targets in his declared war against terrorism, he offered a catchy sound bite for the news media and caused an international controversy. Arab governments in particular as well as Muslim regimes elsewhere distanced themselves from Washington—at least for domestic consumption, and so did traditional friends in Europe—including some who were involved or helpful in the fight against the Taliban and Al Qaeda in Afghanistan. Even Kuwait, which was liberated from the Iraqi occupation by a U.S.-led coalition a decade earlier made clear that its bases were not available for a U.S. attack on Iraq. Most important, 9–11 and the Bush administration's subsequent threats against Saddam Hussein put the Iraqi question once again on the international community's and the United Nations's agenda. Indeed, the attacks of post-9–11 policies provoked the Bush administration to prepare for a war on terrorism well beyond the actions against the Taliban and Al Qaeda's global network of terrorist organizations and cells. The negative reaction on the European continent and especially in the Arab and Muslim world marked one more point on the score card of the 9–11 calculus. Nothing demonstrated this clearer than the embrace between Iraqi and Saudi Arabian representatives at the Arab League's summit in Beirut in the spring 2002 and the signs of a much improved relationship between Kuwait and Iraq.

Finally, the proliferation of the Israeli-Palestinian conflict beginning in late March 2002 widened the gulf between Saudi Arabia's rulers and other Arab governments on one side and the Washington administration on the other. Months earlier, one observer had argued convincingly that it is "disingenuous to suggest that the crisis in the Middle-East is unconnected to bin Laden."[27] Although the staunch U.S. support for Israel has been a perennial source of anti-American sentiment in the Arab world, there is no doubt that 9–11 and Washington's war on terrorism in Afghanistan intensified these feelings and paved the way for a chill in Arab-American relations. First, Al Qaeda's and the Taliban's tough anti-American stance after the attacks on the World Trade Center and the

Pentagon, but far more so the U.S.-led war in Afghanistan mobilized the Arab masses against the American "paper tiger" and against U.S. aggression. This reaction was further proof that the masterminds of the 9–11 attacks achieved their mass-mediated objectives in their own backyard and, in the process, furthered their policy goals. As the recipient of bin Laden's videotapes and text messages and as the preferred media of the Taliban leadership before their fall from power, Al-Jazeera became after 9–11 the Arab CNN, often airing exclusives on bin Laden, Al Qaeda, and the war in Afghanistan. National media organizations in the region became even more pronounced in their anti-American news presentations. In Saudi Arabia, for example, the press took its "cue from top Saudi officials who regularly criticized what they termed 'the media campaign' against the kingdom in the United States. The Saudi press also highlighted the stories of Saudis and other Arabs who were detained in the United States after September 11."[28] Thus conditioned, the Arab street exploded in unprecedented anti-American protests after Israel's Defense Forces launched the largest military incursion into the West Bank and the Bush administration failed to pressure Ariel Sharon to withdraw his troops. From Morocco and Egypt to Saudi Arabia the rulers made no secrets of their unhappiness with Washington and President Bush and thus poured oil into the fires of the anti-American rage in the streets amid fears that the mobilized masses could sooner or later turn against their own governments.

Saudi Arabia's rulers did not kick out the American military or reform their country along bin Laden's ideas; Iraq continued to protest against trade sanctions and the no-fly zone policed by the United States and the United Kingdom; Israel remained on the map of the Middle East. But the multiple cracks in the formerly cozy Saudi-American relationship, the opposition to threatened U.S. military actions against Saddam Hussein far beyond the Arab world, and the Bush administration's willingness to speak for the first time publicly about a Palestinian state shortly after 9–11 were all developments in the direction of bin Laden's spelled-out short- and medium-term objectives.

## McWorld and the Clash of Civilizations?

All of this was facilitated by the more recent advances in communication technology, namely satellite TV, satellite phones, and the Internet, and its spread around the globe. Although technologically tied together in the virtual global village, people of different nationality, ethnicity, religion, and ideology are less inclined to search the readily available global marketplace of ideas for a diversity of information and opinions and are more prone to tune in to narrow, parochial media that reinforce their prejudices and stereotypes. Instead of cultivating better understanding, global communication has been more influential as a web of hate.[29]

These developments have played into the hands of today's hi-tech terrorists. Mocking Americans for suggesting that bin Laden's messages after 9–11 may have contained secret codes to instruct his followers, the Al Qaeda leader said that America "made hilarious claims. . . . It's as if we were living in the time of mail by carrier pigeon, where there are no phones, no travelers, no Internet, no regular mail, no express mail, and no electronic mail. I mean these are very humorous things. They discount people's intellect."[30] Certainly he and other terrorists have demonstrated that they know how to use literally all of the modern communication technologies for their purposes although condemning other aspects of modernity.

In pointing out the contradiction between Jihad in the sense of societal groups in the West, Islamic countries, and elsewhere that defend their traditional values in morals, religion, economics, and politics and the postmodern McWorld in the sense of mass-production, mass-consumption, and mass-entertainment that transcend national borders, Benjamin Barber identified one important source of bin Laden's grievances and motivations[31]: In his 1996 epistle in particular, bin Laden lamented the evils of modernization and globalization:

From here, today we begin the work, talking and discussing the ways of correcting what had happened to the Islamic world in general, and the land of the two Holy Places in particular. We wish to study the means that we could follow to return the situation to its normal path. And to return to the people their own rights, particularly after the large damages and the great aggression on the life and the religion of the people. An injustice that had affected every section and group of the people, the civilians, military and security men, government officials and merchants, the young and the old people as well as school and university students. Hundreds of thousands of the unemployed graduates, who became the widest sections of society, were also affected.

And especially speaking of the situation in Saudi Arabia, he wrote:

More than three hundred forty billions of Riyal owed by the government to the people in addition to the daily accumulated interest, let alone the foreign debt. People wonder whether we are the largest oil exporting country?! They even believe that this situation is a curse put on them by Allah for not objecting to the oppressive and illegitimate behavior and measures of the ruling regime.

He blamed the "American crusader forces for a great deal of the catastrophic policies" imposed on the country, especially in the field of oil industry where production is restricted or expanded and prices are fixed to suit the American economy ignoring the economy of the country." While singling out the United States, modernization and globalization problems were central to this particular catalogue of grievances.

Years before the terror in New York and Washington political scientist Samuel Huntington predicted that the greatest dangers in the post-Cold War era would arise from conflicts between nations and groups of different civilizations, of different cultural backgrounds.[32] Several weeks after the events of 9–11, although rejecting the notion that these attacks signaled such a collision, Huntington was sure that "bin Laden wants it to be a clash of civilizations between Islam and the West."[33] Bin Laden's statements validate this conclusion. In his 1998 declaration of war against "Jews and Crusaders" he listed the wrongdoings of the "crusader-Zionist alliance" and reminded all Muslims that the "jihad is an individual duty if the enemy destroys the Muslim countries" and that

"[n]othing is more sacred than belief except repulsing an enemy who is attacking religion and life." He then called on all Muslims "to kill the Americans and their allies—civilians and military . . . in any country in which it is possible to do. . . ." In October 2001, when the U.S. military commenced military strikes against Al Qaeda and the Taliban in Afghanistan, bin Laden declared:

The events have divided the whole world into two sides. The side of believers and the side of infidels, may God keep you away from them. Every Muslim has to rush to make his religion victorious. The winds of faith have come. The winds of change have come to eradicate oppression from the island of Muhammad, peace be upon him.[34]

Because Muslims did not rise in a massive united front to fight the Christian and Jewish infidels in the holy war that bin Laden had declared, the Al Qaeda leader and his supporters did not realize their most ambitious and ultimate objective. On the contrary, they lost their safe haven, headquarters, training facilities, and weapon arsenals in Afghanistan. In this respect, bin Laden and his comrades in arms underestimated perhaps the resolve of the U.S. government and public and the willingness of many other governments to cooperate with Washington. But it is also doubtful that the Al Qaeda leadership expected to provoke the existential clash of civilizations of which bin Laden spoke simply as a result of the 9–11 operation and the anticipated military response. It is far more likely that the plan was (and probably still is) to move with each additional terror attack closer to a confrontation between "the side of believers" and "the side of infidels."

Certainly, the events of 9–11 increased the tensions between Muslim minorities and Christian majorities in many Western countries—in Europe more so than in the United States. Although singling out Muslim immigrants in the past because of their different cultural and religious preferences, the xenophobic right in France, Austria, Belgium, Denmark, Germany, and elsewhere, became far more popular when people feared that Muslims within their borders could commit violence along the lines of 9–11. These fears were fuelled by reports that terrorist "sleeper cells," ready to be awakened any time to commit violent acts, existed in many Western countries. In this atmosphere populist leaders who made Muslims the scapegoats for all kinds of ills in their societies became bolder and more attractive. In capturing this trend that began well before 9–11 one observer wrote:

> In her best-known campaign poster, Pia Kjaersgaard, the leader of Denmark's People's Party, showed a pretty little blond child with the caption: "By the time you retire, Denmark will be a majority Muslim-nation." Yet in Denmark just 1 person in 15 is of foreign origin and most of these are thoroughly assimilated.[35]

As new antiterrorism laws and profiling criteria in Western democracies targeted Muslims and Arabs in particular, the gap between Muslim minorities and non-Muslim majorities widened. Far from moving rapidly toward the cataclysmic clash of civilizations of which Huntington warned and bin Laden wished, there was certainly increased distrust and hostility between "infidels" and "believers" in many Western countries and perhaps more fertile ground among the Muslim diaspora for bin Laden's divisive agenda and final goal.

In the United States, opinion polls revealed that the public in general viewed American Muslims more favorable after 9–11 than before. Thus, in the last poll before 9–11 (March 2001) 45% of the respondents described their attitude toward American Muslims as very favorable or mostly favorable; in the first poll after 9–11 (November 2001) 59% had a very or mostly favorable view of American Muslims.[36] However, more than six months after the attacks on New York and Washington 44% of the public believed that American Muslims were not doing enough to help authorities track down terrorist cells in the United States; 32% were not sure; and only 24% thought that Muslim Americans cooperated in this respect.[37]

## 9–11 AS A MODEL FOR POST-9–11 TERROR?

Although the attacks on New York and Washington did not realize, or advance significantly, the ultimate goals of the terrorist masterminds, namely a united Muslim front against and the defeat of the "Crusader-Zionist" alliance, it must be kept in mind what the terrorists did achieve with respect to their media-related and short- or medium-term political goals as described in this article. These successes make the 9–11 calculus of terror an attractive model for future terrorism. In the past suicide bombers struck Americans not in their own country but abroad. The events of 9–11 demonstrated the effectiveness of this terror method within the United States and conceivably within other liberal democracies: Without being able to hunt down and apprehend surviving terrorists, as was the case in the first World Trade Center bombing and the Oklahoma City bombing, a target society is deprived of bringing the perpetrators to justice and likely coaxed into responses that might be deemed disproportional at home and abroad. At the same time, terrorists and their supporters get the opportunity to idolize those who committed suicide in order to kill and use their examples to recruit more volunteers as human bombs.

Religiously motivated Palestinian extremists stepped up their suicide bombings in the months following 9–11 and the secular Al-Aksa group embraced this terror method for the first time. After a total of 42 suicide bombing missions against Israelis in the 8 years from 1993 to 2000, Hamas, Islamic Jihad, and the Al-Aksa Martyrs Brigade took responsibility for 36 such bombings in 2001 and an unprecedented 30 in the first four months of 2002. By switching to weapons-grade explosives in early 2002, Hamas and other groups assured that suicide bombers killed more Israelis than in earlier missions. Thus, from March 27, when 28 Israelis were killed in Netanya, to May 7, when at least 15 died as a result of a suicide bombing in Rishon Letzion, 76 Israelis were killed and hundreds injured in 6 separate suicide attacks. Yet, once the Israeli Defense Forces moved into the West Bank, the news media focused barely on Israeli victims of terrorism but mostly, or exclusively, on Palestinian victims of Israel's military might. What the difficult terrain, the political realities on the ground, and a strict censorship imposed by the U.S. military prevented in Afghanistan, namely news reporting and visuals that focused on the civilian casualties in the "war on terrorism," occurred during the incursion of the Israeli military into the West Bank: The media transmitted gruesome images of death, injury, and destruction that resulted in sympathy for the Palestinian cause and hostility against Israelis—and not only among Arabs and Muslims. Moreover, the media reported extensively about the Palestinian predicament that drove young men and women to volunteer for suicide attacks against Israelis without paying similar attention to the Israeli victims of these bombings. No wonder the leaders of Hamas were "almost welcoming of the Israeli attacks in the West Bank," convinced that Israel's actions would result in more Palestinians joining their organizations and in increased prospects "of achieving their goal, the eradication of Israel as a Jewish state."[38]

When Chechen separatists seized a Moscow theater in the fall of 2002 and announced their determination to die for their cause, experts suspected that the terrorists had taken their cue from the terror of 9–11.

Above all, terrorists know that it is very difficult, if not impossible, to prevent suicide terror—whether in the form of simple "human bombs" or sophisticated operations, such as those on 9–11—and certainly not with military means. This became very clear in the latest phase of the Israeli-Palestinian conflict, and this was the lesson of 9–11 as well. Although the possibility of terrorists getting hold of and using weapons of mass destruction some day cannot be ignored, the more immediate concern must be the prospect that 9–11, in one form or another, might well become the most attractive model for terrorism in the near future.

## NOTES

1. The quotes are taken from the translations of a videotape, presumably made in mid-November 2001 in Afghanistan. Available at: (http://www.washingtonpost. com/wp-srv/nation/specials/attacked/transcripts/binladentext_121301.html), retrieved 7 April 2002.

2. Martha Crenshaw, "The logic of terrorism: Terrorist behavior as a product of strategic choice," in Walter Reich, ed., *Origins of Terrorism* (New York, Cambridge University Press, 1990), pp. 7–24.

3. "Transcript of bin Laden's October interview" with Al-Jazeera correspondent Tayseer Alouni. Available at: (http://www.cnn.com/2002/world/-asiapcf/south/02/05/binladen.transcript/index.html).

4. For bin Laden's diminished standing in the Arab and Muslim world, see F. Gregory Gause III, "Be careful what you wish for the future of U.S.-Saudi relations," *World Policy Journal* XIX (Spring 2002), pp. 37–50.

5. Michael Howard, "What's in a name?" *Foreign Affairs* (January/February 2002), pp. 8–13. The quote is from page 11.

6. Paul W. Schroeder, "The Risk of Victory," *The National Interest* (Winter 2001–2002), pp. 14–21. The quote is from page 34.

7. Laura K. Donohue, "Fear Itself: Counter-Terrorism, Individual Rights, and U.S. Foreign Relations Post 9–11." Paper presented at the Annual Meeting of the International Studies Association, 24–27 March 2002, in New Orleans.

8. Updike was quoted in an untitled contribution in "Talk of the Town," *The New Yorker*, 24 September 2001, p. 28.

9. Governor Pataki made the remark on ABC News "Nightline," on 14 September 2000.

10. For more on the idea of politics as communication, see Thomas A. Hollihan, *Uncivil Wars: Political Campaigns in the Media Age* (Boston: Bedford/St. Martins, 2001), especially chapter 1. The quote is from p. 9.

11. Thomas L. Friedman, "No mere terrorist," *New York Times*, 24 March 2002, sect. 4, p. 15.

12. Hamza Hendawi, "Terror Manual advises on targets." Available at: (http://story.news.yahoo.com/news?tmpl=story&u+/ap/20 . . . /afghan_spreading_terror_), retrieved 11 February 2002.

13. Paul Wilkinson, *Terrorism versus Democracy* (London, Frank Cass, 2001), p. 177.

14. Even before Gutenberg invented the printing press terrorists understood the need for publicity and therefore struck their targets in crowded places so that the news spread in a mouth-to-mouth fashion. With the presses in place, terrorists printed their own pamphlets and posters and even their own newspapers. More recently, groups have acquired mobile radio transmitters and television stations. But modern terrorists have mostly relied on the news media for publicity and propaganda.

15. For more about the publicity goals of terrorists see Brigitte L. Nacos, *Terrorism and the Media* (New York: Columbia University Press, 1996).

16. "Text: Bin Laden statement." Available at: (http://www/guardian.co.uk./waronterror/story/0,1361,565069,00html), retrieved 7 April 2002.

17. Donohue, "Fear Itself," p. 1.

18. Quoted in Howard Kurtz, "U.S. doomed, bin Laden says on tape," *Washington Post* (1 February 2002), p. A13.

19. "Transcript of Bin Laden's October interview."

20. Paul Wilkinson, *Terrorism & the Liberal State* (New York: New York University Press, 1986).

21. From bin Laden videotape presumably made in mid-November (see Note 1).

22. The CBS News poll was conducted 24–26 February 2002; the *Los Angeles Times* conducted its poll 18–19 February 1993.

23. Friedman, "No mere terrorist."

24. See, for example, statements made by expert guests on ABC News, "Nightline with Ted Koppel" on 18 March 2002.

25. Unless otherwise indicated descriptions and quotes of bin Laden's objectives are from his 1996 "Ladenese Epistle" and his 1998 "Jihad against Jews and Crusaders." Available at: (http://www.washingtonpost.), retrieved 5 February 2002.

26. This argument was made, for example, by one of the expert guests appearing on "Nightline with Ted Koppel," 18 March 2002.

27. Tony Judt, "America and the War," in Robert B. Silvers and Barbara Epstein, eds., *Striking Terror:*

*America's New War* (New York, New York Review Books, 2002), pp. 17–37. Quote is from page 22.

28. Gause III, "Be careful what you wish for the future of U.S.-Saudi relations," p. 40.

29. For more on this aspect of global communication see Brigitte L. Nacos, *Mass-Mediated Terrorism* (Boulder, CO: Rowman & Littlefield, 2002). See also, Thomas L. Friedman, "Global Village Idiocy," *New York Times,* 12 May 2002.

30. "Transcript of Bin Laden's October interview."

31. Benjamin Barber, *Jihad vs. McWorld* (New York, Ballantine Books, 1995).

32. Samuel P. Huntington, *The Clash of Civilizations and the Remaking of World Order* (New York: Simon & Schuster, 1996).

33. "Q & A; A head-on collision of alien cultures," New York Times, 20 October 2001, p. A13.

34. "Text: bin Laden statement."

35. For more on the European far right's anti-foreigner and anti-immigration stands, see Tony Judt, "America's restive partners." *New York Times,* 28 April 2002, section 4, p. 15.

36. Pew Center for the People & the Press & Pew Forum on Religion and Public Life.

37. Survey was conducted by Fox News, 2–3 April 2002.

38. For more on the reactions by and views of Hamas leaders see, Joel Brinkley, "Bombers gloating in Gaza as they see goal within reach: no more Israel," *New York Times,* 4 April 2002.

---

## Can Terrorists Get the Bomb?

### Gary Milhollin

The story began over a meal in late October. A high British official told a reporter from the London *Times* that Osama bin Laden had the bomb, or at least that he had gotten bomb components, or nuclear materials, and that the source was Pakistan. At about the same time, Pakistan arrested three of its nuclear scientists for questioning about possible ties to the Taliban, bin Laden's Afghan protectors. Then, in early November, bin Laden himself declared that he had nuclear weapons, which he would use as a "deterrent."

Could it be true? Countries do not arrest their nuclear scientists for nothing. By mid-November, Graham Allison, a professor at Harvard and an assistant secretary of defense in the Clinton administration, was predicting in the *Washington Post* that "bin Laden's final act could be a nuclear attack on America." A few weeks later, the *Post*'s Bob Woodward reported that al Qaeda might be making a "dirty" bomb—a radiological device to spread contamination over a wide area. According to Woodward, this could be done by wrapping spent reactor fuel rods around high explosives, which would produce a "zone of intense radiation that could extend several city blocks." A larger bomb, he said, "could affect a much larger area."

In Afghanistan itself, American forces have examined dozens of sites where al Qaeda may have worked on nuclear or radiological weapons. Secretary of Defense Donald Rumsfeld cautioned that while it was "unlikely that they have a nuclear weapon," considering "the determination they have, they may very well."

Despite the reports, and despite the attendant warnings, the risk that a terrorist group like al Qaeda could get the bomb (or a "dirty" substitute) is much lower than most people think. That is the good news. There is also bad news: the risk is not zero.

There are essentially two ways for a terrorist group to lay its hands on a nuclear weapon: either build one from scratch or somehow procure an already manufactured one or its key components. Neither of these is likely.

Building a bomb from scratch would confer the most power: a group that could build one bomb could build several, and a nuclear arsenal would put it front and center on the world stage. But of all the possibilities, this is the unlikeliest—"so remote," in the words of a senior nuclear scientist at the Los Alamos National Laboratory, "that it can be essentially ruled out." The chief obstacle lies in producing the nuclear fuel—either bomb-grade uranium or plutonium—that actually explodes in a chain reaction. More than 80 percent of the effort that went into making America's first bombs was devoted to producing this fuel, and it is no easy task.

To make bomb-grade uranium, a terrorist group would need thousands of high-speed gas centrifuges, machined to exact dimensions, arranged in series, and capable of operating under the most demanding conditions. If they wanted to produce the uranium by a diffusion process, they would need an even greater number of other machines, equally difficult to manufacture and operate. If they followed Saddam Hussein's example, they could try building a series of giant electromagnets, capable of bending a stream of electrically charged particles—a no less daunting challenge. For any of these,

they would also need a steady supply of natural uranium and a specialized plant to convert it to a gaseous form for processing.

Who would sell these things to would-be nuclear terrorists? The answer is: nobody. The world's nuclear-equipment makers are organized into a cooperative group that exists precisely to stop items like these from getting into unauthorized hands. Nor could a buyer disguise the destination and send materials through obliging places like Dubai (as Iran does with its hot cargoes) or Malta (favored by Libya's smugglers). The equipment is so specialized, and the suppliers so few, that a forest of red flags would go up. And even if the equipment could be bought, it would have to be operated in a place that the United States could not find.

If manufacturing bomb-grade uranium is out of the picture, what about making plutonium, a much smaller quantity of which is required to form a critical mass (less than fourteen pounds was needed to destroy Nagasaki in 1945)? There is, however, an inconvenient fact about plutonium, which is that you need a reactor to make enough of it for a workable bomb. Could terrorists buy one? The Russians are selling a reactor to Iran, but Moscow tends to put terrorist groups in the same category as Chechens. The Chinese are selling reactors to Pakistan, but Beijing, too, is not fond of terrorists. India and Pakistan can both build reactors on their own, but, for now, these countries are lined up with the U.S. Finally, smuggling a reactor would be no easier than buying one. Reactor parts are unique, so manufacturers would not be fooled by phony purchase orders.

Even if terrorists somehow got hold of a reactor, they would need a special, shielded chemical plant to chop up its radioactive fuel, dissolve it in acid, and then extract the plutonium from the acid. No one would sell them a plutonium extraction plant, either.

It is worth remembering that Saddam Hussein tried the reactor road in the 1970's. He bought one from France—Jacques Chirac, in his younger days, was a key facilitator of the deal—hoping it would propel Iraq into the nuclear club. But the reactor's fuel was sabotaged in a French warehouse, the person who was supposed to certify its quality was murdered in a Paris hotel, and when the reactor was finally ready to operate, a squadron of Israeli fighter-bombers blew it apart. A similar fate would undoubtedly await any group that tried to follow Saddam's method today.

If making nuclear-bomb fuel is a no-go, why not just steal it, or buy it on the black market? Consider plutonium. There are hundreds of reactors in the world, and they crank out tons of the stuff every year. Surely a dedicated band of terrorists could get their hands on some.

This too is not so simple. Plutonium is only created inside reactor fuel rods, and the rods, after being irradiated, become so hot that they melt unless kept under water. They are also radioactive, which is why they have to travel submerged from the reactor to storage ponds, with the water acting as both coolant and radiation shield. And in most power reactors, the rods are welded together into long assemblies that can be lifted only by crane.

True, after the rods cool down they can be stored dry, but their radioactivity is still lethal. To prevent spent fuel rods from killing the people who come near them, they are transported in giant radiation-shielding casks that are not supposed to break open even in head-on collisions. The casks are also guarded. If terrorists managed to hijack one from a country that had reactors they would still have to take it to a plant in another country that could extract the plutonium from the rods. They would be hunted at every step of the way.

Instead of fuel rods, they would be better advised to go after pure plutonium, already removed from the reactor fuel and infinitely easier to handle. This kind of plutonium is a threat only if you ingest or inhale it. Human skin blocks its radiation: a terrorist could walk around with a lump of it in his front trouser pocket and still have children. But where to get hold of it? Russia is the best bet: it has tons of plutonium in weapon-ready form, and the Russian nuclear-accounting system is weak. Russia also has underpaid scientists, and there is unquestionably some truth behind all the stories one hears about the smuggling that goes on in that country.

But very little Russian plutonium has been in circulation, with not a single reported case of anything more than gram quantities showing up on the black market. This makes sense.

Pure-plutonium is used primarily for making nuclear warheads, it is in military hands, and military forces are not exactly keen to see it come back at them in somebody else's bombs.

One source of pure plutonium that is not military is a new kind of reactor fuel called "mixed oxide." It is very different from the present generation of fuel because it contains weapon-ready material. But precisely because it is weapon-ready, it is guarded and accounted for, and a terrorist group would have to win a gun battle to get close to it. Then they would probably need a crane to move it, and would have to elude or fight off their pursuers.

If terrorists did procure some weapon-ready plutonium, would their problems be over? Far from it: plutonium works only in an "implosion"-type bomb, which is about ten times more difficult to build than the simple uranium bomb used at Hiroshima. In such a device, a spherical shock wave "implodes" inward and squeezes a ball of plutonium at the bomb's center so that it explodes in a chain reaction. To accomplish all this, one needs precision machine tools to build the parts, special furnaces to melt and cast the plutonium in a vacuum (liquid plutonium oxidizes rapidly in air), and high-precision switches and capacitors for the firing circuit. Also required are a qualified designer, a number of other specialists, and a testing program. Considering who the participating scientists are likely to be, the chances of getting an implosion bomb to work are rather small.

The alternative to plutonium is bomb-grade uranium—and here things would be easier. This is the fuel used in the Hiroshima bomb. Unlike the implosion bomb dropped on Nagasaki, this one did not have to be tested: the U.S. knew it would work. The South Africans build six uranium bombs without testing; they knew their bombs would work, too. All these devices used a simple "gun" design in which one slug of uranium was shot down a barrel into another.

The problem with buying bomb-grade uranium is that one would need a great deal of it—around 120 pounds for a gun-type bomb—and nothing near that amount has turned up in the black market. In February 2001 an al Qaeda operative named Jamal Ahmed al-Fadl testified in an American court that he had tried to buy some uranium for $1.5 million in 1993. He had been sent to Khartoum, where he saw a cylinder that supposedly contained uranium from South Africa; he did not know whether the deal went through. South Africa went out of the nuclear-weapon business in 1991, and in 1993 it accounted for all of its bomb-grade uranium to the International Atomic Energy Agency. The deal in Khartoum was probably a scam.

What about getting material from Pakistan? Its centrifuges have been turning out bomb-grade uranium since 1986, and by now there is enough for 30 to 50 nuclear weapons. As it well known, at least some of its nuclear scientists have fundamentalist leanings. Could they spirit out enough for a bomb or two?

The chances are virtually nil. Pakistan's nuclear weapons are its proudest achievement. Every gram of bomb-grade uranium has been produced at the expense of the country's suffering population, and every gram is also part of a continuous manufacturing flow. When uranium leaves the centrifuges, it goes to other plants where it is refined and then to still other plants where it is made into bombs. Pakistan produces enough for about three bombs per year, which means that one bomb's worth is the result of several months' output. If any uranium went missing, it would be as if the assembly workers for Ford Explorers suddenly stopped receiving engines. Someone down the production line would be bound to ask questions, and very quickly.

There is also the fact that Pakistan's nuclear program is controlled by the army, still headed by the country's president, Pervez Musharraf. In response to the September 11 terrorist attack on America, Musharraf created a new military command with direct control over the nuclear-weapons program. In the process, he sidelined officers sympathetic to the Taliban. After all these precautions, Musharraf is unlikely to let any bomb fuel slip through his fingers. The only possibility for terrorists to lay their hands on Pakistan's uranium would be if its government fell under the control of sympathizers; given that Pakistan's army is far and away the most effective and stable organization in the country, there is not much chance of that.

Russia, again, is the best bet. It has tons of bomb-grade uranium left over from the cold war and, in addition to bombs, has used this material to fuel nuclear submarines and research reactors. The result has been to spread it across Russia and several other former members of the eastern bloc.

So Russia and its former satellites are a fat target. This past November, citing a database maintained by the International Atomic Energy Agency, the *New York Times* catalogued a long series of Russian-related smuggling attempts. In 1993, for example, over six pounds of weapon-grade uranium in St. Petersburg was about to go astray before being seized; in 1998, there was a foiled effort to steal more than 40 pounds in the Urals. Russian officials told the *Times* that they had twice discovered terrorists staking out their nuclear-weapon sites. Finally, there was one loss "of the highest consequence" during the past year, about which details were not forthcoming.

There are thus definite prospects in Russia. If terrorist could strike the mother lode, and get enough uranium for a gun-type bomb, they would be on their way.

But the way would still be long. They would have to design the bomb, develop it, and build it, and that would be far from a trivial undertaking. They would have to have a competent bomb designer, who could be a physicist or engineer but would have to come with practical experience in making such things work. High-accuracy machine tools could be dispensed with—implosion not being required, much simpler technologies could be used for firing projectiles down artillery tubes—although someone would have to handle the uranium-235, refine it to metallic form, cast it, and then machine it. Still, with the help of a capable machinist and a chemical laboratory, none of these obstacles is insurmountable.

The main risk would lie in getting caught. True, a uranium bomb would not produce many of the "signatures" that American intelligence agencies look for—the use of a lot of electricity (a sign of a uranium enrichment plant), the presence of contaminated air or water (a sign of a reactor or plutonium extraction plant), a noisy testing program—but a fair number of people would have to be recruited, and one of them could turn the others in. Purchase of equipment might arouse the suspicions of a seller. Above all, what would be needed is a sanctuary—a place in which to assemble the people and the equipment, and keep them together for a period of time. You cannot transport such an operation from cave to cave.

Finding this location would not be easy. A country that was aware of the terrorists' program could end up getting blamed for a nuclear attack on America, and not too many governments would be ready to sign up for that. Better from the terrorists' viewpoint would be a location where the authorities had no idea what they were doing, but even so the theft of the uranium would probably be discovered soon enough, and it might be only a short matter of time before the whole world showed up on their doorstep. Besides, if they only managed to steal enough for one bomb, they would still lack an arsenal—and a single mistake in design could wreck the whole project.

Is there no way around these manufacturing problems? There is: stealing, or buying, a complete bomb. But this presents problems of its own, which are even greater.

All countries, including Russia and Pakistan, take care to safeguard their warheads, and even rogue states, if they should get the bomb, would be highly likely to do the same. Despite press speculation to the contrary, countries maintain careful inventories and employ security measures specifically designed to prevent theft. Warheads are typically stored in bunkers to which access is tightly restricted. They are also protected by alarms and armed guards. Terrorists would have a hard fight on their hands taking over one of these bunkers, and even if they succeeded, they would have a much harder fight getting away with the contents.

Buying is not a great option, either. Since the 1970's, the Libyan dictator Muammar Qaddafi has tried to buy nuclear weapons from China, India, and Pakistan, reportedly offering billions of dollars. So far, there have been no takers. In 1996, General Alexander Lebed, then vying for the presidency of Russia, claimed that a number of "suitcase" bombs—meant to be carried by foot soldiers on demolition missions—had gone missing, but his claim was promptly denied by both the Russian and U.S. governments and has never gained much credibility. In November 2001, President Vladimir Putin said he could certify that no Russian warheads had fallen into terrorist hands.

What options remain? Stymied in their plan to acquire a real nuclear weapon, could a determined group of terrorist at least confirm Bob Woodward's fears by manufacturing a "dirty" bomb? Such a device would be much easier to build than a warhead. Instead of producing a nuclear explosion, it would only have to disperse radioactive particles.

This is a likelier bet. But there is a different problem with these devices: they do not pack much radioactive punch. A bomb that carried enough radiation to injure many people quickly would be too hot to handle. The shielding would have to be many times heavier than the radioactive element—so massive, in fact, that there would be no practical way to transport or deploy the weapon. That is way the Pentagon does not consider such devices useful on the battlefield.

Nor is it easy to bring a sufficient amount of radioactivity into contact with a bomb's human targets. Lacing a high-explosive charge with nuclear waste from a hospital or laboratory, for example, would kill some people immediately from the explosion, but the only radiological effect would be an increased risk of cancer decades later. Once the area around the blast was decontaminated, it would be safer to walk through it than to be a serious smoker.

To inflict a dangerous dose over a broad area requires spewing around large amounts of nuclear waste. The only place to get such waste would be from a reactor, and the problems with that scenario have already been demonstrated. Even if a group of terrorists could somehow procure radioactive fuel rods or any other form of highly radioactive waste, wrapping the rods around "readily available conventional high explosives," as Woodward suggested in the *Post,* would kill the person doing the wrapping. So would transporting such a weapon to its destination, unless the rods were heavily shielded during the entire operation (which would bring us back to the implausible scenario with the giant protective casks). The fact is that it would be a near impossibility to create, in Woodward's words, a "zone of intense radiation that could extend several city blocks."

A research reactor would be a better source. Many countries use such small reactors to irradiate material samples, and it might be possible to insert some material into one of these reactors secretly, irradiate it, and then withdraw it and put it in a bomb. The difficulty would then lie in making the bomb effective. Highly radioactive materials have short half-lives; thus, any bomb would have to be used right away, and one would not be able to build up a stockpile. If enough radioactivity were packed into the bomb to injure a substantial number of victims, the too-hot-to-handle problem would arise. If the radioactive charge were diluted, the bomb would lose its effect. Saddam Hussein actually made and tested such a bomb in the 1980's, but when UN inspectors toured the test site in the 1990's they could find no trace of radiation from it.

What about putting plutonium into a city's drinking water, or into the air? That, too, is a possibility—but according to a 1995 study by the Lawrence Livermore National Laboratory, plutonium dumped into a typical city reservoir would almost entirely sink to the bottom. The little that dissolved would be greatly diluted by the volume of the water, and the people drinking it would get a smaller dose than from natural background radiation. As for plutonium in the air, if an entire kilogram of the stuff were exploded in a city the size of Munich, Germany, and if 20 percent of it became airborne in respirable particles—as with anthrax, the particles would have to be the right size to lodge in the lungs—the effect (according to the same study) would be to produce fewer than ten deaths from cancer.

The main effect of any of these attacks would be panic: people would flee the contaminated zone. This might create a huge economic impact—which would be a victory for the terrorists—and it would be almost certain to create an even huger psychological impact. On the other hand, and unlike anthrax, radiation is something that scientists know how to detect, and at levels far below those that are dangerous. Even the panic might fade quickly as people were reassured that the environment was safe. In any case, there is no chance of achieving anything remotely like the effect of a real nuclear weapon, however small.

In sum, the job of making or procuring a nuclear bomb is a great deal harder than we have been led to believe. From a terrorist's point of view, what is clear above all is that, whether the aim is to build a dirty bomb or a clean one, a sanctuary is needed. The task requires laboratories, equipment, and trained personnel, all of which have to be maintained over a longish period of time.

This in turn underlines the cardinal importance of remaining faithful to our determination to pursue terrorists everywhere, and never leave them in peace. Allowing any group of terrorists to set up shop anywhere puts everyone at risk.

The terrorists' only hope is that we tire of the chase. Then, if they could obtain the bomb, they could deliver it, and anywhere on the globe could become ground zero.

---

## Russia, Islam, and the War on Terrorism: An Uneasy Future

Ariel Cohen

The terrorist attacks on the United States have forced many countries to confront their own Islamic threats. Russia is one country that faces an uncertain future, surrounded by tough neighbors in an unstable geopolitical environment. As the birthrate of ethnic Russians plummets, the Muslim population is growing,[1] and radical Islamic forces are expanding into Russia proper, as well as in its sphere of influence in the former Soviet Central Asia. The challenge for the Russian leadership in the years to come is to develop adequate diplomatic, military, and security tools to halt the rise of the Islamist threat to Russia and its allies. Russia judges that it cannot stem the tide on its own, but its residual mistrust of NATO and the United States, as well as the current incompatibility of the military establishments that have been in place since the cold war era, stands in the way of cooperation. Russia will have to cooperate with the rising giant to the east, China, and with the United States and the European Union to secure its place within the crosscurrents of globalization and the Islamic maelstrom.

In the weeks after the attack on the United States, President Vladimir Putin started to address this challenge, taking Russia closer to the United States and the West in the war against terrorism.[2] Russia launched a supply operation for the Northern Alliance, a mostly Tajik force that was aligned with the pre-Taliban government of Afghanistan. For the first time since World War II, intelligence cooperation between the United States and Russia was exemplary. Moscow was instrumental in securing the agreement of Central Asian leaders to allow U.S. use of military bases in Central Asia. Russia also provided a necessary humanitarian relief operation in the first weeks of the war.[3] But the long-term challenge facing the United States and the EU is whether they can reshape policies to seize this opportunity to integrate Russia into the Euro-Atlantic community.

## VICTIM OF ITS OWN SUCCESS

The Russian two-headed eagle used to soar high in the land of Islam. After the final defeat of the Mongols in 1480, Russian subjugation of Muslim-controlled territories began with expansion against the steppe nomads in the late fifteenth to early sixteenth centuries. It continued with the conquest of the Volga valley under Ivan IV (the Terrible) in the second half of the sixteenth century. In 1552, Ivan took Kazan, the capital of the northern Tatar-Mongol khanate, a remnant of the Mongol Golden Horde that ruled Russia for more than 250 years (1227–1480). "The Mongol yoke" left indelible scars on the Russian national psyche. Ivan then swept down the river and took Astrakhan in the lower Volga, thus establishing the Russian empire, which included Muslims.

Thus, the northern frontier of Islam lies deep in the steppes of the Russian Northern Caucasus and stretches as far north as Kazan, the ancient capital of the Turkic Muslim kingdom in the fourteenth to sixteenth centuries, an hour-plus plane ride from Moscow. There are no geographical barriers, such as mountains, to stop the spread of radical Islam into Russia.

After a long hiatus to fight Poland and Sweden in the west during the second half of the seventeenth and early eighteenth centuries, Russian expansion east and south continued. The Romanovs subjugated the Kazakhs in the steppes east of the Volga, and in the second half of the eighteenth century, Catherine the Great's ex-lover Prince Alexander Potemkin captured the Crimean Tatar khanate on the Black Sea from its Ottoman vassal rulers. This was followed by a series of exceedingly nasty and protracted frontier wars in the Northern Caucasus from the 1780s through the 1850s. The rebellion by Imam Shamil of Daghestan in the eastern part of Northern Caucasus lasted forty-seven years and included "ethnic cleansing" by the Russians, such as the expulsion of half a million mountaineers to the Ottoman Empire. Russia's slow but steady military conquest of the Central Asian khanates of Khoresm, Khiva, and Boukhara continued through the second half of the nineteenth century.

During the expansion phase, Russia surpassed the Muslims educationally and technologically. Slavic birthrates equaled or exceeded those of the Muslims, and Russian military domination was unquestionable. Under the Bolsheviks, centers of Islamic learning in the Muslim world were cut off from the majority of Russian and Soviet Muslims. The links with the global Islamic community, the 'Umma, were difficult at best. Anti-Soviet resisters were either killed or exiled, the most extreme case being the forcible and brutal deportations of the "punished peoples" at the end of World War II. In 1944, Joseph Stalin exiled all Crimean Tatars, Chechens, Meskhetian Turks, and dozens of other ethnic groups to Central Asia and Siberia. All of them were unjustly accused of collaboration with the Nazi invaders, and up to a third died in transit of disease and malnutrition. This was no way for communist Russia to win friends among its Muslim citizens, even after the reversal of most exile decrees and the return of the Chechens and other Caucasus peoples to their ancestral homelands in the second half of the 1950s.

However, Russian domination could not last forever. Ironically, the Russian expansion began almost half a millennium ago in the then-Muslim lands in the Volga, and the beginning of the end of the empire came during an attempt to conquer a Muslim land: Afghanistan. Overextended, fast becoming an economic basket case, and a victim of the U.S.-supported *mujahideen,* the USSR began to collapse as the bodies of Soviet soldiers were flown home in zinc coffins. Islamic propaganda spilled over the northern border into Soviet Central Asia, together with drug trafficking and arms smuggling for the future jihad. The rest is recent history.

As the Soviet Union collapsed, nationalism soared among the Muslim Turkic peoples, Farsi-speaking Tajiks, the Chechens, and other Caucasus inhabitants. The Soviet-era nomenklatura established corrupt and authoritarian secular regimes in the five Central Asian countries, as well as in Tatarstan and Bashkortostan.

## POST-SOVIET DEVELOPMENT: ISLAMIZATION

Direct Russian rule ended in Central Asia only ten years ago, with the collapse of the Soviet Union. The turbulent processes of Islamic revival and radicalization have caused policymakers in Moscow to regard Russia's soft Islamic underbelly as a long-term and serious problem. The nationalist Chechen war of 1994–96 quickly escalated into the Islamic fundamentalist rebellion of 1999–2001.

As far as the Russian Federation and the former Soviet Union are concerned, the geopolitical appetite of radical Muslims is tremendous. For example, the Chechen radical Islamic leaders Shamil Basayev and Jordan-born Khattab, and affiliated organizations called for the establishment of a North Caucasus Islamic republic to include Chechnya, Daghestan, and all the western Muslim autonomies in the area. Such a state would span the area from the Black Sea to the Caspian, would control energy exports from the Caspian basin, and would destabilize oil-rich Azerbaijan. These forces receive ideological and financial support from the conservative Arab states, primarily in the Gulf and Saudi Arabia. Some are the same Islamic "charities" that finance and arm Osama bin Laden and his terrorist networks. The Russian government has been saying for at least five years that there were operational links between al Qaeda and the radical wing of the Chechen nationalist movement.[4]

Russia's allies in Central Asia, secular post-communist autocracies, are also under attack. Radical Muslim movements, such as the Islamic Movement of Uzbekistan, have worked closely with the Taliban, trained hundreds of fighters and terrorists, and infiltrated them into the territory of the Commonwealth of Independent States (CIS) Collective Security Treaty partners, which are Russia's allies.

A broader radical Islamic movement, Hizb-ut-Tahrir (Army of Liberation), established by a Palestinian Arab in Jordan in 1952, calls for the establishment of an Islamic Shari's state in the Fergana valley, which borders Kyrgyzstan, Uzbekistan, and Tajikistan. It also stands for the establishment of a united and absolutist Islamic state, a califate, throughout Central Asia. Such an entity, if established, would command vast natural resources and technical expertise and might have access to weapons of mass destruction (WMD).

If constituted, a Central Asian califate could serve as a platform for the takeover of all Muslim areas within Russia and expansion into the Middle East. However, because Hizb-ut-Tahrir does not openly call for armed struggle, and because the rulers of Central Asia often persecute and prosecute its supporters, it often is defended, not only by the NGO community but also by some U.S. congressional committees dealing with the region. In the longer term, radical Islam could threaten the Volga-Urals region, as the Russian-Kazakh border is not patrolled, and new generations of Tatars and Bashkirs find themselves torn between Westernization and Islamic fundamentalism.

It is difficult to predict how successful the Islamization of Russia and Eurasia will be. Alexei Malashenko, the Islamic affairs expert of the Carnegie Endowment for International Peace in Moscow, believes that Islamists will not achieve their goals and that process of struggle and the image of being fighters for the true faith, standing in opposition to the non-Islamic world, are more important to them than practical politics.[5] However, experience elsewhere in the world, from Algeria to Gaza to Kashmir, indicates that the Russian state and its Central Asian neighbors may well be facing an implacable foe in a decades-long struggle.

In a way, there is little new here; the history of Russian conflict with Islamic forces in the North Caucasus spans two centuries. Two of Russia's nineteenth-century literary icons, Mikhail Lermontov and Leo Tolstoy, wrote some of the best poetry and prose in Russian literature about their military experiences against Muslim fighters in the Caucasus. Today, however, the conflict has escalated beyond cavalry and rifles. The threat of terrorism against civilians and use of unconventional weapons is high indeed.

## THE CHALLENGE OF RISING ISLAM

The world of Islam crosses Russia's southern border, where it claims the allegiance of 20 million citizens of Russia, primarily Tatars, Bashkirs, Chechens, the peoples of Daghestan, and others. Islamic emissaries with new ideas and deep pockets came to Russia through porous post-Soviet borders, with little to stand in their way. Another 80 million Muslims, primarily of Turkie origin, live to the south of the Russian border, from Azerbaijan on the shores of the oil-rich Caspian Sea and farther east to the former Soviet republics of Kazakhstan, Uzbekistan, Kyrgyzstan, Tajikistan, and Turkmenistan.

The Russian security response to the surge of radical Islam in Central Asia and the Northern Caucasus included recognition of the threat in two important documents: the national security doctrine and the defense doctrine. Both were developed during Vladimir Putin's tenure as head of the Russian National Security Council, head of the Federal Security Service (FSB), and then later as prime minister.

The documents single out terrorism and "illegal military formations" (typical of radical, politicized Islam) as threats to the Russian state. The doctrine recognizes the preparation of terrorist groups and organizations in foreign countries and their dispatch against Russia as a specific form of aggression that needs to be countered "with all the might of the Russian state and its armed forces." The doctrine states that the armed forces will be used in the territory of the Russian Federation "if existing conflicts are threatening and destructive" to the state.[6]

As a part of preparing to fight the Islamist threat, Russia and the countries of the Common Security Treaty of the Commonwealth of Independent States have created a CIS Anti-Terrorism Center in Bishkek, the capital of Kyrgyzstan. China decided to join the center at the Shanghai Cooperation Organization meeting in April 2001. Under this arrangement, several countries of the CIS and the Collective Security Treaty will each earmark a battalion to create a rapid deployment antiterrorism force of 1,500–1,700 soldiers.

There are also domestic and legal challenges related to fighting the Islamist security threat. According to Sergey Mel'kov, a Russian security expert at the Military University, Russia proclaims its adherence to the principles of territorial integrity enshrined in the constitution, and the supremacy of federal law in conflict resolution on its territory, and has promulgated a number of laws, including the 1998 Law on Fighting Terrorism.[7] This act provides a definition for "terrorism" and "antiterrorism operations" and puts the government (the cabinet) of Russia, the Ministry of Defense, the FSB, the Foreign Intelligence Service, border guards, and other state institutions in charge of fighting terrorism. In addition, twelve articles of the Criminal Code are relevant and prohibit terrorism, hostage taking, mass rioting, attacks against state and government officials, seizure of power, rebellion, instigation of national and religious hostility, violation of the state border, genocide, illegal changes in state borders, and so on.

However, the challenges posed by the Islamist resurgence go much deeper than the immediate security threat. They could, in fact, result in a clash of juridical values and legal systems that could endanger Russia's very nature as a state. Russia basically is a continental law country, meaning a country whose laws are rooted in the Roman legal system and the Code Napoléon. Although its courts are often inefficient and corrupt, they follow a legal system similar to those of other countries in Europe.

Putin's legal reforms are aimed at harmonizing Russian civil and criminal law with norms accepted in the European Union. This is an important legal and civilizational step, solidifying Russian connections to the West.

Radical Islamists, however, demand the introduction of Islamic law, the *Shari'a,* in their areas of residence. As Muslim consciousness grows, Islamic politicians demand the introduction of Islamic courts as well as Shari'a law. In some areas, supporters of tribal or traditional law want a combination of Shari'a and local customary law.[8]

Experimentation with Shari'a in the territory of the Russian Federation is viewed with concern by experts. In 1992, Islam was pronounced a state religion by the Chechen constitution. In summer 1996, Shari'a-based criminal law was passed by the local parliament in then de facto independent Chechnya. That criminal code was copied from a Sudanese act. In spring 1997, the first public executions took place and were broadcast by Russian television. In 1997–98, a region in Russian-controlled Daghestan influenced by radical Islamists began applying Shari'a law in direct contradiction to the Constitution of the Russian Federation.

Since 1994, President Ruslan Aushev of Ingushetia, a former Soviet general considered loyal to Russia, has issued decrees suspending the application of some parts of Russian federal law and prescribing the introduction of Islamic law, allowing for polygamy and the purchase of brides. He also enacted a law on justices of the peace, who could adjudicate based on "local custom" and "principles of Shari'a" as well as the Russian law.

Although it is conceivable that Muslims may apply principles of their faith-based family law to their personal lives to the extent that it does not contradict the laws of the Russian Federation, the rejection of the secular legal system as a whole by a religious minority is threatening and may lead to alienation and separatism. Moreover, if Shari'a applied, Islamic judges could legitimate the argument that armed struggle against the infidel (*kafir*) state dominated by non-Muslims (Russians), a state that "occupies" lands belonging to Muslims, is a religious duty of the faithful. This is a key dilemma not only in Russia, but also in all those states with significant Muslim minorities. If a radical reading of the Islamic law is applied by Islamic scholars (*ulema*), all such states, from Bosnia to Israel to India, may face a religious-separatist challenge to their sovereignty and territorial integrity.

## GEOPOLITICAL DILEMMA

After the terrorist attacks on the United States on 11 September 2001, perceptions of the violent Islamist threat became clearer on both sides of the Atlantic. The Kremlin and other key Russian players, such as the security services and the military—both potential U.S. allies in the newly declared war on terrorism—began debating the proper course to take to deal with that threat.

Putin recognizes that implacable Islamic fundamentalism is a great threat to Russia. Furthermore, he believes that siding with the West may bring other benefits, such as more foreign investment, a greater share of the global energy market, and more international understanding for Russia's position on Chechnya.

The Russians reacted with great emotion and sympathy to the carnage in America. As of this writing, Putin seems to have placed Russia squarely in the antiterrorist camp. Since the tragic events of 11 September, Putin and Bush have had many telephone conversations, and their October 2001 meeting in Shanghai was positive. According to media reports and personal interviews with high-level Russian officials in Moscow, Putin immediately ordered intelligence on ties between bin Laden and the Taliban to be passed on to the United States. He has stated Russia's willingness to cooperate with the United States on search-and-rescue missions and has encouraged Uzbekistan, Tajikistan, and other Central Asian states to allow the United States to use air corridors and military bases on their territory. Putin appears to have concluded that in the long run it is in Russia's interest to stick with the West.

Putin's cooperative position is supported by both Sergey Lebedev, director of the Foreign Intelligence Service, and Federal Security Service chief Nikolai Patrushev, both long-time Putin confidants. Patrushev claimed that his

Federal Security Service thwarted a plan by Chechen leader Movladi Udugov and a radical Muslim organization, a-Jama'at al-Islami, which has links to the Taliban, to crash a plane into the Kremlin. A number of security-services generals have called for intelligence sharing and cooperation in the fight with Islamic terrorism.

The leaders of Russia believe, in the terrible light of 11 September, that their earlier positions—casting conflicts in locations such as Kosovo, Bosnia, Macedonia, and Chechnya in terms of confrontation with radical Islamist forces—are validated. Russian prosecutor-general Vladimir Ustinov, in a recent meeting with the European Council delegation, repeated claims that Chechen fighters have been trained in terrorist camps in Afghanistan that were run and financed by Osama bin Laden. He stressed that the Taliban regime was one of very few that formally recognized Chechen independence. But although the Kremlin wants more understanding from the West for its position on Chechnya, it in turn understands that uprooting and defeating Islamist terrorist networks, which also target Russia, are very much in its own interests.

But not all of Moscow's leaders have been on the same page. At stake are conflicting approaches to the future of Russia as a Eurasian versus a Euro-Atlantic power. The war against terrorism presents a unique opportunity to integrate Russia with the West and NATO, in terms of security and in other ways, and so to transcend the cold war paradigm. But it will not be easy.

The unreformed military resists efforts to shift Russia's orientation westward and covets Middle Eastern weapons markets. At a conference in Moscow organized by the Adenauer Foundation, which took place after 11 September 2001, representatives of the Russian military were still preoccupied with the alleged threat to Russia of NATO enlargement, instead of focusing on the tasks at hand. And civilian Russian military analysts say that it is high time to abandon the intelligence-gathering approach to all contacts with NATO and Western militaries.

The concerns of the Russian military-industrial complex and the nuclear energy ministry,

Minatom, about the future of their markets in Iran, Iraq, and other rogue states have been publicly aired in the Russian media. Some Russian experts have already claimed that the United States does not really need a ballistic missile defense if the threat is low-tech. Apparently they disregard the possibility that terrorist states and organizations might acquire WMD-tipped missiles along with low-tech weapons.

As long as he holds the portfolio, Defense Minister Sergey B. Ivanov's position is crucial to securing Russia cooperation. Yet after the 11 September terrorist attack, he wavered and seemed out of sync with his own boss, President Putin, who declared that Russia and NATO are prepared to act jointly against terrorism. Later, speaking at the CIS Collective Security Treaty Ministerial in Yerevan, Armenia, Ivanov said that Russia would not allow NATO troops to deploy in the territories of Collective Security Treaty members, nor would it participate in retaliatory ground attacks. Russia may simply not have enough forces to pursue a two-theater engagement: in Central Asia and in Chechnya. The harrowing experience of the Soviet occupation of Afghanistan is still fresh in the memory of Russian generals. However, speaking after the defense minister's speech, Foreign Minister Igor S. Ivanov did not rule out limited and mutually agreed deployment of some elements of the U.S. military for a limited time. This was understood as Russian agreement to deploy U.S. tactical aviation and special forces and to cooperate in support of the Northern Alliance. And, most crucially, Putin supported deployment of U.S. assets into bases in Central Asian CIS states and Georgia.

In Russia, elsewhere, politicians and journalists have tried to shift blame for the assaults on New York and Washington onto the shoulders of the United States, or Israel, or nefarious "international corporations." Two Russian politicians identified in the Russian media as being on the payroll of Saddam Hussein and the Iraqi lobby in Moscow, Vladimir Zhirinovsky and Alexei Mitrofanov, even called for use of the Russian nuclear shield to protect radical Islamic regimes from American ire.[9] Other nationalist and communist politicians have called for Russia to support the Islamic world against Western imperialism. However, persons that I interviewed in Moscow in late September 2001 and February 2002 indicate that the majority of Moscow's political elite rejects such rhetoric. Indeed, Russian elite attitudes were markedly more pro-American than those of the French or liberal-left Germans, Britons, and Italians.

## SIGNIFICANCE OF THE DEBATE

A broad partnership with NATO could be a golden opportunity for the United States to bring Russia into the Euro-Atlantic environment. For Putin, the benefits of supporting a U.S. campaign in Afghanistan are more important than the supposed strategic insecurity that would result from adopting the Eurasianist world view, which includes an anti-Western stance. Eurasianists' idea of insecurity is based on the assumption that Russia and the United States are doomed to be strategic and civilizational competitors, and it traces its roots to the controversies of the nineteenth century between pro-Western reformers and anti-Western Slavophiles.

Russia felt frustrated that with the end of the cold war it lost its great power and prestige and, with it, much of its leverage with the United States. Even with its rusting nuclear weapons, Russia came to be treated as a nuisance, neither friend nor foe. But U.S. operations against the Taliban changed all that. The sustained U.S. campaign to break the back of the Taliban regime included massive Russian support for the Northern Alliance, a coalition of anti-Taliban forces operating south of the old Soviet-Afghan border. This support had both operational and symbolic value. Removal of the Taliban denies sanctuary to the ringleaders of the attacks on the United States while serving as a warning to others who might provide aid and comfort to terrorists. And for the Russian military, it provides some measure of revenge for their losses in Afghanistan.

Russian cooperation allowed the United States to build up an anti-Taliban capability much more quickly than it otherwise could

have. But the U.S.-Russian cooperation may develop beyond the mountains of Hindu-Kush, to the corporate boardrooms of transnational energy companies. Instability in the Middle East provides an opportunity to partially substitute Russian energy for that of the Persian Gulf. Russia wants to be seen as a more dependable source of supply for both natural gas and oil. This cooperation may also lead to a Washington-Moscow understanding that, among other things, would allow Russia once again to ask to reschedule the Soviet-era $100 billion debt. The United States also is likely to spend several billion U.S. dollars sustaining its allies in Central Asia, including the Russians, the Uzbeks, the Kyrgyz, and the Tajiks, paying for air bases and fuel.

The Russians have worked very hard to link the events of 11 September to Chechnya. They have argued that the same radical Islamist circles fund both bin Laden and the Chechen rebels, and that a successful counterattack will require a parallel solution to their Chechen problem. Since the Chechen issue is closely linked to the situation in Georgia's Pankisi Gorge, where several hundred Chechen fighters have established a base, Moscow has suggested U.S.—Russian cooperation in eradicating a terrorist presence there. As Georgia allowed the Chechens to move across its territory into the secessionist Georgian autonomy of Abkhazia, Russia expressed extreme displeasure and reportedly sent aircraft to bomb the rebels. So far, however, the United States has sent military trainers to Georgia and refused offers of Russian cooperation.

Finally, some analysts in Washington suggested that the Kremlin is likely to demand from the Bush administration recognition of its political predominance in the region from the Black Sea to the Chinese border. This would allow Russia to be the decisive voice influencing the outcomes of succession struggles in Tbilisi and Baku and shaping the environment in Central Asia. So far, it has not happened, at least not in the open.

Positioning Russia as an integral part of the Western alliance could bring substantial political dividends for Putin. Certainly, a rich and contented West would be preferable as a partner for Russia than a resource-starved and insecure

China. But so far, Putin has done little to present his case to the Russian voters.

Russia's relatively dovish liberal reformers are Westernizers who took a beating from the communists, the nationalists, and people such as former prime minister Evgeny Primakov. The liberals would see this as an opportunity to revive a Western orientation and alliance with the United States. On the other hand, Russian nationalists are viewing potential rapprochement with a jaundiced eye. Initially, they viewed the war in Afghanistan as an opportunity to revive a Warsaw Pact-like sphere of influence in the Caucasus and Central Asia. However, Putin, knowing more about the real Russian power—or lack thereof—than the chattering classes in Moscow, failed to make a strong pitch to establish such a zone.

The military might have thought of trying to bar further NATO enlargement and preserve the 1972 Anti-Ballistic Missile Treaty in return for Russian cooperation. However, the military is too weak, corrupt, and poorly performing in Chechnya to make any demands. Thus, Putin apparently has come to the conclusion that it is in Russia's interest to support the war against terrorism without preconditions.

## CONCLUSION

The Russian government and political elites face a policy choice. On one hand, many of them reject and fear a world in which American power rules. On the other, the United States came out a decisive victor in Afghanistan and is likely to remove Saddam Hussein in the future, and they want Russian to be on the winning side. Most important, they perceive radical, terrorist Islam as a real threat to their country and to their allies in the region.

Westernizers in Russia argue that this is the moment to lock in their preferred orientation. Some Eurasianists believe that the short-term gain may turn into a long-term loss. If the United States wins, it will quickly forget Russia's interests, they argue. Moscow often complains that the U.S. withdrawal from the 1972 Anti-Ballistic Missile Treaty, the pending NATO enlargement in 2002, and the desire to store, not dismantle, nuclear warheads indicate that the Bush administration is not taking Russian demands seriously. Still, the intensity of U.S.—Russian contacts indicates that the war against the Taliban and Islamic terrorism is yielding some rare U.S.—Russian military and intelligence cooperation.

For the United States and the EU, it is important to recognize that for the first time since the end of World War II there is a natural "fit" between American and Russian interest. This partnership is important for reasons that go well beyond the war against terrorism, and it is imperative that the two sides seize this chance to solidify the relationship. Certainly, cooperation in the fossil and nuclear energy sectors would bring advantages to both sides and would allow the United States to end the tilt of its foreign policy that arises from the need to placate Middle Eastern oil exporters.

The Bush administration can and should address Russian concerns about U.S. involvement in operations in Central Asia by referring to and drawing parallels with the much-revered U.S.—Soviet cooperation in World War II. It also should point to the positive Russian presence in Bosnia and Kosovo. It should engage the Russian military and intelligence services in cooperative operational planning in cases where Russian assets can be involved.

The Bush administration should further increase its efforts to integrate Russia in the antiterrorism coalition. The U.S. intelligence agencies should work for cooperation with their Russian, Uzbek, and other Central Asian counterparts. In addition to the short-term goal of using the intelligence networks of these countries against al Qaeda, the Islamic Movement of Uzbekistan, and other terrorist organizations, there is the long-term need to work against Islamist fundamentalism throughout the region. In addition, Russia and its Central Asian allies have a wealth of language and area expertise, as well as some intelligence assets, that could be very helpful to the CIA and the FBI.

The U.S. military finds the Soviet-era air bases in Central Asia, such as Manas in Kyrgyzstan and Hanabad in Uzbekistan, particularly attractive for flying missions, staging rapid deployment forces, making emergency landings, and refueling. It has already secured overflight rights over Russia, Kazakhstan, and other Central Asian republics. Russia can play a key role in providing safety for elements of the U.S. military in those areas. Moscow already has its 201st Division—eleven thousand strong—in Tajikistan guarding the Tajik-Afghan border. It may provide security and logistical support to the U.S. Air Force and other elements that may be deployed in Central Asia. The U.S. government should also expect to pay the cash-strapped countries in the region for services rendered.

No effort should be spared to destroy opium poppy cultivation and heroin production and storage in Afghanistan. The United States should integrate the Drug Enforcement Administration in fighting drug exports from Afghanistan. Russia and the United States, together with law enforcement agencies from other countries in Europe and Eurasia, should develop and implement a strategy for rolling up the distribution networks that are pushing heroin from Afghanistan.

The true tests of the new U.S.—Russian partnership will arrive when they deal with the countries that are at the nexus of terrorism and that are armed with weapons of mass destruction: Iraq and Iran. Moscow has already signaled that it values its economic interests in Iraq over the survival of the Butcher of Baghdad. A deal can be made recognizing Iraq's Soviet-era debt to Russia and Russian oil majors' contracts signed with the Iraqi energy ministry. Iran did not even graduate from being an irritant in U.S.—Russian relations to being a topic of serious negotiations. But that will happen, too.

A collision of geopolitical and cultural-religious tectonic plates occurred on 11 September when mass murder was committed in America by radical Islamic terrorists. The anti-jihad war of the twenty-first century was forced on the United States, just as the anti-Nazi crusade in which Moscow and Washington cooperated. In the new, upcoming conflict against totalitarian regimes armed with weapons of mass destruction, as well as radical Islamic terrorists, the United States must reach out to new allies, including Russia, to win. And Moscow is beginning to understand that it can secure its own future by closely cooperating

with the West in the field of national security. There will be difficulties along the way. Nevertheless, for the first time in fifty-five years, and now unencumbered by ideology, there exists a real basis for a U.S.—Russian strategic rapprochement.

## NOTES

1. The National Intelligence Council and the Bureau of Intelligence and Research of the U.S. Department of State, "Russia's Physical and Social Infrastructure: Implications for Future Development," December 2000, <http://www.cia.gov/nic/pubs/conference_reports/russia's_infrastructure.html>.

2. "Russia: Putin Backs Antiterrorism Effort, Seeks To Join NATO," *RFE/RL*, 26 September 2001, <http://www.rferl.org/nca/features/2001/09/260926122945.asp>.

3. Ariel Cohen, "Issues 2002: Russia and Eurasia," Heritage Foundation, <http//www.heritage.org/issues/russiaandeurasia/russia_background.html>.

4. Vladimir Bobrovnikov, "Islam na Post-Sovetskom Prostranstve (Dagestan) Mify I Realii" (Islam in the post-Soviet space (Daghestan): Myths and realities), in *Islam na Post-Sovetskom Prostranstve: Vzliad Iznutri (Islam in the post-Soviet space: The view from inside),* ed. Alexei Malashenko and Martha Brill Olcot (Moscow: Carnegie Center, 2001), 76–83.

5. Alexei Malashenko, "Islamskie Orientiry Severnogo Kavkaza" (Islamic orientation points of North Caucasus), Moscow Carnegie Center, 2001; see specifically ch. 5.

6. Sergei Mel'kov, "Transformatsia Voennoy Politiki Rossii pod vliyaniem Islamskogo factora" (Transformation of Russian foreign policy under the influence of the Islamic factor), in *Islam na Post-Sovetskom Prostranstve,* 58–59.

7. Ibid., 60.

8. Leonid Sukiyainen, "Naydetsia li Shariatu Mesto v Rossiiskoi Pravovoi Sisteme?" (Will there be a place for Shari'a in the Russian legal system?), in *Islam na Post-Sovetskom Prostranstve,* 15.

9. Based on the my personal interviews in Moscow 2001–02. Also see Susan B. Glasser, "In Zhirinovsky, Hussein Finds a Russian Partner," *Washington Post,* 10 September 2002.

## REVIEW QUESTIONS

- Did Al Qaeda achieve its goals and objectives in the September 11, 2001 attacks on the American homeland?
- In what ways were the September 11, 2001 attacks successful? How were they unsuccessful?
- How likely is it that terrorists will obtain a nuclear bomb?
- In what way is Russia's security environment a good case study in the new era of terrorism?
- What lessons can be learned from the Russian case?

The following books and articles are suggested for further information about the near-future of terrorism:

### Books

Arquilla, J. and D. Ronfeldt, eds. *Networks and Netwars: The Future of Terror, Crime and Militancy.* Santa Monica, CA: RAND, 2001.

Kushner, Harvey W., ed. *The Future of Terrorism: Violence in the New Millennium.* Thousand Oaks, CA: Sage Publications, 1998.

Reeve, Simon. *The New Jackals: Ramzi Yousef, Osama bin Laden and the Future of Terrorism.* Boston: Northeastern University Press, 1999.

### Articles

Fish, Stanley. "Postmodern Warfare." *Harper's.* (July 2002).

Johnson, Larry C. "The Future of Terrorism." *American Behavioral Scientist.* 44:6 (February 2001).

Hoffman, Stanley. "The Clash of Globalizations." *Foreign Affairs.* 81:4 (July-August 2002).

# Part III

## WHAT IS TO BE DONE?
### Policy Choices in the New Era

*People know we must act, but they worry what might follow. They worry about the economy and talk of recession. And, of course, there are dangers; it is a new situation. But the fundamentals of the U.S., British, and European economies are strong. Every reasonable measure of internal security is being undertaken. Our way of life is a great deal stronger and will last a great deal longer than the actions of the fanatics, small in number and now facing a unified world against them. People should have confidence. This is a battle with only one outcome: our victory, not theirs.*

—Prime Minister Tony Blair
Speech to the [British] Labor Party Conference
October 1, 2001

# 8

# Issues and Challenges for Counterterrorism

C ounterterrorism involves much more than simply selecting alternative courses of action from a menu of policy options. It is a process fraught with political and social considerations that can have unexpected consequences. These consequences are often rooted in the political and moral idiosyncrasies of nations. For example, the detention of hundreds of suspects in the United States after the events of September 11, 2001 stimulated an ongoing debate about the protection of civil liberties during national crises. Similarly, an Israeli campaign to target and eliminate Hamas operatives generated a great deal of international criticism. These controversies were considered to be acceptable by those respective governments because of their analysis of their particular security environments. In essence, governments will often simply "take the heat" for their policy choices. It is apparent that policy makers and other experts must weigh a range of potential consequences and outcomes when formulating counterterrorist options.

The articles in this chapter discuss the question of homeland security and issues arising from the new security environment. Andrew Hurrell explores the role of norms and rules in the war on terrorism in "'There Are No Rules' (George W. Bush): International Order After September 11." He identifies several sources of post-September 11, 2001 influence on the questions of law and morality, and the impact of these factors in the new era of terrorism. A critical evaluation is made of the impact of terrorism and its causes on U.S. hegemonic standing. Stuart Taylor frames a civil liberties-focused analysis of challenges for counterterrorism in "Rights, Liberties, and Security: Recalibrating the Balance After September 11." In his analysis, the modern effort against terrorism is a balance between preserving liberty and assuring security in the face of a clear threat from homicidal terrorists. A provocative and yet critical question is raised by Bruce Hoffman in "A Nasty Business" about the inherent brutality of some counterterrorist options. This contextual discussion raises stark questions about the fundamental necessities of counterterrorist methods in certain environments.

# 'There are No Rules' (George W. Bush): International Order After September 11

Andrew Hurrell
*Nuffield College, Oxford*

In this article I would like to consider these words of President Bush. They may be seen as simply loose remarks from a president hardly known for his careful or precise use of language (his reported words were: 'There's no rules,' press conference, 17 September 2001). Moreover, they were made in the emotional aftermath of the attacks on New York and Washington. However, they do capture a powerful intuition present in much commentary and analysis, either from those who seek to analyse the struggle against terrorism in purely instrumental and strategic terms[1] or from those who deny that rules should apply given the extreme nature of the threat or the character of the opponents. More importantly, asking the question 'which rules?' provides one way of framing the events of September 11 and their aftermath; of evaluating what has changed ('a new, new world order'?, 'a new kind of war'?, 'a new kind of America'?); and of providing a basis for both moral and political judgement. The article is divided into two sections. I will first of all look at legal and moral rules: at what the past seven months tells us about the multiple and complex roles that norms play in world politics; at the processes of institutional and solidarist enmeshment which, on some accounts, have pressed the U.S. to engage with international law and institutions; at the limits to such processes; and at the way in which the nature of the struggle against terrorism and the idea of civilizational conflict have influenced understandings of the roles of legal and moral rules. The second part examines the role of political norms: in terms of the rationality of terrorist violence, the links between terrorism and the conditions from which it arises, and the impact of these events on U.S. power and hegemony and on the idea of a hegemonic political order. The final section examines the ways in which legal rules, moral rules and political rules interact.[2]

## LEGAL AND MORAL RULES

The events that unfolded after September 11 provide an excellent illustration of the complexity of the roles played by norms and rules in international relations. War and conflict often appear to be bereft of all rules. The clash of material forces seems to be all too obviously dominant and decisive. And, yet, war as a particular form of social conflict, its relationship to other forms of violence (including terrorism) and its connection to the practices of politics are impossible to understand outside of a complex set of political, legal and moral norms and rules.

The reactions to September 11 and the unfolding struggle against terrorism should serve to remind us of the multiple roles played by norms, rules and institutions. They may well serve as regulatory rules designed to constrain choices and/or as parameters within which individual agents pursue their own preferences. This is the view of rules that lies behind the common claim that international law regarding the use of force is not able to 'control' what states do. Whilst this may often be true, the critical point is norms and rules have many other roles and do much more than this. In the first place, norms do not simply constrain but also enable and empower action. In Martin Hollis's words: 'They enable not only by making collective action easier but also by creating forms of activity.'[3] Norms are therefore central to understanding the power to mobilize, to justify and to legitimize action. The importance of mobilization, justification and legitimization in the present crisis has been plain for all to see.  Norms and rules also help explain how actors are constituted: who can act and in what kinds of social and political activities. They help us make sense of the identity of actors and hence of the sources of their preferences. Norms can be understood as expressions of what states and other groups are, where they belong and of the kinds of roles they play. In the present conflict, for example, think of the immense political power of normative claims that establish identity: them vs. us, good vs. evil, friends vs. enemies, civilized vs. barbarian.

Second, trying to make sense of the events of September 11, of the responses to those events and of their possible implications also represents an excellent example of the difficulty of insisting on too rigid a divide between a utilitarian logic of consequences and a norm-based logic of appropriateness. Thus Elster contrasts instrumentally rational action that is hypersensitive to consequences with norms understood as internalized Kantian imperatives ('blind, compulsive, mechanical or even unconscious').[4] Krasner distinguishes between consequential action on one hand and 'taken-for-granted,' 'deeply embedded,' 'internalized' norms on the other.[5] And Keohane has written on the differences between instrumental and normative 'optics.'[6] And, yet, the present crisis illustrates very powerfully that how we calculate consequences is often far from obvious, especially in conditions of great uncertainty; it is almost impossible to separate the calculation of consequences from our understanding of legal or moral norms and from the constitutive, mobilizing and legitimizing power of those norms. Moreover, people are not automated, mechanical beings but human beings who make (often very difficult) choices and whose choices have to be explained and justified to others.

Third, norms are central to understanding and explaining action; but they are also central to judging and evaluating action. Thus war and conflict take place within an inherited tradition of ideas that may well have emerged from within the European and indeed Christian world but which have become deeply embedded in the institutions and practices of international society. This is particularly true of war. The continual involvement of individuals and societies in war and conflict, the moral and political necessity of trying to make sense of what war involves, and the limited range of plausible arguments have led over time to the creation of intelligible patterns, traditions and ideologies. These form the core of legal debates over the use of force and also of moral debates, including understandings of what might constitute a just war. As Michael Walzer puts it: 'Reiterated over time, our arguments and judgements shape what I want to call *the moral reality of war*— that is, all those experiences of which moral language is descriptive or within which it is necessarily employed.'[7] Strengthened by globalization and by the embeddedness of this moral reality within both interstate and transnational normative structures, the character of the debates surrounding the events of September 11 and of what should be the correct response to those events illustrates very clearly the inevitability of ethical debate and of moral engagement. The normative agenda is not only set by states. Domestic and transnational civil society groups have played an important role, for example, in pressing humanitarian and refugee issues onto the agenda during the bombing campaign in Afghanistan and the severely negative consequences for human rights in the U.S. and many other countries.

But the events that followed from September 11 and, more particularly, the nature of the U.S. response raise more profound questions about the changing character of the legal and normative order and about the capacity of that order to tame or enmesh even the most powerful state. Hence, especially through the autumn of 2001, a common view was of how an originally strongly unilateralist administration had been forced to engage with international law, and with a range of international and multilateral institutions. The early foreign policy of the Bush administration had stressed the primacy of relations with major powers such as China and Russia, a much repeated critique of the interventionist and nation-building policies of its predecessor ('foreign policy as social work'), and an increasingly antagonist stance towards a range of international legal regimes from global warming, to arms control regimes, to the International Criminal Court. The shift therefore appeared particularly striking. Following the attacks, the U.S. reported measures taken in self-defence to the Security Council, sought endorsement of its response from the UN, from NATO and from the OAS, and engaged in a widespread diplomatic campaign to build an effective and legitimate coalition in the struggle against terrorism.

In terms of both international law and of the politics of international law there is little doubt that the U.S. and its allies were successful in securing good legal 'cover' and that self-defence constituted a very powerful legitimation for the use of armed force and other responses. In previous cases of the use of armed force in response to terrorist attacks the legal situation remained contested, but with doctrine and practice leaning in a restrictionist direction.[8] The U.S. often sought to push for more expansive understandings of self-defence, justifying military strikes against terrorist targets both to punish and to deter states from supporting them. But, whilst sometimes gaining political support, the legal case was far from solidly established. In 1986, the U.S. took military action against Libya in response to terrorist attacks on its forces in Berlin; the U.S. reported its action to the UNSC and claimed that it was both responding to a past terrorist attack for which Libya was responsible and deterring future attacks; many states insisted that such action went beyond legitimate self-defence, although France and Britain joined the U.S. in vetoing a condemnatory resolution in the UNSC. In August 1998, the U.S. attacked Afghanistan and Sudan in response to terrorist attacks on its embassies in Kenya and Ethiopia. It reported its actions to the UNSC arguing that it was acting in response to attacks on its embassies and nationals abroad. There was condemnation from Russia, Pakistan and the Arab states but even those who expressed support made clear that they did not accept the U.S. doctrine of self-defence.

In the case of September 11, by contrast, an armed attack took place on the homeland of the U.S.; not, in other words, on nationals abroad (Grenada 1983 or Panama 1989), nor embassies (Iran 1980), nor on forces abroad (Libya 1986). Moreover, recognition of an armed attack was sought and confirmed under both the Rio and Washington Treaties. In addition, as the bombing campaign in Afghanistan developed, the U.S. was generally successful in arguing that its actions conformed to the standard criteria by which actions taken in self-defence are to be judged: necessity and proportionality.[9] The accuracy of the bombing and the relatively low level of casualties made this a much less politically contentious issue than many had predicted. Finally, it seems very likely that the U.S. actions have helped to crystallize the legality of more expansive notions of self-defence in response to terrorist attacks—providing a clear illustration of the particular power of a hegemonic state to influence the character of customary legal norms.

A great deal of this engagement with rules on the part of the U.S. was obviously strategic: as part of the battle to build coalition support; as part of the thinking about what to do in a post-Taliban Afghanistan and advantages of UN involvement. Beyond the issue of legality, the involvement of the UN reflected important political considerations (especially for the U.S.'s European allies, but also for Russia and China who made clear their desire to see the UN involved); and also practical considerations (above all, the need for a UN or UN-endorsed stabilization force in post-Taliban Afghanistan). Equally, the choice of legal arguments was strategic: going for legal justification in terms of self-defence rather than action under Chapter VII; seeking legal measures that provided freedom of manoeuvre and avoided dangerous or constraining precedents.[10] But, on the optimistic view, that is precisely the point. It demonstrates the extent to which the calculation of options by even the most powerful actors is shaped by the multilateral and legal framework; that that framework provides concrete and tangible benefits; and that even the most powerful need to legitimize their power. As Wight stressed, power is an inherently social phenomenon and the principle problem of power is the legitimation of power.[11]

This pattern of behaviour can be interpreted through two different theoretical lenses. In the first place, it can be seen as a classic example of the sort of institutional enmeshment emphasized by rationalist institutionalists. The logic is familiar, clear and powerful.[12] Globalization creates many kinds of negative externalities, including the reaction of many marginalized groups, the creation of new channels for protest, and, in particular, the facilitation of new patterns of terrorist and other kinds of non-state violence. Institutions provide major benefits for states seeking to respond to these challenges, in terms of (a) cooperative anti-terrorist measures that are both more efficient and more effective than unilateral or bilateral actions; (b) the degree to which duly authorized actions signal credible commitments both to allies and to adversaries; (c) the way in which multilateralism can foster the reciprocity that is necessary to secure effective anti-terrorism strategies across many countries; and (d) the extent to which institutions can provide legitimacy which, in turn, both fosters support amongst friends and delegitimizes the use of violence by adversaries. As is well known, institutions work by affecting the cost calculations of states and the incentives to adopt particular policies. Other liberal writers have also concluded that the character of the terrorist threat and of the necessary responses to that threat (use of military force, deep intrusion into domestic politics of many countries) underlines the inevitability of multilateralism: 'the administration's new ambition to lead a global coalition against terrorism *makes unilateralism untenable.'* [13]

However, there are difficulties in tying the clearly very important idea of legitimacy so closely to a theory that stresses functional benefits, incentives and cost reduction. After all, for the very notion of legitimacy to have any real force, somebody must believe that the legal order is about more than just efficiency, effectiveness, and costs, and that it embodies rules, values and shared purposes that create some sense of felt obligation. Of course, effectiveness is one dimension of legitimacy (in the form of so-called output legitimacy), but only one. A second dimension stays close to the internal realm of the legal order and stresses the systemic coherence of the legal process and of the internal logic and argument that ties that order together. It is this that makes certain sorts of argument simply unpersuasive or even unsayable. A third dimension links specific legal rules and actions judged in accordance with those rules to some broader set of moral goals or shared purposes. A certain action may be legitimate even if it is on the edge of accepted understandings of legality (as with recent debates on humanitarian intervention) provided that it is understood as fulfilling these broader purposes. And a fourth dimension relates rules back to the world of politics and of power, and stresses the fairness of process and of deliberation: how far is law rendered illegitimate by its contamination with the special interests of the powerful, by the selectivity of its application, by the degree to which less powerful states and actors are excluded from the deliberative communities (interstate and transnational) that must be central to the formation and functioning of any legitimate normative order?

Hence a second, alternative, theoretical framework would focus on solidarist legal enmeshment. This would stress the emergence of a more solidarist and normatively ambitious international legal order through the latter part of the 20th century and, especially, since the end of the cold war. It would highlight the way in which both the use of force and other moves towards the coercive enforcement of international norms (via sanctions, conditionalities, etc.) make it very difficult to exclude issues of legitimacy. And it underscores the extent to which the importance of legitimacy has been given a new twist by the structural conditions of globalization. Dealing with problems created or intensified by globalization (of which terrorism is a good example) necessarily involves the creation of deeply intrusive rules and debates about how societies are to be organized domestically. If states are to develop effective policies against terrorism then they need to interact with a wide range of domestic and transnational actors. As with the use of force, this raises the issue of legitimacy in a particularly acute form.

And, yet, both approaches face an obvious difficulty. As the campaign has gone on, the U.S. administration has appeared increasingly resistant to accepting the logic of either of these theoretical positions. Dealing with terrorism in a globalized world might create a structural imperative towards institutions and might underscore the rationality of multilateral engagement. But this rationality and this particular *raison du système* appear eminently resistable; and we clearly need to ask why.

One explanation focuses simply on power and on the sheer extent of American *hegemony.* The United States finds itself in such an unusually dominant power-position that it can resist the constitutionalist pressures of the system. Hegemons have choices in relation to multilateralism: to decide what gets treated within a legal or multilateral framework; to chose (or influence the choice) of forum when questions are addressed multilaterally; and either to walk away or to engage in 'a la carte multilateralism' in ways or on issues that suit its own preferences.

Because weaker states have a stronger interest in multilateral institutions (both because of their limited unilateral options and their need to curb the unilateralism of the strong), they will often make major concessions to keep the hegemon at least partially engaged with international law and institutions. This logic reflects neorealist views of the unilateral character of the contemporary system: U.S. power means that Washington has far less need of allies than in the past and that it can afford to engage and dispense with allies as it sees fit (as with Pakistan or the moderate Arab states who were first courted and then ignored as the U.S. swung back to strong support for Israel); and new military technologies and enhanced power-projection mean that Washington can be far more of a globally engaged but non-regionalist power than in the past. There is far less reliance than in the past on allies for support and on forward-operating bases from which to deploy its military power. And, on this view, it is the successful exercise of power, rather than any reliance on international law and institutions, that will be crucial in restoring the awe that protects American interests abroad and its citizens at home—as current conservative rhetoric would have it.

The second explanation stresses not power in general but rather the specific character of *American hegemony*. This is, of course, a complex subject. However, we can note the long tradition of ambivalence towards international institutions that has been shared by many groups across the political spectrum. This is a tradition that is deeply rooted in American political culture; but it is also the result of the decentralized character of the political system and the fetishization of the U.S. Constitution and of a particular reading of popular sovereignty. We can also note some of the principal characteristics of neoconservative foreign policy thinking which have been clearly visible within this administration:[14] the belief in immutable principles of universal justice that should guide foreign policy, the central importance of religion and of religious values in both domestic and foreign policy, and the commitment to the nation and to patriotic values needed to cement the unity of the nation. All of these features shape the ways in which interest and values come together in

conservative understandings of foreign policy and underpin the tendency towards crusading as the dominant foreign policy tradition (in contrast to the classical realist emphasis on containment against specific threats to specific national interests).

Both these factors, but especially the latter, have pushed the U.S. towards a policy of conservative and nationalist hegemonic leadership which stresses the natural right of the U.S. to dictate the terms of the response to terrorism and to expect unqualified support. It uses institutions when they suit the U.S. ad hoc coalitions of the willing when appropriate and is very happy to be unilateralist when necessary. Although couched in moral language and with many appeals to the values of the international community, it reflects U.S. interests very closely. Moreover, on this view, there is little need, and no justification, for the sorts of broader concessions towards broader-based international decision-making that countries such as Russia seek. As a result, the U.S. stands in increasing tension with many aspects of the international legal order and this tension appears to be growing starker and more serious (although any assessment must be tentative). U.S. understanding of self-defence, for example, are clearly moving in ways that stretch traditional legal interpretations. In the past, it was generally understood that actions taken in self-defence should not be retaliatory, or punitive, or aimed at pre-emption against possible future attacks; but should rather be focused directly at halting or repelling the attack that has taken place. Equally, the issue of timing is becoming more problematic. On the one hand, in responding to an attack, a state may quite legitimately take weeks or months (as in the Gulf War) to put in place the forces needed to repel an attack; but, on the other, justifications for multiple actions in many places over many years based on self-defence against a single, if devastating, attack seem bound to create severe legal and moral doubts. Whilst the case may stand up legally, the use of a self-defence-based argument to justify both repeated uses of coercive power and a broader process of political restructuring seems bound to suffer the same erosion of legitimacy and political support as happened in the case of the repeated U.S. and UK bombing of Iraq. And, of course, it may well be the extension of the war to Iraq that is most likely to lead to such a crisis of legitimacy.

There are two further points that have been very important for understanding the ways in which legal and moral rules have been understood in the context of the war on terrorism. Both of them have to do with the character of the conflict and with the ways in which the conflict has been interpreted.

## Waging War or Pursuing Criminals

One of the most notable features of the aftermath of the attacks has been the blurring of language between waging war and pursuing criminals. The U.S. has been doing both. There are many ways in which these two kinds of activities and these two conceptions of how force and politics are related can coexist quite happily. Indeed, one can argue that, even before last September, the gap between the two had already narrowed significantly. In the first place, the theory of collective security (although far less often the practice of the UNSC) holds that war is to be seen as the result of an aggressor who can be identified and who should be punished as a criminal. Second, the expansion of threats to international peace and security in the 1990s as understood by the UNSC directly involved many activities of an international criminal character (genocide, crimes against humanity). Third, human rights law and international humanitarian law are becoming increasingly interwoven and interconnected.

And, yet, the past months have illustrated the tensions and difficulties that arise. In the first place, the idea of a *war* continues to have distinctive political and legal features. A war involves violence by organized groups (whether states or of other kinds) for political purposes. It is a clash between agents of political groups. This is one of the ways in which terrorists are distinguished from pirates—the group that was classically characterized as the enemies of all mankind—*hostis humani generi*. Speaking in terms of a war does therefore implicitly legitimize the terrorist as having a political cause and as being a political actor. The discourse of war has other implications. It implies that there is an adversary who can be identified and eventually defeated. It also serves to shift the actions

of governments beyond 'normal politics'[15] and to justify actions that might otherwise be hard to justify (most obviously in terms of the curtailing of human rights and legal due process).

Second, there are legal tensions. The idea of pursuing terrorists as criminals and within the bounds of human rights lays emphasis on evidence, trial and punishment. Violence is to be exceptional and in need of special justification. In war, by contrast, violence is the norm and rules are designed to try and limit its scope and consequences. Thus, for example, selective targeting of enemy leaders is permitted (although putting a price on an individual's head is not, nor is assassination of those under your control or leaving prisoners to their fate). Equally, many aspects of the Geneva Conventions (most notably the classification and treatment of prisoners of war) rely for their effectiveness on equality of treatment for both sides and on the cement of reciprocity. Yet such treatment is often in tension with arguments concerning the need to pursue criminals, to prevent further attacks and to enforce justice. Much of the controversy has centred on the treatment by the U.S. of its captives at Guatanamo Bay; and many of the problems have been interpreted as further evidence of a U.S. resistance to abide by international law and norms. Whilst this may indeed be the case, it is also important to note that the structural characteristics of the struggle against terrorism make the tensions amongst different bodies of law inevitable. And they are tensions that the current legal order is singularly ill equipped to deal with.

The other great source of uncertainty concerns the question of how much state involvement in an attack by irregular forces is necessary to justify action taken in self-defence against that state. The U.S. was successful in gaining support for the idea that those 'aiding, supporting, or harbouring the perpetrators, organizers and sponsors of these acts will be held accountable.' Far more dramatically, the early phase of the war saw a switch in emphasis from the enemy being defined as a transnational terrorist network to seeing the Taliban as the enemy. In other ways, the war was redefined in ways that brought it far closer to a traditional interstate model. And, yet, nothing has been said or agreed that clarifies the uncertainty: what are the criterion for judging what aiding, harbouring or supporting might mean? How much of a direct link to a group operating in a particular state needs to be established in order to justify attacks or other forms of intervention? What do we do about weak states unable to control their own territory?

Finally, the distinction between waging wars and pursuing criminals takes us back to the debate about the U.S. as a hegemonic or imperial power. Empires, after all, tend not to wage war within areas that they control. They have consistently defined their own use of force in terms of policing against criminals or putting down rebellions. As Koskenniemi notes 'An empire would hardly wage war on a non-discriminatory basis; it would in fact wage no war at all—it would engage in police action for the punishment of "criminals."'[16] In other words, the particular character of the struggle against terrorism within the context of U.S. hegemony challenges the legal models and understandings that developed in the context of interstate conflicts.

## A Civilizational Conflict?

There has been a great deal of debate and discussion suggesting that we are witnessing a clash between Islam and the West. For many at the time, the attacks and the U.S. response served to make Huntingtonian prophecies about clashing civilizations appear far less abstract and far more plausible.

The counter-arguments to the image of a religious or civilizational conflict are well known and bear constant repetition. First, at a general level, it is difficult to identify clear territorial boundaries to civilizations, and harder still to imbue them with the capacity to act as a coherent unit. The image of clashing civilizations places far too much in the undifferentiated category of 'civilization,' reifying and essentializing cultures and downplaying the multiplicity of trends, conflicts and contradictions within any particular cultural tradition. Cultures are not closed systems of essentialist values and it is difficult to see the world as consisting of a limited number of cultures each with its own indestructible and immutable core, particularly given the expansion of channels, of pressures and of agents through which norms are diffused across the world. Second, and following from this,

there are as many Islams as there are versions of Christianity and only the most mis-informed or malevolent of commentators can see the terrorist attacks as having some representative quality of either an essentialist let alone potentially dominant Islam.

Third, the emergence of traditionalism in the Islamic world and of Islamist movements does not reflect some seamless historical development. As in many other parts of the world, cultural and religious particularism and traditionalism are born out of intimate connection with, and reaction to, the forces of modernity and change, and are not reflective of some inner cultural or religious essence. As with nationalism, it is, if not fully invented, then at least consciously crafted for particular political and social purposes. Fourth, the image of a modern, rational West confronting the fanaticism and irrationality of the Islamic world ignores the extent to which the repudiation of Enlightenment rationalism has been a central part of the western cultural, philosophical and political tradition. Indeed, a vast amount of terror (the greatest part if such an idea of quantity makes any sense) has been directly inspired by this western revolt against reason. Moreover, terrorist attacks against something called modernity have recently taken place in other places and cultural environments (for example Japan). Fifth, the very malleability of western constructions of Islam should give us grounds for scepticism. It was, after all, many of the same figures now in the Bush administration who, in the 1980s, praised the mujahedin as 'freedom fighters' bravely struggling against the atheistic evil empire of the Soviet Union. And, finally, the image of clashing civilization ignores the very important sense in which radical Islamist revolt and Al-Qaeda terrorism is aimed primarily *internally* at governments within the Islamic world for having become corrupted and un-Islamic.

And, yet, despite this list of problems, such views have not receded. On one side, although the actual degree of support for Al-Qaeda in the Islamic world is very hard to judge, the sense that the U.S. stands in deep opposition to Islam has remained powerful. And it has been aided by the U.S. shift back towards solid and uncritical support for the hard-line policies of the Sharon government in Israel and would be boosted still further by the extension of the war to Iraq. Equally, on the U.S. side (and within other western states), the idea of civilizational conflict has undoubtedly shaped views of which norms and rules are applicable and which not. Consider these words from Congressman Tom Lantos:

> But unfortunately we have no option but to take on barbarism which is hell bent on destroying civilization . . . You don't compromise with these people. This is not a bridge game. International terrorists have put themselves outside the bonds of protocols.[17]

What this suggests is the continuing power of a very deep-rooted tradition in western international thought that asserts that the normal rules of international relations should be set aside in certain kinds of conflict or in struggles with certain kinds of states or groups. Thus the rights to be enjoyed by non-Christian and non-European peoples were constantly debated throughout the long and bloody history of European expansion and imperialism. In the encounter between Christianity and Islam, for example, we find the important distinction between a holy war waged outside any framework of shared rules and norms and a just war waged for the vindication of rights within such a shared framework. Moreover, internal to the western tradition, there is also a very powerful tradition of thought that asserts that certain kinds of states and systems cannot be dealt with on normal terms, that the normal rules that govern international relations have to be set aside. This idea has been powerfully asserted by conservatives from Burke onwards in relation to revolutionary states. In the 1980s, for example, many in the Reagan administration argued that a fundamental lack of reciprocity meant that many basic notions of international law had to be set aside in dealing with communist governments. From this conservative tradition, the options are either to contain or to crusade. Such positions clearly continue to resonate within and around the current U.S. administration.

## POLITICAL NORMS

In this section, I would like to contrast the above discussion of legal and moral rules with three common ways of thinking politically about events such as these three aspects of political action and how they help us to make sense of terrorism and its implications. The first builds from the micro-level and from the very powerful, indeed dominant, view in western social science that politics can be understood in terms of the rational pursuit of self-interest. Sometimes this is simply an assumption; at other times it is believed to be revealed in the preferences of actors and the degree to which their actions follow from those preferences. In earlier times (maybe up to the mid-18th century), rationality was a self-conscious goal: how to inject some rationality into statecraft and how to deflect in a certain measure the ever-present power of chance, contingency and fortuna. How far can terrorism be understood in these terms and how far does it challenge or overthrow this deep-rooted way of 'making sense' of politics? The second aspect looks at a different way of 'making sense' of terrorism, namely the relationship between terrorism and some background set of political or economic conditions. And the third aspect looks more at the international systemic level and stresses the importance of the distribution of power. What are the implications of the attacks for the distribution of global power and for the future international role of the United States?

## Terrorism and the Logic of Rational Political Action

Terrorism has been used by states (from the Jacobins to Stalin),[18] by religions (think of the Inquisition) and by many non-state groups. These include not just those we think of as 'terrorists' but others such as the Mafia or the Colombian drug cartels who have used terror for specified aims and purposes. It has been very hard to make much headway by defining terrorism in terms of goals and objectives; hence many have concentrated on terror as means and on understanding terrorism as a particular kind of coercive politics.[19] For Aron, 'an act of violence is labelled "terrorist" when its psychological effects are out of proportion to its purely physical result.'[20] It involves actions which are intended to exploit the psychology of violence and which seek to make deliberate and systematic use of coercive intimidation.

If terrorism is a technique for waging war and thereby for pursuing particular goals, then we can identify different degrees of 'fit' between a terrorist action and some notion of political rationality. In some cases there seems to be a clear connection between the use of terrorism and a set of desired outcomes. However much we may legitimately deplore and condemn them, the actions of the IRA, ETA, the PLO, or the Irgun or Stern can be viewed in this way—as attempts to draw attention to a cause; to demoralize the enemy and force a reassessment of the costs of continuing to fight; to increase the power and position of one group relative to another; and, most importantly, to provoke a response that will create favourable conditions either for negotiation or for gathering greater popular support.[21]

Seen in this way, many cases and instances of terrorism fit within our dominant understandings of political rationality. There are other cases where political rationality and the fit between terrorist action and a clear political framework are much harder to discern. In some cases the goals seem so wholly futile that it is difficult to imagine how anyone believed that terrorist actions might further them—Baader Meinhof, the Weathermen, revolutionary violence in the late 1960s, environmental or other single-issue terrorists, anti-government terrorism in the U.S. in the 1990s. And there are other classes of terrorism where (the line is hard to discern) we are pushed towards the possibility of a pure pathological terrorism, of—to paraphrase Grotius—those who use violence only so that there will be more violence.

And, yet, in thinking about the current situation, it would be wrong to neglect rational political calculation. If the goal is to draw attention to a set of issues, then it has been dramatically successful; if the goal is to provoke the United States into responding in such a way that will increase anti-Americanism in the Islamic world, then again the signs of success are visible. After all, the strategy of provocation is at the heart of most political terrorism; and the chances that anti-American or anti-western feeling will be inflamed are many times greater than, say, that rural guerrilla action in Latin America in the 1960s would ever have incited revolutionary uprisings. Nor is it obvious that the standard

array of concepts in coercive diplomacy has no role—as in the claim that you cannot deter a fanatic. The important point is to avoid assuming that the rationality of violence or the calculus of political consequences looks the same from all perspectives and in all cultural, historical and economic contexts. Analytically what is needed is not a rigid dichotomy between a political rationality that makes sense to us and irrationality and fanaticism; but, rather, a greater understanding of the links between values and action. But, overall, this line of analysis would lead us to doubt how far this should be understood as 'the new terrorism.'

Serious problems come from ignoring the rationality of terrorist action. The current 'war on terrorism' seeks to isolate a single phenomenon labelled 'terrorism' and to declare that the aim of policy should be to smash all terrorism worldwide. But to talk in this way is to risk ignoring or downplaying the underlying political and other disputes from which terrorist acts emerge and the political settlements that will be needed if many forms of terrorism are to be brought to an end. Appropriate tactics will vary. Some degree of coercion was undoubtedly justified in the case of action against Al-Qaeda. But the great damage of this 'one model fits all' approach is already visible from Colombia to Kashmir, but most obviously in the Palestinian conflict.

## Terrorism and Its Origins

Another way of 'making sense' of terrorism is by linking its causes to some background conditions—anti-western resentment in the Islamic world and conditions of globalization are the two that have dominated discussion. It is clearly the case that terrorism arises in a certain cultural and political situation. The origins and the character of Baader-Meinhof may share common features with other terrorists but they are very closely connected with the particular character of post-1945 West German politics. The same is true of anti-government terrorism in the U.S.—it is very hard to think of this set of ideas emerging from within any other country.

In the case of the attacks on America, there is an important degree of connection between the attacks and the multiple resentments felt against the U.S. in many parts of the Islamic world. Palestine and Iraq are routinely stressed. There is a depth of hatred in many parts of the world (shared not just by religious or political radicals) produced by decades of U.S. support for Israel, by the refusal of the U.S. to condemn Israeli actions, and by ignoring or downplaying the hardships and humiliations inflicted on Iraq. But the resentments are wider and it is too simple to believe that solving the Palestinian conflict will undercut such terrorist attacks. It seems plausible to argue that much resentment has to do with the far-reaching and corrosive encroachments of modernization, westernization and globalization. These encroachments have undermined traditional social practices, weakened the political coalitions that it was hoped would underpin developmental nationalism (whether of an allegedly revolutionary socialist or more conservative character); and also, of course, created the conditions and instruments for new forms of social and political mobilization. The attacks of September 11 and the U.S. response reflected a critique of the international order that had been developing in many parts of the Islamic world since the 1970s. To speak in this way is not to condone or to excuse, but simply to explain.

In thinking of these Islamic origins and motivations, it is important to bear in mind the long tradition of such kinds of violent revolt. Note the contemporary force of James Joll's words concerning the anarchist tradition:

> There was simultaneously a sense of desperation, a feeling that there was something hopelessly wrong with the world, and at the same time there was a firm belief in the possibility of putting things right, if only the institutions which hindered the doing of God's will could be destroyed.[22]

Or his description of the infectiousness and prevalence of anarchist violence in the late 19th century when the stream of political assassinations 'were in one way or another the result of the anarchist belief in the immediate, apocalyptic value of an act of self-immolation which would also serve to remove the symbol of the existing order.'[23]

What of the relationship between these terrorist attacks and globalization? This is the source of some of the strongest claims for novelty—namely, as for Braudrillard, that this is the first world war to be connected so intimately to globalization?

Aside from the fact that this is not a world war, these claims should be treated with caution, or at least put in some perspective. It is true, as argued above, that the conditions of revolt and resentment cannot be divorced from the inequities and discontents of globalization. It is also true that social and economic globalization has opened up new targets for attack, new means of attacking them and new opportunities for publicity. But this is not wholly new. Late 19th and early 20th century terrorism was also tied to the great wave of globalization and integration that marked the period from 1870 to 1914—think of the role of immigration and diasporas in facilitating revolutionary movements or the increased range of terrorist targets that followed from new technology and urbanization (bombs, trains, cities). Equally, writing on terrorism in the 1980s was already highlighting the importance of mass communications, increased migration and travel, and new technologies for weapons systems. So, yes, highly destructive technologies and people able to exploit the opportunities of globalization are characteristic of contemporary terrorism, but this is part of a longer-term process of change, not a sudden or revolutionary new development. True transnational terrorism that is genuinely able to undercut the state's monopoly of violence, that is able to exploit the privatization of violence and the instruments of violence, that is able to flourish in areas where state control is weak or non-existent and that is able to move and manoeuvre within the many spaces created by technological globalization and by politically driven deregulation and state retreat would be both practically and conceptually a far more serious threat. But it is not, as yet, clear how far we have arrived at such a reality. How far, for example, is a state base still important for 'network terrorism'?

As with all such debates, the important issue is the dialectic between globalization's challenges and the state's capacity to respond. It is already abundantly clear that this dialectic has been at work over the past months. States, led by the U.S., have sought to react—by reasserting their power over their citizens and over their borders, including the removal or curtailing of basic rights; by making strenuous efforts to remobilize and renationalize politics through the dramatic appeal to an external threat from an alien other; and by shifting early and decisively from defining the threat as a terrorist network to focusing, first, on a regime that controlled much of a state and, then, following the defeat of the Taliban, to concentrating on state supporters of terrorism. It is also notable that the discussion of post-conflict Afghanistan has been conducted in very traditional mode: how to reconstruct the country as a viable nation-state.

## Power and the International Political Order

There is a long and powerful tradition that understands international order principally in terms of the distribution of material power. Balance of power and hegemony constitute the two core ordering mechanisms. A great deal has been written in the period following the end of the cold war on unipolarity, on unipolar politics and on the U.S. as the sole superpower, or hyperpower in the French version. On its own, the distribution of power does not provide an adequate account of either international politics in general or of international order in particular. But it is one very important element. It is therefore critical to ask: what is the likely or possible impact of 11 September on U.S. hegemony and the future of the unipolar world?

On one account, current events suggest that we will see a reinforcement of U.S. power in the world. Four arguments can be noted. First, hegemony is not just about power; it is crucially about purposes and rationales for using that power. Although the sole superpower after the end of the cold war, the purposes of U.S. power were hard to discern. Indeed, the absence of threats, the benign economic environment and the sheer degree of its relative power gave the U.S. the freedom not to have a consistent or coherent project. The attacks will, so it is suggested, provide the U.S. with a sense of purpose; the end of the historical sense of invulnerability will lead to greater involvement and, at least in the short term, make a return to isolationism inconceivable. Second, effective hegemony requires political support. Again, this has been

lacking, or at least uncertain, in post-cold war U.S. foreign policy. The attacks, on the increasing hegemony view, will unleash a durable patriotic fervour and a new self-confidence; they will reinforce both popular and political opinion in recognizing the U.S. goals cannot be achieved by turning inward. It can also plausibly be argued that this sense of purpose will ease the constraints on the use of coercive and military force that have been such a notable feature of U.S. foreign policy since the late 1960s. Thus the unwillingness to bear the military costs of engagement is not (*pace* Luttwak) reflective of a structural change in U.S. society; but has resulted rather from an absence of a convincing national interest that would justify such costs. But now such an interest exists.

Third, effective hegemony requires the acceptance by others of the hegemon's leadership and authority. The attacks, on this view, have already allowed the U.S. to rebuild and tighten relationships with its key allies. In some cases, and especially in the early days following the attacks, the allied coalition reflected shared values, deep human connections so graphically illustrated by the many nationalities of the New York victims, and a powerful sense of equal vulnerability and a 'shared community of fate' far more keenly felt than that created by the shadow of nuclear deterrence. But, beyond its traditional allies, the U.S. had shown a clear capacity to build bridges with other dominant powers such as China and Russia, which had, at least in the former case, been classed as strategic competitors. A fourth reason for stressing the increased dominance of the U.S. concerns the types of power that are most decisive. Whilst the U.S. certainly has a great deal of power relevant to economic globalization (both relational and structural), so too do many others. But, when order and stability are threatened; when the global economy is in clearer need of political management; and when military and coercive power appears to be playing a decisive role, then the particular power resources of the U.S. come into sharper relief—political resources that allow a strong re-engagement of the state in the economy; and military resources in which the U.S. is in a league of its own. Whilst Microsoft may well be useful, in this case it is the marines that matter. Thus, for those who have been sceptical of strong claims about globalization, this crisis provided further grounds for doubting: that the state has somehow definitively retreated from the economy; that military power has become less important.

These are all plausible arguments and events, and continued U.S. success may well press in this direction. But there are powerful forces that pull in the other direction. First, allies. It is true that common interest pulls together and it is also true that U.S. allies (and others) are well aware that a failure to cooperate will engender real antagonism in Washington and risk pushing the U.S. further towards unilateralism. And, yet, whereas traditional security threats push allies together, 'new' security challenges create divisions. This has been visible in many aspects of the new security agenda since the end of the cold war, and the struggle against terrorism is no different. Even more than was the case in dealing with humanitarian emergencies or civil wars, the scope for legitimate disagreement over policy in dealing with terrorism is very large and has been growing more serious. There is also resentment amongst those not closely involved with the 'with us or against us' rhetoric—a curious mixture of Dullesian crusading and the liberal view that in a genuine international community there can be no neutrals (a rhetoric that is particularly resented on the part of those who suffered at the hands of terrorist states actively supported by the U.S. during the cold war).

Second, if hegemony is not just about deploying power but actually about achieving long-term desired outcomes, then there are grounds for doubt. Translating putative power into durable success is often enormously difficult. Think, for example, of the near-total failure of U.S. policy in relation to the 'war on drugs' in Latin America—a region where its relative power is greater than anywhere else in the world. Three points can be made.

First, whilst the bombing of Afghanistan has apparently been very successful in achieving its near-term goals, the task of rebuilding the country and of restoring other failed states that are widely seen as the breeding ground of terrorism remains immense. The paradox, of course, is that an administration that had castigated Clinton's global social welfarism has found

itself involved in the call for restoring the effectiveness and legitimacy of failed states. It insists that it will not become directly involved. But then who will? For how long? And with what success?

Second, as Walt points out, the recent exercise of U.S. hegemony has been extraordinarily 'cheap' for the U.S.[24] One reason for the low costs of the exercise of military power in Afghanistan is the extraordinary technological supremacy. But another was the use of proxies and it is clear that this model is being used extensively from Indonesia to Yemen. And, yet, as the cold war showed all too clearly, the use of proxies is problematic: how to ensure that the conflict reflects your goals rather than theirs (think of all the cold war proxy tails wagging the American dog)? And how to avoid backing deeply disreputable states and groups that attract international human rights criticism, engender political opposition and undermine the legitimacy of support at home in the U.S.?

Third, while this phase of the campaign has indeed seen the successful deployment of coercive force, much of the struggle against terrorism requires deep and intense civilian cross-border cooperation and intelligence sharing. Not only does this require genuine and uncoerced support, but also it can easily be undermined by disagreements over the further use of military force (for example, against Iraq).

## CONCLUSION: POLITICAL ETHICS IN A DIRTY WORLD

One way of thinking about the implications of September 11 is to see in them a return to 'first-order' political questions—in Carl Schmitt's language, the return of 'real' politics after the politics of anti-politics that characterized the liberal moment of the 1990s. Another way of thinking about them is to look not to Schmitt but to Weber. Especially when times get rough, Weber is often a useful guide. For Weber, politics is the arena for struggles amongst differing social and political ideals, and the character of competition for power between these rival views and the manner in which power is deployed will remain the central focus of enquiry.

The past six months have certainly highlighted a number of important Weberian themes. First, and most dramatically visible in the case of the U.S., the idea that the overriding moral responsibility of the political leader is to his or her political community, and not to some notion of a world community. This is not just a reflection of political reality but has a moral significance. In a fragmented and conflictual world, this is ultimately where moral responsibility lies. Second, the extent to which different norms *will* clash with each other. Thus, legal rules (forbidding punitive use of force) have clashed with those who believe that morality justifies punishment and even a legitimate degree of vengeance. Legal rules have clashed with political logic. As we have seen, legal rules stress the need for proportionality; yet political and strategic logic suggests that disproportionate and punitive strikes are most likely to persuade supporting states to desist from their support for terrorist groups. And, third, recent events have highlighted the particular character of moral politics: accepting the inevitability of dirty hands and the need for pragmatic judgement in, for example, deciding when to negotiate with a terrorist group and when to use coercion and force; accepting, too, that politics is about perverse consequences and that conflict develops a logic of its own—as with the way in which the struggle against terrorism has already recast the nature of U.S. relations in the Middle East.

What has the struggle against terrorism done for the post-cold war hopes that a more solidarist international society might be emerging in which the traditional tensions between law, power and morality can be lessened? It suggests, first of all, that there remains a deep tension between the constitutionalist order represented by international law and institutions and the power political structures on which patterned political order rests—in this case the unipolar distribution of power. The easy criticism is of U.S. unilateralism and the exceptionalist ideology that underpins it. The hard Weberian or Schmittian response is that all stable order depends in the last resort on the effective use of coercion for justified and shared ends (as with countering terrorism) that can never be wholly constrained by or contained within a system of legal rules. Second, if the solidarist emphasis on common interests is challenged on one side by the unequal distribution of power, it is challenged on the other by the continued importance of value conflict—and indeed of values and different worldviews as critical determinants of world politics. But, third, and more positively, the character of the struggle against terrorism underscores the limits to the idea of hegemonic order based on U.S. power and coercion alone. The attacks on September 11 did not usher in a new age. They reinforced powerful tendencies that were already visible in the post-cold war order of the 1990s but also exacerbated the tensions and contradictions within that order. On the one hand, the post-September 11 events do bear witness to the extraordinary degree of U.S. relative power and have indeed added purpose and political support to that power. But, on the other hand, they bring into sharper focus the already visible limits to an order based on imposition. Hence the importance of legitimacy as the pragmatic meeting point between political effectiveness and the need for moral consensus.

## NOTES

1. See, for example, Barry R. Posen (2001/02) 'The Struggle Against Terrorism: Grand Strategy, Strategy, and Tactics,' *International Security* 26(3): 39–55.

2. This article was originally written in September 2001 as an early attempt to think through some of the implications of the attacks on the U.S. It was revised in March 2002.

3. Martin Hollis (1991) 'Why Elster is Stuck and Needs to Recover his Faith,' *London Review of Books* 24 January: 13.

4. Jon Elster (1989) *The Cement of Society: A Study of Social Order.* Cambridge: Cambridge University Press.

5. Stephen D. Krasner (1999) *Sovereignty: Organized Hypocrisy.* Princeton, NJ: Princeton University Press.

6. Robert O. Keohane (1997) 'International Relations and International Law: Two Optics,' *Harvard International Law Review* 38(2): 1–13.

7. Michael Walzer (1977) *Just and Unjust Wars: A Moral Argument with Historical Illustrations,* p. 15, emphasis in original. New York: Basic Books.

8. See, for example, Christine Gray (2000) *International Law and the Use of Force,* Chapter 4. Oxford: Oxford University Press.

9. For an evaluation see Adam Roberts (2002) 'Counter-terrorism, Armed Force and the Laws of War,' *Survival* 44(1): 7–32.

10. This strategic use of law is brought out by Michael Byers (2002) 'Terrorism, the Use of Force, and International Law after 11 September,' this issue.

11. Martin Wight (1978) *Power Politics* (edited by Hedley Bull and Carsten Holbraad). Leicester: Leicester University Press.

12. See Robert O. Keohane (2002) 'The Globalization of Informal Violence, Theories of World Politics, and "the liberalization of fear"', available on *Dialog IO* and to be published in Craig Calhoun, Paul Price and Ashley Timmer (eds.) (forthcoming) *Understanding September 11.* New York: New Press/SSRC.

13. G. John Ikenberry (2001) 'American Grand Strategy in the Age of Terror,' *Survival* 43(4): 20, my emphasis.

14. For one view, see Samuel P. Huntington (1999/2000) 'Robust Nationalism,' *The National Interest* (Winter): 31–40.

15. Ole Waever (1995) 'Securitization and Desecuritization,' in Ronnie D. Lipschutz (ed.) *On Security,* pp. 46–86. New York: Columbia University Press.

16. Martti Koskenniemi (2002) *The Gentle Civilizer of Nations. The Rise and Fall of International Law 1870–1960,* p. 419. Cambridge: Cambridge University Press.

17. Interview with Tom Lantos (2001) BBC Radio 4, *Today* programme, 20 November.

18. Note that state-sponsored terrorism does not refer to every bloody or nasty act committed by states but rather to the conscious and targeted use of terror to achieve political purposes whether in Stalin's Russia, Hitler's Germany or Pinochet's Chile. Some actions, such as the fire-bombing of Dresden, straddle the divide between state terrorism and massive destruction inflicted as part of a legitimate war.

19. Cf. Michael Howard: '"Terrorism" is itself simply a technique for waging war, so it makes little sense to talk of "waging war" against it,' *The Times,* 14 September 2001.

20. Quoted in Lawrence Freedman (1976) 'Terrorism and Strategy' in Lawrence Freedman et al. (eds) *Terrorism and International Order,* Chatham House Special Paper, p. 57. London: Routledge and Kegan Paul.

21. Adam Roberts (1976) 'Terrorism and International Order,' in Lawrence Freedman et al. (eds) *Terrorism and International Order,* Chatham House Special Paper, pp. 7–25. London: Routledge and Kegan Paul.

22. James Joll (1979) *The Anarchists,* 2nd edn, p. 6. London: Methuen.

23. Joll (see note 22), p. 111.

24. Stephen M. Walt (2002) 'Beyond Bin Laden: Reshaping U.S. Foreign Policy,' *International Security* 26(3): 58. 'Casualties in the 1991 Persian Gulf War were far lower than expected, and the U.S. Air Force has patrolled the no-fly zone in Iraq and conducted intermittent bombing raids there for nearly a decade without losing a single plane. Subsequent U.S. interventions in Haiti, Somalia, Bosnia, and Kosovo led to fewer than fifty U.S. deaths.'

---

## Rights, Liberties, and Security: Recalibrating the Balance After September 11

Stuart Taylor, Jr.

 When dangers increase, liberties shrink. That has been our history, especially in wartime. And today we face dangers without precedent: a mass movement of militant Islamic terrorists who crave martyrdom, hide in shadows, are fanatically bent on slaughtering as many of us as possible and—if they can—using nuclear truck bombs to obliterate New York or Washington or both, without leaving a clue as to the source of the attack.

How can we avert catastrophe and hold down the number of lesser mass murders? Our best hope is to prevent al-Qaida from getting nuclear, biological, or chemical weapons and smugling them into this country. But we need be unlucky only once to fail in that. Ultimately we can hold down our casualties only by finding and locking up (or killing) as many as possible of the hundreds or thousands of possible al-Qaida terrorists whose strategy is to infiltrate our society and avoid attention until they strike.

The urgency of penetrating secret terrorist cells makes it imperative for Congress—and the nation—to undertake a candid, searching, and systematic reassessment of the civil liberties rules that restrict the government's core investigative and detention powers. Robust national debate and deliberate congressional action should replace what has so far been largely ad hoc presidential improvisation. While the USA Patriot Act—no model of careful deliberation—changed many rules for the (and some for the worse), it did not touch some others that should be changed.

Carefully crafted new legislation would be good not only for security but also for liberty. Stubborn adherence to the civil liberties status quo would probably damage our most fundamental freedoms far more in the long run than would judicious modifications of rules that are less fundamental. Considered congressional action based on open national debate is more likely to be sensitive to civil liberties and to the Constitution's checks and balances than unilateral expansion of executive power. Courts are more likely to check executive excesses if Congress sets limits for them to enforce. Government agents are more likely to respect civil liberties if freed from rules that create unwarranted obstacles to doing their jobs. And preventing terrorist mass murders is the best way of avoiding a panicky stampede into truly oppressive police statism, in which measures now unthinkable could suddenly become unstoppable.

This is not to advocate truly radical revisions of civil liberties. Nor is it to applaud all the revisions that have already been made, some of which seem unwarranted and even dangerous. But unlike most in-depth commentaries on the liberty-security balance since September 11—which argue (plausibly, on some issues) that we have gone too far in expanding government power—this article contents that in important respects we have not gone far enough. Civil

libertarians have underestimated the ne broader investigative powers and exaggerated dangers to our fundamental liberties. Judicious expansion of the government's powers to find suspected terrorist would be less dangerous to freedom than either risking possibly preventable attacks or resorting to incarceration without due process of law—as the Bush administration has begun to do. We should worry less about being wiretapped or searched or spied upon or interrogated and more about seeing innocent people put behind bars—or about being blown to bits.

## RECALIBRATING THE LIBERTY-SECURITY BALANCE

The courts, Congress, the president, and the public have from the beginning of this nation's history demarcated the scope of protected rights "by a weighing of competing interests . . . the public-safety interest and the liberty interest," in the words of Judge Richard A. Posner of the U.S. Court of Appeals for the Seventh Circuit. "The safer the nation feels, the more weight judges will be willing to give to the liberty interest."

During the 1960s and 1970s, the weight on the public safety side of the scales seemed relatively modest. The isolated acts of violence by groups like the Weather Underground and Black Panthers—which had largely run their course by the mid-1970s—were a minor threat compared with our enemies today. Suicide bombers were virtually unheard of. By contrast, the threat to civil liberties posed by broad government investigative and detention powers and an imperial presidency had been dramatized by Watergate and by disclosures of such ugly abuses of power as FBI Director J. Edgar Hoover's spying on politicians, his wiretapping and harassment of the Rev. Martin Luther King, Jr., and the government's disruption and harassment of antiwar and radical groups.

To curb such abuses, the Supreme Court, Congress, and the Ford and Carter administrations placed tight limits on law enforcement and intelligence agencies. The Court consolidated and in some ways extended the Warren Court's revolutionary restrictions on government powers to search, seize, wiretap, interrogate, and detain suspected criminals (and terrorists). It also

etaps and searches of
ress barred warrantless
suspected foreign spies
ly untrammeled presi-
8 Foreign Intelligence
lward Levi, President
general, clamped down on
domestic surveillance by the FBI.

As a result, today many of the investigative powers that government could use to
penetrate al-Qaida cells—surveillance, informants, searches, seizures, wiretaps, arrest, interrogations, detentions—are tightly restricted by a
web of laws, judicial precedents, and administrative rules. Stalked in our homeland by the
deadliest terrorists in history, we are armed with
investigative powers calibrated largely for dealing with drug dealers, bank robbers, burglars,
and ordinary murderers. We are also stuck in
habits of mind that have not yet fully processed
how dangerous our world has become or how
ill-prepared our legal regime is to meet the new
dangers.

## RETHINKING GOVERNMENT'S POWERS

Only a handful of the standard law-enforcement
investigative techniques have much chance of
penetrating and defanging groups like al-Qaida.
The four most promising are: infiltrating them
through informants and undercover agents;
finding them and learning their plans through
surveillance, searches, and wiretapping; detaining them before they can launch terrorist
attacks; and interrogating those detained. All
but the first (infiltration) are now so tightly
restricted by Supreme Court precedents (sometimes by mistaken or debatable readings of
them), statutes, and administrative rules as to
seriously impede terrorism investigators.
Careful new legislation could make these
powers more flexible and useful while simultaneously setting boundaries to minimize overuse
and abuse.

## SEARCHES AND SURVEILLANCE

The Supreme Court's caselaw involving the
Fourth Amendment's ban on "unreasonable
searches and seizures" does not distinguish
clearly between a routine search for stolen
goods or marijuana and a preventive search
for a bomb or a vial of anthrax. To search a
dwelling, obtain a wiretap, or do a thorough
search of a car or truck, the government must
generally have "probable cause"—often (if
incorrectly) interpreted in the more-probable-
than-not sense—to believe that the proposed
search will uncover evidence of crime. These
rules make little sense when the purpose of the
search is to prevent mass murder

Federal agents and local police alike need
more specific guidance than the Supreme Court
can quickly supply. Congress should provide it,
in the form of legislation relaxing for terrorism
investigations the restrictions on searching,
seizing, and wiretapping, including the undue
stringency of the burden of proof to obtain a
search warrant in a terrorism investigation.

Search and seizure restrictions were the main
(if widely unrecognized) cause of the FBI's
famous failure to seek a warrant during the
weeks before September 11 to search the computer and other possessions of Zacarias
Moussaoui, the alleged "20th hijacker." He had
been locked up since August 16, technically for
overstaying his visa, based on a tip about his
strange behavior at a Minnesota flight school.
The FBI had ample reason to suspect that
Moussaoui—who has since admitted to being a
member of al-Qaida—was a dangerous Islamic
militant plotting airline terrorism.

Congressional and journalistic investigations
of the Moussaoui episode have focused on the
intelligence agencies' failure to put together the
Moussaoui evidence with other intelligence
reports that should have alerted them that a
broad plot to hijack airliners might be afoot.
Investigators have virtually ignored the undue
stringency of the legal restraints on the government's powers to investigate suspected terrorists. Until these are fixed, they will seriously
hobble our intelligence agencies no matter how
smart they are.

From the time of FDR until 1978, the
government could have searched Moussaoui's
possessions without judicial permission, by
invoking the president's inherent power to
collect intelligence about foreign enemies. But
the 1978 Foreign Intelligence Security Act

(FISA) barred searches of suspected foreign spies and terrorists unless the attorney general could obtain a warrant from a special national security court (the FISA court). The warrant application has to show not only that the target is a foreign terrorist, but also that he is a member of some international terrorist "group."

Coleen Rowley, a lawyer in the FBI's Minneapolis office, argued passionately in a widely publicized letter last May 21 to FBI Director Robert S. Mueller III that the information about Moussaoui satisfied this FISA requirement. Congressional investigators have said the same. FBI headquarters officials have disagreed, because before September 11 no evidence linked Moussaoui to al-Qaida or any other identifiable terrorist group. Unlike their critics, the FBI headquarters officials were privy to any relevant prior decisions by the FISA court, which cloaks its proceedings and decisions in secrecy. In addition, they were understandably gunshy about going forward with a legally shaky warrant application in the wake of the FISA court's excoriation of an FBI supervisor in the fall of 2000 for perceived improprieties in his warrant applications. In any event, even if the FBI had done everything right, it was and is at least debatable whether its information about Moussaoui was enough to support a FISA warrant.

More important for future cases, it is clear that FISA—even as amended by the USA Patriot Act—would not authorize a warrant in any case in which the FBI cannot tie a suspected foreign terrorist to one or more confederates, whether because his confederates have escaped detection or cannot be identified or because the suspect is a lone wolf.

Congress could strengthen the hand of FBI terrorism investigators by amending FISA to include the commonsense presumption that any foreign terrorist who comes to the United States is probably acting for (or at least inspired by) some international terrorist group. Another option would be to lower the burden of proof from "probable cause" to "reasonable suspicion." A third option—which could be extended to domestic as well as international terrorism investigations—would be to authorize a warrantless "preventive" search or wiretap of anyone the government has reasonable grounds to suspect of preparing or helping others prepare for a terrorist attack. To minimize any temptation for government agents to use this new power in pursuit of ordinary criminal suspects, Congress could prohibit the use in any prosecution unrelated to terrorism of any evidence obtained by such a preventive search or wiretap.

The Supreme Court seems likely to uphold any such statute as consistent with the ban on "unreasonable searches and seizures." While the Fourth Amendment says that "no warrants shall issue, but upon probable cause," warrants are not required for many types of searches, are issued for administrative searches of commercial property without probable cause in the traditional sense, and arguably should never be required. Even in the absence of a warrant or probable cause, the justices have upheld searches based on "reasonable suspicion" of criminal activities, including brief "stop-and-frisk" encounters on the streets and car stops. They have also upheld mandatory drug-testing of certain government employees and transportation workers whose work affects the public safety even when there is no particularized suspicion at all. In the latter two cases, the Court suggested that searches designed to prevent harm to the public safety should be easier to justify than searches seeking evidence for criminal cases.

## EXAGGERATED FEAR OF BIG BROTHER

Proposals to increase the government's wiretapping powers awaken fears of unleashing Orwellian thought police to spy on, harass, blackmail, and smear political dissenters and others. Libertarians point out that most conversations overheard and e-mails intercepted in the war on terrorism will be innocent and that the tappers and buggers will overhear intimacies and embarrassing disclosures that are none of the government's business.

Such concerns argue for taking care to broaden wiretapping and surveillance powers only as much as seems reasonable to prevent terrorist acts. But broader wiretapping authority is not all bad for civil liberties. It is a more accurate and benign method of penetrating terrorist cells than the main alternative, which is planting and recruiting informers—a dangerous, ugly, and unreliable business in which the government is already free to engage without limit. The narrower the government's surveillance powers, the more it will rely on informants.

Moreover, curbing the government's power to collect information through wiretapping is not the only way to protect against misuse of the information. Numerous other safeguards less damaging to the counterterrorism effort—inspectors general, the Justice Department's Office of Professional Responsibility, congressional investigators, a gaggle of liberal and conservative civil liberties groups, and the news media—have become extremely potent. The FBI has very little incentive to waste time and resources on unwarranted snooping.

To keep the specter of Big Brother in perspective, it's worth recalling that the president had unlimited power to wiretap suspected foreign spies and terrorists until 1978 (when FISA was adopted); if this devastated privacy or liberty, hardly anyone noticed. It's also worth noting that despite the government's already-vast power to comb through computerized records of our banking and commercial transactions and much else that we do in the computer age, the vast majority of the people who have seen their privacy or reputations shredded have not been wronged by rogue officials. They have been wronged by media organizations, which do far greater damage to far more people with far less accountability.

Nineteen years ago, in *The Rise of the Computer State,* David Burnham wrote: "The question looms before us: Can the United States continue to flourish and grow in an age when the physical movements, individual purchases, conversations and meetings of every citizen are constantly under surveillance by private companies and government agencies?" It can. It has. And now that the computer state has risen indeed, the threat of being watched by Big Brother or smeared by the FBI seems a lot smaller than the threat of being blown to bits or poisoned by terrorists.

## THE CASE FOR COERCIVE INTERROGATION

The same Zacarias Moussaoui whose possessions would have been searched but for FISA's undue stringency also epitomizes another problem: the perverse impact of the rules—or what are widely assumed to be the rules—restricting interrogations of suspected terrorists.

"We were prevented from even attempting to question Moussaoui on the day of the attacks when, in theory, he could have possessed further information about other co-conspirators," Coleen Rowley complained in a little-noticed portion of her May 21 letter to Mueller. The reason was that Moussaoui had requested a lawyer. To the FBI that meant that any further interrogation would violate the Fifth Amendment "*Miranda* rules" laid down by the Supreme Court in 1966 and subsequent cases.

It's not hard to imagine such rules (or such an interpretation) leading to the loss of countless lives. While interrogating Moussaoui on September 11 might not have yielded any useful information, suppose that he had been part of a team planning a second wave of hijackings later in September and that his resistance could have been cracked. Or suppose that the FBI learns tomorrow, from a wiretap, that another al-Qaida team is planning an imminent attack and arrests an occupant of the wiretapped apartment.

We all know the drill. Before asking any questions, FBI agents (and police) must warn the suspect: "You have a right to remain silent." And if the suspect asks for a lawyer, all interrogation must cease until the lawyer arrives (and tells the suspect to keep quiet). This seems impossible to justify when dealing with people suspected of planning mass murder. But it's the law, isn't it?

Actually, it's not the law, though many judges think it is, along with most lawyers, federal agents, police, and cop-show mavens. You do *not* have a right to remain silent. The most persuasive interpretation of the Constitution and the Supreme Court's precedents is that agents and police are free to interrogate any suspect without *Miranda* warnings; to spurn requests for a lawyer; to press hard for answers; and—at least in a terrorism investigation—perhaps even to use hours of interrogation, verbal abuse, isolation, blindfolds, polygraph tests, death-penalty threats, and other forms of psychological coercion short of torture or physical brutality. Maybe even truth serum.

The Fifth Amendment self-incrimination clause says only that no person "shall be compelled in any criminal case to be a witness against himself." The clause prohibits forcing a defendant to testify at his trial and also making him a witness against himself indirectly by using compelled pretrial statements. It does not prohibit compelling a suspect to talk. *Miranda* held only that in determining whether a defendant's statements (and information derived from them) may be used against him at his trial, courts must treat all interrogations of arrested suspects as inherently coercive unless the warnings are given.

Courts typically ignore this distinction because in almost every litigated case the issue is whether a criminal defendant's incriminating statements should be suppressed at his trial; there is no need to focus on whether the constitutional problem is the conduct of the interrogation, or the use at trial of evidence obtained, or both. And as a matter of verbal shorthand, it's a lot easier to say "the police violated *Miranda*" than to say "the judge would be violating *Miranda* if he or she were to admit the defendant's statements into evidence at his trial."

But the war against terrorism has suddenly increased the significance of this previously academic question. In terrorism investigations, it will often be more important to get potentially life-saving information from a suspect than to get incriminating statements for use in court.

Fortunately for terrorism investigators, the Supreme Court said in 1990 that "a constitutional violation [of the Fifth Amendment's self-incrimination clause] occurs only at trial." It cited an earlier ruling that the government can obtain court orders compelling reluctant witnesses to talk and can imprison them for contempt of court if they refuse, if it first guarantees them immunity from prosecution on the basis of their statements or any derivative evidence. These decisions support the conclusion that the self-incrimination clause "does not forbid the forcible extraction of information but only the use of information so extracted as evidence in a criminal case," as a federal appeals court ruled in 1992.

Of course, even when the primary reason for questioning a suspected terrorist is prevention, the government could pay a heavy cost for ignoring *Miranda* and using coercive interrogation techniques, because it would sometimes find it difficult or impossible to prosecute extremely dangerous terrorists. But terrorism investigators may be able to get their evidence and use it too, if the Court—or Congress, which unlike the Court would not have to wait for a proper case to come along—extends a 1984 precedent creating what the justices called a "public safety" exception to *Miranda.* That decision allowed use at trial of a defendant's incriminating answer to a policeman's demand (before any *Miranda* warnings) to know where his gun was hidden.

Those facts are not a perfect parallel for most terrorism investigations, because of the immediate nature of the danger (an accomplice might pick up the gun) and the spontaneity of the officer's question. And as Rowley testified, "In order to give timely advice" about what an agent can legally do, "you've got to run to a computer and pull it up, and I think that many people have kind of forgotten that case, and many courts have actually limited it to its facts."

But when the main purpose of the interrogation is to prevent terrorist attacks, the magnitude of the danger argues for a broader public safety exception, as Rowley implied in her letter.

Congress should neither wait for the justices to clarify the law nor assume that they will reach the right conclusions without prodding. It should make the rules as clear as possible as soon as possible. Officials like Rowley need to know that they are free to interrogate suspected terrorists more aggressively than they suppose. While a law expanding the public safety exception to *Miranda* would be challenged as unconstitutional, it would contradict no existing Supreme Court precedent and—if carefully calibrated to apply only when the immediate purpose is to save lives—would probably be upheld.

Would investigators routinely ignore *Miranda* and engage in coercive interrogation—perhaps extorting false confessions—if told that the legal restraints are far looser than has been supposed? The risk would not be significantly greater than it is now. Police would still need to comply with *Miranda* in almost all cases for fear of jeopardizing any prosecution. While that would not be true in terrorism investigations if the public safety exception were broadened, extreme abuses such as beatings and torture would violate the due process clause of the Fifth Amendment (and of the Fourteenth Amendment as well), which has been construed as barring interrogation techniques that "shock the conscience," and is backed up by administrative penalties and the threat of civil lawsuits.

## BRINGING PREVENTIVE DETENTION INSIDE THE LAW

Of all the erosions of civil liberties that must be considered after September 11, preventive detention—incarcerating people because of their perceived dangerousness even when they are neither convicted nor charged with any crime—would represent the sharpest departure from centuries of Anglo-American jurisprudence and come closest to police statism.

But the case for some kind of preventive detention has never been as strong. Al-Qaida's capacity to inflict catastrophic carnage dwarfs any previous domestic security threat. Its "sleeper" agents are trained to avoid criminal activities that might arouse suspicion. So the careful ones cannot be arrested on criminal charges until it is too late. And their lust for martyrdom renders criminal punishment ineffective as a deterrent.

Without preventive detention, the Bush administration would apparently have no solid legal basis for holding the two U.S. citizens in military brigs in this country as suspected "enemy combatants"—or for holding the more than 500 noncitizens at Guantanamo Bay. Nor would it have had a solid legal basis for detaining any of the 19 September 11 hijackers if it had suspected them of links to al-Qaida before they struck. Nor could it legally have detained Moussaoui—who was suspected of terrorist intent but was implicated in no provable crime or conspiracy—had he had not overstayed his visa.

What should the government do when it is convinced of a suspect's terrorist intent but lacks admissible evidence of any crime? Or when a criminal trial would blow vital intelligence secrets? Or when ambiguous evidence makes it a tossup whether a suspect is harmless or an al-Qaidan? What should it do with suspects like Jose Padilla, who was arrested in Chicago and is now in military detention because he is suspected of (but not charged with) plotting a radioactive "dirty-bomb" attack on Washington, D.C.? Or with a (hypothetical) Pakistani graduate student in chemistry, otherwise unremarkable, who has downloaded articles about how terrorists might use small planes to start an anthrax epidemic and shown an intense but unexplained interest in crop-dusters?

Only four options exist. Let such suspects go about their business unmonitored until (perhaps) they commit mass murders; assign agents to tail them until (perhaps) they give the agents the slip; bring prosecutions without solid evidence and risk acquittals; and preventive detention. The latter could theoretically include not only incarceration but milder restraints such as house arrest or restriction to certain areas combined with agreement to carry (or to be implanted with) a device enabling the government to track the suspect's movements at all times.

As an alternative to preventive detention, Congress could seek to facilitate prosecutions of suspected "sleepers" by allowing use of now-inadmissible and secret evidence and stretching the already broad concept of criminal conspiracy so far as to make it almost a thought crime. But that would have a harsher effect on innocent terrorism suspects than would preventive detention and could weaken protections for all criminal defendants.

As Alan Dershowitz notes, "[N]o civilized nation confronting serious danger has ever relied exclusively on criminal convictions for past offenses. Every country has introduced, by one means or another, a system of preventive or administrative detention for persons who are thought to be dangerous but who might not be convictable under the conventional criminal law."

The best argument against preventive detention of suspected international terrorists is history's warning that the system will be abused, could expand inexorably—especially in the panic that might follow future attacks—and has such terrifying potential for infecting the entire criminal justice system and undermining our Bill of Rights that we should never start down that road. What is terrorist intent, and how may it be proved? Through a suspect's advocacy of a terrorist group's cause? Association with its members or sympathizers? If preventive detention is okay for people suspected of (but not charged with) terrorist intent, what about people suspected of homicidal intent, or violent proclivities, or dealing drugs?

These are serious concerns. But the dangers of punishing dissident speech, guilt by association, and overuse of preventive detention could be controlled by careful legislation. This would not be the first exception to the general rule against preventive detention. The others have worked fairly well. They include pretrial detention without bail of criminal defendants found to be dangerous, civil commitment of people found dangerous by reason of mental illness, and medical quarantines, a practice that may once again be necessary in the event of bioterrorism. All in all, the danger that a preventive detention regime for suspected terrorists would take us too far down the slippery slope toward police statism is simply not as bad as the danger of letting would-be mass murderers roam the country.

In any event, we already have a preventive detention regime for suspected international terrorists—three regimes, in fact, all created and controlled by the Bush administration without congressional input. First, two U.S. citizens—Jose Padilla, the suspected would-be dirty bomber arrested in Chicago, and Yaser Esam Hamdi, a Louisiana-born Saudi Arabian captured in Afghanistan and taken first to Guantanamo—have been in military brigs in this country for many months without being charged with any crime or allowed to see any lawyer or any judge. The administration claims that it never has to prove anything to anyone. It says that even U.S. citizens arrested in this country—who may have far stronger grounds than battlefield detainees for denying that they are enemy combatants—are entitled to no due process whatever once the government puts that label on them. This argument is virtually unprecedented, wrong as a matter of law, and indefensible as a matter of policy.

Second, Attorney General John Ashcroft rounded up more than 1,100 mostly Muslim noncitizens in the fall of 2001, which involved preventive detention in many cases although they were charged with immigration violations or crimes (mostly minor) or held under the material witness statute. This when-in-doubt-detain approach effectively reversed the presumption of innocence in the hope of disrupting any planned followup attacks. We may never know whether it succeeded in this vital objective. But the legal and moral bases for holding hundreds of apparently harmless detainees, sometimes without access to legal counsel, in conditions of unprecedented secrecy, seemed less and less plausible as weeks and months went by. Worse, the administration treated many (if not most) of the detainees shabbily and some abusively. (By mid-2002, the vast majority had been deported or released.)

Third, the Pentagon has incarcerated hundreds of Arab and other prisoners captured in Afghanistan at Guantanamo, apparently to avoid the jurisdiction of all courts—and has refused to create a fair, credible process for determining which are in fact enemy combatants and which of those are "unlawful."

These three regimes have been implemented with little regard for the law, for the rights of the many (mostly former) detainees who are probably innocent, or for international opinion. It is time for Congress to step in—to authorize a regime of temporary preventive detention for suspected international terrorists, while circumscribing that regime and specifying strong safeguards against abuse.

## CIVIL LIBERTIES FOR A NEW ERA

It is senseless to adhere to overly broad restrictions imposed by decades-old civil-liberties rules when confronting the threat of unprecedented carnage at the hands of modern terrorists. In the words of Harvard Law School's Laurence H. Tribe, "The old adage that it is better to free 100 guilty men than to imprison one innocent describes a calculus that our Constitution—which is no suicide pact—does not impose on government when the 100 who are freed belong to terrorist cells that slaughter innocent civilians, and may well have access to chemical, biological, or nuclear weapons." The question is not whether we should increase governmental power to meet such dangers. The question is how much.

## A Nasty Business

Bruce Hoffman

"Intelligence is capital," Colonel Yves Godard liked to say. And Godard undeniably knew what he was talking about. He had fought both as a guerrilla in the French Resistance during World War II and against guerrillas in Indochina, as the commander of a covert special-operations unit. As the chief of staff of the elite 10th Para Division, Godard was one of the architects of the French counterterrorist strategy that won the Battle of Algiers, in 1957. To him, information was the sine qua non for victory. It had to be zealously collected, meticulously analyzed, rapidly disseminated, and efficaciously acted on. Without it no anti-terrorist operation could succeed. As the United States prosecutes its global war against terrorism, Godard's dictum has acquired new relevance. Indeed, as is now constantly said, success in the struggle against Osama bin Laden and his minions will depend on good intelligence. But the experiences of other countries, fighting similar conflicts against similar enemies, suggest that Americans still do not appreciate the enormously difficult—and morally complex—problem that the imperative to gather "good intelligence" entails.

The challenge that security forces and militaries the world over have faced in countering terrorism is how to obtain information about an enigmatic enemy who fights unconventionally and operates in a highly amenable environment where he typically is indistinguishable from the civilian populace. The differences between police officers and soldiers in training and approach, coupled with the fact that most military forces are generally uncomfortable with, and inadequately prepared for, counterterrorist operations, strengthens this challenge. Military forces in such unfamiliar settings must learn to acquire intelligence by methods markedly different from those to which they are accustomed. The most "actionable," and therefore effective, information in this environment is discerned not from orders of battle, visual satellite transmissions of opposing force positions, or intercepted signals but from human intelligence gathered

mostly from the indigenous population. The police, specifically trained to interact with the public, typically have better access than the military to what are called human intelligence sources. Indeed, good police work depends on informers, undercover agents, and the apprehension and interrogation of terrorists and suspected terrorists, who provide the additional information critical to destroying terrorist organizations. Many today who argue reflexively and sanctimoniously that the United States should not "over-react" by over-militarizing the "war" against terrorism assert that such a conflict should be largely a police, not a military, endeavor. Although true, this line of argument usually overlooks the uncomfortable fact that, historically, "good" police work against terrorists has of necessity involved nasty and brutish means. Rarely have the importance of intelligence and the unpleasant ways in which it must often be obtained been better or more clearly elucidated than in the 1966 movie *The Battle of Algiers*. In an early scene in the film the main protagonist, the French paratroop commander, Lieutenant Colonel Mathieu (who is actually a composite of Yves Godard and two other senior French army officers who fought in the Battle of Algiers), explains to his men that the "military aspect is secondary." He says, "More immediate is the police work involved. I know you don't like hearing that, but it indicates exactly the kind of job we have to do."

I have long told soldiers, spies, and students to watch *The Battle of Algiers* if they want to understand how to fight terrorism. Indeed, the movie was required viewing for the graduate course I taught for five years on terrorism and the liberal state, which considered the difficulties democracies face in countering terrorism. The seminar at which the movie was shown regularly provoked the most intense and passionate discussions of the semester. To anyone who has seen *The Battle of Algiers,* this is not surprising. The late Pauline Kael, doyenne of American film critics, seemed still enraptured seven years after its original release when she described *The Battle of Algiers* in a 900-word review as "an epic in the form of a 'created documentary'"; "the one great revolutionary 'sell' of modern times"; and the "most impassioned, most astute call to revolution ever." The best reviews, however, have come from terrorists—members of the IRA; the Tamil Tigers, in Sri Lanka; and 1960s African-American revolutionaries—who have assiduously studied it. At a time when the U.S. Army has enlisted Hollywood screenwriters to help plot scenarios of future terrorist attacks, learning about the difficulties of fighting terrorism from a movie that terrorists themselves have studied doesn't seem farfetched.

In fact, the film represents the apotheosis of *cinéma vérité.* That it has a verisimilitude unique among onscreen portrayals of terrorism is a tribute to its director, *Gillo Pontecorvo,* and its cast—many of whose members reprised the real-life roles they had played actually fighting for the liberation of their country, a decade before. Pontecorvo, too, had personal experience with the kinds of situations he filmed: during World War II he had commanded a partisan brigade in Milan. Indeed, the Italian filmmaker was so concerned about not giving audiences a false impression of authenticity that he inserted a clarification in the movie's opening frames: "This dramatic re-enactment of The Battle of Algiers contains NOT ONE FOOT of Newsreel or Documentary Film." The movie accordingly possesses an uncommon gravitas that immediately draws viewers into the story. Like many of the best films, it is about a search—in this case for the intelligence on which French paratroops deployed in Algiers depended to defeat and destroy the terrorists of the National Liberation Front (FLN). "To know them means we can eliminate them," Mathieu explains to his men in the scene referred to above. "For this we need information. The method: interrogation." In Mathieu's universe there is no question of ends not justifying means: the Paras need intelligence, and they will obtain it however they can. "To succumb to humane considerations," he concludes, "only leads to hopeless chaos."

The events depicted on celluloid closely parallel those of history. In 1957 the city of Algiers was the center of a life-and-death struggle between the FLN and the French authorities. On one side were the terrorists, embodied both on screen and in real life in Ali La Pointe, a petty thief turned terrorist cell leader; on the other stood the army, specifically the elite 10th Para Division, under General Jacques Massu, another commander on whom the Mathieu composite was based. Veterans of the water to preserve France's control of Indochina, Massu and his senior officers—Godard included—prided themselves on having acquired a thorough understanding of terrorism and revolutionary warfare, and how to counter both. Victory, they were convinced, would depend on the acquisition of intelligence. Their method was to build a meticulously detailed picture of the FLN's apparatus in Algiers which would help the French home in on the terrorist campaign's masterminds—Ali La Pointe and his bin Laden, Saadi Yacef (who played himself in the film). This approach, which is explicated in one of the film's most riveting scenes, resulted in what the Francophile British historian Alistair Horne, in his masterpiece on the conflict, *A Savage War of Peace,* called a "complex *organigramme* [that] began to take shape on a large blackboard, a kind of skeleton pyramid in which, as each fresh piece of information came from the interrogation centres, another [terrorist] name (and not always necessarily the right name) would be entered." That this system proved tactically effective there is no doubt. The problem was that it thoroughly depended on, and therefore actively encouraged, widespread human-rights abuses, including torture.

Massu and his men—like their celluloid counterparts—were not particularly concerned about this. They justified their means of obtaining intelligence with utilitarian, cost-benefit arguments. Extraordinary measures were legitimized by extraordinary circumstances. The exculpatory philosophy embraced by the French Paras is best summed up by Massu's uncompromising belief that "the innocent [that is, the next victims of terrorist attacks] deserve more protection than the guilty." The approach, however, at least strategically, was counterproductive. Its sheer brutality alienated the native Algerian Muslim community. Hitherto mostly passive or apathetic, that community was now driven into the arms of the FLN, swelling the organization's ranks and increasing its popular support. Public opinion in France was similarly outraged, weakening support for the continuing struggle and creating profound fissures in French civil-military relations. The army's achievement in the city was therefore bought at the cost of eventual political defeat. Five years after victory in Algiers the French withdrew from Algeria and granted the country its independence. But Massu remained forever unrepentant: he insisted that the ends justified the means used to destroy the FLN's urban insurrection. The battle was won, lives were saved, and the indiscriminate bombing campaign that had terrorized the city was ended. To Massu, that was all that mattered. To his mind, respect for the rule of law and the niceties of legal procedure were irrelevant given the crisis situation enveloping Algeria in 1957. As anachronistic as France's attempt to hold on to this last vestige of its colonial past may now appear, its jettisoning of such long-standing and cherished notions as habeas corpus and due process, enshrined in the ethos of the liberal state, underscores how the intelligence requirements of counterterrorism can suddenly take precedence over democratic ideals.

Although it is tempting to dismiss the French army's resort to torture in Algeria as the desperate excess of a moribund colonial power, the fundamental message that only information can effectively counter terrorism is timeless. Equally disturbing and instructive, however, are the lengths to which security and military forces need often resort to get that information. I learned this some years ago, on a research trip to Sri Lanka. The setting—a swank oceanfront hotel in Colombo, a refreshingly cool breeze coming off the ocean, a magnificent sunset on the horizon—could not have been further removed from the carnage and destruction that have afflicted that island country for the past eighteen years and have claimed the lives of more than 60,000 people. Arrayed against the democratically elected Sri Lankan government and its armed forces is perhaps the most ruthlessly efficient terrorist organization-cum-insurgent force in the world today: the *Liberation Tigers of Tamil Eelam,* known also by the acronym LTTE or simply as the Tamil Tigers. The Tigers are unique in the annals of terrorism and arguably eclipse even bin Laden's al Qaeda in professionalism, capability, and determination. They are believed to be the first nonstate group in history to stage a chemical-weapons attack when they deployed poison gas in a 1990 assault on a Sri Lankan military base—some five years before the nerve-gas attack on the Tokyo subway by the apocalyptic Japanese religious cult Aum Shinrikyo. Of greater relevance, perhaps, is the fact that at least a decade before the seaborne attack on the U.S.S. *Cole,* in Aden harbor, the LTTE's special suicide maritime unit, the Sea Tigers, had perfected the same tactics against the Sri Lankan navy. Moreover, the Tamil Tigers are believed to have developed their own embryonic air capability—designed to carry out attacks similar to those of September 11 (though with much smaller, noncommercial aircraft). The most feared Tiger unit, however, is the Black Tigers—the suicide cadre composed of the group's best-trained, most battle-hardened, and most zealous fighters. A partial list of their operations includes the assassination of the former Indian Prime Minister Rajiv Gandhi at a campaign stop in the Indian state of Tamil Nadu, in 1991; the assassination of Sri Lankan President Ranasinghe Premadasa, in 1993; the assassination of the presidential candidate Gamini Dissanayake, which also claimed the lives of fifty-four bystanders and injured about one hundred more, in 1994; the suicide truck bombing of the Central Bank of Sri Lanka, in 1996, which killed eighty-six people and wounded 1,400 others; and the attempt on the life of the current President of Sri Lanka, Chandrika Kumaratunga, in December of 1999. The powerful and much venerated leader of the LTTE is *Velupillai Prabhakaran,* who, like bin Laden, exercises a charismatic influence over his fighters. *The Battle of Algiers* is said to be one of Prabhakaran's favorite films.

I sat in that swank hotel drinking tea with a much decorated, battle-hardened Sri Lankan army officer charged with fighting the LTTE and protecting the lives of Colombo's citizens. I cannot use his real name, so I will call him Thomas. However, I had been told before our meeting, by the mutual friend—a former Sri Lankan intelligence officer who had also long fought the LTTE—who introduced us (and was present at our meeting), that Thomas had another name, one better known to his friends and enemies alike: Terminator. My friend explained how Thomas had acquired his sobriquet; it actually owed less to Arnold Schwarzenegger than to the merciless way in which he discharged his duties as an intelligence officer. This became clear to me during our conversation. "By going through the process of laws," Thomas patiently explained, as a parent or a teacher might speak to a bright yet uncomprehending child, "you cannot fight terrorism." Terrorism, he believed, could be fought only by thoroughly "terrorizing" the terrorists—that is, inflicting on them the same pain that they inflict on the innocent. Thomas had little confidence that I understood what he was saying. I was an academic, he said, with no actual experience of the life-and-death choices and the immense responsibility borne by those charged with protecting society from attack. Accordingly, he would give me an example of the split-second decisions he was called on to make. At the time, Colombo was on "code red" emergency status, because of intelligence that the LTTE was planning to embark on a campaign of bombing public gathering places and other civilian targets. Thomas's unit had apprehended three terrorists who, it suspected, had recently planted somewhere in the city a bomb that was then ticking away, the minutes counting down to catastrophe. The three men were brought before Thomas. He asked them where the bomb was. The terrorists—highly dedicated and steeled to resist interrogation—remained silent. Thomas asked the question again, advising them that if they did not tell him what he wanted to know, he would kill them. They were unmoved. So Thomas took his pistol from his gun belt, pointed it at the forehead of one of them, and shot him dead. The other two, he said, talked immediately; the bomb, which had been placed in a crowded railway station and set to explode during the evening rush hour, was found and defused, and countless lives were saved. On other occasions, Thomas said, similarly recalcitrant terrorists were brought

before him. It was not surprising, he said, that they initially refused to talk; they were schooled to withstand harsh questioning and coercive pressure. No matter: a few drops of gasoline flicked into a plastic bag that is then placed over a terrorist's head and cinched tight around his neck with a web belt very quickly prompts a full explanation of the details of any planned attack.

I was looking pale and feeling a bit shaken as waiters in starched white jackets smartly cleared the china teapot and cups from the table, and Thomas rose to bid us good-bye and return to his work. He hadn't exulted in his explanations or revealed any joy or even a hint of pleasure in what he had to do. He had spoken throughout in a measured, somber, even reverential tone. He did not appear to be a sadist, or even manifestly homicidal. (And not a year has passed since our meeting when Thomas has failed to send me an unusually kind Christmas card.) In his view, as in Massu's, the innocent had more rights than the guilty. He, too, believed that extraordinary circumstances required extraordinary measures. Thomas didn't think I understood—or, more to the point, thought I never could understand. I am not fighting on the front lines of this battle; I don't have the responsibility for protecting society that he does. He was right: I couldn't possibly understand. But since September 11, and especially every morning after I read the *"Portraits of Grief" page* in the *New York Times,* I am constantly reminded of Thomas—of the difficulties of fighting terrorism and of the challenges of protecting not only the innocent but an entire society and way of life. I am never bidden to condone, much less advocate, torture. But as I look at the snapshots and the lives of the victims recounted each day, and think how it will take almost a year to profile the approximately 5,000 people who perished on September 11, I recall the ruthless enemy that America faces, and I wonder about the lengths to which we may yet have to go to vanquish him.

The moral question of lengths and the broader issue of ends versus means are, of course, neither new nor unique to rearguard colonial conflicts of the 1950s or to the unrelenting carnage that has more recently been inflicted on a beautiful tropical island in the

Indian Ocean. They are arguably no different from the stark choices that eventually confront any society threatened by an enveloping violence unlike anything it has seen before. For a brief period in the early and middle 1970s Britain, for example, had something of this experience—which may be why, among other reasons, Prime Minister Tony Blair and his country today stand as America's staunchest ally. The sectarian terrorist violence in Northern Ireland was at its height, and had for the first time spilled into England in a particularly vicious and indiscriminate way. The views of a British army intelligence officer at the time, quoted by the journalist Desmond Hamill in his book *Pig in the Middle* (1985), reflect those of Thomas and Massu.

> Naturally one worries—after all, one is inflicting pain and discomfort and indignity on other human beings . . . [but] society has got to find a way of protecting itself . . . and it can only do so if it has good information. If you have a close-knit society which doesn't give information then you've got to find ways of getting it. Now the softies of the world complain—but there is an awful lot of double talk about it. If there is to be discomfort and horror inflicted on a few, is this not preferred

to the danger and horror being inflicted on perhaps a million people?

It is a question that even now, after September 11, many Americas would answer in the negative. But under extreme conditions and in desperate circumstances that, too, could dramatically change—much as everything else has so profoundly changed for us all since that morning. I recently discussed precisely this issue over the telephone with the same Sri Lankan friend who introduced me to Thomas years ago. I have never quite shaken my disquiet over my encounter with Thomas and over the issues he raised—issues that have now acquired an unsettling relevance. My friend sought to lend some perspective from his country's long experience in fighting terrorism. "There are not good people and bad people," he told me, "only good circumstances and bad circumstances. Sometimes in bad circumstances good people have to do bad things. I have done bad things, but these were in bad circumstances. I have no doubt that this was the right thing to do." In the quest for timely, "actionable" intelligence will the United States, too, have to do bad things—by resorting to measures that we would never have contemplated in a less exigent situation?

## REVIEW QUESTIONS

- How have norms and rules for security been affected by the new security environment and the modern war on terrorism?
- How did the September 11, 2001 attacks affect fundamental notions of law and morality? Is this acceptable when societies are confronted with severe terrorist threats?
- How can a society beset by terrorism preserve the liberty of its citizens while at the same time assure their security?
- Should civil libertarians temper their criticism of enhanced security measures and laws?
- Are some of the more violent and brutal counterterrorist methods necessary under certain circumstances?

The following books and articles are suggested for further information about issues and challenges for counterterrorism:

## Books

Heymann, Philip B. *Terrorism and America: A Commonsense Strategy for a Democratic Society.* Cambridge, MA: The MIT Press, 1998.

Pillar, Paul R., and Michael H. Armacost. *Terrorism and U.S. Foreign Policy.* Washington, D.C.: Brookings Institution, 2001.

Rubin, Barry and Judith Colp Rubin, eds. *Anti-American Terrorism and the Middle East: A Documentary Reader.* New York: Oxford University Press, 2002.

## Articles

Dallmayr, Fred. "Lessons of September 11." *Theory, Culture, & Society.* 19:4 (2002).

Note: "Responding to Terrorism: Crime, Punishment, and War." *Harvard Law Review.* 115:4 (February 2002).

Roth, Kenneth. "Misplaced Priorities: Human Rights and the Campaign Against Terrorism." *Harvard International Review.* (Fall 2002).

# 9

---

# Counterterrorist Options
# in the New Era

E ffective counterterrorism requires the selection of correct responses to unique situations. No single counterterrorist measure can be applied in the same manner to every terrorist environment. This is logically and pragmatically impossible. Fortunately, policymakers have the opportunity to select counterterrorist measures from among a wide range of options. These options may be categorized in many ways, but a good approach might include the following categories: The use of force; repressive operations other than war; conciliatory options; and legalistic responses. When considering which counterterrorist method is advisable, it is instructive for policy makers to bear in mind that although hardline options send a powerful message (and can certainly be effective), other measures may be more suitable in some circumstances.

The articles in this chapter discuss perspectives on counterterrorist options. In "Terrorism and the Use of Force," Geir Ulfstein provides an analysis of the international legal implications of the use of force in the U.S.-led war on terrorism. Focusing on a discussion of the war against the Taliban, he investigates the role of the United Nations in sanctioning military intervention vis-à-vis the United States' right of self defense under international law. The discussion raises critical implications for further military actions in the aftermath of the invasion and occupation of Iraq by the U.S. and its coalition allies. In "A New Strategy for the New Terrorism," Paul Bremer explains the fundamental shift toward the new era of terrorism, its features, and how counterterrorist doctrine must adapt. The essay argues that several objectives must be pursued to reduce the threat from the New Terrorism, including the denial of safe havens, vigorous responses, and ending state sponsored terrorism. John Deutch and Jeffrey Smith discuss the adaptation of intelligence to the new era of terrorism in "Smarter Intelligence." The authors present a framework for how intelligence can be used as an effective counterterrorist measure.

## Terrorism and the Use of Force

Geir Ulfstein
*Department of Public and International Law, University of Oslo, Norway*

Terrorism is new neither as a political phenomenon nor as a problem within international law. Physical force has been used for political motives throughout history, while the concept of terrorism can be traced back at least to the period of the French Revolution and Robespierre. In the last century, the assassinations of a number of statesmen during the inter-war period led to negotiations within the League of Nations. A convention on the prevention and prosecution of terrorism was adopted in 1937, though this never came into force.[1]

Today, we have 12 important global conventions for the suppression of terrorism, as well as a number of regional terrorist conventions. Common to these is that acts of terrorism are treated as criminal offences, to be dealt with by national courts of law. The conventions define the offences that they cover and impose on states a duty to investigate such offences and either bring the perpetrators to justice or extradite suspects. However, the prevention of terrorism has not been unproblematic in international law. There has been disagreement both about what ought to be deemed to be terrorism and about whether states may respond with force if they are subjected to a terrorist attack originating from inside the borders of another state.

The events of 11 September 2001 represent a new element within terrorism, in terms of both the objects of the terrorist attacks and the extent of the damage caused. In addition, these attacks were presumed to have come from terrorists with bases in another country, and the attacks were made upon the world's only superpower, one with the capacity and will to strike back.

In this article, I shall first discuss whether the UN Security Council has approved the USA's use of military force against other states in the wake of these attacks and whether the USA might be able to base its use of force on the right of self-defence. In the concluding section, emphasis is given to the need for preservation of the general prohibition against the use of force in international law.[2]

## HAS THE SECURITY COUNCIL APPROVED THE USA'S USE OF FORCE?

Under Chapter VII of the United Nations Charter, the UN Security Council may adopt binding measures against states or authorize the use of military force where it finds that international peace and security are threatened. In connection with acts of terrorism, the Security Council has previously implemented sanctions against Libya, Sudan and Afghanistan.[3] However, the council has not previously approved the use of military force in the fight against international terrorism.

UN Security Council Resolution 1368 (2001) strongly condemned the terrorist attacks on the USA and declared that such acts were a threat to international peace and security. But does Resolution 1368 recognize the USA's right to exercise force against Afghanistan and other states that may be deemed to have contributed to terrorism? Here, reference may be made to the fact that the resolution acknowledges the right of self-defence: 'Recognizing the inherent right of individual and collective self-defence in accordance with the Charter . . . '. However, it should be noted that the right of self-defence follows from general international law and from Article 51 of the UN Charter. Consequently it does not require approval by the Security Council. The Security Council has been given no role in the exercise of the right of self-defence, other than that this right only applies under Article 51 until the council has 'taken measures necessary to maintain international peace and security.'

Furthermore, the resolution makes no reference to Chapter VII of the UN Charter, and it contains no explicit approval of the use of force. In addition, the formulation concerning self-defence is part of the preamble to the resolution, not its operative part. This is in contrast, for example, to UN Security Council Resolution 678, adopted in 1990 after Iraq's invasion of

Kuwait, which in the operative part of the resolution 'authorises' all member-states cooperating with Kuwait to use 'all necessary means' to force Iraq to implement the council's resolutions and restore international peace and security in the region.

The wording of Resolution 1368 has been taken word for word from Article 51 of the UN Charter, and the resolution makes particular reference to the right of self-defence that exists under the terms of the Charter. This can only mean that the Security Council did not take a position on whether the Charter's conditions for the use of force in self-defence had been satisfied in the case then under consideration, in contrast to UN Security Council Resolution 661 (1990), which also made reference to the right of self-defence but at the same time linked this right to 'the armed attack by Iraq against Kuwait.'

It is also relevant that Resolution 1368 was passed on the day following the terrorist attacks, at a time when it was not possible to know with certainty who was behind the attacks or whether they had been planned from abroad. It has the presumption against it that the council should at this time have given unlimited authority for the USA to use force against any state that had connections with terrorism in general or this attack in particular. Nor were either the right of self-defence or the design of the resolution touched upon in statements made in the Security Council in connection with the resolution's adoption, though the USA as the final speaker declared that no distinction would be made between terrorists and those who 'harbor them' in terms of responsibility (United Nations, 2001a). Finally, it may be argued that the use of force is a far-reaching intrusion into state sovereignty and thus ought to require clear legal authority.

Given these arguments, it must be clear that, legally speaking, Resolution 1368 does not in itself approve the use of force on the part of the USA.[4] It may be claimed, though, that the resolution represents political acceptance of the idea that the use of force in exercise of the right of self-defence may be appropriate in cases of terrorism. However, it is difficult to see that the Security Council could have been expressed its opinion on the right of self-defence in a more noncommittal way than through a simple reference to Article 51 of the UN Charter.

UN Security Council Resolution 1373 (2001) deals with the financing of terrorism and places on member-states a duty to prevent and criminalize such financing. Since this resolution also refers in its preamble to the right of self-defence, it may be asked whether the Security Council therein approved the USA's right to use force in exercise of the right of self-defence. The relevant formulation is: '*Reaffirming* the inherent right of individual or collective self-defence as recognized by the Charter of the United Nations as reiterated in resolution 1368 (2001). . . '.

In contrast to the earlier Resolution 1368, this resolution was adopted under Chapter VII, though this may be explained by the fact that the resolution places demands on the member-states that are binding in international law, inter alia with regard to the prevention of the financing of terrorism. Furthermore, in this resolution too the formulation concerning self-defence is found in the preamble, not in the resolution's operative part. The wording of Resolution 1373 is just as general as that of Resolution 1368 and provides no explicit acknowledgement of a right on the part of the USA to use force against a particular state or states in exercise of the right of self-defence. And since no debate took place in the Security Council in connection with the adoption of Resolution 1373, there is no guidance to be found there with regard to how the resolution is to be interpreted (United Nations, 2001b).

It could be claimed that, 17 days after the attacks on the USA, it was clearer who was behind them and that the clues pointed in the direction of Osama bin Laden and Afghanistan. This might suggest that the council approved the right to use force in self-defence against Afghanistan. Here again, however, it is pertinent to point out that it is not part of the Security Council's function to approve the right of self-defence and that, if any such approval were to be given, it ought at any rate to be stated clearly. In any case, legally speaking, to claim such approval would be to read too much into a resolution that, in terms of its wording, exclusively refers to the right of self-defence as it is formulated in Article 51 of the UN Charter (Kirgis, 2001).[5] The use of such general wording also limits the significance of the resolution as a political ground for legitimizing the use of force by the USA against states other than Afghanistan.

In letters of 7 October 2001, the USA and the UK informed the Security Council, in accordance with Article 51, that actions had been implemented against Afghanistan in self-defence.[6] In the letter from the USA, however, it was stated that the issue of self-defence might also be relevant with regard to organizations other than Al-Qaeda and states other than Afghanistan. In a press statement from the president of the Security Council, it was announced that the council met at the request of the USA and the UK to be informed of measures that had been taken. The Security Council took note of the letters from the two countries, and its members 'were appreciative of the presentation' (United Nations, 2001d). It has since been claimed that this should be taken as agreement by the council that the two states were acting in self-defence (Randelzhofer, 2002). However, the president did not explicitly state that the Security Council endorsed the actions taken. Furthermore, a press statement by the president is not equivalent to a decision by the council, nor even equivalent to a formal presidential statement adopted by consensus and read out at a formal meeting of the council. Accordingly, this press statement should not be seen as a formal recognition by the Security Council of the lawfulness of the military actions in Afghanistan.

In UN Security Council Resolution 1377 (2001), the council adopted at the ministerial level a declaration in which reference was made to previously adopted resolutions and the need for implementing measures against terrorism, though without any mention of the use of force. In UN Security Council Resolution 1378 (2001) we also find a formulation that may be relevant in relation to the right of self-defence: '*Supporting* international efforts to root out terrorism, in keeping with the Charter of the United Nations, and *reaffirming* also its resolutions 1368 (2001) of 12 September 2001 and 1373 (2001) of 28 September 2001 . . .'. However, Resolution 1378 was not adopted under Chapter VII, and once again the relevant formulation is not actually part of the resolution's operative part. Also, what particularly distinguishes this formulation from the previous

ones is that here no actual reference is made to the right of self-defence. Instead, the resolution states that the Security Council supports 'international efforts to root out terrorism.'

It could be argued that since this resolution was adopted after the USA had commenced its military operations against Afghanistan, that use of force must be considered as a part of the international efforts referred to in the resolution. Also, it could be argued that 'to root out' is a very strong term—stronger than, for example, 'to combat'—and that referring to the previous resolutions implies that Resolution 1378 builds on and goes further than them. On the other hand, supporting international efforts is not the same as authorizing them. Nor does the Security Council specifically mention the use of force, either in Afghanistan or elsewhere. Instead, it expresses itself in general terms in relation to 'international efforts' in the plural, with no definite article. And the term 'to root out terrorism' need not be taken to imply the use of force, since it is conceivable that this goal could be achieved without resort to force. Thus, both because this resolution was not adopted under Chapter VII and because authorization of the use of force ought to have a reasonably clear legal basis, Resolution 1378 should not be considered as providing such authorization. In addition, the reference to the UN Charter indicates that the Security Council took no standpoint on whether the conditions for the exercise of the right to use force in self-defence as they are formulated in Article 51 were satisfied.

Politically speaking, however, Resolution 1378 does provide clearer support for the USA's use of force. Yet, here as well it is significant that the resolution does not state precisely which international efforts are to be supported. Nor can the resolution be said to provide support for measures that are of a different nature than those that were in progress against Afghanistan at the time the resolution was adopted: the resolution does not, for example, provide support for the use of force against states other than Afghanistan, be they Iraq or Somalia.

UN Security Council Resolution 1390 (2002) was adopted under Chapter VII, and the wording of its preamble corresponds with that of Resolution 1378 in terms of supporting 'international efforts to root out terrorism.' This resolution, therefore, provides nothing new for an evaluation of whether the Security Council has expressed support for the use of force in exercise of the right of self-defence in efforts directed against terrorism.

In view of the above, it may be concluded that, legally speaking, the Security Council has not *approved* the USA's use of force in exercise of the right of self-defence—neither against Afghanistan nor against other states—in any of its resolutions, (Greenwood, 2002: 309; Charney, 2001: 835; Franck, 2001: 840; Delbrück, 2001: 13–14; Mégret, 2002: 375). Nor has the council authoritatively taken a standpoint on whether the conditions for the exercise of the right of self-defence in accordance with Article 51 of the UN Charter have been satisfied. However, the resolutions may have legal significance as expressions of the Security Council's view that the right of self-defence has not been *impaired* through the council's having taken 'measures necessary to maintain international peace and security' in pursuance of Article 51. Furthermore, the resolutions' coupling of terrorism and self-defence may be a relevant interpretation factor in an evaluation of the right of states to use force on the basis of terrorist acts (see below).

The USA, however, has not asked for legal approval of its military actions. It has preferred to act without formal international recognition. This is consistent with increasing unilateralism on its part, seen in its rejection of the Kyoto Protocol on climate change, the International Criminal Court and other multilateral agreements. All the same, the political support from other states represented by the Security Council resolutions with regard to military measures taken against Afghanistan is welcomed by the USA. But this support has not been given in an explicit form: the Security Council has chosen to make general references to the right of self-defence and measures against terrorism. At the same time, no countries—not even Afghanistan—are specifically mentioned, and explicit reference is made to the provisions of the United Nations Charter concerning the use of force. These resolutions therefore cannot be seen as support for absolutely any military measure against Afghanistan. Nor do they provide political support for the implementation of military measures against states other than Afghanistan.

## THE RIGHT OF SELF-DEFENCE

International law lays down a prohibition against the use of force between states. This prohibition is expressed in Article 2(4) of the UN Charter. Above, it was concluded that the Security Council has not approved the use of force in response to the attacks of 11 September 2001 under Chapter VII of the Charter. Therefore, if the use of force in such a case is to be lawful, this must be based on the right of self-defence under Article 51 of that charter. However, disagreement has been voiced about whether terrorist attacks give rise to the right of self-defence.[7]

Article 51 states that the right of self-defence may be exercised if a state has suffered an armed attack. Here, however, we must consider whether the attacks of 11 September were directed against the USA as a state. Damage to buildings, hijacking of aircraft and killings perpetrated by private individuals are normally considered criminal acts, not armed attacks against a state. In terms of the goals behind the attacks - namely, to protest against US policy - it is perhaps true that the attacks on Washington and New York were directed against the USA as a state. However, most terrorist activities have similar aims. In this instance, though, there is a further reason to deem the attacks as directed against the USA as a state: one of the targets of the attacks was the Pentagon, that is to say the USA's defence ministry. Also, the attack on the World Trade Center may in a certain sense also be seen as directed against the USA as a state on account of the symbolic significance of those buildings for the country's economic power.

However, not every instance of the use of force against a state is deemed to be an armed attack under Article 51. There is a requirement that the level of force involved be of a certain magnitude. In the *Nicaragua* case—where the International Court of Justice (ICJ) examined the question of whether the USA was responsible for acts performed by the US-financed contras in Nicaragua—one of the court's rulings was that border incidents could not be deemed to constitute an armed attack upon the state.[8] On the other hand, several thousand people were killed in the case of the terrorist acts of 11 September 2001, and the attacks were of such a nature that the USA implemented comprehensive defense measures in their wake. This would suggest that the actions ought on account of their nature and extent to be deemed an armed attack under Article 51 (Delbrück, 2001:16; Mégret, 2002: 372).

Article 51 does not explicitly say anything about from where an armed attack must have come if it is to give rise to the right of self-defence. The actions against the USA have been seen as an example of a new kind of threat (asymmetric threat), in which attacks are not necessarily carried out by states but by non-state groups. It may be asked whether it shall be deemed necessary that another state can be connected to such an action in order to give rise to the right of self-defence. Because acting in self-defence entails the right to use force against another state, notwithstanding the general prohibition in Article 2(4) of the UN Charter, such a connection should be required (Mégret, 2002: 379).[9]

A state is not usually considered responsible for acts performed by individuals who are not in the service of that state. Nevertheless, there may be instances in which a state ought to be identified with actions carried out by certain groups, even when the latter are not formally affiliated to the state concerned. The question here is what type and level of control over such individuals or groups must a state have in order for them to be deemed to represent that state, with the result that the state is held responsible for their actions under international law.

Returning to the *Nicaragua* case, here the ICJ formulated the issue of responsibility as a question of whether the USA had 'effective control' of what the contras were doing in Nicaragua.[10] However, the requirement of effective control was criticized by the Appeals Chamber of the International Criminal Tribunal for former Yugoslavia (ICTY) in the *Tadic* case, where the questions were whether Serbia was responsible for acts committed by Serbs in Bosnia and, if so, whether events in Bosnia constituted an international conflict. Here, the tribunal took the view that the ICJ's requirement for effective control was in conformity neither with provisions relating to state responsibility nor with court and state practice.[11] The tribunal came to the conclusion that effective control was not required: 'overall control' was sufficient.[12]

In Article 8 of its draft provisions relating to state responsibility (3 August 2001), the UN International Law Commission (ILC) proposed that the condition for state responsibility for the acts of groups of persons is that these groups are acting under the 'instruction,' 'direction' or 'control' of the state in carrying out the acts concerned.[13] The commission took its point of departure in the requirement for control established by the ICJ's ruling in the *Nicaragua* case. It disagreed with the ICTY's criticism of this judgement on the grounds that the questions of law and fact were different in that case, in that the ICTY's role is to apply humanitarian law, not to take a view on the question of state responsibility (International Law Commission, 2001: 196–197).

Another of the ILC's draft provisions that may allow for responsibility on the part of groups of persons is Article 4(2), which provides that bodies that de facto act on behalf of a state should also be considered as organs of that state, and that the state concerned should thereby be held responsible for the actions of such organs (International Law Commission, 2001: 90).

That noted, the exact relationship between Al-Qaeda and the Afghan authorities is somewhat unclear. There is nothing to suggest that the organization was formally a part of the Afghan state apparatus. On the other hand, it is clear not only that Afghan authorities tolerated Al-Qaeda's activities on Afghan territory, but also that there were close ties between the authorities and the organization. However, it is more difficult to argue that Afghanistan 'directed or controlled the specific operation and the conduct complained of was an integral part of that operation' in accordance with the commentary to the ILC's Article 8, or that Al-Qaeda ought to be considered as a de facto organ of the Afghan state pursuant to Article 4(2). Nor are there grounds for asserting that the Afghan authorities recognized and accepted Al-Qaeda's terrorist actions as their own pursuant to the commission's draft Article 11. There is even less reason to consider Al-Qaeda or individuals connected with that organization as part of the state apparatus of states other than Afghanistan. This suggests that neither Afghanistan nor any other states ought to be deemed responsible for the attacks on the USA on the basis of the argument that the terrorists, under the terms of international law, were acting on behalf of such states.

Nevertheless, states may be held responsible for failing to prevent certain actions carried out by individuals, including terrorist acts. UN General Assembly Resolution 2625 (XXV) (1970) - the 'Friendly Relations' resolution—lays down that member-states shall not tolerate the use of their territory for terrorist acts.[14] UN General Assembly Resolution 49/60 (1994), on 'Measures to Eliminate International Terrorism,' also contains a prohibition against allowing the preparation of terrorist acts that are to be carried out on the territory of other states.[15]

It is true that UN Security Council Resolution 1269 (1999) on international cooperation against terrorism was not adopted under Chapter VII and is therefore not binding. However, it refers to UN General Assembly Resolution 49/60 and 'calls upon' the member-states to implement appropriate measures, among these being to prevent the preparation of acts of terrorism within their territory. We also have the Security Council resolutions that were specially directed against Afghanistan:[16] two of these were adopted under Chapter VII[17] and specify that Afghanistan's territory should not be allowed to constitute a free area for terrorists.

Support for terrorism or allowing the use of a state's territory by terrorists must on this basis be deemed to be contrary to international law, and it may also be contrary to the UN Charter's prohibition against the use of force. (In the case of Afghanistan, such conduct would also be contrary to binding Security Council resolutions.) However, this does not necessarily entail that the breach of international law constituted by such support means that a state may be attacked by virtue of the right of self-defence that exists under Article 51 of the UN Charter. This distinction between a state's responsibility under international law for providing such support and the right of other states to use force against such a state is not often made clear in the literature on international law (Greenwood, 2002: 313; Franck, 2001: 841; Delbrück, 2001: 15).[18]

In the *Nicaragua* case, the ICJ stated that 'substantial involvement' in sending irregular forces into another country may be deemed an armed attack giving rise to the right of self-defence.[19] It must also be firmly kept in mind that failure to respect the prohibition against accepting the presence of terrorists on a state's own territory does not necessarily mean that the actions of such groups can be considered as an armed attack that might constitute grounds for the use of force in the form of self-defence. Even though in the case of Afghanistan there was close contact between the authorities and Al-Qaeda, there is little to suggest that the terrorists who attacked the United States were sent by the authorities, that they were acting on behalf of those authorities or that the authorities were substantially involved in sending them in the manner required in the Nicaragua judgement.[20]

But have other conditions been set for exercise of the right of self-defence since 11 September 2001?[21] It might be argued that the Security Council, through its linking of the attacks against the USA and the right of self-defence in Resolution 1368 and subsequent resolutions, has authoritatively stated that support for terrorists in the form of allowing the use of a state's own territory for planning and training for terrorist actions may give rise to the right of self-defence. It is true that the Security Council does not have a formal role in interpreting the UN Charter, but the council does have a special function in preserving peace and security in the world community. Reference may also be made to the fact that the USA's right to exercise the right of self-defence in the wake of the attacks of 11 September 2001 has been approved both by NATO and by a large number of other states in the world.[22] Finally, there are sound equitable grounds to support the view that a state ought in certain instances to be able to use force if another state does not have the will or ability to address acts of terror originating from its own territory.

But, even so, this cannot be taken to grant an open right for any state that wishes to exercise the right of self-defence against any other state that does not take sufficient steps to combat terrorism on its territory. Such a right would undermine the general prohibition against the use of force in international law. A right of humanitarian intervention, as in Kosovo, is open for abuse, but the danger of undermining the general prohibition is no less if states are permitted to respond to terrorist attacks with armed force. It has been claimed that approximately 60 countries support terrorists, and US officials have designated certain countries as 'rogue states.' [23] Worryingly, since the USA has opened up for the possibility of 'pre-emptive action,' the threshold for the use of force by the USA appears to be lower than the requirements of international law.[24]

In questions concerning the use of force, the legal point of departure must be the general prohibition against the use of force unless such use has been approved by the Security Council. This means that an argument of self-defence ought to be applicable only in extreme situations. And, even in response to the attacks of 11 September 2001, the USA and its allies cannot simply call on the right of self-defence to legitimize the use of force against states other than Afghanistan. It was Afghanistan that housed Al-Qaeda and it was Afghanistan alone that was made the object of the binding resolutions discussed above (Schrijver, 2001: 271, 286; see also Farer, 2002: 359).

The right of self-defence is subject to further limitations that follow from international customary law. In this connection, reference is usually made to the classic *Caroline* case from 1837, where the US secretary of state formulated the requirements of burden of proof, immediacy, necessity and proportionality.[25] Even though this case goes back to a time before there was any prohibition against the use of force in international law, these conditions are still considered to be legally valid (Dinstein, 2001: 183).

To begin with, it is the USA that must bear the burden of proof in terms of establishing that the factual basis for being able to exercise the right of self-defence is present (Charney, 2001: 836; Mégret, 2002: 380–381).[26] Furthermore, force may not be used for purposes of revenge or punishment, only self-defence. International law does not permit the use of force as a reprisal.

However, in the present instance, there is a great deal of evidence to support the view that the USA was involved in a conflict with those behind the actions of 11 September 2001, and that this conflict was not brought to an end with the attacks on the USA. Hence, the US actions may be regarded as defence against an ongoing attack.

The requirements of necessity and proportionality are supported in the *Nicaragua* judgment[27] and in the ICJ's advisory opinion on the legality of the threat or use of nuclear weapons (the *Nuclear Weapons* case).[28] The requirement of necessity means that force may only be used if no other means are available. The requirement of proportionality means that, even though the actions carried out against the USA were heinous, there are limits to the type and degree of military action that can be justified by this: the USA does not have a free hand to respond however it sees fit, regardless of civilian casualties and irrespective of damage to the property of civilians. In the *Nicaragua* case, the court was of the opinion that assistance from Nicaragua to the revolutionary movement in El Salvador did not provide grounds for the USA's mining of Nicaraguan harbours and its attacks on harbours, oil installations, etc.[29] In addition, the law of war sets further restrictions on the measures that may be implemented (Greenwood, 2002: 313–316).[30]

In relation both to necessity and to proportionality, it may be asked whether invasion of a country like Afghanistan with the purpose of over-throwing its government—true enough, with local support—is in conformity with international law. Here, the point of departure must be that an external state only has the right to 'neutralize' individuals or groups responsible for attacks made upon that state, in this instance Al-Qaeda. However, in this particular instance, there do exist grounds for arguing that the Afghan authorities' extensive cooperation with Al-Qaeda justified the extension of the use of force to include them.[31]

## EVALUATION

As far as possible, we should stick firmly to the view that terrorist acts are criminal offences. It is up to states to prevent terrorism, inter alia by means of prosecution. The more effective the efforts to combat terrorism through combating crime, the less pressure there will be to use military force. Alongside ongoing negotiations on a general convention on terrorism in the UN,[32] the EU has adopted a Framework Decision on Combating Terrorism,[33] and a number of countries have passed, or are in the process of producing, more effective legislation against terrorism. The difficult weighing and balancing in this work is to avoid encroachment on fundamental human rights, such as freedom of expression and guarantees of legal safeguards.

The use of force should to the greatest possible extent be brought under international—that is to say UN—control. This is in the interests of the international community, while the USA also needs an effective UN in order to secure political support and legitimacy for the use of force. In contrast to the case of Kosovo, there is every reason to suppose that the Security Council would have been willing to authorize the use of force in Afghanistan. However, the USA clearly preferred a strategy of trying to secure the political support of the UN without having its use of force anchored in and brought under the control of the UN (Charney, 2001: 835–837; Delbrück, 2001: 21–22; Mégret, 2002: 395–396).

Furthermore, resolutions of the Security Council should be designed and interpreted in such a way that the general prohibition against the use of force is not undermined. If force is used on the basis of an implicit or extended interpretation of a Security Council resolution, this may have the additional effect of making it more difficult to achieve agreement on future resolutions in the council. The continual bombing of Iraq by the USA and the UK since 1991 may serve as an example of the use of force on a dubious basis in international law (Lobel & Ratner, 1999: 154; Gray, 2002: 11; Byers, 2002: 23–27, 40).

Finally, it is important that the prohibition against the unilateral use of force is not weakened. While on the one hand, it should be appreciated that a state cannot passively accept that terrorists can freely use bases in other countries for attacks on their territory, any dilution of the restrictions on the use of force in international law may in itself constitute a threat to international peace and security and may open the door to misuse of military force (Farer, 2002: 363; Mégret, 2002: 384, 397–399; Byers, 2002: 36, 38–39).

## NOTES

1. For the historical background, see König (1995).

2. An earlier version of this article was published in Norwegian (Ulfstein, 2002). The article was revised and brought up to date for publication in *Security Dialogue.*

3. UN Security Council Resolutions 748 (1992), 1054 (1996), 1267 (1999) and 1333 (2000).

4. Antonio Cassese (2001) characterizes the resolution as 'ambiguous and contradictory.'

5. See also Bring (2001–02).

6. See United Nations (2001c); a similar letter was sent by the United Kingdom.

7. See, for example, Gray (2000: 115–119) and Alexandrov (1996: 182).

8. See International Court of Justice, 1986: 103.

9. On the other hand, Franck argues that '[if] the Council can act against Al-Qaeda, so can an attacked state' (Franck, 2001: 840), and Greenwood argues that 'it would be a strange formalism which regarded the right to take military action against those who caused or threatened such consequences as dependent upon whether their acts could somehow be imputed to a state' (Greenwood, 2002: 307).

10. International Court of Justice, 1986: 65, para. 115; see also paras 109 and 110.

11. *Prosecutor v. Tadic,* 38 International Legal Materials 1999: 1540–1546.

12. *Prosecutor v. Tadic,* 38 International Legal Materials 1999: 1546, para. 145.

13. International Law Commission, 2001: 104. See also Crawford (2002). The ILC's proposal was noted by the UN General Assembly in Resolution 56/83 of 28 January 2002, and the draft provisions appear in an accompanying Annex to the resolution.

14. See also UN General Assembly Resolution 42/22 (1987) ('Declaration on the Enhancement of the Effectiveness of the Principle of Refraining from the Threat or Use of Force in International Relations'), chapter I, para 6.

15. See also UN General Assembly Resolution 51/210 (1996) ('Measures to Eliminate International Terrorism'), chapter I, para 5.

16. UN Security Council Resolutions 1189 (1998), 1214 (1998), 167 (1999) and 1333 (2000).

17. UN Security Council Resolutions 167 (1999) and 1333 (2000).

18. But see Mégret (2002: 382–383).

19. See International Court of Justice, 1986: 103, para. 195.

20. See also Randelzhofer (1994: 674) on the view that the Nicaragua judgement's 'substantial involvement' should be interpreted restrictively.

21. See Cassese (2001: 997); see also Bring (2001/02: 251): 'En ny supplementärände självförsvarsnorm är på väg att etableras' [A new supplemental self-defence norm is in the process of being established].

22. The North Atlantic Treaty Council (2001) resolved on 12 September 2001 that if the attack against the USA 'was directed from abroad,' this should be deemed to trigger collective self-defence under Article 5 of the North Atlantic Treaty. On 2 October 2001, NATO's Secretary General announced that, on the basis of information provided by the USA, the NATO Council had ascertained that the attack 'was directed from abroad.' See also the resolution passed by the foreign ministers of the member-states of the Inter-American Treaty of Reciprocal Assistance on 21 September 2001, which declared that the attacks were to be considered as 'attacks against all American states' (Inter-American Treaty of Reciprocal Assistance, 2001).

23. In a speech entitled 'Beyond the Axis of Evil,' US Under-Secretary of State John Bolton added Cuba, Libya and Syria to the list of so-called rogue states—Iraq, Iran and North Korea (BBC News, 6 May 2002; available at http://news.bbc.co.uk/2/hi/world/americas/1971852.stm [28 August 2002]).

24. President George W. Bush at the US Military Academy at West Point, New York on 1 June 2002; see http://usinfo.state.gov/topical/pol/terror/02060201.htm (21 August 2002). See also Kirgis (2002).

25. The relevant diplomatic note from the USA has been reproduced in Dixon & McCorquodale (2000: 562).

26. On the other hand, see Franck (2001: 842) on the view that 'a victim state and its allies' may exercise 'their own, sole judgments in determining whether an attack has occurred and where it originated.'

27. See International Court of Justice, 1986: 94, para. 176.

28. See International Court of Justice, 1996: 226, para. 41.

29. See International Court of Justice, 1986: 122, para. 237.

30. On the USA's use of 'military commissions' to try individuals accused of terrorism, see *American Journal of International Law* 96(2): 320–359, which contains contributions from Daryl A. Mundis, Ruth Wedgwood, Harold Hongju Koh, Joan Fitzpatrick and Michael J. Matheson.

31. See Schrijver (2001:290): 'But targeting the overthrow of the Taliban regime would be beyond the scope of self-defence and hence unlawful.' Cassese argues: 'Force *may not* be used to wipe out the Afghan leadership or destroy Afghan military installations and other military objectives that have nothing to do with the terrorist organizations, unless the Afghan central authorities show by words or deeds that they approve and endorse the action of terrorist organizations' (2001: 999).

32. Under the terms of UN General Assembly Resolution 56/88, adopted on 12 December 2001, the Ad Hoc Committee on the drafting of a terrorism convention shall continue to elaborate a comprehensive convention on international terrorism as a matter of urgency; see http://www.un.org/law/terrorism/index.html (28 August 2002).

33. Council Framework Decision of 13 June 2002 on combating terrorism (2002/475/JHA); available at http://ue.eu.int/jai_Jo/EN/ST006128_02ORIEN.PDF (11 March 2003).

## REFERENCES

Alexandrov, Stanimir A., 1996. *Self-Defense Against the Use of Force in International Law.* The Hague: Kluwer Law International.

Bring, Ove, 2001–02. 'En rätt till väpnat självförsvar mot internationell terrorism?' [A Right to Armed Self-Defence Against International Terrorism?], *Juridisk tidskrift vid Stockholms universitet* 2: 241–251.

Byers, Michael, 2002. 'The Shifting Foundations of International Law: A Decade of Forceful Measures against Iraq,' *European Journal of International Law* 13(1): 21–43.

Cassese, Antonio, 2001. 'Terrorism Is Also Disrupting Some Crucial Legal Categories of International Law,' *European Journal of International Law* 12(5): 993–996.

Charney, Jonathan I., 2001. 'The Use of Force Against Terrorism and International Law,' *American Journal of International Law* 95(4): 835–839.

Crawford, James, 2002. *The International Law Commission's Articles on State Responsibility: Introduction, Text and Commentaries.* Cambridge: Cambridge University Press.

Delbrück, Jost, 2001. 'The Fight Against Global Terrorism: Self-Defense or Collective Security as International Police Action? Some Comments on the International Legal Implications of the "War Against Terrorism"', *German Yearbook of International Law* 44: 9–24.

Dinstein, Yoram, 2001. *War, Aggression and Self-Defence,* 3rd edn. Cambridge: Cambridge University Press.

Dixon, Martin & Robert McCorquodale, 2000. *Cases & Materials on International Law,* 3rd edn. London: Blackstone.

Farer, Tom J., 2002. 'Beyond the Charter Frame: Unilateralism or Condominium,' *American Journal of International Law* 96(2): 359–364.

Franck, Thomas M., 2001. 'Terrorism and the Right of Self-Defense,' *American Journal of International Law* 95(4): 839–843.

Gray, Christine, 2000. *International Law and the Use of Force.* Oxford: Oxford University Press.

Gray, Christine, 2002. 'From Unity to Polarization: International Law and the Use of Force against Iraq,' *European Journal of International Law* 13(1): 1–21.

Greenwood, Christopher, 2002. 'International Law and the "War Against Terrorism,"' *International Affairs* 78(2): 301–317.

Inter-American Treaty of Reciprocal Assistance, 2001. OEA/Ser.F/II.24 RC.24/RES.1/01; available at http://www.oas.org/juridico/english/sigs/b-29.html (11 March 2003).

International Court of Justice, 1986. *Military and Paramilitary Activities in and Against Nicaragua,* Reports of Judgments, Advisory Opinions and Orders. The Hague: International Court of Justice.

International Court of Justice, 1996. *Legality of the Threat or Use of Nuclear Weapons,* Reports of Judgments, Advisory Opinions and Orders. The Hague: International Court of Justice.

International Law Commission, 2001. *Report of the International Law Commission.* UN General Assembly Official Records, Fifty-Sixth Session, Supplement No. 10, A/56/10.

Kirgis, Frederic L., 2001. 'Addendum: Security Council Adopts Resolution on Combating International Terrorism,' *ASIL Insights,* 1 October; available at http://www.asil.org/insights/insigh77.htm#addendum7 (17 February 2003).

Kirgis, Frederic L., 2002. 'Pre-Emptive Action To Forestall Terrorism,' *ASIL Insights,* June; available at http://www.asil.org/insights/insigh88.htm (19 August 2002).

König, Doris, 1995. 'On Terrorism,' in Rüdiger Wolfrum, ed., *United Nations: Law, Policies and Practice,* vol. 2. Dordrecht: Martinus Nijhoff (1220–1229).

Lobel, Jules & Michael Ratner, 1999. 'Bypassing the Security Council: Ambiguous Authorizations To Use Force, Cease-Fires and the Iraqi Inspection Regime,' *American Journal of International Law* 93: 124–155.

Mégret, Frédéric, 2002. '"War"? Legal Semantics and the Move to Violence,' European Journal of International Law 13(2): 361–401.

North Atlantic Treaty Council, 2001. 'Statement by the North Atlantic Council,' Press Release 124; available at http://www.nato.int/docu/pr/2001/p01–124e.htm (11 March 2003).

Randelzhofer, Albrecht, 1994. 'Article 51,' in Bruno Simma, ed., *The Charter of the United Nations: A Commentary,* Vol. I. Oxford: Oxford University Press (661).

Randelzhofer, Albrecht, 2002. 'Article 51,' in Bruno Simma, ed., *The Charter of the United Nations: A Commentary,* Vol. I, 2nd edn. Oxford: Oxford University Press (802).

Schrijver, Nico, 2001. 'Responding to International Terrorism: Moving the Frontiers of International Law for "Enduring Freedom"?,' *Netherlands International Law Review* XLVIII(3): 271–291.

Ulfstein, Geir, 2002. 'Terror og folkerett' [Terror and International Law], *Lov og Rett* 2: 67–82.

United Nations, 2001a. Provisional Verbatim Records Security Council, 12 September, S/PV.4370.

United Nations, 2001b. Provisional Verbatim Records Security Council, 28 September, S/PV.4385.

United Nations, 2001c. Security Council, 7 October, S/2001/946.

United Nations, 2001d. 'Press Statement on Terrorist Threats by Security Council President, 8 October,' AFG/152 SC/7167.

# A New Strategy for the New Face of Terrorism

L. Paul Bremer, III
*Marsh Crisis Consulting*

"The third World War was begun on Tuesday, September 11, on the East Coast of the United States"—so began the French magazine *L'Express* two days later. Whether these words turn out to be prediction or exaggeration will depend on how the world now reacts to the new face of terrorism represented by the vicious attacks of that day.

The September 11 atrocities made for the most dramatic day in American History, dwarfing even the events at Pearl Harbor sixty years ago. Three times as many Americans died in New York and Washington as died at Pearl Harbor. And this time innocent civilians, not military men, were the intended targets. But this was not just an attack on America. Citizens of at least eighty countries died in the collapsed World Trade towers. We are all, in a direct way, victims of the new terrorism.

## THE CHANGING NATURE OF TERRORISM

While the attacks were shocking for their audacity and effectiveness, they should have surprised no serious student of terrorism. A large-scale attack on American soil has been widely predicted by experts. For years they have drawn attention to a disturbing paradox: while the number of international terrorist incidents has been declining over the past decade, the number of casualties has risen. This trend reflects the changing motives of terrorists.

During the 1970s and 1980s, most terrorist groups had limited political motives. For them, terrorism was a tactic mainly to draw attention to their "cause." These groups reasoned that many people would sympathize with that cause if only they were made aware of it. Designing their tactics to support this objective, these "old-style" terrorists rarely engaged in indiscriminate mass killing. They rightly concluded such

attacks would disgust the very audiences they were trying to convert to their cause. So most terrorist groups designed their attacks to kill enough people to draw in the press but not so many as to repel the public. Often they used terror to force negotiations on some issue, such as the release of jailed comrades. As one terrorism expert put it, these groups were seeking a place at the negotiating table.

Eventually, most terrorist groups in Europe overplayed their hands and the publics turned against them. But anti-terrorism policies helped win the day. With vigorous American leadership, European countries and the United States developed a counter-terrorist strategy to deal with this threat. At the heart of that strategy were three principles: make no concessions to terrorists; treat terrorists as criminals to be brought to justice; and punish states that support terrorism. On balance, this strategy worked.

Over the past decade, however, it has become clear that many terrorist groups are motivated less by narrow political goals and more by ideological, apocalyptic or religious fanaticism. Sometimes their goal is simply hatred or revenge, and tactics have changed to reflect these motives. Rather than avoiding large-scale casualties, these terrorists seek to kill as many people as possible. They are unconstrained by the respect for human life that undergirds all the world's great religions, including Islam.

Beginning with the downing of Pan Am Flight 103 in December 1988, through the first World Trade Center bombing in 1993, to the chemical attacks in the Tokyo subways in 1995 and the attacks on two U.S. embassies in East Africa in 1998, terrorist actions have resulted in increasing numbers of casualties. The September 11 attacks killed more than 5,000 people, making it the single worse terrorist attack in world history.

Things could get even worse. During the 1990s, concerns arose that terrorists might use chemical, biological, radiological or nuclear agents. In the 1980s, terrorist groups could have developed such weapons, but they did not do so, apparently calculating that their use would make public support for their causes less likely. But far from steering away from such agents, the new terrorists might find these weapons attractive precisely because they can kill tens of thousands. This was the goal, fortunately unrealized, of Aum Shinrikyo's chemical attack on the Tokyo subway. Indeed, there is evidence that some new terrorist groups, including bin Laden's Al-Qaeda, have tried to acquire nuclear, biological and chemical agents. It is known that the terrorist states of North Korea, Iraq, Iran, Libya and Syria all have tried to develop nuclear, chemical and biological weapons. Moreover, in the 1990s, information about chemical and biological agents became widely available on the Internet. The recent anthrax attacks may foreshadow a major escalation to bioterrorism by Islamist and perhaps other terrorists.

The changed motives of these "new-style" terrorists mean that at least two-thirds of the West's old strategy is out-moded. One pillar of that strategy, not making concessions to terrorists, remains valid. But it may be irrelevant when faced with groups like Al-Qaeda. Such groups are not trying to start negotiations. They make no negotiable "demands" that the West can comply with to forestall further attacks. These men do not seek a seat at the table; they want to overturn the table and kill everybody at it.

It is an honorable reflection of the basic friendliness of the American people that most of us find it difficult to believe that anybody hates Americans. Many find it especially confusing that men who lived among us, sometimes for years, attending our schools and shopping in our malls, should hate the very society whose freedoms they enjoyed. That they somehow must not understand us is the first reaction of many.

But this reaction reflects a misunderstanding about the new terrorists. They hate America precisely because they *do* understand our society; they hate its freedoms, its commitment to equal rights and universal suffrage, its material successes and its appeal to so many non-Americans. Thus, the question of whether or not to make concessions in the face of such hatred is simply irrelevant. Nothing America can say or do, short of ceasing to exist, will satisfy these terrorists.

Our long-standing objective of "bringing terrorists to justice," the second pillar of U.S. strategy, is also irrelevant to the new fight. During the past decade, an increasing percentage of terrorist attacks, especially those conducted by Middle Eastern groups, have involved suicides. This underscores the perpetrators' extraordinary commitment to terror, but it also shows the futility of relying on the concept of using criminal justice to punish them. Men who are prepared to die in an airplane crash are not going to be deterred by the threat of being locked in a prison cell. We need to revise our thinking; now our goal should be, as President Bush has suggested, "bringing justice to the terrorists."

## Terrorism—The New Face of War

In the broader sense, the September 11 attacks preview the kind of security threat America will face in the 21st century. Terrorism allows the weak to attack the strong. It is relatively inexpensive to conduct, and devilishly difficult to counter.

Relative to all the other powers in the world, America is stronger than any country has ever been in history. The Gulf War showed that even a lavishly equipped conventional force (at the time, Iraq possessed the world's fifth largest army) was no match for America. The lesson for would-be tyrants and terrorists was clear: America could only be attacked by unconventional means, and terrorism is a fundamental tactic of asymmetrical warfare.

Terrorists take advantage of two important asymmetries. First, in the fight against terrorism, defenders have to protect all their points of vulnerability around the world; the terrorist has only to attack the weakest point. This lesson was brought home to the U.S. government when Al-Qaeda attacked the American embassies in Nairobi and Dar es Salaam in August 1998, two embassies thought to be in little danger and thus ill-protected.

Secondly, the costs of launching a terrorist attack are a fraction of the costs required to defend against it. To shoot up an airport, a terrorist needs only an AK-47 assault rifle; defending that same airport costs millions of dollars. The September 11 attacks probably cost less than $2 million and caused over $100 billion in damage and business interruption. Thus, the new terrorism reverses the conventional wisdom that, in military operations, the offense must be three times as strong as the defense.

How, then, are we to fight this new and increasingly dangerous threat?

The proper objective of a counter-terrorist policy is to prevent attacks before they happen. So, more than in any other field of foreign and national security affairs, success in the fight against terrorism depends on having good intelligence. But there is no more difficult or dangerous kind of intelligence to collect. The surest way to know about an attack ahead of time is to have somebody tell you the plans. That means having a spy in the terrorist group itself.

Inserting an agent inside a terrorist group is among any intelligence agency's most difficult task. These groups are by nature clandestine and suspicious, even paranoid. Membership is often based on ethnic, tribal, clan or family ties, so Western intelligence agencies can rarely use their own nationals to infiltrate such groups.

There are two other possibilities for getting this valuable "human intelligence." Our agencies can, and do, work with friendly intelligence agencies in the Middle East. Often those organizations can use their own nationals to infiltrate terrorist cells. And if we handle such a relationship properly, our government can get useful and timely information about terrorist plans that enables us to disrupt them before they can be carried out. Such a relationship helped foil Al-Qaeda's planned millennium celebration attacks.

The second path is for the CIA itself to recruit a member of the group. This is exceptionally dangerous since the penalty, if caught spying, is certain death. We have also made the task more difficult for ourselves. Over the past 25 years, the United States has seriously undermined its capability to acquire "human intelligence." In the mid-1970s, politicized attacks by Congress damaged CIA operations and morale. In the late 1970s, a large number of the Agency's best officers specializing in collecting human intelligence were fired. These trends were exacerbated when, in 1995, the Clinton Administration imposed rigid and bureaucratic procedures governing the Agency's recruitment of spies who themselves have been involved with terrorist organizations. These new guidelines had the effect of making such recruitments even more difficult than they already were.

The bipartisan National Commission on Terrorism, which I chaired, carefully investigated the effect of these 1995 "guidelines." During our work in 2000, we heard testimony from serving CIA officers, at home and abroad, from first-tour case officers to station chiefs. Their testimony was unambiguous, unanimous and conclusive: the "guidelines" were an obstacle to the recruitment of effective spies in the struggle against terrorism. We strongly recommended their immediate cancellation.

The CIA's response to this recommendation was curious. Its leaders stated that they had never turned down a proposal *presented to them* to recruit a terrorist spy. But this entirely misses the point. By the time a proposed recruitment makes it to the CIA's leadership, it has already passed through a welter of rules, regulations, procedures, committees and lawyers that essentially guarantees that only the least suspect person will be suggested (assuming that after this tortuous and time-consuming process the terrorist is still around to recruit).

As the Bremer Commission noted, the major problem with the "guidelines" is the effect they have in the field. Officer after officer confirmed to our commissioners that the prospect of having to navigate Washington's bureaucratic jungle-gym was a clear disincentive even to begin the process of such recruitments. Many officers told us that they simply decided to go after easier targets. The "guidelines" have become an effective, though undesirable, bureaucratic prophylactic against risk-taking. They must be changed.

## A New Strategy for Countering Terrorism

The elements of a new strategy to deal with the new threat are at hand. We need only the will to implement that strategy.

## WHAT IS TO BE DONE?

Our strategic objective must be to deny terrorist groups safe havens from which they can operate and garner various kinds of support from governments. As President Bush stated in his September 20 address, America intends to punish not just the terrorists but any group or state that has in any way supported them.

We must apply this strategy ruthlessly and creatively. Our tactics should range across the entire spectrum of activity from diplomacy, political pressure and economic measures, to military, psychological and covert operations. As the President has emphasized, this will be a long campaign demanding patience and cunning. The battle will be less like an American football game, with its fixed "battle lines" and clearly defined moves (as in the Gulf War), and more like European football: open, fluid and improvisational.

American actions must move beyond the episodic and limp-wristed attacks of the past decade, actions that seemed designed to "signal" our seriousness to the terrorists without inflicting any real damage on them. Naturally, their feebleness demonstrated the opposite. This time the terrorists and their supporters must be eliminated.

Our strategy should operate in three concentric circles. In the first and innermost circle, we must deal decisively with those most immediately responsible for the September attack. This means destroying all the terrorist camps, personnel and infrastructure in Afghanistan and getting rid of the Taliban regime. We must avoid thinking that the fight is only about bin Laden. It is one of the habitual failings of U.S. policy to over-emphasize one individual terrorist and ignore the broader dangers. In the late 1970s, Libya's Muammar Qaddafi was America's enemy number one. In the mid-1980s, Abu Nidal took his place. Ten years later, it was, and remains today, bin Laden.

There are two dangers with this approach. First, it tends to build up the terrorist leader, in his own eyes and in the eyes of his supporters. The concentration on one individual may thus paradoxically make it easier for him to find new recruits. Secondly, over-emphasis on one man may mislead the public into thinking that if only the "bad guy" could be eliminated, the terrorist problem would go away. It's just not so. Even if bin Laden were to die today, our problems would not end, for Afghanistan has become a cesspool of terrorism, much as Lebanon was in the 1980s. At least a half dozen other terrorist groups have training camps and facilities in the country, all welcomed by the Taliban. That is why our initial actions must go beyond destroying the terrorist camps. As long as the Taliban rule in Afghanistan, the terrorists' infrastructure can be quickly reconstituted.

It would be preferable if the Afghan people, who have suffered greatly under the harsh rule of the Taliban, could throw that regime out themselves. Certainly, the West should encourage this by supporting the exiled king, Mohammed Zahir, in his call for an uprising. Still popular among the Afghan people, the King is a Pashtun and thus has a crucial role to play in the establishment of a credible alternative government (though we must respect his need to avoid being seen as an American puppet).

This political strategy must be wedded to a three-pronged military plan. Our military forces and those of our allies must first degrade the Taliban's military capabilities. This will bring about a new balance of forces on the ground. Then we must encourage the creation and arming of an effective Pashtun military force, using as its core those Taliban commanders who have already defected. Finally, we and our allies should support the Northern Alliance, which still controls 10 to 15 percent of the country and which has support among the Tajik, Uzbek and Hazara communities.

The harsh reality is that any campaign that does not result in a change of regime in Kabul will be a failure. This is the *sine qua non* of our entire strategy. We therefore cannot exclude the possibility that it may be necessary to introduce ground troops into this hostile topography.

America's seriousness of purpose in the new war on terrorism will be demonstrated by U.S. and allied actions in this first phase. If we are weak, hesitant or ineffective, we will pay a heavy price later.

## ENDING STATE SUPPORT FOR TERRORISM

The second objective of our strategy must be to deny terrorists operating bases. This means rooting out terrorist camps, bases and cells wherever they are, including in the United States. It is likely that some of the Al-Qaeda terrorists will escape us in Afghanistan. They will try to relocate elsewhere, perhaps seeking out friendly governments or weak states in the Middle East, Central Asia or in Africa. We must pursue them and destroy them, with or without the help of the relevant governments.

The President made clear in his address to the American people on September 20 that any state that harbors or supports terrorist groups will be henceforth considered "a hostile regime." This statement has important implications beyond the obvious countries of Iran and Iraq. Syria, with which our European allies and we have regular diplomatic relations, still hosts over a dozen terrorist groups. So do Sudan and Lebanon.

Yet for too long American policy has contented itself with merely identifying states that support terrorism without forcing any serious consequences upon them in turn. Our European allies have been even less forceful, seeming to ignore state involvement in terrorism, often in the hopes of winning commercial advantage. For example, the European Union's long running "constructive dialogue" with Iran may have won European firms handsome contracts to develop Iranian energy resources, but it has not in any respect altered Iran's continued and open support for Middle East terrorist groups. Iran remains the world's leading state sponsor of terrorism. Groups such as Hamas, the Palestinian Islamic Jihad and Hizballah, which regularly target innocent civilians, all depend on Iranian support. In fact, as the State Department has pointed out, Iranian involvement in terror has actually increased since the election of Mohammad Khatemi as president four years ago.

Some commentators argue that the new terrorism is caused by discontent with America's role in supporting Israel. The implication is that if America would just weaken that support, the terrorism would end. This argument is wrong on two counts. First, bin Laden has made clear in his own words, for years, that he attacks America because he hates who we are, not because of whom we support. Secondly, dealing effectively with radical Islam is the prerequisite to moving toward a broader regional peace, not the other way around. It was America's decisive

(though incomplete) victory over Iraq in 1991 that was the necessary precondition for the Oslo peace process. Now as then, countries in the Middle East and Europe will pay attention to American ideas for regional security when we have shown that we are prepared to act decisively against threats to that security.

## A War on Islam?

President Bush and all his senior advisors have been clear: We do not consider the American response to the September 11 attacks to be a war against Islam. He is right. Bin Laden and his allies in the Taliban are a fringe minority far removed from the teachings of mainstream Islam. But there is a real danger now that "moderate" Muslims are allowing these radicals to hijack Islam, and thus to define Islam as an enemy of the West. Until now, we have heard too few voices of restraint from the Islamic world. Quite the contrary. For example, through their controlled media, the Palestinians and even some "moderate" Arab governments have spewed out anti-American hatred with impunity for years. On the very day of the suicide attacks, the newspaper of the Palestinian Authority, *al-Hayat al-Fadida,* praised suicide bombers as "noble . . . the salt of the earth, the engines of history. . . . They are the most honorable among us." Inflammatory articles like this have contributed to an environment that made possible the appalling spectacle of schoolchildren in Gaza and Ramallah cheering the news of the American tragedies.

Europeans, who provide the bulk of money to the Palestinians, should make clear that until such inflammatory rhetoric stops, there will be no more euros for Yasir Araft. Nor should American taxpayers be expected to send another penny to the Palestinian Authority until Arafat roots out, expels or imprisons the Hamas, Hizballah and Islamic Jihad terrorists who operate from his territory.

In Pakistan, Islamic *madrassas* regularly indoctrinate young boys to hate America. At one school, after the September 11 attack, eight year-old boys vied with one another to be the one who would grow up to bring down the Sears Tower in Chicago. Here in America, some

...amic leaders have said that the September 11 attacks violate the Quran. But several have then made the astonishing statement that, this being the case, Israelis or Americans themselves must have conducted the attacks.

Moderate Islam is on the front line now. Its leaders have a solemn responsibility to make clear, in public, that the purposeful slaughter of innocent civilians is anathema to Islamic beliefs and that those who commit such acts are apostates who will go to hell, not to heaven. Unless they speak out now, there is a real risk that Islam will be defined by the radicals at war with the West. And then this *will* become a war with Islam, declared *by* Islam.

## DELEGITIMIZING TERROR

Finally, American strategy must have as a broader objective rebuilding the international consensus against terrorism that flourished briefly during the 1980s, but then fell into neglect. If done effectively, this can delegitimize terror.

There are many areas where better cooperation will prove useful. Intelligence cooperation is the most urgent need. Clearly, no matter how good its intelligence organization, no one nation alone can hope to gather enough specific information on a worldwide terrorist network. In the wake of the September 11 attacks, it has become clear that America's intelligence failure was mirrored in many other countries: none seemed to be taking seriously enough the clear declarations of war by bin Laden, and none was sufficiently attentive to the activities of suspicious people. Sharing intelligence with friendly countries is an essential step in developing a common strategy. As noted, during the 1980s America and its European partners found ways to deepen cooperation in this vital area. This effort must not be accelerated and broadened to include cooperation with friendly Muslim states.

There must also be more vigorous and persistent efforts to track terrorist funds. Too often, terrorist groups have been able to use front organizations, non-governmental organizations and willing dupes to raise and distribute money. Out of ignorance, laziness or cowardice, most governments have looked the other way.

The recent U.S. decision to seize terrorist assets is a good first step. So is the UN Security Council resolution calling on all states to take robust action against terrorist finances.

To maintain broad support for the struggle against terrorism, the United States will have to accept that the problem goes beyond those terrorist groups with a "global reach." While such groups are the proper objective of our initial strategy, we will have to show that we share the concerns of our allies who are subjected to Irish and Basque terrorism, for example, if we are to get continuing support from Britain and Spain in the fight.

As to legal matters, no doubt there will be proposals for new international conventions and treaties concerning terrorism and state support for it. Each of these should be examined on its merits and pursued where useful. But we should not let the search for an illusive international legal consensus stop us from vigorous action against known terrorist groups or states.

We have seen the face of the new threat to our security in the 21st century. Under Article 51 of the United Nations Charter, the United States is fully justified in taking any and all means of self-defense against that threat. The United States has made clear that it welcomes the assistance of any country in anti-terrorist military operations, and so far the American government has done a masterful job of assembling broad support for the initial phase of the campaign in Afghanistan. The challenge will be to sustain that support as the battle wears on, and especially when the campaign enters, the second phase, after we have dealt with Afghanistan.

We must destroy the terrorists before they destroy us. They hate us and are so dangerous that they must be stopped before they can take the battle to a still higher plane of lethality. We must disrupt, dismantle or destroy terrorist groups wherever they are and deny them safe heavens. Americans should therefore be under no illusions about the campaign we have embarked upon. There will be war with more than one country. As in all wars, there will be civilian casualties. America will win some battles but lose others. More Americans will die. But neither our allies nor our enemies should be in any doubt: We shall prevail.

## Smarter Intelligence

John Deutch and Jeffrey H. Smith

The terrorist attacks on the World Trade Center and the Pentagon understandably provoked two reactions—that this was the worst intelligence failure in recent U.S. history and that U.S. intelligence gathering and analysis must be vastly improved. Many proposals have been put forward to improve U.S. intelligence capabilities. In order to sort those that make sense from those that do not, it is important first to understand the constrains the intelligence community has inherited.

The framework for U.S. intelligence was created in a different time to deal with different problems. The National Security Act of 1947, which established the Central Intelligence Agency (CIA), envisioned the enemy to be states such as the Soviet Union and also recognized the importance of protecting citizens' rights [see sidebar on page 67]. The result was organizations and authority based on distinctions of domestic versus foreign threats, law enforcement versus national security concerns, and peacetime versus wartime. The Federal Bureau of Investigation (FBI) was responsible for the former, and the intelligence community—comprising the CIA, the National Security Agency (NSA), the Defense Intelligence Agency (DIA), and other agencies—was responsible for the latter.

Law enforcement's focus is to collect evidence *after* a crime is committed in order to support prosecution in a court of law. The FBI is reluctant to share with other government agencies the information obtained from its informants for fear of compromising future court action. On the other hand, the CIA collects and analyzes information in order to forewarn the government *before* an act occurs. The CIA is reluctant to give the FBI information obtained from CIA agents for fear that its sources and methods for gaining that information will be revealed in court.

Clearly, the current structure is ill-suited to deal with catastrophic terrorism. Decision on intelligence reform will revolve around this question of the proper balance between national security and law enforcement goals. Meanwhile, historical boundaries between organizations remain, stymieing the collection of timely intelligence and warnings of terrorist activity. This fragmented approach to intelligence gathering makes it quite possible that information collected by one U.S. government agency before an overt act of terrorism will not be shared and synthesized in time to avert it.

A word about intelligence "failures" is in order. By the most obvious criterion—the success of Osama bin Laden's operatives on September 11—intelligence and law enforcement failed to protect the public. But only time will tell if the information necessary to predict and stop the attacks was in government hands in advance or reasonably could have been. At some point it will be appropriate to analyze this question. For now, however, such an inquiry would only distract government agents and analysts from the critical task of identifying and preventing *future* attacks.

### GIVING THE CIA THE LEAD

The FBI and CIA have been working to overcome the fragmentation of counterterrorism intelligence efforts through personnel exchanges and joint training. Yet the FBI and the intelligence community still have separate counterterrorism centers. This duplication hardly makes sense. In an era when national security must be the preeminent concern, the director of central intelligence (DCI) should manage a single National Counterterrorism Center that plans intelligence collection for all agencies and produces analysis derived from all sources of intelligence. A committee chaired by the DCI and including the national security advisor, the director of the new Office of Homeland Security, and the attorney general should set the agenda for these activities.

The security services of friendly nations are important sources of information for U.S.

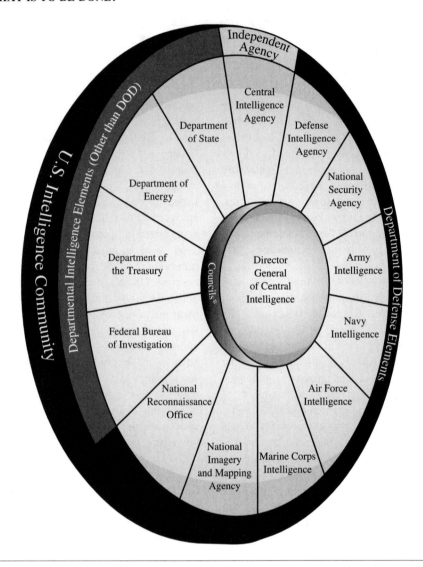

**Figure 9.1**

Source: CIA Web site

*Special committees counsel the DCI on community wide concerns

intelligence; they know their neighborhoods and have access that U.S. agencies do not. At present, the CIA, NSA, DIA, FBI, and the Drug Enforcement Administration have separate agreements with foreign counterpart organizations to obtain information. These efforts should be coordinated. The DCI's authority and responsibility to plan, monitor, and approve arrangements between all intelligence agencies and their foreign counterparts on all intelligence matters, including counterterrorism matters, should be clarified and strictly enforced.

Judging by their recent articles, some editorial writers apparently believe the collection of intelligence through technical means such as communications intercepts and imagery is not important in the fight against terrorist organizations. In fact, cooperation between human and technical intelligence, especially communications intelligence, makes both stronger. Human sources, or HUMINT, can provide access to valuable signals intelligence, which incorporates primarily voice and data communications intelligence. Communications intercepts can validate information provided by a human source. Any operation undertaken in a hostile environment is made safer if communications surveillance is possible. Currently, the NSA, which is under the authority of the secretary of defense, carries out communications intelligence, and the CIA carries out human intelligence, which is under the authority of the DCI. The secretary of defense and the DCI share authority for setting foreign collection priorities. In the case of foreign threats within the United States, the FBI has primary responsibility for setting collection priorities. Here again, the fragmentation makes no sense when considering the global terrorist threat. The new antiterrorism law took a good first step toward remedying this problem by clarifying the DCI's lead role in setting priorities for wiretaps under the Foreign Intelligence Surveillance Act (FISA) and disseminating the resulting information.

In addition, the Bush administration's current review of intelligence, under the leadership of former National Security Advisor Brent Scowcroft, should recommend greater centralization of intelligence collection and analysis under the DCI. Inevitably, strengthening the authority of the DCI will raise the question of whether this position should be separated from the position of head of the CIA. If the DCI is given budgetary, planning, and management authority over the agencies that are responsible for national-level intelligence, then the positions should be separated, just as the secretary of defense sits above the individual services.

## Drags on Covert Action

Fragmentation also impairs covert action—activities the United States undertakes to achieve objectives without attribution. Such action has been associated with past CIA efforts to overthrow, in peacetime, political regimes considered a threat to the United States. The future purpose of covert action will be quite different: to destroy terrorist cells and facilities that may produce or store weapons of mass destruction. The distinction between CIA-sponsored covert action and military special operations will become much less relevant, if it

is relevant at all. For larger paramilitary operations, a permanent planning staff under the leadership of the secretary of defense, including CIA and FBI staff members, should be put in place to strengthen counterterrorism covert action.

Current law requires both a presidential finding and reporting to Congress of all CIA covert action. No such rule governs covert military operations. In the fight against terrorists, the CIA and the military will be called to conduct joint covert operations, but the differing approval and reporting requirements of these organizations can hamper cooperation. Congress should consider streamlining the law to remove the artificial distinction.

The September 11 attacks renewed questioning about the adequacy of U.S. human intelligence capability. Use of spies is an essential aspect of combating terrorism, and the intelligence community has neither ignored human intelligence nor neglected to target terrorist groups such as Osama bin Laden's al Qaeda organization. Indeed, there have been notable successes in penetrating terrorist groups and preventing planned terrorist acts, but because they were successes they did not come to the public's attention.

Strengthening human intelligence has been a priority of all DCIS. But human intelligence collection is not a silver bullet that can be separated from other intelligence activities and improved overnight. It takes a long time to build a team of experts who understand the language, culture, politics, society, and economic circumstances surrounding terrorist groups. Furthermore, neither bin Laden nor any other terrorist is likely to confide a full operational plan to a single individual, no matter how carefully placed as a source. Spying requires great skill and discipline, something that cannot be achieved quickly or by throwing money at it. To be sure, the morale of the operations directorate hit an acceptable low in the early and mid-1990s. But this was not due to reduced budgets or lack of presidential support. The poor morale was due to the discovery within the CIA's ranks of Soviet spy Aldrich Ames in 1994, the revelation of CIA activity in Paris in 1995, frequent investigations by Congress and the CIA's own inspector general, and other events that indicated that professional standards had slipped badly.

HUMINT depends critically on other intelligence efforts. It is generally not decisive by itself, but must be combined with all other sources of information. A prerequisite for good human intelligence is a thorough understanding of the sources of terrorism, and much of this kind of information can be obtained from open sources such as local newspapers in the communities that spawn and protect terrorist organizations. Such analytic information is essential for planning collection strategies, successfully penetrating terrorist groups, and mounting covert operations to disrupt terrorist activities and facilities. Successful human intelligence operations rely critically on intelligence analysis to target their efforts. Thus, rather than creating a separate clandestine service, as some have proposed, the United States should support a stronger, seamless partnership between the CIA's operations and intelligence directorates.

---

### Coming Full Circle

A dramatic attack on the United States—Pearl Harbor—provided the backdrop to the last major reorganization of intelligence, which led to creation of the Central Intelligence Agency (CIA) in 1947. "I have often thought," wrote President Harry Truman in his memoirs, "that if there had been something like coordination of information in the government it would have been more difficult, if not impossible, for the Japanese to succeed in the sneak attack at Pearl Harbor."

Key administration officials agreed about the failures of wartime intelligence: "Inadequate operations have resulted in failure to anticipate intelligence needs, in failure to recognize trends, in lack of perspective, and in inadequate pooling of intelligence," wrote Bureau of the Budget Director Harold Smith in a 1945 memorandum to President Truman.

Policymakers' perceptions of intelligence also posed a problem. "There still is widespread misunderstanding of what intelligence is, how it is produced, and in what way it relates to and serves the action and policymaking people," Smith wrote in his memo to Truman. "For example, many persons whose active participation in developing an effective post-war operation is essential are still thinking narrowly in terms of spies and intrigue, in terms of current developments and the latest news, or in terms, solely, of the development of new or special sources of information."

There was no consensus on how to fix the deficiencies of wartime intelligence. The 1945 debate about what sort of intelligence operation to create focused on the question of which was the worst evil: too much centralization or too much compartmentalization. Truman complained to CIA employees in 1952 that when he took office "each Department and each organization had its own information service, and that information service was walled off from every other service." Key military officials argued for one central agency to deal with this problem. Smith, however, argued that most intelligence operations should be organized at a departmental level, and he wanted the State Department to coordinate the departments' intelligence operations.

The forces of centralization won. The 1947 National Security Act established the CIA for a peacetime world in which it was not yet clear what an intelligence agency should do and in which past intelligence failures were foremost in policy-makers' minds. In 1999 the Hart-Rudman Commission called for rethinking the way the 1947 act organized intelligence in a report called "New World Coming: American Security in the 21st Century." Yet the discussion surrounding the CIA's birth makes it clear: much of the debate remains the same.

—FP

## Changing the Rules

The recent terrorist attacks gave new momentum to a debate over three controversial rules governing CIA operations. The first of these governs how CIA case officers in the field may recruit agents. In 1995, the CIA established a policy requiring the Directorate of Operations headquarters to approve the recruitment of sources believed to have serious criminal or abusive human rights records. The officials apply a simple balancing test: Is the potential gain from the information obtained worth the cost that might be associated with doing business with a person who may be a murderer, rapist, or the like? Some believe this rule has constrained case officers from recruiting agents inside terrorist groups and therefore made it harder to predict and preempt terrorist acts, although senior CIA officials maintain that the rules have not reduced the quality or quantity of counterterrorism intelligence. Congress recently considered legislation directing the DCI to revoke the rule, but it ultimately enacted a "sense of the Congress" provision, as part of the new antiterrorism law, encouraging intelligence officers to "make every effort" to "establish relationships" with such individuals.

There are two reasons such rules are necessary. First and most important, case officers have been and will continue to be vulnerable when they enter arrangements with agents who do not necessarily produce valuable or accurate information and later are found to have committed atrocities against U.S. citizens or others. These case officers may be investigated by the CIA inspector general, the Department of Justice, and congressional committees. The overriding purpose of the 1995 recruiting guidelines was to keep case officers from worrying about just this possibility of prosecution, Clearance by the Directorate of Operations protected the case officer in the field. The rules did the opposite of what was feared; they gave case officers the incentive to take risks because approval from Washington meant that headquarters had to stand behind field decisions. It is a sad irony that Congress, while passing one piece of legislation that encourages case officers to take risks in recruiting agents, in another authorized the DCI to pay for personal liability insurance for case officers. Congress seems to be saying, "Go take risks, but if later we don't like the risks you took, you will be investigated. And the government will pay your legal bills." This seems an old way to motivate case officers in the field.

The second reason for the 1995 rule governing recruiting is efficiency. The CIA should focus on recruiting agents that have access to genuinely important information and reward case officers' efforts for the quality of information collected, not just the quantity. It can be difficult to judge the appropriate balance between recruiting numbers of agents that may be valuable and recruiting a few agents that will be vital. In some cases, one can rely on the judgement of experienced station chiefs. But both prudence and experience suggest that officials at headquarters need to review these judgments.

Another contentious rule has been President Gerald Ford's 1976 executive order barring U.S. intelligence agencies from assassinating foreign political leaders. The horror of the September 11 attacks on civilians prompted many to call for a reversal of this ban to allow assassination of a terrorist leader or a political leader who supports terrorism. This move would be unwise. The United States will win the war on terrorism, but one result of this victory should not be a world in which assassination of political leaders is an acceptable norm of international law—a precedent that could be established by U.S. action.

Moreover, assassination is rarely effective in defeating motivated groups. For example, the murder of bin Laden would not necessarily remove the threat from al Qaeda. However, the executive order does not and should not prohibit targeting individual political or military leaders, including leaders of terrorist organizations, in the process of military operations, which take place during *overt* hostilities where opposing forces and their political leadership know they are at risk.

A third change in rules concerns wiretaps on foreigners in the United States and U.S. citizens (especially those in U.S. corporations set up as front organizations) who are associated with suspected terrorist groups. In addition to clarifying the DCI's role under FISA, Congress also relaxed the conditions under which courts may authorize warrants for national security wiretaps and searches. The intelligence community must have access to telecommunications and databases so it can track the movements and associations of suspected terrorists operating in the United States. Similarly, corporations such as banks and airlines will increasingly be asked or required to cooperate with authorities to trace suspected terrorists. Vigilance will be required to prevent improper spying on Americans, but it is possible to devise a system to collect large amounts of information without compromising the privacy and rights of American citizens.

## Unreasonable Expectations

A larger question underlying discussions of intelligence reform is, how much should Americans expect from the intelligence community? Over the past two decades, despite organizational handicaps and conflicting authorities, the intelligence community has built up a considerable counterterrorism capability that has resulted in many successes and, as is now apparent, some spectacular failures. Clearly,

Congress and the executive branch are ready to grant the intelligence community greater authority to pursue the paramount mission of national security. And there are dedicated, talented men and women who will make every effort to reduce the threat of catastrophic terrorism. But while the American people can be better protected, they should be under no illusion that the intelligence community can remove all risk. Even if we destroy al Qaeda, other terrorist groups could also mount acts of catastrophic terrorism, including attacks on our information infrastructure and the use of biological agents such as anthrax, chemical nerve agents, and perhaps even nuclear weapons.

Fortunately, there are not hundreds of such organizations but perhaps only a few dozen, which makes the intelligence task feasible. But it is unreasonable to expect 100 percent success. Thus, while intelligence is the first line of defense, other counterterrorism efforts are also important, including prevention by deterrence or interdiction, bioweapons defense, and managing the consequences of a catastrophic terrorist attack whenever and wherever it occurs.

---

### Want to Know More?

Many authors have ruminated on the changing nature of intelligence since the spies came in from the cold. Prominent works include *Reshaping National Intelligence for an Age of Information* (Cambridge: Cambridge University Press, 2001) by Gregory F. Treverton, *Fixing the Spy Machine* (Westport: Praeger, 1999) by Arthur S. Hulnick, *On Intelligence: Spies and Secrecy in the Open World* (Fairfax: AFCEA International Press, 2000) by Robert David Steele, and *Best Truth: Intelligence in the Information Age* (New Haven: Yale University Press, 2000) by Bruce D. Berkowitz and Allan E. Goodman.

Recent articles on the shortcomings of the CIA and proposals for reform include Bobby R. Inman's **"Spying for a Long, Hot War"** (*New York Times,* October 9, 2001), Frederick P. Hitz's **"Not Just a Lack of Intelligence, a Lack of Skills"** (*Washington Post,* October 21, 2001), and Seymour M. Hersh's **"What Went Wrong: The CIA and the Failure of American Intelligence"** (*New Yorker,* October 8, 2001). In **"The Counterterrorist Myth"** (*Atlantic Monthly,* July/August 2001), former CIA operative Reuel Marc Gerecht explains the difficulties of mounting covert operations in Pakistan.

A number of recent books and articles on terrorism also deal with counterterrorism intelligence issues. Notable among these are Philip B. Heymann's *Terrorism and America: A Commonsense Strategy for a Democratic Society* (Cambridge: MIT Press, 1998); Richard A. Falkenrath, Robert D. Newman, and Bradley A. Thayer's *America's Achilles' Heel: Nuclear, Biological, and Chemical Terrorism and Covert Attack* (Cambridge: MIT Press, 1998); Ashton B. Carter, John M. Deutch, and Philip Zelikow's **"Catastrophic Terrorism: Tackling the New Danger"** (*Foreign Affairs,* November/December, 1998); and John Deutch's **"Think Again: Terrorism"** (*Foreign Policy,* Fall 1997).

The U.S.A. **Patriot Act of 2001**, which includes a number of provisions relevant to counterterrorism intelligence, became law on October 26, 2001, and can be found on the Library of Congress's Thomas Legislative Information Web site (Public Law No. 107–56). Likewise, the State Department posts its annual terrorism report, *Patterns of Global Terrorism,* on its Web site.

The discussion of the CIA's origins is derived from an article posted on the CIA's Web site titled **"Salvage and Liquidation: The Creation of the Central Intelligence Group,"** by CIA historian Michael Warner, and from a set of National Archives records posted on the State Department Web site, **"Founding of the National Intelligence Structure: August 1945 Through January 1946."**

- For links to relevant Web sites, as well as a comprehensive index of related *Foreign Policy* articles, access www.foreignpolicy.com.

## REVIEW QUESTIONS

- Can the ideal of United Nations cooperation be reconciled with the United States' (or any nation's) right of self-defense?
- Were the invasions of Afghanistan and Iraq legitimate options in a war being waged against shadowy terrorist movements?
- Are current counterterrorist recommendations adequate for the task of rooting out the new terrorists?
- How effective has intelligence been in the war on terrorism? How effective can it ever be?
- What are the policy criteria for adopting hardline or other counterterrorist measures?

The following books and articles are suggested for further information about counterterrorist options in the new era:

## Books

Baer, Robert. *See No Evil: The True Story of a Ground Soldier in the CIA's War on Terrorism.* New York: Crown, 2002.

Katz, Samuel M. *The Hunt for the Engineer: How Israeli Agents Tracked the Hamas Master Bomber.* New York: Fromm International, 2001.

Lesser, Ian O., Bruce Hoffman, John Arquilla, David Ronfeldt, and Michele Zanini. *Countering the New Terrorism.* Santa Monica, CA: RAND, 1999.

## Articles

Luft, Gal. "The Logic of Israel's Targeted Killing." *Middle East Quarterly.* 10:1 (Winter 2003).

Maas, Peter. "Dirty War: How America's Friends Really Fight Terrorism." *The New Republic.* (November 11, 2002).

Walt, Stephen M. "Beyond Bin Laden: Reshaping U.S. Foreign Policy." *International Security.* 26:3 (Winter 2001/2002).

# 10

## Forging Alliances in the New Era

The United States and other nations responded to the events of September 11, 2001 with a declared "war on terrorism." This war was to be waged in a manner unlike other wars–often covertly, usually using elite forces, and in conjunction with civilian security forces. These small scale and frequently secret measures were intended to harden targets and disrupt potentially pre-positioned cells. On a larger scale, the invasions and subsequent occupations of Afghanistan and Iraq were launched with the avowed purpose of disrupting and eliminating terrorist networks and the state sponsors of those networks. The attempts to neutralize alleged state sponsorship tested the cohesion of the anti-terrorist alliance. In particular, the invasion of Iraq created significant fissures in a previously collegial Western alliance. Outside of the West, the war in Iraq caused major domestic problems for governments allied with the West in the war on terrorism. Consequently, the problem of building and sustaining anti-terrorist alliances became a central issue in the new era.

The articles in this chapter discuss debates and other considerations arising out of the war on terrorism. We return to the question of unipolarity and hegemony in Steve Smith's "The End of the Unipolar Moment? September 11 and the Future of World Order." In this analysis, written prior to the invasion of Iraq, Smith discusses the ramifications which the American shift away from multipolarity toward unipolarity are likely to have for U.S. power and the future of world politics. He warns that unipolarity may have grave implications for the U.S. in the long term. Paul Dibb assesses the needed elements for constructing counterterrorist cooperative regimes in "The Future of International Coalitions: How Useful? How Manageable?" Factors affecting the quality and cohesion of international alliances are identified, as are the risks and benefits of participating in these alliances. An important discussion from the perspective of the Muslim world is presented by Azar Nafisi in "They the People: Our Abandoned Muslim Allies." A critical challenge is made to academic and political conventional wisdom in this essay.

# The End of the Unipolar Moment? September 11 and the Future of World Order

Steve Smith
*University of Wales, Aberystwyth*

In this article I want to look at the impact of the events of September 11 on the structure of the international political system. Initially, like many others, I thought that the main effect would be to bring to an end a period in international relations known as the unipolar moment, replacing it with a more multilateral, though not multipolar, world order. But six months after the events it seems to be becoming increasingly clear that the world order likely to emerge will be one of both increased U.S. power and increased U.S. unilateralism; this carries with it the risk of an unconstrained superpower pursuing foreign policy for narrowly defined domestic interests, and of the further development of a regressive world order unsympathetic to calls for an end to inequality. This world order is likely to be unable to bring to an end many of the key conflicts in world politics, notably the dispute between Israel and the Palestinians: indeed, this order seems set to exacerbate existing tensions, and, by virtue of a probable attempt to overthrow Saddam Hussein, to create an entire set of political and economic problems for the West generally, but also, paradoxically, for the U.S. itself.

## The Unipolarity Thesis

I want first to say something about the debates over the form of world order that replaced the Cold War bipolar structure. The end of the Cold War brought to an end a period of international bipolarity and since then academics, journalists and policy-makers have tried to work out exactly what kind of power structure would replace it. There were two main views: first that the United States would withdraw from international entanglements since there was no longer any great enemy, no global cause, to structure U.S. foreign policy, nor any clear reason for the U.S. to continue to spend so much money acting as world policeman. Add to this the changing nature of U.S. internal politics, and specifically the shifts within its ethnic mix, and one clear possibility was for the U.S. to reduce its commitments to its old alliances, notably towards Europe where the development of the European Union implied to some the possibility of a united European defence and foreign policy effort that did not require U.S. involvement. The second, and opposite, view was that the U.S. would be able to influence world politics like never before: it was a unipolar moment, in which the U.S. was the world's only remaining superpower. According to this view, no one power or group of powers could challenge U.S. hegemony for the foreseeable future. And, of course, there were those who saw some kind of self-interested combination of these two positions being the likely outcome, with the U.S. pulling back from international commitments that were not seen as central to its interests while aggressively pursuing other interests through its overwhelming economic, political, cultural and military power.

Within the academic debate, one of the first main statements was by Charles Krauthammer, in his 1991 article 'The Unipolar Moment.'[1] Krauthammer argued that bipolarity was not being replaced by multipolarity but by unipolarity: 'The most striking feature of the post-Cold War world is its unipolarity. No doubt, multipolarity will come in time . . . But we are not there yet, nor will we be for decades. Now is the unipolar moment.'[2] In language that would not seem out of place from current U.S. leaders, Krauthammer outlined how the U.S. should act in the unipolar moment:

> . . . there is no alternative to confronting, deterring and, if necessary, disarming states that brandish and use weapons of mass destruction. And there is no one to do that but the United States, backed by as many allies as will join the endeavor . . . Our best hope . . . is in American strength and will— the strength and will to lead a unipolar world,

unashamedly laying down the rules of world order and being prepared to enforce them.[3]

Within two years the U.S. Defense Department had developed a strategy to prevent any rival state from threatening the position of the U.S. as the undisputed sole superpower. According to a leaked version:

> Our first objective is to prevent the re-emergence of a new rival, either on the territory of the former Soviet Union or elsewhere, that poses a threat . . . Our strategy must now refocus on pre-cluding the emergence of any potential future global competitor.[4]

This claim that there was a unipolar moment led to spirited debate in the literature over whether this was a durable position for the U.S. and whether unipolarity was itself war-prone. Samuel Huntington argued that U.S. unipolarity was good for the world for two reasons: first the U.S. was the only power able to act as the world's cop—'If the United States is unable to maintain security in the world's trouble spots, no other single country or combination of countries is likely to provide a substitute.'[5] Second, the U.S. was the only power in the world whose identity was defined by a set of universal political and economic values. Taking the two together:

> A world without U.S. primacy will be a world with more violence and disorder and less democracy and economic growth than a world where the United States continues to have more influence than any other country in shaping global affairs.[6]

As to whether unipolarity was durable, William Wohlforth has argued that U.S. dominance is durable because no other state is likely to be able to challenge U.S. power in any of the main dimensions for several decades, and the likely challengers (Russia, Germany, China and Japan) can only do so in a context that will be likely to set off local or regional counterbalancing behaviour by others.[7] By way of contrast, Christopher Layne argued that unipolarity is merely a geo-political interlude, and that it will give way to multipolarity sometime between 2000 and 2010 as a result of systemic imperatives

to create balancers to U.S. dominance. Other great powers would seek to balance U.S. power and this would lead to a new multipolarity.[8]

The events of September 11, and their aftermath, seem to support those who claim that U.S. unipolarity is durable. This is because the U.S. has emerged stronger, and will thus be more in a position to influence world events. In part this is because the U.S. has already considerably increased its military and intelligence expenditure, but it also reflects the ability of the U.S. to impose leadership on allies under the theme of a war on terrorism. In that sense, fighting terrorism becomes the new 'grand cause' underlying U.S. foreign policy, and such a cause assists in the creation and unification of alliances. In other words the U.S. will be in a stronger position to provide leadership in world politics either by getting together a group of allies, or, more likely, by having the sheer military power, and will, to go it alone. The public reaction in the U.S. to the events of September 11 seems likely to license a very unilateral foreign policy, which roughly translates as saying to U.S. allies that they can join with the U.S. on U.S. terms, or leave the U.S. to act alone. This has been made plain by the statements of Rumsfeld, Wolfowitz and Perle, each of whom has made it clear that the U.S. will act as it sees fit, with or without the support of its allies.

## BARBER, FUKUYAMA, AND HUNTINGTON

As well as these debates about unipolarity, there was also a set of extremely influential articles and books about the more general question of the emerging world order, chief amongst them Samuel Huntington's *The Clash of Civilizations and the Remaking of World Order* (1996), Benjamin Barber's *Jihad vs McWorld* (1996) and Francis Fukuyama's *The End of History and the Last Man* (1992).[9] Of the three views, the one that has, since September 11, received the most attention is Huntington's notion of the clash of civilizations, and at first it seems to have much to recommend it, certainly over Fukuyama's more optimistic notion of the end of history, and a future world order dominated by a growing liberal zone of peace. Fukuyama seems to have been far too ethnocentric when he asked whether 'it makes sense for us once again to speak of a coherent and directional History of mankind that will eventually lead the greater part of humanity to liberal democracy? The answer I arrive at is yes.'[10] The motivations of those involved in the terrorist attacks on September 11 could hardly have been further from this liberal ideal; and Fukuyama's reliance on the twin mechanisms of economic development and the struggle for personal recognition to push the world towards liberalism seems irrelevant to the concerns not just of those involved in the attacks but in a far more extensive part of humanity which opposed military action against Afghanistan, and is, as I write, currently opposing Israeli action in Palestine and the prospect of a US-led overthrow of Saddam Hussein. Adherents of these views are not part of the liberal project; indeed, it is precisely this project that they oppose, not least because of the kinds of Islamic regimes that liberalism promotes and supports. In this light, attacking bin Laden was exactly what he wanted since it would open up exactly this split between modernizing and traditional Islam, thereby radicalizing Muslim opinion and (hopefully in his view) leading to the overthrow of pro-Western, pro-modernizing Islamic regimes. No amount of economic development and no amount of personal recognition under liberalism can alter this view since it is liberalism and modernization themselves that are the enemies.

Huntington's argument has been referred to constantly since September 11, and of course there is a sort of common-sense reason for this. At first sight the current crisis can seem as if it is one between civilizations, and of course in his book Huntington discussed at length the conflict between the Western and Muslim worlds as being one of the main fault lines for future war. Huntington sees two possible future world orders. The first is a major inter-civilizational war 'most likely involving Muslims on one side and non-Muslims on the other';[11] the second, which he prefers, is for the U.S. (and other core civilizational states) to abstain from involvement in conflicts in other civilizations, and to negotiate amongst each other so as to contain wars at the fault lines between civilizations. My overwhelming worry about Huntington's argument follows from my view that the social

world is something that we constitute by our theories, and that Huntington's language is self-fulfilling since the analysis creates exactly the kinds of identities and ultimately the very foreign policy mindsets that bring such world orders into existence. Thankfully, neither of Huntington's alternatives seems to have guided U.S. policy since September 11. On the one hand, the U.S. has found out that it is unavoidably involved in the Muslim world, and that staying out of the politics of faraway places is not an option. On the other hand, the Bush administration has said loudly and repeatedly that this is not a clash between the West and Islam, that it is not a clash of civilizations; indeed, the main weakness in Huntington's thesis is that neither states nor civilizations are anything like as united and monolithic as his account logically requires. The current conflict pits members of the same civilization against one another, in both the Muslim and the non-Muslim worlds. Having said which, the clash of civilizations seems to be exactly how Osama bin Laden defines the current conflict.

Barber's portrayal of the future world order seems most in accord with the world order that is most likely to emerge from the current crisis. Barber sees a world in which two forms of international order coexist: the first 'rooted in race holds out the grim prospect of a retribalization of large swaths of humankind . . . in which culture is pitted against culture . . . a Jihad . . . against modernity itself.' The second is 'a busy portrait of onrushing economic, technological, and ecological forces that demand integration and uniformity . . . one McWorld tied together by communications, information, entertainment, and commerce.'[12] It is exactly this duality that has characterized the response to the events of September 11. Take as one example the question of proving bin Laden's guilt: most Western observers believe that the evidence leads to bin Laden and to al-Qaeda, yet large parts of the world's populations do not accept the evidence, and, critically, there may be no information that would lead them to accept his guilt. Thus, just as there are clear globalizing trends in world politics and economics, so there remain (and may even be strengthening) sets of cultural lenses that undermine and literally prevent the emergence of common global norms.

## US Foreign Policy After September 11: Multilateralist or Unilateralist?

For the first month or so after September 11, it seemed to many (myself included) that the United States had abruptly ended its brief experiment with unilateralism. For the initial eight months of the new Bush administration observers in many parts of the world worried that the U.S. was simply not interested in developing multilateral responses to world problems, and instead seemed to be acting alone. The most high-profile example of this was the U.S. withdrawal from the Kyoto agreement, but there were also the following actions: the administration rejected the protocol on inspection for the Biological Weapons Convention; diluted a UN agreement to limit small arms trade; stated that it would not ratify the treaty on an international criminal court; refused to ratify the Comprehensive Test Ban Treaty; and restated its opposition to a ban on landmines.

After September 11, the U.S. initially spent considerable time building exactly the kind of multilateral response that it had previously eschewed. The terrorist attacks brought home in the most awful way the fact that, although the U.S. may not be interested in what happens in faraway places, those faraway places are interested in it. Some thought that this indicated that the future world order would be marked by a far more active U.S. foreign policy than seemed likely on September 10. Not only that, but the clear interconnectedness between the security of citizens in the U.S. and events in areas such as the Middle East seemed to imply that the U.S. was more likely to see a need to try and solve some of the most intractable problems in the world. For many observers, then, the events of September 11 could have led to a change in the Bush administration's policy towards unilateralism, and the Israeli—Palestinian dispute appeared to be the acid indicator of the extent of this change. In early October, U.S.—Israeli relations were said to be at their lowest ebb for many years, as the U.S. appeared willing to push the Israeli government towards compromise with the Palestinian leadership.

However, that optimism has now vanished totally. In both the specific-issue area of the Middle East and the more general orientation of U.S. foreign policy, there has been a significant return to unilateralism, and a persistent unwillingness to see the connections between the 'war on terrorism,' against first al-Qaeda and then the 'axis of evil,' and events in the Middle East. Thus Bush has given his tacit approval to the Sharon administration's expansion of settlements and war against the Palestinians, thereby making it far more difficult for Arab regimes in the region to support his proposals for the expansion of the 'war on terrorism' to countries such as Iraq. This widening of the 'war on terrorism' to include an attack on Iraq threatens to undermine any prospects for a settlement in the Israeli—Palestinian dispute, and could also have significant effects on the world economy, if, as seems probable, oil prices rise in the lead up and duration of a war. Such a widening of the 'war' would also see a significant split emerging between most members of the European Union and the Bush administration. In these respects unilateralism seems to be the dominant strain in the U.S. leadership, despite Tony Blair's attempts to present a picture of consultation and multilateralism.

More generally, the U.S. has, since September 11, embarked on a series of measures that seem decidedly unilateralist. The most obvious examples are: first, the decision of the administration to withdraw from the ABM Treaty, which has been greeted with almost universal condemnation since withdrawal, seems to indicate a significant change of heart about the possibility of using nuclear weapons, possibly even using them first; second, the leak in March 2002 of the new nuclear posture review, which both adds countries (Iran, Iraq, North Korea, Syria and Libya) to the list of potential nuclear targets and also proposes the development of 'limited' nuclear weapons for use against deep, hardened targets;[13] third, the imposition of tariffs as high as 30 percent on steel imports from Europe and Asia, which flew in the face of Bush's stated commitment to free trade and which was denounced by the U.S. Treasury Secretary; fourth, the 'axis of evil' segment of the President's 2002 State of the Union Address, which suddenly, and to the evident surprise of even close U.S. allies, linked Iran, Iraq and North Korea to the 'war on terrorism' that followed the events of September 11, and which struck many allies as perversely ill-timed given the Israeli crackdown on Palestinians in the West Bank; fifth, there has been the massive increase in the proposed U.S. defence budget. This would boost military spending by more than 14 percent to $379 billion, the largest percentage increase for 20 years; by 2008 the U.S. defence budget would increase by a total of $120 billion, taking it to the same peak, taking into account inflation, as the Reagan administration spent in 1985; finally, there is the prospect of a war against Iraq, or, as Kenneth Pollack puts it in the title of a recent article, 'Next Stop Baghdad?'[14] Such an action would be bitterly opposed by nearly all European and Middle Eastern countries, officially if not unofficially, and would undermine any coalition against terrorism. Added to all of these is the rise of racial profiling in U.S. immigration procedures, and a significant pattern of harassment against Muslims in the U.S.[15]

## THE IMPLICATIONS OF SEPTEMBER 11 FOR WORLD ORDER

What, then, are likely to be the main implications of the events of September 11 for future world order regardless of whether it is unipolar or multipolar? There are nine main ones; the first is that states are no longer, if they ever were, the key actors in major international arenas. al-Qaeda is a very different type of organization to the state, both in its identity and in its structure. Its structure is the antithesis of the hierarchical modern state, and its identity is correspondingly amorphous. International terrorism does not map onto state structures, it works in the spaces between them. Fundamentally, globalization results in a world in which many of the most important political actions take place between non-state actors in arenas as diverse as the internet, banking, global civil society and international terrorism.

Second is the realization that actors in contemporary world politics do not follow some kind of overarching logic, be it of security, military, political or economic. This shatters the assumptions of the main theories of international relations, and makes identity, which has been traditionally assumed to follow from interests, of primary analytical significance.

Third, the future world order will be marked by asymmetrical conflict in which the weapons of the powerful can no longer defeat the weapons of the weak. In this sense power is less fungible than ever, as the images of million-dollar missiles destroying piles of rubble whilst creating thousands of future martyrs demonstrates.

Fourth, more than ever, this is a time of virtual war, a war in which the propaganda battle is as, if not more, important than the military campaign. Humanitarian considerations will assume considerable, maybe literally decisive, importance, and can thus snatch political defeat out of the jaws of military victory.

Fifth, military force is becoming less and less easily related to political effects. Achieving military objectives is one thing, but achieving political goals is much more difficult, especially when wars such as the present one rely on coalitions. Portraying the conflict as one between good and evil may sound persuasive, but it cannot serve as the glue to hold together the kind of coalition necessary to wage a sustained conflict.

Sixth, it becomes more and more difficult to answer the question of what is victory. Compared to conflicts such as the Vietnam war, the Falklands war, the Gulf conflict and Kosovo, victory is a much more nebulous concept in the current conflict. Was victory achieved when the Taleban were overthrown, and a new government installed in their place, or would victory require a much longer-term project to bring stability to the country through economic regeneration? Is victory now defined as capturing bin Laden? Killing him? Destroying al-Qaeda? (What would that entail, and how would we conceivably know that we had achieved this even a few years after the end of the military conflict?) Or is victory the defeat of terrorism (which sorts qualify?) and the replacement of the regimes of the countries comprising the 'axis of evil'? Critically, the trade offs between these goals and likely effects in the rest of the world are almost impossible to estimate. Put most simply, each and every one of these goals could be achieved, and yet the coalition could see a humanitarian tragedy in Afghanistan, a fundamentalist revolution in

Pakistan resulting in radical Islamic hands on its nuclear weapons, the end of hope for any negotiated settlement in Israel/Palestine, the overthrow of pro-western regimes in the Middle East, as well as the creation of a new generation of future suicide bombers.

Seventh, one of the most basic problems will be how the West negotiates with opponents who hold such different views of the world. For the Taleban the conflict is not about narrowly defined foreign policy interests that can be traded off against other policy goals; rather their aim is to reverse modernization and to impose a form of society diametrically opposed to western notions. How do you negotiate with someone who is not interested in financial aid, in most favoured nation status, or in development, and instead wants to destroy exactly your kind of society?

The eighth implication is that the events of September 11 shatter the key assumption of many proponents of globalization that the conveyor belt of economic development and the spread of liberal democracy were in some way inevitable, irreversible and universal. They are not, and notions of a direction, even a teleology, to history are simply wrong.

Finally, the current conflict shows all too clearly the dangers of seeing the world in terms of stark alternatives, such as those represented by notions of good versus evil and the clash of civilizations. Such dichotomies create the kind of oppositional thinking that will make coalition building difficult, especially in those parts of the world where 'other civilizations' dominate.

## The Future of U.S. Foreign Policy

The main political problem facing U.S. leaders is how to steer a path between these features of the current and future world order. The danger is that the impulse to eradicate terrorism, and thereby make the U.S. safer from attack, could run counter to the need for the U.S. to develop multinational coalitions. Specifically, if the views expressed by Donald Rumsfeld concerning widening the war to deal with other terrorist groups (for example in Iraq) win the day, then it is impossible to think of the coalition holding together. For many key members of the Bush administration, the U.S. does not need any coalition to win the war against terrorism, and many would prefer the U.S. to act alone than be held back by the requirement to hold a coalition together. In this sense the military dimension of world order may be far easier for the U.S. to dominate than the political one. If it transpires that the war against terrorism either leads to significant civilian casualties and/or is extended to countries other than Afghanistan then it is difficult to see any coalition surviving. On current indications, Blair will continue to stand shoulder to shoulder with the Bush administration, but few other European leaders, let alone leaders of U.S. allies in the Middle East, will be openly supportive of any widening of the conflict to countries such as Iraq. A related challenge is for the U.S. to present the current war as one against specific terrorist groups and their supporters, and to do all it can to prevent it being characterized as a war against Islam, which could usher in exactly the kind of clash of civilizations that bin Laden explicitly said he wanted in his video released on the day the attacks commenced. Failure on either of these two grounds would significantly undermine U.S. security and would lead to the construction of a world order that would make the achievement of U.S. foreign policy goals more difficult.

In this emerging world order, the U.S. will be the leading world power, but, as Joe Nye has recently noted, assessing U.S. power is complex.[16] On the one hand, it is the only superpower, and no other state, or even group of states, can match its military power: 'the United States is the only country with both nuclear weapons and conventional forces with global reach. American military expenditures are greater than those of the next eight countries combined.'[17] In this sense the U.S. presides over a unipolar world order. But this power may turn out to be less useful than military power in earlier eras. This is because politically and economically the world is not unipolar. Economically, the U.S. has 31 percent of world product, equalling the total of the next four countries (Japan, Germany, the UK and France), but this dominance is to a considerable extent offset by the extent of integration by the EU countries, which results in a world economic order in which the U.S. has to deal with the EU as a roughly equal partner. Politically, the U.S. faces an emerging world order in which there are increasing challenges to the dominance of its model of liberal democracy, and there are large areas of the world in which the 'American way' is precisely what is rejected. Put simply, if the world order is unipolar, then this has to coexist with much more multipolar economic and political world orders. This creates a friction between U.S. military might and its ability to impose its political will. Nowhere is this juxtaposition clearer than in the Middle East, where the U.S. has the military power to impose settlements but does not have the political will or desire to impose them on all conflicts and on all proponents of terrorism and aggression.

Nye likens the current structure of world power to a three-dimensional chessboard.[18] On the top, military, board the world remains unipolar, but on the second, economic, chessboard 'power is multi-polar, with the United States, Europe and Japan representing two-thirds of world product, and with China's dramatic growth likely to make it the fourth big player. On this economic board, the United States is not a hegemon.'[19] The third chessboard relates to 'transnational relations that cross borders outside government control . . . On this [board] power is widely dispersed, and it makes no sense to speak of uni-polarity, multi-polarity or hegemony.'[20] Crucially, and in contrast to many American views of U.S. power, Nye notes that:

> Those who recommend a hegemonic American foreign policy based on . . . traditional descriptions of American power are relying on woefully inadequate analysis. When you are in a three-dimensional game, you will lose if you focus only on the top board and fail to notice the other boards and the connections among them.[21]

As he has argued in his recent book *The Paradox of American Power: Why the World's Only Superpower Can't Go It Alone,*[22] the connections between these three levels means that, if the U.S. pursues a self-interested unilateralist foreign policy, based on its military power, then it will contribute to its own decline by undermining its ability to influence world events. Nye argues persuasively that the U.S. needs to work with its allies to create legal frameworks and alliances so as to create a world order in which other states will be more willing to work with, rather than against, U.S. power. This implies that the U.S. must give up some freedom of manoeuvre in order to develop more cooperative and predictable relations with other states. But, even then he notes that transnational relations will remain outside the control of the U.S., or any other state for that matter.

In the contemporary world order, what matters are not so much the 'old' military and economic tools of foreign policy, but the growing influence of what Nye has termed 'soft power.' He originally coined this term in the late 1980s to characterize the situation at the end of the Cold War, with the thought, encapsulated in the title of his 1990 book, that U.S. dominance in the area of soft power meant that the U.S. was *Bound to Lead.*[23] In this book he opposed the argument of the theorists of U.S. decline and instead argued that the U.S. dominated in terms of soft as well as hard (traditional, military) power and that this dominance was sufficient to ensure that the U.S. would continue to be the leading world power regardless of changes in the more traditional measures of state power. This analysis has stood the test of time, and so, in 2002, Nye continues to argue that U.S. soft power, defined as the ability 'to get others to want what you want,' continues to reinforce the U.S.'s position as the world's most powerful state: 'American popular culture has a global reach . . . there is no escaping the influence of Hollywood, CNN and the Internet.'[24] This soft power, centred on ideology and cultural attraction, is particularly important in dealing with the issues raised by the transnational chessboard. For Nye, the key task for U.S. foreign policy is how to make 'soft' and 'hard' power reinforce each other and ensure that U.S. 'hard' power does not undermine U.S. 'soft' power. This could occur if the U.S. acted unilaterally and in an overbearing way, thereby reducing the appeal to others of its way of life and ideology.

This analysis implies that the U.S. needs to steer a careful path between exercising its power and taking into account the views of its partners. The danger is that the U.S. will act increasingly unilaterally, whereas in fact this is unlikely to strengthen the U.S.'s position in the long run.

This is because, first, as Nye puts it, 'military power alone cannot produce the outcomes Americans want'[25]; second, acting alone cannot achieve all U.S. international goals. Thus the success of the 'war on terrorism' will depend far more on diplomatic negotiations to develop cooperation than it will on any military victories. Indeed, the military victories could even undermine the attempts by the U.S. to build a political and diplomatic coalition against al-Qaeda, which after all has cells in some 50 countries, thus Nye calls for a policy of engagement with other countries in order to achieve long-term U.S. interests by legitimizing and making more acceptable U.S. power. This policy will require the U.S. to define its national interest in a broader way than currently favoured by sizeable sections of the Bush administration and by the unilateralists. If such a policy of engagement was followed then the U.S. could continue to be the leading world power for the medium-term future. As Mick Cox argues, at the start of the new century the U.S. is in fact in a stronger international position than it was even after the Second World War, is essential to international order and is in a position to continue that dominance. As he puts it:

> ... there is little to indicate that things will change over the long term, so long as the United States exercises its hegemony in a relatively benign way, and where the benefits of cooperation within an American-led world system continue to make it an attractive option for competitors and allies alike.[26]

Fox Cox, as for Nye, the U.S. can continue to be the leading world power for the current century, but both persuasively argue that the U.S. can only achieve this by acting multilaterally. As Cox argues:

> Hegemony ... requires the U.S. to listen to its allies. Indeed, historically it has been at its most effective when it has done precisely that. The process may be noisy, tedious, and slow. In the end, though, it is likely to lead to more positive outcomes than unilateral actions emanating from what many non-Americans—rightly to wrongly— already perceive to be an overly powerful giant always seeking to get its own way.[27]

The problem of course is that these wise words may not prevail. There remain very powerful forces promoting a unilateral U.S. foreign policy, often strangely allied to a form of isolationism, as if the world didn't really exist except where it significantly affected immediate U.S. interests. In his review of U.S. strategy after September 11, Stephen Walt notes four lessons for U.S. foreign policy in its aftermath. These are: 1) U.S. foreign policy is not cost free; 2) the U.S. is less popular than it thinks; 3) failed states are a national security problem; and 4) the U.S. cannot go it alone.[28] Walt thinks that the jury is still out on the last of these issues, and in many ways this is the single most important question concerning U.S. foreign policy. As we have seen above, the U.S. has engaged in a series of unilateral foreign policy acts and, as the dust settles, it looks as if the multilateralism in the immediate aftermath of September 11 was indeed only an interlude. As of this writing (April 2002) the unilateralists in the Bush administration seem to have won out and, despite hope based on some readings of current strategy towards Israel, my view is that this president is going to pursue unilateralist, mainly military, policies for the remainder of his time in office. As I have argued above, this concerns me greatly since it seems likely to undermine long-term U.S. interests and sustain a world order that is very much in the interests of the few. As Walt puts it: 'If the United States wants to make its position of primacy more palatable to others, in short, it will have to use its wealth and power in ways that serve the interests of others as well as its own.'[29]

## CONCLUSION

All of this causes me to reflect on the literature of my academic specialization, International Relations. I have spent a lot of the last 20 years working on the nature of agency and social action, both in its philosophy of social science context, and in terms of its policy implications. Contrary to the dominant tendency in the U.S. in International Relations, which remains committed to treating international (and all social) structures in such a way as to downplay agency, I remain convinced of the role of human agency.

I think the events since September 11 reaffirm the importance of human agency as illustrated by the almost constant round of diplomatic activity. States are not actors, humans are; interests clearly influence behaviour but they have to be mediated through identity; and discourse and language are crucially important in constructing identity and framing interests. That is why the future of world order depends on the choices our leaders make and what values we think they should promote. World orders always reflect dominant values, are always partial and may well hinder the search for global justice and peace. They are not given, they are not natural—they reflect our conscious or unconscious choices. That is how domestic and international debates interact, and that is why an informed, questioning and diverse civil society is essential to the debate now more than ever.

## NOTES

1. Charles Krauthammer (1991) 'The Unipolar Moment,' *Foreign Affairs* 70(1): 23–33.

2. Krauthammer (see note 1), pp. 23–24.

3. Krauthammer (see note 1), pp. 32–3.

4. 'Excerpts from Pentagon's Plan: "Prevent the Re-emergence of a New Rival"', *New York Times,* 8 March 1992, p. 14.

5. Samuel Huntington (1993) 'Why International Primacy Matters,' *International Security* 17(4): 82.

6. Huntington (see note 5), p. 83.

7. William Wohlforth (1999) 'The Stability of a Unipolar World,' *International Security* 24(1): 5–41.

8. Christopher Layne (1993) 'The Unipolar Illusion: Why New Great Powers Will Rise,' *International Security* 17(4): 5–51.

9. Samuel Huntington (1996) *The Clash of Civilizations and the Remaking of World Order.* New York: Simon and Schuster; Benjamin Barber (1996) *Jihad vs McWorld: How Globalism and Tribalism are Reshaping the World.* New York: Ballantine Books; Francis Fukuyama (1992) *The End of History and the Last Man.* New York: Free Press.

10. Fukuyama (see note 9), p. xii.

11. Huntington (see note 9), p. 312.

12. Barber, (see note 9), p. 4.

13. See 'What's New?,' *The Economist,* 16 March 2002, p. 35.

14. Kenneth Pollack (2002) 'Next Stop Baghdad?,' *Foreign Affairs* 81(2): 32–47.

15. See George Monbiot (2002) 'War on the Third World,' *The Guardian,* 5 March, p. 15.

16. Joseph Nye (2002) 'The New Rome Meets the New Barbarians,' *The Economist,* 23 March, pp. 23–5.

17. Nye (see note 16), p. 23.

18. Nye (see note 16), p. 24.

19. Nye (see note 16), p. 24.

20. Nye (see note 16), p. 24.

21. Nye (see note 16), p. 24.

22. Joseph Nye (2002) *The Paradox of American Power: Why the World's only Superpower Can't Go It Alone.* New York: Oxford University Press.

23. Joseph Nye (1990) *Bound to Lead: The Changing Nature of American Power.* New York: Basic Books.

24. Nye (see note 16), p. 25.

25. Nye (see note 16), p. 24.

26. Michael Cox (2002) 'September 11th and U.S. Hegemony—Or Will the 21st Century Be American Too?,' *International Studies Perspectives* 3(1): 67.

27. Cox (see note 26), p. 67.

28. Stephen Walt (2001) 'Beyond Bin Laden: Reshaping U.S. Foreign Policy,' *International Security* 26(3): 58–63.

29. Walt (see note 28), p. 76.

---

## The Future of International Coalitions: How Useful? How Manageable?

### Paul Dibb

The most dramatic political result of the September 11 terrorist attacks on the United States has been the construction of a global coalition against terrorism. The diversity of this coalition is unprecedented. It includes the United States' NATO allies, Japan, and

Australia. It also involves such unexpected partners as China and Russia, as well as Pakistan and India. Major international organizations, specifically the United Nations and the leaders of the Asia-Pacific Economic Cooperation forum, have condemned the terrorist attacks, as has the Conference of the Islamic Organization.

For the first time in its 52-year history, NATO has invoked Article 5, under which an attack on one alliance member is considered an attack on all members. Also for the first time, the Australian government has invoked Article 4 of the 1951 ANZUS Treaty (a security treaty among Australia, New Zealand, and the United States) in order to meet this common danger. Great Britain, Canada, and Australia committed military forces to the coalition's operations against Osama bin Laden's terrorist network and the Taliban regime. France, Germany, and Italy have indicated that they may contribute military support personnel to a peace stabilization force in Afghanistan, as have several Muslim countries. Japan, in a major departure from its past reluctance to send military units overseas, has deployed naval warships in a support role.

This coalition is remarkable not only because of the large number of countries involved from all around the world, but also the apparent recognition that the fight against terrorism will be a prolonged one—one that will involve diplomatic pressure and financial sanctions, as well as military force. Never in world history have so many countries combined together against a common threat in this manner.

The war against terrorism will be unprecedented as it spreads across a wide range of countries, not only in the Middle East. It will require patience and close coordination. Victories will not be readily apparent in the traditional sense of battlefield successes. As President George W. Bush has said, the collective efforts of the coalition will require "the patient accumulation of successes." Even bin Laden's death will not be the end of the matter by any means. In his book about bin Laden, Yossef Bodansky observes, "Ultimately the quintessence of bin Laden's threat is his being a cog, albeit an important one, in a large system that will outlast his own demise. . . ."[1]

Can this unprecedented coalition against terrorism hang together under such difficult circumstances? A coalition, by definition, is a temporary combination of parties that retain distinctive principles. Already, views have differed over the bombing campaign in Afghanistan. Opinions vary—not least within the United States itself—about whether the war should extend to Iraq. The installation of a new regime in Kabul to replace the Taliban is a step fraught with danger, as is the wooing of the military regime in Islamic Pakistan. Although the coalition members do share a common fear of terrorism, the fact remains that only the United States has suffered a severe terrorist attack. This possibility, and the risk that the war may widen, will put intense pressure on the coalition.

The events that led to the brokering of the coalition must be examined, as well as the performance of the coalition's military, diplomatic, and financial coordination. Finally, what are the risks for the future of the coalition, especially if the war widens? What are the limits of the international coalition against terrorism?

## A SEMINAL EVENT?

The assertion that the events of September 11 initiated a fundamentally new era in world politics has become commonplace. The spectacular building of the coalition against terrorism is cited as evidence, as is the almost universal condemnation of the terrorist attacks. On September 12, the prominent French newspaper *Le Monde* proclaimed, "We are all Americans now." Attendees at the International Institute for Strategic Studies' annual conference, held in Geneva, coincidentally the day after the attacks, came to the conclusion that the world had passed through a defining moment. A war on terrorism had to be waged, a broad coalition needed to be established for this purpose, and the war would have to be conducted with both diplomatic and military means. The will to fight this war would need to be sustained over a very long haul, and risks would have to be taken to ensure a chance for success. Building a coalition would not be easy and would involve unprecedented cooperation.

Conference attendees also believed that, if the United States fails in its task of freeing the world from the scourge of terrorism, the concept of world order would be relegated to the realm of imaginative literature. The task for the United States, as the custodial power in the international system, is immense. The United States will have an enormous challenge before it to keep its allies and newfound friends focused on a war that may appear to conform to a purely U.S. agenda. Maintaining a coalition against a virtual and hidden enemy will be difficult. New coalition building that has no institutional base such as NATO is a huge task. The United States will have to work hard to keep just NATO behind the effort; a wider coalition will require an intensity of diplomacy and degree of cooperation with culturally different countries that is without precedent. The coexistence of a broad political coalition and a narrow military one will strain diplomatic support for the overall campaign. Maintaining the strength of the coalition will be difficult when disagreements over other elements of U.S. foreign policy intrude. The coalition has an awesome agenda, offering as much scope for disagreement as for cooperation.

As Avery Goldstein has observed, believing that the terrorist attacks of September 11 so transformed the post-Cold War world that they have heralded the beginning of an age whose only defining feature will be the global struggle against terrorism would be a mistake. For this realignment to occur, the international community would need to present a united front among almost all states and mute their disagreements on less pressing matters.

A second possibility would be to formulate policy based on the belief that September 11 did not fundamentally alter the strategic priorities of the United States. Under this view, the United States must of course take steps to counter pressing terrorist threats but should not allow this necessity to obscure potentially more serious threats to U.S. vital interests. Fundamentally reconfiguring U.S. policy in the wake of September 11 would be seen as a dangerous mistake from this perspective. While fighting terrorism, the United States should not lose sight of the strategic priorities that guided the

Quadrennial Defense Review and that placed a greater emphasis on security challenges in Asia. This perspective would therefore suggest that the United States should recognize that the more serious challenge in coming decades is from a hostile great power, such as China, rather than from nonstate actors who are able to inflict damage but maybe not jeopardize U.S. national survival.[2]

A third possibility, and the one that seems to be shaping the Bush administration's thinking, is to formulate policy based on the belief that the September 11 attacks were neither a historical turning point nor a tragedy of transient significance, but instead a momentous event that has helped clarify national interests long muddied by arcane speculation about the nature of the post-Cold War era.[3] Under this view, the Bush administration's initial attitude toward such issues as multilateralism, the utility of allies, missile defense, and the threat from weapons of mass destruction has now been modified from a unilateralist stance to one that recognizes the need for international cooperation. This change in U.S. posture reflects the seriousness of the terrorist threat it faces and the need to put together an international coalition that can be sustained over a considerable period of time. This effort has involved significant policy trade-offs and adjustments to previous U.S. policy stances with countries such as Pakistan and Russia. The global balance of power remains unchanged, however, leaving the United States in a dominant position. As a result, dismissive unilateralism characterizes its attitude to binding treaties, such as the Anti-Ballistic Missile (ABM) Treaty, and its resistance to multilateral commitments, such as the Biological Weapons Convention.

Robert Zoellick, now the U.S. trade representative, argued at the beginning of 2000 that a modern Republican foreign policy emphasizes building and sustaining coalitions.[4] Until September 11, however, the Bush administration showed precious little interest in this aspect of its foreign policy. Instead, it seemed to be heading down the path of unilateralism. Prominent U.S. commentators, such as William Kristol and Robert Kagan, argued the case for U.S. hegemony. Others, such as Deputy

Secretary of State Richard Armitage, talked about U.S. preeminence as a force for good. Whether these labels were accurate or not, with the collapse of the Soviet Union the United States had certainly lost its clear sense of national purpose, and the U.S. alliance system risked losing what had been its compelling rationale. Lacking a clear enemy, the United States grew confused about whether expanding its costly global engagement was really necessary after the end of the Cold War.[5] Allies, including NATO, Japan, and Australia, sensed a lack of focus and attention in Washington. Russia was treated as if it was unimportant, and China was regarded with hostility. Both India and Pakistan were punished for their nuclear weapons programs.

With the events of September 11, all this has now changed. Constructing the antiterrorism coalition has involved important U.S. policy concessions to Russia, Pakistan, and India, as well as to China to get it on the coalition's side if not actually within it. The general expectation of U.S. allies that the United States would be the one to come to their assistance has been reversed; instead, the NATO and ANZUS alliances have been invoked in defense of the United States. Although the diplomatic aspects of coalition building have been impressive, the countries willing to contribute combat forces have been the usual U.S. allies: Great Britain, Canada, and Australia. Other countries were apparently willing to contribute military forces but were turned away. Unlike the 1991 Persian Gulf War and even the Kosovo conflict, the military coalition against terrorism has been a "shadow coalition," which is particularly disappointing, given the perception in much of the Middle East that the U.S.-led war on terrorism is a Western crusade against Islam.

As the war enters a new phase involving peacekeeping and stabilization operations in Afghanistan, the participation of non-Anglo-Saxon countries is vital. France, Germany, and Italy seem to have committed to these efforts—against some strong domestic political opposition. Other countries that have indicated a commitment include important Muslim countries such as Indonesia, Turkey, Jordan, and Bangladesh.

Leading the coalition effectively requires clear-eyed judgments about priorities, an appreciation of others' interests, constant consultations among partners, and a willingness to compromise on some points but to remain focused on core objectives.[6] So far, the United States has fared well in this regard: in just four weeks, before it decided to use military power, it assembled an impressive diplomatic coalition. The military coalition has been less impressive: the United States, with some assistance from the United Kingdom, has almost completely dominated it. At the time of writing, Australian and Canadian military operations were still very limited, as were those of Germany and France. Washington has found it difficult to manage the military operations in Afghanistan as a true coalition, as distinct from a dominant U.S. military force with subordinate allies expected to do what is demanded of them. Much of this situation was unsurprising, given the need to quickly punish the Taliban for their harboring of bin Laden. The management of this aspect of the coalition, however, will require much more finesse in the future, particularly if the war against terrorism expands.

## THE COALITION: WINNERS AND LOSERS

Some U.S. commentators argue that establishing a broad coalition is "nothing less than an invitation for paralysis."[7] Even the individual members of a coalition of Western governments will insist on having their say before decisions are made. A coalition is never stronger than its weakest link and, so the argument goes, this coalition will consist of many weak links. Walter Laqueur argues that the United States' most effective course of action would have been to retaliate within a day or two after the attacks indiscriminately against any of the governments suspected of aiding international terrorism. He reasons that terrorism is not based on common sense and elementary logic, and neither is effective counterterrorism. This proposal, however, ignores the uniqueness of the strategy of terrorism: it achieves its goal not through its acts but through the response to its acts.

From what we know of bin Laden, the supposition that he actually wanted to provoke indiscriminate strikes by the United States against certain Middle Eastern Muslim countries is fairly made. As argued more than 25 years ago, terrorism is violence used in order to create fear; but it is aimed at creating fear in order that the fear, in turn, will lead somebody else to embark on some quite different program of action that will accomplish whatever it is that the terrorist really desire.[8] Terrorism is an indirect strategy that wins or loses only based on how one responds to it. If one chooses not to respond at all, or else to respond in a way that diverges from the desires of the terrorists, they will fail to achieve their objectives. The important point here is that the choice is yours—and that is the ultimate weakness of terrorism as a strategy.[9] In this context, the U.S. strategy so far seems correct. Despite extreme provocation, it has not lashed out. Its use of force has been both discriminate and proportionate and, contrary to expectations, has resulted in the collapse of the Taliban.

The United States is leading a moral campaign. In World War II, the firm conviction that evil was being fought greatly simplified the Allied effort.[10] The image of a "just war" nourished the Allies' willingness to fight the war to the bitter end. The difference between the war against terrorism and World War II, of course, is that in World War II the Allied powers were all the victims of aggression, simplifying the task of constructing a wartime consensus. Until and unless terrorists attack other Western powers, maintaining the coalition in the longer term will be difficult. The sense of moral outrage, however, has certainly led to the view that this war is just.

Some believe that political solutions must be given priority over military solutions for the global campaign against terrorism to be successful. The only thing that can undercut bin Laden's brand of global terrorism is a sustained political effort to address the issues that have fueled extremism. In this view, priority must be given to finding a sustainable solution to the Israeli-Palestinian conflict and removing the debilitating economic sanctions against Iraq. This line of reasoning holds that "[t]he link that

currently exists between historical grievances, contemporary political injustices, social and economic hardship, closed political opportunity structures, and politicized religion must be broken."[11] Military actions, they argue, are only likely to strengthen these links.

The problem is that this approach to the immediate demands of decisionmaking is unrealistic, particularly when the United States has suffered such a devastating terrorist attack on its homeland. The Israeli-Palestinian conflict can only be resolved in the longer term. Asking the United States to desist from military action and concentrate on the long-term and well-nigh impossible task of solving the underlying grievances in the Middle East is not a practical course in the shorter term. It leads to the entirely unacceptable view of moral equivalence between what bin Laden did and the defects that may or may not exist in U.S. Middle East policy.

Arising out of all of this debate has been a useful clarification of the United States' international policy stance. For much of the last decade—since the end of the Cold War—the United States had become more unpredictable because it lost the focus provided by its enemy for the previous 50 years: the USSR. The end of the Cold War removed a clear and simple rationale for devising foreign policy in Washington. Francois Heisbourg described this development as the great risk of entropy, of growing inconsistency in the construction of U.S. foreign and security policy.[12] His despair that foreign policy and security studies in the United States were no longer given the same priority as they received during the Cold War has been reversed.

The question now is, Can Washington devise a new organizing principle of the international system for the twenty-first century? This principle, however, cannot only be "you are with us or you are with the terrorists." China's rise to power, the continuing risk of war across the Taiwan Straits as well as on the Korean Peninsula, nuclear competition between India and Pakistan, and instability in Russia and parts of the former Soviet Union are all hazards to world peace. They will need Washington's careful attention while it fights the new war against terrorism and avoids, if possible, a wider war in the Middle East.

Problematically, cobbling together the coalition against terrorism has resulted in some risky trade-offs in other key aspects of U.S. national security policy. National security adviser Condoleezza Rice believes that U.S. foreign policy should be firmly grounded in national interests, "not [in] the interests of an illusory international community."[13] Arguably, the United States now needs such an international community. This realization does not deny Rice's view that the United States must focus on being able to meet powerfully and decisively the emergence of any hostile military power in the Asia-Pacific region, the Middle East, the Persian Gulf, and Europe—areas where not only U.S. interests but also those of its key allies are at stake. The war against terrorism, however, will require some short-term tactical adjustments.

For example, both Pakistan and India are winners in this new situation in a way that before would have been inconceivable. Pakistan and India were nuclear pariah states. Now, Pakistan is crucial to U.S. military operations in Afghanistan and to U.S. efforts to pursue bin Laden. India's support has been important as the world's largest democracy and a key Asian power with a large Muslim population. As a result, the sanctions applied against Pakistan and India because of their nuclear weapons programs have been lifted, and Washington's diplomatic focus on both of these countries has become much more intense. The question becomes, Can the United States use its new-found leverage with India and Pakistan to broker a resolution to their dangerous military confrontation in Kashmir?

Russia too is a winner. Its relations with the United States have improved dramatically. During President Vladimir Putin's visit to the United States in November 2001, Bush announced a unilateral reduction in U.S. strategic nuclear forces from about 6,000 warheads to 2,200 or less. Russia facilitated U.S. access to military bases in Central Asia. In return, the Russians have made plain their regard for the Chechnyans as terrorists and their belief in "a right to expect that double standards will not be applied."[14] A decade after the end of the Cold War, Russia finally feels that the United States

is treating it as a friend and important power, if not a global power, once again.

Japan has improved its status as a U.S. ally. Its historic decision to deploy naval ships to the Indian Ocean in support of the war against terrorism should not be underestimated. In the 1991 Gulf War, Japan incurred U.S. displeasure because of its reluctance to contribute military forces (minesweepers) until after the war had finished. Its contribution this time has involved considerable domestic debate. The Japanese now seem willing to reinterpret the peace constitution that was imposed on them in 1947. In October 2001, the Japanese Diet passed an antiterrorism special law that authorizes, under strict conditions, a military response to assist the U.S.-led war against terrorism. This historic naval deployment has attracted the ire of China and South Korea; the United States must firmly rebuff any such criticism.

The country that has gained most in its status with the United States is the United Kingdom (UK). Once again, the UK has proven that it is the only ally with credible military forces and sufficient diplomatic clout to stand by the side of the United States. In the bombing and missile attacks on Afghanistan, the UK was the only other country to contribute to the U.S. military mission. In bringing together the coalition, Prime Minister Tony Blair has exhibited diplomatic skills that eclipse those of Bush. Blair's help has been crucial in shoring up support not only among Europeans but also with Middle Eastern countries, Pakistan, and Russia. Australia, by comparison, has contributed significant but token military forces. Additionally, Prime Minister John Howard has been unable to exert any influence with either Indonesia or Malaysia—Australia's Muslim neighbors.

Who are the losers? The most obvious is China. Beijing has seen the United States assume notable influence in Pakistan—a country in which China has invested considerable military and economic assistance. It has also seen the United States gain access to military bases in Central Asia—a region that China considers within its natural sphere of influence. Before the events of September 11, China had developed an important relationship with Russia because both countries were concerned about what they viewed as the new Bush administration's hard-line stance toward them. Russia now is seizing the chance to be accepted as a friend of the West, and it seems ready to pay less attention to its relations with China. Although China says that it supports the war against terrorism, it has contributed nothing to the coalition other than general diplomatic support. Arguably, China has gained something by losing its status as the United States' number one enemy: Taiwan also seems to have gone off the boil in Washington. Bush's announcement in December 2001 that the United States will rescind the ABM Treaty, however, is a severe blow to China's security.

The other loser is Israel. Israel's hard-line military actions against the Palestinians are an embarrassment and potential danger to the coalition against terrorism. Washington may have initially urged Israel to keep its head down while the United States mounted sensitive military operations against bin Laden and the Taliban, but some Arab regimes no doubt believe, rightly or wrongly, that the United States has now allowed Israel freer rein because of its own successful strategy against the Taliban. Statements by the United States that it approves Palestinian statehood in principle, however, are a worrisome development for Tel Aviv. If the war against terrorism should widen to include U.S. attacks on Iraq, Israel's position will become even more delicate. The United States simply cannot afford to be seen as pursuing a war against Islam in the Middle East in cahoots with Israel.

As this war develops, Saudi Arabia may find itself in an increasingly untenable position. It is a friend of the United States, a critical supplier of oil to the West, and host to U.S. military bases that have drawn the anger of bin Laden and other Islamic fundamentalists. The majority of the terrorists who hijacked the aircraft involved in the attacks on September 11 came from Saudi Arabia, bin Laden himself was born there, and Riyadh was one of only three governments to have extended diplomatic relations to the Taliban. The autocratic regime in Saudi Arabia is trying to walk a fine line between its orthodox support for Islam and its friendship with the United States.

Indonesia is the largest Muslim and the fourth most populous country in the world. It occupies an archipelago that stands across narrow straits that control half of the world's maritime traffic. President Megawati Sukarnoputri has equivocated in her support for the United States: a week after the attacks of September 11, she was in Washington giving fulsome support, but once the bombing of Afghanistan started, she implicitly criticized the United States. Although she clearly must keep a careful eye on her domestic Islamic credentials, Washington is now disenchanted with her.

What states support bin Laden? The Taliban regime in Afghanistan is now finished. Although the attitudes of most Arab states, including pro-Western ones, "range from lukewarm to ice-cold,"[15] supporters of terrorism such as Iraq, Iran, and Syria are keeping remarkably quiet. As Charles Krauthammer has observed, on the enemy's side are fanatical but weak forces, supported and sheltered by not a single major power. On the U.S. side, for all near-term practical purposes at least, are NATO, Japan, Canada, Australia, Russia, China, India, Pakistan, and scores of other countries.

## WHAT IF WAR EXPANDS?

What happens to the coalition if the war expands? There are three main dangers. The first raises the specter of the coalition becoming bogged down in Afghanistan in a Vietnam-style counterinsurgency war. The second involves the war expanding beyond Afghanistan to other supporters of terrorism, such as Iraq. The third possibility involves another major terrorist attack on the United States, only this time using weapons of mass destruction.

The defeat of the Taliban should minimize the risks of another Vietnam. At the beginning of the bombing campaign, skeptics predicted that the only way to defeat the Taliban involved a U.S. ground force of 500,000. Yet, the combination of precision air strikes (which were much more effective than in the Gulf War), ground offensives by the Northern Alliance, and special operations forces has worked well. The withdrawal of Pakistan's support for the Taliban was a fatal blow. The retreat of Taliban remnants into remote mountainous areas in the south of Afghanistan need not demand a debilitating ground force operation by the coalition. Afghanistan will not become another Vietnam.

A more serious prospect for the coalition is a possible U.S. decision to widen the war to include other countries, such as Iraq, Iran, Syria, Sudan, Somalia, and Yemen, that host either bin Laden's Al Qaeda terrorist network or other dangerous terrorist movements. Influential people in the Bush administration, such as Rice and Deputy Secretary of Defense Paul Wolfowitz, are keen to pursue unfinished business from the 1991 Gulf War with Saddam Hussein. A widening of the war to include Iraq would undoubtedly strain the coalition, particularly with European countries such as France and Germany, as well as Russia. Many in the Middle East would probably regard it as confirmation that the United States is fighting a war against Islam. If evidence implicates Saddam's regime, however, the coalition must agree to punish him. Otherwise, this so-called war against terrorism will falter.

A more dangerous situation would arise if Islamic fundamentalists overthrew General Pervez Musharraf's regime in Pakistan. Unlike Iraq or Iran, Pakistan has developed operational nuclear ballistic missiles. It could easily target U.S. military bases in the Middle East or threaten to widen the conflict to include India— also in possession of nuclear weapons and ballistic missiles—which would raise the war on terrorism to an entirely different level of conflict. Under such conditions, how much of the coalition would remain and what price would U.S. partners demand to stay in it?

The third possibility involves the use by Al Qaeda or some other terrorist group of a nuclear weapon against the United States. The outrage in the United States would show no bounds; the urge to retaliate in kind against some target associated with the terrorists would be strong. This response would break a tacitly agreed norm of international behavior since the end of World War II not to use nuclear weapons. Holding the coalition together in such an apocalyptic situation would be nigh impossible.

These scenarios are speculative. Perhaps the more serious immediate task is to keep the coalition together in the face of increasing accusations that it is waging a war against Islam. To counter this sentiment, the international stabilization force in Afghanistan must include personnel from Muslim countries such as Turkey, Jordan, Bangladesh, and Indonesia— and exclude U.S. troops.

As the Economist observed, "[T]he West can live in peace with Islam. What is unclear is whether Islam can live in peace with the West."[16] Muslims in many parts of the world flatly say it cannot. When they consider the comparative failure, in material terms, of their once mighty civilization, they feel a deep sense of humiliation.[17]

This issue is complex and must be handled with the utmost sensitivity if the world is not to slide into a confrontation between Islam and the West. We should not commit the error of typing all Islamic countries with the same homogeneous attitudes, as we did, incorrectly, with "world communism." Samuel Huntington asserts that the collapse of communism removed a common enemy of the West as well as Islam and left each the perceived major threat to the other.[18] He predicts "a civilizational war" between Islam and the West. This prophecy must not become self-fulfilling.

## Concluding Observations

Predicting how the war against terrorism will unfold is obviously very difficult. So far at least, the United States has handled the situation well. Who would have predicted such an impressive array of countries supporting the United States, including every major power? Additionally— contrary to much media speculation—the United States has acquitted itself exceptionally well in bringing about the defeat of the Taliban in Afghanistan. The death of bin Laden, however, will not be the end of the matter. The war against terrorism will demand infinite patience and satisfaction with incremental successes that are not measured in terms of historical battlefield victories. Maintaining pressure in the financial, legal, and diplomatic war against terrorism over a prolonged period of time will be far from easy.

There is a risk that the coalition will fray at the edges, particularly if the war expands. That danger should be no excuse for a U.S. retreat or a reversion to isolationist sentiment. Ten years after the end of the Cold War, the United States has a new organizing principle to help define its interests. The United States must not define those interests in narrow terms. If anything, the events of September 11 have increased the global commitment to democracy democracy as well as open economic systems and have decisively limited the unilateral and aggressive use of force and violence.[19] The United States can expect its major allies to stand by it in this context, but it must involve them in the coalition's decisionmaking more than it has done so far.

Crises other than terrorism will naturally arise, engaging U.S. national interests. Whenever they arise, the United States must not revert to its previous unilateral, U.S.-first instincts and recognize that, as powerful as it is, it needs to work with other countries to achieve its aims. At times, this reality will demand some uncomfortable trade-offs and concessions. Washington will need to ensure that its current emphasis on greater domestic security does not undermine its traditional international support for human rights and democracy.

This historic coalition must not be discarded if the going gets tough, as it will. The United States is no longer an invulnerable country.

## Notes

1. Yossef Bodansky, Bin Laden: *The Man Who Declared War on the United States* (Rocklin, Calif.: Prima Publishing, 1999), p. 406.

2. I owe the thoughts in this paragraph to Avery Goldstein, "September 11, The Shanghai Summit, and the Shift in U.S.-China Policy," in *E-Notes* (Philadelphia: Foreign Policy Research Institute, November 9, 2001), http://www.fpri.org/enotes/americawar.20011109.goldstein.sept11china.html (accessed January 8, 2002).

3. Ibid.

4. Robert B. Zoellick, "A Republican Foreign Policy," *Foreign Affairs* 79, no. 1 (January/February 2000): 69.

5. William Pfaff, "The Question of Hegemony," *Foreign Affairs* 80, no. 1 (January/February 2001): 228.

6. Zoellick, "A Republican Foreign Policy," p. 69.

7. Walter Laqueur, "Let the Eagle Strike Free," *Australian,* October 2, 2001, p. 13.

8. David Fromkin, "The Strategy of Terrorism," in James F. Hoge Jr. and Fareed Zakaria, eds., *The American Encounter: The United States and the Making of the Modern World* (New York: Basic Books, 1997), p. 345. This article was first published in *Foreign Affairs* in July 1975 and addresses "how to drain the swamps of misery in which hatred and fanaticism breed."

9. Ibid., p. 348.

10. Richard Overy, *Why the Allies Won* (London: Pimlico, 1995), p. 290.

11. Christian Reus-Smit, "The Return of History," in *The Day the World Changed? Terrorism and World Order* (Canberra: Australian National University, 2001), pp. 5–6.

12. Francois Heisbourg, "U.S. Hegemony? Perceptions of the United States Abroad," *Survival* 41, no. 4 (winter 1999–2000), p. 17.

13. Condoleezza Rice, "Promoting the National Interest," *Foreign Affairs* 79, no. 1 (January/February 2000): 62.

14. *Nezavisimaya Gazeta,* October 23, 2001 (quoting Russian first deputy minister of foreign affairs Vyacheslav Trubnikov).

15. *Economist,* November 17–23, 2001, p. 18.

16. "Muslims and the West: The Need to Speak Up," *Economist,* October 13–19, 2001, p. 14.

17. Ibid.

18. Samuel P. Huntington, *The Clash of Civilizations and the Remaking of World Order* (New York: Simon & Schuster, 1996), p. 211.

19. Adam Garfinkle, "September 11: Before and After," in *FPRI Wire* 9, no. 8 (Philadelphia: Foreign Policy Research Institute, November 9, 2001), http://www.fpri.org/fpriwire/0908.200110.garfinkle.sept11.html (accessed January 8, 2002).

## They the People: Our Abandoned Muslim Allies

Azar Nafisi

A few days after the September 11 attacks, I received a note from a former student in Tehran. "[Y]ou won't believe it," she wrote, "but the whole country is in mourning. You should have been here for the demonstrations and candle-light vigils for America, it's all true: the tears, the long-stemmed roses, the candles, . . . and then of course the hoodlums attacked and started beating us, especially the young kids, and arresting them. . . . The funny thing about it is that those bastards felt betrayed by the love we showed 'the imperialist Zionist enemy.' . . . Ever since that night I keep asking myself, what is it that makes us in this God forsaken place to feel so orphaned and so filled with grief for what happened in a city we have never seen, except in dreams?"

To understand the love of which she speaks, you have to understand the hate coming from exactly the same part of the world—the hate that killed 3,000 on September 11, 2001. The source of this hatred does not lie in the wreckage at the World Trade Center or at the Pentagon but in other ruins: in cities in the Muslim world. It lies in the terror in a sports stadium turned into execution grounds in Kabul, in the villages of Algeria, in the slave trade in Sudan, in the bloody diamond mines of Sierra Leone, and in the homes and streets of Saudi Arabia, Iraq, and Iran. The Islamists' hatred of the United States is based on fear, and that fear is rooted in their fear of the woman in Algeria who, at the risk of having her throat cut, refuses to wear the veil; or the writer who is murdered in Tehran while translating the Declaration of Human Rights; or the Afghan crowds who flooded the streets of their ruined cities as the Taliban fled. The fear is not merely of American might but of the influence of American culture on people in their countries. They are afraid of the innumerable people, such as my former student, who feel closer to strangers living thousands of miles away than to the despots who rule their land in the name of their religion. And so the Islamists hate them and their supposed allies across the oceans.

Thus terrorized, their existence in danger, the Islamists turn to violence. The worst forms have been against progressive men and women—Muslim and non-Muslim—in their own countries who have become critical of the reactionary norms, who today ask for reform and a different way of viewing Islam. The more critical the people in Muslim societies become, the more vicious the Islamists will be. The Islamists see that the only true alternative to their system is democracy, which they identify with the West. That is why they are afraid of the West and why they want to destroy it.

Whether in power or in opposition, Islamists target Western culture in the name of whole peoples. But, if this claim were true, if all Muslims desired to be ruled by religious laws, then there would have been no need for states like Afghanistan and Iran to arm themselves against their own citizens: against unveiled women; unruly youths holding hands in public; against novels, films, music. Today, there is not one country in the Muslim world where there does not exist conflict and tension, not just between moderate and fundamentalist versions of Islamic rule but between the proponents of secularism and democracy and the supporters of theocracy and Islamism. In Egypt, democratic-minded individuals such as Saad Eddin Ibrahim are jailed, and human rights organizations are closed down. In Bahrain and Kuwait, there is the ongoing struggle over the right of women to vote. In Iran, former radical Islamist revolution-aries, progressive students, and secular intellec-tuals are jailed for quoting Western liberal thinkers such as Hannah Arendt and Karl Popper. In countries from Pakistan to Malaysia there are daily debates, and at times bloody battles, over the Muslim soul.

Still, commentators in the West seldom differentiate between the people of the "Muslim world" and their self-proclaimed representa-tives. So crimes committed against these people are repeated three times: once when they are forced into submission, once when they are rep-resented through the very forces that oppress them, and once when the world talks about them in the same language and through the same images as their oppressors. And it is that last crime that helps explain why Muslim anti-Americanism has been growing. As in all great tragedies, we must also look to our own hubris.

For two decades, questions of Islam and terror, us and them, who hates us and who likes us have been posed in the wrong context—on the assumption that the enemy of my enemy is my friend—and have led us to the wrong solutions. If the Americans have not treated the more democratic-minded people in the Muslim world as their allies, then who did they choose? This story is fraught with ironies: Today's predicament, after all, is partly the result of America's success in creating a Muslim "green belt" against communism in the Middle East in the 1980s. The United States, caught by a false sense of immediacy and crass pragmatism, helped the Muslim fundamentalists it now confronts in the wastelands of Afghanistan. America's new allies, such as Russia, and old friends, such as Pakistan and Saudi Arabia—which have helped fund the fundamentalists—are directly responsible for the present tragedy.

This alliance with dubious friends has forced Western governments to close their eyes not only to these transient allies' brutality against their own people but also to their acts of terror against Americans and other democracies in the West. Over the past two decades, European governments have reacted to terrorist regimes like those in Iran and Iraq with mild rebukes and critical "dialogues." The United States has also underestimated threats of terrorism against Americans and others. The most obvious examples are Lebanon in 1982, the Khobar Towers in 1996, the World Trade Center bombing in 1993, and the bombing of U.S. embassies in Africa in 1998. In all these cases, Americans either took hasty, insufficient action or no action at all.

Such weakness has dismayed the democratic-minded people within the Muslim world and created contempt for the United States among its enemies, who felt bold enough to publicly boast of their actions without fear of reprisals. In 1987, Mohsen Rafiq-Doust, then head of Iran's revolutionary guards, articulated this contempt when he publicly boasted that "both the TNT and ideology that blasted four hundred U.S. officers and soldiers to hell in Lebanon were ours." After the September 11 attacks, Osama bin Laden was quoted in *The Washington Post* with a similar boast: "'We believe that the defeat of America is possible, with the help of God, and is even easier for us—God permitting—than the defeat of the Soviet Union was before.'"

The problem, of course, goes deeper than America's short-sighted policies. It is rooted in a cynical attitude toward those whom Harvard's Samuel Huntington calls "the rest," as opposed to those who are privileged to be born in the "West." This attitude is prevalent not just in government but in the media, academic, and policy worlds. Namely, that the United States should not support democratic forces in the Muslim world because people in the region don't really aspire to democracy. This assumption allows Western governments and businesses to justify their relations with the most oppressive regimes. They can live with such allies and their abuses because they know that these allies are basically different from them, that what they share are not common values but common interests. Human rights have no place in such dealings. It is not enough that people in those countries should be robbed, but they should be robbed because they deserve it.

Afghanistan is a good example. The United States has had three recent openings to help move that traumatized country toward pluralism. The first was when, after the September 11 attacks, the United States had to choose as its main political ally either the Northern Alliance—greatly hated and feared by the majority of Afghans for its atrocities against them in the 1990s—or the more democratic forces gathered around the former king. Given the Northern Alliance's military power, the United States could not completely rule it out, so the wisest move would have been to support an alliance of the two; instead, the United States chose the Northern Alliance alone. The second opportunity came during the *loya jirga* in June 2002, when 80 percent of the delegates supported the democratic forces. Again, the United States capitulated to the extremists. Although Hamid Karzai was elected, key Cabinet seats, including Defense and Judiciary, have gone to the extremist forces. Many brutal warlords have taken advantage of the situation and are responsible for numerous murders, assassinations, and fatwas against women and progressive forces. The third opportunity to effect democratic change is taking place now, during the debate over the creation of a new constitution. Because of the presence of so many extremists in the government, the possibility of a democratic constitution is severely compromised.

Similarly, the United States in the '80s encouraged and supported Iraq in its war against Iran, not considering that, no matter how terrible the Iranian regime, Iran was still a more open and flexible society than the one created by Saddam Hussein. It was obvious that a semi-victory for Saddam would not make him more open to the West. But the United States still fanned the flames of old animosities between the Arabs and Iranians, ultimately leading the United States itself to fight two wars against Saddam.

But elite America's refusal to believe in the possibility of genuine democracy in the Muslim world is only part of a larger, flawed Western vision. Equally bad is the fact that the Islamists, more or less in the same manner as the communists before them, have become popular among America's intellectual leaders, most emphatically in the field of Middle Eastern studies. Unlike realpolitik American policymakers and businessmen, who merely ignore fundamentalists' cruelty, these leftists often proclaim solidarity with the Islamists' anti-American impulse. In the strange world of Middle Eastern studies, any attempt to condemn gender apartheid is branded an imposition of Western values, the voices of prominent clerics who oppose the politicization of religion are ignored, and the secular dissidents are dismissed as Westernized and therefore inauthentic. A return to roots has become fashionable, but those roots have been redefined not as poetry and philosophy but as stoning and flogging women. A Saudi princess advises us to mind our own business, this is how Arab women like it; an Iranian despot tells us about Western decadence; and an American professor at Duke University, Miriam Cooke, comments that "when men are traumatized [by colonial rule], they tend to traumatize their women." Dominant theories on colonization exploit the guilt of the victors and resentment of

the victims to form a new and more dangerous form of neocolonialism, denying the victims freedom in the name of Asian values, Islamic democracy, and cultural relativism. According to these experts, people living in countries with a majority Muslim population have no choice but to live under some form of the Islamic law. At best, these laws could be modified under what they claim to be an Islamic democracy. One could of course ask them, "If you wish to implement the Sharia law in moderate form, how do you more moderately stone a woman to death?"

The truth is not as the academics say, Islam today is used as a political tool and an ideology by Islamists against their own peoples, and as such has little to do with real Islamic traditions and culture. What we call Islamic fundamentalism, for lack of a better word, is a modern phenomenon, in the same way that fascism and communism, both products of the West, are modern. It takes its language, goals, and aspirations as much from the crassest forms of Marxism as it does from religion. Its leaders are as influenced by Lenin, Sartre, Stalin, and Fanon as they are by the Prophet. Today, fundamentalism's main targets are women, culture, and minorities, whose suppression it justifies in the name of Islam, thereby proving that both totalitarianism and democracy know no cultural or national boundaries.

I should have told my former student in Iran not to be surprised at the solidarity demonstrated by the Iranian people for the Americans. They understand who their true allies are. Democratic values and principles, for which so many millions of lives have been lost, did not always exist, and there is no guarantee they will always remain. Like hothouse flowers, they are fragile and need the right kind of light and nourishment to survive. Every time you deny this right to another, you deny it to yourself. The existence of the average American citizen, like the average citizen of Tehran or Kabul, depends on a vague concept she cannot fully define called democracy. But how can you exchange the gifts of culture and principles with others when you do not believe they deserve or understand them? To win this war, the Americans need the courage of their convictions, the belief that the Declaration of Human Rights is not a

Western conspiracy to impose its values upon others. They also need to recognize that today, as in the Soviet bloc before, the people living under totalitarian rule are democracy's most important potential allies. Not only should they and their representatives be supported, but their human rights must be at the center of negotiations with their governments.

No one knows whether democratic objectives will be realized. The "ordeal of freedom," to borrow from Saul Bellow, is very difficult to face. But the fact that these aspirations have been desired and imagined—not only now but for more than a century and a half—by the peoples living in the different Muslim societies, means they have a chance to be actualized. No one can take a people's dreams of a better life away from them without paying a high price. Democracies in the West have to support the aspirations of those fighting for democracy in the Muslim world, and, if Americans have become too cynical to do so out of idealism and compassion, then they should do it for the urgently pragmatic reason that their own survival, it is now unmistakably clear, is also at stake.

## REVIEW QUESTIONS

- Has the United States truly shifted away from multipolarity to unipolarity in its international behavior?
- Does the United States, as the world's remaining superpower, always need to accommodate the opinions of its allies? What are the ramifications of not accommodating them?
- How should alliances be forged? Are counterterrorist coalitions viable in the new era of terrorism?
- What elements are needed to accommodate the perspective of Arab societies in the formation of counterterrorist alliances?
- Can counterterrorist coalitions remain viable in the long term despite fundamental differences about how to wage the war on terrorism?

The following books and articles are suggested for further information about forging alliances in the new era:

### Books

Alexander, Yonah, ed. *Combating Terrorism: Strategies of Ten Countries.* Ann Arbor: University of Michigan Press, 2002.

Booth, Ken and Tim Dunne, eds. *Worlds in Collision: Terror and the Future of Global Order.* New York: Palgrave Macmillan, 2002.

Huntington, Samuel P. *The Clash of Civilizations: Remaking of World Order.* New York: Simon & Schuster, 1996.

### Articles

Gordon, Philip H. "Bridging the Atlantic Divide." *Foreign Affairs.* 82:1 (January/February 2003).

Rees, Wyn. "Transatlantic Relations and the War on Terror ." *Journal of Transatlantic Studies.* 1:1 (Spring 2003 Supplement).

Solana, Javier. "The Transatlantic Rift: U.S. Leadership After September 11." *Harvard International Review.* (Winter 2003).

# INDEX

# About the Editor

**Clarence Augustus Martin, J.D., Ph.D.,** is Associate Professor and Chair, Public Administration Department, School of Business and Public Administration, California State University, Dominguez Hills. He is also Coordinator of the Criminal Justice Administration program. Martin previously sat on the faculty of the Graduate School of Public and International Affairs, University of Pittsburgh. Teaching and research fields of specialization include Administration of Justice, Terrorism and Extremism, Juvenile Justice, Fair Housing, and Urban Affairs. He received his AB from Harvard College; JD from Duquesne Law School; and PhD from the Graduate School of Public and International Affairs at the University of Pittsburgh.

Martin was a public interest/civil rights attorney prior to joining academia. His professional practice included: Legislative Assistant to Congressman Charles B. Rangel of New York, Executive Associate for Legal Affairs to the American Psychological Association, Special Counsel to the Attorney General of the U.S. Virgin Islands, Managing Attorney of the Fair Housing Partnership of Greater Pittsburgh, and Director of the Fair Housing Services Center created under a consent decree to desegregate public and assisted housing in Allegheny County, New York. Martin is a guest lecturer and presenter for academic panels, workshops, classes, and private agencies. He is the author of *Understanding Terrorism* (2003).